ISRAEL

7th Edition

Fodor's Travel Publications   New York, Toronto, London, Sydney, Auckland
www.fodors.com

Be a Fodor's Correspondent

Share your trip with Fodor's

Our latest guidebook to Israel—now in full color—owes its success to travelers like you. Whether they're floating in the Dead Sea, visiting ancient ruins, or observing religious traditions, our members share their experiences with us and other travelers at Fodors.com. Facing this page is a montage of snapshots submitted to our "Show Us Your . . . Israel" photo contest. On page 53 you'll see the grand prize–winning photograph, taken by member Nicole_Pappas during her visit to Jerusalem's Church of the Holy Sepulcher. We've also included tips and suggestions from travelers who have shared their experiences with others in our forums, as a part of our "Word of Mouth" features.

We are especially proud of this color edition. No other guide to Israel is as up to date or has as much practical planning information, along with hundreds of color photographs and illustrated maps. If you're inspired and can plan a better trip because of this guide, we've done our job.

We invite you to join the travel conversation: Your opinion matters to us and to your fellow travelers. We encourage you to come to Fodors.com to plan your trip, share an experience, ask a question, submit a photograph, post a review, or write a trip report. Tell our editors about your trip; they want to know what went well and how we can make this guide even better. Share your opinion at our feedback center at fodors.com/feedback, or email us at editors@fodors.com with the subject line "Israel Editor." You might find your comments published in a future Fodor's guide. We look forward to hearing from you.

Nesi'ah tovah! (Happy Traveling!)

Tim Jarrell, Publisher

FODOR'S ISRAEL
Editors: Linda Cabasin, Rachel Klein

Editorial contributor: Mark Sullivan
Writers: Benjamin Balint, Judy Balint, Sarah Bronson, Phyllis Glazer, Judy Stacey Goldman, Shelly Paz, Lisa Perlman, Mike Rogoff, Adeena Sussman, Miriam Feinberg Vamosh, Gil Zohar

Production Editors: Evangelos Vasilakis, Carrie Parker
Maps & Illustrations: Henry Colomb and Mark Stroud, Moon Street Cartography; David Lindroth, *cartographers*; Bob Blake, Rebecca Baer, *map editors*; William Wu, *information graphics*
Design: Fabrizio La Rocca, *creative director*; Guido Caroti, Siobhan O'Hare, *art directors*; Tina Malaney, Chie Ushio, Ann McBride, Jessica Walsh, *designers*; Melanie Marin, *senior picture editor*
Cover Photo: (Western Wall at Dusk, Jerusalem): SIME s.a.s/eStock Photo
Production Manager: Amanda Bullock

7th Edition

ISBN 978-1-4000-0898-8

ISSN 0071-6588

SPECIAL SALES
This book is available at special discounts for bulk purchases for sales promotions or premiums. Special editions, including personalized covers, excerpts of existing books, and corporate imprints, can be created in large quantities for special needs. For more information, write to Special Markets/Premium Sales, 1745 Broadway, MD 6-2, New York, New York 10019, or e-mail specialmarkets@randomhouse.com.

AN IMPORTANT TIP & AN INVITATION
Although all prices, opening times, and other details in this book are based on information supplied to us at press time, changes occur all the time in the travel world, and Fodor's cannot accept responsibility for facts that become outdated or for inadvertent errors or omissions. So **always confirm information when it matters,** especially if you're making a detour to visit a specific place. Your experiences—positive and negative— matter to us. If we have missed or misstated something, **please write to us.** We follow up on all suggestions. Contact the Israel editor at editors@fodors.com or c/o Fodor's at 1745 Broadway, New York, NY 10019.

PRINTED IN SINGAPORE

10 9 8 7 6 5 4 3 2 1

CONTENTS

1 EXPERIENCE ISRAEL 8
  Israel Today. 10
  What's Where 12
  Israel Planner 14
  Israel Made Easy. 16
  Israel's Top Attractions 18
  Quintessential Israel. 20
  If You Like 22
  Israel: People, Religion,
  and State. 24
  Israel's Top Experiences 28
  Where to Stay in Israel 29
  Israeli Cuisine 30
  Israel with Kids. 32
  Israel's Markets. 34
  Israel's Best Beaches 35
  Israel and the Performing Arts . . 36
  Israel's Major Holidays 38
  Great Itineraries 41

2 JERUSALEM **53**
  Welcome to Jerusalem 54
  Jerusalem Planner 56
  Exploring Jerusalem. 59
  Where to Eat 117
  Best Bets for Jerusalem
  Dining 118
  Holiday Foods in Israel. 122
  Where to Stay. 133
  Best Bets for Jerusalem
  Lodging. 135
  Nightlife and the Arts. 149
  Sports and the Outdoors 155
  Shopping. 157

**3 AROUND JERUSALEM
  AND THE DEAD SEA** **165**
  Welcome to Around Jerusalem
  and the Dead Sea 166
  Around Jerusalem and the
  Dead Sea Planner. 168

Fodor's Features

Israel Through the Ages. 47
Jerusalem: Keeping the Faith 66
Masada: Desert Fortress. 180
The Dead Sea: A Natural Wonder 194
Tel Aviv After Dark 267
The Wines of Israel 326
Jesus in the Galilee 378
Adventures in the Negev. 462

  Masada and the Dead Sea. 171
  West of Jerusalem 200
  Bethlehem 209

4 TEL AVIV **217**
  Welcome to Tel Aviv. 218
  Tel Aviv Planner 220
  Center City 223
  Neveh Tzedek 230
  Jaffa 232
  The Tel Aviv Port and
  Northern Tel Aviv 236
  Where to Eat 239
  Best Bets for Tel Aviv Dining . . . 240
  Street Food In Israel. 242
  Where to Stay. 253
  Best Bets for Tel Aviv Lodging. . 254
  Nightlife and the Arts. 264
  Sports and the Outdoors 274
  Shopping. 277

CONTENTS

5 HAIFA AND THE NORTHERN
  COAST.................... 281
    Welcome to Haifa and the
    Northern Coast.............. 282
    Haifa and the Northern
    Coast Planner............... 284
    Haifa..................... 287
    The Northern Coast......... 306
    The Wine Country and
    Mt. Carmel................ 318
    Akko to Rosh Hanikra........ 336

6 LOWER GALILEE 351
    Welcome to Lower Galilee..... 352
    Lower Galilee Planner........ 354
    Jezreel and Jordan Valleys..... 357
    Nazareth and the Galilee Hills.. 369
    Tiberias and the
    Sea of Galilee............... 386

7 UPPER GALILEE AND THE
  GOLAN 407
    Welcome to Upper Galilee
    and the Golan.............. 408
    Upper Galilee and the Golan
    Planner.................... 410
    Tzfat (Safed) and Environs..... 413
    Upper Hula Valley........... 430
    The Golan Heights.......... 436

8 EILAT AND THE NEGEV....... 445
    Welcome to Eilat and the
    Negev.................... 446
    Eilat and the Negev Planner... 448
    The Heart of the Negev....... 451
    Beersheva and the Northern
    Negev.................... 470
    Eilat and Environs........... 477
    Side Trip to Petra........... 496
    Petra Planner 498

  VOCABULARY 507

  TRAVEL SMART ISRAEL 518

INDEX...................... 538
ABOUT OUR WRITERS 548

MAPS

The Old City 60–61
East Jerusalem................ 96
West Jerusalem 103
Center City 112
Where to Eat and Stay in
Jerusalem................120–121
Masada and the Dead Sea....... 173
West of Jerusalem............. 201
Bethlehem 213
Center City and Neveh Tzedek.... 224
Jaffa 233
Tel Aviv Port and Northern
Tel Aviv 237
Where to Eat in Tel Aviv......... 241
Where to Stay in Tel Aviv........ 255
Haifa...................290–291
Where to Eat and Stay in Haifa... 299
The Northern Coast to
Rosh Hanikra 308
Caesarea 312
Akko–Old City............... 338
Lower Galilee 359
Nazareth................... 371
Sea of Galilee............... 387
Where to Eat and
Stay in Tiberias.............. 389
Tzfat (Safed) 414
Tzfat and Environs 423
Upper Hula Valley and the
Golan Heights............... 431
The Heart of the Negev........ 451
Beersheva to Ein Bokek........ 470
Eilat and Environs............ 478
Where to Eat and Stay in Eilat ... 483
Petra...................... 497

ABOUT THIS BOOK

Our Ratings

Sometimes you find terrific travel experiences and sometimes they just find you. But usually the burden is on you to select the right combination of experiences. That's where our ratings come in.

As travelers we've all discovered a place so wonderful that its worthiness is obvious. And sometimes that place is so unique that superlatives don't do it justice: you just have to be there to know. These sights, properties, and experiences get our highest rating, **Fodor's Choice**, indicated by orange stars throughout this book.

Black stars highlight sights and properties we deem **Highly Recommended**, places that our writers, editors, and readers praise again and again for consistency and excellence.

By default, there's another category: any place we include in this book is by definition worth your time, unless we say otherwise. And we will.

Disagree with any of our choices? Care to nominate a place or suggest that we rate one more highly? Visit our feedback center at www. fodors.com/feedback.

Budget Well

Hotel and restaurant price categories from ¢ to $$$$ are defined in the opening pages of each chapter. For attractions, we always give standard adult admission fees; reductions are usually available for children, students, and senior citizens. Want to pay with plastic? **AE, D, DC, MC, V** following restaurant and hotel listings indicate whether American Express, Discover, Diners Club, MasterCard, and Visa are accepted.

Restaurants

Unless we state otherwise, restaurants are open for lunch and dinner daily. We mention dress only when there's a specific requirement and reservations only when they're essential or not accepted—it's always best to book ahead.

Hotels

Hotels have private bath, phone, TV, and air-conditioning and operate on the European Plan (aka EP, meaning without meals), unless we specify that they use the Continental Plan (CP, with a Continental breakfast), Breakfast Plan (BP, with a full breakfast), or Modified American Plan (MAP, with breakfast and dinner) or are all-inclusive (including all meals and most activities). We always list facilities but not whether you'll be charged an extra fee to use them, so when pricing accommodations, find out what's included.

Many Listings
- ★ Fodor's Choice
- ★ Highly recommended
- ⊠ Physical address
- ✢ Directions
- ⌂ Mailing address
- ☎ Telephone
- 🖷 Fax
- ⊕ On the Web
- ✉ E-mail
- 🗎 Admission fee
- ☉ Open/closed times
- ▭ Credit cards

Hotels & Restaurants
- 🏨 Hotel
- 🛏 Number of rooms
- ♿ Facilities
- ۴🍴 Meal plans
- ✗ Restaurant
- 🪑 Reservations
- 🚭 Smoking
- 🍶 BYOB

Outdoors
- 🏌 Golf
- ⛺ Camping

Other
- ☁ Family-friendly
- ⇨ See also
- ✉ Branch address
- ☞ Take note

Experience
Israel

ISRAEL TODAY

Israel and Its Neighbors

The Arab-Jewish conflict here predates the establishment of the State of Israel, and the political, ethnic, religious and territorial issues involved are far beyond the scope of this book. Many Israelis feel torn between their desire to make peace with their Arab neighbors—even with concessions of land—and their not-unfounded fear that concessions may worsen, rather than improve, their safety and security.

Currently, Israel is concerned about military threats at four borders: Lebanon and Syria to the north, Gaza (which Israel occupied from 1967 to 2005) to the west, and the West Bank (which Israel has occupied since 1967) to the east. In contrast, Egypt and Jordan have diplomatic ties, and a "cold" peace, with Israel since signing peace treaties in 1978 and 1994, respectively.

At this writing, there are 1.5 million Palestinians living in Gaza, and an additional 2.4 million in the West Bank, along with 187,000 Israelis. Some Israelis view the West Bank occupation as a military necessity, citing Hamas' use of Gaza as a rocket-launching pad. Others see it as immoral or, conversely, as a religious mandate. A pullout in the near future seems unlikely for three reasons: the removal of Israeli forces from Gaza has resulted in continued conflict; a large number of Israeli Jews still live in the West Bank; and Arab states' ongoing refusal to recognize Israel's right to exist.

The current Israeli government—like those before it—will have to grapple with these issues, along with all the social and economic challenges that face the country.

Diversity Through Immigration

One of Israel's most unique features—and one that accounts for its diverse social mosaic—has been its amazing absorption of immigrants.

The first waves of immigrants came in the late 19th century, when Jews fled Russian pogroms. Later, despite harsh British quotas, tens of thousands escaped the rising tide of Nazism in the years before and during World War II.

Since its founding in 1948, Israel has provided refuge to persecuted Jews. The country's Law of Return affords any Jew the right to immigrate and take Israeli citizenship. More than half a million, including many Holocaust survivors, came to Israel just after its founding.

Immigration from the ghettos and shtetls of Europe is only half the story. Israel gave shelter to hundreds of thousands of Jews from Arab lands and to Ethiopian Jews. And since the demise of the Soviet Union, a million Soviet Jews have emigrated to Israel. While integration and acculturation are not easy, they remain a top national priority.

Israel and the European Union

In 2008, after a year of intensive negotiations, the EU-Israel Association Council announced upgraded relations between Israel and the EU, ushering in a new era for the country. This entailed closer diplomatic cooperation; Israel's participation in European environmental, educational, agricultural, banking, and space programs; and an examination of possible future Israeli integration into the European single market. The upgrade also reinforced a growing friendship. The country started to enjoy stronger ties with France under Nicolas Sarkozy, Britain under Gordon

Brown, Germany under Angela Merkel, and Italy under Silvio Berlusconi.

But the upgrade took on its deepest significance in light of the EU's role as a Quartet member, and the increased leverage with which Israel could encourage the Europeans to take a firmer stand against Hamas and Iran.

The upgrade was also welcome for the economic fruits it promised to bring to an already robust partnership, with reciprocal tariff-free exports and concessions in industrial and agricultural goods. In terms of total trade, which in 2006 amounted to more than 23.5 billion euros, the EU is Israel's major partner.

A Vibrant Economy

It may be too early to tell, but at this writing Israel has been largely insulated from the effects of the American credit crisis, in part because its banks were always heavily regulated—a paradoxical legacy of Israel's socialist past. Yet there are economic issues, including that the country's income inequality rate is one of the highest in the developed world, with wealth concentrated in the hands of the few.

But the country has one of the world's fastest-growing emerging markets, as the gross domestic product has remained above 3% for the past four years, and hosts the greatest number of NASDAQ-listed companies after the United States and Canada. Export earnings are up. Tourism is up. So are property prices. In 2008, Forbes magazine rated Israel as the world's most "up-and-coming" real-estate market.

Israel's economy is powered by its leadership in research and development spending for science and technology. Among other top-tier companies, the country is home to Teva Pharmaceuticals, the largest maker

of generic drugs, and to Intel's advanced chip production facilities. "Silicon Wadi," the corridor of high-tech industries that runs from Tel Aviv to Haifa, is one of the world's strongest technology clusters.

In a relatively short time, the country has managed to build an economy that is both well-cushioned against political instability, and well-positioned to lead the nation into greater prosperity.

The Jewish Divide

While three-quarters of Israel's population is Jewish, a tangle of divisions and sub-divisions complicates the scene.

Two major rifts run through Israeli Jewish society. The first divides ultra-Orthodox (in Hebrew, Haredim) and secular Israelis. Bound to a strict interpretation of Jewish law, and distinguished by their black hats and garb, the ultra-Orthodox accept the yoke of all 613 of the Torah's commandments. They've also achieved increasing political clout, both on the national level, where coalitions rely on ultra-Orthodox parties to attain Knesset majorities, and on the municipal level. From 2003 to 2008, for instance, Jerusalem had an ultra-Orthodox mayor. Many secular Israelis, however, resent the ultra-Orthodox monopoly on conversion and marriage, as well as the fact that most of their ultra-Orthodox countrymen do not serve in the army.

A second fault line is marked by the often uneasy relationship between an elite dominated by Ashkenazi Jews (those whose origins are in Europe) and the often under-privileged Sephardic Jews who came to Israel from Arab lands. To this day, Sephardic immigrants and their children argue that the Ashkenazi establishment discriminates against traditional Sephardic families.

WHAT'S WHERE

Tel Aviv

The following numbers refer to chapters.

2 Jerusalem. The walls of the Old City embrace sites sacred to Judaism, Christianity, and Islam, but Israel's capital is more than its ancient places. Shop in the souk or relax in a bustling café and savor the city's unique atmosphere. It's a heady mix of sensations both worldly and emotional.

3 Around Jerusalem and the Dead Sea. If you love the desert, explore it east of Jerusalem at the remains of Herod's palace atop Masada, or float in the Dead Sea at Ein Bokek. Day trips to Bethlehem and to wineries west of Jerusalem are other options.

4 Tel Aviv., Tel Aviv's beautiful beaches and seaside promenade, vibrant with cafés and good times, hug the Mediterranean. The city is also Israel's economic and cultural center. Don't miss its Bauhaus architecture, busy markets, and strolling its charming neighborhoods.

5 Haifa and the Northern Coast. Although you're never far from a Mediterranean beach, take time to see the sights in Haifa, including the Baha'i Shrine and Gardens, and in the Old City in Akko. South of Haifa are Roman Caesarea and the Mt. Carmel wine country.

6 Lower Galilee. Verdant valleys, rolling hills, and the freshwater Sea of Galilee are counterpoints to the historical riches in Israel's northeast corner. Hike Mt. Gilboa, explore archaeology at Beit She'an and Zippori, and visit Nazareth and the famed sites of Jesus's ministry. At night, enjoy dinner by the lake.

Capernaum

7 Upper Galilee and the Golan. Historical treasures, quaint bed-and-breakfasts, and the great outdoors are just a few reasons to visit Israel's northernmost region. The sacred hilltop city of Tzfat (Safed) and Rosh Pina, a delightful restored village, are two top sites.

8 Eilat and the Negev. Visiting the Negev is about experiencing the desert's stunning geological treasures and enjoying Eilat's gorgeous beaches. Take a side trip to Petra, nearby in Jordan, to see its temples and tombs carved out of sandstone cliffs.

Negev desert

Mediterranean Sea

LEBANON

Dan
Kiryat Shmona
Rosh Hanikra
Nahariya
Meron
Ma'alot
Tzfat
Akko
7
Gamla
HAIFA
Haifa
5
Tiberias
Sea of Galilee
Ein Hod
Nazareth
6
Afula
Umm el Fahm
Bet She'an
Jenin
2
Netanya
6
Tulkarm
Herzlia Pituach
Qalqilya
5
Nablus/Shechem
Ramat Gan
Petah Tikva
Tel Aviv
4
4
Lod
Ramallah
Rishon Lezion
6
7
2
Jericho
Ashdod
Ashkelon
★ JERUSALEM
Bethlehem
WEST BANK
Gaza
Kiryat Gat
Hebron
Ein Gedi
GAZA
Beersheva
3
Masada
Ein Bokek
Mashabei Sadeh
Dimona
Nizzana
Sde Boker
Hatzeva
Ein Yahav
Mitzpe Ramon
Petra
EGYPT
Lotan
8
Eilat
Aqaba
Gulf of Eilat

GOLAN HEIGHTS
UNDOF Zone (U.N. Disengagement Observer Force)
SYRIA
Yarmuk River
Jordan River
★ Amman
JORDAN
Dead Sea

0   30 miles
0   30 km

ISRAEL PLANNER

Getting Here

International flights land at Ben Gurion International Airport, about 10 miles from Tel Aviv and about 27 miles from Jerusalem.

Security checks on airlines flying to Israel are stringent. Be prepared for what might sound like personal questions about your itinerary, packing habits, and desire to travel to Israel. Remember that the staff is concerned with protecting you, and be patient.

Taxis to Tel Aviv cost NIS 140 ($35), and can take up to 45 minutes during rush hour. The train is a money-saver for NIS 13 ($3.50), and takes about 25 minutes.

A taxi is recommended for travel to Jerusalem; it costs 280 NIS ($70) for the 45-minute trip. The 10-passenger Nesher shuttles cost NIS 50 ($12); book at least a day in advance.

Getting Around

You can get almost anywhere in Israel by bus, and the Central Bus Station is a fixture in most towns: ask for the *tahana merkazit*. Egged handles all of the country's bus routes; in Tel Aviv there's also Dan. Both intercity and urban buses run from 5:30 AM to 12:30 AM Sunday–Thursday.

Public transportation is generally suspended during the Jewish Sabbath (Shabbat), from about two hours before sundown Friday to sundown Saturday, although some lines run minibuses in Tel Aviv. Haifa, with a large Arab population, also has some Shabbat service.

Taxis can be a good option on Shabbat—they're plentiful, relatively inexpensive, and can be hailed on the street. Drivers must use the meter according to law. *Sherut* are shared taxis or minivans that run fixed routes at a set rate; some can be booked in advance.

The train from Tel Aviv to Jerusalem is a scenic, 75-minute trip. Commuter trains run between other cities; the majority of service runs along the coast, from Nahariya south and then inland to Beersheva. Signs at train stations are posted in English. Reservations are not accepted.

⇨ *For more information on getting here and around, see Travel Smart Israel.*

Driving Distances in Israel

Eilat to Tel Aviv	220 miles (354 km.)
Tel Aviv to Jerusalem	36 miles (58 km.)
Jerusalem to Ben-Gurion International Airport	27 miles (43 km.)
Ben Gurion International Airport to Tel Aviv	10 miles (16 km.)
Tel Aviv to Haifa	52 miles (84 km.)
Haifa to Tiberias	35 miles (56 km.)
Tiberias to Jerusalem	109 miles (175 km.)
Jerusalem to Eilat	190 miles (306 km.)

Dining

Unless otherwise noted, the restaurants listed in this guide are open daily for lunch (*arukhat tzohorayim*) and dinner (*arukhat erev*), and prices are in Israeli shekels (NIS). In Israel, many restaurants are *kosher*, and serve dishes that include either dairy products or meat—but neither is ever served together. Fish can be served with either dairy products or meat, except shellfish, which is a non-kosher food and is not served in kosher restaurants. In the cities, cafés are generally open Sunday–Thursday 8 AM–midnight. Kosher cafés close two hours before the Sabbath; non-kosher places keep regular hours. Restaurants serving lunch and dinner usually open at noon and close around midnight or 1 AM. Israelis eat dinner fairly late, and it's not uncommon to wait for a table at 10 PM.

Lodging

Nearly all hotel rooms in Israel have private bathrooms with a combined shower and tub. The best hotels have a swimming pool, a health club, and tennis courts; and with rare exceptions in major cities, most hotels have parking facilities. Almost all the large Israeli hotels are certified kosher, and most include a traditional Israeli breakfast. The lodgings we list are the cream of the crop in each price category. We always list the facilities that are available— but we don't specify whether they cost extra: when pricing accommodations, always ask what's included and what costs extra. Price-category information is given in each chapter. Prices are in dollars, as paying bills at hotels in foreign currency eliminates the Value-Added Tax (VAT). Unless otherwise noted, all lodgings have a private bathroom, air-conditioning, a room phone, and a television.

WHAT IT COSTS					
	¢	$	$$	$$$	$$$$
Restaurants	Under NIS 32	NIS 32–49	NIS 50–75	NIS 76–100	Over NIS 100
Hotels	Under $120	$120–$200	$201–$300	$301–$400	Over $400

Restaurant prices are per person for a main course at dinner in NIS (Israeli shekels). Hotel prices are in US dollars, for two people in a standard double room in high season. Non-Israeli citizens paying in foreign currency are exempt from the 15.5% VAT tax on hotel rooms.

When to Go

Israel has several high seasons, but each attracts different types of visitors. The Jewish New Year (Rosh Hashanah) usually falls in September or October, bringing those wanting to celebrate in the Holy Land. The same goes for April or March, when Passover and Easter attract Christian and Jewish tourists. July and August are the hottest months, and Israel becomes swamped with beachgoers. The weather is perfect in September and October, and from April to mid-June, when days are warm enough without being too hot, and nights are comfortable. May and June are in between high seasons and prices are more affordable. The weather is still splendid across country, and historical sites and other attractions are yet to be filled with tourists.

Renting a Car

Renting a car is a good idea only if you plan to thoroughly explore the country but not within big cities. At press time, gas costs NIS 6.50 per liter. (self service is always cheaper). Before taking insurance from the rental car agency, always check to see what coverage you already have. Most importantly, double check if coverage applies if you plan to drive in the West Bank.

ISRAEL MADE EASY

Customs of the Country

"Etiquette" is not a key word in the Israeli vocabulary. In this highly informal society, there are many traditions but few rules. That said, both Jewish and Arabic cultures have their own social customs and strictures. Visitors (particularly women) to ultra-Orthodox neighborhoods must wear modest dress. Local women keep their knees and elbows covered and do not wear pants; married women also keep their heads covered. In Jerusalem's Old City, where the major sites holy to Christianity, Islam, and Judaism are located, women will feel more comfortable if they keep a scarf handy to cover the shoulders when entering a synagogue or other important religious institutions.

Eating Out

Restaurants that abide by "kosher" dietary regulations, to satisfy a particular clientele, close for Friday dinner and Saturday lunch (Sabbath ends at dark). Kosher hotel eateries remain open, but will not offer menu items that require cooking on the spot. "Kosher" has nothing to do with particular cuisines but with certain restrictions (no pork or shellfish, no dairy and meat products on the same menu). Kosher restaurants today have to compete with a growing number of non-kosher restaurants, so the variety of kosher food is growing. Tipping (in cash) is 12% minimum. There is great coffee all over Israel. Latte is called "hafooch"; and if you want black coffee, ask for "filter" coffee. Tap water is safe throughout Israel.

Greetings

Israelis do not stand on ceremony, and greet each other warmly with either a slap on the back (for men) or an air-kiss on both cheeks (for women). Tourists are usually greeted with a handshake.

Women won't be acknowledged by ultra-Orthodox Jewish men, and very religious Jews of either gender do not shake hands or mingle socially with members of the opposite sex.

Israelis are renowned for their bluntness and won't hesitate to ask how much you earn or what you paid for your hotel room or a piece of jewelry. That openness extends to discussions on religion and politics, too, so don't be afraid to speak your mind.

The Jewish Sabbath

The Sabbath extends from sundown Friday until sundown Saturday every week. During this time period you can expect the majority of shops and restaurants in Jerusalem to be closed. Life in Tel Aviv doesn't grind to a halt in quite the same way although public transportation is suspended in both cities. Sunday is the first day of the regular work week.

Language

Hebrew is the national language of Israel, but travelers can get by speaking English only. Virtually every hotel has English-speaking staff; as do restaurants and shops in the major cities. In smaller towns and rural areas it might take a little longer to find someone who speaks English. If you have learned a few words of Hebrew, such as toda (thank you), bevakasha (please), and shalom (hello and goodbye), your efforts will be warmly appreciated.

Arabic is Israel's other official language, spoken by Arabs as well as many Jews (especially those with origins in Arab lands). Because Israel is a nation of immigrants, mistakes and various accents are tolerated cheerfully.

Israelis use a lot of hand gestures when they talk. A common gesture is to turn the palm outward and press the thumb

and three fingers together to mean "wait a minute"; rest assured that this has no negative connotations. Just as harmless is the Israeli who says "I don't believe you" to express that something is unbelievably wonderful.

Money and Shopping

The Israeli shekel (designated NIS) is the currency, but the U.S. dollar is widely accepted. At press time, $1 is equal to NIS 4.20. Rates for hotels, guiding services, and car rentals are always quoted and paid for in foreign currency, thus avoiding the 15.5% local VAT. Many better stores offer a government VAT refund on purchases above U.S. $100, claimable at the airport duty-free. Currency Exchange: For the most favorable rates, change money through banks. Although ATM transaction fees may be higher abroad than at home, ATM rates are excellent because they're based on wholesale rates offered only by major banks. A word of advice: avoid buying gold, silver, gemstones, and antiquities in bazaars (like Jerusalem's Old City souk), where things aren't always what they seem and prices fluctuate wildly.

Safety

On the security front, Israel has been the subject of such intense media attention over the years that, ironically, many would-be visitors are confused about where to go and what regions to avoid. Despite the country's small size, trouble in one area does not necessarily influence travel in another. In Jerusalem, the Old City can be thronged during the day and relatively empty at night, when almost everything there is closed. Spend your evenings elsewhere. In times of particular political unrest, it is generally best to avoid shopping areas, public buses and bus stops, and other crowded areas. The Arab neighborhoods of East Jerusalem have become less hospitable of late, but unless there are general security problems at the time, the daytime wanderer should not encounter any problems. If you want to visit Palestinian autonomous areas such as Bethlehem and Jericho, a Palestinian guide must accompany you, as Israeli citizens are not allowed to enter. Some Israeli guides may be able to provide a reference. There are standard security checks along the roads to the West Bank, but the routes are open except in periods of particular political tension.

Expect to have your handbags searched as a matter of course when you enter bus and train terminals, department stores, places of entertainment, museums, and public buildings. These checks are generally fast and courteous.

Visiting Sacred Sites

Muslim sites are closed for tourists on Friday, the Muslim holy day. Avoid the Muslim Quarter of Jerusalem's Old City between 12 noon and 2 PM on Fridays, when the flow of worshippers in the streets can be uncomfortable or even rowdy. Some Christian sites close on Sunday; others open after morning worship. Jewish religious sites, and some museums and historical sites, close midday Friday and remain closed through Saturday (the Jewish Sabbath).

ISRAEL'S TOP ATTRACTIONS

Old City, Jerusalem
(A) Within the golden stone walls of the Old City are thousands of years of history and a number of sites cherished by Jews, Christians, and Muslims. A day spent exploring its winding alleyways, arched gateways, Arab market, and storied buildings is both a fascinating history primer and a lesson in the challenges of coexistence.

Masada
(B) Whether you hike the steep Snake Path or take the faster cable car, ascending the rocky mountain to view the remains atop Masada, south of Jerusalem, is a memorable journey. The site was one of King Herod's palace-fortresses and also where the Jews made their last stand against the Romans. It's an amazing vantage point from which to witness sunrise over the Judean desert.

The Sea of Galilee
(D) This shimmering body of water—known in Hebrew by its Old Testament name, the Kinneret—is linked to many events during the life of Jesus. Pilgrims flock to its shores to be baptized at the point where it flows into the Jordan River. The lake is also a recreation destination for Israelis.

Makhtesh Ramon
(C) Part of a larger nature reserve in the Negev, the Ramon Crater—formed when an ancient ocean above it migrated northward—includes stunning multicolored rock formations, breathtaking hills and valleys, wadis (mostly dry river beds), fossil formations, and many flora and fauna unique to the region.

Baha'i Shrine and Gardens
(E) Adherents of the Baha'i faith, which believes in the unity of humankind, built this showpiece in Haifa, combining a show-stopping acre of manicured grounds

with an ornate, gold-domed shrine sure to impress visitors and true believers alike.

Caesarea

(F) This seaside town half an hour north of Tel Aviv owes its name to King Herod, who dedicated it to Caesar Augustus. Highlights include the still-functional Roman amphitheater and the remains of Herod's port. There's also a beach with a Roman aqueduct.

Western Wall

(G) Jews the world over flock to the only remaining relic of the complex that housed the ancient Holy Temple in Jerusalem. Every day, hundreds of handwritten paper notes covered with personal prayers are stuffed into the wall's cracks.

Church of the Holy Sepulcher

(H) Five of the fourteen Stations of the Cross—including the site of Jesus's crucifixion and burial—are found within this Crusader-era church in Jerusalem's Old City. Four denominations of Christianity are represented here, each with distinct chapels and religious rites.

Dome of the Rock

(J) In Jerusalem an enormous plaza, on the site of the Temple Mount, holds the Al-Aqsa mosque, the third-holiest site in Islam and an active house of worship, and the gold-topped Dome of the Rock. Both were built over 1,300 years ago.

Old City, Akko

(I) This coastal city has borne witness to history, watching everyone from the Greeks to the Ottomans sweep through. In the walled Old City, explore Crusader remains, Turkish bathhouses, and port, and visit the British-era jail where Jewish resistance fighters were imprisoned in the 1940s.

QUINTESSENTIAL ISRAEL

Falafel

Falafel sandwiches are a fast-food staple in Israel, and stands are found from the busy streets of downtown Tel Aviv to the ultra-Orthodox areas of Jerusalem and the Eilat beach promenade.

It starts with a scoop of seasoned chickpeas mashed into small spheres that are quickly fried in oil, then thrust—six or so—into a pita. Patrons give a nod or a "no thanks" to some hummus or *harif* (hot sauce), and to each of the colorful accompaniments: cubed cucumbers and tomatoes, pickled turnip and eggplant, shredded cabbage, parsley, pickles, and even french fries stuffed on top. Discerning diners then drizzle their creation with self-serve sauces: *amba* (spicy pickled mango) and tahini.

And about that drizzling—diners should have a few extra napkins ready, and assume the falafel position before taking their first bite: leaning forward well away from clothing and shoes.

The Sabra Personality

Israelis are known to have prickly personalities. Although the most popular word in the country is *savlanut* (patience), natives don't seem to be blessed with an overabundance of that quality.

An old saying tries to explain the character of Israelis, masters of the short retort, by comparing it to the pear cactus, known as a *sabra*, a fruit that has prickles all over the outside but is sweet on the inside. Native-born Israelis are known as sabras. Fortunately, this national tendency toward abruptness is tempered with a dose of Mediterranean warmth. But there's a trick to dealing with the perceived cold-shoulder: persevere. A welcome thaw is likely to be close at hand.

Israel is more than holy sites and turbulent politics; to get a sense of the country, familiarize yourself with some of the features in daily life.

Markets and Bargaining

Israel's open-air markets are just the place to soak up local culture while shopping for snacks to stock your hotel room. Most produce markets also have stalls selling cheap clothing and other textiles—the 100% cotton socks and tablecloths made in Israel are often economical and high quality. Machaneh Yehuda in Jerusalem and Tel Aviv's Carmel Market are famous. For markets that sell decorative brass, ceramic and glass items, beads, embroidered dresses, and jackets or secondhand funky clothes, head to Jerusalem's Old City or the Jaffa Flea Market.

Bargaining can be a fun part of any market experience—but there are some useful pointers to keep in mind: never answer the question "how much do you want to pay?" When the seller names a price, come back with about half. If the seller balks, be prepared to walk out; if you're called back, they want to make a sale. If you're in a hurry, vendors will know it and won't drop the price. Know, too, that not every vendor will be in the mood for the bargaining game.

Café Culture

Café-sitting is an integral part of Israeli life, especially in the cities where it seems as if there's one on every corner. The locals particularly love their *café hafuch* (cappuccino: literally, "upside-down coffee").

Unlike Parisian or European cafés where the waiters get antsy if you stay too long, at Israeli cafés you can sit un-hassled. Most are inexpensive places to stop for Mediterranean-style sandwiches, maindish salads, or soup. There are also upscale bistro-cafés, great for everything from a glass of wine to a heartier meal.

IF YOU LIKE

Nature Reserves

Think green. After a tour of the cities and sites, visit one or more of Israel's tranquil nature reserves to mellow-out and commune with the flora and fauna.

If cave exploration interests you, those in the **Nahal Me'arot Nature Reserve** were settled by five different prehistoric cultures for 200,000 continuous years. A great time to visit is from late winter to spring, when the entire Reserve comes alive with flowers. The **Hai Bar Nature Reserve** is a haven for animals with biblical roots and endangered desert species, like the addax, the oryx, and the fennec. At this park you tour in your own car, together with one of the center's guides. Every type of stalactite formation known can be seen at the **Sorek Cave** near Jerusalem. Some of the stalactites are 300, 000 years old, others are even older.

Throughout history, the Hula Valley was an important pied-à-terre for migrating birds from Europe and Africa, and home to magnificent flora and fauna. At the **Hula Nature Reserve,** drop in for a bird's-eye view of cranes, storks, pelicans, cormorant, and more. The **Tel Dan Nature Reserve** is a fairyland of brooks and streams that lead to the remnants of the ancient Canaanite city of Laish, captured by the Tribe of Dan. The **Gamla Nature Reserve** is home to eagles and Griffin vultures. There are canyon views, a lovely waterfall, and remains of the earliest known synagogue in the world as well as the ancient settlement of Gamla. Springs and grottoes, and one of the most beautiful waterfalls in Israel can be found at the **Hermon River (Banias) Nature Reserve**; the Banias were a strategic site during the reign of Herod.

Desert Adventures

In antiquity, Israel's deserts were the stomping grounds for everyone from ancient prophets and hermits to traders. Today, there are several ways you can experience the rocky, spring-studded hills and dales of Israel's two deserts—the Judean and the Negev—and your excursion can be as short as a few hours or as long as a day, or several days. You can book tours through travel agents or through your hotel, but some tours don't operate in the summer, when it's very hot. Whatever you do, take plenty of water and a hat.

It's not advised to go off into the desert by yourself, but for a convenient, short exploration on foot, you can visit springs like **Ein Gedi** and the adjacent **Nahal Arugot** on the eastern edge of the Judean Desert southeast of Jerusalem. In the Negev, the trek to **Ein Avdat** is easy and begins at the end of a short drive from Ben-Gurion's tomb. Any of these is only a few minutes' walk from the road. If you're looking for something more intense, join an organized hike, like the ones led by guides from the **Society for the Protection of Nature in Israel.**

If you prefer to travel by other means than by foot, you can sign up to see the desert by jeep, with **Jeep See** in Eilat or **Israel Adventure Tours** in Jerusalem, or join a camel trip into the Negev mountains northwest of Eilat through the **Camel Ranch.** If horseback riding is your thing, **Texas Ranch,** also in Eilat, takes riders on trails through Wadi Shlomo (Solomon's Valley) and into the desert.

Hands-on Archaeology

If you've ever been to a museum and wondered what it would be like to dig up one of those ancient artifacts, Israel has many options to feed the fantasy. Digs are under way all over the country, and volunteer programs range from a half-day to a week or longer. Most take place during spring or summer, and charge a fee to participants; some offer package deals that include accommodations. Current top options are listed below, and a list of digs looking for volunteers is updated on the Israel Ministry of Foreign Affairs Web site (www.mfa.gov.il) under "Our Bookmarks."

If getting your hands dirty for half a day sounds like fun, Archaeological Seminars has a year-round Dig-for-a-Day program, with three-hour excavations at **Bet Guvrin–Maresha National Park**, outside of Jerusalem. **Ramat Rachel**, almost *in* Jerusalem, is the site of a First Temple–era royal palace whose remains can be seen in the small archaeological park near the hotel; excavation has resumed and volunteers can sign up for one-week-long periods in the summer. A week is also the minimum to sign on with the 10-year-long project underway in **Tiberias** (for more information, visit ⊕*www.tiberiasexcavation.com*), which has the advantage of being right on the Sea of Galilee, a great location for free-time touring and water fun. If you can make a longer commitment, the excavation at **Megiddo**, the traditional Armageddon, in the Jezreel Valley, offers accommodations at a nearby kibbutz and has three- or four-week dig options.

Sacred Spaces

It's close to the same size as New Jersey, but Israel probably has more sacred places per square mile than anywhere else on earth. Some are so full of hustle and bustle that it can be hard to focus on matters of the spirit, but it does make it easy to appreciate the impact of the places they have drawn believers for millennia.

For the Jewish faith, the holiest place in the world is the **Western Wall**, the only remnant of the ancient Great Temple in Jerusalem. Farther afield, the country is dotted with tombs traditionally thought to be the resting places of biblical characters and Talmudic sages, such as the tombs of the prophet Elijah in Haifa and Rabbi Shimon Bar Yochai on **Mt. Meron** in Upper Galilee.

Just above Jerusalem's Western Wall, Muslims flock to the silver-domed **Al-Aqsa Mosque**, considered to be the third-holiest place in Islam. The adjacent golden **Dome of the Rock** shrine is built on the spot where Prophet Mohammed is believed to have ascended to the heavens on his horse al-Buraq.

For Christians of every denomination, Israel offers the unique opportunity to follow in the very footsteps of Jesus. From Capernaum and Tabgha on the shores of the **Sea of Galilee** to the Jordan River and Nazareth with its many churches, the Bible comes alive as visitors gaze at the landscape where Jesus walked and preached. In Jerusalem, the **Garden of Gethsemane**, the **Via Dolorosa**, and the **Church of the Holy Sepulcher** evoke the moving scenes of Jesus's final days.

ISRAEL: PEOPLE, RELIGION, AND STATE

One of the most fascinating aspects of Israel is not its rich history or its complex political situation, but its incredibly varied population. The 7.2 million people who live in this tiny country represent a startlingly wide array of ethnicities, nationalities, religious beliefs, and lifestyles. The diversity of Israel's population is one of the country's greatest strengths.

What comes with this, however, is often the struggle to define national identity, as people in Israel feel rooted in the Middle East, yet take pride in their Western values. Diversity may also help explain why 60 years has not been enough time to work out the conflicting needs and desires of different groups.

Creating a Nation

Israel's founding generation saw the country as a modern reincarnation of the ancient Jewish nation-state. Israel was the "Promised Land" of Abraham and Moses, the Israelite kingdom of David and Solomon, and the home of Jesus of Nazareth and the Jewish Talmudic sages. Although the Jewish presence in the country has been unbroken for more than 3,000 years, several massive exiles—first by the Babylonians in 586 BC and then by the Romans in AD 70—created a diaspora, a dispersion of the Jewish people throughout the world. The sense of historical roots still resonates for many, probably most, Jewish Israelis; and bringing their brethren home has been a national priority from the beginning.

The attachment to the ancient homeland, and a yearning for the restoration of "Zion and Jerusalem," weaves through the entire fabric of Jewish history and religious tradition. Over the centuries, many Jews trickled back to Eretz Yisrael (the Land of Israel) while others looked

forward to fulfilling their dream of return in some future—many felt imminent—messianic age. Not all were prepared to wait for divine intervention, however, and in the late 19th century, a variety of Jewish nationalist organizations emerged, bent on creating a home for their people in Israel (then Palestine). Zionism was founded as a political movement to give structure and impetus to that idea.

Some early Zionist leaders, like founding father Theodor Herzl, believed that the urgent priority was simply a Jewish haven safe from persecution, wherever that haven might be. Argentina was suggested, and Great Britain offered Uganda. In light of Jewish historical and emotional links to the land of Israel, most Zionists rejected these "territorialist" proposals.

The establishment of the State of Israel did not, of course, meet with universal rejoicing. To the Arab world, it was anathema, an alien implant in a Muslim Middle East. Palestinian Arabs today mark Israel's independence as the *Nakba*, the Catastrophe, when their own national aspirations were thwarted. To many ultra-Orthodox Jews, the founding of Israel was an arrogant preempting of God's divine plan; and to make matters worse, the new state was blatantly secular, despite its concessions to religious interests. This internal battle over the character of the Jewish state, and the implacable hostility of Israel's neighbors—which has resulted in more than half a century of almost constant conflict—have been the two main issues engaging the country since its birth.

The Israeli People

Roughly 5.4 million of Israel's citizens—a little more than 75%—are Jewish. Some trace their family roots back many generations on local soil; others are first- to

fourth-generation *olim* (immigrants) from dozens of different countries. The first modern pioneers arrived from Russia in 1882, purchased land, and set about developing it with romantic zeal. A decade or two later, inspired by the socialist ideas then current in Eastern Europe, a much larger wave founded the first *kibbutzim*— collective villages or communes. In time, these fiercely idealistic farmers became something of a moral elite, having little financial power but providing a greatly disproportionate percentage of the country's political leadership, military officer cadre, and intelligentsia. "We are workers," they liked to say, "but not working-class!"

Individual kibbutz members may still wield some influence in one area or another, and the movement as a whole is still a factor in the Israeli economy, but the ideology has pretty much run out of steam. A more personally ambitious younger generation has increasingly eschewed the communal lifestyle in favor of the lures of the big city; and in almost all the hundreds of kibbutzim across the country, modern economic realities have undermined the old socialist structure, and some degree of privatization is the order of the day.

The State of Israel was founded in 1948, just three years after the end of World War II, in which the Nazis annihilated fully two-thirds of European Jewry in the Holocaust. In light of the urgency of providing a haven for remnants of those shattered communities, the Law of Return was passed in 1949 granting any Jew the automatic right to Israeli citizenship.

Most of the immigrants before Israel's independence in 1948 were Ashkenazi Jews (those of Central or Eastern European descent), but the biggest wave in the first decade of statehood came when Sephardic Jews immigrated from the Arab lands of North Africa and the Middle East. From the 1940s through the 1960s, almost one million Jews were exiled from, fled, or left Morocco, Algeria, Libya, Egypt, Syria, Lebanon, Iran, Iraq, Yemen, and other countries in the region. Israel's Jewish population—600,000 at the time of its independence—doubled within 3 ½ years and tripled within 10.

In the 1990s, a wave of about 700,000 thousand Jews moved to Israel from the former Soviet Union, bringing a huge Russian influence. Around the same time, most of the Jews from Ethiopia, almost 22,000 people, also immigrated to Israel—often on foot.

The vast majority of Israel's 1.5 million Arabic-speaking citizens are Muslims (among them about 100,000 Bedouin), followed by about 100,000 Christian Arabs, and a similar number of Druze (a separate religious group). Most Israeli Arabs live in metropolitan Jerusalem, Haifa, or the Galilee. The extent to which they are integrated with Israeli Jews depends largely on location. In Haifa, for example, there is little tension between the two ethnic groups, whereas in Jerusalem the situation is more fraught. All Israeli Arabs are equal under the law, and vote for and may serve in the *Knesset*, the Israeli parliament. (Not included are the 2.5–3 million Palestinian Arabs of the partly autonomous West Bank and the completely autonomous Gaza who are not Israeli citizens.)

What may not be equal are the social and economic gaps that exist between the Arab and Jewish sectors. Arab complaints of government neglect and unequal allocation of resources have sometimes spilled into angry street demonstrations and other

ISRAEL: PEOPLE, RELIGION, AND STATE

anti-establishment activity. Although the Muslims in Israel, mainstream Sunnis, are regarded as both politically and religiously moderate by the standards of the region, there has been considerable radicalization in recent years of the community's youth, who identify politically with the Palestinian liberation movement and/or religiously with the Islamic revival that has swept the Middle East.

Of the Christian Arabs, most belong to the Greek Catholic, Greek Orthodox, or Roman Catholic church; a handful of Eastern denominations and a few tiny Protestant groups account for the rest. The Western Christian community is minuscule, consisting mainly of clergy, and temporary sojourners such as diplomats and foreign professionals on assignment.

The Druze, though Arabic-speaking, follow a separate and secret religion that broke from Islam about 1,000 years ago. Larger kindred communities exist in long-hostile Syria and Lebanon, but Israeli Druze have solidly identified with Israel, and the community's young men are routinely drafted into the Israeli army. The Arab community itself is not liable for military service, in order to avoid the risk of battlefield confrontations with kinsmen from neighboring countries.

Judaism in Israel

The myth that Israelis are overwhelmingly fundamentalist could not be less true. In surveys, the majority of Israeli Jews call themselves secular; many are atheist or agnostic. A third identify themselves as "traditional," which often means that they observe Jewish customs to some extent, either as a nod to Jewish heritage or out of a sense of family duty.

Only about 15 percent of the country's Jews are "religious." They share certain beliefs,

such as the divine origin of the Torah (Five Books of Moses) and the obligatory nature of rabbinic laws. They also share certain lifestyle choices, such as refraining from driving on the Sabbath, and strict adherence to kosher dietary laws.

Of religious Israelis, there are those who consider themselves either "nationally religious," or "haredi." The haredim—ultra-Orthodox—are easily recognized by the men's black hats and suits, or the Chassidic garb of black robes and, sometimes, white knee socks. The haredi community, though relatively significant in numbers, is fairly marginalized in Israeli society, partly because they do not typically pursue university studies (choosing instead, often, to study full-time in Talmudic academies throughout their lives) and partly because they do not usually serve in the army.

The nationally religious population, in contrast, is extremely patriotic and considers army service as a sacred undertaking. They are likely to attend college and to work in business environments with secular Israelis. Nationally religious men can be recognized by their crocheted *kippot* (skullcaps), which often also signal, through their size and colors, the wearer's political orientation. A woman who is wearing a headscarf, knee-length skirt, and sandals (as opposed to closed-toed shoes) probably considers herself nationally religious, not haredi. Ultra-Orthodox married women are even more modestly dressed, covering their knees and elbows, and often wear wigs to cover their hair.

Israeli Government

There is no firm separation of religion and state in Israel. Matters of personal status—marriage, divorce, adoption, and burial—are the preserve of the religious

authorities of the community concerned. For this reason there is no civil marriage; if one partner does not convert to the faith of the other, the couple must marry abroad. Within the Jewish community, such functions fall under the supervision of the Orthodox chief rabbinate, much to the dismay of members of the tiny but growing Conservative and Reform movements (many of whom are American expatriates) and of the large number of nonobservant Jews.

The confrontation between secular Israelis and the hard-line ultra-Orthodox has escalated over the years, as the religious community tries to impose on what it considers an apostate citizenry its vision of how a Jewish state should behave. One volatile issue is the Orthodox contention that only someone who meets the Orthodox definition of a Jew (either born of a Jewish mother or converted by strict Orthodox procedures) should be eligible for Israeli citizenship under the Law of Return. Disagreements about public observance of the Sabbath and of dietary laws are old sources of tension as well. For many nonreligious Israelis, already irked by what they consider religious coercion, the fact that most ultra-Orthodox Jewish men avoid military service on the grounds of continuing religious studies just rubs salt in the wound.

Israel prides itself on being the only true democracy in the Middle East, and it sometimes seems bent on politically tearing itself apart in the democratic process. This is how the system works (or doesn't): once every four years, prior to national elections, every party publishes a list of its candidates for the 120-member Knesset. There are no constituencies or voting districts; each party that breaks the minimum threshold of 2% of the national vote gets in, winning the same percentage of Knesset seats as its proportion of nationwide votes (hence the term "proportional representation").

The good news is that the system is intensely democratic. A relatively small grouping of like-minded voters countrywide (currently about 60,000) can elect an M.K. (Member of the Knesset) to represent its views. The largest party able to gain a parliamentary majority through a coalition with other parties forms the government, and its leader becomes the prime minister. The bad news is that the system spawns a smattering of small parties, whose collective support the government needs in order to rule. Since no party has ever won enough seats to rule alone, Israeli governments have always been based on compromise, with small parties exerting a degree of political influence often quite out of proportion to their actual size. Attempts to change the system have been doomed to failure, because the small parties, which stand to lose if the system is changed, are precisely those on whose support the current government depends.

ISRAEL'S TOP EXPERIENCES

Shopping in the Souk

A walk through one of Israel's souks (markets) may occasionally feel like a contact sport, but this is hands-down the best way to experience real commerce that combines authentic Middle Eastern–style salesmanship with top-quality products. Fragrant spices, dried fruits, nuts, produce, cheeses, and meats are sold from the bastot (stalls) crowded one up against the other, and it's truly a feast for every sense.

Floating in the Dead Sea

Named for the fact that no living thing can survive in its salty brew, the Dead Sea has become a mecca for those who believe its mineral-rich compounds can cure virtually any ailment.

The sodium content of the water makes humans extra buoyant, and you'll find the young and old, healthy and infirm, floating serenely on what appear to be invisible rafts, often reading newspapers.

Eating Israeli Breakfast

The traditional Israeli breakfast is served at most hotels. Vast buffets typically include bowls of salads, platters of cheeses, piles of fresh fruit, breads and baked goods, smoked fish, made-to-order eggs, cereals, juices, and pancakes (locals pour on chocolate sauce). Country lodgings such as B&B's offer homemade versions, and city coffee houses specialize in the Israeli breakfast, accompanied by croissants and cappuccino with the daily paper, often served 'til 1 PM

Exploring Tel Aviv's Old Neighborhoods

From Old Jaffa's dramatic port and flea market to the winding streets and cobblestoned charm of Neveh Tzedek, Tel Aviv's old neighborhoods—situated largely in the south—tell the tale of the development of a modern city that celebrated its 100th anniversary in 2009. Now gentrifying after years of neglect, these storied streets offer an unmatched fusion of architectural preservation and modern progress, dotted with some of the city's best ethnic cuisine—and some of its most thrilling nightspots.

Touring a Winery

Israeli grape-growing and wine production can be traced to biblical times, and there's no better way to sample the country's vintages than tour its wineries, from large operations with dozens of varieties to boutique, limited-production establishments. Hit the road with a map and a sense of adventure, but note that reservations need to be made for tours and tastings at all but the largest wineries.

Checking out the Beach Scene in Eilat

The bikinis, the Speedos, the sarongs, the sunglasses—it's the Riviera with local flair. Eilat is a respite for on-the-go Israelis who love nothing more than to spend a few days sucking on popsicles, eating chips (french fries), and dipping into the Red Sea—all set to the *plonk-plonk* soundtrack of matkot, the Israeli paddleball game which may as well be a national sport.

Taking a Side Trip to Petra

This ancient Nabatean city, now a UNESCO World Heritage site, is just across the Jordanian border. Hop on a donkey to begin your journey traversing through narrow canyons, and prepare to be amazed at the magnificent, age-old architectural facades carved right into the gorgeous red-stone rocks.

WHERE TO STAY IN ISRAEL

Israel has plenty of hotels belonging to major international hotel chains and smaller national networks, as well as independently run lodgings. Options such as kibbutz guest houses and bed-and-breakfasts offer a glimpse into local life.

Keep in mind that there is no official hotel rating system.

Apartment and House Rentals

Short-term rentals are popular, particularly in Jerusalem and Tel Aviv. Options range from basic studios to mansions, and most are privately owned.

Agents give you the biggest selection, but it's also possible to find accommodations through listing services.

Good Morning Jerusalem (☎02/623–3459 ⊕ www.accommodation.co.il). **Israel Holiday Apartments** (☎09/772–7163 ⊕ www.holiday apartments.co.il).**Kleiman Real Estate**(☎052/238– 0638 ⊕ www.kleimanrealestate.com).

Bed-and-Breakfasts

Over the past decade, dozens of *zimmers* (B&Bs) have sprung up, especially in the Galilee and the Golan. These are intimate cabins, usually featuring one or two bedrooms, a kitchenette, a hot tub, and an outdoor lounging area. Prices are not necessarily lower than hotels, but if it's peace and quiet you're after, these may be just the thing.

Many of Israel's *kibbutzim* (communal settlements) have opened B&Bs. Private-home owners are also increasingly opening their doors to guests.

Contacts Bed and Breakfast in Israel (⊕ www.b-and-b.co.il). **Home Accommodation Association of Jerusalem** (☎02/645–2198 ⊕ www.bnb.co.il).

Camping

Campgrounds in Israel are more rustic than in the United States. They're known as *khenonyanei layla* (night parking) and may be found in national parks everywhere around the country except for the central region around Tel Aviv.

It's illegal to set up camp outside of parks, but despite this, Israelis like to camp on the beaches. Camping on the shores of the Sea of Galilee is ideal in late spring and fall.

Christian Hospices

Christian hospices (meaning hostelries, not facilities for the ill) provide lodging and sometimes meals; these are mainly in Jerusalem and the Galilee.

Some hospices are real bargains, while others are merely reasonable; facilities range from spare to luxurious. They give preference to pilgrimage groups, but almost all will accept secular travelers when space is available. A full list of hospices is available from the Israel Government Tourist Office.

Kibbutz Guest Houses

Kibbutz guest houses, popular in Israel for years, are similar to motels; guests are taken in as a source of extra income for the kibbutz and are not involved in its social life (with the possible exception of having meals in the communal dining room).

Unlike motels, though, most kibbutz lodgings offer rustic settings. Most kibbutzim have large lawns, swimming pools, and athletic facilities. Some offer lectures and tours of the settlement.

Contacts Kibbutz Hotels Chain (☎03/527– 8085 ⊕ www.kibbutz.co.il).

ISRAELI CUISINE

Most Israelis divide the day into at least six excuses to eat. There's breakfast, a 10 AM snack, a quick lunch, a 5 PM coffee break (around the time that the Western world is calling for a cocktail), a full dinner, and a snack before bed, just for good measure.

A good number of Israel's restaurants are kosher, and conform to Jewish dietary laws. Essentially, kosher restaurants do not serve food that mixes milk and meat. Fish can be served with either, although note that shellfish is not kosher. Some restaurants that identify themselves as kosher may not be open on the Jewish Sabbath. The majority of hotels countrywide serve kosher food. Bon appétite, or *betayavon*!

Israeli Breakfast

The classic "Israeli Breakfast" is legendary; but these days you will mostly find it at hotels, B&Bs, and cafés across the country. Hotel buffets will include bowls of brightly-colored "Israeli" salads, platters of cheeses, piles of fresh fruit, granola, hot and cold cereals, baskets of various breads and baked goods ranging from cinnamon or chocolate twists to quiche, smoked fish, fresh fruit juices, made-to-order eggs (*betza ayin*, or "egg-like-an-eye," means a fried egg), and pancakes (locals pour on chocolate sauce). Country lodgings such as B&Bs offer homemade versions and city coffee houses specialize in the Israeli breakfast, accompanied by croissants and cappuccino with the daily paper, often served until 1 PM.

The Essential Cup of Coffee

Gone are the days when the only coffee available was a tiny cup of *botz*, or mud. You can have that too (ask for "café Turki") but you can also have a usually robust and flavorful cappuccino (known as *hafuch*, or upside-down); an "Americano" should you be homesick; espresso; and in the summer, iced coffee or barad, a slushy iced coffee made with crushed ice. Soy milk is often available, as is decaf (*natoul* in Hebrew). In the Old City of Jerusalem, espresso is made with the addition of a pinch of cardamom, or *hel*.

Israeli Salad

There are several different kinds of chopped salads in Israel, but there's one classic, and there's no question that this is a trademark dish. Its origins probably lie with Arab cuisine; basically it's a combination of fresh cucumbers, tomatoes, and onion but the secret's in the chopping— each ingredient must be chopped small and evenly. Cooks who fly in the face of tradition might add chopped parsley and mint, or bits of chopped lemon. Then the salad is dashed with quality olive oil and fresh lemon juice and a sprinkle of salt and pepper. It can be eaten on its own with white cheese and bread before work, spooned into a pita with falafel and hummus any time of day, and accompanying the main dish at most every meal.

Grilled Meats and Steaks

Virtually every town has at least one Middle Eastern grill restaurant, where you can find kebab, skewered grilled chicken, lamb, beef, mixed grill or spit-grilled shawarma, generally prepared with turkey seasoned with lamb fat, cumin, coriander, and other spices.

If you want a good steak, don't worry: order entrecote and see for yourself. Hard to believe, but true, you can even get a good hamburger these days. In Jerusalem, around the open fruit and vegetable market, are grilled-meat eateries famous for their chicken and beef on skewers, called *shipudim*. A gourmet treat to be found in

these basic restaurants is a skewer of melt-in-the-mouth duck or goose liver.

Seafood

There are fish restaurants all over the country, but locals say the best ones are in cities and towns that border the Mediterranean (like Tel Aviv, Jaffa, Ashdod, Haifa, and Akko), around the Kinneret (Sea of Galilee), and in Eilat.

Salatim

The world *salat* in Hebrew means salad. But many small dishes, served cold, as an appetizer, are called salatim. It's basically a mezze. In less fancy restaurants, and often in fish and grilled-meat places, these are slung onto the table along with a basket of pita before you've managed to get comfortable. Dig into selections such as two or three types of eggplant, hot Turkish condiments in red or green, tehini hummus, fish roe, fried cauliflower, pickled vegetables, and cracked-wheat salad (tabbouleh), but leave room for the main course, too.

Cheeses

Holyland cows are hard at work providing milk for cheeses, and these top the list, closely followed by goat and sheep milk cheese and, last but not least, the healthy buffalo cheese—mostly mozzarella. Soft white cheeses reign supreme and are to be found in cheese shops, supermarkets, outdoor produce markets and on hotel breakfast buffet tables.

An Israeli favorite is "gvina levana", simply a spreadable white cheese, perhaps topped with a slice of ripe tomato or strawberry jam. A few famous cheeses: "Bulgarit" (goat), on the salty side; "Brinza" (half goat, half sheep), more crumbly; "Tzfatit", originally made in the northern city of Tzfat, not too salty; the ubiquitous goat cheese, feta; and "Tom" (goat), a harder, zingy white cheese.

Wines

There's a surfeit of choice when it comes to excellent wine in Israel, made from all the major international grape varieties in five main wine regions from north to south. Waitstaff in restaurants know what they're talking about (high-end dining places have sommeliers) and can help you make a choice that will complement your sandwich or your steak. Reds are especially delicious. You can easily spend a day or two visiting the multitude of boutique (and large, old established) wineries in Israel. *For more information, see the Wines of Israel feature in Chapter 5.*

World Cuisine

The last decade or so has brought fusion cuisines to Israel—a superb blend of local flavors and ingredients with French-Italian-Asian or Californian influences—uniquely designed by young Israeli chefs, many of whom have studied abroad.

Although gourmet restaurants dot the Galilee, Golan, Jerusalem, and other parts of the country, it's definitely worth saving up to eat at one of Tel Aviv's top establishments. These restaurants are most often pricey. The locals also adore sushi, and Japanese restaurants and fast-food sushi joints abound. If you like to poke around, try some home-cooked ethnic foods—like Moroccan, Persian, Bucharian, or Tripolitan (Libyan) fare, generally served in inexpensive "workers" restaurants off the beaten track and mostly open just for lunch.

ISRAEL WITH KIDS

It's not hard to keep the kids busy in Israel. Let them expend energy exploring Crusader castles, caves in nature reserves, or climbing man-made climbing walls. For fun on the water, try rafting on the Jordan River or, for a mellower outing, pedal-boating in Yarkon Park in Tel Aviv. And then there are the beaches, of course.

Check the Friday papers' entertainment guides (they have a children's section) for up-to-date information.

Eating Out

Restaurants are almost always happy to accommodate those seeking super-simple fare, and fast food is both easily accessible and doesn't have to be junk. Kebabs; cheese or potato-filled pastries called bourekas; even baked potatoes with sauce are often available in cafés. Israeli kids, like their counterparts the world over, will rarely say no to a plate of spaghetti or french fries, so these are readily available too.

Nature

Israel's nature reserves and national parks (⊕*www.parks.org.il*) have plenty for the whole family to do. In the north, there's cycling around Hula Lake, or you can explore **Nimrod's Castle** or eagle-watch at ancient Gamla. In the Galilee, kayak or raft the cool waters of the Jordan River as you swish through one of the country's lushest areas. Still in the Galilee—or down south in the arid Negev desert—jeep tours will have you bouncing around some awesome landscapes. You can self-drive a 4x4 or book a tour with a driver.

In the south, check out Ein Gedi oasis or the wondrous **Masada**—Herod's mountain-top palace is a real treat and can be reached by foot along the steep Snake Trail (most people start the walk at sunrise) or via

the faster cable car. The trail is best for older kids.

Walking is a lively and easy activity to do anywhere. In Jerusalem, consider the **Ramparts Walk,** which offers views of the Old City as well as of Jerusalem beyond the city gates. Smaller kids can do part of it. In Tel Aviv, the **Tel Aviv Port** is great for coffee and a stroll—and even little kids can run freely while you enjoy iced drinks and the balmy weather.

Museums

A dirty word among kids? Maybe so, but the following museums might change some minds.

JERUSALEM

A walk through the ancient **City of David** near the Old City may be better than any museum or history lesson; it's not for the smallest kids, though, as at one point you wade through an ancient tunnel. In West Jerusalem, the **Israel Museum's Youth Wing** has outdoor play areas as well as exhibitions, often interactive, and a "recycling room" where children can use their creative energy freely.

TEL AVIV

The **Eretz Israel Museum** (⊕*www.eretz museum.org.il*) has a series of pavilions on its vast campus, each dedicated to a different theme, ranging from archeology to anthropology to Israel's cultural history and modern identity; it also has a planetarium—replete with moon rocks.

The **Azrieli Observatory** isn't a museum, but has lots to gaze at and analyze. Head to the 49th floor of the Azrieli Towers for a panoramic view of the whole city. On a clear day, it's possible to see the coastline stretching from Ashkelon in the south to Hadera in the north.

HAIFA

The **National Science Museum of Science and Technology (Technoda)**, the **Railway Museum**, and the **National Maritime Museum** are all geared to young and curious minds.

THE NEGEV

The **Israel Air Force Museum**, at the Hatzerim Air Force base (west of Beersheba), houses a huge collection of IAF airplanes and helicopters—Spitfires, Cobras, and more. There is no English Web site, but guided tours in English can be arranged (☎08/990–6855). This could be a stop on the way to or from Eilat.

At One with the Animals

In addition to the wonderful **Tisch Family Zoological Gardens** in Jerusalem, with its emphasis on fauna that feature in the Bible or that are native to Israel (⊕*www.jerusalemzoo.org.il*), the **Ramat Gan Safari** (; ⊕*www.safari.co.il*), near Tel Aviv, and the small but delightful **Haifa Educational Zoo**, there are numerous other options for time out with animals.

The **Jerusalem Bird Observatory** (⊕*www.jbo.org.il*), perched above the Knesset, offers "close encounters" with ringed birds, bird-watching tours, and other tidbits about bird life; night safaris are recommended.

In the Beit Shean Valley in the Galilee, **Gan Garoo Park** (☎04/648–8060) specializes in native Australian wildlife—kangaroos and wallabies, cockatoos, flying foxes, laughing kookaburras, cassowaries, and emus. It is even recognized by the Australian Wildlife Protection Authority.

Far from the Andes mountains, at the **Alpaca Farm** (⊕*www.alpaca.co.il*) near Mitzpe Ramon you can handfeed the critters as well as learn about the whole process of raising them and spinning their wool.

Horseback riding is an option pretty much throughout the country these days. In the Galilee, end a trail—of a few hours or a couple of days—with hot apple pie at **Vered Hagalil** or with a chunky steak at **Bat Yaar**, in the Biriya Forest near Tzfat (Safed). Down near **Eilat** you can even go camel riding.

Beaches

You're never too far from a beach in Israel—but check for a lifeguard at the one you choose before you slap on the sunscreen. This is a given at city beaches, but not at those off the beaten track. Considering it's such a tiny country, the range of different beach experiences is amazing, from the Mediterranean to the Red Sea, to the Sea of Galilee and even the super-salty Dead Sea, where you can float but not swim!

Etc.

The whole family will enjoy getting their hands dirty at **Dig for a Day** (⊕*www.archesem.com*)—a chance to dig, sift, dust, and discover what it's like to be part of an archeological excavation.

Off the Tel Aviv–Jerusalem highway at Latrun is **Mini Israel** (⊕*ww.minisrael.co.il*)—hundreds of exact replica models of the main sites around the country, historical, archeological, and modern. It's great for an all-of-Israel orientation.

In Eilat, venture out to the biblical theme park, **Kings City**, which comes replete with Pharaohs' palaces and temples, Solomon's mines, mazes, and optical illusions.

ISRAEL'S MARKETS

Israel's main markets are found in Jerusalem and Tel Aviv. As for bargaining—sure, give it a go, but these days it's a hard drive, so decide if you want to have fun playing the game, or not. The difference in price is likely to be less than you think.

JERUSALEM

The **Machaneh Yehuda Market** offers produce that is as colorful as it is flavorful. Recent additions to this collection of alleys running off the main market street include a sprinkling of boutiques and boutique cafés, and stalls selling clothes and rugs from India. The market, a tad cheaper than the supermarket, is a great place to grab some goodies while on the go or for the hotel room later. Think globally: start the fun with an Indian lassi (yogurt drink); ask the fishmongers to slice you a sliver of salmon sashimi; and try the French cheeses and hearty whole grain bread that are just an olive-pit's-throw away. Then you must—but must—end such a meal with a chunk of sweet sesame halva.

Weaving through the **Old City market** (the souk) will cast you even further back in time. Lavish rugs and fabrics, oriental ceramics, blown-glass items, not-so-antique antiques, beads, embroidered kaftans, and leather thongs line the stone alleyways that bring to life the Old and New Testaments. Almost all the "salespeople" here speak English but a quip or two thrown at them in Arabic or Hebrew will bring a wonderful smile—and perhaps a little discount. There's hummus and pickles, Arabic coffee and honey-dripping pastries to buy. Go to the Austrian Hospice (actually a guesthouse) on the Via Dolorosa for real Wiener schnitzel and apple strudel. Well-established stores can handle shipping of items.

TEL AVIV

The **Carmel Market**, or Shuk Hacarmel, begins, at its top end (Allenby Road), with stalls of clothes and housewares and then becomes the city's primary produce market, extending almost down to the sea. The scents are sensational—fresh greens (mint, parsley, basil), lemons and other citrus fruit, salty herring, and more. It can get packed in here—hold onto your belongings, though pick-pocketing is not usually a problem in Israel. The shuk borders the Yemenite Quarter, with a host of small eateries offering down-home cooking, Yemenite style, of course.

Primarily a crafts market, you'll find some true artisans at the **Nahalat Binyamin Market,** along with often unsung peddlers of imported goods. It's lively, with street performers sharing space with shoppers and strollers. Because it is only open on Tuesdays and Fridays, it gets pretty crowded—especially on Fridays and as holidays approach—though the vibe is always cheery. Nahalat Binyamin is a great place to pick up original and reasonably priced gifts.

The **Jaffa Flea Market** in Jaffa is another such shopping option. In the warren of small streets you can shop for—or just take in the view of—rugs, Mideast finjan coffee sets (with the tiny cups for that strong, strong coffee), clothes from India, jewelry, retro lamps, and other junk-mixed-with-bargains. Along with the stores and stalls, some of whose wares spill right out onto the sidewalk, are many small workshops—tinsmiths and carpenters, for example.

ISRAEL'S BEST BEACHES

Whether you'd like to take a dip, jog along the boardwalk at dawn or sunset, have a glass of wine or beer at a beachfront café, or just commune with nature, this little country's beaches have something to offer at the Mediterranean, the Red Sea, and the Dead Sea (known locally as "The Med, the Red, and the Dead"), and inland on the shores of Sea of Galilee.

The Med: City Beaches

All the major cities along the coastline like Akko, Haifa, Herzlia, and Tel Aviv have their own licensed beaches with lifeguards, locals, and varying amenities like showers, changing rooms, beachside cafés, restaurants, and sometimes even a boardwalk.

Tel Aviv's beaches are particularly colorful, with a popular boardwalk for children of all ages, and a diverse local and international crowd of singles and families. Along the way you'll find "Chinky" Beach (with a retro-hippie crowd), a gay beach (to the right of the Hilton hotel), and slightly farther north, a segregated beach for those of the religious persuasion with separate days for men and women. In summer, there are free movies, concerts, and meditation and yoga classes right on the beach.

The Red and the Dead

There are beaches and water sports galore in the Red Sea kissing the southernmost city of Eilat, but don't miss The Coral Beach Reserve, with a reef so close you can walk right in with your fins on and snorkel among more than 100 types of stony coral and 650 species of fish. The Dead Sea draws people from all over the world who luxuriate in its waters, hot springs, and black medicinal mud. It's shores—the lowest point of dry land on earth—are filled with hotels that offer spas and beach access. On the northern part of the Sea, there are five laid-back beaches—Biankini, Kalya, Neve Midbar, and Minerali—where you can swim and soak up the sun.

The Sea of Galilee

Placid and shimmering in the sunlight, the Sea of Galilee, or *Kinneret* in Hebrew, is Israel's only natural freshwater lake, and the backdrop for some of the most important sites in the New Testament. Scenery includes the Galilee's lovely mountains and foothills and a spectacular view of the Golan Heights in the distance. Beaches range from soft sand to rocky, many are camper-friendly, there are large water-parks at Gai Beach and Luna Gal, and beach concerts at Tzemach and Ein Gev.

Beach Basics

■ Sun in this region is stronger than in Europe and most of North America. Don't overdo exposure.

■ Don't leave valuables unattended on blankets, in lockers, or in your car.

■ Observe the flags at the lifeguard stations: white means bathing is safe, red means swim with caution, and black means bathing forbidden. Take them seriously.

■ Don't swim at beaches without lifeguards. There are seasons with dangerous undertows.

■ At some time during July and August there is a short jellyfish invasion. Stay out of the water.

■ The Israeli national beach game is called matkot—a kind of table tennis with bigger paddles but no table. Fervent players often usurp prime territory just at the shoreline and are oblivious to passersby, so duck to avoid getting hit with the ball!

ISRAEL AND THE PERFORMING ARTS

For such a small country, Israel has a wealth of cultural activity that reflects both the extraordinary diversity of its population and the fact that the state is just over 60 years old. Innovation and experimentation meld with traditional art forms, creating an exciting Israeli art scene in which classical western meets the new Middle East.

Apart from the top venues in Tel Aviv, Jerusalem, and Haifa, many towns in Israel have a performing arts center where you can catch flagship performers as well as up-and-coming local talent.

DANCE

The main venue for Israeli dance of all kinds is the beautiful **Suzanne Dellal Center for Dance and Theater** (⊕*www.suzanne dellal.org.il*), in Tel Aviv's historic Neveh Tzedek neighborhood.

All the other companies perform at Israel's large concert halls—check the calendar section of the Jerusalem Post or Haaretz newspaper for schedules.

For classical ballet, look for performances of Israel's veteran classical ballet company, the **Israel Ballet Company** (☎*03/ 604–6610*). The **Panov Ballet Theater Company** (☎*08/854–5180*) founded in 1998, features a repertoire of both classical and contemporary dance under the direction of former Kirov ballet star and company founder, Valery Panov.

If it's strictly modern dance you're looking for, try to catch the **Batsheva Dance Company** in Tel Aviv (☎*03/510–4037*)—one of Israel's most respected modern dance companies, founded by Martha Graham and Baroness Batsheva De Rothschild—or the **Kibbutz Contemporary Dance Company** (☎*09/954–0403*).

In Jerusalem, the **Vertigo Dance Company** (☎*02/624–4176*), based at the Gerard Behar Center, takes the audience into new and unexpected territory through their modern dance interpretations.

MUSIC

CLASSICAL AND OPERA

Israel's classical orchestras are world renowned and often host the best soloists and conductors from around the world. See if you can catch the **Israel Philharmonic Orchestra** (⊕*www.ipo.co.il*), directed by Zubin Mehta, during one of their many performances in Tel Aviv, Haifa, or Jerusalem.

The **Jerusalem Symphony** (⊕*www.jso. co.il*) under the direction of Leon Botstein appears regularly all over the country.

In Haifa it's the **Haifa Symphony Orchestra** (⊕*www.haifasymphony.co.il*) that brings classical music to the north, while music lovers in the center of the country can enjoy the **Israel Symphony Orchestra of Rishon Lezion** (⊕*www.isorchestra.co.il*), which also serves as the resident orchestra of the Israeli Opera.

The **Tel Aviv Performing Arts Center** (⊕*www. israel-opera.co.il*) is the place to enjoy the Israel Opera, which stages several series of classical operas and operettas throughout the season, which runs from November to July.

POPULAR MUSIC

Israeli popular music ranges from rock groups with an international following such as Hadag Hanachash to singers of modern Israeli ballads like Eviatar Banai, who are well known to locals only. Both will appear at places such as **The Lab** (HaMa'abada) (☎*02/629–2001*), in Jerusalem, or the **Goldstar Zappa Club** (☎*03/649–9550*), in Tel Aviv.

The best popular music festival of the year is the **Ein Gev Festival** in April on the shores of the Sea of Galilee (⊕*www.ein gev.com*).

JAZZ, ETHNIC, AND WORLD MUSIC

There are Israelis with origins in almost every country in the world, and ethnic music is an extremely important part of Israel's musical culture.

Jazz has grown in popularity over the past decade with an influx of accomplished immigrant musicians from Russia and America. Stars like the Idan Raichel Project with his Ethiopian influenced sound and the Yemenite flavored Zafa have put Israel on the world music map. Performances are at a variety of venues including **Jerusalem's Confederation House** (☏*02/642–5206*).

Every November Jerusalem hosts the **International Oud Festival** that highlights ensembles featuring music of the Middle Eastern lute (⊕*www.confederationhouse.org*).

For aficionados of vocal music, the village of Abu Ghosh just west of Jerusalem is the place to be in October and May when the beautiful local churches provide the best acoustics for the **Abu Ghosh Music Festival** (⊕*www.agfestival.co.il*).

THEATER

Theater in Israel is almost exclusively staged in Hebrew, with the exception of Tel Aviv's **Cameri Theater Company** (⊕*www.cameri.co.il*), which presents its most popular productions three times a week with screened simultaneous English translation.

The **Israel Festival** in Jerusalem is the place to take in an array of the best of the performing arts over two weeks in May. Both Israeli artists and performers from all over the world converge on the capital to showcase the best in music, dance, and theater (⊕*www.israel-festival.org.il*).

FILM

Israel has a sophisticated and thriving film industry with Israeli movies consistently being nominated for prestigious awards worldwide.

The best places to see the most interesting Israeli films are the **Cinematheques** in Tel Aviv, Haifa, Jerusalem, and Sderot (⊕*www.jer-cin.org.il*). Most Israeli films have English subtitles.

For real film buffs, plan your visit to Israel to coincide with the prestigious two-week-long **Jerusalem International Film Festival** that takes place in mid-July every year.

ISRAEL'S MAJOR HOLIDAYS

Time is figured in different ways in Israel. The Western Gregorian calendar—the solar year from January to December—is the basis of day-to-day life and commerce, but the school year, for example, which runs from September through June, follows the *Hebrew* lunar calendar. Jewish religious festivals are observed as national public holidays, when businesses and some museums are closed (on Yom Kippur, the Day of Atonement, *all* sites are closed).

The Muslim calendar is also lunar, but without the compensatory leap-year mechanism of its Hebrew counterpart. Muslim holidays thus drift through the seasons and can fall at any time of the year.

Even the Christian calendar is not uniform: Christmas in Bethlehem is celebrated on different days by the Roman Catholic ("Latin") community, the Greek Orthodox Church, and the Armenian Orthodox Church.

Major Jewish Holidays

The phrase "Not religious" in the text indicates that the holiday might be part of the religious tradition, but few or no public restrictions apply. On holy days, when the text indicates "Religious," most of the Sabbath restrictions apply.

Shabbat (Sabbath) The Day of Rest in Israel is Saturday, the Jewish Sabbath, which begins at sundown Friday and ends at nightfall Saturday. Torah-observant Jews do not cook, travel, answer the telephone, or use money or writing materials during the Shabbat, hence the Sabbath ban on photography at Jewish holy sites like the Western Wall. In Jerusalem, where religious influence is strong, the downtown area clears out on Friday after-

noon, and some religious neighborhoods are even closed to traffic.

Kosher restaurants close on the Sabbath, except for the main hotel restaurants, where some menu restrictions apply. In the Holy City itself, your dining choices are considerably reduced. Outside Jerusalem, however, you'll scarcely be affected; in fact, many restaurants do their best business of the week on the Sabbath because nonreligious Israelis take to the roads.

In Arab areas, such as East Jerusalem and Nazareth, Muslims take time off for the week's most important devotions at midday Friday, but the traveler will notice this much less than on Sunday, when most Christian shopkeepers in those towns close their doors. Saturday is market day, and these towns buzz with activity.

There is no public intercity transportation on the Sabbath, although the private *sherut* taxis drive between the main cities. Urban buses operate only in Nazareth and, on a reduced schedule, in Haifa. Shabbat is also the busiest day for nature reserves and national parks—indeed, anywhere the city folk can get away for a day. Keep this in mind if you fancy a long drive; the highways toward the main cities can be choked with returning weekend traffic on Saturday afternoon.

Rosh Hashanah (Jewish New Year) Sept. 19, 2009, Sept. 9, 2010 Yom Kippur and this two-day holiday are collectively known as the High Holy Days. Rosh Hashanah traditionally begins a 10-day period of introspection and repentance. Observant Jews attend relatively long synagogue services and eat festive meals, including apples and honey to symbolize the hoped-for sweetness of the new year. Nonobservant Jews

often use this holiday to picnic and go to the beach.

Yom Kippur (Day of Atonement) Sept. 28, 2009, Sept. 18, 2010. Yom Kippur is the most solemn day of the Jewish year. Observant Jews fast, wear white clothing, and avoid leather footwear. There are no radio and television broadcasts. All sites, entertainment venues, and most restaurants are closed. Much of the country comes to a halt, and in Jerusalem and other cities the roads are almost completely empty aside from emergency vehicles. It is considered a privilege to be invited to someone's house to "break fast" as the holiday ends, at nightfall.

Sukkoth (Feast of Tabernacles) Oct. 3, 2009, Sept. 23, 2010. First and last days religious. Jews build open-roof "huts" or shelters called *sukkot* (singular *sukkah*) on porches and in backyards to remember the makeshift lodgings of the biblical Israelites as they wandered in the desert. The more observant will eat as many of their meals as possible in their sukkah, and even sleep there for the duration of the holiday.

Simhat Torah Oct. 11, 2009, Oct. 1, 2010. The last day of Sukkoth, this holiday marks the end—and the immediate recommencement—of the annual cycle of the reading of the Torah, the Five Books of Moses. The evening and morning synagogue services are characterized by joyful singing and dancing (often in the street) as people carry the Torah scrolls.

Hanukkah Dec. 12, 2009, Dec. 2, 2010. Not religious. A Jewish rebellion in the 2nd century BC renewed Jewish control of Jerusalem. In the recleansed and rededicated Temple, the tradition tells, a vessel was found with enough oil to burn for a day. It miraculously burned for eight days,

hence the eight-day holiday marked by the lighting of an increasing number of candles (on a candelabrum called a *hanukkiah*) from night to night. Schools take a winter break. Shops, businesses, and services all remain open.

Purim Feb. 28, 2010, March 20, 2011. Not religious. Children dress up in costumes on the days leading up to Purim. In synagogues and on public television, devout Jews read the Scroll of Esther, the story of the valiant Jewish queen who prevented the massacre of her people in ancient Persia. On Purim day, it's customary to exchange gifts of prepared foods with neighbors and friends. Many towns hold street festivals.

Pesach (Passover) March 30, 2010, April 19, 2011. First and last days religious; dietary restrictions in force throughout. Passover is preceded by vigorous spring cleaning to remove all traces of leavened bread and related products from the household. During the seven-day holiday itself, no bread is sold in Jewish stores, and the crackerlike matzo replaces bread in most hotels and restaurants. On the first evening of the holiday, Jewish families gather to retell the ancient story of their people's exodus from Egyptian bondage and to eat a festive and highly symbolic meal called the seder (Hebrew for "order"). Hotels have communal seders, and the Ministry of Tourism can sometimes arrange for tourists to join Israeli families for Passover in their homes.

Yom Ha'atzma'ut (Independence Day) April 19, 2010, May 9, 2011. Not religious. Israel achieved independence in May 1948; the exact date of Yom Ha'atzma'ut follows the Hebrew calendar. Although there are gala events, fireworks displays, and military parades all over the country,

ISRAEL'S MAJOR HOLIDAYS

most Israelis go picnicking or swimming. Stores and a few tourist sites are closed, but public transportation runs.

Shavuot (Feast of Weeks) May 19, 2010, June 8, 2011. This holiday, seven weeks after Passover, marks the harvest of the first fruits and, according to tradition, the day on which Moses received the Torah ("the law") on Mt. Sinai. Many observant Jews stay up all night studying the Torah. It is customary to eat meatless meals with an emphasis on dairy products.

Christian Holidays

Easter April 4, 2010, April 24, 2011. This major festival celebrates the resurrection of Jesus. The nature and timing of its ceremonies and services are colorfully different in each Christian tradition represented in the Holy Land—Roman Catholic, Protestant, Greek Orthodox, Armenian Orthodox, Ethiopian, and so on. The dates above are for the Western Easters, which are the basis for public holidays, and are the dates observed by the Western churches—Roman Catholic and Protestant. Check the dates for different groups such as the Orthodox Armenian, Greek, and Russian churches, who base their holidays on the Julian calendar, converted to the Gregorian calendar now commonly in use.

Christmas Except in towns with a large indigenous Christian population, such as Nazareth and Bethlehem, Christmas is not a high-visibility holiday in Israel. The Christmas of the Catholic and Protestant traditions is, of course, celebrated on December 25, but the Greek Orthodox calendar observes it on January 7, and the Armenian Orthodox wait until January 19. Shuttle buses from Jerusalem run to Bethlehem's Manger Square on Christmas Eve (December 24) for the annual international choir assembly and the Roman Catholic midnight mass.

Muslim Holidays

Muslims observe Friday as their holy day, but it's accompanied by none of the restrictions and far less of the solemnity than those of the Jewish Shabbat and the Christian Sabbath (in their strictest forms). The noontime prayer on Friday is the most important of the week and is typically preceded by a sermon, often broadcast from the loudspeakers of the mosques.

The dates of Muslim holidays vary widely each year because of the lunar calendar.

Ramadan Aug. 22, 2009; Aug. 11, 2010. This month-long fast commemorates the month in which the Koran was first revealed to Muhammad. Devout Muslims must abstain from food, drink, tobacco, and sex during daylight hours; the conclusion of the period is then marked by the three-day festival of Id el-Fitr. The dates are affected by the sighting of the new moon and can change slightly at the very last moment. The Muslim holy sites on Jerusalem's Temple Mount (Haram esh-Sharif) offer only short morning visiting hours during this time and are closed to tourists during Id el-Fitr.

Eid al-Adha Nov. 27, 2009; Nov. 16, 2010. This festival commemorating Abraham's willingness to sacrifice his son marks the end of the annual Haj, or pilgrimage to Mecca. Muslim families throughout Israel celebrate Eid al-Adha by slaughtering a sheep or goat.

GREAT ITINERARIES

1

BEST OF ISRAEL, WITH THE NEGEV AND EILAT, 11–19 DAYS

Israel is a small but varied country. This itinerary lets you see the high points of Jerusalem and the northern half of the country; you can add the desert if you have the time and inclination.

Jerusalem, 3–4 days

You could spend a lifetime in Jerusalem, but 3 days is probably a good minimum to get a feel for the city and environs. First, spend a day getting an overview of the holy sites of Judaism, Christianity, and Islam by moving through the Jewish Quarter to the Western Wall, then seeing the mosques on the Temple Mount, the Via Dolorosa, and the Church of the Holy Sepulcher. Stop for a Middle Eastern–style lunch at one of the restaurants in the Old City's Jaffa Gate square.

On your second day, you can venture farther afield: many consider the Israel Museum and the Yad Vashem Holocaust Museum and Memorial essential if you're visiting Jerusalem, and Mt. Herzl National Memorial Park is also a pleasant excursion. (Note: the Israel Museum is closed Sunday; Yad Vashem and Mt. Herzl are closed Saturday.)

Your third day can be devoted to sites within an hour of Jerusalem: perhaps a wine tour in the Judean Hills. Or join a dig at Bet Guvrin–Maresha National Park with Archaeological Seminars—and on your way back, visit Mini Israel, with its hundreds of models of Israeli sites.

The 3 days suggested for Jerusalem are the bare minimum; a fourth day gives you time to relax and absorb the city—and shop.

The Dead Sea region, 2 days

After getting an early start in your rental car, head east through the stark Judean desert to Qumran, where the Dead Sea Scrolls were discovered. You can spend an hour or so touring the ruins and seeing the audiovisual presentation. About 45 minutes south of Qumran on the road parallel to the Dead Sea is Ein Gedi, where a leisurely hike to the waterfall and back should take about two hours. End the day with a float in the Dead Sea, and spend the night at one of Ein Gedi's fine hotels or at the Kibbutz Ein Gedi Guest House. A highlight for many are the spa treatments featuring the famously curative Dead Sea mud.

In the morning, hike the Snake Path—or take the cable car—up Masada. The gate to the path opens at first light so you can catch the sunrise on the way up. Later, head back to Jerusalem to spend a night on your way to the Galilee, stopping a few miles north of the Dead Sea–Jerusalem highway at the oasis town of Jericho, the world's oldest city. It's almost worth a trip through this lush city—adorned with date palms, orange groves, banana plantations, bougainvillea, and papaya trees—just to be able to say "I was there," but there are also some significant archaeological sites at Tel Jericho, where you can stop for baklava and orange juice. Jericho is in the Palestinian Authority, so check the daily newspaper for political conditions and use common sense.

The Galilee, 3 days

From Jerusalem, where you've spent the night, make an early start to allow time for all the sites on today's schedule. Take the Jordan Valley route (Route 90) to the Galilee so you can stop at the springs of Gan Hashelosha for a swim, then visit the

GREAT ITINERARIES

vast Roman-Byzantine ruins at Beit She'an, where you can have lunch in town or take a sandwich to the site. The Crusader castle of Belvoir will round out the day and then you can enjoy a lakeside fish dinner in Tiberias, where you'll spend the night.

The next day, spend an hour or two at the Dan Nature Reserve, with its rushing water and biblical archaeology. Spend the afternoon hiking, kayaking, or horseback riding at Bat Ya'ar (call ahead to reserve if you want to go trail riding), or kayak at Hagoshrim or Kfar Blum (no need to reserve). Overnight in Tiberias again, or better yet, farther north in a Hula Valley B&B.

On your third day, you can explore the treasures of Tzfat, with its beautiful vistas, old synagogues, and art and Judaica galleries. Depending on how you spend your day, you can also visit the Golan Heights Winery or do some hiking or bird-watching at Gamla. Overnight in Tiberias or at your Hula Valley B&B.

The Mediterranean Coast and Tel Aviv, 3 days

From Tiberias or your Hula Valley B&B, head west to the coast. Your first stop can be the cable car ride to the white caverns of Rosh Hanikra. Then travel to Akko, with its Crusader halls and picturesque harbors. This is also an excellent place for a fish lunch. Then drive to Haifa for a view from the top of Mt. Carmel from the Panorama. Spend the night in Haifa.

The next day, visit Haifa's Baha'i Shrine and its magnificent gardens, then continue down the coast to visit the city of Zichron Ya'akov and the Carmel Mizrachi Wine Cellars or the Bet Aaronson Museum. Have lunch and then head to Tel Aviv, stopping at the Roman ruins of Caesarea

on the way. In Tel Aviv, you can enjoy a night on the town.

On your third day, take in Tel Aviv's museums, shop, and enjoy a dip in the Mediterranean. From here you can head to the airport if it's time to go home. If you're proceeding on to the desert, spend another night in Tel Aviv and get an early start in the morning.

Add on: The Negev, 2 days

From Tel Aviv, head south toward Beersheva and Road 40. If you're doing this on a Thursday, leave early enough to get to the Beersheva Bedouin market, which is most colorful in the morning (Beersheva is about a two-hour drive from Tel Aviv). Driving south, stop at Sde Boker, where you can have lunch and see David Ben-Gurion's house and gravesite overlooking the biblical Wilderness of Zin. Near Sde Boker is Ein Avdat, a wilderness oasis that has a trail with stone steps and ladders leading up the magnificent white chalk canyon. Drive on to Mitzpe Ramon, on the edge of the immense Ramon Crater. Stop at the Israel Nature and Parks Authority visitor center, where you can find out the best places to hike, or how to see the sites by car. Spend the night here, then enjoy the natural wonders of the Ramon Crater the next day. Spend a second night here as well.

Eilat and environs, 2–5 days

Eilat is about a three-hour drive from Mitzpe Ramon. Drive south on Road 40 to where it joins Road 90 and continue south on the Arava Road, which runs along the border with Jordan. Stop at Timna Park for a hike and a view of Solomon's Pillars, and at the Hai Bar Nature Reserve, arriving in Eilat in the late afternoon. A minimum of 2 days here allows you to see all the highlights; 3 to 5 days

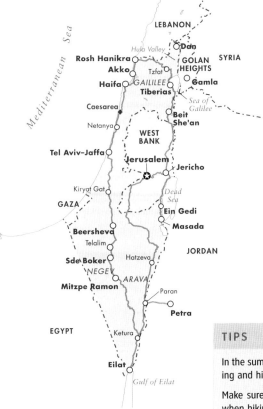

In the summer, plan to do most of your walking and hiking by midday to avoid the heat.

Make sure to take lots of water, and a hat, when hiking or walking.

Consider flying back to Tel Aviv from Eilat—or fly round-trip to Eilat if you don't have the time or inclination to drive.

Make your hotel/B&B reservations ahead of time, especially in summer and on weekends year-round, when hotels and B&B's are crowded with vacationing Israelis.

Most hotels in the Dead Sea area and Eilat have spas with a host of treatments; call ahead or book one when you arrive.

You won't need a rental car in the Old City of Jerusalem; navigating and parking can be a challenge, so save the rental car for trips out of town.

means you can have some serious beach or diving time, and take a side trip to Petra in Jordan. You'll probably want to pick one hotel in Eilat as a base.

The lunar-like red-rock canyons in the hills behind Eilat are great for hiking, and there are also plenty of options if you want to take to the water: you can snorkel, parasail, or arrange a boat trip to prime dive spots. To see Petra properly, plan on 2 full days, leaving Eilat early the first day and returning on the late afternoon of the second day. You can make the return drive from Eilat to Jerusalem via the Arava— leave yourself a full day to allow for stops along the way.

GREAT ITINERARIES

IN THE FOOTSTEPS OF JESUS, 6 DAYS

Visit the Holy Land, they say, and you'll never read the Bible the same way; the landscapes and shrines that you'll see, and your encounters with local members of Christian communities at the landmarks of Jesus' life, will have a profound and lasting impact.

Jerusalem and Bethlehem, 2 days

Spend your first day retracing the climax of the story of Jesus in Jerusalem, starting at the Mount of Olives. This is where Jesus taught, and wept over the city (Luke 19:41), and it is commemorated by the tear-shaped Dominus Flevit church. The walk down the Mount of Olives road, also known as the Palm Sunday road, leads to the ancient olive trees in the Garden of Gethsemane, where you can contemplate Jesus' arrest. Following the Via Dolorosa, walk the Stations of the Cross to the Church of the Holy Sepulcher, where most Christians believe Jesus was crucified, buried, and resurrected. The Garden Tomb—the site of Calvary for many Protestants—offers a spot of tranquillity. Take your time contemplating the sites; this will not be a rushed day.

The next day, you can explore the Southern Wall excavation's at the Jerusalem Archeological Park, adjacent to the Old City's Dung Gate. Scholars believe Jesus could have walked the stones of the ancient street here, and climbed the Southern Steps to the Temple—and if this is, as believed, the Gate Beautiful (Acts 3:10), Peter almost certainly did so. Down the hill in the City of David, excavations have revealed the steps of the pool of Siloam, where a blind man healed by Jesus washed (John 9:7–11). Add a visit to the Room of the Last Supper on Mt. Zion, up the hill from the Dung Gate, and then have lunch. In the afternoon, you can drive, political climate permitting (read the daily paper and use common sense), to Bethlehem, Jesus's birthplace, to visit the Church of the Nativity, one of the oldest churches in the world—or you can opt to stay in Jerusalem, checking out the Old Testament sites of the City of David, including Area G, Warren's Shaft, and Hezekiah's Tunnel. Bethlehem is in the Palestinian Authority, so bring your passport, and even if you have a car, it's best to take a taxi to the border crossing south of Jerusalem's Gilo neighborhood. The crossing for tourists is usually uncomplicated, and there are Palestinian taxis waiting on the other side to take you to the church.

On the way to the Galilee, 1 day

Making an early start, head east into the barren Judean Desert to Qumran, where the Dead Sea Scrolls were found. Some scholars believe John the Baptist may have passed through here, and a visit to the site—you can spend an hour here or longer—is an opportunity to learn about the desert in which Jesus (along with many Jews of that time) sought solitude, purity, and inspiration. Then head up the Jordan Valley (Route 90), passing through (depending on political conditions) or near Jericho, through which Jesus also passed when he healed a blind man (Mark 10:46) and had a meal with the tax collector Zaccheaus (Luke 19:1–5). If the security situation isn't favorable, the Israeli soldiers at the checkpoint at Jericho won't allow you in (again, read the newspaper and use common sense). If Jericho is a no-go or you decide to skip it, a detour allows you to bypass. In Jericho, though, a visit to Tel Jericho, the first conquest of the Israelites in the Holy Land (Joshua

6) is a must. You can have lunch at the restaurant next to the tell, or at a truck stop on the way north from Jericho. Then it's on to the ruins at Beit She'an, including the ancient main street, a bathhouse, and mosaics. Not only is this an important Old Testament site, it was also the capital of the Decapolis, the alliance of 10 Roman cities, among which Jesus taught and healed (Mark 7:31). Farther north, pilgrims go to Yardenit to be baptized in the Jordan River, to remember the baptism of Jesus in these waters. Spend the night in Tiberias.

Sea of Galilee, 1 day

Start the day heading north to the ancient wooden boat at Ginosar, which evokes Gospel descriptions of life on the lake—see, for example, Matthew 9:1. Then, after meditating on Jesus' famous sermon (Matthew 5) in the gardens of

the Mount of Beatitudes and its chapel (off Route 90 north of the Sea of Galilee), descend to Tabgha to see the mosaics of the Church of the Multiplication of Loaves and Fishes. From a lakeshore perch at the nearby Church of the Primacy of St. Peter, where Jesus appeared to the disciples after the resurrection (John 21), you can marvel at how Scripture and

GREAT ITINERARIES

landscape blend before your eyes. Farther east, the ruins of ancient Capernaum—the center of Jesus's local ministry—include a magnificent pillared synagogue and Peter's house. The massive ancient mound across the Jordan River, north of the Sea of Galilee, is believed to be Bethsaida, where the Gospels say Jesus healed and taught (Luke 9:10, 10:13)—to get there, continue east of Capernaum, cross the Jordan River north of the Sea of Galilee, turn left onto Route 888, and follow the signs to Bethsaida in the Jordan River Park. From there, head back down to the lake and continue to Kursi National Park and the ruins of an ancient church where Jesus cast out demons into a herd of pigs that stampeded into the water (Matthew 8:28–30). A good idea for lunch is the fish restaurant at Kibbutz Ein Gev, after which you can join a cruise across the lake and back (the kibbutz also has a boat company). Spend the night in Tiberias, or at one of the kibbutz guesthouses or B&Bs in the Hula Valley.

The Hula Valley and Banias (Caesarea Philippi), 1 day
The next day, drive through the Hula Valley; it's especially remarkable in the spring when the flowers bloom and bring alive Jesus's famed teaching from the Sermon on the Mount: "Consider the lilies of the field, how they grow" (Matthew 6:28). At the base of Mt. Hermon (which some scholars point to as an alternative identification for the site of the transfiguration, as described in Mark 9:2–8), northeast of the Hula Valley, is Banias (Caesarea Philippi), where Jesus asked the disciples, "Who do people say I am?" (Mark 8:27), and where the remains of Roman temples are a powerful backdrop for contemplation of that message. Dan, the capital of the biblical Northern Kingdom, has a beautiful nature reserve. Stay overnight at your B&B or kibbutz hotel in the Hula Valley.

The Galilee Hills and the Coast, 1 day
Head for the hills, connecting to Route 77 and turning south onto Route 754 to Cana to see the church that marks the site where Jesus changed water into wine (John 2:1–11), on your way to Nazareth, Jesus' childhood town. Here, the massive modern Church of the Annunciation houses depictions of Mary from around the world, and the city's spring, now in the Greek Orthodox church, is believed to be where the Angel Gabriel appeared to her (Luke 1:26–38). A drive through the lush Jezreel Valley, via Route 60 then north on Route 65 (the New Testament Valley of Armageddon), brings you to Mt. Tabor, long identified as the Mount of Transfiguration. The valley is named Armageddon (Revelation 16:16) after the archaeological site of Megiddo, now a national park south of Afula on Route 65, with many sights to see. The drive back to Jerusalem from Megiddo is about two and a half hours, or you can spend the night in Haifa and return to Jerusalem the next day.

ISRAEL
THROUGH THE AGES

Where else in the world can you find the living history of three major religions that have been intertwined for more than 1,000 years? Israel is the crossroads for Christianity, Islam, and Judaism, and many of the remarkable sites here help to tell this country's unique story. One of the best examples can be found in Jerusalem's Old City, where you can visit the Church of the Holy Sepulcher, the Dome of the Rock, and the Western Wall all within a short walk of one another.

(top left) The Bible—David playing the harp while bringing the Ark of the Covenant from Kirjath-Jearim with other musicians. (bottom) The goddess Asherah was worshipped by some in ancient Israel as the consort of El and in Judah as the consort of Yahweh (the Hebrews baked small cakes for her festival). (right) Artist's depiction of Solomon's court (Ingobertus, c. 880).

Prehistory

1.2 million BC

The land that Israel now occupies served as a land bridge for Homo Erectus on his epic journey out of Africa. The oldest human remains found outside that continent, 1.4 million years old, were unearthed at Ubediya near Lake Kinneret (Sea of Galilee). It was in the Carmel Caves in northern Israel that the only indication of direct contact between Neanderthal Man and Homo Sapiens, 40,000 years ago, has been found, lending credence to the theory that they lived contemporaneously.

■ Visit: Museum at Degania Alef (⇨Ch.6), Carmel Caves (⇨Ch.5)

Biblical Period

2000–1000 BC

The arrival of Abraham, Isaac, and Jacob marked the beginning of the Patriarchal Age, dated to around 1800 BC. The Israelite exodus from Egypt took place in the 13th century BC. It was at this time that Israel was divided into Canaanite city-kingdoms. As the Israelites established themselves in the hill country, the Philistines, originating in the Aegean, were landing on the coastal plain. In 1150, the Philistines invaded and established a league of five city-states. A place name deriving from their presence endures to this day—Palestine.

■ Visit: Valley of Ellah (⇨Ch.3)

United Monarchy

1000–928 BC

David conquered Jerusalem in 1000 BC, and united the Israelite tribes into one kingdom and established his capital here. David's son, Solomon, became king in 968 BC. In 950 BC, Solomon built the First Temple in Jerusalem and the city became the new religious center. Shortly after Solomon's death in 928 BC, the kingdom split in two—the northern tribes, which seceded and formed the Kingdom of Israel, and the southern tribes, now known as the Kingdom of Judah.

■ Visit: City of David (⇨Ch.2), Temple Mount (⇨Ch.2).

721 BC Assyrians conquer Israel	586 BC Babylonian rule	538 BC Cyrus the Great of Persia conquers Babylonia. Second Temple rebuilt	AD 26 Jesus's Galilean ministry takes place	AD 73 Romans destroy Second Temple. Masada falls
	600 BC	300 BC	0	AD 300

1

IN FOCUS ISRAEL THROUGH THE AGES

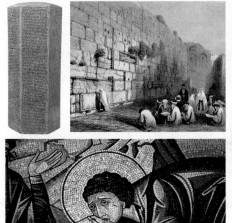

(top left) Hexagonal cylinder of King Sennacherib of Assyria inscribed with an account of his invasion of Palestine and the siege of Jerusalem in the reign of Hezekiah, King of Judah, dated 686 BC. (top center) 1860 engraving of the Western Wall. (top right) Masada. (bottom left) Fragment of the Church of the Holy Sepulcher, Jerusalem.

The Divided Kingdom

928–587 BC

After initial conflict, the Kingdom of Israel and the Kingdom of Judah lived in prosperity alongside each other. But in 721 BC, the Assyrian army, which at the time already dominated the region, conquered Israel and took its residents eastward into captivity. The fate of these "ten lost tribes" would be a subject of speculation by scholars thereafter. In 586 BC, the Assyrians were defeated by a new power, the Babylonians. Their king, Nebuchadnezzar, conquered Judah and destroyed Jerusalem and the temple. Those who survived were exiled to the "rivers of Babylon."

Second Temple Period

538 BC–AD 73

This exile ended after only 50 years when Cyrus the Great of Persia conquered Babylonia and permitted the exiles to return to Judah. Jerusalem was rebuilt and a new temple erected. The Persian Empire continued to gain strength until 333 BC, when it was defeated by Alexander the Great. Judah the Maccabee claimed victory over Hellenistic armies in 165 BC and rededicated the then-desecrated temple. Judean independence brought the Hasmonean dynasty in 142 BC, which the Romans put an end to in 63 BC when they annexed the country.

Jesus was born in Bethlehem, and 26 years later began his ministry, teaching mostly around the Sea of Galilee. In AD 29, Jesus and his disciples celebrated Passover in Jerusalem; he was arrested, put to trial, and crucified soon after.

In AD 66, the Jews rose up against Roman rule. Their fierce revolt failed and Jerusalem and the temple were destroyed in the process. A vestige of the temple compound, the Western Wall, is venerated by Jews to this day. In AD 73, the last Jewish stronghold, Masada, fell.

■ Visit: Sea of Galilee (⇨ Ch.6), Via Dolorosa (⇨ Ch.2), Masada (⇨ Ch.3).

(immediate left) Bar Kokhba's coin: top, the Jewish Temple facade with the rising star; reverse: A lulav, the text that reads: "to the freedom of Jerusalem." (top left) Saladin, commander of Muslim forces, battles Christians in the 3rd Crusade. (top right) Richard the Lionheart In battle during the Crusades.

Late Roman & Byzantine Period

AD 73–640

In 132, Roman emperor Hadrian threatened to rebuild Jerusalem as a pagan city and another Jewish revolt broke out, led by Bar-Kochba. In retribution, Hadrian leveled Jerusalem in 135 and changed the name of the country to Syria Palestina. Most of the remaining Jews went into exile for the next two millennia.

It wasn't until the 4th century AD that the Roman emperor Constantine made Christianity the imperial religion. This revived life in the Holy Land, making it a focus of pilgrimage and church construction that included the present Church of the Nativity in Bethlehem. In spite of persecution, a vibrant Jewish community still existed.

Muhammad's *hejira* (flight) from Mecca to Medina in Arabia took place in 622, marking the beginning of Islam. This became Year One on the Muslim calendar. When Muhammad died in 632, his followers burst out of Arabia and created a Muslim empire that within a century would extend from India to Spain.

■ Visit: Jerusalem's Cardo (⇨ Ch.2); Caesarea (⇨ Ch.5)

Medieval Period

640–1516

The Dome of the Rock was constructed in Jerusalem in 691 by Caliph Abd al-Malik. In 1099, the Crusaders conquered the city and massacred Jews and Muslims living there. Akko (also called Acre) and Belvoir, in the Lower Galilee, were built around 1100. Muslim reconquest of the land under the Mamluks began in 1265. Finally in 1291, Akko fell marking the end of the Crusades. An outstanding period of architecture followed, especially in Jerusalem's Temple Mount (Haram esh-Sharif) and in the Muslim Quarter.

■ Visit: Dome of the Rock (⇨ Ch.2); Aqsa Mosque (⇨ Ch.2)

1265 Muslim reconquest begins	Akko falls in 1291, marking the end of the Crusader kingdom	1516 Mamlucks defeated in Syria by the Ottoman Turks	1897 First World Zionist Conference
1300	**1500**	**1700**	**1900**

1

IN FOCUS ISRAEL THROUGH THE AGES

(top left) Jewish settlers known as Biluim, in Palestine, 1880s. The 38th Zionist congress, 1933. (bottom right) *Palestine Post* headline announcing declaration of independence in 1948.

Modern Period

1516–1917

In 1516, the Mamluks were defeated in Syria by the Ottoman Turks. Egyptian nationalists took control of Israel in 1832, but were expelled in 1840 with help from European nations. The country's population shifted in the 19th century, when the steamship made access easy.

The first World Zionist Conference, organized by Theodor Herzl, took place in 1897, fueling the idea of a Jewish homeland. In 1909, Tel Aviv was founded, and Degania, the first kibbutz, was established on the southern shore of the Sea of Galilee.

■ Visit: Akko (⇨ Ch. 5); Walls of Jerusalem (⇨ Ch. 2)

Creation of a Jewish State

1917–1948

The conquest of Palestine by the British in the First World War ushered in many critical changes. In 1917, the British government expressed support in the Balfour Declaration for creation of a Jewish homeland. Arab nationalism began to rise around 1920 in the post-Ottoman Middle East after Ottoman Turkey, which sided with Germany during the first World War, abandoned Palestine. This marked the point at which tension between Jews and Arabs began to increase, peaking in the massacre of Jews in 1920, 1929, and again in 1936. Various Jewish militias formed to counter the violence.

In view of growing clashes between Arabs and Jews, a British commission in 1937 recommended partitioning the land into two states, and in 1939 Britain issued a "White Paper" restricting Jewish immigration and purchase of land in Palestine. With the end of the British mandate in May 1948, David Ben-Gurion, the Palestinian Jewish leader who would later become Israel's first prime minister, declared Israel a Jewish state. Immediately thereafter, Israel survived invasions by the armies of seven Arab countries.

■ Visit: Tel Hai (⇨ Ch. 7), Independence Hall, Tel Aviv (⇨ Ch. 4), Jordan Valley Kibbutzim (⇨ Ch. 5)

(left) David Ben-Gurion in 1918. (top right) Knesset, Israeli parliament, Jerusalem. (bottom right) Israeli flag.

The First 50 Years

1948–1998

Fighting ended January, 1949, and a U.N.-supervised cease-fire agreement was signed. Transjordan annexed the West Bank and East Jerusalem; Egypt annexed the Gaza Strip. Palestinian Arabs who fled or were expelled were housed in neighboring countries; those who stayed became citizens. The first elections to the Knesset took place, and David Ben-Gurion was elected prime minister. In 1950, the Knesset enacted the Law of Return, giving any Jew the right to Israeli citizenship.

Around 1964, the Palestine Liberation Organization (PLO) was founded, which sought an independent state for Palestinians and refused to recognize Israel as a state. In 1967, the Six-Day War broke out; Israel occupied territory including the Golan Heights. A coalition of Arab states attacked Israel on Yom Kippur in 1973. The Lebanon War in 1982 met with unprecedented Israeli opposition. In 1987, the *intifada* (uprising) brought sustained Palestinian Arab unrest. The Oslo Accords, completed in 1994, mutually recognized Israel and the PLO, as well as Palestinian autonomy in the Gaza Strip.

Israel Today

1998–Present

After Ehud Barak was elected prime minister in 1999, Israel withdrew from Lebanon. The second *intifada* began in 2001 and subsided in 2005, costing more than 3,000 Israeli and Palestinian lives. Current concern is the rise of Hamas, which unexpectedly celebrated a landslide victory in Palestinian elections in January, 2006. Shortly thereafter, the kidnapping of two Israeli soldiers by Hezbollah sparked a 34-day war. Hezbollah's increasing power as well as peace with Lebanon remain difficult issues Israel faces. Despite all this, however, Israel continues to enjoy a strong economy and healthy tourism.

Jerusalem

WORD OF MOUTH

"My family was visiting Israel with a group of other families, and as our tour guide was explaining the amazing history of the Church of the Holy Sepulcher, this little boy separated himself and silently went and lit a candle, symbolizing a prayer, all by himself."

—photo by nicole_pappas, Fodors.com member

WELCOME TO JERUSALEM

TOP REASONS TO GO

★ **The Old City:** For an astonishing montage of religions and cultures, the heart of Jerusalem—with the Holy Sepulcher, Arab bazaar, and Western Wall—has few equals anywhere in the world.

★ **City of David:** Here you can plunge underground to explore Jerusalem's most ancient remains, and wade the 2,700-year-old water tunnel that once saved the besieged city.

★ **Mt. of Olives:** This classic panorama puts the entire Old City, with the golden Dome of the Rock, squarely within your lens. The view is best with the morning sun behind you.

★ **Machaneh Yehuda:** You can munch a falafel as you watch shoppers swirl and eddy through West Jerusalem's outstanding produce market.

★ **Israel Museum:** The museum is still a winner, with its Dead Sea Scrolls; its stunning collection of art, archaeology, and ethnography should be top of your list when other sections reopen after massive renewal in mid-2010.

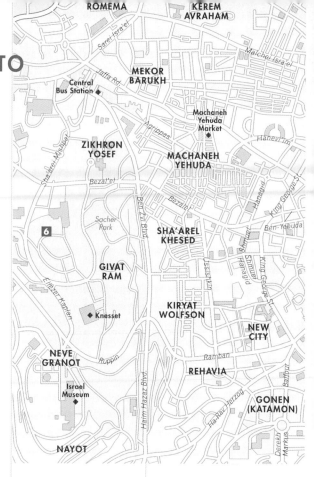

1 Old City Classic Sights. The walled Old City, with its narrow streets, is what Jerusalem is all about. It is a labyrinth of memories, a bewitching flicker-show of colors and cultures, best epitomized by the souk, or bazaar. But it is also the Holy Sepulcher, the Western Wall, and the Dome of the Rock, redolent with religion and seething with history.

2 Jewish Quarter. Excavations in the 1970s unearthed a handful of interesting ancient sites (notably the Herodian Quarter), now integrated into this reconstructed neighborhood in the Old City. Good stores and lots of eateries complete the picture.

3 Tower of David and Mt. Zion. Stretching south from Jaffa Gate, this area is a potpourri of interesting minor sights. The Tower of David Museum is the most notable.

4 City of David. At the very core of ancient Jerusalem, outside the Old City walls, this largely underground

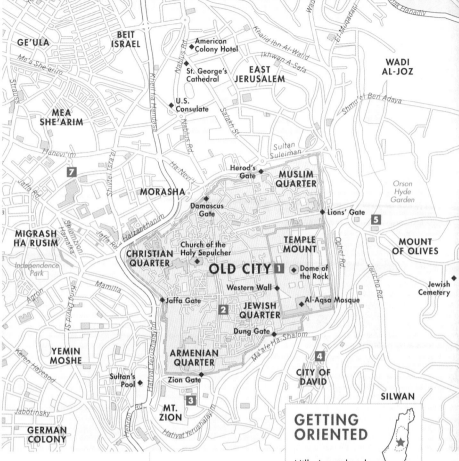

6 West Jerusalem. Within this extensive side of Jerusalem are several great but unrelated sights, some a few miles apart. Savor the extraordinary Israel Museum and Yad Vashem.

7 Center City. West Jerusalem's downtown areas have more subtle attractions than the city's postcard snapshots. Check out the Yemin Moshe and Nahalat Shiva neighborhoods, Ben-Yehuda Street, and the Machaneh Yehuda market.

archaeological adventure would be a banner-headline site anywhere else; in Jerusalem, however, it gets unjustly overshadowed by the famous shrines.

5 Mount of Olives and East Jerusalem. Most visitors, particularly Christians, will identify with two or three particular sites—Gethsemane and the Garden Tomb are the obvious ones. Pick your way down the Mount of Olives. Rockefeller Museum is a gem.

GETTING ORIENTED

Hilly Jerusalem has two centers—the Old City, on the east side; and the modern downtown triangle of King George, Ben-Yehuda, and Jaffa streets on the west. Jerusalem is Israel's capital, and home to its national institutions, most in Jewish West Jerusalem. East Jerusalem, including the Old City, is largely (but not entirely) Arab. Coexistence is sometimes fragile, and the two communities tend to keep to themselves.

JERUSALEM PLANNER

When to Go

Jerusalem, like Israel in general, is a year-round destination, but the very best months are late March through April, and October. Winter is colder than in Tel Aviv, but gloomy winter days are often followed by gorgeous sunny ones. Jerusalem gets its own back in the hot, rainless summer months; the inland capital is dry and cools off toward evening.

Avoid the main Jewish holidays, when hotels charge peak prices and many sights are on a different schedule. Many sights have shorter visiting hours (or close) on Fridays, Saturdays, or Sundays because of the sabbaths of the communities that operate them.

Visitor Information

The Tourist Information Office is open Sunday–Thursday 8:30–5. The Christian Information Center is open Monday, Wednesday, and Friday 8:30–5:30; Tuesday and Thursday 8:30–4; Saturday 8:30–12:30.

Contacts Christian Information Center (✉ Jaffa Gate ☎ 02/627–2692 ⊕ 198.62.75.1/ www1/ofm/cic/CICmainin.htm). **Tourist Information Office** (✉ Jaffa Gate ☎ 02/627–1422 ⊕ tour.jerusalem.muni.il).

Getting Here

⇨ See Getting Here and Around in Travel Smart Israel for information about air travel to Israel.

Taking the bus from Ben Gurion Airport to Jerusalem is cheap but tedious. Board the Egged shuttle (line #5, fare NIS 4.80) for a 10-minute ride to the Airport City complex, and wait for the Egged bus (line #947, fare NIS 21). It runs to Jerusalem's Central Bus Station. As an easier alternative, ten-seat sherut taxis (limo-vans) depart from Ben Gurion Airport when they fill up and drop passengers at any Jerusalem address for NIS 50.

By car, Route 1 is the chief route to Jerusalem from both the west (Tel Aviv, Ben Gurion Airport, Mediterranean coast) and the east (Galilee via Jordan Valley, Dead Sea, Eilat).

Getting Around

Bus Travel: Egged operates the extensive bus service within Jerusalem. The fare is NIS 5.70; you do not need exact change. There are no transfers. A cab is more time-effective, and for a group often more cost-effective as well. Egged operates Route 99, a two-hour circle tour of Jerusalem for visitors with 29 stops. The route begins at the Central Bus Station; cost is NIS 60 for one full trip.

Bus Contacts Egged (⊕ www.egged.co.il/Eng).

Car Travel: In Jerusalem, a combination of walking and taking cabs or a guide-driven tourist limo-van is often more time-effective than a rental car.

Light Rail Travel: Jerusalem's much-delayed light rail has an opening date in 2010. Check the Web site, www.rakevetkala-jerusalem.org.il.

Taxi Travel: Taxis can be flagged on the street, ordered by phone, or picked up at a taxi stand or at major hotels. The law requires taxi drivers to use their meters.

Train Travel: Train service between Jerusalem and the coast takes about an hour and 20 minutes—good at rush hour, but 50 minutes slower than the bus at other times. The fare to or from Tel Aviv is NIS 36 round-trip.

⇨ For more information, see Travel Smart Israel. For tours, see the box on Sightseeing Tours in Exploring Jerusalem.

Travel Precautions

The anxiety over personal safety that characterized the early 2000s has largely dissipated at this writing. Individual violence is rare and tourists are not specific targets. Nevertheless, avoid Muslim Quarter back streets, and be cautious walking the Old City at night (when almost everything is closed anyway). The important weekly Muslim prayers around midday Friday sometimes get passionate if there is a particularly hot Palestinian-Israeli issue in the news. Emotions can spill into the streets of the Muslim Quarter as the crowds leave the Al-Aqsa Mosque.

As in any major tourist destination, pickpockets can be a problem: keep purses closed and close to you, and wallets in less accessible pockets. Don't leave valuables (especially passports) in parked cars, and use hotel safes.

⇨ *For information about medical care, see Travel Smart Israel.*

Dining and Lodging

While the range of Jerusalem eateries will never rival that of cosmopolitan Tel Aviv, you can eat very well in the holy city. Middle Eastern food (sometimes mistranslated as "oriental") is a strong suit. Proportionately, there are far more kosher establishments than in Tel Aviv, but fear not: the food can be just as varied and delicious, and the dietary restrictions often hardly noticeable.

Lodgings range from cheap and simple to high-end deluxe in a variety of settings, from city center to the almost-rural periphery. Where possible, avoid Jewish holidays—especially the one-week holidays of Passover (March–April) and Sukkot/Tabernacles (September–October), when hotels are full and prices peak.

WHAT IT COSTS

	¢	$	$$	$$$	$$$$
Restaurants	Under NIS 32	NIS 32– NIS 49	NIS 50– NIS 75	NIS 76– NIS 100	over NIS 100
Hotels	Under $120	$120–$200	$201–$300	$301–$400	over $400

Restaurant prices are per person for a main course at dinner in NIS (Israeli shekels). Hotel prices are in US dollars, for two people in a standard double room in high season. Non-Israeli citizens paying in foreign currency are exempt from the 15.5% VAT tax on hotel rooms.

Planning Your Time

Israel itineraries tend to favor Jerusalem. The Old City alone offers an absorbing two days. Beyond its religious shrines are ancient sites, panoramic walks, and museums. Allow time for poking around the Arab market and the stores of the Jewish Quarter. The immediate environs—the City of David, Mount of Olives, Mount Zion, and a few sites north of the Old City walls—can add a day or more. West Jerusalem's spread-out museums, institutions, and attractions take time. Add leisure time and shopping, and you're quickly up to a five- to six-day stay. Jerusalem is also a convenient base for day trips to Masada and the Dead Sea, and even Tel Aviv.

A few tips for maximizing your time: Make a list of must-see sights. Pay attention to opening times and geography, to minimize backtracking. Mix experiences each day, to avoid overdosing on museums, shrines, or archaeology. Above all, take time to let your senses absorb the city: Jerusalem is as much about atmosphere as it is a checklist of world-class sights.

By Mike
Rogoff

Jerusalem is a city suspended between heaven and earth, east and west, past and present—parallel universes of flowing caftans and trendy coffee shops. For some people, Jerusalem is a condition, like being in love; for others, it is a state of mind, a constant tension between rival flags and faiths, or members of the same faith. You may feel moved, energized, or swept into the maelstrom of contemporary issues—but the city will not leave you unaffected.

The word "unique" is easy to throw around, but Jerusalem has a real claim on it. The 5,000-year-old city is sacred to half the human race, and its iconic Old City walls embrace primary sites of the three great monotheistic religions. For Jews, Jerusalem has always been their spiritual focus and historical national center; the imposing Western Wall is the last remnant of the ancient Temple complex. For almost 2,000 years, Christians have venerated Jerusalem as the place where their faith was shaped—through the death, burial, and resurrection of Jesus of Nazareth—and the candlelit Church of the Holy Sepulcher is where the greater part of Christendom recognizes those events. Islamic tradition identifies Jerusalem as the *masjid al-aqsa,* the "farthermost place," from which Mohammad ascended to Heaven for his portentous meeting with God: the dazzling, gold-top Dome of the Rock marks the spot.

The Old City is far more than shrines, however. Its arches, hidden courtyards, and narrow cobblestone alleyways beckon you back in time. The streets are crowded with travelers, pilgrims, and vendors of everything from tourist trinkets and leather sandals to fresh produce, embroidered fabrics, and dubious videocassettes. Your senses are assaulted by intense colors and by the aromas of turmeric, fresh mint, wild sage, and cardamom-spiced coffee. The blare of Arabic music and the burble of languages fill the air.

Step outside the Old City and you'll be transported into the 21st century—well, at least the 20th: quaint neighborhoods, some restored, embody an earlier simplicity. West Jerusalem forms the bulk of a modern metropolis of 750,000, Israel's largest city. It is not as cosmopolitan as Tel Aviv, to be sure, but it does have good restaurants, fine hotels, cultural venues, vibrant markets, and high-quality stores. The downtown triangle of Jaffa Road, King George Street, and Ben-Yehuda Street is a natural gathering place.

The city prides itself on its historical continuity. A municipal bylaw dating back to 1918 makes it mandatory to face even high-rise commercial buildings with the honey-colored "Jerusalem stone," the local limestone that has served Jerusalem's builders since, well, forever. Watch the stone walls glow at sunset—the source of the by-now clichéd but still compelling phrase "Jerusalem of Gold"—and understand the mystical hold Jerusalem has had on so many minds and hearts for so many thousands of years.

EXPLORING JERUSALEM

Immerse yourself in Jerusalem. Of course you can see the primary sights in a couple of days—some visitors claim to have done it in less!—but don't short-change yourself if you can help it. Take time to wander where the spirit takes you, to linger longer over a snack and people-watch, to follow the late Hebrew poet, Yehuda Amichai, "in the evening into the Old City / and . . . emerge from it pockets stuffed with images / and metaphors and well-constructed parables . . ." The poet struggled for breath in an atmosphere "saturated with prayers and dreams"; but the city's baggage of history and religion need not weigh you down. Decompress in the markets, the jewelry and art stores, the eateries and coffee shops and pubs of both the Old City and the newer areas.

Jerusalem beyond its ancient walls is a city of neighborhoods. Several are picturesque or quaint enough to attract the casual daytime visitor, but hold little interest once the sun sets: the upscale Talbieh-Yemin Moshe area and the lower-end Machaneh Yehuda-Nahlaot area are good examples. Two hives of activity after dark are the downtown complex of the Ben-Yehuda Street pedestrian mall ("midrachov") and Nahalat Shiva, and Emek Refa'im, the main artery of the German Colony.

Let's put Jerusalem on the map. The city is built on a series of hills, part of the country's north–south watershed. To the east, the Judean Desert tumbles down to the Dead Sea, the lowest point on earth, less than an hour's drive away. The main highway to the west winds down through the pine-covered Judean Hills toward the international airport and Tel Aviv. North and south of the city—Samaria and Judea, respectively—is what is known as the West Bank. Since 1967, this contested area has been administered largely by Israel, though the major concentrations of Arab population are currently under autonomous Palestinian control.

OLD CITY: THE CLASSIC SIGHTS

Drink in the very essence of Jerusalem as you explore the city's primary religious sites in the Muslim and Christian Quarters, and at the Western Wall, and touch the different cultures that share it. The Old City's

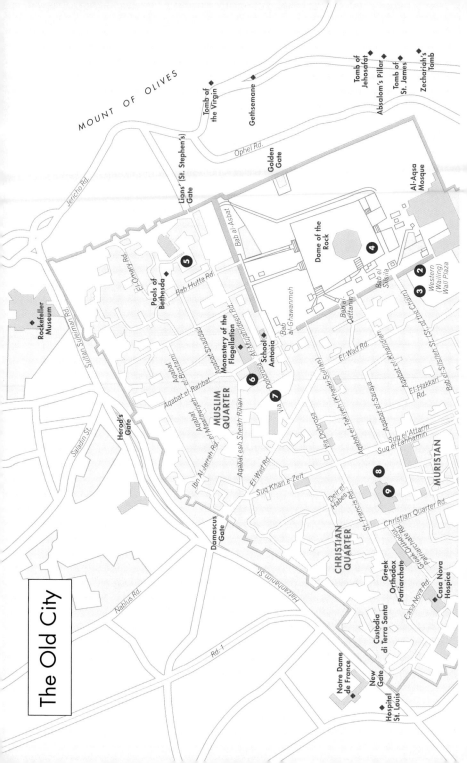

The Old City

MOUNT OF OLIVES

Jericho Rd.

Ophel Rd.

Tomb of the Virgin

Gethsemane

Tomb of Jehosafat

Absalom's Pillar

Tomb of St. James

Zechariah's Tomb

Lions' (St. Stephen's) Gate

Golden Gate

Al-Aqsa Mosque

Rockefeller Museum

Sultan Suleiman Rd.

Saladin St.

El-Omary Rd.

Pools of Bethesda

Bab Hutta Rd.

❺

Dome of the Rock

❹

Bab al-Asbat

Western (Wailing) Wall Plaza

❷

❸

Bab el-Silsila

Bab el-Qettanin

Aqabat Shaddad

Aqabat el-Bustami

Monastery of the Flagellation

Al-Mujahideen Rd.

School Antonia

Bab al-Ghawanmeh

Herod's Gate

Aqabat el-Rahbat

Aqabat el-Mawlawieh

Ibn Al Jarrah Rd.

MUSLIM QUARTER

❻

Via Dolorosa

❼

Aqabat esh. Sheikh Rihan

Bab al-Qettanin

El-Wad Rd.

Aqabat el-Saraya

Aqabat el-Khalideh

Aqabat el-Takiyeh (Khalek Sultan)

El-Hakkari Rd.

Via Dolorosa

El-Wad Rd.

Suq Khan e-Zeit

Deir el Habes

St. Francis Rd.

❽

❾

Suq el-Attarin

Suq el-Lahhamin

MURISTAN

Damascus Gate

Nablus Rd.

CHRISTIAN QUARTER

Christian Quarter Rd.

Greek Orthodox Patriarchate

Greek Orthodox Patriarchate Rd.

Casa Nova Rd.

Casa Nova Hospice

Custodia di Terra Santa

Hazzanham St.

Notre Dame de France

New Gate

Hospital St. Louis

Rd. 1

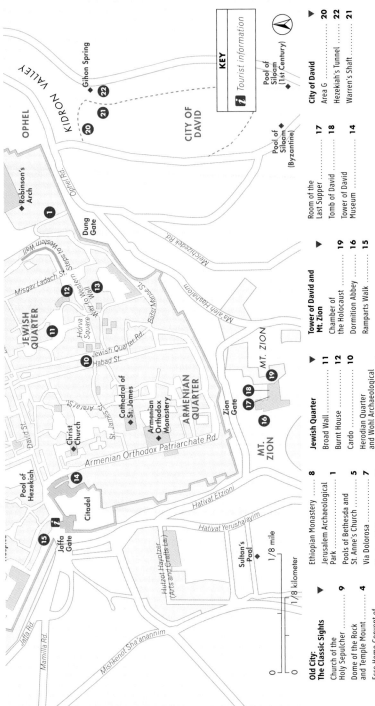

Old City:
The Classic Sights

Church of the Holy Sepulcher	9
Dome of the Rock and Temple Mount	4
Ecce Homo Convent of the Sisters of Zion	6

Ethiopian Monastery	8
Jerusalem Archaeological Park	1
Pools of Bethesda and St. Anne's Church	5
Via Dolorosa	7
Western Wall	2
Western Wall Tunnel	3

Jewish Quarter

Broad Wall	11
Burnt House	12
Cardo	10
Herodian Quarter and Wohl Archaeological Museum	13

Tower of David and Mt. Zion

Chamber of the Holocaust	19
Dormition Abbey	16
Ramparts Walk	15
Room of the Last Supper	17
Tomb of David	18
Tower of David Museum	14

City of David

Area G	20
Hezekiah's Tunnel	22
Warren's Shaft	21

KEY

i Tourist Information

35,000 inhabitants jostle in the cobblestone lanes with an air of ownership, at best merely tolerating the "intruders" from other quarters. Devout Jews in black and white scurry from their neighborhoods north and west of the Old City, through the Damascus Gate and the Muslim Quarter, toward the Western Wall. Arab women in long embroidered dresses flow across the Western Wall plaza to Dung Gate and the village of Silwan beyond it. It is not unusual to stand at the Western Wall, surrounded by the sounds of devotions, and hear the piercing call to prayer of the Muslim *muezzin* above you, with the more distant bells of the Christian Quarter providing a counterpoint.

Sites such as the Western Wall, Calvary, and the Haram esh-Sharif bring the thrill of recognition to ancient history. The devout cannot fail to be moved by the holy city, and its special, if sometimes dissonant, moods and modes of devotion tend to fascinate the nonbeliever as well.

GETTING HERE AND AROUND

To do this tour in one day, keep in mind opening times and geography, and plan accordingly. Dung Gate first thing in the morning will get the Western Wall area and the Temple Mount (Muslim shrines) off the list. Exit the northern end of the Mount to the Via Dolorosa and Holy Sepulcher. Jaffa Gate will take you right to the Holy Sepulcher and on to the Western Wall, but poses logistical issues for the Via Dolorosa and the Temple Mount. Lions' Gate is best for beginning with the Via Dolorosa, and fine for everything else except the Temple Mount. With some initial walking through the bazaar, Damascus Gate allows you to choose your preferred sequence of sights. Of course, you can spread the sights over more than one day!

TIMING AND PRECAUTIONS

Best to avoid the Via Dolorosa, which largely runs through the Muslim Quarter, between noon and 2 PM Fridays, the time of important weekly Muslim prayers. All the holy places demand modest dress: no shorts and no sleeveless tops.

TOP ATTRACTIONS

9 ★ **Church of the Holy Sepulcher.** *For information about the church, see the feature Jerusalem: Keeping the Faith in this chapter.*

4 ★ **Dome of the Rock and Temple Mount.** *For information about these sites, see the feature Jerusalem: Keeping the Faith in this chapter.*

1 **Jerusalem Archaeological Park.** Overlooked by many casual visitors, the site still referred to as the Western and Southern Wall Excavations was a historical gold mine for Israeli archaeologists in the 1970s and '80s. Interesting Byzantine and early Arab structures came to light, but by far the most dramatic and monumental finds were from the Herodian period, the late 1st century BC. Walk down to the high corner facing you. King Herod the Great rebuilt the Second Temple on the exact site of its predecessor, where the Dome of the Rock now stands. He expanded the sacred enclosure by constructing a massive, shoebox-shaped retaining wall on the slopes of the hill, the biblical Mt. Moriah. The inside was filled with thousands of tons of rubble to create the huge plaza, the size of 21 football fields, still known today as the Temple Mount. The great stones near the corner, with their signature precision-cut borders, are not held together with mortar; their sheer weight gives the structure its stability. The original wall would have been at least one-third higher than it is today.

Exposed to the left of the corner is the white pavement of an impressive main street and commercial area from the Second Temple period. The protrusion left of the corner and high above your head is known as **Robinson's Arch.** Named for a 19th-century American explorer, it is a remnant of a monumental bridge to the Temple Mount which was reached by a staircase from the street where you now stand: look for the ancient steps. The square-cut building stones heaped on the street came from the top of the original wall, dramatic evidence of the Roman destruction of AD 70.

Return to the higher level and turn left (east). Fifty yards over, a modern spiral staircase descends below present ground level to a partially reconstructed labyrinth of Byzantine dwellings, mosaics and all; from here you reemerge outside the present city walls. Alternatively, go straight, passing through the city wall by a small arched gate. The broad, impressive **Southern Steps** on your left, a good part of it original, once brought hordes of Jewish pilgrims through the now-blocked southern gates of the Temple Mount. The rock-hewn ritual baths near the bottom of the steps were used for the purification rites once demanded of Jews before they entered the sacred temple precincts. (On Friday, this section of the site closes at noon April through September, and at 11 AM October through March.) The air-conditioned **Davidson Visitors Center** offers visual aids, some artifacts, two interesting videos (which continuously alternate between English and Hebrew), and toilet facilities. It's a good place to start your visit if you're on your own. Allow 30 minutes for the center and another 40 for the site. ⊠*Dung Gate, Western Wall* ☎*02/627–7550* ⊕*www.archpark.org.il* ✍*NIS 30* ⊙*Sun.–Thurs. 8–5, Fri. and Jewish holiday eves 8–2.*

❼ Via Dolorosa. The Way of Suffering—or Way of the Cross, as it's more commonly called in English—is venerated as the route Jesus walked, carrying his cross, from the place of his trial and condemnation by Pontius Pilate to the site of his crucifixion and burial. The present tradition is essentially medieval or later, but it draws on older beliefs. Some of the incidents represented by the 14 "Stations" of the Cross are scriptural; others (III, IV, VI, VII, and IX) are not. Tiny chapels mark a few of the stations; the last five are inside the Church of the Holy Sepulcher. Catholic pilgrim groups, or the Franciscan-led Friday afternoon procession, take about 45 minutes to wind their way through the busy market streets of the Muslim and Christian quarters, with prayers and chants at each station.

Here are the 14 stations on the Via Dolorosa that mark Jesus's route, from trial and condemnation to crucifixion and burial.

Station I. Jesus is tried and condemned by Pontius Pilate.

Station II. Jesus is scourged and given the cross.

Station III. Jesus falls for the first time. (The chapel was built after World War II by soldiers of the Free Polish Forces.)

Station IV. Mary embraces Jesus.

Station V. Simon of Cyrene picks up the cross.

Station VI. A woman wipes the face of Jesus, whose image remains on the cloth. (She is remembered as Veronica, apparently derived from the words *vera* and *icon*, meaning true image.)

Station VII. Jesus falls for the second time. (The chapel contains one of the columns of the Byzantine Cardo, the main street of 6th-century Jerusalem.)

Station VIII. Jesus addresses the women in the crowd.

Station IX. Jesus falls for the third time.

Station X. Jesus is stripped of his garments.

Station XI. Jesus is nailed to the cross.

Station XII. Jesus dies on the cross.

Station XIII. Jesus is taken down from the cross.

Station XIV. Jesus is buried.

✉ *Muslim and Christian Quarters.*

NEED A BREAK?

Between the sixth and seventh stations of the Via Dolorosa is the very good **Holy Rock Café** (✉ *Muslim Quarter*). The name may be a little hokey, but there's nothing wrong with its freshly squeezed orange and pomegranate juice (in season), Turkish coffee, mint tea, and superb bourma, a round Arab confection filled with whole pistachio nuts. An Internet café is only a few steps away.

②★ **Western Wall.** *For information about this sight, see the Jerusalem: Keeping the Faith feature in this chapter.*

③ **Western Wall Tunnel.** The long tunnel beyond the men's side (north of the plaza) is not a rediscovered ancient thoroughfare, but was deliberately dug in recent years with the purpose of exposing a strip of the Western Wall along its entire length. One course of the massive wall revealed two building stones estimated to weigh an incredible 400 and 570 tons, respectively. Local guided tours are available and are recommended— you can visit the site only as part of an organized tour—but the times change from week to week (some include evening hours). The tour takes about 75 minutes; you see a kinetic model of the Western Wall, as well as incredible building stones and other things, and hear about history (some of it modern). Tours end, during daylight hours, at the beginning of the Via Dolorosa, in the Muslim Quarter. After dark, that exit is closed, and the tour retraces its steps through the tunnel. The ticket office is under the arches at the northern end of the Western Wall plaza. ✉ *Western Wall* ☎ *02/627–1333* ⊕ *english.thekotel.org* ✉ *NIS 25* ☉ *Sun.–Thurs. 8* AM*–late evening (changing schedules), Fri. and Jewish holiday eves 8–12:30. Call ahead for exact times.*

WORTH NOTING

⑥ **Ecce Homo Convent of the Sisters of Zion.** The arch that crosses the Via Dolorosa, just beyond Station II, continues into the chapel of the adjacent convent. It was thought to have been the gate of Herod's Antonia

Continued on page 82

CLOSE UP

A Walk on the Via Dolorosa

The Old City's main Jewish and Muslim sites can be visited individually, but the primary Christian shrines—the Via Dolorosa (or "Way of the Cross") and the Holy Sepulcher—are best experienced in sequence. This walk will keep you oriented in the confusing marketplace through which the Via Dolorosa picks its way. (Beware of slick pickpockets.) The route takes about an hour; plan additional time if you want to linger.

About 300 yards up the road from St. Anne's Church (near Lions' Gate), look for a ramp on your left leading to the blue metal door of a school. On Friday afternoons at 4 (April to September; at 3 from October to March), the brown-robed Franciscans begin their procession of the **Via Dolorosa** in the school courtyard. This is Station I; Station II is across the street. Just beyond it, on the right, is the entrance to the **Ecce Homo Convent of the Sisters of Zion,** with a Roman arch in the chapel. The continuation of the arch crosses the street outside.

The Via Dolorosa runs down into El-Wad Road, one of the Old City's most important thoroughfares. To the right, the street climbs toward the Damascus Gate; to the left, it passes through the heart of the Muslim Quarter and reaches the Western Wall. Arab matrons sail by; black-hatted Hasidic Jews hurry on divine missions; nimble local Muslim kids in T-shirt, jeans, and sneakers play in the street; and Christian pilgrims pace out ancient footsteps.

As you turn left onto El-Wad Road, Station III is on your left. A few steps beyond, also on the left, is Station IV and, on the corner, Station V. There the Via Dolorosa turns right and begins its ascent toward Calvary. Halfway up the street, a brown wooden door on your left marks Station VI.

Facing you at the top of the stepped street, on the busy Suq Khan e-Zeit, is Station VII. The little chapel preserves one of the columns of the Byzantine Cardo, the main street of 6th-century Jerusalem. Step to the left, and walk 30 yards up the street facing you to Station VIII, marked by nothing more than an inscribed stone in the wall on the left. Return to the main street and turn right. (If you skip Station VIII, turn left as you reach Station VII from the stepped street.) One hundred yards along Suq Khan e-Zeit from Station VII, turn onto the ramp on your right that ascends parallel to the street. At the end of the lane is a column that represents Station IX.

Step through the open door to the left of the column into the courtyard of the **Ethiopian Monastery** known as Deir es-Sultan. From the monastery's upper chapel, descend through a lower one and out a small wooden door to the court of the **Church of the Holy Sepulcher.** Most Christians venerate this site as that of the death, burial, and resurrection of Jesus—you'll find Stations X, XI, XII, XIII, and XIV within the church—but many Protestants are drawn to Skull Hill and the Garden Tomb, north of the Damascus Gate. A good time to be here is in the late afternoon, after 4 PM, when the different denominations in turn chant their way between Calvary and the tomb.

For more information on the sights in bold, see the listings in the Old City.

2

JERUSALEM: KEEPING THE FAITH

✡ ✝ ☪

Unforgotten and unforgettable, the city of Jerusalem is holy ground for the three great monotheistic religions, whose numbers embrace half the world's population. Its Old City is home to some of the most sacred sites of Judaism, Christianity, and Islam: the Western Wall, the Temple Mount/Haram esh-Sharif, the Church of the Holy Sepulcher, and the Dome of the Rock and Al-Aqsa Mosque. Some travelers visit them to find their soul, others to seek a sense of communion with ancient epochs. Whether pilgrim or tourist, you'll discover that history, faith, and culture commingle here as perhaps nowhere else on earth.

By Mike Rogoff

(right) The Western Wall, (opposite left) Dome of the Church of the Holy Sepulcher, (opposite right) The Dome of the Rock

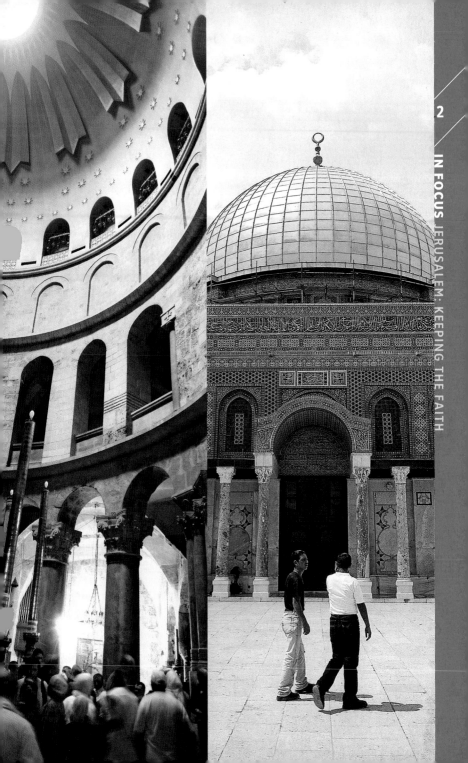

ONE CITY UNDER GOD

Jerusalem is a composite of three faith-civilizations: Jewish, Christian, and Muslim. They cohabit the Old City uneasily, burdened by centuries of struggle with each other for rights and real estate. But at the level of day-to-day routine, each draws its adherents to, respectively, the Western Wall, the Church of the Holy Sepulcher, and the Al-Aqsa Mosque. To the visitor, the collage of spiritual traditions is often bewildering, sometimes alien, always fascinating. The intricate choreographies of devotion have been known to move nonbelievers as well as the devout.

HISTORY AND HOLY STONES

Wander the cobblestone lanes of historical Jerusalem and you can hear in your mind's ear the echoes of King David's harp, trace the revered footsteps of Jesus of Nazareth, and sense the pres-

(left) Woman praying, (top right) Miracle of Holy Fire, Church of the Holy Sepulcher, (bottom right) Men praying near the Dome of the Rock

ence of the Prophet Muhammad. In the space of just a few hours, you can visit the tomb of Jesus at Golgotha, gaze at the shrine where Islam's founder rose to "the farthermost place," and stand before the only extant remnant of the Second Temple compound. Not without reason do some visitors imagine their fold-out atlases to be road maps leading to heaven itself.

Great dramas played out on these stones—occasionally, it is claimed, on the very same stone. The rock capped by the gold dome is the summit of Mt. Moriah, identified in Jewish tradition with the biblical site where Abraham erected an altar and prepared to sacrifice his son Isaac. It was here on the Temple Mount that the "First" and "Second" Jewish Temples stood for a total of one thousand years. In the same rock, devout Muslims point to the imprint of a foot, regarded as that of Muhammad himself, as evidence that it was here that the Prophet ascended to heaven for his meeting with God. The Dome of the Rock and the nearby Al-Aqsa Mosque enshrine that tradition.

On the one hand, Jerusalem is a layer-cake of time, each period leaving discernible sediments. The biblical kings David and Solomon transformed a small and already-ancient Jebusite town into an important metropolis. The march of history proceeded through destruction and the Babylonian captivity, Hellenization, Roman rule and another destruction, Byzantine Christianity, the Muslim invasions, the 12th-century Crusades, the Muslim reconquest, European rediscovery of the Holy Land and British control, and down to Jerusalem's contemporary status as the capital (though some dispute it) of the State of Israel.

At another level—change the metaphor—Jerusalem is a complex tangle, a Gordian knot of related but competing faith traditions, historical narratives, and national dreams. The knot seems fated to be around for a while yet, with no hero in sight to slice it through with one bold stroke.

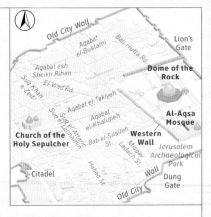

Israelites enslaved during the Babylonian Captivity after the fall of Jerusalem in 586 BC

FINDING YOUR FEET

Each of the three religious sites is infused with its own unique tradition. Making a connection between these stone structures of the past and the wellsprings of religious faith or cultural identity can be uplifting. Many pilgrims focus on their own shrines; some take the time to explore the others so close at hand. The Western Wall is just steps from the Jerusalem Archaeological Park, where excavations turned up remnants of King Herod the Great's grand structures that Jesus almost certainly knew. The ramp between the Western Wall and the park leads up to the vast plaza—the Temple Mount or Haram esh-Sharif—now dominated by the Muslim shrines. Any of the gates at its far northern end will deposit you on the Via Dolorosa. A twenty-minute stroll through the bustling bazaar brings you to the Church of the Holy Sepulcher, revered as the site of Jesus's death and burial.

Whichever site you start with (this feature lists them in historical order: Wall, Church, Dome), a tour of all three unfailingly provokes a powerful appreciation of Jerusalem as an epicenter of faith.

THE WESTERN WALL

No Jewish shrine is holier than the Western Wall, the remains of the ancient Second Temple compound, whose stones are saturated with centuries of prayers and tears.

The status of the Western Wall as the most important existing Jewish shrine derives from its connection with the ancient Temple, the House of God. The 2,000-year-old Wall was not itself part of the Temple edifice, but of the massive retaining wall King Herod built to create the vast plaza now known as the Temple Mount.

After the destruction of Jerusalem by the Romans in AD 70, and especially after the dedication of a pagan town in its place 65 years later, the city became off-limits to Jews for generations. The precise location of the Temple—

in the vicinity of today's Dome of the Rock—was lost. Even when access was regained, Jews avoided entering the Temple Mount out of fear of trespassing on the most sacred, and thus forbidden, areas of the ancient sanctuary. With time, the closest remnant of the period took on the aura of the Temple itself, making the Western Wall a kind of holy place by proxy.

Jewish visitors often just refer to the site as "the Wall" (*Kotel* in Hebrew); "Wailing Wall" is a Gentile term, describing the sight—once more common—of devout Jews grieving for God's House. For many Jews, the ancient Temple was as much a national site as a religious one, and its destruction as much a national trauma as a religious cataclysm.

(top) Jewish man praying at the Western Wall,
(right) Western Wall

VISITING THE WALL

The swaying and praying of the devout reveal the powerful hold this place has on the hearts and minds of many Jews.

On Monday and Thursday mornings, the Wall bubbles with colorful bar-mitzvah ceremonies, when Jewish families celebrate the coming of age of their 13-year-old sons. The excitement is still greater on Friday evenings just after sunset, when the young men of a nearby yeshiva, a Jewish seminary, sometimes come dancing and singing down to the Wall to welcome in the "Sabbath bride." The fervor reaches its highest point three times a year during the three Jewish pilgrimage festivals—Passover, Sukkot (Feast of Tabernacles), and Shavuot (Feast of Weeks), when many Jews come to pray. But many people find that it's only when the crowds have gone (the Wall is floodlit at night and always open), and you share the warm, prayer-drenched stones with just a handful of bearded stalwarts or kerchiefed women, that the true spirituality of the Western Wall is palpable.

The Wall precinct functions under the aegis of the rabbinic authorities, with all the trappings of an Orthodox synagogue. Modest dress is required (men must cover their heads in the prayer area), there is segregation of men and women in prayer, and smoking and photography on the Sabbath and religious holidays are prohibited. Expect a routine check of your bags. ✉ In the southeast corner of the Old City; accessible from Dung Gate, the Jewish Quarter, and the Muslim Quarter's El-Wad St. ⊕ http://english.thekotel. org ⊙ 24 hrs daily.

NOTES IN THE WALL

The cracks between the massive stones of the Western Wall are stuffed with slips of paper bearing prayers and petitions. "They reach their destination more quickly than the Israeli postal service," it has been said, with a mixture of serious faith and light cynicism. The cracks are cleared several times a year, but the slips are never simply dumped. Since the slips often contain God's name, and are written from the heart, they are collected in a sack and buried with reverence in a Jewish cemetery.

THE TEMPLE MOUNT, OR HARAM ESH-SHARIF

The size of 21 football fields, the Temple Mount is the vast plaza constructed around the Second Temple, rebuilt by King Herod "the Great" in the late 1st century BC.

In order to rebuild the Temple on a grand scale, and significantly expand the courts around it, Herod leveled off the top of Mt. Moriah with thousands of tons of rubble. The massive retaining walls include some of the largest building stones known. Structurally, the famous Western Wall is simply the western side of the huge shoebox-like project.

Some scholars regard the Temple Mount as perhaps the greatest religious enclosure of the ancient world, and the

(top) Aerial view of the Jewish Quarter and the Temple Mount, (top left) Al-Aqsa Mosque, (top right) Drawing of a reconstruction of the First Temple

splendid Temple, the one Jesus knew, as an architectural wonder of its day. The Romans reduced the building to smoldering ruins in the summer of AD 70, in the last stages of the Great Revolt of the Jews (AD 66–73), carting off to Rome many of its treasures, including the gold menorah of the Temple.

Jewish tradition identifies the great rock at the summit of the hill—now under the golden Dome of the Rock—as the foundation stone of the world, and the place where Abraham bound and almost sacrificed his son Isaac (Genesis 22). With greater probability, this was where the biblical King David made a repentance offering to the Lord (II

Samuel 22), and where his son Solomon built "God's House," the so-called First Temple. The Second Temple stood on the identical spot, but the precise location of its innermost holy of holies is a question that engages religious Jews and archaeologists to this day.

Christian tradition adds the New Testament dimension. Here Jesus disputed points of law with other Jewish teachers, angrily overturned the tables of money changers, and, looking down at the Temple precinct from the Mount of Olives, predicted its destruction. The Byzantines seem to have ignored the place (perhaps believing it cursed); the medieval Templars took their name from the area in which they set up their headquarters.

Muslims identify it as "the farthermost place," from which Muhammad rose to heaven, and call this area Haram esh-Sharif, the Noble Sanctuary. (*See section on the Muslim shrines in this feature.*)

✉ Access between the Western Wall and Dung Gate, Temple Mount ☎ 02/628–3292 or 02/628–3313 ☉ Apr.–Sept., Sun.–Thurs. 7:30 AM–11 AM and 1:30 PM–2:30 PM; Oct.–Mar., Sun.–Thurs. 8 AM–10 AM and 12:30 PM–2 PM, subject to change. Last entry 1 hr before closing.

THE JERUSALEM ARCHAEOLOGICAL PARK

Immediately south of the Western Wall, in the shadow of the Temple Mount, is an important archaeological site, still popularly known as the Western and Southern Wall excavations. Precious little was found from the Old Testament period, but archaeologists unearthed some impressive structures from the Byzantine and Arab periods (4th–8th centuries). Robinson's Arch, named for a 19th-century American explorer, once supported a monumental stairway leading up to the Temple Mount. Also discovered were numerous "mikva'ot" (singular "mikveh," a Jewish ritual bath) and a Herodian street, once lined with shops. In the southern part of the site is the low-rise Davidson Visitors Center; its exhibits range from ancient artifacts to computer-animated recreations of the Second Temple. *For complete information, see the separate entry for Jerusalem Archaeological Park in this chapter.*

THE CHURCH OF THE HOLY SEPULCHER

Follow the footsteps of Jesus along the Via Dolorosa to the hallowed church that enshrines Golgotha—the hillside of Jesus's crucifixion, burial, and resurrection.

Vast numbers of Christians, especially adherents of the older "mainstream" churches, believe that this church marks the place where Jesus was crucified by the Romans, buried by his followers, and then rose from the dead three days later. Some claim that the antiquity of the Holy Sepulcher tradition argues in favor of its authenticity, since the fervent early Christian community would have striven to preserve the memory of such an important site. The church is outside the city walls *of Jesus's day*—a vital point, for no executions or burials took place within Jerusalem's sacred precincts.

The site was officially consecrated, and the first church built here, following the visit in AD 326 by Helena, mother of the Byzantine emperor Constantine the Great. The present imposing structure, the fourth church on the site, was built by the Crusaders in the 12th century. Interior additions over the years have distorted the Gothic plan, but look for the Norman-style vault at the far end of the Greek Orthodox basilica (facing the tomb), and the ceiling of the dim corridor leading to the adjacent Catholic chapel. After a fire in 1808, much of the church was rebuilt in 19th-century style.

(top) Church of the Holy Sepulcher, (top right) Greek Orthodox chapel, Calvary, (bottom right) Monk kissing the Stone of Unction

HOLIEST LANDMARKS

On the floor just inside the entrance of the church is the rectangular pink **Stone of Unction**, where, it is said, the body of Jesus was cleansed and prepared for burial. Pilgrims often rub fabric or religious trinkets on the stone to absorb its sanctity, and take them home as mementos. Nearby steep steps take you up to **Golgotha**, or Calvary, meaning "the place of the skull," as the site is described in the New Testament. The chapel on the right is Roman Catholic: a window looks out at Station X of the Via Dolorosa, a wall mosaic at the front of the chapel depicts Jesus being nailed to the cross (Station XI), and a bust of Mary in a cabinet to the left of it represents Station XIII where Jesus was taken off the cross. The central chapel—all candlelight, oil lamps, and icons—is Greek Orthodox. Under the altar, and capping the rocky hillock on which you stand, is a silver disc with a hole, purportedly the place—Station XII—where the cross actually stood.

The **tomb** itself (Station XIV), encased in a pink marble edifice, is in the rotunda to the left of the main entrance of the church, under the great dome that dominates the Christian Quarter. The only hint of what the tomb must have been like 2,000 years ago is the ledge in the inner chamber (now covered with mar-

ble) on which Jesus's body would have been laid. You can see a more pristine example of an upscale Jewish tomb of the period in the gloomy Chapel of St. Nicodemus, opposite the Coptic chapel in the back of the sepulcher.

SHARING THE CHURCH

An astonishing peculiarity of the Holy Sepulcher is that it is shared, albeit unequally and uncomfortably, by several Christian denominations. Centuries of sometimes-violent competition for control of key Christian sites culminated in the Status Quo Agreement of 1852. Under the pressure of Orthodox

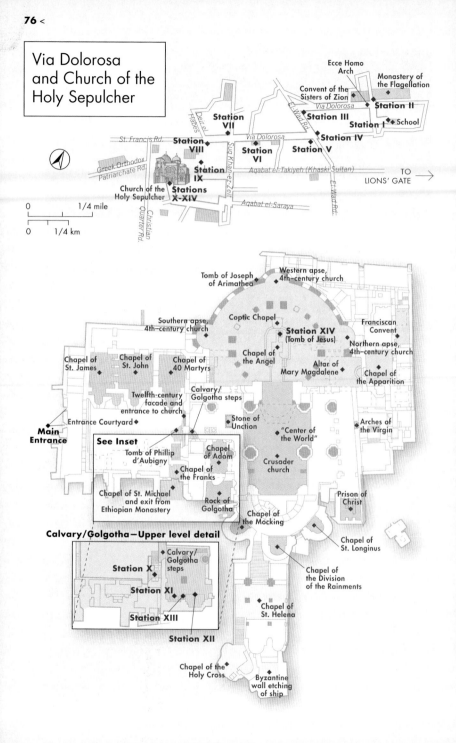

Via Dolorosa and Church of the Holy Sepulcher

Ecce Homo Arch
Monastery of the Flagellation
Convent of the Sisters of Zion
Via Dolorosa
Station II
Station III
Station I
School
Via Dolorosa
Station VII
Station IV
St. Francis Rd.
Station VIII
Station VI
Station V
Greek Orthodox Patriarchate Rd.
Suq Khan-ezz-eit
Station IX
Aqabat el-Takiyeh (Khaski Sultan)
TO LIONS' GATE
Church of the Holy Sepulcher
Stations X–XIV
El Wad Rd.
Aqabat el-Saraya
Christian Quarter Rd.
Deir el-Habes
El Wad Rd.

0   1/4 mile
0   1/4 km

Tomb of Joseph of Arimathea
Western apse, 4th-century church
Southern apse, 4th-century church
Coptic Chapel
Station XIV (Tomb of Jesus)
Franciscan Convent
Northern apse, 4th-century church
Chapel of the Angel
Altar of Mary Magdalene
Chapel of the Apparition
Chapel of St. James
Chapel of St. John
Chapel of 40 Martyrs
Calvary/Golgotha steps
Twelfth-century facade and entrance to church
Stone of Unction
"Center of the World"
Arches of the Virgin
Main Entrance
Entrance Courtyard
See Inset
Tomb of Phillip d'Aubigny
Chapel of Adam
Crusader church
Prison of Christ
Chapel of the Franks
Chapel of St. Michael and exit from Ethiopian Monastery
Rock of Golgotha
Chapel of the Mocking
Chapel of St. Longinus

Calvary/Golgotha—Upper level detail

Calvary/Golgotha steps
Station X
Station XI
Station XIII

Chapel of the Division of the Rainments
Chapel of St. Helena
Station XII

Chapel of the Holy Cross
Byzantine wall etching of ship

Mosaic of Jesus near the Stone of Unction

Russia, the Ottoman Turks recognized the precedence of the Greek Orthodox as on-the-ground representatives of the Eastern Rite churches.

Each denomination guards its assigned privileges, and minor infringements by one of its neighbors can flare up into open hostility. At the same time, the phenomenon gives the place much of its color. Try visiting in the late afternoon (the exact time changes with the seasons), and watch each group in turn—Greek Orthodox, Latins (as Roman Catholics are known in the Holy Land), Armenians, and Egyptian Copts—in procession from Calvary to the tomb. The candlelight and swinging censers are passingly similar; the robes and lusty hymn-singing are different.

A modern agreement among the Greeks, the Latins, and the Armenians on the interior restoration of the great dome was hailed as a breakthrough in ecumenical relations, and it was rededicated in January, 1997 in an unprecedented interdenominational service. ⊠ Between Suq Khan e-Zeit and Christian Quarter Rd., Christian Quarter ☎ 02/627–3314 ⊕ http://198.62.75.5/www1/jhs/TSspmenu.html ☒ Free ☽ Apr.–Sept., daily 5 AM–9 PM; Oct.–Mar., daily 4 AM–8 PM

SUGGESTIONS FOR YOUR VISIT

While the first nine Stations of the Cross are to be found along the Way of the Cross—the Via Dolorosa—the final and most holy ones are within the Church of the Holy Sepulcher itself. The best time to visit may be around 4 o'clock when many denominations are found worshipping. *For more information, see the separate entry for the Via Dolorosa elsewhere in this chapter.*

As in many religious sites, modest dress and discreet behavior are required here, but it's difficult for the clergy of any particular community to assert authority. Come early or late to avoid the worst crowds; be patient, too. A small flashlight or some candles will help you explore the small tomb of St. Nicodemus, an authentic Jewish tomb of the period.

Entrance of the Church of the Holy Sepulcher

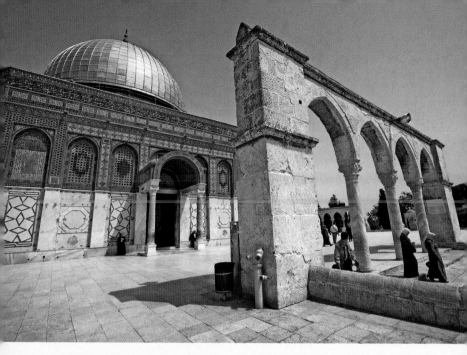

THE DOME OF THE ROCK AND AL-AQSA MOSQUE

The focal point of these sanctuaries, whose interiors are currently open only to Muslims, is the Rock—the place from which Muhammad is believed to have ascended to heaven to be given the divine precepts of Islam.

The magnificent golden **Dome of the Rock** dominates the vast 35-acre Temple Mount, the area known to Muslims as Haram esh-Sharif (the Noble Sanctuary). This is the original octagonal building, completed in AD 691. It enshrines the great rock—the summit of Mt. Moriah—from which the prophet Muhammad is said to have risen to heaven. Jerusalem is not mentioned in the Koran, but Muhammad's "Night

Ride" is. Awakened by the archangel Gabriel, he was taken on the fabulous winged horse el-Burak to the *masjid al-aqsa*, the "farthermost place." From there he rose to heaven, met God face to face, received the teachings of Islam, and returned to Mecca the same night. Tradition has it that the *masjid al-aqsa* was none other than Jerusalem, and the great rock the very spot from which the prophet ascended.

To be sure, Muhammad's triumphant successors venerated Jerusalem's biblical sanctity; but some modern scholars suggest they did not like the feeling of being Johnnies-come-lately in the

(top) Eight *qanatirs* (arcades) stand by sets of steps leading to the Dome of the Rock, (top right) The rock, the Dome's central shrine

holy city of rival faiths. The impressive Dome of the Rock, built by the Ummayad caliph Abd el-Malik, was almost certainly intended to proclaim the ascendancy of the "true faith."

A SPLENDID SHRINE

Considering the original builders and craftsmen adopted the artistic traditions of their Byzantine predecessors, it's hardly surprising that the plan of the shrine resembles those of its Christian contemporaries, like the Byzantine Church of San Vitale in Ravenna, Italy. Take a close look at the bright exterior tiles in variegated shades of blue. The marvelous gold dome was restored in the 1990s, with 176 pounds of 24-carat gold electroplated on copper.

At the time of this writing, non-Muslims were denied entry to the interior of the building, with its beautiful granite columns supporting arches, some of which bear the original green-and-gold mosaics set in arabesque motifs. In obedience to Islamic religious tradition, no human or animal forms appear in the artwork. The mosaics were restored in 1027, but preserved much of the original work.

All this splendor was designed to emphasize the importance of the rock itself, directly under the great dome. The faithful reach out and touch an inden-

tation which, they believe, was nothing less than the Prophet's footprint, left there as he ascended to heaven.

THE THIRD-HOLIEST OF ALL

At the southern end of the Haram, immediately in front of you as you enter the area from the Western Wall plaza (the only gate for non-Muslims), is the large, black-domed **Al-Aqsa Mosque**. The Dome of the Rock is a shrine, the place where a hallowed event is believed to

THE DOME'S MOSAICS

Some of the Arabic inscriptions in the mosaics are quotations from the Koran; others are dedications. One of the latter originally lauded Abd el-Malik, caliph of the Damascus-based Ummayad dynasty, who built the shrine. Some 140 years later, the caliph of a rival dynasty removed el-Malik's name and replaced it with his own, but he neglected to change the date.

have taken place. Individuals go there to pray, but Al-Aqsa is a true mosque, attracting thousands of worshippers on Fridays and Muslim holidays. It is third in holiness for Muslims everywhere, after the great mosques of Mecca and Medina, both in Saudi Arabia.

First built by the Ummayad dynasty in the early 8th century AD, it has been destroyed and restored several times. In the 12th century, the Al-Aqsa Mosque became the headquarters of the Templars, a Crusader monastic order that took its name from the ancient site itself. The spot has been the setting for more recent dramas, though—most importantly the assassination of King Abdullah I of Jordan (the present king's great-grandfather) in 1951.

EXPLORING THE HARAM
The Haram today is a Muslim preserve, a legacy that dates back to AD 638, when the Arab caliph Omar Ibn-Khatib seized Jerusalem from the Byzantines.

At the time of this writing, the Muslim shrines were closed to non-Muslims indefinitely, leaving the faithful alone to enjoy their wondrous interiors.

Even if you can't get inside, the vast plaza is visually and historically arresting, and worth a visit. Fifteenth-century Mamluk buildings line the western edge. Overlooking the plaza at its northwestern corner is a long building, today an elementary school, built on the artificial scarp that protected Herod's Antonia fortress. Christian tradition, very possibly accurate, identifies the site as the praetorium where Jesus was tried.

Security check lines to enter the Haram esh-Sharif are often long; it's best to come early. Note that the Muslim attendants prohibit Bibles in the area. ✉ Access between the Western Wall and Dung Gate, Haram esh-Sharif, Temple Mount ☎ 02/628–3292 or 02/628–3313 ☉ Apr.–Sept., Sun.–Thurs. 7:30 AM–11 AM and 1:30 PM–2:30 PM; Oct.–Mar., Sun.–Thurs. 8 AM–10 AM and 12:30 PM–2 PM, subject to change. Last entry 1 hr before closing.

(top) Parts of columns on the Haram, (right) Mosaics and arches grace the Dome's interior

Fortress, perhaps the spot where the Roman governor Pontius Pilate presented Jesus to the crowd with the words "*Ecce homo!*" ("Behold, the man!"). Recent scholarship suggests otherwise: it was a triumphal arch built by the Roman emperor Hadrian in the 2nd century AD.

The basement of the convent has two points of interest: an impressive reservoir with a barrel-vault roof, apparently built by Hadrian in the moat of Herod's older Antonia Fortress, and the famous *lithostratos,* or stone pavement, etched with games played by Roman legionnaires. The origin of one such diversion—the notorious Game of the King—called for the execution of a mock king, a sequence tantalizingly reminiscent of the New Testament description of the treatment of Jesus by the Roman soldiers. Contrary to tradition, however, the pavement of large, foot-worn brown flagstones is apparently not from Jesus's day, but was laid down a century later. ⊠ *Via Dolorosa, Muslim Quarter* ☎ *02/627–7292* ⊕ *www.eccehomoconvent.com* ⊠ *NIS 8* ⊙ *Daily 8:30–5.*

❽ Ethiopian Monastery. Stand in the monastery's courtyard beneath the medieval bulge of the Church of the Holy Sepulcher, and look around. Views of the churches of Christendom crowd in. The adjacent Egyptian Coptic monastery peeks through the entrance gate, and the skyline is broken by a Russian Orthodox gable, a Lutheran bell tower, and the crosses of Greek Orthodox, Armenian, and Roman Catholic churches.

The robed Ethiopian monks live in tiny cells in the rooftop monastery. One of the modern paintings in their small, dark church depicts the visit of the Queen of Sheba to King Solomon. Ethiopian tradition holds that more passed between the two than is related in the Bible—she came to "prove" his wisdom "with hard questions" (I Kings 10)—and that their supposed union produced an heir to both royal houses. The prince was met with hostility by Solomon's legitimate offspring, says the legend, and the king was compelled to send him home—with the precious Ark of the Covenant as a gift! To this day (say the Ethiopians) it remains in a sealed crypt in their homeland. The script in the paintings is Gehz, the ecclesiastical language of the Ethiopian church. ⊠ *Roof of the Church of the Holy Sepulcher, access from Suq Khan e-Zeit, Christian Quarter* ⊠ *Free* ⊙ *Daily during daylight.*

❺ Pools of Bethesda and St. Anne's Church. The transition is sudden and complete, from the raucous cobbled streets and persistent vendors to the pepper trees, flower patches, and birdsong of this serene Catholic cloister. The Romanesque Crusader **St. Anne's Church,** built in 1140, was restored in the 19th century, and with its austere and unadorned stone interior and extraordinarily reverberant acoustics, it is one of the finest examples of medieval architecture in the country. According to local tradition, the Virgin Mary was born in the grotto over which the church is built, and the church is named for her mother.

In the same compound are the excavated **Pools of Bethesda,** a large, double public reservoir in use during the 1st century BC and 1st century AD. The New Testament speaks of Jesus miraculously curing a lame man by "a pool, which is called in the Hebrew tongue Bethesda" (John 5).

The Via Dolorosa often teems with pilgrims but can sometimes offer a quiet path.

The actual bathing pools were the small ones, east of the reservoir, but it was over the big pools that both the Byzantines and the Crusaders built churches, now ruined, to commemorate the miracle. ✉ *Al-Muja-hideen Rd., near Lions' Gate, Muslim Quarter* ☎ 02/628–3285 💲 NIS 7 🕙 *Apr.–Sept., Mon.–Sat. 8–12 and 2–6; Oct.–Mar., Mon.–Sat. 8–12 and 2–5.*

JEWISH QUARTER

This is at once the Old City's oldest quarter and its newest neighborhood. The Quarter, abandoned for a generation, was restored and resettled after the 1967 Six-Day War, and the subsequent archaeological excavations exposed artifacts and structures that date back 27 centuries and more. If you have a photographer's eye, get off the main streets and stroll at random. The limestone houses and alleys—often counterpointed with a shock of bougainvillea or palm fronds and ficus trees—offer pleasing compositions.

If you like to people-watch, find a shaded café table and sip a good latte while the world jitterbugs by. The population of the Jewish Quarter is almost entirely religious, roughly split between "modern" Orthodox (devout, but integrated into contemporary Israeli society at every level) and the more traditional ultra-Orthodox (men in black frock coats and black hats, in many ways a community apart). The locals, especially the women, tend to dress very conservatively. Several religious study institutions attract a transient population of young students, many of them from abroad. Religious Jewish families tend to have lots of kids, and little ones here are given independence at an astonishingly early age. It's quite common to see 3- and 4-year-olds toddling home from preschool alone, or shepherded by a one-year-more-mature brother or sister. And if you see a big group of Israeli soldiers, don't assume the worst. The army maintains a center for its educational tours here, and the recruits are more likely than not boisterously kidding around with each other as they follow their guide. Shopping is good here—jewelry, Judaica, gift items—and there are decent fast-food options when hunger strikes.

GETTING HERE AND AROUND

It's best to approach the Jewish Quarter on foot. From Jaffa Gate, you can plunge into the Arab bazaar and follow David Street until it becomes a T-junction: the right turn becomes Jewish Quarter Street. Alternatively, after you enter Jaffa Gate, follow the vehicle road to the right and through a small tunnel, then turn left (on foot) onto St. James Street and down to the quarter. A third idea is to begin your tour on Mt. Zion, and then continue to the Jewish Quarter through Zion Gate.

TIMING AND PRECAUTIONS

Allow two hours to explore the Jewish Quarter, not counting shopping and eating. If you're pressed for time, absorb the scene over the rim of a glass or mug, and take time to visit the Herodian Quarter. Avoid visiting on Saturday, when everything is closed, and some religious locals may resent you taking pictures on their sabbath. Paid sites close by midday Friday.

TOP ATTRACTIONS

12 **Burnt House.** "We could almost smell the burning and feel the heat of the flames," wrote archaeologist Nahman Avigad, whose team uncovered vivid evidence of the Roman devastation of Jerusalem in AD 70. Charred cooking pots, sooty debris, and—most arresting—the skeletal hand and arm of a woman clutching a scorched staircase in a futile attempt to escape the flames recaptured the full poignancy of the moment. Stone weights inscribed with the name Bar Katros—a Jewish priestly family known from ancient sources—suggested that this may have been a basement industrial workshop, possibly for the manufacture of sacramental incense used in the Temple. A video presentation recreates the bitter civil rivalries of the period, and the city's tragic end. ⊠ *Tiferet Israel St., Jewish Quarter* ☎ *02/626–5900* 💻 *NIS 25; combined ticket with Herodian Quarter NIS 35* ⊙ *Sun.–Thurs. 9–5, Fri. and Jewish holiday eves 9–1 (last entry 40 mins before closing).*

13 **Herodian Quarter and Wohl Archaeological Museum.** Excavations in the
★ 1970s exposed the Jewish Quarter's most visually arresting site: the remains of sumptuous mansions from the aristocratic Upper City of the Second Temple period. Preserved in the basement of a modern Jewish seminary—but entered separately—the geometrically patterned mosaic floors, still-vibrant frescoes, and costly glassware, stone objects, and ceramics provide a peek into the life of the wealthy in the days of Herod and Jesus. Several small stone cisterns have been identified as private *mikva'ot*, (Jewish ritual baths); holograms depict their use. Large stone water jars are just like those described in the New Testament story of the wedding at Cana. Rare stone tables resemble the dining-room furniture depicted in Roman stone reliefs found in Europe.

CLOSE UP

Jews in the Old City

The history of Jewish life in the Old City has been marked by the trials of conflict and the joys of creating and rebuilding community. Here are some highlights from the medieval period on.

1099. Crusaders conquer Jerusalem, followed by wholesale massacre. Jews lived at the time in today's Muslim Quarter.

1267. Spanish rabbi Nachmanides ("Ramban") reestablishes Jewish community. (His synagogue is on Jewish Quarter Road.)

1517. Ottoman Turks conquer Palestine and allow Sephardic Jews (expelled from Spain a generation earlier) to resettle the country. They develop four interlinked synagogues in the quarter.

1700. Large groups of Ashkenazi Jews from Eastern Europe settle in Jerusalem.

1860. The first neighborhood is established outside the walls (Mishkenot Sha'ananim). Initially, very few Old City Jews had the courage to move out.

1948. Israel's War of Independence. Jewish Quarter surrenders to Jordanian forces and is abandoned. By then, the residents of the quarter represent only a tiny percentage of Jerusalem's Jewish population.

1967. Six-Day War. The Jewish Quarter, much of it ruined, is recaptured. Archaeological excavations and restoration work begin side by side.

1980s. Section after section of the Quarter becomes active again as the restoration work progresses—apartments and educational institutions, synagogues and stores, restaurants and new archaeological sites.

On the last of the site's three distinct levels is a mansion with an estimated original floor area of some 6,000 square feet. None of the upper stories have survived, but the fine, fashionable stucco work and the quality of the artifacts found here indicate an exceptional standard of living, leading some scholars to suggest this may have been the long-sought palace of the high priest. The charred ceiling beam and scorched mosaic floor and fresco at the southern end of the reception hall bear witness to the Roman torching of the neighborhood in the late summer of AD 70, exactly one month after the Temple itself had been destroyed. ✉*Hakara'im Rd., Jewish Quarter* ☎*02/626–5900* ✆*NIS 15; combined ticket with Burnt House NIS 35* ⏱*Sun.–Thurs. 9–5, Fri. and Jewish holiday eves 9:30–1 (last entry 30 mins before closing).*

WORTH NOTING

⓫ Broad Wall. The discovery in the 1970s of the rather unobtrusive 23-foot-thick foundations of an Old Testament city wall was hailed as one of the most important archaeological finds in the Jewish Quarter. The wall was built in 701 BC by Hezekiah, King of Judah and a contemporary of the prophet Isaiah, to protect the city against an impending Assyrian invasion. The unearthing of the Broad Wall—a biblical name—resolved a long-running scholarly debate about the size of Old Testament Jerusalem: a large on-site map shows that the ancient city was far larger than was once thought. ✉*Jewish Quarter Rd., Jewish Quarter.*

⑩ Cardo. Today it's known for shopping, but the Cardo has a long history. In AD 135, the Roman emperor Hadrian built his town of Aelia Capitolina on the ruins of Jerusalem, an urban plan essentially preserved in the Old City of today. The *cardo maximus* (the generic name for the city's main north-south street) began at the strategic Damascus Gate, in the north, where sections have been unearthed. With the Christianization of the Roman Empire in the 4th century, access to Mt. Zion and its important Christian sites became a priority, and the main street was eventually extended into today's Jewish Quarter. The original width—today you see only half—was 73 feet, about the width of a six-lane highway. A strip of good stores (jewelry, art, Judaica, T-shirts, and souvenirs) occupies the Cardo's medieval reincarnation. ⊠ *Jewish Quarter Rd., Jewish Quarter.*

TOWER OF DAVID AND MT. ZION

When you've "done" the main sights, take a leisurely few hours to dip into lesser-known gems on the periphery of the Old City. Most of the city walls were built in the 16th century by the Ottoman sultan Suleiman the Magnificent. According to legend, his two architects were executed by the sultan and buried behind the railings just inside the imposing Jaffa Gate. One version relates that they angered Suleiman by not including Mt. Zion and the venerated Tomb of David within the walls. Another version has it that the satisfied sultan wanted to make sure they would never build anything grander for anyone else.

Jaffa Gate got its name from its westerly orientation, toward the once-important Mediterranean harbor of Jaffa, now part of Tel Aviv. Its Arabic name of Bab el-Halil, Gate of the Beloved, points you south, to the city of Hebron, where the biblical Abraham, the "Beloved of God" in Muslim tradition, is buried. The vehicle entrance is newer, created by the Ottoman Turks in 1898 for the visit of the German emperor, Kaiser Wilhelm II. The British general, Sir Edmund Allenby, took a different approach when he conquered the city from the Turks in December 1917: he and his staff officers dismounted from their horses to enter the holy city with the humility befitting pilgrims.

The huge stone tower on the right as you enter Jaffa Gate is the last survivor of the strategic fortress built by King Herod 2,000 years ago. Today it is part of the so-called Citadel that houses the Tower of David Museum—well worth your time as the springboard for exploring this part of the historical city. Opposite the museum entrance (once a drawbridge) is the neo-Gothic Christ Church (Anglican), built in 1849 as the first Protestant church in the Middle East. Directly ahead is the souk (Arab bazaar), a convenient route to the Christian and Jewish Quarters. To reach Mt. Zion, follow the vehicle road inside the walls to Zion Gate, or take the Ramparts Walk.

GETTING HERE AND AROUND

Jaffa Gate, the logical entry point for this area and tour, is an easy walk from the downtown or King David Street areas. City bus routes 20, 38, and 99 take you right there, but any downtown dropoff is within striking distance.

2

TIMING AND PRECAUTIONS
Sunday through Thursday is when everything is open. Some sites have limited hours or are closed Friday or Saturday. Modest dress is required at shrines.

TOP ATTRACTIONS

⑮ Ramparts Walk. The narrow stone catwalks of the Old City walls provide an interesting perspective and an introduction to the area. It's an innocent bit of voyeurism as you look down into gardens and courtyards and become, for a moment, a more intimate partner in the secret domestic life of the different quarters you pass. Across the rooftops, the domes and spires of the three religions that call Jerusalem holy compete for the skyline, just as their adherents jealously guard their territory down below. Peer through the shooting niches—just like the long-ago watchmen—and take in the broad vistas beyond the walls: the hotels and high-rises of the new city to the west and south, the bustle of East Jerusalem to the north, and the quiet churches and cemeteries of Mount of Olives to the east. There are many high steps on this route; the railings are secure, but small children should not walk alone.

The two sections of the walk are disconnected from each other (though the same ticket covers both). The shorter southern section is accessible only from the end of the seemingly dead-end terrace outside Jaffa Gate (at the exit of the Tower of David Museum). Descent is at Zion Gate. The longer and more varied walk begins at Jaffa Gate (up the stairs immediately on the left as you enter the Old City), with descent at New, Damascus, Herod's, or Lions' gates. In terms of timing, allow 30 minutes to walk south-southeast to Zion Gate for the shorter section, with an extra 10 minutes to Dung Gate. For the longer section, it takes 30 minutes to walk north-northeast to New Gate, another 20 minutes east to Damascus Gate, and then 15 minutes each to get to Herod's Gate and then Lion's Gate. ✉ *Jaffa Gate* ☎ *02/625–4403* 💲 *NIS 16 (for both sections); combined ticket with Ophel Archaeological Garden, Damascus Gate, and Zedekiah's Cave (on same day only) NIS 55* ☉ *Apr.–Sept., Sat.–Thurs. 9–5, Oct.–Mar., Sat.–Thurs. 9–4. Short route also open Fri. 9–2, long route closed Fri. Zedekiah's Cave and Damascus Gate are closed Fri. Routes are open Saturday but tickets must be purchased in advance.*

⑰ Room of the Last Supper. Tradition has enshrined this spare, 14th-century second-story room as the location of the "upper room" referred to in the New Testament (Mark 14). Two thousand years ago, when Jesus and his disciples celebrated the ceremonial Passover meal that would become known as "the Last Supper," the site would have been *inside* the city walls. Formally known as the Cenacle or the Coenaculum, the room is also venerated by a second New Testament tradition as the place where Jesus' disciples, gathered on Pentecost seven weeks after his death, were "filled with the Holy Spirit," and began to speak in foreign "tongues."

A little incongruously, the chamber has the trappings of a mosque as well. There are restored stained-glass Arabic inscriptions in the Gothic windows, and one window is blocked by an ornate *mihrab* (an alcove indicating the Muslim direction of prayer, toward Mecca). There are also two Arabic plaques in the wall and a Levantine dome. The Muslims were not concerned with the site's Christian traditions but with the supposed Tomb of King David—the "Prophet" David in their tradition—on the level below. ⊠*Mt. Zion* 🕮*Free* ◷*Sat.–Thurs. 8–5, Fri. 8–1.*

⓮ **Tower of David Museum.** Many visi-
★ tors find this museum invaluable in mapping Jerusalem's often-confus-ing historical byways. Housed in a series of medieval halls, known locally as the Citadel ("Hametzuda" in Hebrew), the museum tells the city's four-millennia story through models, maps, holograms, and videos. The galleries are organized by historical period around the Citadel's central courtyard, where the old stone walls and arches add an appropriately antique atmosphere. Walk-ing on the Citadel ramparts provides unexpected panoramas. You'll need about 90 minutes to do justice to the museum. Be sure to inquire about the next screening of the animated introductory film (which has English subtitles), and don't miss the spectacular view from the top of the big tower. Take the guided tour if the timing works for you. There are sometimes special night shows in the summer months. ⊠*Jaffa Gate* 🕾*02/626–5333, 02/626–5310 for recorded info* ⊕*www.towerofdavid. org.il* 🕮*NIS 30* ◷*Apr.–Oct., Sun.–Thurs. 10–5, Fri. call ahead or check Web site, Sat. 10–2; Nov.–Mar., Mon.–Thurs. 10–4, Sat. 10–2. Free guided tour in English with cost of admission, on weekdays at 11 (call ahead).*

WORTH NOTING

⓳ **Chamber of the Holocaust.** Not to be confused with Yad Vashem in West Jerusalem, this small museum is also dedicated to the memory of the 6 million European Jews annihilated by the Nazis in the Second World War. Among the artifacts salvaged from the Holocaust are items that the Nazis forced Jews to make out of sacred Torah scrolls (the biblical Five Books of Moses). With grim humor, one Jewish tailor fashioned the inscribed parchment into a jacket, choosing sections that contained the worst of the biblical curses. Plaques commemorate many of the 5,000 European Jewish communities destroyed from 1939 to 1945. ⊠*Near Tomb of David, Mt. Zion* 🕾*02/671–5105* ⊕*www.holocaustchamber. org* 🕮*NIS 12* ◷*Sun.–Thurs. 9–3:45, Fri. 9–1:30.*

⓰ **Dormition Abbey.** This round, black-domed Roman Catholic church, distinctive in its ornamented turrets and landmark clock tower, was built on land given by the Turkish sultan to the German kaiser Wil-helm II when the kaiser visited Jerusalem in 1898. The echoing main church, with its Byzantine-style apse and mosaic floors, was dedicated in 1910 by the German Benedictines. The lower-level crypt houses a cenotaph with a carved-stone figure of Mary in repose ("dormitio"),

A bicycle is one way anyone can avoid Jerusalem's often intense traffic.

reflecting the tradition that she fell into eternal sleep. Among the adjacent little chapels is one donated by the Ivory Coast, with wooden figures and motifs inlaid with ivory. The premises include a bookstore and a coffee shop. ⊠ *Near the Room of the Last Supper, Mt. Zion* ☎ *02/565-5330* ⊕ *www.hagia-maria-sion.net* ☜ *Free* ⊙ *Weekdays 8:30–11:45 and 12:40–5:30; Sat. 8:30–noon, 12:40–2:45, and 3:30–5:30; Sun. 10:30–11:45 and 12:30–5:30.*

 Tomb of David. According to the Bible, King David, the great Israelite king of the 10th century BC, was buried in "the City of David," one of the contemporary names for his capital, Jerusalem. The actual site of the city has been identified and excavated on the small ridge east of here, but medieval Jewish pilgrims erroneously placed the ancient city on this hill, where they sought—and supposedly found—the royal tomb. Its authenticity may be questionable, but some nine centuries of tears and prayers have sanctified the place.

The tomb itself is capped by a cenotaph, a massive stone marker draped with velvet cloth and embroidered with symbols and Hebrew texts traditionally associated with David. Behind it is a stone alcove, which some scholars think may be the sole remnant of a synagogue from the 5th century AD, the oldest of its kind in Jerusalem. More stringent regulations by Jewish religious authorities have recently divided the shrine into a men's and a women's side. Modest dress is required; men must cover their heads. ⊠ *Mt. Zion* ☎ *02/671-9767* ☜ *Free* ⊙ *Apr.–Sept., Sun.–Thurs. 8–6, Fri. and Jewish holiday eves 8–2; Oct.–Mar., Sun.–Thurs. 8–5, Fri. and Jewish holiday eves 8–1.*

CITY OF DAVID

Indiana Jones would have loved this archaeological adventure. Plunge underground to sense Jerusalem's primal pulse—the Spring of Gihon, the life-blood of the ancient city and the primary reason for its settlement, over four millennia ago. The Israelite king David captured this modest ridge from the Jebusites around 1000 BC, and made it his capital. David's son Solomon, who was anointed at the spring, subsequently expanded the city northward to Mt. Moriah, where he built the Temple of God (on the site of today's Dome of the Rock). In time, Jerusalem spread farther west and north; but in recent years, the name "City of David" has been revived to describe the city's ancient core. If you thrill to the thought of standing where the ancients once stood, you'll be in your element in this city of memories, from its Old Testament walls and water systems to its Second Temple streets and stones.

GETTING HERE AND AROUND

At the time of this writing, the limited legal parking nearby was eliminated by a new archaeological dig. Best come by cab, or walk down from the Old City by way of Dung Gate.

TIMING AND PRECAUTIONS

Allow yourself enough time for an unhurried tour of, say, two hours, noting that the site is closed Friday afternoon and all Saturday. There is a minibus (fare NIS 5) to shuttle you up the steep hill from the exit to the Visitors Center. The site is in the heart of the predominantly Arab Silwan neighborhood, where friction between veteran Palestinians and newly ensconced Jewish settlers is not unknown. The layout of the site and the guards on duty dispel any security concerns, however.

TOP ATTRACTIONS

㉒ **Hezekiah's Tunnel.** Wading through a 2,700-year-old tunnel that once
Fodor'sChoice supplied water to the city is a great adventure for those who like a little
★ exercise with their history. The Assyrians invaded Judah in 701 BC, 20 years after they had destroyed its sister-kingdom of Israel to the north. According to the Bible, King Hezekiah attempted to protect Jerusalem's precious water supply in order to meet the imminent assault on the capital. He instructed his men to "stop the water of the springs that were outside the city" (II Chronicles 32). Racing against time, they dug a water tunnel a third of a mile long through solid rock, one team starting from the Gihon Spring and the other from a new inner-city reservoir. Miraculously, considering the serpentine course of the tunnel, the two teams met in the middle. The chisel marks, the ancient plaster, and the zigzags near the halfway point as each team sought the other by sound bear witness to the remarkable project. With the water now diverted into the city, the original opening of the spring was blocked to deny the enemy access. Hezekiah, says the same biblical chapter, "closed the upper outlet of the waters of Gihon and directed them down to the west side of the city of David."

In the 19th century, an inscription in ancient Hebrew (since removed) was found chiseled into the tunnel wall near the exit. "This is the story of the boring through . . ." it began, echoing the biblical account; "the tunnelers hewed the rock, each man toward his fellow . . . And the

CLOSE UP

A Walk in the City of David

A walk-through-time adventure, this walk is a heady combination of mysterious tunnels and ancient remains. The climax is wading through the 2,700-year-old Hezekiah's Tunnel (water is knee- to thigh-deep; bring appropriate clothing, water shoes or sandals, and a flashlight; not recommended for very small children), though there is a dry exit from the site for nonwaders. Plan 1½ hours for the walk, and an additional 45 minutes to wade the tunnel. Note that you can tour the sites on your own or, for a larger admission fee, on a guided tour.

A platform at the City of David Visitors Center gives a fine view of the Kidron Valley, which drops sharply to the east, and gave ancient Jerusalem its best protection. Steps descend to the excavation site **Area G**, and from there halfway down the hill to **Warren's Shaft** (small sign on the right). At the entrance to the shaft are enlargements of remarkable clay seals. A

tunnel slopes down to the top of a shaft that drops 40 feet to the Gihon Spring. Conventional wisdom identifies this as the point where King David's commandos penetrated the city in 1000 BC, but recent excavations near the spring have suggested an alternative route.

A short flight of steps and a tunnel take you down through a cavernous structure with the massive foundations of 18th-century BC towers that once guarded the Gihon Spring, the original water supply of ancient Jerusalem. **Hezekiah's Tunnel**, also known as the Shiloah or Siloam Tunnel, was cut through the hill to secure the city's water supply in the face of the Assyrian invasion of 701 BC. It emerges at a small pool long identified as the New Testament "Pool of Siloam" where a blind man had his sight restored (John 9).

⇨ *For more information on the sights in bold, see the bulleted listings in City of David.*

---

water flowed from the spring toward the reservoir for 1,200 cubits [577 yards]."

If you don't want to get your feet wet, you can still view the spring and marvel at the ingenuity of the ancient engineers, and then exit the site through a narrow but dry Canaanite tunnel. If you do decide to enter the spring and wade the long narrow tunnel, you can easily imagine the dull digging of the ancient teams, and relive the electrifying moment when the last chunk of rock was removed, the water flowed, and the city saved. The tunnel emerges in the Pool of Siloam, mentioned in the New Testament as the place where a blind man had his sight restored (John 9). What you see today is a modest Byzantine construction; but the current exit takes you over the large flagstones of a Second Temple street to the original, impressive 1st-century reservoir, only recently discovered and partially exposed. ⊠*Off Ophel Rd., Silwan* ☎*02/626–2341* ⊕*www.cityofdavid.org.il* ✆*NIS 23, add NIS 5 for 3D film, guided tour NIS 50 (includes admission and film)* ☉*Apr.–Sept., Sun.–Thurs. 8–7, Fri. and Jewish holiday eves 8–3; Oct.–Mar., Sun.–Thurs. 8–5, Fri. and Jewish holiday eves 8–1, last entrance 2 hrs before closing.*

㉑ ★ **Warren's Shaft.** Charles Warren was an inspired British army engineer who explored Jerusalem in 1867. In the City of David he discovered

SIGHTSEEING TOURS

Jerusalem's guides and tour operators offer everything from orientation tours by bus to thematic walks. If your time is limited or you have a special interest, tours are useful.

ORIENTATION

Veteran nation-wide tour operators Egged Tours and United Tours offer almost identical half-day Jerusalem orientation tours, including a panoramic view and Old City highlights. The full-day tour adds the Yad Vashem Holocaust memorial (except on Saturday) and either a second panorama (Egged) or Mt. Zion shrines (United).

Prices are usually quoted in U.S. dollars so that visitors are exempt from the V.A.T. The approximate cost is $42 for the half-day tour, $62 for the full day. The price includes pickup at your hotel but ends at the Old City's Jaffa Gate. You can reserve directly or through your hotel concierge.

Zion Walking Tours is best known for its topic-focused Old City walking tours, but some of its seven routes venture well beyond the walls as well (biblical Jerusalem; Christian sites on Mt. of Olives; old Jewish neighborhoods).

Another option is Egged's Route 99 bus, a two-hour circle tour of Jerusalem. ⇨ *See Bus Travel in Getting Here and Around in Travel Smart Israel for information.*

Tour Contacts Egged Tours (☎ 1700/70-75-77 *or* 03/920-3919 ⊕ *www. egged.co.il/Eng/*). **United Tours** (☎ 02/625-2187 ⊕ *www.unitedtours.co.il*). **Zion Walking Tours** (✉ *Inside Jaffa Gate, opposite police station, Jaffa Gate* ☎ 02/628-7866 ⊕ *zionwt.dsites1. co.il*).

PERSONAL GUIDES

At this writing, the daily rate for a private guide with an air-conditioned car, limousine, or van was $400–$500, depending on the size of the vehicle; half-days start at $300. Many guides will offer their services without a car for $220–$280 per day, and $150–$190 for a half day. For private guiding, approach Genesis 2000 or Eshcolot Tours.

Guide Contacts Eshcolot Tours (✉ *17 Ya'ari St., Gilo* ☎ 02/566-5555 ✐ *advantag@netmedia.net.il*).

Genesis 2000 (☎ 052/286-2650, 052/381-4484, 02/676-5868 ✐ *genesis4@netvision.net.il*).

SPECIAL-INTEREST TOURS

The Sonia and Marco Nadler Institute of Archaeology in Tel Aviv University runs week-long programs in the summer for volunteers who want to join the excavations of the First Temple-era royal palace near Ramat Rachel, on the edge of Jerusalem.

Tour Contacts Ramat Rachel (⊕ *www. ramatrachel.co.il/archeology/ VolunteerPrograms.htm*).

WALKING TOURS

Zion Walking Tours offers both classic and off-the-beaten-path itineraries. Tours last three to three-and-a-half hours and cost $25–$35, depending on the sites visited. Both Egged Tours and United Tours do half-day walking tours of Old City highlights. (⇨ *See Orientation Tours, above, for contact information.*)

this spacious, sloping access tunnel—note the ancient chisel marks on the walls—which burrowed under the city wall to a point 40 feet above the Gihon Spring, in the valley. A narrow vertical shaft dropped into the spring, giving access to ancient water-drawers. The presumption was that it was pre-Davidic, and perhaps the actual biblical *tzinnor* (gutter or water shaft) of II Samuel 5 through which David's warriors penetrated the city, ca. 1000 BC. Archaeologists now believe that the space at the head of the shaft was only created in a later era; and a recent dig around the Gihon Spring at the bottom of the hill has uncovered a different access to the spring, protected by two huge towers that date back to the Middle Bronze Age, centuries before David. The biblical story remains intact for the moment, but the famous Warren's Shaft may not have been the exact place where it occurred. ⊠ *Off Ophel Rd., Silwan* ☏ *02/626–2341* ⊕ *www.cityofdavid.org.il* ✎ *NIS 23, add NIS 5 for 3D film, guided tour NIS 50 (includes admission and film)* ⊙ *Apr.– Sept., Sun.–Thurs. 8–7, Fri. and Jewish holiday eves 8–3; Oct.–Mar., Sun.–Thurs. 8–5, Fri. and Jewish holiday eves 8–1, last entrance 1 hr before closing, but ticket office closes 2 hrs before the site.*

WORTH NOTING

㉗ Area G. This open-air dig-site comes with the territory and your ticket. Archaeologists have dug up bits of the City of David for well over a century—notably Charles Warren in the 1860s, and Kathleen Kenyon a hundred years later. The most thorough expedition, however, was led by Israeli archaeologist Yigal Shiloh from 1978 to 1985. In this locale, he confirmed Kenyon's assertion that the angular pieces of the city wall, seen at the top, were indeed part of the 2nd-century BC construction that the historian Josephus Flavius dubbed the "First Wall." On the other hand, he redated the sloping "stepped structure" to at least the 10th century BC, the time of Israelite kings David and Solomon, when it apparently supported a palace or fortification on the crest of the ridge. In the 7th century BC, a house (now partially restored on a platform) was built against it.

The most intriguing artifacts found were 51 bullae, clay seals used for documents, just as hot wax might be used today, with personal names impressed on them in ancient Hebrew script. All of the seals were found in one chamber, suggesting that it was used as an archive or a royal office. This idea was reinforced by the biblical name on one of the seals: Gemariah ben Shafan, the royal secretary in the days of the prophet Jeremiah. The clay seals were baked into pottery by a massive fire, apparently during the Babylonian destruction of Jerusalem in 586 BC. ⊠ *Off Ophel Rd., Silwan* ☏ *02/626–2341* ⊕ *www.cityofdavid. org.il* ✎ *NIS 23, add NIS 5 for 3D film, guided tour NIS 50 (includes admission and film)* ⊙ *Apr.–Sept., Sun.–Thurs. 8–7, Fri. and Jewish holiday eves 8–3; Oct.–Mar., Sun.–Thurs. 8–5, Fri. and Jewish holiday eves 8–1, last entrance 1 hr before closing, but ticket office closes 2 hrs before the site.*

MOUNT OF OLIVES AND EAST JERUSALEM

Loosely speaking, "East Jerusalem" refers to the Arab neighborhoods controlled by Jordan in the years when the city was divided (1948–1967). That includes Mount of Olives, the areas north of the Old City, and in fact the Old City itself (though those sights are covered elsewhere in the chapter).

The sights in this area are for the most part distinctly Christian. A few are a little off the beaten path, and the best way to explore them—if you're energetic enough—is on foot. If you're driving, however, you can find parking at the Seven Arches Hotel on the Mount of Olives, and at the American Colony Hotel; or take a cab.

GETTING HERE AND AROUND

The Route 99 circle tour has a stop near the Hebrew University campus. If you enjoy a bit of a walk and the weather is fine, it's no more than 20 minutes across to Mount of Olives (with a bonus of a panoramic view of the Judean Desert to the east). A cab ride is an alternative, but if you skip the top of the mountain, the rest of the sights are accessible by foot from the Old City.

TIMING AND PRECAUTIONS

Morning views are best from Mount of Olives. Some of the sites are closed on Sundays. Watch out for pickpockets on Mount of Olives and the road down to Gethsemane, and the Nablus Road outside the Garden Tomb.

TOP ATTRACTIONS

❻ Garden of Gethsemane. After the Last Supper, the New Testament relates, Jesus and his disciples came to a "place" called Gethsemane. There he agonized and prayed, and there, in the end, he was betrayed and arrested. Gethsemane derives from the Aramaic or Hebrew word for "oil press," referring to the precious olive that has always flourished here. The enormous, gnarled, and still-productive olive trees on the site may be older than Christianity itself, according to some botanists.

The **Church of All Nations,** with its brilliantly colorful, landmark mosaic façade, was built in the garden in 1924 on the scanty remains of its Byzantine predecessor. The prolific architect, Antonio Barluzzi, filled the church's interior domes with mosaic symbols of the Catholic communities that contributed to its construction. The seal of the United States is in the first dome on the right as you enter the church; Canada is two up in the same line; and the English dome is the first, nearest the door, in the middle line. The windows are glazed with translucent alabaster in somber browns and purples, creating a mystical feeling in the dim interior. At the altar is the so-called Rock of the Agony, where Jesus is said to have endured his Passion; this is the source of the older name of the church, **the Basilica of the Agony.**

A popular approach to Gethsemane is walking down the steep road from the top of Mount of Olives, perhaps stopping in on the way at the Dominus Flevit church where, tradition has it, Jesus wept as he foretold the destruction of the city (Luke 19). The entrance to the well-tended garden at the foot of the hill is marked by a small platoon of vendors

CLOSE UP

Jerusalem Through the Ages

The first known mention of Jerusalem is in Egyptian "hate texts" of the 20th century BC, but archaeologists give the city a founding date of up to 1,000 years earlier. Abraham and the biblical Joshua may have been here, but it was King David, circa 1000 BC, who captured the city and made it his capital, thus propelling it onto the center stage of history. His son Solomon built the "First" Temple, giving the city a preeminence it enjoyed until its destruction by the Babylonians, and the exile of its population, in 586 BC.

They returned 50 years later, rebuilt the Temple (the "Second"), and began the slow process of revival. By the 2nd century BC, Jerusalem was again a vibrant Jewish capital, albeit one with a good dose of Hellenistic cultural influence. Herod the Great (who reigned 37 BC–4 BC) revamped the Temple on a magnificent scale and expanded the city into a cosmopolis of world renown.

This was the Jerusalem Jesus knew, a city of monumental architecture, teeming—especially during the Jewish pilgrim festivals—with tens of thousands of visitors. It was here that the Romans crucified Jesus (circa AD 29), and here, too, that the Great Jewish Revolt against Rome erupted, ending in AD 70 with the total destruction (once again) of the city and the Temple.

The Roman emperor Hadrian redesigned Jerusalem as the pagan polis of Aelia Capitolina (AD 135), an urban plan that became the basis for the Old City of today. The Byzantines made it a Christian center, with a massive wave of church building (4th–6th centuries AD), until the Arab conquest of AD 638 brought the holy city under Muslim sway. Except during the golden age of the Ummayad dynasty, in the late 7th and early 8th centuries, Jerusalem was no more than a provincial town under the Muslim regimes of the early Middle Ages. The Crusaders stormed it in 1099 and made it the capital of their Latin Kingdom. With the reconquest of Jerusalem by the Muslims, the city again lapsed into a languid provincialism for 700 years under the Mamluk and Ottoman empires. The British conquest in 1917 thrust the city back into the world limelight as rising rival nationalisms vied to possess it.

Jerusalem was divided by the 1948 war: the much larger Jewish western sector became the capital of the State of Israel, while Jordan annexed the smaller, predominantly Arab eastern sector, which included the Old City. The Six-Day War of 1967 reunited the city under Israeli rule, but the concept of an Arab "East" Jerusalem and a Jewish "West" Jerusalem still remains, even though new Jewish neighborhoods in the northeastern and southeastern sections have rendered the distinction somewhat oversimplified.

The holy city continues to engage the attention of devotees of Christianity, Islam, and Judaism. Between Jews and Arabs it remains the subject of passionate debate and occasional violence as rival visions clash for possession of the city's past and control of its future. It is widely recognized that any peace negotiations between Israel and the Palestinians will fail unless the thorny issue of sharing Jerusalem is resolved.

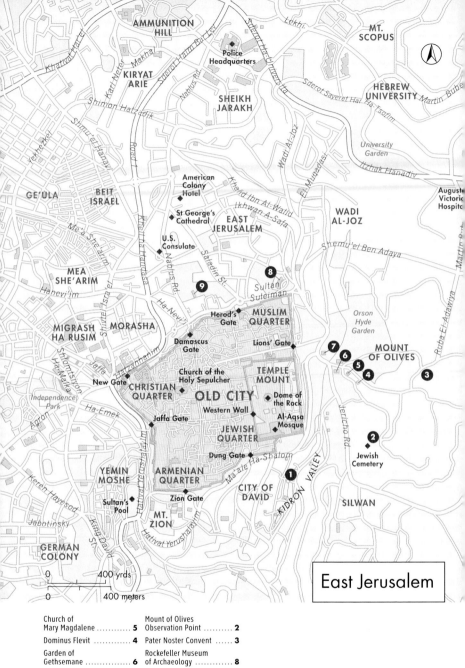

East Jerusalem

0 _____ 400 yards
0 _____ 400 meters

Church of
Mary Magdalene 5

Dominus Flevit 4

Garden of
Gethsemane 6

Garden Tomb 9

Kidron Valley 1

Mount of Olives
Observation Point 2

Pater Noster Convent 3

Rockefeller Museum
of Archaeology 8

Tomb of the Virgin 7

outside. ⊠*Jericho Rd., Kidron Valley* ☏*02/626–6444* ✉*Free* ☉*Apr.–Sept., daily 8–12 and 2–6; Oct.–Mar., daily 8–12 and 2–5.*

➒ Garden Tomb. A beautifully tended English-style country garden makes
★ this an island of tranquillity in the hurly-burly of East Jerusalem. What Christian pilgrims come for, however, is an empty ancient tomb, and a grand opportunity to ponder the Gospel account of the death and resurrection of Jesus. It is a favorite site for the many Protestant visitors who respond less or not at all to the ornamentation and ritual of the Holy Sepulcher.

The theory identifying this site with Calvary and Jesus' burial place goes back to 1883, when the British general Charles Gordon (of later Khartoum fame) spent several months in Jerusalem. From his window looking out over the Old City walls, Gordon was struck by the skull-like features of a cliff face north of the Damascus Gate. He was convinced that this, rather than the traditional Calvary in the Church of the Holy Sepulcher, was "the place of the skull" (Mark 15) where Jesus was crucified. His conviction was infectious, and after his death, a fundraising campaign in England resulted in the purchase of the adjacent site in 1894. An ancient rock-cut tomb had already been uncovered there, and subsequent excavations exposed cisterns and a wine press, features typical of an ancient garden.

All the elements of the Gospel account of Jesus' death and burial seemed to be in evidence, and the newly formed Garden Tomb Association was jubilant. According to the New Testament, Jesus was buried in the fresh tomb of the wealthy Joseph of Arimathea, in a garden close to the execution site, and archaeologists identified the tomb as an upper-class Jewish burial place of the Second Temple period. Recent research has challenged that conclusion, however. The tomb might be from the Old Testament period, making it too old to have been Jesus', since his was freshly cut. The gentle guardians of the Garden Tomb do not insist on the identification of the site as that of Calvary and the tomb of Christ, but are keen to provide a contemplative setting for the pilgrim, in a place that just might have been historically significant. ⊠*Conrad Schick St., East Jerusalem* ☏*02/627–2745* ⊕*www.gardentomb.com* ✉*Free* ☉*Mon.–Sat. 9–noon and 2–5:30.*

NEED A BREAK?
The upscale **American Colony Hotel** (⊠ *23 Nablus Rd., American Colony* ☏*02/627–9777*) is an elegant 19th-century limestone building with cane furniture, Armenian ceramic tiles, and a delightful courtyard. The food is generally very good, and a light lunch or afternoon tea in the cool lobby lounge, at the poolside restaurant, or on the patio under the trees can make for a well-earned break.

➋ Mount of Olives Observation Point. This is the classic panoramic view of
★ the Old City: looking across the Kidron Valley over the gold Dome of the Rock. It's best in the early morning, with the sun at your back, or at sunset on days with some clouds, when the golden glow can compensate for the glare.

DID YOU KNOW?

Many graves in the Jewish cemetery on the slope below the Mount of Olives have stones on them. It's customary for Jews to place a stone on graves to indicate they have visited.

The Mount of Olives has been bathed in sanctity for millennia. On the slope beneath you, and off to your left, is the vast **Jewish cemetery,** reputedly the oldest still in use anywhere in the world. For more than 2,000 years, Jews have been buried here to await the coming of the Messiah and the resurrection to follow. The raised structures over the graves are merely tomb markers, not crypts; burial is below ground.

In the Old City wall facing you, and just to the right of the Dome of the Rock, is the blocked-up, double-arched Gate of Mercy, or Golden Gate. Jewish tradition holds that the Messiah will enter Jerusalem this way; Christian tradition says he already did, on Palm Sunday. To the south of the Dome of the Rock is the black-domed Al-Aqsa Mosque, and behind it the stone arches of the Jewish Quarter. Some distance behind the Dome of the Rock is the large, gray dome of the Church of the Holy Sepulcher. To the left of the Old City, the cone-roof Dormition Abbey and its adjacent tower mark the top of Mt. Zion, today outside the walls but within the city of the Second Temple period. ⊠ *E-Sheikh St., opposite Seven Arches Hotel, Mt. of Olives.*

❽ Rockefeller Museum of Archaeology. The Rockefeller's octagonal white stone tower is an East Jerusalem landmark. Built in the 1930s, its echoing stone halls and somewhat old-fashioned display techniques recall the British Mandate period, when it was in its prime. The finds are all from this country, dating from prehistoric times to around AD 1700. Among the most important exhibits are cultic masks from Neolithic Jericho, ivories from Canaanite (Bronze Age) Megiddo, the famous Israelite "Lachish Letters" (6th century BC), Herodian inscriptions, and decorative reliefs from Hisham's Palace, in Jericho, and from the Church of the Holy Sepulcher. On Mondays and Wednesdays at 11 AM (except on eves of Jewish holidays), a free shuttle bus takes visitors from the Israel Museum to the Rockefeller for a guided tour. (There is no addition to the cost of the entry fee, but it is necessary to reserve a place.) The museum has no parking within its grounds. ⊠ *27 Sultan Suleiman St., East Jerusalem* ☎ *02/628–2251, 02/670–8811 to reserve shuttle bus from Israel Museum* ⊕ *www.imj.org.il/rockefeller/eng/index.html* ☎ *NIS 26; combined ticket with Israel Museum (good for 2 wks) NIS 37* ☉ *Sun., Mon., Wed., and Thurs. 10–3, Sat. 10–2.*

WORTH NOTING

❺ Church of Mary Magdalene. This Russian Orthodox church, with its sculpted white turrets and gold onion domes, looks like something out of a fairytale. It was dedicated in 1888, when the competition among European powers for influence in this part of the world was at its height. The church has limited hours, but its icon-studded interior and tranquil garden are well worth a visit if your plans bring you to the area at the right time. ⊠ *Above Gethsemane, Mt. of Olives* ☎ *02/628–4371* ☎ *Free* ☉ *Tues. and Thurs. 10–noon.*

❹ Dominus Flevit. Designed by Antonio Barluzzi in the 1950s, the tear-shape church—its name means "the Lord wept"—preserves the New Testament story of Jesus' sorrowful prophecy of the destruction of Jerusalem (Luke 19). The remarkable feature of its simple interior is a picture window facing west, the iron cross on the altar silhouetted against a superb view of the Old City. Many small archaeological items were found here, but the tradition that holds this as the site of the story is no older than the Crusader period. The courtyard is a good place to enjoy the view in peace between waves of pilgrim groups. (Equally worthy of mention are the rest rooms, rare in this area!) The church is about one-third of the way down the steep road that descends to Gethsemane from the Mount of Olives observation point. Beware of pickpockets on the street outside. ⊠ *Below Mount of Olives observation point, Mt. of Olives* ☎ *02/626–6450* ⊕ *www.christusrex.org* 🖾 *Free* ☉ *Daily 8–11:45 and 2:30–5.*

❶ **Kidron Valley.** This deep valley separates the Old City and the City of David from the high ridge of the Mount of Olives and the Arab neighborhood of Silwan. In the cliff face below the neighborhood are the symmetrical openings of tombs from both the First Temple (Old Testament) and Second Temple (Hellenistic-Roman) periods. You can view the impressive group of 2,200-year-old funerary monuments from the lookout terrace at the southeast corner of the Old City wall, down and to your left, or wander down into the valley itself and see them close up. The huge, square, stone structure with the conical roof is known as **Absalom's Pillar.** The one crowned by a pyramidal roof, a solid block of stone cut out of the mountain, is called **Zachariah's Tomb.** The association with those Old Testament personalities was a medieval mistake, and the structures more probably mark the tombs of wealthy Jerusalemites of the Second Temple period who wished to await in style the coming of the Messiah and the resurrection that would surely soon follow. To see the structures up close, access is best from Jericho Road, just south of Gethsemane. ⊠ *Kidron Valley.*

❸ **Pater Noster Convent.** The focal point of this Carmelite convent is a grotto, traditionally identified as the place where Jesus taught his disciples the so-called Lord's Prayer: "Our Father [*Pater Noster*], Who art in Heaven . . ." (Matthew 6). The site was purchased by the Princesse de la Tour d'Auvergne of France in 1868, and the convent was built on the site of earlier Byzantine and Crusader structures. The ambitious basilica, begun in the 1920s, was designed to follow the lines of a 4th-century church, but was never completed: its aisles, open to the sky, are now lined with pine trees. The real attractions of the site, however, are the many ceramic plaques adorning the cloister walls and the small church, with the Lord's Prayer in over 100 different languages. (Look for the high wall and metal door on a bend 200 yards before the Seven Arches Hotel.) ⊠ *E-Sheikh St., Mt. of Olives* ☎ *02/626–4904* 🖾 *NIS 7* ☉ *Mon.–Sat. 8:30–noon and 2:30–4:30.*

❼ **Tomb of the Virgin.** The Gothic facade of the underground Church of the Assumption, which contains this shrine, clearly dates it to the Crusader era (12th century). However, tradition has it that this is where the Virgin Mary was interred and then "assumed" into heaven. In an otherwise gloomy church—hung with age-darkened icons and brass lamps—the marble sarcophagus, thought to date from the 12th century, remains illuminated. The Status Quo Agreement in force in the Church of the Holy Sepulcher and Bethlehem's Church of the Nativity pertains here, too: the Greek Orthodox, Armenian Orthodox, and even the Muslims

On the Mount of Olives, the stunning mosaic facade of the Church of All Nations is a city landmark.

control different parts of the property. The Roman Catholic Franciscans were expelled in 1757, a loss of privilege that rankles to this day. The shrine is a few steps away from the Garden of Gethsemane. ✉ *Jericho Rd., adjacent to Gethsemane, Kidron Valley* ☎ *02/628–4613* ⊕ *www.christusrex.org* 💲 *Free* 🕙 *Daily 6–noon and 2:30–5.*

WEST JERUSALEM

Visitors tend to focus, naturally enough, on the historical and religious sights on the eastern side of town, especially in the Old City; but West Jerusalem houses the nation's institutions, is the repository for its collective memory, and—together with the downtown—gives more insight into contemporary life in Israel's largest city. The world-class Israel Museum and Yad Vashem are located here, as well as poignant Mt. Herzl and the picturesque neighborhood of Ein Kerem. These attractions, which are spread out, are most easily accessible by car or by a combination of buses and short cab rides.

GETTING HERE AND AROUND

There are good city bus services in this part of town (ask at each site how to get to the next), but a few $10 cab rides will be a much better use of limited time. Remember that Route 99 serves a good number of sights in this part of town.

TIMING AND PRECAUTIONS

Pay attention to the closing times of sites: several are not open on Saturdays and close early on Fridays. Some museums have evening hours on particular days—a time-efficient option. Avoid burnout by staggering visits to the museums, and combining them with different kinds of experiences.

TOP ATTRACTIONS

8 Bible Lands Museum. Most archaeological museums group artifacts according to their place of origin (Egyptian, Babylonian, and so on), but the curators here have abandoned this method in favor of a chronological display. The museum was the brainchild of the late Elie Borowski, whose personal collection of ancient artifacts forms its core. The display method allows a comparison of objects of neighboring cultures of the same period, the better to explore cross-cultural interactions and influences. The exhibits cover a period of more than 6,000 years—from the prehistoric Neolithic period to that of the Byzantine Empire—and sweep geographically from Afghanistan to Nubia (present-day Sudan). Rare clay vessels, fertility idols, cylinder seals, ivories, and sarcophagi fill the soaring, naturally lighted galleries. Look for the ancient Egyptian wooden coffin, in a stunning state of preservation.

The concept of the museum is intriguing, but some have criticized its methodology. A concept was imposed on a largely preexisting collection, rather than a collection being created item by selected item to illustrate a concept. Join the guided tour to get the most out of the place.

The museum runs a Saturday night concert series, with cheese and wine served in the foyer. The NIS 75 ticket includes access to the exhibition areas for 30 minutes before and after the concert. ⊠*25 Granot St., Givat Ram* ☎*02/561–1066* ⊕*www.blmj.org* ☜*NIS 32* ☉*Sun.–Tues. and Thurs. 9:30–5:30, Wed. 9:30–9:30, Fri. and Jewish holiday eves 9:30–2. Guided tours in English Sun.–Fri. at 10:15 (Wed. at 5:30 in addition); call ahead to verify.*

2 Chagall Windows and Hadassah Hospital. Some remarkable stained glass draws travelers to Hadassah, one of the leading general hospitals in the Middle East and the teaching hospital for Hebrew University's medical and dental schools. When the U.S.-based Hadassah women's organization approached the Russian-born Jewish artist Marc Chagall in 1959 about designing stained-glass windows for the synagogue at the new hospital, he was delighted and contributed his work for free. Taking his inspiration from the Bible—Jacob's deathbed blessings on his sons and, to a lesser extent, Moses' valediction to the tribes of Israel—the artist created 12 vibrant windows in primary colors, with an ark full of characteristically Chagallian beasts and a scattering of Jewish and esoteric symbols. The innovative techniques of the Reims glassmakers give the wafer-thin windows an astounding illusion of depth in many places. Buses 19 and 27 serve the hospital. The recorded explanations in the synagogue alternate languages. ⊠*Hadassah Hospital, Henrietta Szold Rd., Ein Kerem* ☎*02/677–6271* ⊕*www.hadassah.org.il/english* ☜*NIS 10* ☉*Sun.–Thurs. 8–4; call ahead to verify times.*

1 Ein Kerem. The neighborhood of Ein Kerem (sometimes Ein "Karem") ★ still retains much of its old village character. A couple of hours is enough time to explore it, though you could spend more if you take time out for a coffee or a meal. Tree-framed stone houses are strewn across its hillsides with a pleasing Mediterranean nonchalance. Many

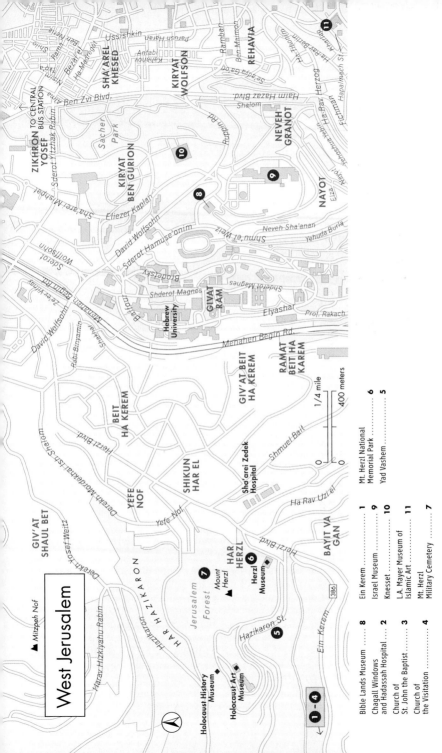

West Jerusalem

Mitzpeh Nof

GIV'AT SHAUL BET

HAR HAZIKARON

Holocaust History Museum

Holocaust Art Museum

Jerusalem Forest

Mount Herzl

HAR HERZL

Herzl Museum

Hazikaron St.

Ein Kerem

386

BAYIT VA GAN

Herzl Blvd.

Ha Rav Uzi'el

Sha'arei Zedek Hospital

Shmuel Bait

SHIKUN HAR EL

YEFE NOF

Yefe Nof

BEIT HA KEREM

GIV'AT BEIT HA KEREM

RAMAT BEIT HA KAREM

Menahem Begin Rd.

Elyashar

Prof. Rakach

GIVAT RAM

Hebrew University

Shderot Magnes

Shderot Magnes

Bradetsky

Sderot Wolffsohn

David Wolfsohn

Rabi Binyamin

Shahar

Menahem Begin Rd.

Ze'ev Vilnay

Derekh Mordekhai Ish-Shalom

Herzl Blvd.

Yosef Weitz

Harav Hizkiyahu Rabin

Shmu'el Weiz

Neveh Sha'anan

Yehuda Buria

NAYOT

Elza

Nayot

Sderot Hamuse'onim

David Wolfsohn

Eliezer Kaplan

KIRYAT BEN GURION

Sha'arei Mishpat

Sderot Yitzhak Rabin

ZIKHRON YOSEF

TO CENTRAL BUS STATION

Ben Zvi Blvd.

Sacher Park

Ruppin Rd.

Shalom

Haim Hazaz Blvd.

NEVEH GRANOT

REHAVIA

Se'adya Ga'on

Ben-Maimon

Ramban

Parush Haran

Ussishkin

Ha-Rav Berlin

Khabad

Ha-Rav Herzog

Hapalmach St.

Fichman

Yehoshua Bin-Nun

Antabi

Kahoneh

SHA'AREL KHESED

KIRYAT WOLFSON

Bezal'el

Ha-Madregot

Alfasi

Nissim

Keren Ha-Yesod

Ha Rav Rami

Shaul

Ben Netta

8

10

9

11

1-4

Bible Lands Museum 8

Chagall Windows and Hadassah Hospital.... 2

Church of St. John the Baptist......... 3

Church of the Visitation 4

Ein Kerem 1

Israel Museum 9

Knesset 10

L.A. Mayer Museum of Islamic Art 11

Mt. Herzl Military Cemetery 7

Mt. Herzl National Memorial Park 6

Yad Vashem................. 5

0   1/4 mile

0   400 meters

The Shrine of the Book at the Israel Museum dramatically displays delicate sections of the Dead Sea Scrolls.

homes have been marvelously renovated by artists and professionals who have joined the older working-class population over the last 40 years. Back alleys provide an off-the-beaten-path feel, and occasionally a serendipitous art or craft studio. Though not mentioned by name in the New Testament, Ein Kerem is identified as the home of John the Baptist, and indeed the orange-roofed **Church of St. John the Baptist** in the heart of the village, and the **Church of the Visitation** *(see below for these listings)* up the hillside above the Spring of the Virgin, are its most prominent landmarks.

The road down to the valley begins at the big Mt. Herzl intersection. Alternatively, if you're driving and you've just visited the Chagall Windows, turn right as soon as you leave the hospital grounds, and descend to where the road joins Route 386. Turn right again, reentering Jerusalem through the bottom of Ein Kerem. The neighborhood is served by city bus 17. ⊠*Ein Kerem.*

❾ **Israel Museum.** An eclectic treasure trove, the museum is a world-class don't-miss. At the time of this writing, its entire main complex was

Fodor's Choice closed for an $80 million "renewal," with a reopening date of June

★ 2010. New exhibits, fresh ideas, and state-of-the-art presentations will enhance the three main specialties of art, archaeology, and Judaica. Meanwhile, take time to explore what *is* open: the Dead Sea Scrolls in the white-domed Shrine of the Book, the 1:50 scale model of 1st-century-AD Jerusalem, the sculpture garden, and fascinating changing exhibits in the Youth Wing.

The **Dead Sea Scrolls** are certainly the Israel Museum's most famous—and most important—collection. The first of the 2,000-year-old scrolls were discovered by a Bedouin boy in 1947 in a Judean Desert cave, overlooking the Dead Sea. The adventures of these priceless artifacts before they found a permanent home are the stuff of which Indiana Jones movies are made (*see Masada and the Dead Sea in Chapter 3*). The shape of the pavilion was inspired by the lids of the clay jars in which the first scrolls were found.

The scrolls were written in the Second-Temple period by a fundamentalist Jewish sect, conventionally identified as the Essenes, as they are referred to by contemporary historians. All archaeological, laboratory, and textual evidence dates the earliest of the scrolls to the 2nd century BC; none could have been written later than AD 68, the year in which their home community, known today as Qumran, was destroyed by the Romans. Written on parchment, and still in an extraordinary state of preservation because of the exceptional dryness of the Dead Sea region, the scrolls contain the oldest Hebrew manuscripts of the Old Testament ever found, authenticating the almost identical Hebrew texts still in use today. Sectarian literature includes "The Rule of the Community," a sort of constitution of this ascetic group, and "The War of the Sons of Light Against the Sons of Darkness," a blow-by-blow account of a final cataclysmic conflict that would, they believed, presage the messianic age.

The quarter-acre **scale model**, adjacent to the Shrine of the Book, represents Jerusalem as it was on the eve of the Great Revolt against Rome (AD 66). For 40 years, the huge, intricate reconstruction was a popular attraction in its original home, on the grounds of West Jerusalem's Holyland Hotel. It moved to the Israel Museum in 2006, when the hotel was overtaken by high-end property development.

When the model was originally built in the mid-1960s, its designer, the late Professor Michael Avi-Yonah, relied on considerable data gleaned from Roman-period historians, important Jewish texts, and even the New Testament. Later archaeological excavations have sometimes confirmed and sometimes contradicted his inspired guesswork, and the model has been updated occasionally to incorporate new knowledge. The available audioguide is a worthwhile asset in deciphering the site.

The open-air **Art Garden** was designed against a Judean Hills cityscape by the landscape architect Isamu Noguchi. Crunch over the gravel amid works by Daumier, Rodin, Moore, and Picasso.

BRIDGE OF STRINGS

Designed by Spanish architect Santiago Calatrava, the new "Bridge of Strings" suspends the new light rail over the intersection at Jerusalem's western (Tel Aviv highway, Route 1) entrance. The commission was intended to provide the city with a contemporary icon. "What do we need it for?" complained some residents. Judge for yourself from the best angle, not as you enter the city but from the sidewalk outside the International Convention Center (*Binyanei Ha'ooma, Zalman Shazar Blvd.*). The first phase of the light rail, years behind schedule and millions over budget, is slated for completion in 2010.

Israel's Electoral System

Take two Israelis," runs the old quip, "and you've got three political parties!" The saying is not without truth in a nation where everyone has a strong opinion and usually will not hesitate to express it. The Knesset reflects this rambunctious spirit, sometimes to the point of paralyzing the parliamentary process and driving the public to distraction.

Israel's electoral system, based on proportional representation, is a legacy of the dangerous but heady days of Israel's War of Independence, in 1948–49. To avoid an acrimonious and divisive election while the fledgling state was still fighting to stay alive, the founding fathers developed a one-body parliamentary system that gave representation to rival ideological factions in proportion to their comparative strength in the country's *pre*-State institutions.

Instead of the winner-takes-all approach of the constituency system, the Israeli system grants any party that wins 2% of the national vote its first seat in the Knesset. The good news is that even fringe parties can have their voices heard. The bad news is that the system spawns a plethora of political parties,

making it virtually impossible for one party to get the majority needed to govern alone.

Consequently, Israeli governments have always consisted of a coalition of parties, inevitably making them governments of compromise. The smaller coalition partners have been able to demand a price for their crucial parliamentary support—influential political positions, budgets for pet projects, and so on—which is often beyond what a minor party deserves, and sometimes at odds with the good of the nation at large.

Israel also has a President, chosen by the members of the Knesset for one term of seven years; these elections are held at a different time than the national elections.

After the elections for the Knesset, the President consults with every party that made the 2% cut, and entrusts the party leader who seems to have the best coalition options with the job of forming a government. If successful within a designated period, he or she becomes Prime Minister.

Once a year, when the **youth wing** is not substituting for closed exhibition wings, it mounts a new exhibition, delightfully interactive and often adult-friendly, designed to encourage children to appreciate the arts and the world around them, or be creative in a crafts workshop. Parents with restless kids will also be grateful for the outdoor play areas. A cafeteria (only one at this writing, and closed Saturday) and a museum store complete the site. ⊠*Ruppin Rd., Givat Ram* ☎*02/670–8811* ⊕*www.imj.org.il* ⊠*NIS 42 (includes audioguide); half price for return visit within one month (keep your ticket)* ☉*Sun., Mon., Wed., Thurs., Sat., and Jewish holidays 10–5, Tues. 4–9, Fri. and Jewish holiday eves 10–2.*

❿ **Knesset.** Both the name of Israel's one-chamber parliament and its number of seats (120) were taken from *Haknesset Hagedolah*, the Great Assembly of the Second Temple period, some 2,000 years ago. The 40-minute public tour held on Sunday and Thursday includes the

2

session hall as well as three enormous, brilliantly colored tapestries designed by Marc Chagall on the subjects of the Creation, the Exodus, and Jerusalem. On other days, when in session, the Knesset is open to the public—call ahead to verify but note that all the proceedings are of course conducted in Hebrew. Allow at least 1½ hours for the visit (perhaps more in summer, when the lines are longer), arrive at least 30 minutes before the tour, and be sure to bring your passport.

Across the road from the Knesset main gate is a 15-foot-high bronze menorah, based on the one that once graced the ancient temple in Jerusalem. The seven-branch candelabra was adopted soon after independence as the official symbol of the modern State of Israel. This one, designed by artist Bruno Elkin, and given as a gift by the British Parliament to the Knesset in 1956, is decorated with bas-relief depictions of events and personages in Jewish history, from biblical times to the modern day. Behind the menorah is the Wohl Rose Garden (enter from outside the Knesset security barrier), which has hundreds of varieties of roses, many lawns for children to romp on, and adult-friendly nooks in its upper section. ⊠ *Kiryat Ben-Gurion, Givat Ram* ☎ *02/675–3416* ⊕ *www. knesset.gov.il* ☐ *Free* ☉ *Guided tours Sun. and Thurs. 8:30–2:30. Call ahead to verify tour times in English.*

❻ **Mt. Herzl National Memorial Park.** Cedars of Lebanon and native pine and cypress trees surround the entrance to the memorial and cemetery, which has a section with the graves of Zionist Theodor Herzl and many Israeli leaders. Immediately to the left is the **Herzl Museum** (⊠ *Mt. Herzl* ☎ *02/632–1515* ⊕ *www.herzl.org* ☉ *Sun.–Thurs. 8:45–3:15, Fri. 8:45–12:15*), a strongly engaging, interactive introduction to the life, times, and legacy of Israel's early visionary. Tours take an hour and cost NIS 25. Call ahead to verify times of tours in English. In 1894, the Budapest-born Theodor Herzl was the Paris correspondent for a Vienna newspaper when the Dreyfus treason trial hit the headlines. The anti-Semitic outbursts that Herzl encountered in cosmopolitan Paris shocked him. Dreyfus, a Jewish officer in the French army, had actually been framed and was later exonerated. Herzl devoted himself to the problem of Jewish vulnerability in "foreign" host countries and to the need for a Jewish state. The result of his activities was the first World Zionist Congress, held in Basel, Switzerland, in 1897. That year Herzl wrote in his diary: "If not in five years, then in 50, [a Jewish state] will become reality." True to his prediction, the United Nations approved the idea exactly 50 years later, in November 1947. Herzl died in 1904, and his remains were brought to Israel in 1949. His simple grave marker, inscribed in Hebrew with just his last name, caps the hill.

To the left (west) of the grave site, a gravel path leads down to a section containing the graves of Israeli national leaders, among them prime ministers Levi Eshkol, Golda Meir, and Yitzhak Rabin, and presidents Zalman Shazar and Chaim Herzog. Bear down and right through the military cemetery, exiting back on Herzl Boulevard, about 250 yards below the parking lot where you entered. ⊠ *Herzl Blvd., Mt. Herzl* ☎ *02/643–3266* ☐ *Free* ☉ *Apr.–Sept., Sun.–Thurs. 8–6:45, Fri. and Jewish holiday eves 8–12:45; Oct.–Mar., Sun.–Thurs. 8–4:45, Fri. and Jewish holiday eves 8–12:45.*

Tisch Family Zoological Gardens. Spread over a scenic 62-acre ridge in the Judean Hills, this zoo has many of the usual species that delight zoo visitors everywhere: monkeys, snakes, and birds, for example. But it goes much further, focusing on two groups of wildlife. The first is creatures mentioned in the Bible that have become locally extinct, some as late as the 20th century. Among these are Asian lions, bears, cheetahs, the Nile crocodile, and the Persian fallow deer. Plaques on the enclosures give biblical references and modern information. The second focus is on endangered species worldwide, among them the Asian elephant and rare macaws. This is a wonderful place to let kids expend some energy (and adults to have some down-time from regular touring!). Early morning or late afternoon are the best hours in summer; budget 2½ hours for a really full visit. A wagon-train does the rounds of the zoo, at a nominal fee of NIS 2 (not on Saturdays and Jewish holidays). The Noah's Ark Visitors Center has a movie and computer programs. The zoo is served by the Circle Tour bus (line 99), and by city routes 26 (from Central Bus Station) and 33 (from Mt. Herzl). ⊠*Near the Jerusalem (Malcha) Mall, Malcha* ☎*02/675–0111* ⊕*www.jerusalemzoo.org.il* ⊠*NIS 42* ⊙*June–Aug., Sun.–Thurs. 9–7, Fri. 9–4:30, Sat. 10–6; Sept., Apr., and May, Sun.–Thurs. 9–6, Fri. and Jewish holiday eves 9–4:30, Sat. 10–6; Oct.–Mar., Sun.–Thurs. 9–5, Fri. and Jewish holiday eves 9–4:30, Sat. 10–5. Call ahead to verify closing times and possible guided tours. Last entrance 1 hr before closing.*

⑤ Yad Vashem. The experience of the Holocaust—the annihilation of 6 million Jews by the Nazis during World War II—is so deeply seared into the Jewish national psyche that understanding it goes a long way toward understanding Israelis themselves. The institution of Yad Vashem, created in 1953 by an act of the Knesset, was charged with preserving a record of those times. The name "Yad Vashem"—"a memorial and a name (a memory)"—comes from the biblical book of Isaiah (56:5). The Israeli government has made a tradition of bringing almost all high-ranking official foreign guests to visit the place.

The riveting **Holocaust History Museum**—a 200-yard-long triangular concrete prism—is the centerpiece of the site. Powerful visual and audiovisual techniques in a series of galleries document Jewish life in Europe before the catastrophe and follow the escalation of persecution and internment to the hideous climax of the Nazi's "Final Solution." Video interviews and personal artifacts individualize the experience. Note that children under 10 are not admitted; large bags have to be checked.

Near the exit of the museum is a film center, a computer center, and an art museum. The older, small **Art Museum** presents a permanent, poignant exhibition of children at play in the Holocaust.

In Yad Vashem's Holocaust History Museum, the Hall of Names includes 600 photos of Jews who perished.

The small **Children's Memorial** is dedicated to the 1.5 million Jewish children murdered by the Nazis. Architect Moshe Safdie wanted to convey the enormity of the crime without numbing the visitor's emotions or losing sight of the victims' individuality. The result is a single dark room, lit by five candles infinitely reflected in some 500 mirrors. Recorded narrators intone the names, ages, and countries of origin of the known victims. The effect is electrifying. There are no steps, and guide rails are provided throughout.

The **Avenue of the Righteous** encircles Yad Vashem with several thousand trees marked with the names of Gentiles in Europe who risked and sometimes lost their lives trying to save Jews from the Nazis. Raoul Wallenberg, King Christian X of Denmark, Corrie ten Boom, and Oskar Schindler are among the more famous honorees. The **Hall of Remembrance** is a heavy basalt-and-concrete building that houses an eternal flame, with the names of the death and concentration camps in relief on the floor.

At the bottom of the hill, large rough-hewn limestone boulders divide the **Valley of the Communities** into a series of small, man-made canyons. Each clearing represents a region of Nazi Europe, laid out geographically. The names of some 5,000 destroyed Jewish communities are inscribed in the stone walls, with very large letters highlighting those that were particularly important in prewar Europe.

There is an information booth (be sure to pick up a map of the site), a bookstore, and a cafeteria at the entrance to Yad Vashem. Photography is not permitted within the exhibition areas. Allow about two hours to see the Holocaust History Museum; if your time is short, be sure to see the Children's Memorial and the Avenue of the Righteous in addition to the museum. The site is an easy 10-minute walk or a quick free shuttle from the Mt. Herzl intersection, which in turn is served by many city bus lines. The Egged sightseeing bus 99 takes you right into Yad Vashem. ⊠ *Hazikaron St., near Herzl Blvd., Mt. Herzl* ☎ *02/644–3565* ⊕ *www.yadvashem.org* 🖃 *Free* ⊘ *Sun.–Wed. 9–5, Thurs. 9–8 (late closing for History Museum only), Fri. and Jewish holiday eves 9–2. Last entrance 1 hr before closing.*

WORTH NOTING

❸ Church of St. John the Baptist. The orange tile roof of this large, late-17th-century Franciscan church is a landmark in Ein Kerem. Though not mentioned by name in the New Testament, the village has long been identified as the birthplace of John the Baptist, a tradition that apparently goes back to the Byzantine period (5th century AD). Apart from the grotto where John the Baptist is said to have been born, the church's old paintings and glazed tiles alone make it worth a visit. ⊠ *Ein Kerem St., Ein Kerem* ☎ *02/632–3000* 🖃 *Free* ⊘ *Apr.–Sept., daily 8–noon and 2:30–6; Oct.–Mar., daily 8–noon and 2:30–5.*

❹ Church of the Visitation. Built over what is thought to have been the home of John the Baptist's parents, Zechariah and Elizabeth, this church sits high up the hillside in Ein Kerem, with a wonderful view of the valley and the surrounding wooded hills. It is a short but stiff walk up from the spring at the center of the village. When Mary, pregnant with Jesus, came to visit her pregnant cousin, the aging Elizabeth, "the babe leaped in [Elizabeth's] womb" with joy at recognizing the unborn Jesus, and Mary pronounced the paean to God known as the Magnificat ("My soul doth magnify the Lord . . ." [Luke 1]). One wall of the church courtyard is covered with ceramic tiles quoting the Magnificat in 41 languages. The upper church is adorned with large wall paintings depicting the mantles with which Mary has been endowed—Mother of God, Refuge of Sinners, Dispenser of All Grace, Help of Christians—and the Immaculate Conception. Other frescoes depict Hebrew women of the Bible also known for their "hymns and canticles," as the Franciscan guide puts it. ⊠ *Above Spring of the Virgin, Ein Kerem* ☎ *02/641–7291* 🖃 *Free* ⊘ *Apr.–Sept., daily 8–noon and 2:30–6; Oct.–Mar., daily 8–noon and 2:30–5. Gates closed Sat., ring bell.*

⓫ L. A. Mayer Museum for Islamic Art. The institution prides itself on being a private Jewish initiative (opened 1974) that showcases the considerable and diverse artistic achievements of Islamic culture worldwide. Its rich collections—ceramics, glass, carpets, fabrics, jewelry, metal-work, and painting—reflect a creativity that spanned half a hemisphere, from Spain to India, and from the 7th century to modern times. Unconnected to the main theme is a unique collection of European clocks, the pride of the founder's family. ⊠ *2 Hapalmach St., Hapalmach* ☎ *02/566–1291* ⊕ *www.islamicart.co.il/default-eng.asp* 🖃 *NIS 20 (free on Sat.)* ⊘ *Sun., Mon., Wed., Thurs. 10–3; Tues. 10–6; Fri., Sat., holidays, and holiday eves 10–2.*

❼ Mt. Herzl Military Cemetery. The tranquillity and well-tended greenery of Israel's largest military cemetery almost belie its somber purpose.

Different sections are reserved for the casualties of each of the wars the nation has fought. The large number of headstones, all identical, is a sobering reminder of the price Israel has paid for its national independence and security. Note that officers and privates are buried alongside one another—lost lives are mourned equally, regardless of rank. ⊠*Herzl Blvd., Mt. Herzl* ☎*02/643–7257* ☑*Free* ☙*Daily.*

2

CENTER CITY

West Jerusalem's downtown and near-downtown areas, just west of the Old City, are a mix of old neighborhoods, new limestone edifices, monuments, and markets. There are plenty of hotels and restaurants here, too. Few of the attractions appear on a Jerusalem don't-miss checklist, but you'll rub shoulders with the locals in the Machaneh Yehuda produce market, breathe the atmosphere of day-to-day life on Ben-Yehuda and Jaffa Streets, get a feel for the city's more recent history in Nahalat Shiva and Yemin Moshe—in short, for a few brief hours be a bit less of a tourist.

GETTING HERE AND AROUND
Avoid driving into the center city, at least until the new light rail starts running and the dust on the attendant chaotic road-works has settled. Walk if you can; otherwise use cabs or ride city buses: lines 18, 20, 21, and 23 from Mt. Herzl via the Central Bus Station (where other lines join the route); 4, 18, and 21 from the German Colony and Talbieh; 9 from the Knesset and the Israel Museum.

TIMING AND PRECAUTIONS
Jaffa Street, Ben-Yehuda Street, and Machaneh Yehuda are ghostly quiet late Friday and on Saturday because of the Jewish Sabbath. Morning through midday Friday is the most bustling, as Jerusalemites meet friends for coffee or lunch, and do their weekend shopping.

TOP ATTRACTIONS
8 **Ben-Yehuda Street.** Most of the street is an open-air pedestrian mall, in the heart of the downtown, forming a triangle with King George Street and Jaffa Street. It is known locally as the **Midrachov,** a term concocted from two Hebrew words: *midracha* (sidewalk) and *rechov* (street). The street is named after the brilliant linguist Eliezer Ben-Yehuda, who in the late 19th century almost single-handedly revived Hebrew as a modern spoken language; he would have liked the clever new word. Cafés have tables out on the cobblestones; vendors display cheap, arty items like funky jewelry and prints; and buskers are usually out in good weather, playing tunes old and new. It's a great place to sip coffee or munch falafel and watch the passing crowd. ⊠*Downtown* ☙*A few restaurants but nothing else open Sat. and Jewish holidays.*

9 **Machaneh Yehuda.** This block-long alley and a parallel wider street are

Fodor'sChoice
★
filled with the brilliant colors of the city's best-quality and lowest-price fruit, vegetables, cheeses, confection stalls, falafel stands, fresh fish, and poultry. It's fun to elbow your way through anytime, but it's riotously busy on Thursday and Friday in particular, when Jewish Jerusalem shops for the Sabbath, and the hawkers' cries get more passionate as closing time approaches. Look for the excellent coffee shop called

Ben-Yehuda
Street **8**

Bet Ticho **7**

Hinnom Valley ...**4**

Independence
Park **5**

Machaneh
Yehuda **9**

Montefiore's
Windmill **1**

Nahalat Shiva ...**6**

Yemin Moshe **3**

YMCA **2**

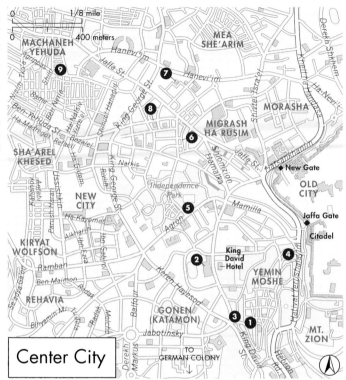

Center City

"Mizrachi / Hakol le'ofeh Ve'gam Kafeh" (sign in Hebrew only), on Shazif Street, third lane on the left as you enter from the Agrippas Street end. The market links Jaffa Street and Agrippas Street, parallel to and just a five-minute walk up from King George Street (as you go west). Most of the downtown bus lines stop on Jaffa Street, or at least on King George, and there is paid parking close to the market. ⊠*Machaneh Yehuda* ⊘ *Sun.–Thurs. 8* AM*–sunset, Fri. and Jewish holiday eves 8* AM*– 2 hrs before sunset.*

❶ Montefiore's Windmill. Sir Moses Montefiore was a prominent figure in the financial circles of mid-19th-century London—a rare phenomenon for a Jew at the time. It didn't harm his fortunes that he married into the legendary Rothschild family, and became the stockbroker of its London branch. The larger-than-life philanthropist—he stood a remarkable 6'3" or 1.90 meters—devoted much of his long life, and his wealth, to aiding fellow Jews in distress, wherever they might be. To this end he visited Palestine, as this district of the Ottoman Empire was then known, seven times. He had the limestone windmill built in 1857 to provide a source of income for his planned neighborhood of Mishkenot Sha'ananim, but it was poorly located for harnessing the prevailing winds, and it was anyway soon superseded by newfangled steam-driven mills. At the time of this writing, it was reported that the city plans to reactivate the mill, though powered by electricity, as a tourist attraction. The restored carriage in which Montefiore once traveled the country was on display until torched by vandals in the 1980s; the one you see now is an exact replica. ⊠ *Yemin Moshe St., Yemin Moshe.*

❻ ★ Nahalat Shiva. This small downtown neighborhood has a funky feel, with worn flagstones, wrought-iron banisters, and defunct water cisterns. Its name translates roughly as "the Estate of the Seven," so called by the seven Jewish families that founded the quarter, only the second to be established outside the Old City walls, in 1869. The parallel narrow arteries of Salomon and Rivlin Streets stretch from Jaffa Street to Hillel Street. Their in-between alleys and courtyards have

> **GERMAN COLONY**
>
> Israelis have discovered the Old World charms of "the Moshava" (the Colony). Eateries, cafés, and stores proliferate in this neighborhood south of Downtown. Come daytime Friday, or on warm evenings (except Friday). Look for the (irregular) Friday food and flea-market at the Adam School at 22 Emek Refai'm. German inscriptions on 19th-century stone houses along the main drag, Emek Refai'm Street, recall the Templers (not medieval), breakaway Lutherans who believed their presence in the Holy Land would hasten the Second Coming. The British exiled their pro-Nazi descendants during World War II.

been refashioned as a pedestrian district, offering equal opportunities to the keen photographer, the eager shopper, and the gastronome. An eclectic variety of eateries, from Israeli to Italian, Asian to Arabic, tempt you to take a break from the jewelry and ceramics. ⊠ *Nahalat Shiva* ⊗ *Many establishments closed Sat. and Jewish holidays.*

❷ YMCA. The high-domed landmark bell tower thrusts out of the palatial white-limestone facade of the YMCA, offering superb, long-range views in all directions. For NIS 5 you can ride the small elevator to the grille-protected balconies, 150 feet above ground, and get an unsurpassed view over the roof of the famous King David Hotel toward the Old City and farther east. The complex often surprises visitors who associate the YMCA with modest buildings and sports facilities. The Jerusalem "Y" has those, too, as well as an auditorium with a Levantine-inspired dome and excellent acoustics, a hotel, and a bilingual Arabic-Hebrew preschool. A bit of trivia: the building, dedicated in 1933, was designed by Arthur Loomis Harmon, one of the architects of New York City's Empire State Building. ⊠ *26 King David St.* ☎ *02/569–2692* ⊕ *www. jerusalemymca.org* ☞ *Free; elevator NIS 5* ⊗ *Tower: Mon.–Thurs. 8–8, Fri. 8–5, Sat. 8–12.*

WORTH NOTING

❼ Bet Ticho *(Ticho House).* The handsome two-story historical building is part museum, part restaurant, and part concert venue. Dr. A. A. Ticho was a renowned ophthalmologist who immigrated to Jerusalem from Austria in 1912. His cousin, Anna, a trained nurse, followed the same year, to assist him in his pioneering struggle against the endemic scourge of trachoma. They were soon married, and in 1924 bought and renovated this fine 19th-century stone house. Anna's artistic talent gradually earned her a reputation as a brilliant chronicler—in charcoal, pen, and

A Good Walk in Center City

Jerusalem is a good city to stroll. Beyond its shrines and antiquities, the limestone buildings, shaded courtyards, and colorful peoplescapes of the center city make for an absorbing experience. The first part of the walk—up to the YMCA—is good anytime; avoid the rest of it late Friday and on Saturday, when the downtown area shuts down for the Jewish Sabbath. The route will take 1½ hours to walk, not counting stops.

Begin at the landmark **Montefiore's Windmill**, across the valley from Mount Zion. Immediately below the adjacent patio is the long crenelated roof of Mishkenot Sha'ananim, the first neighborhood outside the walls of Jerusalem, built by Sir Moses (Moshe) Montefiore in 1860.

Separating you from Mt. Zion and the Old City is the deep **Hinnom Valley,** the biblical border between the Israelite tribes of Judah (to the south) and Benjamin (to the north), and the site of human sacrificial rites in the 7th century BC. A few hundred yards off to your right is the fortress-like St. Andrew's Scots Church, right above the bend in the valley known as Ketef Hinnom (the Hinnom Shoulder). An excavation in the late 1970s on the rock scarp below the church uncovered rock-hewn tombs and a treasure trove of archaeological finds.

Stroll through the attractive cobblestone streets of the **Yemin Moshe** neighborhood, abutting the windmill, and up through the small park that separates it from King David Street. The landmark King David Hotel is a handsome, rectangular limestone building with a back terrace overlooking the Old City walls. Drinks and desserts are not cheap, but the location and Hollywood echoes (Paul Newman and Eva Marie Saint in

Exodus) count for something. Across the street is the **YMCA**: its tower has stunning panoramas.

Turn onto Abraham Lincoln Street, alongside the YMCA and opposite the gas station. From the intersection 70 yards beyond it, a pedestrian lane (George Eliot Street) continues in the same direction, emerging at Agron Street, next to the U.S. Consulate-General. Cross Agron and walk over the lawns of **Independence Park.** The park's crossroad, 50 yards to your right, emerges at Hillel Street, where there are excellent coffee shops.

Across Hillel is Yoel Moshe Salomon Street, and to the right and parallel to it is Yosef Rivlin Street, named after two of the seven founders of **Nahalat Shiva,** the second neighborhood built outside the city walls, in 1869. Hidden courtyards, funky stores, and eateries make this a fun time-out option. At the other end of Salomon Street is Zion Square, where Jaffa Road, Jerusalem's main thoroughfare, is met by **Ben-Yehuda Street,** a pedestrian-only commercial street.

At the top of Ben-Yehuda Street, cross King George Street, turn right, and take your first left onto Agrippas Street. (The corner falafel stand is your landmark.) A five-minute walk up the street, on your right, is the entrance to the colorful **Machaneh Yehuda** produce market. It extends for one city block, to Jaffa Road. *For more information on the sights in bold, see the bulleted listings in Center City.*

brush—of the landscape around Jerusalem. Set among pine trees, just a few steps off the busy downtown streets, Bet Ticho displays a selection of Anna Ticho's works, offers changing intimate art and photography exhibitions, and has a very good nonmeat restaurant. Chamber music concerts are held regularly on Friday mornings, in the upper gallery. ✉*Ticho La., at 7 Harav Kook St., Downtown* ☎*02/624–5068* ⊕*www.imj.org.il* ✉*Free* ☉*Sun., Mon., Wed., and Thurs. 10–5, Tues. 10–10, Fri. and Jewish holiday eves 9–2 (upper gallery closed for concert Fri. 10:30–12:15* PM).

OFF THE BEATEN PATH

Haas Promenade. Get your bearings in Jerusalem by taking in the panorama from the Haas Promenade, an attractive 1-km (2/3-mi) promenade ("tayelet" in Hebrew) along one of the city's highest ridges. Hidden behind a grove of trees to the east (your right as you pan the view) is a turreted limestone building, the residence of the British High Commissioner for Palestine in the 1930s and '40s. In Hebrew, the whole ridge is known as Armon Hanatziv, the Commissioner's Palace. The building became the headquarters of the U.N. Truce Supervision Organization (UNTSO), charged with monitoring the 1949 armistice line that divided the city. It remained a neutral enclave between Israeli West Jerusalem and Jordanian-controlled East Jerusalem until the reunification of the city in the Six-Day War of 1967. West Jerusalem is off to your left, its downtown area easily distinguishable by the high-rises. The walls of the Old City and the golden Dome of the Rock are directly in front of you. To the right of it is the ridge of Mt. Scopus–Mt. of Olives, with its three towers (from left to right, Hebrew University, Augusta Victoria Hospital, and Russian Church of the Ascension), separated from the Old City by the deep Kidron Valley. South of the Old City walls (between your location and the black-domed al-Aqsa Mosque) is a blade-shaped strip of land, between the valley and a steep asphalt road. That was the original nucleus of ancient Jerusalem, established over 4,000 years ago, and captured by King David ca. 1000 BC (whence came the biblical name "the City of David"). You can reach the promenade by car from Hebron Road—consult a map, and look for signs to East Talpiot and the Haas Promenade—by bus #8, or of course by cab. If the traffic flows well, it's a 10-minute drive from downtown, 5 minutes from the German Colony. ✉*Daniel Yanovsky St., East Talpiot.*

❹ **Hinnom Valley.** The Hinnom Valley achieved notoriety in the 7th century BC during the long reign of the Israelite king Menasseh (697–640 BC). He was an idolater, the Bible relates, who supported a cult of child sacrifice by fire in the Valley of the Son of Hinnom. Over time, the biblical Hebrew name of the valley—Gei Ben Hinnom, contracted to Gehennom or Gehenna—became a synonym for hell in both Hebrew and New Testament Greek.

In the late 1970s, Israeli archaeologist Gabriel Barkai discovered a series of Old Testament–period rock tombs at the bend in the valley, below the fortress-like St. Andrew's Scots Church. A miraculously unplundered pit yielded "grave goods" like miniature clay vessels and jewelry. The most spectacular finds, however, were two tiny rolled strips of silver designed to be worn around the neck as amulets. When unrolled, the fragile pieces revealed a slightly condensed version of the biblical priestly benediction,

Me'a She'arim

The name of this neighborhood just north of Downtown is the biblical "hundredfold," the bountiful blessing received by Isaac (Genesis 26). It was regarded as a good omen when the neighborhood was founded in 1874. This is 24/7 ultra-Orthodox Judaism. The community is insular and uncompromising—residents have no TVs; some reject the legitimacy of modern Israel; people speak Yiddish rather than the "sacred" Hebrew as the conversational language—and clings to an Old World lifestyle.

Modesty in dress and behavior is imperative for anyone entering the neighborhood. Visitors (best in tiny groups) must avoid male-female contact; women should wear long skirts, long sleeves, and nothing exposed below the neck. It's a voyeuristic experience, but avoid the Sabbath and photograph discreetly other times if you choose to go.

Me'a She'arim is traversed by Me'a She'arim Street, and most of the historic neighborhood is on the slope above it (in the direction of Hanevi'im Street and the downtown area). To the west it is more or less bounded by Strauss Street; to the east it almost touches Road No. 1.

---

inscribed in the ancient Hebrew script. (The original, in Numbers 6, reads: "The Lord bless you and keep you; the Lord make his face to shine upon you and be gracious to you; the Lord lift up his countenance upon you and give you peace.") The 7th-century BC text is the oldest biblical passage ever found. The tombs are an open site, behind the Menachem Begin Heritage Center. Access is through the premises of the center, but you don't enter the building. ⊠ *Hinnom Valley.*

❺ Independence Park. This is a great area for lounging around, throwing Frisbees, or eating a picnic lunch in warm weather. Some of the Muslim graves at the bottom of the park date from the 13th century. The large defunct reservoir nearby, known as the Mamilla Pool, is probably medieval, though it may have much earlier origins. ⊠ *Between Agron and Hillel Sts., Downtown* ⊙ *Daily.*

❸ ★ Yemin Moshe. This now-affluent neighborhood, with its attractive old stone buildings, bursts of greenery and bougainvillea, and well-kept cobblestone streets, grew up a century ago alongside the older Mishkenot Sha'ananim, and was named for that project's founder, Sir Moses (Moshe in Hebrew) Montefiore. In the 1950s and '60s, the area overlooked the jittery armistice line that gashed through the city, and was dangerously exposed to Jordanian sniper positions on the nearby Old City walls. Most families sought safer lodgings elsewhere, leaving only those who couldn't afford to move, and the neighborhood ran to seed. The reunification of Jerusalem under Israeli rule after the Six-Day War in 1967 changed all that. Developers bought up the area, renovated old buildings, and built new and spacious homes in a compatible style. Yemin Moshe is now a place to wander at random, offering joy to photographers and quiet nooks for meditation. A couple of restaurants are added bonuses. ⊠ *Yemin Moshe.*

WHERE TO EAT

Jerusalem is less chic and cosmopolitan than Tel Aviv—no question about it—but you can still eat very well in the Holy City. Inexpensive eateries serving Middle Eastern standards, fast-food favorites, or sandwiches and salads remain popular; but travel abroad by Israelis has whetted the appetite of both cooks and customers for more interesting food. The excellence of local produce and the endurance of ethnic or family culinary traditions have been fertilized by imported new ideas and individual inspiration.

The result—common enough to sniff a trend in it—is a joyfully rich menu of palate-pleasers. Some of the new restaurants clearly identify themselves by cuisine—French or Spanish, for example—while others defy easy labeling. Not quite Mediterranean, not quite European (though clearly influenced by both), they are, well, Israeli enough to deserve a new sobriquet: modern Israeli. How ground-breaking the trend is remains to be seen—categorizing cuisines is not an exact science—but there is no doubt that the new restaurants have markedly changed the culinary map of Jerusalem.

Some cuisine designations are self-explanatory, but other terms may be less so. A restaurant advertising itself as "dairy" will serve meals without meat; many such places do fish, in addition to pasta, soup, and salads. "Oriental" on a sign is usually a literal translation of *mizrachi,* suggesting Middle Eastern (in contrast to Western).

"Kosher" does not imply a particular style of cooking, only that certain religious restrictions are adhered to in the selection and preparation of the food. The half-truth that you can't find a decent kosher steak has been well and truly buried. Choose the right place, and your fillet will be as good as it gets. Remember that kosher restaurants are closed for Friday dinner and Saturday lunch in observation of the Jewish Sabbath.

Dress codes are pretty much nonexistent in Jerusalem's restaurants (as in the rest of Israel). People tend to dress very casually—jeans are perfectly appropriate almost everywhere anytime. A modicum of neatness and modesty (trousers instead of jeans, a button-down shirt instead of a T-shirt) might be expected in a hotel dining room on the Sabbath, for example. Still, if you've taken the trouble to bring your dressy duds, you won't be out of place in a more exclusive establishment.

WHAT IT COSTS IN ISRAELI SHEKELS					
	¢	$	$$	$$$	$$$$
Restaurants	under NIS 32	NIS 32–NIS 49	NIS 50–NIS 75	NIS 76–NIS 100	over NIS 100

Prices are for a main course at dinner.

BEST BETS FOR JERUSALEM DINING

With hundreds of restaurants to choose from, how will you decide where to eat? Fodor's writers and editors have selected their favorite restaurants by price, cuisine, and experience in the lists below. In the first column, Fodor's Choice properties represent the "best of the best" across price categories. You can also search by area for excellent eats—just check out our complete reviews in the following pages.

Fodor's Choice ★

Ima, $$$, p. 126
Little Jerusalem, $$ p. 127
Mona, $$$, p. 127

By Price

¢

Abu Shukri, p. 129
Pinati, p. 127

$

Angelo, p. 119
Focaccia, p. 126
Spaghettim, p. 128
Te'enim, p. 132
Village Green, p. 129

$$

Ima, p. 126
Little Jerusalem, p. 127
Paradiso, p. 132
Sakura, p. 127
T'mol Shilshom, p. 129

$$$

Angelica, p. 119
Chakra, p. 124
Dolphin Yam, p. 125
Ima, p. 126
Mona, p. 127
Sol, p. 128
Terra, p. 128

$$$$

Canela, p. 124
Darna, p. 125

By Cuisine

MEAT LOVERS

Angelica, $$$, p. 119
Black Burger & Bar, $$, p. 124
Burgers Bar, $, p. 124
El Gaucho, $$$, p. 125
Olive, $$$, p. 129

MIDDLE EASTERN

Ima, $$$, p. 126
Nafoura, $$, p. 130

MODERN ISRAELI

Angelica, $$$, p. 119
Chakra, $$$, p. 124
Mona, $$$, p. 127
Scala, $$$$, p. 132

DAIRY AND FISH

Angelo, $, p. 119
Little Jerusalem, $$, p. 127
T'mol Shilshom, $$, p. 129

VEGETARIAN

Te'enim, $, p. 132
Village Green, $, p. 129

By Experience

CHILD-FRIENDLY

Burgers Bar, $, p. 124
Keshet, $, p. 130
Little Jerusalem, $$, p. 127
Spaghettim, $, p. 128
T'mol Shilshom, $$, p. 129

OUTSIDE DINING

Barood, $$, p. 119
Chakra, $$$, p. 124
Keshet, $, p. 130
Little Jerusalem, $$, p. 127
Nafoura, $, p. 130
Village Green, $, p. 129

LOCAL FAVORITES

Abu Shukri, ¢, p. 129
Chakra, $$$, p. 124
Focaccia, $, p. 126
Ima, $$$, p. 126
Mona, $$$, p. 127
Paradiso, $$, p. 132
Pinati, ¢, p. 127
Sol, $$$, p. 128
Spaghettim, $, p. 128

GREAT VIEWS

Chakra, $$$, p. 124
Lavan, $$, p. 130
Te'enim, $, p. 132

CENTER CITY

The area extends from the Machaneh Yehuda market and Nahlaot neighborhood, through the central Downtown triangle, to Nahalat Shiva and the junction with King David Street (which is a stone's throw from the Old City), a walk of 15 minutes from end to end. The range is vast, from funky budget or takeaway joints to upscale fine-dining specialists, from Middle-Eastern food to European cuisine, and several surprises in between. Non-kosher restaurants do a roaring trade on Friday night, after the Sabbath begins, when their kosher counterparts are closed and the city streets quiet.

$$$
MODERN ISRAELI
✕ **Angelica.** The proprietor-chef trained in fine dining, and it shows; wonderfully fresh and perfectly cooked ingredients add the dimension of texture to an explosion of great flavors. The clean lines and aqua tints of Angelica's modern decor add an extra touch of class. Don't fill up on crusty bread as you sample starters of gazpacho, marinated sardines, salads, or veal cheek ravioli. Main courses are carnivore heaven: superb lamb shoulder osso buco, tender top-quality steaks, and goose confit with apples and chestnuts. If that's not your style, choose one of the tempting fish or pasta dishes. Changing fruit tarts are the house dessert specialty. ⊠ *7 Shatz St., Downtown* ☎ *02/623–0056* ⌕ *Reservations essential* ⊟ *AE, DC, MC, V* ⊘ *Closed Fri., no Sat. lunch.* ✛ *2A*

$
ITALIAN
✕ **Angelo.** The chef-owner is from Rome, and it shows in the authenticity of this non-meat establishment. The decor is simple: lower walls of deep burgundy and the rest in sandy beige conjure up Italian hill towns. Angelo is not interested in trendy variations on an already-great traditional cuisine: homemade pasta, high-quality fresh ingredients, and a sure hand produce simply flavorsome food. Start with (but don't fill up on) the antipasti and focaccia. House specialties are the ravioli and the delicious salmon cannelloni, but other good choices are lemon tagliolini, and gnocchi Angelo (olive oil, garlic, pesto, cheese, cherry tomatoes, fresh basil, and mushrooms). Homemade ice cream is worth waiting for. ⊠ *9 Horkanos St., Downtown* ☎ *02/623–6095* ⊟ *AE, DC, MC, V* ⊘ *Closed Fri. No lunch Sat.* ✛ *1C*

$$
MIDDLE EASTERN
✕ **Barood.** Tenth-generation Jerusalemite Daniella Lerer fiercely preserves her family's Sephardic culinary traditions: casserole dishes; *pastilla* filled with beef, pine nuts, and grilled eggplant; *sufrito* (braised dumplings cooked with Jerusalem artichoke); and a beef and leek dish in lemon juice. For dessert, look for the traditional *sutlach,* a cold rice pudding topped with cinnamon, nuts, and jam. Barood's other face is its well-stocked bar, with more familiar fare like spareribs and sausages. Reservations are a must for dinner Friday night. ⊠ *In courtyard off 31 Jaffa Rd., Downtown* ☎ *02/625–9081* ⊟ *AE, MC, V* ⊘ *Closed Sun.* ✛ *2C*

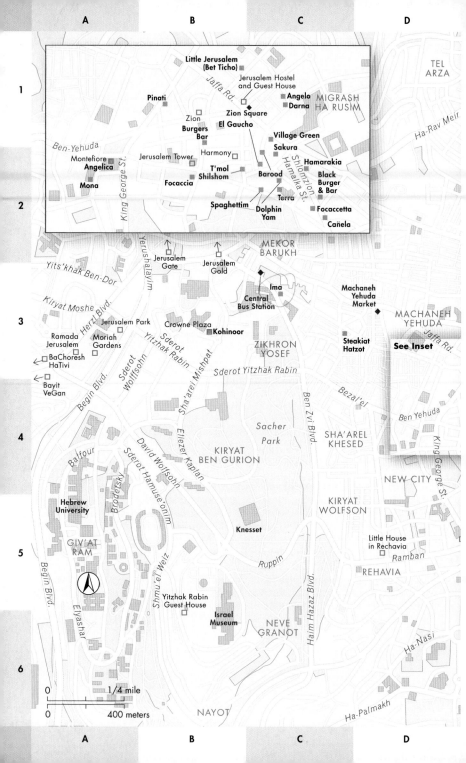

A   **B**   **C**   **D**

1

Little Jerusalem
(Bet Ticho)
Jerusalem Hostel
and Guest House
Pinati
Angelo
Darna
MIGRASH
HA RUSIM
Zion Square
Zion
Burgers
Bar
El Gaucho
Ben-Yehuda
Village Green
Sakura
Montefiore
Angelica
Jerusalem Tower
Harmony
Hamarakia
Mona
T'mol
Shilshom
Barood
Black
Burger
& Bar
Focaccia
Terra
Focaccetta
Spaghettim
Dolphin
Yam
Cañela

2

Yits'khak Ben-Dor
Jerusalem
Gate
Jerusalem
Gold
MEKOR
BARUKH
Kiryat Moshe Blvd.
Ima
Machaneh
Yehuda
Market
Jerusalem Park
Crowne Plaza
Central
Bus Station
MACHANEH
YEHUDA

3

Ramada
Jerusalem
Moriah
Gardens
Kohinoor
ZIKHRON
YOSEF
Steakiat
Hatzot
See Inset
BaChoresh
HaTivi
Bayit
VeGan
Sderot Yitzhak Rabin
Bezal'el
Ben Yehuda

4

Balfour
Sderot Hamuse'onim
Eliezer Kaplan
Sacher
Park
KIRYAT
BEN GURION
SHA'AREI
KHESED
NEW CITY
David Wolfsohn

5

Hebrew
University
GIV'AT
RAM
Knesset
KIRYAT
WOLFSON
Little House
in Rechavia
Ramban
REHAVIA
Begin Blvd.
Yitzhak Rabin
Guest House
Israel
Museum
NEVE
GRANOT
Ha-Nasi

6

Elyashar
0   1/4 mile
0   400 meters
NAYOT
Ha-Palmakh

A   **B**   **C**   **D**

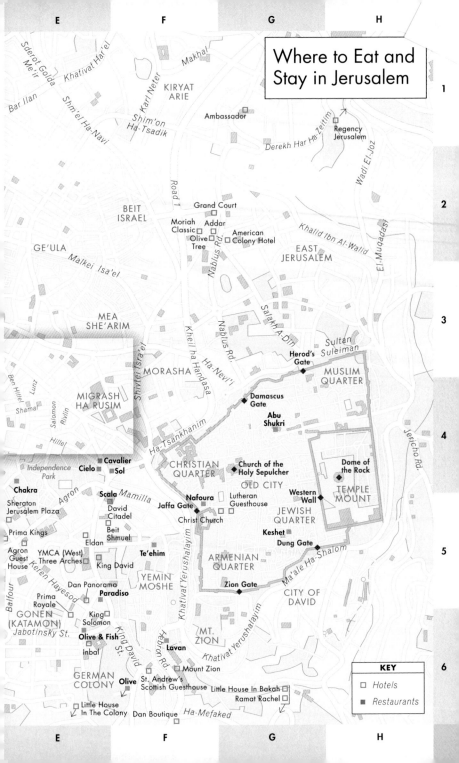

Where to Eat and Stay in Jerusalem

E   F   G   H

1

Sderot Golda Me'ir
Bar Ilan
Khativat Har'el
Karl Neter
Makhal
Shm'el Ha-Navi
KIRYAT ARIE
Shim'on Ha-Tsadik
Ambassador
Derekh Har Ha-Ze'itim
Regency Jerusalem
Wadi El-Joz

2

Road 1
BEIT ISRAEL
Grand Court
Moriah Classic
Addar
Olive Tree
American Colony Hotel
Nablus Rd.
EAST JERUSALEM
Khalid Ibn Al-Walid
El-Muqadasy
GE'ULA
Malkei Isa'el

3

MEA SHE'ARIM
Kheil ha Handasa
Nablus Rd.
Ha-Nevi'i
Salakh A-Din
MORASHA
Shivtei Isra'el
Sultan Suleiman
Herod's Gate
MUSLIM QUARTER
Jericho Rd.

4

Ben Hillel
Lunz
Shamal
Salomon
Rivlin
Hillel
MIGRASH HA RUSIM
Ha-Tsankhanim
Damascus Gate
Abu Shukri
CHRISTIAN QUARTER
Church of the Holy Sepulcher
OLD CITY
Dome of the Rock
TEMPLE MOUNT

Independence Park
Cavalier
Cielo
Sol
Agron
Chakra
Scala
Mamilla
Nafoura
Lutheran Guesthouse
Western Wall
Sheraton Jerusalem Plaza
David Citadel
Jaffa Gate
Christ Church
JEWISH QUARTER
Prima Kings
Beit Shmuel
Keshet
Agron Guest House
Eldan
YMCA (West) Three Arches
Te'ehim
King David
Dung Gate
Ma'ale Ha-Shalom

5

Balfour
Keren Hayesod
Dan Panorama
Prima Royale
Paradiso
King Solomon
YEMIN MOSHE
ARMENIAN QUARTER
Zion Gate
CITY OF DAVID
GONEN (KATAMON)
Jabotinsky St.
Olive & Fish
King David St.
Khativat Yerushalayim

6

Inbal
Lavan
MT. ZION
Hagdud Rd.
GERMAN COLONY
Olive
St. Andrew's Scottish Guesthouse
Mount Zion
Khativat Yerushalayim
Little House In Bakah
Ramat Rachel
Little House In The Colony
Dan Boutique
Ha-Mefaked

E   F   G   H

KEY

☐	Hotels
■	Restaurants

HOLIDAY FOODS IN ISRAEL

PASSOVER MATZAH

The journey from slavery in Egypt to freedom, remembered during the week-long Passover holiday each spring, inspires the preparation of unleavened bread called matzah. Why unleavened? The Hebrew people left Egypt in a hurry and had no time for bread to rise. Today it is rare to find bread or any foods made with leavening agents for sale during Passover, especially in Jerusalem. Matzah is a flat, crisp—and bland on its own—square of crunchiness. Modern times have produced chocolate-coated versions and matzah flavored with onion and made richer with eggs. Cooks get creative with fried matzah, sweet or savory pies, and baked treats.

You know it's a holiday when special treats suddenly appear in bakeries, street stalls, supermarkets, and restaurants. Round doughnuts dabbed with jelly at Hanukkah, cheese blintzes bursting with raisins at Shavuot, or triangles of filled pastry at Purim: foods symbolize each holiday's historical event or theme.

On holidays, families and friends sit down to festive meals of favorite foods eaten in time-honored tradition. Tu b'Shevat, the winter New Year of Trees celebration, has everyone munching juicy dried fruit such as tart apricots, golden raisins, and sweet dates and figs, accompanied by nuts and pumpkin or sunflower seeds. On Independence Day in spring, people head to the countryside or city park for a barbecue, and the scent of sizzling steak or skewers of meat wafts throughout Israel.

Shabbat, the Jewish sabbath, is observed each Friday night and Saturday. Friday dinner is when families eat traditional fare reflecting their ethnic origins. Pride of place goes to a golden-crusted, braided, soft *challah* bread; look for these in bakeries each week.

ROSH HASHANAH

During the New Year holiday each fall, "sweet" is the byword, indicating wishes for a sweet year: apple slices dipped in honey are nibbled, and ruby-red pomegranate seeds decorate salads and are eaten with the hope that good deeds performed in the coming year will be as plentiful as the seeds of this fruit. Plump dates hang in bunches at markets; Sephardi Jews end the holiday meal with them. Bakeries and restaurants feature dark honey cake enhanced with ginger and cinnamon.

HANNUKAH

As winter approaches, Hannukah celebrates a 2nd-century BC victory over the Greeks; the story includes a miraculous amount of oil for the Temple menorah, or candelabrum. Foods fried in oil are the order of the day. Round, deep-fried jelly doughnuts called sufganiyot—browned to a crisp on the outside and pillowy soft inside—appear all over town. Fillings get more creative every year, from caramel or chocolate to lemon cream or halvah.

PURIM

This early spring holiday commemorates a victory in which food helped win the day, the 6th-century BC triumph over the evil Haman. On Purim, everyone eats triangular pastries called hamantashen or, in Hebrew, oznai Haman—Haman's ears. The treats are

filled with jam, poppy seeds, dates, or chocolate. It's a tradition, known as mishloach manot, to exchange gifts of foods, and you'll see children on the streets carrying little baskets of goodies as well as the ubiquitous "ears."

SHAVUOT

The Feast of Weeks, a spring holiday, marks the giving of the Torah at Mount Sinai. Explanations for the connection with eating dairy foods are many; one is that just as milk sustains the body, so the Torah provides spiritual nourishment for the soul. Look for rich, creamy cheesecakes with sour-cream toppings and cheese blintzes with raisins. Try cheeses from Israel's boutique goat and sheep farms, from perfect cottage cheese to sharp blue and chunky tom.

RAMADAN

The holiest month of the Islamic year is Ramadan, when believers fast from sunrise to sunset every day. Special sweets are enjoyed at family meals in the evening and at the feast of Eid el-Fitr, at the end of Ramadan. A favorite delicacy is attayif, puffy little pancakes folded over a filling of cheese or nuts and doused in syrup. Look for these at bakeries or on outdoor griddles in the Old City of Jerusalem, Nazareth, Haifa, and Akko's Old City.

—by Judy Stacey Goldman

$$ ✕ **Black Burger & Bar.** This trendy establishment—black and crimson
AMERICAN upholstery; a mirrored ceiling; white backlights behind the liquor bot-
tles—serves hamburgers, but the resemblance to fast-food joints ends
there. Apart from the wide selection of burgers including beef, lamb,
chicken, and veggie, the menu lists entrées such as steak and schnitzel
(pan-fried slices of turkey or chicken). Gluten-free options are available.
The bar, with its good range of drinks, exudes cool. ⊠*18 Shlomzion
Hamalka St., Downtown* ☎*02/624–6767* ▭*AE, DC, MC, V.* ✛*2C*

$ ✕ **Burgers Bar.** The menu bears a passing resemblance to that of the big
FAST FOOD hamburger chains, but the product is a different creature altogether.
☺ Hamburgers of different weight are more like cakes than patties, come
with good sauces, and all are made to order. Chicken offerings and
robust salads reflect Israeli tastes. Even those who generally oppose
the fast-food experience have been happy here. The traditional bun/
sandwich averages NIS 30, the meal version closer to NIS 50. Other
branches of this expanding chain are in the German Colony and the Old
City's Jewish Quarter. ⊠*12 Shammai St., Downtown* ☎*02/622–1555*
▭*No credit cards* ☾*No dinner Fri. No lunch Sat.* ✛*1B*

$$$$ ✕ **Canela.** The parquet flooring, upholstered chairs, diaphanous drapes,
FRENCH and flower arrangements hint at class, not trendiness; the cream-col-
ored baby grand confirms it. The restaurant sees itself as a pioneer in
kosher fine dining (no contradiction anymore). That will hardly affect
your meal, but your fellow diners may include religiously observant
Jews celebrating a night out. Great starters include the sea-fish sashimi,
the thinly sliced grilled veal tongue and beef carpaccio, the ox-tail
ravioli, and the artichoke and grilled zucchini risotto. The deliberately
restrained entrée menu offers a pasta dish and a couple of interesting
fish dishes, but more variety for meat-eaters. The duck breast glazed
in honey and dried roses with Calvados sauce and potato confit is
among the more creative, but there is an entrecôte steak or a seared
beef fillet to satisfy the true carnivore. ⊠*8 Shlomzion Hamalka St.,
Downtown* ☎*02/622–2293* ▭*AE, DC, MC, V* ☾*Closed Fri. No
lunch Sat.* ✛*2C*

$$$$ ✕ **Cavalier.** Stone balconies overhung with wisteria, gently lit yellow and
FRENCH cream walls, wood ceiling beams, and alcoves filled with racks of wine
offer a warm welcome. The predominantly French menu is modified by
Mediterranean influences. Don't fill up on the great crusty whole-wheat
bread; look for starters like crab ravioli or goose liver crème brûlée
made with truffles, apples, and caramel. There is a tempting range of
fish and shrimp dishes, and several steak and veal options. A standout
is the lamb sirloin served on couscous with pine nuts, a light curry, and
sweet sauce. Top it off with a tarte tatin or the red fruit (mostly ber-
ries) vacherin (based on a meringue core). ⊠*1 Ben Sira St., Downtown*
☎*02/624–2945* ✐*Reservations essential* ▭*AE, DC, MC, V.* ✛*4E*

$$$ ✕ **Chakra.** Despite its new central location (below Cup o' Joe) and more
MODERN ISRAELI sophisticated ambience, Chakra still pretends to anonymity: the name
of the restaurant is nowhere in sight. It draws a lively thirty-something
crowd that appreciates the good fare coming out of the open kitchen.
The bistro-bar layout includes a large semicircular counter but plenty
of table seating, some on sofas; golden tones on the walls and picture

2

frames are offset by dark wood fixtures. The patio (for fine-weather dining) enjoys a park view. Daily specials enhance the expansive menu, and some good starters are beef or red tuna carpaccio, summer salad with sliced beef fillet and fruit, or a shrimp dish; ask for bread and baba ghanoush dip. Fish and beef dishes are excellent—but avoid the goulash soup. Share a dessert of ice cream in tahini and date honey sauce. The tasting menu is a tempting way to go. Reservations are essential for dinner Thursday and Friday. ✉ *41 King George St., Downtown* ☎ *02/625–2733* ✁ *AE, DC, MC, V.* ✛ *4E*

$$$ ✗ **Cielo.** Chef Adi maintains his family's tradition of good Italian fare.
ITALIAN The soft lighting is easy on the eye, and the lack of decoration is not a shortcoming in the very intimate setting: large, tastefully framed wall mirrors add depth to the room. Service is professional and friendly. The starter menu includes great traditional dishes like ravioli (the stuffings change: look for seafood or truffles), and a superb lasagna/cannelloni combination. Especially interesting among the entrées—beef, chicken, and fish are also options—are the tender *piccatina con funghi* (thinly sliced veal with lemon and mushrooms), and the succulent veal marsala. ✉ *18 Ben Sira St., Downtown* ☎ *02/625–1132* ✍ *Reservations essential* ✁ *AE, DC, MC, V* ✎ *No lunch Fri.* ✛ *4E*

$$$$ ✗ **Darna.** A vaulted tunnel sets you down in a corner of Morocco, complete
MOROCCAN with imported floor tiles and decorative artifacts. The high-end fixed-price menus (NIS 175 and NIS 240 per person, respectively) are a veritable banquet; ordering à la carte, though, offers more flexibility. Don't over-order. The salads are quite different from the local Arab meze, but don't miss the *harira* soup of meat, chickpeas, and lentils, flavored with cumin, or the *pastilla fassia,* phyllo pastry stuffed with almonds, cinnamon, and Cornish hen (nonmeat versions are usually available). The *tagines,* or Moroccan stews, are excellent entrées, but the house specialty is the more expensive roast baby lamb shoulder with almonds, served on couscous. Finish with refreshing mint tea (served with fine ceremony) and the wonderful *toubkal* delight, sweet phyllo layers in cinnamon and (nondairy) almond milk. ✉ *3 Horkonos St., Downtown* ☎ *02/624–5406* ✁ *AE, DC, MC, V* ✎ *Closed Fri. No lunch Sat.* ✛ *1C*

$$$ ✗ **Dolphin Yam.** Also known in translation as Sea Dolphin, this is where
SEAFOOD you'll find the city's best seafood. The decor is pleasant enough—pale yellow stucco, recessed wine racks, stone-arched windows, a central wooden counter—but it's not a place for intimacy. Food is what draws the mixed clientele, including families. Start with a meze of refillable dishes; the green salad and the eggplant in tomato sauce are excellent. Try the shrimp in cream and mushroom sauce or the *musar baladi* (drum fish) with ginger and black olives. Beef, poultry, and pasta are other options. ✉ *9 Ben Shetach St., Downtown* ☎ *02/623–2272* ✍ *Reservations essential* ✁ *AE, DC, MC, V.* ✛ *2C*

$$$ ✗ **El Gaucho.** Red meat reigns at this Argentinian grill in the downtown
ARGENTINE Nahalat Shiva neighborhood. The stone building with interior arches and a flagstone floor has wooden tables and ceiling beams. Nibble on great chicken wings while you wait for your steak: try the entrecôte or the chorizo (a sirloin cut; no relation to the sausage of the same name,

though that's also available) with a parsley-based *chimichurri* sauce. A house specialty is the long-cooking "asado," a boneless rib. There are chicken options, a kids' menu, and (for non-carnivores) salad, a couple of pasta dishes, and a vegetarian platter. ⊠*22 Rivlin St., Nahalat Shiva* ☎*02/624–2227* ▭*AE, DC, MC, V* ⊘*Closed Fri. No lunch Sat.* ✛*2C*

$$
ITALIAN

✕**Focaccetta.** Enforcement of no-smoking regulations has cost this bar-restaurant some of its liveliest young customers. It's quiet at midday, but the clubby atmosphere still comes alive in the evening. Focaccia, with an extraordinary variety of toppings to choose from, is the house specialty, and the earth oven seems to give it and the pizza options a special flavor. The Italian influence is felt as well in the seafood fettuccine with cream sauce, and other salt-water delectables. Mexican dishes—try the chicken fajita—are part of Focaccetta's eclecticism. Reservations are essential on weekends. ⊠*4 Shlomzion Hamalka, Downtown* ☎*02/624–3222* ▭*AE, DC, MC, V.* ✛*2C*

$
ITALIAN

✕**Focaccia.** The smallish interior in an old stone building is pleasant enough, but the spacious patio just off the street is much livelier. A popular haunt for twenty- and thirtysomethings (but patronized by all ages), this "focaccia bar" offers good value. There are many toppings (don't miss the black olive spread), and some tasty starters (try the fried mushrooms stuffed with sheep's cheese). Chicken livers stir-fried with apples, shallots, and nuts are delicious. There are great sandwich options, like sirloin strips, and several salads and pasta dishes. ⊠*4 Rabbi Akiva St., Downtown* ☎*02/625–6428* ▭*AE, DC, MC, V.* ✛*2B*

¢
ISRAELI

✕**Hamarakia.** Housed in a slightly dilapidated old building, this is a funky hangout for young, impecunious students. The name means "soup pot," and a changing menu of hearty soups served with half-loaves of crusty bread, butter, and pesto make it a satisfying alternative to the conventional three-course meal. *Shakshuka* (a tangy simmering dish of eggs, tomatoes, and onions) and a dessert pie complete the menu. There's a piano in the corner, a box of old records, and a chandelier made of spoons. Late-evening drinkers can hear jazz two nights a week, usually Mondays and Wednesdays. ⊠*4 Koresh St., Downtown* ☎*02/625–7797* ⊘*No lunch. Closed Fri.* ✛*2C*

$$–$$$
MIDDLE EASTERN
Fodor's Choice
★

✕**Ima.** It's pronounced "*ee*-mah," means "mom," and is named for Miriam, the owner's Kurdish-Jewish mother, who still cooks some of the excellent traditional Middle Eastern food. In the Nahla'ot neighborhood, opposite Sacher Park, the restaurant has a more diverse clientele than the fast-food diners up the street. The floor plan of the century-old stone house, with its arched doorways and niched windows (what locals call "very Jerusalemite"), create different-size dining areas that create a feeling of intimacy. First courses include a modest but quality meze of some half-dozen salads, such as hummus and baba ghanoush (eggplant dip), as well as the wonderful *kibbeh* (seasoned ground meat deep fried in a jacket of bulgur wheat) and stuffed grape leaves. The selection of stuffed vegetables is an excellent choice if you're sharing: it's easy to over-order. Try one of the tangy kibbeh soups, full of dumplings—it's almost a meal in itself. Entrées, like shashlik, chicken or a Jerusalem mixed grill, are often accompanied by *majadra* (rice and lentils). ✉*189 Agrippas St., Nahla'ot* ☎*02/624–6860* ▭*AE, DC, MC, V* ✕*No dinner Fri. Closed Sat.* ✛*3C.*

$$ ✕**Little Jerusalem** *(Bet Ticho).* This imposing old stone building, in a tranquil rustic setting, was once the home of artist Anna Ticho, whose evocative drawings of Jerusalem adorn its walls. House specialties include excellent salmon blintzes, quiches, onion soup served inside a crusty loaf of bread, and sea bream in fresh ginger sauce. The generous portions are often large enough to share, and desserts are sinful: diet tomorrow. On Tuesday night, there is a wine-and-cheese buffet accompanied by jazz music. Friday morning you can hear a chamber music concert in the upstairs gallery for a separate fee. Angle for a table on the patio in good weather. ✉*7 Harav Kook St., Downtown* ☎*02/624–4186* ⊕*www.go-out.com/ticho* ▵*Reservations essential* ▭*AE, DC, MC, V* ✕*No dinner Fri. No lunch Sat.* ✛*1B*

ISRAELI

☾

Fodor'sChoice

★

FAST FOODS TO TRY

Falafel and hummus are ubiquitous, and Israeli cheeses are worth a try, but if meat is what you hunger for, try these local favorites. Me'oorav yerushalmi (Jerusalem mixed grill) is a specialty of the grills on Agrippas Street, near the Machaneh Yehuda market. It's a deliciously seasoned meal of grilled chicken hearts and other organ meats in pita.

Shawarma is grilled meat (lamb or turkey), also served in pita bread. Try the stands in the Ben- Yehuda Street open-air mall, and near the Machaneh Yehuda produce market.

$$$ ✕**Mona.** You cross the austere stone hall of the Artists' House to get here: but it's another world inside. The atmosphere envelops you at the door—flagstone floors, an open fire in winter, yesteryear artifacts, quirky wall decorations, a great bar. Start your exploration of modern Israeli fare with the sublime cream of vegetable roots soup or a carpaccio. Meat-eaters and piscatorians have plenty to choose from; vegetarians have a variety of large salads (share) and a couple of pasta dishes (try the ravioli). Wonderful mains are the richly flavored butcher's cut stew with chestnuts and red wine, and the well-blended spiciness of the calamari and shrimp in ginger, chili pepper, and sesame oil. The strawberry mascarpone (in season) is the house dessert of choice. ✉*12 Shmuel Hanagid, Downtown* ☎*02/622–2283* ▵*Reservations essential* ▭*AE, DC, MC, V.* ✛*2A*

MODERN ISRAELI

Fodor'sChoice

★

¢ ✕**Pinati.** When aficionados of local standards like hummus, skewered shish kebab, and bean soup argue hotly about the merits of *their* favorite eateries, Pinati comes up as a leading contender. In the very heart of the downtown, this simple spot is a convenient place to take the weight off your feet and rub shoulders with the locals. Not for long, though: your table will soon be in demand. ✉*13 King George St., Downtown* ☎*02/625–4540* ▵*Reservations not accepted* ▭*No credit cards* ✕*No dinner Fri. Closed Sat.* ✛*1B*

MIDDLE EASTERN

$$ ✕**Sakura.** Many consider Jerusalem's veteran Japanese restaurant the best of its kind in the country, with its authentic (specially imported) ingredients and high standard of food and presentation. The sushi/ sashimi combination is a must for enthusiasts, or try the salmon teriyaki, jumbo shrimp tempura, or chicken yakitori. Vegetarian options

JAPANESE

are also available. Cleverly renovated, the old structure preserves and illuminates its honey limestone through a glass facade by day and soft lighting by night. An intimate loft-like upstairs room, a sushi bar, and a few tables in the entrance courtyard give a range of options. ⊠ *31 Jaffa Rd. (Finegold Court), Downtown* ☎ *02/623–5464 or 02/623–5244* ⌖ *Reservations essential* ⊟ *AE, DC, MC, V.* ✛ *2C*

$$$ ✕ **Sol.** Here is a place to linger, with wood floors, soft lighting, terra-
SPANISH cotta, and a big wood counter that exude warmth. Sol is about tapas, though there's a respectable if limited main-course menu (steak, chicken, seafood, and ravioli). Go for the black tiger shrimp and calamari duet in a cream-based sauce; leek and chard fritters; chicken livers with confiture; mushrooms stuffed with goat cheese and deep fried; and the beef fillet and smoked goose medallion combo. Around 11, the place transmogrifies into a popular bar, with a different tapas menu. ⊠ *15 Shlomzion Hamalka St., Downtown* ☎ *02/624–6938* ⌖ *Reservations essential* ⊟ *AE, DC, MC, V* ⊘ *No lunch.* ✛ *4F*

$ ✕ **Spaghettim.** Although pizza and other pasta dishes are available, spa-
ITALIAN ghetti is the thing here—the name of the restaurant weds the Italian
⟳ term to a Hebrew plural form—with more than 40 sauces and toppings grouped by base (olive oil, tomato, and cream or butter). Look for traditional combinations as well as variations like the carbonara, a tempting mixture of smoked meat, sausage, white wine, butter, nutmeg, ground pepper, and cream. Among the reasonably priced meat and fish options, try the salmon grilled in a brick oven with garlic confit and sun-dried tomatoes. Whole-wheat pasta and tofu substitutes are available. The high ceiling and sleek metallic lines are trendy elements; the clientele here is a mix of families and young patrons. ⊠ *35 Hillel St. (in Beit Agron), Downtown* ☎ *02/623–5547* ⊟ *AE, DC, MC, V.* ✛ *2C*

$$ ✕ **Steakiat Hatzot.** Agrippas Street, down the street from the Machaneh
MIDDLE EASTERN Yehuda produce market, has some of Jerusalem's best-known blue-collar "mizrahi" (Middle Eastern) diners. Loyalists claim that Steakiat Hatzot (which means "midnight grill," though nobody uses the translation) actually pioneered the *me'oorav yerushalmi*—Jerusalem mixed grill—a substantial and delicious meal-in-a-pita of cumin-flavored bits of chicken hearts and other organ meats. Certainly that is its specialty; for other traditional Middle Eastern dishes, you might prefer the more comfortable surroundings of Ima, across the street. Make sure of prices before you order to avoid unasked-for side dishes. ⊠ *123 Agrippas St., Machaneh Yehuda* ☎ *02/624–4014* ⌖ *Reservations not accepted* ⊟ *No credit cards* ⊘ *Closed Fri. and Sat.* ✛ *3C*

$$$ ✕ **Terra.** A tasteful combination of Jerusalem stone, gentle lighting,
FRENCH unobtrusive music, and soothing modern fabrics sets the mood. Attentive service and an impressive wine list complete the picture. The creative menu tempts with a tomato-based interpretation of bouillabaisse, seared foie gras in mango martini and caramel sauce, and lamb osso buco slow-cooked in cognac and root vegetables. Seafood and veal specialties are another way to go. Reservations are essential Friday and Saturday. ⊠ *3 Ben Shetach, Downtown* ☎ *02/623–5001* ⊟ *AE, MC, V* ⊘ *No lunch Sun.–Thurs.* ✛ *2C*

2

$$ ✕**T'mol Shilshom.** The name—a Hebrew literary phrase that translates
ISRAELI roughly as "yesteryear"—is a clue to the character of the place. This
funky café-restaurant and used bookstore occupies two separate rooms
on the upper floor of a mid-19th-century house. Hosting Hebrew (and
occasionally English) poetry readings and modest book launches, it's
long been a popular spot with intellectuals and folks who just enjoy
lingering over a book. No meat is served, but choose from a tempting
selection of salads, pasta, and fish dishes such as salmon fillet in white
wine and fig sauce. Desserts have taken a serious turn for the better.
⊠*Off 5 Yoel Solomon St., Nahalat Shiva* ☎*02/623–2758* ▭*AE, DC,
MC, V* ⊘*No dinner Fri. No lunch Sat.* ✛*2B*

$ ✕**Village Green.** Right near Zion Square, this airy vegetarian restau-
VEGETARIAN rant prides itself on the quality of its offerings. There's a good variety
of soups, quiches, lasagnas, fresh vegetable salads, and more. Many
ingredients are organic, and this is a great choice for vegans as well.
Salads and the hot buffet are self-service (charged by weight); every meal
comes with a choice of homemade bread rolls. For a coffee-time option,
take a fine latte and a slice of home-baked cake or pie (gluten-free and
sugar-free options available) out to a table on the shaded sidewalk.
⊠*33 Jaffa Rd., Downtown* ☎*02/625–3065* ▭*AE, DC, MC, V* ⊘*No
dinner Fri. Closed Sat.* ✛*1C*

GERMAN COLONY

South of Downtown, the Colony is a hot spot for eateries, cafés, and
little shops. It's a fun spot to pass an evening.

$$$ ✕**Olive.** This place is a veteran landmark among the German Colony's
STEAK rash of new restaurants. The largely older crowd seems to prefer the
comfortable atmosphere of the glass-enclosed, split-level enclosed front
yard to the back room, with its arched windows, bar, and stronger
acoustics. At this happy hunting ground for carnivores, beef and lamb
kebabs are superb, and the steaks and chicken combos very good. Veg-
gies can keep starvation at bay with a soup (try the tomato-based lentil,
if available), some appetizers, and a hearty salad or a Thai dish. Save
room for a dessert pie or the delicious passion fruit sorbet. A full taster's
menu is available by prior arrangement. ⊠*36 Emek Refaim St., German Colony* ☎*02/561–1102* ✑*Reservations essential* ▭*AE, DC, MC,
V* ⊘*No dinner Fri. No lunch Sat.* ✛*6F*

OLD CITY

The walled Old City pretty much shuts down at night, so most watering
holes cater for the lunch custom. There are several falafel-and-shawar-
ma places and Middle Eastern eateries in the Muristan area of the Christian Quarter, very few in the Muslim Quarter, and a more numerous
and broader range of stands and restaurants (falafel, pizza, sandwiches,
burgers, and some fuller-menu options) in and near the Jewish Quarter's
Hurva Square, and on the route to the Western Wall.

¢ ✕**Abu Shukri.** In the heart of the Old City, right at Station V on the Via
MIDDLE EASTERN Dolorosa, this place has an extraordinary and well-deserved reputation

for the best hummus in town. Don't expect decor. This is a neighborhood eatery, and a look at the clientele—Palestinian Arabs and Jewish Israeli insiders—confirms that you have gone local. Enjoy the excellent fresh falafel balls, *labaneh* (a dairy item somewhere between tart yogurt and cream cheese), baba ghanoush, tahini, and fresh vegetable salad; no meat is served. Eat family-style, and don't over-order: you can get additional portions on the spot. ⊠ *63 El-Wad (Hagai) St., Muslim Quarter* ☎ *02/627–1538* ⚞ *Reservations not accepted* ▭ *No credit cards* ◷ *No dinner.* ⊹ *4G*

$
CAFÉS
◷

✕**Keshet.** With wooden tables in its cool interior and tables under the trees in the square outside, this daytime-only eatery is a very good lunch option but also a place to take the weight off your feet and sip a beer, or grab a latte and a crêpe. The menu offers a modest variety of soups, pasta, lasagna, quiches, *latkes* (potato fritters), and salads—try the deliciously fresh (and virtuously healthy) Earth Salad. ⊠ *2 Tiferet Israel St., Jewish Quarter* ☎ *02/628–7515* ▭ *MC, V* ◷ *Closed Sat. No dinner.* ⊹ *5G*

$$
MIDDLE EASTERN
◷

✕**Nafoura.** Just inside the Jaffa Gate (up the first street on the left), Nafoura offers an attractive tranquil courtyard for alfresco lunchtime dining, where your table might lean against the Old City's 16th-century wall. The pleasant if unremarkable interior is a comfortable refuge in inclement weather. Start with the traditional meze, an array of salads: the smaller version is enough for two people. Insist on the excellent local dishes only (hummus, eggplant dip, tahini, carrots, and so on) and skip the mushrooms and corn. Ask particularly for the *kibbeh,* delicacies of cracked wheat and ground beef, or the *lahmajun,* the meat-topped "Armenian pizza." From the typical selection of entrées, try the lamb cutlets or the sea bream (called "denise"). Smaller portions are available for many items. The NIS 50 buffet (chicken, kebab, side dishes, and fruit) is an excellent value. ⊠ *18 Latin Patriarch Rd., Christian Quarter* ☎ *02/626–0034* ▭ *AE, DC, MC, V* ◷ *No dinner* ⊹ *5F.*

TALBIEH, KING DAVID STREET, AND YEMIN MOSHE

These upscale neighborhoods, some of them an easy walk south from Downtown, are home to a good number of the city's hotels, and most of the top ones. While that fact explains the presence of at least some of the restaurants, don't write them off as tourist traps: some have a very good local reputation.

$$
CAFÉS

✕**Lavan.** At the in-house eatery of the popular Cinematheque, coffee and drinks satisfy film buffs, but the superb prospect of greenery and Old City walls from the glassed-in patio draws other locals as well. For the tourist, big pluses are proximity to Jaffa Gate and the fact that it's open Saturday. The fare is light: fresh fish of the day, soup, and pasta, sandwiches, pizza, and salads. The chef's more inventive dishes have mixed success, but one winner is gnocchi with chestnuts and sautéed onions, topped with parmesan slices. Do try the unusual ice cream made with tahini and halva. ⊠ *11 Hebron Rd., Yemin Moshe* ☎ *02/673–7393* ▭ *AE, MC, V* ⊹ *6F.*

$$$
MEDITERRANEAN

✕**Olive & Fish.** The location, near major hotels, is part of its success, but Olive & Fish pleases locals on its own merits. With no trendy

JERUSALEM'S CAFÉS

Sitting down for coffee and cake in one of Jerusalem's fine cafés is something of a tradition. Yeast cakes and strudels recall the past, but today's palate craves cheesecake and fruit pies. Italian coffee machines have become almost universal, driving a rise in quality and in demand for the beverage.

The downtown Midrachov, the open-air mall of Ben-Yehuda Street, has several venerable hangouts, but the newer cafés offer a more sophisticated menu—and better coffee. The Mamilla strip mall, outside Jaffa Gate, embraces that trend; but the "in" neighborhood mecca is Emek Refa'im Street, in the German Colony.

Most popular watering holes serve decent light, affordable meals for lunch and dinner as well, and courtyard seating gets full in fine weather and on summer evenings. Coffee and a pastry are about NIS 30—NIS 40; sandwiches, salads, quiche, and pasta will cost NIS 16—NIS 46.

Coffee Mill (⊠ *23 Emek Refa'im, German Colony* ☎ *02/566-1665*) is a must for coffee devotees, with its dizzying selection of blends. You can get a light meal, too.

Gulindo (⊠ *17 Shamai St., Downtown* ☎ *02/624-6663*) is a tiny coffee and home-baked goods establishment that spills into the nearby alley. Pizza and quiches are also on the menu.

Hillel (⊠ *8 Hillel St., Downtown* ☎ *02/624-7775* ⊠ *1 Helene Hamalka St., Downtown* ☎ *02/625-6552* ⊠ *50 EmekRefai'm,GermanColony* ☎ *02/566-7187*) is a popular chain. This is a favorite with locals for breakfast, with its good food and good prices.

Jan's (⊠ *20 Marcus St., Talbieh* ☎ *02/561-2054*), literally under the plaza of the Jerusalem Theater (access at the corner with Chopin Street), is a special place of pillows and rugs, low lights, Asian ornaments, and a good vegetarian menu.

Kadosh (⊠ *6 Shlomzion Hamalka St., Downtown* ☎ *02/625-4210*) is one place locals are reluctant to share, lest it lose its intangible "Jerusalemite" character. Home-baked goods and delicacies, and '30s-style decor are part of the draw.

Mizrahi (⊠ *12 Hashezif St., Machaneh Yehuda* ☎ *02/624-2105*), still subtitled Hakol La'ofeh Ve'gam Cafe (though the name is only in Hebrew), makes a good stop while you're enjoying the produce market. It serves some of the best coffee around, as well as tasty light meals. Come for live music and tapas Sunday nights in summer.

Modus (⊠ *31 King George St., Downtown* ☎ *02/624-4215*) has a loyal following due to the homemade sandwiches, apple strudel, bourekas, and early opening hours.

Shamai-12 (⊠ *12 Shamai St., Downtown* ☎ *02/623-2421*) offers good coffee, the usual pastries, and generous sandwiches.

YMCA–Three Arches (⊠ *26 King David St., King David St.* ☎ *02/569-2692*) has known better days as a dinner option. However, its ambience—relax on the flagstone patio across from the King David Hotel in fine weather—and the fact that it's open Friday night and Saturday make it good for coffee, a beer, or a light lunch.

pretensions, the restaurant draws an older crowd. The glass-enclosed front porch is popular; the interior, with pale yellow walls, framed prints, and unintrusive lighting is a warm and inviting, if not memorable, setting. For starters, try the grilled eggplant in tahini sauce or the excellent sirloin salad. Great fish options are the freshwater St. Peter's fish (tilapia), done with artichokes, sun-dried tomatoes, white wine, and lemon, or the sea bass fillet. Other temptations are delectable lamb and beef kebabs, or tender *pargiyot* (spring chicken chunks) in date honey sauce or Middle Eastern seasonings. Save room for one of the pies or chocolate creations. ⊠*2 Jabotinsky St., Talbieh* ☎*02/566–5020* ⌕*Reservations essential* ☰*AE, DC, MC, V* ⊘*Closed Fri. No lunch Sat.* ✛*5E*

$$ ✕**Paradiso.** You may be suspicious of its strategic location near major
MEDITERRANEAN hotels, but the food is excellent and much of the clientele local. Although the white stucco and dark wood touches are pleasant, decor is not the big attraction. You can eat light—breakfasts, sandwiches, salads, soup—but the main menu tempts you with unusually flavored appetizers (dolmades and stuffed vegetables; a seasonal salad of fresh figs, blue cheese, and greens), grilled steaks and imaginative meat combinations, tasty pasta dishes, and some child-friendly options. Mullet fillet baked with rosemary, olive oil, white wine, and garlic is recommended, but also ask about other seafood dishes on the constantly changing menu. Desserts are unexceptional. For fine-weather dining, there is a small deck over the sidewalk. Reservations are essential Friday night but are not accepted otherwise. ⊠*36 Keren Hayesod St., Talbieh* ☎*02/563–4805* ☰*AE, DC, MC, V* ✛*5E.*

$$$$ ✕**Scala.** The concept has something to recommend it: instead of a
MODERN ISRAELI selection of appetizers followed by a full main-course menu, Scala has created intriguing dishes in middle-size portions. For two people, the way to go is to choose three or four (served one at a time) and share. Creations are not equally successful, but worth trying are the yellowtail ceviche; onion layers stuffed with lamb and herbs, and served with black lentils and root vegetables; and the complex niçoise, built around fresh anchovy, spices, and vegetables. A few individual entrées are available. The chocolate desserts are delicious (but skip the nondairy ice cream). Service is informed and attentive. Dark wood, thoughtful lighting, and jazzy background music enhance the sophisticated atmosphere. ⊠*David Citadel Hotel, 7 King David St., King David St.* ☎*02/621–1111* ⌕*Reservations essential* ☰*AE, DC, MC, V* ⊘*No lunch. Closed Fri. and Sat.* ✛*5E*

$ ✕**Te'enim.** Comfortably ensconced in the classic limestone Confedera-
VEGETARIAN tion House—stone arches and flagstones, with tantalizing views (from the right tables) of the Old City walls—Te'enim ("Figs" in Hebrew) finds a delicate balance between traditional and innovative in its vegetarian fare. Share the large green salad, with goat cheese, fruit, and nuts; or the salad with portobello mushrooms, polenta, and arugula. Standard mains include a mushroom, polenta, olive, garlic, and red wine bake; and the successful *Maharajah majadra,* with bulgur, onion, ginger chutney, and yogurt. Daily specials are repeated on a weekly cycle: Mexican chili, an Indian dish, couscous, and so on. The homemade

sorbets are excellent, but try the surprising mini-eggplant in date honey and almonds. ⊠*12 Emile Botta St., Yemin Moshe* ☎*02/625–1967* ▭*AE, DC, MC, V* ☾*No dinner Fri. Closed Sat.* ✛*5F*

WEST JERUSALEM

The "cultural mile" in West Jerusalem is not known for fine dining—lunch-time cafeterias is the best you can hope for—but one superb Indian restaurant is a shining exception.

$$
INDIAN
✗**Kohinoor.** Gracious hospitality and Moghul-influenced decor immediately set a tone of quiet, informal elegance. *Naan* breads, piquant dips, and slightly spicy lamb samosas are great starters; fresh salad is untraditional but a refreshing foil. The cuisine is the less-fiery northern Indian: among the best entrées are the superb lamb *rogan gosht* and the subtle, tender, tandoori-baked chicken tikka. Curries or the flavorsome *dhal makham* (beans, lentils, and onions in a spicy sauce) are vegetarian options. Finish with fragrant *kulfi* ice cream or the exotic *elaichi kheer* rice pudding. The lunch buffet is an excellent value. ⊠*Crowne Plaza Hotel, 1 Ha'aliyah St., Givat Ram* ☎*02/658–8867* ⟶*Reservations essential* ▭*AE, DC, MC, V* ☾*No dinner Fri. No lunch Sat.* ✛*3B*

WHERE TO STAY

Some travelers insist on a hotel in a central location; others prefer to retreat to a haven at the end of the day, with ambience more important than accessibility. Jerusalem has more of the first kind than the second, and even hotels once considered remote are really no more than 10 minutes by cab from the city center. Most hotels are contemporary and modern, but a few have retained an Old World charm.

The majority of Jerusalem's better hotels are in West Jerusalem, the Jewish/Israeli side of the old "Green Line" that divided the city between 1948 and 1967. Some Israelis still avoid Arab "East Jerusalem," but the term is as much a matter of perception as of political geography: three large Israeli-run hotels (Olive Tree, Grand Court, and Moriah Classic) are just over the old line, sharing the "seam" where East meets West with the Palestinian-run American Colony and Addar.

The less-expensive hotels in East Jerusalem were seriously affected by Palestinian street violence in the late 1980s and early '90s, and again in the early 2000s. The ensuing shrinkage of hotel occupancy led to a widespread decline in standards as well.

Defining "high season" is not an exact science. Some hotels may talk about "peak" periods in addition to or instead of high season, typically the week-long Jewish holiday of Passover (March–April), and a similar period over the Sukkoth (Tabernacles) holiday in October. Depending on the hotel, rates may go up during other Jewish holidays, as well as Christmas. Because of variations in hotel policy, and because the dates of Jewish holidays shift annually in accordance with the Hebrew calendar, the difference in room rates can be significant. Shop around and check online for the best deals.

New construction in Jerusalem tends to be high-end (the Harmony Hotel is a refreshing exception). An eagerly-awaited new development is the Waldorf Astoria, built in the shell of a historic building, at the bottom of Agron Street. It is due to be managed by Hilton, and advertised as setting a new standard for luxury hotels in Jerusalem when it opens in late 2010.

All West Jerusalem hotels, with the exception of the YMCA, are Kosher.

WHAT IT COSTS IN U.S. DOLLARS					
	¢	$	$$	$$$	$$$$
Hotels	Under $120	$120–$200	$201–$300	$301–$400	over $400

Prices are for two people in a standard double room in high season. Non-Israeli citizens paying in foreign currency are exempt from the 15.5% V.A.T tax on hotel rooms.

CENTER CITY

This section embraces an area from the Rehavia neighborhood northeast down to Zion Square in the heart of Downtown. It's more about central locations than leafy retreats. Parking is at a premium: this is discouraging territory for rental cars.

¢   🏨**Agron Guest House.** The Israel Youth Hostel Association has reinvented itself in the last couple of decades, upgrading its properties to simple but comfortable and well-designed guesthouses, and Agron is no exception. The hostel is all light and limestone, with ground-floor courtyards and a large second-floor pergola-covered patio that offers a great city view. Its location is excellent: a less than 10-minute walk from downtown, and just 15 minutes from the Old City. **Pros:** strategic touring location; free Internet access; large late-night supermarket across the street. **Cons:** sometimes noisy when exuberant youth groups come to stay; most rooms only available February–August. ⊠6 *Agron St., Downtown* ☎*02/621-7555* ⊕*www.iyha.org.il* ⤴*55 rooms* ⌂*In-room: refrigerator, Internet. In-hotel: restaurant, laundry facilities, Internet terminal, parking (free), no-smoking rooms* ▭*AE, DC, MC, V* ⊙*Sept.–Jan.* †⊚*BP.* ✛*5E*

$$ 🏨**Harmony.** The seemingly sudden appearance of a new boutique hotel
Fodor'sChoice   in the heart of downtown Jerusalem created a buzz in tourism circles.
★   The cleverly arranged furniture and ceilings covered with silk-screened historical Jerusalem photos make for a comfortable intimacy; full-length mirrors on the walls enhance the sense of space. The modern feel is carried over into the guest rooms, with off-white, dove-gray, red, and blue accents. The daily happy hour (5–7 PM) includes free glasses of wine, arak, hot drinks, fruit, and cookies. The location, in the heart of the historic Nahalat Shiva neighborhood, is as downtown as you can get. **Pros:** free Internet access; heart of where it's happening; free leaflets for self-guided theme tours. **Cons:** parking difficult and/or expensive; downtown noise when you open windows. ⊠6 *Yoel Salomon St., Downtown* ☎*02/621-9999* ⊕*www.atlas.co.il* ⤴*50 rooms*

BEST BETS FOR JERUSALEM LODGING

2

Fodor's writers and editors have selected their favorite hotels and other lodgings by price and experience. Fodor's Choice properties represent the "best of the best" across price categories. You can also search by area for excellent places to stay—just check out our complete reviews on the following pages.

Fodor's Choice ★

David Citadel, $$$$, p. 139
Harmony, $$, p. 134
Inbal, $$$, p. 139

By Price

¢

Lutheran Guesthouse, p. 147
Mount Zion, p. 146
Yitzhak Rabin Guest House, p. 144

$

Addar, p. 147
Ambassador, p. 148
Little House in the Colony, p. 145
Moriah Gardens, p. 144
Regency Jerusalem, p. 149
St. Andrew's Scottish Guesthouse, p. 146

$$

Crowne Plaza, p. 143
Dan Boutique, p. 145
Dan Panorama, p. 138

Harmony, p. 134
Ramada Jerusalem, p. 144
Ramat Rachel, p. 146

$$$

Inbal, p. 139
Mount Zion, p. 146
Prima Royale, p. 140

$$$$

American Colony Hotel, p. 148
David Citadel, p. 139
King David, p. 140

By Experience

BEST ISRAELI BREAKFAST

American Colony Hotel, $$$$, p. 148
Inbal, $$$, p. 139
King David, $$$$, p. 140
Sheraton Jerusalem Plaza, $$$$, p. 137

BEST SPA

David Citadel, $$$$, p. 139
Inbal, $$$, p. 139
Ramada Jerusalem, $$, p. 144
Regency Jerusalem, $, p. 149

BEST FOR KIDS

Inbal, $$$, p. 139
Ramada Jerusalem, $$, p. 144
Ramat Rachel, $$, p. 146
Yitzhak Rabin Guest House, ¢, p. 144
YMCA (West)—Three Arches, $, p. 141

BEST VIEWS

Crowne Plaza, $$, p. 143
Ramat Rachel, $$, p. 146
Regency Jerusalem, $, p. 149
Sheraton Jerusalem Plaza, $$$$, p. 137

BEST POOL

King David, $$$$, p. 140
Mount Zion, $$$, p. 146
Ramada Jerusalem, $$, p. 144
Ramat Rachel, $$, p. 146

BEST FOR HISTORY BUFFS

American Colony Hotel, $$$$, p. 148
Christ Church, $, p. 147
King David, $$$$, p. 140

BEST HOTEL BAR

American Colony Hotel, $$$$, p. 148
King David, $$$$, p. 140

BEST ROOF DECK

Dan Boutique, $$, p. 145
Lutheran Guesthouse, ¢, p. 147

BEST FOR ROMANCE

American Colony Hotel, $$$$, p. 148
Little House in the Colony, $, p. 145
Mount Zion, $$$, p. 146

⚴ *In-room: safe, refrigerator, Wi-Fi. In-hotel: laundry service, Internet terminal, Wi-Fi, no-smoking rooms* ▭*AE, DC, MC, V* ⦿|*BP.* ✛*2B*

¢ 🏨 **Jerusalem Hostel and Guest House.** Overlooking Zion Square, this is as downtown as you can get. Don't look for frills—this is for the budget traveler—but you do get double-glazed windows and (somewhat frayed) wall-to-wall carpeting, keeping the noise level down. Dormitory beds (eight in a room) are $21 a night; larger private rooms sleep parents and two kids; children under 12 are free. There's air-conditioning at certain hours. **Pros:** good value; free Internet access. **Cons:** noisy street; a bit down at the heel. ✉*44 Jaffa Rd., Downtown* ☎*02/623–6102* ⊕*www.jerusalem-hostel.com* ⇆*20 rooms, 3 dormitories* ⚴*In-room: no phone. In-hotel: laundry facilities, Internet terminal, Wi-Fi, some pets allowed, no-smoking rooms* ▭*AE, DC, MC, V* ⦿|*room-only arrangement.* ✛*1B*

$ 🏨 **Jerusalem Tower.** The choice location, right in the center of downtown, makes this hotel a great option for those who enjoy being close to the action. Guest rooms are smallish, but have large wall mirrors above the wood-panel headboards to enhance the sense of space. Furnishings are a pleasing blend of beige, gold, and dark blue. Ask for an east-facing room above the sixth floor to guarantee a view. The dining room, which has private seating nooks and arched stained-glass windows, is an unexpected attraction. **Pros:** free Wi-Fi; renovations expected in 2009. **Cons:** guest rooms ready for renovation; rooms not spacious. ✉*23 Hillel St., Downtown* ☎*02/620–9209* ⊕*www.jthotels.com* ⇆*120 rooms* ⚴*In-room: safe. In-hotel: restaurant, bar, laundry service, Internet terminal, Wi-Fi, parking (free)* ▭*AE, DC, MC, V* ⦿|*BP.* ✛*2B*

$ 🏨 **Little House in Rechavia.** For quick walks to the Old City, lots of green space, and pleasant strolling, Rechavia is a good choice. The hotel makes no pretensions to a full-service facility, but it is comfortable and good value. There is some street noise, but double-glazed windows help. Some of the rooms are notably roomier, especially the quads and family units. At times (not predictable), the hotel has a very religious Jewish clientele. **Pros:** some sizable rooms; uncommercial neighborhood feel. **Cons:** devout clientele makes for interesting but not cool atmosphere; only breakfast available. ✉*20 Ibn Ezra St., Rehavia* ☎*02/563–3344* ⊕*www.o-niv.com/Rechavia* ⇆*32 rooms* ⚴*In-room: Wi-Fi. In-hotel: restaurant, Wi-Fi, no-smoking rooms* ▭*AE, DC, MC, V* ⦿|*BP.* ✛*5D*

$ 🏨 **Montefiore.** The side-street location smack in the center of town— shops and restaurants abound within yards of the front door—doesn't seem to trouble the hotel's serenity. The lobby is an aesthetic blend of rough limestone walls, parquet and flagstone floors, and faux-leather sofas. Off-white bedcovers and large mirrors enhance light and space in the modest guest rooms (those facing the street are larger; windows are double-glazed). After breakfast, the dining room is transformed into Angelica, the excellent new fine-dining restaurant, with independent access from the street. **Pros:** renovations expected with change of management in 2009; easy walking distance from Old City. **Cons:** the sole suite has an exceptionally ugly non-view; no in-house restaurant serving lighter fare. ✉*7 Shatz St., Downtown* ☎*02/622–1111* ⊕*www.*

Ancient arches and minarets are both part of the distinctive landscape of the Old City.

montefiorehotel.com ✆*47 rooms, 1 suite* ♿*In-room: Wi-Fi (some). In-hotel: restaurant, laundry service, Internet terminal, Wi-Fi, no-smoking rooms* ▭*AE, DC, MC, V* ⦶*BP.* ✛*2A*

$$ **Prima Kings.** The Kings—the name by which it's still known—is on a busy intersection (but insulated from the noise), less than a 10-minute walk from the city center. Cane furniture and deep sofas create comfortable, if not particularly intimate, public areas. Most of the guest rooms are fairly large, the deluxe ones are done in tones of burgundy and green, with touches of leather. If your budget allows, upgrade to a junior suite with a balcony; check for lower online rates. Especially large family rooms are also available. **Pros:** 15 minutes from Old City; late-night supermarket across the street. **Cons:** overpriced; traffic noise when windows are open. ✉*60 King George St. (entrance on Ramban St.), Rehavia* ☎*02/620–1201* ⊕*www.prima.co.il* ✆*217 rooms* ♿*In-room: safe, Wi-Fi (some). In-hotel: 2 restaurants, room service, bar, laundry service, Internet terminal, Wi-Fi, parking (paid), no-smoking rooms* ▭*AE, DC, MC, V* ⦶*BP.* ✛*5E*

$$$$ **Sheraton Jerusalem Plaza.** Near the lively downtown area set on a hill, the 22-story Sheraton looks like a big business hotel, but the terrific views, especially from upper floors (the top two have balconies) remind you where you are. The hotel is popular with high-end religious Jewish clientele. All guest rooms have been recently renovated, in gold and dark blue, with Starwood's signature beds as well as a coffee corner. Primavera, the nonmeat Italian restaurant presided over by acclaimed chef Shalom Kadosh, has won kudos locally for its good food and elegance. In addition, an outdoor barbecue is offered Sunday through Thursday in summer. The small pool, surrounded by unaesthetic concrete,

encourages quick dips, not prolonged relaxation. **Pros:** minutes away from downtown; plenty to eat. **Cons:** chain hotel feel; pricey. ✉ *47 King George St., Downtown* ☎ *02/629–8666* ⊕ *www.sheraton.com* ⇨ *300 rooms* ⟳ *In-room: safe, Wi-Fi. In-hotel: 4 restaurants, room service, bar, pool, children's programs (occasional), laundry service, Internet terminal, Wi-Fi, parking (paid), no-smoking rooms* ⊟ *AE, DC, MC, V* ⑩ *BP.* ⊹ *5E*

¢ 🏨 **Zion.** With little balconies overlooking a pedestrian street off the downtown Ben-Yehuda mall, this 19th-century stone building has an Old World feel to it. Front rooms get some street noise until late hours, though air-conditioning and double-glazed windows have eased the problem. Furnishings are simple; ask for a "good room" if you want less minimalistic surroundings. Ten rooms have showers only. The lobby, reception area, and a few rooms are up a single flight of stairs (other rooms are up farther still—there is no elevator). Breakfast is not included, but a good coffee shop is downstairs. The manager speaks five languages, but not English. **Pros:** fun downtown location; inexpensive; European character. **Cons:** a little dingy; some communication issues; not for guests with physical disabilities. ✉ *10 Dorot Rishonim St., Downtown* ☎ *02/623–2367* ⇨ *25 rooms* ⟳ *In-room: refrigerator. In-hotel: laundry service, Wi-Fi* ⊟ *No credit cards.* ⊹ *1B*

TALBIEH AND KING DAVID STREET

These are desirable residential neighborhoods (good for jogging and after-dinner strolls), their prime locations just 10 to 20 minutes' walk from both the Old City and Downtown. Alongside the city's high-end hotels are several budget-friendly options.

$–$$ 🏨 **Beit Shmuel.** This is a limestone complex, with cool inner courtyards and fabulous Old City views from the roof. The new wing has better-grade hotel rooms: ask for one facing the private inner courtyard and lawn; the Old City view is somewhat obstructed. The guesthouse (superior hostel) rooms are bright and pleasant, if utilitarian. They can sleep six when bunk beds are lowered from the walls. Request a street-facing room to avoid the noise of fine-weather evening events in the inner courtyard. The location is excellent: only 5 minutes' walk to Jaffa Gate, 10 minutes to downtown. **Pros:** free Internet; great coffee in the snack bar. **Cons:** no frills; only street parking. ✉ *13 King David St. (entrance on Sham'a St.), King David St.* ☎ *02/620–3456* ⊕ *www.beitshmuel. com* ⇨ *41 rooms* ⟳ *In-room: no phone or TV in hostel rooms, Wi-Fi. In-hotel: restaurant, laundry service, Internet terminal, Wi-Fi* ⊟ *AE, DC, MC, V* ⑩ *BP.* ⊹ *5E*

$$ 🏨 **Dan Panorama.** The copper ceiling, palm-tree planters, and dark polished-stone floors and columns enhance the pleasantly muted feel of the reception area. The newer guest rooms are a bit compact, but good lighting and interesting old prints on the walls make a difference; the similarly smallish bathrooms are tiled with pleasing sand-colored ceramics. Rooms in the older wing are larger but less well appointed; depending on availability, the front desk is usually happy to accommodate your preference. **Pros:** excellent location; pleasant

2

staff. **Cons:** wannabe deluxe hotel. ✉*39 Keren Hayesod St., Talbieh* ☎*02/569–5695* ⊕*www.danhotels.com* ⤸*283 rooms, 8 suites* ⬧*In-room: safe, refrigerator (some), Wi-Fi. In-hotel: 2 restaurants, room service, bar, pool, gym, spa, children's program (all ages), laundry service, Internet terminal, Wi-Fi, parking (free), no-smoking rooms* ▤*AE, DC, MC, V* ⊙|*BP.* ⊕*5E*

$$$$
Fodor'sChoice
★

🛉**David Citadel.** Stonework and arches at this hotel, just five minutes from Jaffa Gate and 10 minutes from downtown, make a powerful first impression. The lobby—a monument to the architect—is somewhat cold, though offset by the comfortable, bright lounge and terrace one floor above. Views of the Old City walls from many rooms and public areas remind you that this is more than a good business hotel. The aesthetics are carried over into the spacious guest rooms, with furnishings in soft tones of beige and cream, decorative old-style mosaic wall-pieces, and well-appointed bathrooms. The new Scala specialty restaurant may tempt guests to stay in for dinner. **Pros:** friendly staff; great location; year-round outdoor pool. **Cons:** feel of a large business hotel; events sometimes intrusive. ✉*7 King David St., King David St.* ☎*02/621–1111* ⊕*www.thedavidcitadel.com* ⤸*381 rooms* ⬧*In-room: safe, Internet, Wi-Fi. In-hotel: 3 restaurants, room service, bar, pool, gym, spa, laundry service, Internet terminal, Wi-Fi, parking (paid), no-smoking rooms* ▤*AE, DC, MC, V* ⊙|*BP.* ⊕*5E*

$

🛉**Eldan.** Its central location in the heart of a prestigious hotel district—just a 10- minute walk from downtown or from Jaffa Gate—is a major draw. Rooms are bright and decorated in cheerful colors. Those over the side-street main entrance are smaller but quieter. Rooms facing King David Street (from some you can see the Old City) are more spacious, but expect traffic noise when the double-glazed windows are open. The rental-car company that owns the property often offers good deals. **Pros:** prime location; cheerful. **Cons:** few frills; busy street. ✉*24 King David St., King David St.* ☎*02/567–9777* ⊕*www.eldanhotel. com* ⤸*76 rooms* ⬧*In-room: safe, refrigerator, Wi-Fi. In-hotel: 2 restaurants, laundry service, Internet terminal, Wi-Fi, parking (free), no-smoking rooms* ▤*AE, DC, MC, V* ⊙|*BP.* ⊕*5E*

$$$
Fodor'sChoice
★
☺

🛉**Inbal.** The low-rise building of Jerusalem stone wrapped around a central courtyard and atrium makes an eye-pleasing first impression; and the Inbal's energetic spirit complements the picture. In warm weather, an excellent outdoor breakfast in the shaded courtyard makes a great start to the day. The guest rooms, decorated in shades of brown and beige, are comfortable; bathrooms are compact. Many deluxe rooms have balconies and fine views of a park next door as well as the Old City, and the heated pool in winter is an added bonus. The hotel's location next to the playgrounds of Liberty Bell Garden is convenient for families. **Pros:** good location with nearby restaurants; business center. **Cons:** smallish bathrooms; too family-friendly for guests seeking quiet intimacy. ✉*3 Jabotinsky St., Talbieh* ☎*02/675–6666* ⊕*www.inbal-hotel.co.il* ⤸*282 rooms, 26 suites* ⬧*In-room: safe, refrigerator, DVD (some), Internet, Wi-Fi. In-hotel: 3 restaurants, room service, bar, pool, gym, spa, children's programs (summer), laundry service, Internet, Wi-Fi, parking (paid), no-smoking rooms* ▤*AE, DC, MC, V* ⊙|*BP.* ⊕*6E*

$$$$ 🛏 **King David.** The grande dame of Israeli luxury hotels opened in 1931 and has successfully (and self-importantly) defended its title ever since. The ceilings, columns, and walls of the bustling lobby-lounge are decorated in "ancient Mesopotamian" geometrics. Airy guest rooms are elegantly orchestrated in cream and gold, with old-fashioned writing tables a gracious addition. Pricier rooms have views of the Old City, and suites have balconies facing the same direction. The landscaped pool area is a winner. An in-house French-style restaurant, La Régence, completes the picture. **Pros:** great pool and garden; terrific location; historic building. **Cons:** lingering reputation for snobbish staff; limited guest parking. ✉23 King David St., King David St. ☎02/620–8888 ⊕www.danhotels. com ⇆202 rooms, 35 suites ⚬In-room: safe, kitchen (some), refrigerator (some), DVD (some), Wi-Fi. In-hotel: 4 restaurants, room service, bar, tennis court, pool, gym, spa, children's programs (holidays), laundry service, Internet terminal, Wi-Fi, parking (free), some pets allowed, no-smoking rooms ⊟AE, DC, MC, V ⊙BP. ✛5E

$–$$ 🛏 **King Solomon.** The centerpiece of the lobby is a huge, spherical sculpture of Jerusalem by renowned sculptor Frank Meisler. A split-level atrium reveals shops half a floor down and the dining room a floor below that. The standard guest rooms are average-sized, but the more deluxe ones are quite large. The decor is attractive, with matching drapes and bedcovers, dark wood, translucent glass tabletops, and prints above the beds. The small pool (on an upper floor) offers a stunning view of southeast Jerusalem. The hotel has a large religious Jewish clientele, especially on Friday and Saturday and Jewish holidays. Over the weeks of Passover (spring) and Sukkoth (October), room rates soar, but regular rates are a good value. **Pros:** excellent location with restaurants close by; comfortable lobby-bar area; great views from many rooms. **Cons:** hotel ripe for renovation; reception sometimes understaffed. ✉32 King David St., Talbieh ☎02/569–5555 ⊕www.kingsolomon-hotel.com ⇆142 rooms, 6 suites ⚬In-room: safe, refrigerator, Wi-Fi. In-hotel: 2 restaurants, room service, bar, pool, laundry service, Internet terminal, Wi-Fi, parking (free), no-smoking rooms ⊟AE, DC, MC, V ⊙BP. ✛6E

$$$ 🛏 **Prima Royale.** The old landmark Windmill Hotel was gutted and reinvented in admirable taste. The well-lighted, golden-marble lobby—with potted palms, brightly colored armchairs and cushions, and touches of leather—augurs well. Guest rooms are very compact, but burgundy drapes and cushions and colorful accents in the bathrooms offer some compensation. Ask for a room with a view. The chain has designated the Royale as its cultural flagship: Chopin and champagne for breakfast, art in the dining room, live jazz, and more. The location is good, too: a 15- to 20-minute walk from the city center or the Old City. **Pros:** free culture and drinks; tasteful decor. **Cons:** small rooms; pricey for what it is. ✉3 Mendele St., off Keren Hayesod, Talbieh ☎02/560–7111 ⊕www.prima.co.il ⇆126 rooms, 7 suites ⚬In-room: safe, refrigerator, DVD (some), Wi-Fi (some). In-hotel: 2 restaurants, room service, bar, gym, spa, laundry service, Internet terminal, Wi-Fi, parking (free), no-smoking rooms ⊟AE, DC, MC, V ⊙BP. ✛6E

2

$ 🏨 **YMCA (West)–Three Arches.** Built in 1933, this limestone building with
😊 its famous domed bell tower is a Jerusalem landmark. Stone arches,
exotic murals, latticed cupboards, Armenian tiles, and the front patio
give the place charm and character. The guest rooms are comfortably
spacious for this grade, and attractively fitted in beige with patterned
burgundy touches and prints of landscape artist Anna Ticho on the walls.
The atmosphere, the excellent sports facilities, and a great location make
the "Y" an attractive deal. **Pros:** Old World feel; great strategic location;
free sports facilities. **Cons:** poor restaurant. ✉26 King David St., Box
294, King David St. ☎02/569–2692 ⊕www.ymca3arch.co.il ⤆52
rooms, 4 suites ♿In-room: refrigerator (some). In-hotel: restaurant,
bar, pool, gym, laundry service, Internet terminal, Wi-Fi, parking (free),
no-smoking rooms ☐AE, DC, MC, V ⊠BP. ♦5E

WEST JERUSALEM

This cluster of hotels in Givat Ram and Romema is near the point where
the Tel Aviv Highway (Route 1) enters Jerusalem. Some properties are
right at the Central Bus Station, others closer to the Israel Museum and
the Knesset. Ein Kerem, a leafy enclave, is included here, too, along
with Mt. Herzl. Downtown is some distance away, the Old City even
farther—a long walk, but 10–15 minutes by cab or bus, and bus lines
are plentiful. If it's hotel deals you're after or if other places in town
are booked, this area makes a great option.

$ 🏨 **BaChoresh HaTivi.** The exuberantly lush garden and sweeping view
of the valley are your first hint that you've found the perfect hideaway;
the well-appointed pine-and-tile suites with kitchenettes confirm it. Two
of the three units are of superior standard, one with a kid-friendly
loft. Private patios and garden furniture extend the living area into
the outdoors. Wine and a classical guitarist can be booked for warm
evenings.**Pros:** Ein Kerem itself is a joy; whirlpool baths in the better
suites; massages available. **Cons:** parking can be remote; 60 steps to
the place; far from the rest of Jerusalem. ✉Ein Kerem G7, Ein Kerem
☎02/643–6586, 054/235–5660 ⊕www.bachti.co.il ⤆3 suites ♿In-
room: no phone, DVD. In-hotel: parking (no fee), no-smoking rooms
☐No credit cards ⊠ BP. ♦3A

¢ 🏨 **Bayit VeGan.** The setting, opposite Mt. Herzl in West Jerusalem, has
sweeping views of the Judean Hills, yet is only a 15-minute cab ride
(there's a taxi stand next door) or a 25-minute bus ride from downtown.
Upgraded from a youth hostel to a guesthouse, it offers two levels of
accommodations. The new wing is essentially an economy hotel: 78
spacious, well-laid-out rooms (light wood furnishings; most with tubs,
some shower only) that sleep four. The 53 older hostel rooms (some
sleep six) are simpler, though still with carpets and en-suite bathrooms.
Always ask for a view. Meals are substantial and cheap. **Pros:** free Internet access; good falafel stand nearby. **Cons:** remote location; sometimes
noisy local groups. ✉8 Hapisgah St., Bayit VeGan, Box 16350, Mt.
Herzl ☎02/642–0990 ⊕www.bvh.co.il ⤆115 rooms ♿In-room: no
phone, safe, no TV. In-hotel: restaurants, Wi-Fi, parking (free), no-
smoking rooms ☐AE, DC, MC, V ⊠BP. ♦3A

The Inbal Jerusalem Hotel

The David Citadel Hotel

$$ ⊞**Crowne Plaza.** Although this landmark tall building with sweeping city views is a classic business hotel, it's also a comfortable vacation option. Pale salmon wallpaper and white duvets make a pleasing combination in guest rooms; bathrooms, though aesthetic, are small. The lobby-level bar–coffee shop is well laid out, with discreet alcoves, and the Kohinoor Indian restaurant is a real treat. The pool, and its adjacent lawns and playground, provide a welcome refuge for all ages at the end of a hot day. (The pool is covered and heated in winter.) **Pros:** away from city noise; spa and sports facilities; an ATM in the lobby. **Cons:** few attractions within walking distance; limited parking. ⊠*1 Ha'aliyah St., Givat Ram* ☎*02/658–8888* ⊕*www.crowneplaza.com* ⊅*380 rooms, 17 suites* ⌂*In-room: safe, Wi-Fi. In-hotel: 3 restaurants, room service, bar, tennis courts, pool, gym, spa, children's programs, laundry service, Internet terminal, Wi-Fi, parking (paid), no-smoking rooms* ▭*AE, DC, MC, V* ❙◯❙*BP.* ✛*3B*

$ ⊞**Jerusalem Gate.** Its main clientele is tour groups, but the good value of this hotel attracts individual tourists and budget-minded families as well. The location near the Central Bus Station makes transportation simple. Guest rooms have solid-wood furniture (a rarity) and duvets; ask for a high floor with a cityscape view. An attractive bar with a reflective copper ceiling looks down onto the open and airy lobby from an unobtrusive mezzanine. The rooftop sundeck offers great panoramas while you work on your tan. **Pros:** a spacious place to stay; direct access to Center One mall; on major bus routes. **Cons:** far from downtown; large groups mean less intimacy; sun-deck undeveloped. ⊠*43 Yirmiyahu St., Romema* ☎*02/500–8500* ⊕*www.jerusalemgatehotel. com* ⊅*294 rooms, 4 suites* ⌂*In-room: refrigerator (some), Wi-Fi. In-hotel: 2 restaurants, room service, bar, children's programs (summer), laundry service, Internet terminal, Wi-Fi, parking (paid), no-smoking rooms* ▭*AE, DC, MC, V* ❙◯❙*BP.* ✛*2B*

$ ⊞**Jerusalem Gold.** Owner-manager Ariella Shmida Doron's home-maker's touch is felt in the well-coordinated guest-room decor: some rooms are done in burgundy, others in bottle green. Bathrooms are small, but very light cream tiles enhance the sense of space. Double-glazed windows allow guests to ignore the very urban surroundings. **Pros:** bus lines to everywhere; Center One mall conveniently close. **Cons:** crowded seating in lobby-lounge; grungy neighborhood; few attractions nearby. ⊠*234 Jaffa St., Romema* ☎*02/501–3333* ⊕*www.jerusalemgold.com* ⊅*163 rooms, 35 suites* ⌂*In-room: safe, kitchen (some), refrigerator, Wi-Fi. In-hotel: 2 restaurants, room service, bar, laundry service, Internet terminal, Wi-Fi, parking (paid), no-smoking rooms* ▭*AE, DC, MC, V* ❙◯❙*BP.* ✛*2B*

$ ⊞**Jerusalem Park.** This West Jerusalem hotel (until recently the Park Plaza; cabbies still know it as the even older Sonesta) clings to its good local reputation. The bar-lounge offers comfortable sofas, deeply upholstered in burgundy or bottle green. Guest rooms are better than adequate, with pastel duvets and dark carpets; a tasteful touch in the small bathrooms is aqua accents on the light tiles. At this writing, two designated business floors were to be thoroughly renovated in 2009. Breakfast is served in a roofed stone courtyard. Guests have free access to Hebrew University's sports center, a 15-minute walk away (gym, tennis, squash, year-round pool). **Pros:** friendly; good aesthetics; intimate atmosphere. **Cons:** sports facilities not on-site; guest rooms small. ⊠ *2 Vilnai St., Givat Ram* ☎ *02/658–2222* ⊕ *parkplazajerusalem.co.il* ⟿ *210 rooms, 7 suites* ⬥ *In-room: refrigerator, Wi-Fi. In-hotel: 2 restaurants, room service, bar, tennis courts, pool, gym, laundry service, Internet terminal, Wi-Fi, parking (free), no-smoking rooms* ⊟ *AE, DC, MC, V* ⍾⃝*BP.* ✛*3A*

$–$$ 🏨 **Moriah Gardens.** Even cabbies cannot keep up with the hotel's many reincarnations (tell 'em "next to the Ramada"). It's a standout in its price category, with good-size guest rooms (ask for one with a view), larger family rooms (with a little kitchenette and a refrigerator on request), and notable recreational facilities. The outdoor and indoor pools, saunas, and whirlpool bath are free to guests; the gym is extra. A comfortably landscaped pool area provides a relaxing environment at the end of an intense day of summertime sightseeing. **Pros:** coffee-making kit in guest rooms; good value. **Cons:** slightly impersonal service; gym not free. ⊠ *4 Vilnai St., Givat Ram* ☎ *02/655–8888* ⊕ *www.azorim-hotels.co.il* ⟿ *172 rooms, 8 suites* ⬥ *In-room: safe, Wi-Fi (some). In-hotel: restaurants, room service, bar, pools, gym, spa, laundry service, Internet terminal, Wi-Fi, parking (free), no-smoking rooms* ⊟ *AE, DC, MC, V* ⍾⃝*BP.* ✛*3A*

$$ 🏨 **Ramada Jerusalem.** The marble lobby, with its reflecting copper ceiling
🄲 and potted palms, is elegant in a grand sense. Rooms are comfortably large and warmly designed with duvets, beige wallpaper, and pastel drapes; the bathrooms, however, are small. Most have fine city views and open spaces, some with small balconies—insist on one from the fifth floor up. The well-landscaped pool area with kids' playground equipment is a great asset. **Pros:** good value; great spa and gym; wonderful kiddie spaces. **Cons:** a ride from downtown and Old City; no tennis equipment provided. ⊠ *Ruppin Bridge at Herzl Blvd., Givat Ram* ☎ *02/659–9999* ⊕ *www.ramada.com* ⟿ *350 rooms, 10 suites* ⬥ *In-room: safe, refrigerator, Wi-Fi. In-hotel: 3 restaurants, room service, bar, tennis court, pools, gym, spa, children's programs (some holidays and Aug.), laundry service, Internet terminal, Wi-Fi, parking (free), no-smoking rooms* ⊟ *AE, DC, MC, V* ⍾⃝*BP.* ✛*3A*

¢ 🏨 **Yitzhak Rabin Guest House.** Part of the official Youth Hostel Associa-
🄲 tion, this place is an example of how good budget accommodations can get. The large, airy, stone-and-aluminum lobby is a gathering place that opens out to flower-filled patios, with a view of Hebrew University's abundantly green Givat Ram campus. Guest rooms are spacious enough (they sleep from two to five, two in fold-up bunks), with private showers and toilets; furnishings are functional. The Israel Museum is a short walk away, and there is a bus route to the downtown and the Central Bus Station. Meals are substantial and good. **Pros:** big on aesthetics; great place to meet travelers. **Cons:** no-frills rooms; closest bus line a bit infrequent. ⊠ *1 Nahman Avigad St., Givat Ram* ☎ *02/678–0101* 🖷 *02/679–6566* ⊕ *www.youth-hostels.org.il/english.html* ⟿ *77 rooms* ⬥ *In-room: no phone, refrigerator. In-hotel: restaurant, laundry service, Internet terminal, Wi-Fi, parking (free)* ⊟ *AE, DC, MC, V* ⍾⃝*BP.* ✛*6B*

GERMAN COLONY, HEBRON ROAD, AND ENVIRONS

This area lies in Jerusalem's south-east quadrant, due south of Jaffa Gate. Bakah is some distance away, but all other listed properties are a fairly easy walk from the Old City. The German Colony has become a popular leisure-time neighborhood, with numerous restaurants and coffee shops.

The slightly rustic kibbutz location of Ramat Rachel is technically south of the city limits, but geographically part of Jerusalem—enjoying the best of both worlds, as locals would say.

$$ **Dan Boutique.** The new onyx-black, red, and copper reception area and bright lobby lounge say it all: the veteran group-oriented Ariel Hotel has changed management and character, its recent, contemporary makeover intended to please the individual traveler. Room decor is a tasteful balance, done up in a similar, but gentler, color scheme than previously. About one-quarter of the rooms are classified as "superior Old City" regardless of size: you pay for the excellent views of Mt. Zion and the more distant Mt. of Olives. A third-floor sun-deck offers a 180-degree panorama. **Pros:** inviting public area; close to Ma'abada complex of restaurants and bars. **Cons:** trendy look not to everyone's taste; video screens in public areas intrusive. ⊠ *31 Hebron Rd., Hebron Rd.* ☎ *02/568–9999* ⊕ *www.danhotels.com* ↦ *125 rooms, 4 suites* ⌂ *In-room: safe, refrigerator, DVD, Wi-Fi. In-hotel: 2 restaurants, room service, bar, gym, laundry service, Internet terminal, Wi-Fi, parking (free), no-smoking rooms* ⊟ *AE, DC, MC, V* ❢⃝*BP.* ✦*6F*

$ **Little House in Bakah.** An attractive, stone-arched building on the edge of a residential neighborhood, with good bus lines and many eateries and shops just a short walk away, is not a bad recipe for the budget-conscious. Some rooms are a little cramped, others feel less-so: ask for an upper floor if stairs don't bother you. The renovated rooms have dark wood furniture and gold-hued curtains and carpets. Family units, with refrigerator and a balcony, sleep five. A sunken room with vaulted ceiling and wooden floor serves as an inviting bar, coffee shop, and Italian-inspired restaurant, spilling out into a shaded courtyard. **Pros:** intimacy; good value; nice neighborhood. **Cons:** a bit dowdy; no elevator. ⊠ *1 Yehuda St., corner of 80 Hebron Rd., Bakah* ☎ *02/673–7944* 🖷 *02/673–7955* ⊕ *www.o-niv.com/bakah* ↦ *34 rooms* ⌂ *In-room: refrigerator (some), Wi-Fi. In-hotel: restaurant, bar, Internet terminal, Wi-Fi, parking (free), no-smoking rooms* ⊟ *AE, DC, MC, V* ❢⃝*BP.* ✦*6G*

$ **Little House in the Colony.** The "smallest hotel in Jerusalem" (as its Web site calls it) shares a historic lot with the landmark Semadar Cinema and a restaurant, on a quiet narrow street just steps away from the German Colony's bubbling main drag. Room decor is simple but aesthetically pleasing (dark wood headboards; bathrooms tiled in a tranquil beige), and wood floors add to the charm. **Pros:** very quiet and intimate; shops and eateries nearby. **Cons:** a bit expensive for what you get; only breakfast provided. ⊠ *4a Lloyd George St., German Colony* ☎ *02/566–2424* ⊕ *www.o-niv.com/melonit* ↦ *22 rooms* ⌂ *In-room: Wi-Fi. In-hotel: restaurant, Wi-Fi* ⊟ *AE, DC, MC, V* ❢⃝*BP.* ✦*6E*

$$$ ⛰ **Mount Zion.** Columns, arched doorways, and windows in Jerusalem stone all frame ethereal views of Mt. Zion and create attractive nooks filled with wall hangings, Armenian tiles, and plants. The core of the hotel is a 19th-century building that later served as a British hospital. A new wing was added in the 1970s, but the older "Citadel" rooms are more interesting and roomy. While the architectural adaptations are inspired, the decor in some rooms suffers from clashes of colors and patterns. The beautiful pool area enjoys views over the Hinnom Valley; the Turkish steam bath spa complex, decorated with traditional blue tiles, is a great addition. **Pros:** wonderful aesthetics in public areas; inviting pool area surrounded by flowers and greenery; easy walk to Old City. **Cons:** staff could be cheerier; pricey. ⊠ *17 Hebron Rd., Hebron Rd.* ☏ *02/568–9555* ⊕ *www.mountzion.co.il* ⏎ *116 rooms, 14 suites* ⚭ *In-room: safe, refrigerator, DVD (some), Wi-Fi. In-hotel: 2 restaurants, room service, bar, pool, gym, spa, laundry service, Internet terminal, Wi-Fi, parking (free)* ═*AE, DC, MC, V* ⏏❘*BP.* ✛*6F*

$$ ⛰ **Ramat Rachel.** The relaxed, informal atmosphere is great. Rooms in
☺ the older South Wing have stunning views of Bethlehem and the Judean Desert. Recent renovations have introduced light-colored wood furniture offset by colorful throw-cushions and bed-covers. A long sofa hugging the rooms' picture windows can be folded out to sleep up to three kids. Bathrooms are very compact but well appointed. West Wing guest rooms, facing the pool, are decorated in tasteful aquamarines. With its fine pool (including a giant waterslide) and other sports facilities, all free to guests, Ramat Rachel feels like an isolated resort. Cheaper hostel rooms are also available. **Pros:** rustic location; tennis courts open 6 AM–10 PM; children's playground and petting farm. **Cons:** remote location, requiring car, cab, or city bus; sometimes crowded with events and lunch-time tour groups; no tennis equipment provided. ⊠ *Kibbutz Ramat Rachel, Ramat Rachel* ☏ *02/670–2555* ⊕ *www.ramatrachel. co.il* ⏎ *164 rooms* ⚭ *In-room: safe, refrigerator, Wi-Fi (some). In-hotel: 2 restaurants, bar, tennis courts, pool, gym, spa, laundry service, Internet terminal, Wi-Fi, parking (free), no-smoking rooms* ═*AE, DC, MC, V* ⏏❘*BP.* ✛*6G*

$ ⛰ **St. Andrew's Scottish Guesthouse.** Built in the early 1930s as part of the St. Andrew's (Presbyterian) Church complex, the guesthouse is as much a retreat as a place to stay overnight—"feeling like you're home," is the way they like to put it. The comfortable library, the garden, and the lounge with stuffed chairs and stone arches framing Old City views define the character of the place. Some of the guest rooms—tiled floors, gold-and-orange bedcovers and curtains—have tubs, others showers only. Bigger rooms have less of a view; some rooms have balconies. **Pros:** serene; close to German Colony; interesting "ethnic" gift shop. **Cons:** no meals other than breakfast; only one room for guests who can't do steps. ⊠ *1 David Remez St., Hebron Rd.* ☏ *02/673–2401* ⊕ *www. scotsguesthouse.com* ⏎ *17 rooms, 1 suite, 1 apartment* ⚭ *In-room: no TV, kitchen (some), Wi-Fi. In-hotel: Wi-Fi, parking (free)* ═*AE, DC, MC, V* ⏏❘*BP.* ✛*6F*

OLD CITY

The Old City, the historic walled heart of Jerusalem, includes the Armenian Quarter, the Christian Quarter, the Jewish Quarter, and the Muslim Quarter. Lodging options here are limited.

$ 🛏 **Christ Church.** This is the guesthouse of the adjacent Anglican church, the oldest Protestant church (1849) in the Middle East. Pinkish limestone floors and light furnishings in the guest rooms make for a pleasing aesthetic. Rooms in the newer Nicolayson Block are air-conditioned. The courtyard is a good retreat, and there is a library and a comfortable common room with cane chairs and cable TV. The location, in the Old City just inside Jaffa Gate, is excellent for sightseeing. **Pros:** tranquil haven; Internet cafés and convenience stores close by. **Cons:** some distance from West Jerusalem; many rooms without air-conditioning; ministry-oriented atmosphere not always comfortable for non-Christian guests. ⊠ *Jaffa Gate Jaffa Gate* ☎*02/627–7727 or 02/627–7729* ✍*christch@netvision.net.il* 🛏*32 rooms* &*In-room: no a/c (some), no TV, Wi-Fi. In-hotel: restaurant, laundry service, Wi-Fi, parking (free), no-smoking rooms* ☐*AE, MC, V* ⦿|*BP.* ✛*5G*

¢ 🛏 **Lutheran Guesthouse.** Tucked into an Old City alley, between Jaffa Gate and the Jewish Quarter, the guesthouse is a maze of stone buildings and courtyards. The tranquil roof garden offers sweeping views of Jerusalem's holy places. Single rooms are very small; triples are ample. Angle for double room #25 with its own balcony. The new top-floor addition (nearing completion at press time) will include an indoor-outdoor coffee-shop. **Pros:** free Internet access; wonderful leaf-framed panoramas; free hot drinks. **Cons:** far from West Jerusalem sites; Old City atmosphere not for everyone. ⊠*St. Mark's Rd., Old City* ☎*02/626–6888* ⊕*www.evangelisch-in-jerusalem.org/guesthouse* 🛏*34 rooms* &*In-room: no a/c, Wi-Fi. In-hotel: restaurant, Internet terminal, Wi-Fi, no-smoking rooms* ☐*AE, MC, V* ⦿|*BP.* ✛*5G*

EAST JERUSALEM AND THE "SEAM LINE"

The cluster of hotels here, some Israeli-run, some Palestinian, are within yards of each other, and of the old "seam" (as it's sometimes called) that once divided Jerusalem into East and West. At some levels, the old divisions remain, but the seam area itself has become a comfortable middle ground.

In splendid isolation on the northeast side of town, with long views southwest toward the Old City, Mount Scopus is home to the original Hebrew University and Hadassah Hospital campuses. The Regency Jerusalem hotel here abuts the French Hill neighborhood, at the northern end of the ridge.

$ 🛏 **Addar.** Elegantly intimate, this boutique hotel is on the seam between East and West Jerusalem. The red marble floor, gilded columns, wooden lattices, wrought-iron work, and plush burgundy upholstery of the lobby suggest other eras, and somehow manage to avoid gaudiness. The suites were freshly renovated in 2008; in-room whirlpool tubs are standard in the marble bathrooms. **Pros:** free Internet access;

personable, English-speaking manager; reasonable à la carte meals and snacks. **Cons:** not inviting neighborhood to stroll; dead at night. ✉*10 St. George Rd., Seam Line* ☎*02/626–3111* ⊕*www.addar-hotel.com* ↘*7 rooms, 23 suites* 🛁*In-room: safe, kitchen (some), refrigerator, DVD, Internet, Wi-Fi. In-hotel: restaurant, room service, gym, laundry service, Internet terminal, Wi-Fi, parking (free), some pets allowed, no-smoking rooms* ☰*AE, DC, MC, V* ⫚*BP* ✥*2F*

$ ◫ **Ambassador.** One of East Jerusalem's veteran hotels, the Ambassador has been transformed by thorough, tasteful renovations, and the use throughout of Jerusalem limestone. Rooms are airy and well appointed; for extra space, upgrade to a junior guest room, and ask for an Old City view. In fine weather, the somewhat eclectic Al-Diwan à la carte restaurant—Middle Eastern and Italian, mostly—expands to the patio and the Bedouin tent in the inviting garden. **Pros:** in-house patisserie; comfortable rooms. **Cons:** far from attractions and restaurants; staff lack warmth. ✉ *Nablus Rd., Sheikh Jarrah, East Jerusalem* ☎*02/541–2222* 🖶*02/582–8202* ⊕*www.jerusalemambassador.com* ↘*120 rooms* 🛁*In-room: safe, refrigerator, Wi-Fi. In-hotel: 2 restaurants, room service, bar, gym, laundry service, Internet terminal, Wi-Fi, parking (free), no-smoking rooms* ☰*AE, DC, MC, V* ⫚*BP.* ✥*1E*

$$$$ ◫ **American Colony Hotel.** Once a pasha's palace, this cool limestone oasis with its flower-filled inner courtyard has been a hotel for more than a century. It's a 10-minute walk from the Damascus Gate, in East Jerusalem, but worlds away from the hubbub of the Old City. A favorite haunt of American and British expats, foreign journalists, and diplomats, the hotel (Swiss-run and affiliated with The Leading Small Hotels of the World) is famous for its ambience: turquoise-and-blue tilework, Damascene wood inlay, potted palms. The best, exceptionally large rooms breathe elegance, with rug-strewn flagstone floors and vaulted or antique painted-wood ceilings. At press time, the hotel was being renovated, one wing at a time, with some guest rooms redesigned in an antique style. **Pros:** Old World aesthetics and international atmosphere; good English bookstore; free Internet access. **Cons:** dead neighborhood at night; a cab ride to most attractions and restaurants. ✉*23 Nablus Rd., Box 19215, Seam Line* ☎*02/627–9777* ⊕*www.americancolony. com* ↘*73 rooms, 13 suites* 🛁*In-room: safe, DVD (some), Internet, Wi-Fi. In-hotel: 3 restaurants, room service, bar, pool, gym, spa, laundry service, Internet terminal, Wi-Fi, parking (free), no-smoking rooms* ☰*AE, DC, MC, V* ⫚*BP.* ✥*2G*

$$ ◫ **Grand Court.** This huge hotel is a celebration of light and space: from the large, airy lobby, with its limestone walls and marble arches, to the well-lighted, comfortable guest rooms, with their soft-color decor and light-tile bathrooms. The suites are impressively large. Guests have free access to Hebrew University's sports center. **Pros:** cheerful natural lighting; well-decorated rooms. **Cons:** remote location; sports facilities off-site; neighborhood dead at night. ✉*15 St. George St., Seam Line* ☎*02/591–7777* ⊕*www.grandcourt.co.il* ↘*427 rooms, 15 suites* 🛁*In-room: safe, refrigerator, Wi-Fi (some). In-hotel: 3 restaurants, room service, bar, tennis courts, pool, gym, children's programs (August),*

laundry service, Internet terminal, Wi-Fi, parking (free), no-smoking rooms ⊟*AE, DC, MC, V* ⦾*BP.* ⊹*2F*

2

$$ ⛱**Moriah Classic.** The huge sky-lit atrium in the middle of the lobby has a comfortable if not intimate coffee-shop. The light-colored guest-room furniture and parquet floors are offset by blues in the decor. "Superior" is the house term for standard rooms; the better "deluxe" rooms are on the eighth floor and have balconies. (The hotel is often still known as the Novotel—its former identity.) **Pros:** a sense of spaciousness. **Cons:** a drive from most places; neighborhood dead at night; hotel has no distinctive character. ⊠*9 St. George St., Hebron Rd.* ☎*02/232–0000* ⊕*www.azorim-hotels.co.il* ⇆*382 rooms, 18 suites* ⟡*In-room: safe, refrigerator, Wi-Fi. In-hotel: 2 restaurants, room service, bar, pool, gym, children's programs (August and Jewish holidays), laundry service, Internet terminal, Wi-Fi, parking (free), no-smoking rooms* ⊟*AE, DC, MC, V* ⦾*BP.* ⊹*2F*

$$ ⛱**Olive Tree.** Aesthetics are the strong point of this property. Stone arches, wood latticework, and bronze ornaments in the reception area, old flagstones in the sky-lit atrium, and polished floorboards in the comfortable lounge all combine to create a distinctly regional ambience. Guest rooms are not huge, but are comfortable. Black and gold touches, and framed old prints, give them some class. **Pros:** Internet access through TV; superior sports facilities free; ATM. **Cons:** sports facilities are a 5-minute cab ride away; neighborhood is dead at night. ⊠*23 St. George St., Seam Line* ☎*02/541–0410* ⊕*www.olivetreehotel. com* ⇆*300 rooms, 4 suites* ⟡*In-room: safe, refrigerator, Internet, Wi-Fi. In-hotel: 2 restaurants, room service, bar, tennis courts, pool, gym, spa, laundry service, Internet terminal, Wi-Fi, parking (free), no-smoking rooms* ⊟*AE, DC, MC, V* ⦾*BP.* ⊹*2F*

$ ⛱**Regency Jerusalem.** Cascading down Mt. Scopus, the Regency (still called the "Hyatt" by cabbies) has a dramatic setting and a bold design. The lobby is a stylish combination of stone and greenery; one-third of the guest rooms have Old City views; and the pool area, with an adjacent playground, is a cool enclave of palms and plants. The large, sophisticated spa, popular among Jerusalemites, includes an authentic marble Turkish bath, imported piece by piece. **Pros:** impressive architecture; great panoramic view. **Cons:** needs renovation; spa facilities not free for guests; very remote location. ⊠*32 Lehi St., Mt. Scopus* ☎*02/533–1234* ⊕*www.regency.co.il* ⇆*455 rooms, 50 suites* ⟡*In-room: safe, refrigerator, Wi-Fi (some). In-hotel: 2 restaurants, room service, bar, pool, gym, spa, children's programs (August), laundry service, Internet terminal, Wi-Fi, parking (free), no-smoking rooms* ⊟*AE, DC, MC, V* ⦾*BP.* ⊹*1H*

NIGHTLIFE AND THE ARTS

The Holy City is not as staid as you might think, even though over half its residents—ultra-Orthodox Jews and the Arab community—do not partake in Western-style entertainment and arts. You can combine a great meal or tasty snack with a concert, pub, or dance bar for a lively evening out on the town. Thursday and Friday nights are the hot times for bars and clubs and late-night shows; classical music and dance performances tend to avoid Friday nights, and take place over the rest of the week. Check out listings in English-language publications and free booklets, which you can find in hotels.

NIGHTLIFE

While Jerusalem can't compete with Tel Aviv in terms of the number of nightlife attractions, locals insist that what the city lacks in quantity it more than makes up for in quality. Pubs, bars, and nightclubs in Jerusalem tend to be more relaxed than those in Tel Aviv—they're friendlier, more informal, and often less expensive. As in Tel Aviv, the nightlife scene in Jerusalem starts very late: some places only begin to fill up after midnight, and most pubs are open until the early hours of the morning.

BARS AND PUBS

If you want to break away from hushed hotel bars and pre-meal restaurant counters, look for local color in the downtown area's watering holes.

Ha'taklit (⊠ *7 Helene Hamalka St., Downtown* ☎*02/624–4073*) means "The Record," a nostalgic tribute to the vinyl predecessor to CDs and MP3s. This is a great place for beer and music, with frequent live acts, occasional dance parties, and a back room where international soccer games are screened.

Slow Moshe (⊠*6 Nissim Bahar St., Downtown* ☎*02/623–2602*) is a homey neighborhood pub in the old Nahlaot neighborhood, near the Machaneh Yehuda market. It's a good place to top off the day with a cold one, but note that it's closed on Friday night.

★ The long-standing **Stardust** (⊠*6 Rivlin St, .Nahalat Shiva* ☎*02/622–2196*) occupies a 19th-century stone building, has a warm, intimate atmosphere, and is open until 5 AM.

Tuvia (⊠*6 Shushan St., Downtown* ☎*02/624–0949*) offers a wide variety of imported beers, good bar food, and good background music.

As a sort of inside joke, **Uganda** (⊠*4 Aristobulus St., Downtown* ☎*02/623–6087*) is named for the African country once proposed as an alternative home for the Jewish state, and "alternative" is what the pub is all about. It also sells comic books and vinyl records, hosts live music, and is quite popular with art students.

RESTAURANT BARS

More mature customers who find the pubs too loud or frenetic can retreat to one of several good restaurants where latecomers are welcome to order just drinks.

Adom (⊠*Feingold Courtyard, off 31 Jaffa St., Downtown* ☎*02/624–6242*) has a reputation for good shrimp and other seafood. **Barood** (⊠*Feingold Courtyard, off 31 Jaffa St., Downtown* ☎*02/625–9081*) serves a unique variety of meat dishes and has a pub atmosphere and a good bar. **Chakra** (⊠*41 King George St., Downtown* ☎*02/625–2733*) has a large, diverse menu as well as soft lighting and good background

You can join Jerusalemites as they unwind at the movies at the popular Jerusalem Cinematheque.

music. **Link** (⊠*3 Hama'a lot St., Downtown* ☎*02/625–3446*) is popular with legal and other professionals. The deck's a great spot on warm evenings and the grilled chicken wings are terrific. **Mona** (⊠*12 Shmuel Hanagid St., Downtown* ☎*02/622–2283*), in the old stone Artists' House, is a place to be seen. The food is excellent, but you must wait until late in the evening if you want to order just drinks.

DANCE CLUBS
Discos have declined; for young partiers, dance bars are where it's at.

★ **Bar Shva-esray** (⊠*17 Ha'oman St., Talpiot Industrial Zone* ☎*02/678–1658*) means "Bar 17"—the establishment's street number. The place has reinvented itself as a hip, nicely styled "mega dance bar," with a different genre of music each night of the week (closed Sunday; private events Wednesday). Hum along with Israeli hits Tuesday, break loose to rock and disco on Thursday, enjoy an older, more mellow atmosphere Saturday.

Bass Dance Club (⊠*1 Hahistadrut St., Downtown* ☎*077/512–3056* 🎬*NIS 35*) is quickly becoming one of the hottest spots in Jerusalem, while maintaining its underground appeal. It specializes in techno/electro/drum and bass, but other styles of music are played as well. Admission is often waived for pre-midnight early arrivals.

Hakatzeh ("the Edge") (⊠*4 Shushan St., Downtown*) is another drink-and-dance pub. Music styles vary considerably from night to night, but the atmosphere is always lively. It operates as a gay bar one night a week.

★ **Sira** (✉*4 Ben-Sira St., Downtown* ☎*02/624–2298*) is a great watering hole and the small dance floor, variety of music spun by DJs, and late hours make this one of the most fun places in the city to dance. Here you'll find a Bohemian hodgepodge of students and internationals.

FOLK-MUSIC CLUBS

Jerusalem has a modest folk scene, with performances by local artists and occasional visits by international performers. Watch for listings, usually under "Entertainment" in the *Jerusalem Post, Ha'aretz,* and elsewhere. You can email **Carol Fuchs** (✎*israelfolkstuff@gmail.com*), who edits the Israel Folkstuff e-newsletter and calendar, to link up with the local folk community.

JAZZ CLUBS

Apart from performances in auditoriums and other more conservative venues, you can sometimes find jazz at smaller places around town.

Both international and local musicians play at **The Lab** (*The Jerusalem Performing Arts Laboratory or, in Hebrew, Hama'abada* ✉*28 Hebron Rd., Hebron Rd.* ☎*02/629–2000 or 02/629–2001*). You can sit at the bar and just enjoy the DJ's offerings, or pay extra for a specific performance. Check listings ahead of time.

Yellow Submarine (✉*13 Ha'rechavim St., Talpiot Industrial Zone* ☎*02/570–4646*) is a multi-disciplinary, not-for-profit music center (with a strong program to nurture young musicians), and jazz is one of its strong suits. Occasional festivals and individual gigs by both international and local artists make it a venue worth checking.

THE ARTS

Classical music is the capital's strong suit: it's worth checking schedules of ensembles and main venues ahead of time. Artists in other musical genres pass through from time to time, but Jerusalem is seldom their main focus. Dance performances are infrequent, and English theater is very rare.

For English-language schedules of performances and other cultural events, consult the Friday weekend section of the *Jerusalem Post* and its insert *In Jerusalem*; Friday's "The Guide" of *Ha'aretz*'s English edition; and the free weekly and monthly booklets available at hotels and information bureaus.

There are three **main ticket agencies** for performances in Jerusalem. Student discounts are sometimes available; present your card at the ticket office: **Ben-Naim** (✉*38 Jaffa Rd., Downtown* ☎*02/623–1273*), **Bimot** (✉*8 Shammai St., Downtown* ☎*02/623–7000*), and **Kla'im** (✉*12 Shammai St., Downtown* ☎*02/622–2333*).

DANCE

The better-known Tel Aviv–based troupes seldom make it to Jerusalem, but you can watch the listings and hope. Look out for two excellent Jerusalem contemporary dance companies: **Vertigo** (⊕*www.vertigo.org.il*), and the more innovative **Kolben** (named for its founder and director; ⊕ *www.kolbendance.com*), which are both based at the **Gerard Behar Center** (✉*11 Bezalel St., Downtown*).

FESTIVALS

Top Israeli and international orchestras, choirs, singers, theater companies, dance troupes, and street entertainers participate in the **Israel Festival** (☏*1700/702015 or 02/623–7000* ⊕*www.israel-festival.org.il*), usually held in late May or early June. All the performing arts are represented, and offerings range from the classical to the avant-garde. The Jerusalem Theater is the main venue, but a dozen secondary locations around the city get some of the smaller, more "fringe" acts.

FILM

Many new films, American and otherwise, reach Israel screens very quickly, while some are mysteriously delayed. Israeli films have been garnering international praise in recent years; they and other non-English-speaking movies are almost always subtitled in English. Check newspaper listings for showtimes.

The **Jerusalem Cinematheque** (✉*11 Hebron Rd., Hinnom Valley* ☏*02/565–4333* ⊕*www.jer-cine.org.il*) specializes in old, rare, and art films, but its many programs often include current offerings. Its monthly programs focus on specific directors, actors, or subjects, and its annual **Jerusalem Film Festival,** held in July, is a must for film buffs. The theater is open Friday night.

Jerusalem Mall (Kenyon Malcha) (✉*Malcha* ☏*02/678–9077*) has a cluster of cinemas run by the Globus Group. Note that these theaters are closed Friday night.

The veteran **Lev Smadar** (✉*4 Lloyd George St., German Colony* ☏*02/561–8168* ⊕*www.lev.co.il*), in the German Colony, is a bit of a throwback to yesteryear's movie atmosphere. It's a single cinema in an older building on a narrow lane.

Rav Chen (✉*19 Ha'oman St., Talpiot Industrial Zone* ☏*02/679–2799*) is a multi-auditorium cinema group that shares a building with a large supermarket.

MUSIC

Classical music abounds in Jerusalem, with Israeli orchestras and chamber ensembles performing year-round and a trickle of international artists passing through. There's other interesting programming around town, too.

The **International Convention Center** (✉*Zalman Shazar Blvd., Givat Ram* ☏*02/655–8558*), located opposite the Central Bus Station and still known locally by its old name, Binyanei Ha'ooma, is the local venue for the subscription series of the world-renowned, Tel Aviv–based **Israel Philharmonic Orchestra** (☏*1700/703–030* ⊕*www.ipo.co.il*). For tickets, contact the orchestra's office or one of the local ticket agencies.

The **Jerusalem Theater** (✉*20 Marcus St., Talbieh* ☏*02/560–5755*) houses four auditoriums of different sizes. It's officially named the Jerusalem Center for the Performing Arts, though nobody calls it that. The 750-seat Henry Crown Auditorium is the home base of the Jerusalem Symphony Orchestra, and the venue for the popular **Etnachta** series of free concerts produced by Israel Radio's classical station and broadcast live Monday at 5PM, generally from October through June (check by phone first).

A Friday-night Oneg Shabbat series is presented at **Beit Shmuel** (✉ *6 Eliyahu Shama'a St., off King David St., King David St.* ☎ *02/620–3455 or 02/620–3456* ⊕ *www.beitshmuel. com*), which typically hosts some of the most popular Israeli pop performers. The evening will be in Hebrew, catering to the predominantly local audience, but the music may speak a universal language.

> ## MUSIC IN CHURCHES
>
> Hearing music in one of Jerusalem's many churches can be a moving experience. The **Church of the Redeemer** (✉ *Muristan, Christian Quarter* ☎ *02/627–6111*) is a favorite venue. **Dormition Abbey** (✉ *Mt. Zion, Mt. Zion* ☎ *02/ 565–5330*) offers concerts, mostly on Saturday, late morning. The **Mormon campus** (✉ *Mt. Scopus* ☎ *02/626–5666*) hosts a Sunday evening classical concert series in its fine auditorium.

Bet Ticho (*Ticho House* ✉ *9 Harav Kook St., near Zion Sq., Downtown* ☎ *02/624–5068*) holds intimate recitals on Friday mornings in a serene setting.

The **Bible Lands Museum** (✉ *25 Granot St., next to the Israel Museum, Givat Ram* ☎ *02/561–1066* ⊕ *www.blmj.org*) puts on Saturday-evening concerts for most of the year. Programs include chamber music, jazz, gospel, folk music, country-and-western, and more. Each concert is preceded by cheese and wine in the foyer; and the museum's galleries are open to concertgoers for half an hour before and after the performance at no extra charge.

The concert hall at the **Jerusalem International YMCA (West)** (✉ *26 King David St., King David St.* ☎ *02/569–2692, 050/523–3210 for folk information*) is the permanent home of fine Israeli ensembles when they appear in the city. It's also the venue for the much-acclaimed **Jerusalem International Chamber Music Festival** (⊕ *www.jcmf.org.il/EN/*) in late August. At a different level, the "Y" hosts a rousing Israeli folklore performance—mostly singing and folk dancing—usually on Monday, Thursday, and Saturday evenings. Schedules may change with the seasons and demand: call ahead. Reservations are advised; arrive early, as the 500-seat hall is generally inundated by tour groups and seats are unmarked. The cost is about NIS 100.

The **Targ Music Center** (✉ *29 Hama'ayan St., Ein Kerem* ☎ *02/641–4250 or 02/561–7075*), 7 km (4½ mi) from the city center, often holds noontime chamber-music performances on Fridays and Saturdays. The surroundings have a rustic charm.

THEATER

The **Israel Festival,** held in May or June in the Jerusalem Theater, is your best bet for quality non-Hebrew productions. English theater in Jerusalem throughout the rest of the year is too rare to predict, but it is still worth checking listings. The **Khan Theater** (✉ *2 David Remez Sq., Hebron Rd.* ☎ *02/671–8281 Ext. 1*) has mostly Hebrew productions. **The Lab** (*The Jerusalem Performing Arts Laboratory or, in Hebrew, Hama'abada* ✉ *28 Hebron Rd., Hebron Rd.* ☎ *02/629–2000 or 02/629–2001*) is a place to call about possible English productions.

SPORTS AND THE OUTDOORS

Most visitors who like to exercise regularly, or want to atone for eating their way through Israel, make do with the hotel gym or a jog through the neighborhood. You might also want to try joining an informal soccer or basketball game in Sacher Park (on Ben-Zvi Boulevard, below the Knesset complex), particularly on Friday afternoons. There are other options, however.

BIKING

The **Jerusalem Bicycling Club** (☎052/253–1667) leads mountain bike rides on Saturday morning at 7 AM, starting from the International Convention Center, Binyanei Ha'ooma (opposite the Central Bus Station). This informal club is a good source for information on bike rentals and can recommend routes within the city.

Every Tuesday night a town ride organized by **Ofnei Nitzan (Nitzan Bicycles)** (✉137 Jaffa St., Downtown ☎02/625–2741 or 02/623–5976) sets out at 9 PM from the store. You can also rent bicycles here. The shop is closed Saturday.

HEALTH CLUBS

The best fitness clubs in Jerusalem are in hotels. All welcome health seekers who are not hotel guests.

The **Crowne Plaza Hotel** (✉1 Ha'aliyah St., Givat Ram ☎02/658–8888) has a gym, dry and wet saunas, and a year-round pool. The cost is NIS 90 Sunday to Thursday, NIS 110 on Friday and Saturday.

The **Ramada Jerusalem** (✉6 Wolfson St., Givat Ram ☎02/659–9999) charges NIS 90 Sunday through Friday, and NIS 120 Saturday, for use of its gym, saunas, inside pool, outside pool (seasonal), and even participation in a work-out class.

The sophisticated complex at the **Regency Jerusalem Hotel** (✉32 Lehi St., Mt. Scopus ☎02/533–1234) has a great range of facilities—a gym, Turkish bath, whirlpool bath, saunas, indoor and outdoor pools (in season)—all for NIS 80. It's open daily from 6:15 AM–9 PM (opens on Saturday at 8:45 AM).

HORSEBACK RIDING

Stables offer lessons and trail rides, including ones suitable for children, as well as longer (and more interesting) trails. Rates vary, so call ahead.

King David's Riding Stables (✉Shoresh ☎057/739–8866), in the wooded Judean Hills, is 16 km (10 mi) west of Jerusalem. The basic rate is NIS 120 for a 45-minute session. Rides require a minimum of 3 people, but call ahead to see if you can join a group. The **Riding Club** (✉no street address, behind Angel's Bakery, Kiryat Moshe ☎02/651–3585) breeds Arabians. A 50-minute session costs NIS 140.

SQUASH

The **Hebrew University** (✉*Ruppin Blvd., Givat Ram* ☎*02/658–4286 or 02/658–4293*) has two squash courts in its on-campus Cosell Center (opposite the Science Museum), open Sunday noon–10 PM, Monday–Thursday 7 AM–10 PM, Friday 7–5, and Saturday 8–5. Reservations can be made by phone from 7 AM–noon and 3 PM–9:30 PM. The cost is NIS 30 per session, and rackets can be rented for NIS 15 each.

The **YMCA (West)** (✉*26 King David St., King David St.* ☎*02/569–2692 or 02/569–2684* ⊕*www.jerusalemymca.org*) has two squash courts for rental. They're available for NIS 70 for 45 minutes, 6 AM–9 PM, Monday–Saturday. Non-members are advised to book a court a day ahead, though you may find an open court if you just turn up. The price includes use of the gym, sauna, and swimming pool.

SWIMMING

The enthusiast can swim year-round at several pools. (Those at hotels welcome nonguests.) Check opening hours, as some pools provide specific hours for mixed or single-sex swimming. In addition to outdoor pools, the following hotels provide winter swimming as well.

The **Inbal Hotel** (✉*3 Jabotinsky St., Talbieh* ☎*02/675–6666*) has an outdoor pool that is covered and heated in winter. The fee of NIS 100 Sunday through Thursday, NIS 120 on Friday and Saturday, includes use of the gym.

It costs NIS 80 to swim at the **Jerusalem Regency Hotel** (✉*32 Lehi St., Mt. Scopus* ☎*02/533–1234*), and access to the gym and spa facilities is included.

The **Moriah Gardens Hotel** (✉*4 Wolfson St., Givat Ram* ☎*02/655–8888*) has attractive facilities that are NIS 75 for the day, Sunday through Friday, and NIS 90 on Saturday, including access to the health club.

Swimming at the **Ramada Jerusalem Hotel** (✉*6 Wolfson St., Givat Ram* ☎*02/659–9999*) costs NIS 90 (NIS 120 on Saturday), and gives you access to the health club.

PUBLIC POOLS

Public pools provide a more colorful local experience, at a lower price. The **Jerusalem Pool** (✉*43 Emek Refa'im St., German Colony* ☎*02/563–2092*) has a public outdoor pool that is covered in winter. It gets very crowded in July and August, but it's one of the most reasonable places around, at NIS 50 for the day.

TENNIS

Tennis has become increasingly popular in Israel. In addition to the courts below, a few major hotels have their own courts, but may restrict usage to guests or club members. Ask your concierge to make inquiries if you want to play at a particular hotel. At all venues, advance reservations are always required.

The **Hebrew University at Mt. Scopus** (⌧*1 Churchill St., Mt. Scopus* ☎*02/588–2796 or 02/582–6960*) has 10 lighted courts and rental equipment. Courts go for NIS 35 an hour in daylight and NIS 45 an hour in evenings, and are open Sunday 11 AM–10 PM, Monday–Thursday 6:30 AM–10 PM, Friday 7–4, and Saturday 8–4. You can rent a racket for NIS 20, and buy three balls for NIS 30. Call ahead to book, especially during campus recess.

The **Israel Tennis Center** (⌧*5 Almaliach St., Katamon Tet* ☎*02/679–1866 or 02/679–2726*) has 18 lighted courts, available for NIS 40 per hour, Sunday–Thursday, 7 AM–3 PM; NIS 55 per hour Sunday–Thursday, 7 PM–10 PM, Friday 7 AM–6 PM (Oct.–Mar. until 5 PM), and Saturday 8 AM–noon. Equipment rental is sometimes available; call ahead.

SHOPPING

Jerusalem offers distinctive ideas for gifts—for yourself or others—from jewelry and art to traditional crafts, items of a religious nature, and souvenirs. The several shopping areas make it easy to plan expeditions. Prices are generally fixed in the city center and the Jewish Quarter of the Old City, though you can sometimes negotiate for significant discounts on expensive art and jewelry. Shopping in the Old City's colorful Arab bazaar, or souk (pronounced "shook" in Israel—rhymes with "book"), is fascinating but can be a trap for the unwary.

Stores generally open by 8:30 AM or 9 AM, and some close between 1 PM and 4 PM. A few still close on Tuesday afternoon, a traditional but less and less observed half day. Jewish-owned stores (that is, all of West Jerusalem—the "New City"—and the Old City's Jewish Quarter) close on Friday afternoon by 2 PM or 3 PM, depending on the season and the kind of store (food and souvenir shops tend to stay open later), and reopen on Sunday morning. Some stores geared to the tourist trade, particularly downtown, reopen on Saturday night after the Jewish Sabbath ends, especially in summer. Arab-owned stores in the Old City and East Jerusalem are busiest on Saturday and quietest on Sunday, when many (but not all) Christian storekeepers close for the day.

SHOPPING STREETS AND MALLS

Arts and Crafts Lane (*Hutzot Hayotzer* ⌧*Yemin Moshe*), opposite and downhill from the Jaffa Gate, is home to goldsmiths and silversmiths specializing in jewelry, fine art, and Judaica, generally done in an ultramodern, minimalist style. The work is of extremely high quality and priced accordingly. Look for the exquisite designs of **Sari Srulovitch** (⌧*Hutzot Hayotzer, Hinnom Valley* ☎*02/628–6699* ⊕*www.sarisrulovitch.com*).

Stores along the narrow streets of the souk in the Old City tempt passersby with food, fabrics, and ceramics.

The **Cardo** (⊠*Jewish Quarter Rd., Jewish Quarter*), in the Old City's Jewish Quarter, began life as the main thoroughfare of Byzantine Jerusalem, was a commercial street during the Crusader era, and has now been converted into an attractive shopping area. Beyond discovering souvenirs and Judaica, you'll find good-quality jewelry and art here.

Emek Refai'm (⊠*German Colony*), in the German Colony, has become the funkiest area in which to shop, eat, and people-watch from early morning to late at night. Gifts and jewelry are easy to find in a rainbow of styles and tastes to meet different budgets.

The **Jerusalem Mall** (⊠*Malcha* ☎*02/679–1333*), known locally as Kenyon Malcha, is—at 500,000 square feet, not counting parking—one of the largest in the Middle East. It includes a department store, a supermarket, eight cinemas, and almost 200 shops and eateries (Pizza Hut and Burger King among them). The interior is an attractive mix of arched skylights and wrought-iron banisters in a quasi–art deco style. The mall is clearly signposted from the Begin Boulevard, via Eliyahu Golomb Street, and from the Pat Junction–Gilo Road. It's open Sunday to Thursday from 9:30 AM–9:30 PM, Friday from 9:30–2:30, and Saturday dusk–11 PM.

King David Street (⊠*King David St.*) is lined with prestigious stores, most with an emphasis on art, Judaica, antiquities, or high-end jewelry.

The pedestrian-only **Midrachov** (⊠*Downtown*) is simply downtown Ben-Yehuda Street, the heartbeat of West Jerusalem (the New City). The selection of clothing, shoes, jewelry, souvenirs, T-shirts, and street food here makes for a fun shopping experience. Street musicians serenade the passersby, and the human parade is best appreciated from one of the many outdoor cafés. Summer evenings are lively, as the mall fills with peddlers of cheap jewelry and crafts, and young admiring shoppers.

Salomon Street (✉ *Nahalat Shiva*), in the old neighborhood of Nahalat Shiva, just off Zion Square, has also been developed as a pedestrian mall. Between the restaurants, you'll find several crafts galleries and arty jewelry and clothing shops, both on the main drag and in the adjacent alleys and courtyards.

STREET MARKETS

★ Jerusalem's main market is the **souk** (✉ *Christian and Muslim Quarters*) in the Old City, spread over a warren of intersecting streets. This is where much of Arab Jerusalem shops. It's awash with color and redolent with the clashing scents of exotic spices. Village women's baskets of produce vie for attention with hanging shanks of lamb, fresh fish on ice, and fresh-baked delicacies. Food stalls are interspersed with purveyors of fabrics and shoes. The baubles and trinkets of the tourist trade often seem secondary, except along the well-trodden paths of the Via Dolorosa, David Street, and Christian Quarter Road.

Haggling with merchants in the Arab market—a time-honored tradition—is not always the good-natured experience it once was. It is not always easy to identify the honest merchants among the many whose jewelry, antiquities, leather, and embroidery are often not what they claim. Unless you know what you want, know how much it's *really* worth, and enjoy the sometimes aggressive give-and-take of bargaining (but stay polite), you're better off just enjoying the local color (stick to the main streets, and watch your wallet or purse) and doing your shopping in the more modern and familiar New City. Note that women are advised to dress discreetly.

Fodor's Choice Off Jaffa Road, near the commercial Clal Center, is the produce market
★ **Machaneh Yehuda** (✉ *Machaneh Yehuda*), a block-long alleyway that becomes a blur of brilliant primary colors as the city's best-quality fruit and vegetables, pickles and cheeses, fresh fish and poultry, confections, and falafel await inspection. The busiest days are Thursday and Friday, when Jews shop for the Sabbath; the market is closed on Saturday along with the rest of Jewish West Jerusalem. Combine your visit with lunch or a snack at one of the many Middle Eastern restaurants in the neighborhood, or grab a cup of excellent coffee at a Western-style café.

SPECIALTY STORES

ART GALLERIES
Several galleries representing Israeli artists are close to the city's premier hotels, on King David Street.

Udi Merioz, the artist and owner of **Blue and White Art Gallery** (✉ *Cardo, Jewish Quarter* 📞 *02/628–8464* 🌐 *www.gift-museum.com*), does "soft painting," a special appliqué technique that uses cloth on cloth. The gallery also represents Israeli artist Yaacov Agam.

Motke Blum (✉ *Hutzot Hayotzer [Arts and Crafts Lane], Hinnom Valley* ☎ *02/623–4002* ⊕ *www.motke.com*) does fine soft-colored oils and minimalist landscapes.

BEAUTY PRODUCTS

The **Ahava Center** (✉ *5 Ben Yehuda St., Downtown* ☎ *02/625–2592*) stocks all the Ahava products that use minerals from the Dead Sea, but at less attractive prices than elsewhere. The **Dead Sea Gallery** (✉ *17 Jaffa Rd., corner of King Solomon St., Downtown* ☎ *02/622–1451*) stocks Ahava skincare products. Their Dermud line with Dead Sea minerals is particularly worth trying. The helpful staff and the competitive prices make this visit a particular pleasure. Mail-order service is also available.

CLOTHING

Clothing can be expensive in Israel, but Jerusalem is now home to the boutiques of several relatively affordable Israeli designers. Once, it seemed, you could only find clothes for impossibly thin teenagers or full-figured women, but the new stores offer classy and fashionable items for in-between sizes as well. Another unsuspected innovation: if you're looking for that special wedding gown, you may well find it in the Holy City.

A.B.C (✉ *25 King George St., Downtown* ☎ *050/849–2029*) is a home-grown label that has developed popular, well-made women's lines.

Bella Buchman (✉ *29 Keren Kayemet St., Downtown* ☎ *02/566–0319*) caters to the more mature woman, with a range of classic clothing from Italy and other foreign climes.

Cheder Mishelach (A Room of Your Own) (✉ *8 Emek Refa'im St., German Colony* ☎ *02/561–7174*) is funky, even quirky, with a range of vintage-style clothes and accessories for a range of sizes, as well as—yes—wedding dresses.

Hemp Shop (✉ *27 Ben-Yehuda St., Downtown* ☎ *02/623–0668*) brings you items made from, well, hemp. The fabrics are both gentle on your skin and environmentally friendly. It's pricey but worth a look.

Israeli fashion designer **Kedem Sasson** (✉ *21 King George St., Downtown* ☎ *02/625–2602* ⊕ *www.kedem-sasson.com*) caters to the fuller figure, with clothes in soft fabrics, some of them in decidedly quirky styles.

Naama Bezalel (✉ *27 King George St., Downtown* ☎ *02/625–5611* ✉ *26 King George* ☎ *02/622–3479*) specializes in decidedly feminine lines for a range of ages, as well as a selection of distinctly beautiful bridal dresses. The second store across the street carries discounted leftovers from past seasons.

Ronen Chen (✉ *Alrov Mamilla Ave., Mamilla* ☎ *02/624–2881* ✉ *Jerusalem Mall, Malcha* ☎ *02/679–4280* ⊕ *ronenchen.com*) designs simple, classic styles in very comfortable fabrics.

Sigal Dekel (✉ *Alrov Mamilla Ave., Mamilla* ☎ *0732/150–115* ⊕ *www.sigaldekel.com*) is trendy and expensive, with clothes in interesting fabrics others don't use.

Ceramic creations large and small are among the many lovely crafts worth seeking out around Jerusalem.

Tali Imbar (✉ *Designers' Gallery, Jerusalem Mall, Malcha* ☎ *02/679–3890* ⊕ *www.talimbar.com*) creates casually elegant clothes that are a pleasure to wear.

Tashtari (✉ *25 King George St., Downtown* ☎ *02/625–3282*) is an exclusive boutique that features imported handmade evening bags (including a line made of recycled materials), owner Amos Sadan's own outstanding "wearable art"—much of which is influenced by Japanese aesthetics—and feather or crystal hair accessories.

T-SHIRTS

Tourist shops all stock the same range of machine-stamped merchandise, but many stores will also custom-decorate shirts from a selection of designs. There are several around the Ben-Yehuda pedestrian mall.

Lord Kitsch (✉ *42 Jaffa Rd., Downtown* ☎ *02/625–2595* ✉ *Jerusalem Mall, Malcha* ☎ *02/678–0576* ✉ *Achim Yisrael Mall, 18 Yad Harutzim, Talpiot Industrial Zone* ☎ *02/673–3106*) stocks a range of casual clothes, including T-shirts in a full range of colors.

Sweet (✉ *2 Ben-Yehuda St., Downtown* ☎ *02/625–4835*) has a good selection of T-shirts ready for custom-decoration.

CRAFTS

Charlotte (✉ *4 Coresh St., Downtown* ☎ *02/625–1632*) carries colorful items of high quality: ceramics, weavings, painted silks, jewelry, and fashion accessories.

Danny Azoulay (✉ *5 Salomon St., Nahalat Shiva* ☎ *02/623–3918*) offers delicate items in fine porcelain, all hand-painted in rich shades of blue, red, and gold. Many are traditional Jewish ritual objects—some pricey—but you can also find less expensive items, such as napkin rings and bottle stoppers.

Hoshen (⊠ *32 Emek Refa'im, German Colony* ☎*02/563–0966* ⊕*www.hoshenshop.com*) offers attractive items in wood, ceramics, fabric, and jewelry.

Gans (⊠*8 Rivlin St., Nahalat Shiva* ☎*02/625–1159* ⊕*www.gans.co.il*) proudly sells art and crafts made only in Israel. Choose from good-quality Judaica, glassware, weaving, jewelry, painted silk, wood, and ceramic ornaments.

Klein (⊠*3 Ziv St., off Bar Ilan St., Tel Arza* ☎*02/538–8784*) produces some of the highest-quality olive-wood objects in Israel. This is the factory showroom, off the tourist route. It stocks everything they make, from bowls and yo-yos to attractive trays of Armenian pottery tiles set in olive wood, picture frames, boxes, and desktop paraphernalia.

Jerusalem Experience (⊠*17 Jaffa St., opposite Safra Square, Downtown* ☎*02/622–3030*) is the place for items of Christian interest and hand-made Judaica. The friendly staff are happy to show you Israeli perfumes, skincare products, ceramics, glassware, and textiles, but also books about Jerusalem and other aspects of the Holy Land.

The **Jerusalem House of Quality** (⊠*12 Hebron Rd., Hebron Rd.* ☎*02/671–7430* ⊕*www.art-jerusalem.com*) showcases the work of some excellent Israeli craftspeople in the media of ceramics, glass, jewelry, sculpture, wooden ornaments, and ritual objects. You can often see them at work in their studios on the second floor.

Ruth Havilio (⊠*Ein Kerem D/4, Ein Kerem* ☎*02/641–7912*) makes hand-painted tiles with a more modern feel, for both decorative and practical purposes. Her sense of color and fun (whimsical clay animals, for instance) play alongside more traditional styles. You can have tiles personalized, but keep in mind that this cannot be done on the spot. To get there, take the alley to the left of St. John's Church. Part of the charm of the gallery is its evocative setting in a courtyard.

Set (⊠*34 Emek Refa'im, German Colony* ☎*02/566–3366*) can solve your gift problems with an array of different objects in both traditional and modern styles.

Sunbula (⊠*St. Andrew's Scottish Guesthouse, 1 David Remez St., Hebron Rd.* ☎*02/673–2401* ⊕*www.sunbula.org*) sells high-quality, traditional Palestinian embroidery. Colorful cushion covers and decorative cloths are particularly good value for the money, but there are smaller items and gift ideas for limited budgets as well.

ARMENIAN POTTERY

Armenian hand-painted pottery—geometric or stylized natural motifs, in blues and greens, with somewhat non-Western brown, yellow, or mauve accents—is a good and well-priced idea for gifts.

The standouts in Armenian **Hagop Antreassian's** studio (⊠*near Zion Gate, Armenian Quarter* ☎*02/627–2584* ⊕*hagopceramics.com*) are his wonderful large bowls. They won't fit in your carry-ons, but Hagop ships. You can often catch him painting or firing his clay creations in his studio just inside Zion Gate.

Jerusalem Pottery (✉*15 Via Dolorosa, Muslim Quarter* ☎*02/626–1587* ⊕*www.jerusalempottery.biz*), at the VI Station of the Cross, is the store of one of the best local artisans: Stefan Karakashian. His particularly high-quality work includes plates, bowls, tiles, and plaques.

Sandrouni (✉*Armenian Orthodox Patriarchate Rd., Armenian Quarter* ☎*02/628–3567* ⊕*www.sandrouni.com*) stocks a variety of utilitarian pieces in many colors and styles.

COOPERATIVE STORES

Whether you like the unpredictable shapes of contemporary ceramics or more conservative items, local artists present a rich choice at three cooperative stores, all on the same street.

Cadim (✉*4 Salomon St., Nahalat Shiva* ☎*02/623–4869*) presents a decidedly contemporary selection. The **Guild of Ceramicists** (✉*27 Salomon St., Nahalat Shiva* ☎*02/624–4065*) beckons you in with its delightful serendipity of colorful tiled steps, though the decorated pottery on sale inside, both functional and ornamental, is entirely different.

Shemonah Beyachad (✉*11 Salomon St., Nahalat Shiva* ☎*02/624–7250*) has grown to become a group of 11 individual ceramicists (even though the name means "8 Together"), one of whom is usually on duty in the store.

PAPER-CUTS

Paper-cutting is a traditional and well-established Jewish art form. These pieces make unusual gifts—to say nothing of being both light and easy to pack.

Archie Granot (✉*1 Agron St., Downtown* ☎*02/625–2210 or 054/464–1568* ⊕*www.archiegranot.com*) has evolved his own complex, multilayered style of paper-cut Judaica inspired by traditional motifs. Some of his high-end creations are displayed in museum collections around the world. Call ahead; the store is by appointment only.

Judaicut (✉*21 Yoel Salomon St., Nahalat Shiva* ☎*02/623–3634* ⊕*www. judaicut.co.il*) sells more traditional and affordable paper-cuts, which can be customized with your name.

HARPS

The **House of Harrari** (✉*Ramat Raziel* ☎*02/570–9075* ⊕*www.harrariharps.com*) is in the village of Ramat Raziel, a 25-minute drive from downtown Jerusalem, west of Ein Kerem. The small decorative door harps and graceful 10- and 22-string folk instruments are inspired (the makers say) by the Bible. The workshop displays the instruments in different stages of production. There are many kinds of ornamentation, and the door harps can be decorated with an inscription. The gallery will ship your purchase home. Call for directions.

JEWELRY

Jewelry in Israel is of a high international standard. You can choose between conservative styles; sleek, modern pieces inspired by different ethnicities; and the increasingly popular bead jewelry of Michal Negrin and other current Israeli stars of both the local and international scene.

Adipaz (✉ *20 Pierre Koenig St., Talpiot Industrial Zone* ☎ *02/678–3887* ⊗ *Sun.–Thurs. 11–5*) cuts diamonds and makes its own jewelry, much of it without precious stones.

★ **Daniel Alsberg** (✉ *Hinnom Valley* ☎ *02/627–1430* ⊕ *www.studioalsberg. com*), in the Arts and Crafts Lane (Hutzot Hayotzer), outside Jaffa Gate, is a particularly outstanding and original craftsman of modern pieces, mostly in gold and silver.

Hedya (✉ *7 Ma'alot St., Nahalat Shiva* ☎ *02/622–1151*) carries the collections of both Ze'ev Tammuz and Sarah Einstein: necklaces and earrings made from antique silver, amber, and other materials that retain a feel of the past.

H. Stern (✉ *7 King David St., King David St.* ☎ *02/624–3606*) has its main store at the **David's Citadel Hotel,** with branches at many of the other major hotels in town. The international company offers high-quality, expensive pieces.

Idit (✉ *23 King George St., Downtown* ☎ *02/622–1911* ⊕ *www.idit jewelry.com*) offers an intriguing range of in-house designs. The family business is still run by veteran craftsman Chaim Paz.

Keo (✉ *25 Emek Refa'im, German Colony* ☎ *02/563–7026*) specializes in delicate, modern pieces at reasonable prices.

Michal Negrin (✉ *2 HaMelitz St., on the corner of Emek Refa'im, German Colony* ☎ *02/563–3080* ✉ *Alrov Mamilla Ave., Mamilla* ☎ *02/624–2112* ✉ *Jerusalem Mall, Malcha* ☎ *02/648–0067* ✉ *Yoel Salomon St., Nahalat Shiva, Downtown* ☎ *02/622–3573* ⊕ *www. michalnegrin.com*), has become a remarkable success story with her whimsical, vintage-inspired jewelry and fashion accessories. Each branch has a slightly different selection.

Sheshet (✉ *34 Emek Refa'im, German Colony* ☎ *02/566–2261*) has high-quality merchandise at accessible prices.

Stav (✉ *40 Emek Refa'im, German Colony* ☎ *02/563–7059* ⊕ *www. stav.us*) is a standout, offering exquisite (and expensive) pieces in a graceful mix of both ethnic and modern influences.

Around Jerusalem and the Dead Sea

WITH MASADA AND BETHLEHEM

WORD OF MOUTH

"This was taken on my trip to Israel and the Dead Sea. There were only a few of us on this stretch of beach, and I captured this lone paddler, with Jordan visible in the distance."

—photo by markdewd, Fodors.com member

WELCOME TO AROUND JERUSALEM AND THE DEAD SEA

TOP REASONS TO GO

★ **Ein Gedi:** At this oasis rich in flora, fauna, and archaeological remains, you can hike near waterfalls and canyons. Swimming in the Dudim Cave, also known as Lover's Cave, is a romantic experience.

★ **Masada:** The spectacular remains of this mountaintop palace with desert views recall its history as a retreat for Herod the Great and the site of the last stand of the Jewish rebels against Rome in AD 73.

★ **Dead Sea:** This body of water is so saturated with salt and minerals that you easily float on the surface. In Ein Bokek, cover yourself with the mud, exported as a beauty treatment.

★ **Bethlehem:** The location of Jesus's manger is believed to be beneath the Byzantine-era Church of the Nativity.

★ **Judean Hills wineries:** Close to Jerusalem, this area is home to more than two dozen wineries that produce some excellent Cabernet Sauvignons, Merlots, and Chardonnays.

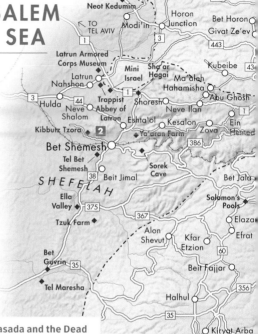

1 Masada and the Dead Sea. Herod the Great's desert retreat would be an extraordinary archaeological site even if it had never made it into the history books. But Masada is also famous for being where hundreds of Jews committed suicide rather than submit to Rome. Combine a visit with a trip to Ein Gedi or Ein Bokek, both near the Dead Sea, for unforgettable desert adventures whether you are hiking or floating in the salty sea.

Ein Gedi oasis

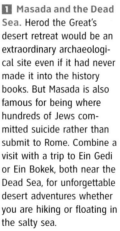

2 West of Jerusalem. The Judean Hills west of Jerusalem are dotted with natural springs, nature reserves, filigreed forests, and picturesque villages—as well as some excellent wineries. The Sorek Cave is one attraction; the antiquities of Bet Guvrin are another. Pack a picnic, turn onto a winding road, and you'll find yourself embraced by peace and quiet.

3 Bethlehem. Just a few miles south of Jerusalem in the West Bank, this largely Muslim city is filled with meaning for Christians. The Church of the Nativity on Manger Square is a highlight.

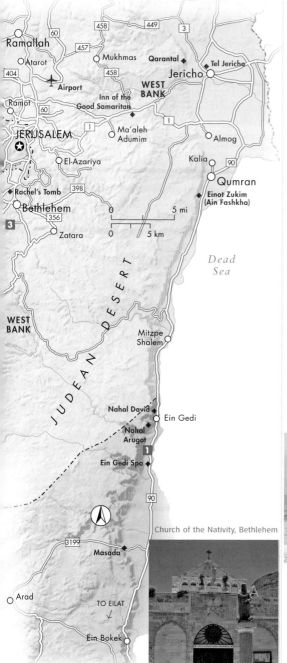

Ramallah
60
458 449 3
457
Atarot Mukhmas Qarantal Tel Jericho
404 458 Jericho
Airport WEST BANK
Inn of the
Good Samaritan
Ramot 60
1
JERUSALEM Ma'aleh
Adumim Almog
El-Azariya Kalia 90
Rachel's Tomb 398 Qumran
Bethlehem Einot Zukim
356 (Ain Fashkha)
Zatara 0 5 mi
0 5 km

*Dead
Sea*

J U D E A N   D E S E R T

WEST
BANK
Mitzpe
Shalem

Nahal David
Ein Gedi
Nahal
Arugot
1
Ein Gedi Spa
90

Church of the Nativity, Bethlehem

3199
Masada

Arad
TO EILAT

Ein Bokek

GETTING
ORIENTED

The wealth of beautiful landscapes, historical treasures,
and biblical sites within
an easy drive of Jerusalem
make a number of good
day trips. To the west lie
the Judean Hills, covered
with vineyards and farms.
To the south is Bethlehem,
a pilgrimage site for many
of the faithful. And to the
east is the Judean Desert,
graced with heavenly oases
like Jericho and Ein Gedi.
Descending from Jerusa-
lem's peaks, you quickly
arrive at the Dead Sea—the
lowest point on the face of
the Earth. Ein Bokek, near
the Dead Sea's southern
end, is a good place to
float in its salty water.

3

סכנת טביעה
خطر الغرق
DANGER OF
DROWNING

Near the Dead Sea

AROUND JERUSALEM AND THE DEAD SEA PLANNER

When To Go

The Dead Sea region is pleasant between October and April but very hot the rest of the year. Beginning the day with a tour of Masada can help beat the heat and the crowds. Ein Bokek, with its unique hotels and spas by the Dead Sea, attracts visitors even in broiling hot summer. Bethlehem is best early or late in the day if you want to avoid the crowds. Before you set out, check the hours for the Church of the Nativity. The area to the west of Jerusalem is pleasant any time of the year.

Do some homework if you want to visit this region during a religious holiday. Many celebrations, including those on the Jewish and Muslim calendars, vary from year to year. Similarly, Christmas is celebrated three times in Jerusalem and Bethlehem, according to the Western, Orthodox, and Armenian rites.

Getting Here and Around

Bus Travel: Egged buses are modern, air-conditioned, and reasonably priced. Service is dependable on main routes but infrequent to outlying rural districts. Buses do not run on Saturday (a few routes resume after sunset).

From the Beersheva Central Bus Station, buses depart four times a day for Arad, Ein Bokek, and other southern points. For Ein Bokek, there's also a daily 8:30 AM bus from Tel Aviv's Central Bus Station and several buses from Jerusalem. Buses can be crowded, especially on Friday and Sunday. You cannot buy tickets or reserve seats by phone for the above routes; go to the bus station, and arrive early.

Car Travel: Driving is much better than relying on public transportation here, as many sights are on secondary roads where bus service is scarce. Highway conditions are good, and most destinations are marked. The steep road between Arad and Ein Bokek has one hairpin turn after another. Unless otherwise posted, stick to the inter-city speed of 90 kph (56 mph). Budget extra time for leaving Jerusalem during rush hours. Gas stations are plentiful, and some are open 24 hours a day. Still, play it safe and keep the tank at least half full at all times. Pay special attention to keeping the radiator topped off in the torrid summer months.

Note: In times of political unrest, check with authorities to confirm safety of roads that pass through the West Bank.

Sherut Travel: A *sherut*, or shared taxi seating up to nine passengers, runs along a set route. Usually, it follows a major bus route and charges a nominally more expensive fare. Arab sheruts to Bethlehem and Jericho are available from East Jerusalem's Damascus Gate. An Arab taxi may be delayed at military checkpoints, however.

Train Travel: Israel Railways provides regular—but slow—train service between Jerusalem and Tel Aviv via Bet Shemesh on an hourly basis from 6 AM to 8 PM. Trains depart from the southern neighborhood of Malcha, opposite the Jerusalem Mall. There are also occasional departures from the Jerusalem Biblical Zoo. Many people take the beautiful 40-minute ride through the forested hills to the Judean Lowlands merely for the scenery.

⇨ *For more information on getting here and around, see Travel Smart Israel.*

Dining

Some Judean Hills wineries offer fancy meals along with their tastings, but these should be reserved in advance. Abu Ghosh, on the way to Latrun, is known for its hummus and kebab restaurants. There are also some passable cafeterias west of Jerusalem, but few really tempting restaurants for lunch or dinner. An alternative is to take a packed lunch or have a picnic west of Jerusalem with wine and cheese. On the Dead Sea, it's always a good idea to make reservations in Ein Bokek restaurants, especially on Friday and Saturday night.

Lodging

The lodgings in the Dead Sea region are heavily used by visitors, both national and international, who come to "take the waters" and enjoy the desert scenery. Facilities range from youth hostels to kibbutz inns. Although they might conjure up visions of Spartan plainness, the kibbutz inns are surprisingly comfortable. They also offer a chance to see life on the communal settlements firsthand.

Hotels in sunny Ein Bokek, the resort on the Dead Sea, run from family-style to huge and luxurious. Shuttle buses link hotels with each other and the center of town. A beautiful and luxurious spa with a wide range of facilities is an important feature of each large hotel, and many smaller hotels as well. High season is mid-March to mid-June and mid-September to the end of November.

People typically explore the area west of Jerusalem on a day trip, so lodgings are few and far between. The only decent lodgings here are some fine guesthouses, known in Hebrew as *zimmeren*, and most are just 15 or 20 minutes outside the capital.

WHAT IT COSTS

	¢	$	$$	$$$	$$$$
Restaurants	under NIS 32	NIS 32– NIS 49	NIS 50– NIS 75	NIS 76– NIS 100	over NIS 100
Hotels	under $120	$120–$200	$201–$300	$301–$400	over $400

Restaurant prices are per person for a main course at dinner in NIS (Israeli shekels). Hotel prices are in US dollars, for two people in a standard double room in high season. Non-Israeli citizens paying in foreign currency are exempt from the 15.5% VAT tax on hotel rooms.

Planning Your Time

This area offers several day-trip options. The Dead Sea has the richest fare and takes the most time—it's worth an overnight if it appeals—but some sights there can be visited en route to the Galilee via the Jordan Valley. The area west of Jerusalem has sights that can be visited together; check with wineries about visiting. Bethlehem (⇨*see that section for information about traveling to this West Bank city*) can be a separate trip and could take at least half a day.

Sightseeing Tours

Bus tours are convenient for this area; they pick you up and return you to your hotel in Jerusalem. Egged Tours and United Tours offer full-day tours of Masada, the Dead Sea, and Ein Gedi. Tours depart daily and cost about $70 per person from Jerusalem. For a private guided tour, try Jerusalem-based Eshcolot Tours.

Tour Information Egged Tours (☎ *03/694–8888 or *2800 ⊕ www.egged.co.il/eng*). **Eshcolot Tours** (✉ *36 Keren Hayesod St., Talbieh, Jerusalem* ☎ *02/563–5555*). **United Tours** (☎ *02/625–2187 ⊕ www.unitedtours.co.il*).

Updated by
Gil Zohar

The Judean Hills spreading north, west, and south of Jerusalem, and the wilderness sloping eastward to the Dead Sea, offer an astonishing range of scenery. Passing from forest to desert in minutes, you encounter springs and oases, biblical sites and ancient monasteries, hiking trails and historic sites such as Masada. West of the city, nature reserves and wineries offer other worthwhile excursions from Jerusalem.

The most dramatic sights are in the Judean Desert–Dead Sea area, a moonscape of barren hills where Bedouin eke out a living in encampments little changed from when Abraham wandered here from Ur with his flocks. The barren, desert landscapes contrast sharply with the lush greenery of the oases of Ein Gedi, Ain Fashka, and the verdant city of Jericho. The route along the Dead Sea shore is hemmed in by fractured brown cliffs over 1,600 feet high, and is often cut by (mostly dry) wadis, or dry riverbeds. Ein Gedi has two of the most spectacular of these wadis, Nahal David and Nahal Arugot. In Ein Bokek, near the southern end of the Dead Sea, you can settle into one of the numerous health and beauty spas that make use of the Dead Sea waters and medicinal mud.

Masada, Herod the Great's mountaintop palace-fortress built over 2,000 years ago, was named a UNESCO World Heritage Site in 2001. Overlooking the Dead Sea, the king's extravagant architectural feat has ingenious water systems, wall frescoes, mosaic floors, bathhouses, and a fresh-water swimming pool. Add the human drama of the last Jewish defense against Rome during the Great Revolt, and it is easy to understand why this is one of the most visited sights in Israel.

You'll find echoes of Joshua (though not his walls) at the oasis of Jericho to the east and in the Ayalon Valley to the west, where Joshua ordered the sun and moon to stand still so that he could vanquish the Canaanites. The Ella Valley to the west was the dueling ground of David and Goliath, and where Judah met Tamar.

The reforested hills west of Jerusalem in the Judean Lowlands are full of delightful views, picnic spots, and nature reserves. Don't miss the Sorek Cave, a fantastic cavern of stalagmites and stalactites, or the extraordinary ancient man-made caves of Bet Guvrin and Maresha. The area is becoming more popular with Israelis as well as tourists, thanks to its thriving wineries and cheese and olive oil producers.

Adjacent to Jerusalem, Bethlehem is a major site of Christian pilgrimage. The Church of the Nativity, the oldest church in the country, erected in the 4th century, is built over the grotto where Christian tradition holds Jesus was born. The West Bank Arab city of almost 40,000 sits on the ancient highway through the rocky Judean Hills.

3

MASADA AND THE DEAD SEA

The 4,000-foot descent from Jerusalem to the Dead Sea is only 24 km (15 mi), creating interesting weather patterns. Annual precipitation plummets from 22 inches in Jerusalem to 2 inches at the Dead Sea. The desert's proximity has always made it part of that city's consciousness. Refugees fled here; hermits sought its solitude; and when the Temple stood, on the Day of Atonement a scapegoat bearing the sins of the Jewish people was symbolically driven off its stark precipices.

Nomadic Bedouin still cling to their tribal ancestral way of life, herding sheep and goats. They have made some concessions to modernity: pickup trucks are parked beside camels, and synthetic fabrics flapping on clotheslines from tents bear witness to a culture in flux.

INN OF THE GOOD SAMARITAN

20 km (13 mi) east of Jerusalem on Rte. 1, 500 yds east of the junction with Rte. 458.

GETTING HERE AND AROUND
Follow Route 1 east from Jerusalem for 20 km (13 mi). The site is clearly signposted on the south side of the road.

EXPLORING
The **Inn of the Good Samaritan,** a lone one-story building, sits on the strategic spot that marks the halfway point between Jerusalem and Jericho, as well as the border between the biblical Israelite tribes of Benjamin, to the north, and Judah, to the south. Although no 1st-century remains have been found, the restored Ottoman-period *caravanserai* (inn) likely sits in the same place as the inn mentioned in the New Testament (Luke 10) parable of a man ambushed on the Jericho road and helped by a Samaritan.

If you're energetic, turn away from the inn, cross the highway *very, very* carefully, and climb the dirt track to the top of the hill opposite. Amid the scanty ruins of the small 12th-century Crusader fort of Maldoim— from which the outskirts of Jerusalem and Jericho are visible—the Gospel passage comes alive. ⊠ *Rte 1.*

JERICHO

35 km (22 mi) east of Jerusalem on Rte. 1, and north 5 km (3 mi) on Rte. 90.

The sleepy oasis of Jericho is immortalized as the place where "the walls came tumblin' down" at the sound of Joshua's trumpets. Those ramparts haven't been found, but the ruins of Hisham's Palace will give you an idea of the devastating power of an earthquake at a time when cities were built of mud, wood, and stone. Jericho—adorned with date palms, orange groves, banana plantations, bougainvillea bushes, and papaya trees—is the oldest city in the world. The Arab population of about 25,000 is mostly Muslim, but the tiny Christian minority is well represented by a number of landmark churches and monasteries. It's these biblical and archaeological sites that draw most tourists today.

GETTING HERE AND AROUND

Follow Route 1 east from Jerusalem for 35 km (13 mi), then turn north on Old Route 90. Jericho is clearly signposted. While Egged bus drivers will drop you off at the side of Route 1, it's still 5 km (3 mi) to Jericho.

TIMING

Jericho is very pleasant during the winter months, but swelteringly hot in the summer.

SAFETY AND PRECAUTIONS

Jericho has been under Palestinian Authority control since 1994. Check the current political situation before visiting. While there are no restrictions on tourists in private cars visiting the town, you will need to present your foreign passport to re-enter Israeli-controlled territory. Note that your car rental insurance may be void in this area; check. Israeli citizens are currently prohibited from visiting Jericho and other Area A parts of the Palestinian Authority.

EXPLORING

As you enter Jericho from Route 1, take the left fork at the traffic island. A few hundred yards farther, the road swings sharply to the left. To the right of the bend and one block down a no-entry street is a fenced-off **sycamore tree,** which tradition (and the postcard vendors) identifies as the very one Zacchaeus the chief tax collector climbed to get a better look at Jesus (Luke 19:4).

Tel Jericho is the mound of accumulated strata that entombs the legendary ancient city. Although it's been extensively excavated, archaeologists have not found the walls that fell to the blast of Israelite rams' horns when Joshua stormed the city in the mid-13th century BC. The most impressive ruins that have been unearthed are a massive tower and a wall, remains of the world's oldest walled city, which predates the invention of pottery. Carbon-14 tests have placed human skulls and bones found here in the Neolithic period (Late Stone Age) between 7800 and 6500 BC. Little is known about these early urbanites, or why they needed such fortifications thousands of years before they became common in the region, but a wealth of artifacts, displayed in the Israel

Masada and the Dead Sea

and Rockefeller Museums in Jerusalem, helps us imagine their domestic life and customs.

From the top of the tell, there is a sweeping view of Jericho, the biblical "City of Palms." Across the road, capped by a pump house, is **Ain as-Sultan,** or the Sultan's Spring. The name comes from the prophet Elijah's miracle of sweetening the water with a bowl of salt (II Kings 2:19–22). To the east in Jordan are the mountains of the biblical kingdoms of Ammon and Moab, among them the peak of Mt. Nebo, from which Moses viewed the Promised Land before dying at the ripe old age of 120.

To the south, among the banana trees some 3 km (2 mi) away and not far from the IDF checkpoint at the south end of Jericho, are a number of small but distinctive mounds on both banks of Wadi Kelt. This is **Telul Abu 'Alayiq,** where the remains of the royal palace of the Hasmonean dynasty (2nd–1st centuries BC) have been uncovered. In the 1st century BC, Mark Antony gave the valuable oasis of Jericho to his beloved Cleopatra; the humiliated King Herod, Antony's local vassal, was then forced to lease the property back from the Egyptian queen. Herod expanded and improved the palace, turning it into a winter retreat. He died there in 4 BC. The site is not developed; there is no entrance fee and you can wander here during daylight.

To the west is the **Mount of Temptation,** identified by tradition as the "exceedingly high mountain" from which Satan tempted Jesus with dominion over "all the kingdoms of the world" (Matthew 4). Halfway down the mountain sits the remarkable Greek Orthodox monastery of Qarantal, the name being a corruption of *quarantena*—a period of 40 days (the source of the English word "quarantine")—the period of Jesus's temptation. Built into the cliff face in 1895 on Byzantine and Crusader remains, it is flanked by many caves which once housed hermits. From a ticket booth facing Tel Jericho, a **cable car** offers round-trip rides up the mountain for NIS 45. The cable car's upper station, from which stairs lead up to the monastery, is served by the Jericho Heights Restaurant with a spectacular view.

To get to the tell by car, drive along Old Route 90, the main road through Jericho, and turn left at the traffic circle onto Ain as-Sultan Street. The parking lot is about 2 km (1 mi) down the road. ✉ *Ain as-Sultan St.* ☎ *02/232–1590 or 02/232–2240* 🎫 *NIS 10* ⊙ *Oct.–Mar., daily 8:30–5; Apr.–Sept., daily 8:30–6.*

The remains of **Hisham's Palace,** known as Khirbet al-Mafjar in Arabic, have interesting stonework and a spectacular mosaic floor. Hisham was a scion of the Ummayad dynasty, which built the Dome of the Rock and al-Aqsa Mosque in Jerusalem. Although the palace was severely damaged by the great earthquake of AD 749 while still under construction, the surviving mosaics and stone and plaster reliefs are evidence of its splendor.

A small gatehouse leads into a wide plaza dominated by a star-shape stone window that once graced an upper floor. Several sections of the fine geometric mosaics have been left exposed; others are covered by sand. The most impressive part of the complex is the reception room, off the plaza. Its intricate mosaic floor, depicting a lion hunting gazelles, is one of the most beautiful in the country. The balustrade of an ornamental pool reflects the artistic influences of both East and West. Fragments of ornate stucco reliefs are still visible on some of the walls, but the best examples that were found here are now in Jerusalem's Rockefeller Museum.

To get here go north from the traffic circle that constitutes downtown Jericho, following Hisham's Palace Road for 4 km (2½ mi) and turn right at the sign to Hisham's Palace immediately after the Police Intelligence Building. After that, the left turn toward the site itself is another 1 km (½ mi) down a road marked only by a low stone pillar on the right. ⊠ *Hisham's Palace Rd.* ☎ *02/232–2522* 🖅 *NIS 23* ⊘ *Daily 8–5.*

↻ **Banana Land,** 4 km (2½ mi) north of Tel Jericho along Canaanite Dulok Street, is the only water park in the West Bank. Around the swimming pools you'll encounter Palestinian families enjoying a day off. ⊠ *Canaanite Dulok St.* ☎ *02/232–445* ⊕ *www.jericho-jit.com* 🖅 *NIS 10* ⊘ *Oct.–Mar., daily 8:30–5; Apr.–Sept., daily 8:30–6.*

WHERE TO EAT

$$ ✕ **Jericho Heights.** Reachable by cable car, this hilltop restaurant offers
MIDDLE EASTERN a spectacular view of the oasis below, as well as of the Dead Sea in the distance. The pleasant dining room has blissfully cool air-conditioning. The cuisine is Middle Eastern, and the Turkish coffee is delicious. ⊠ *Qarantal St.* ☎ *02/232–1590* ☰ *AE, MC, V.*

$ ✕ **Temptation Restaurant.** The closest restaurant to Tel Jericho (it even
MIDDLE EASTERN shares a parking lot), Temptation has excellent *bourma*, a honey-rolled pastry filled with whole pistachio nuts. The lunches are a good value, with tasty meat dishes and *mezzes* (Middle Eastern salads). The nearby fruit stands tend to overcharge, but try the pomelo (related to the grapefruit), in season from December to March. ⊠ *Ain as-Sultan St.* ☎ *02/232–2614* ☰ *AE, MC, V.*

QUMRAN

13 km (8 mi) south of the Almog Junction on Rte. 90, 20 km (13 mi) south of Jericho, 50 km (31 mi) east of Jerusalem.

GETTING HERE AND AROUND
Follow Route 1 east from Jerusalem for 50 km (31 mi), turning south on Route 90. Qumran is on the right. The town is inside the Palestinian Authority, but cars are routinely waved through the two checkpoints, making travel here uneventful. Around Qumran are some Dead Sea beaches worth a stop; you need a car.

SAFETY AND PRECAUTIONS
Check the weather forecast before hiking in the winter. Flash floods are a danger.

EXPLORING
Although the remains of **Qumran** are not especially impressive, caves in the cliffs west of the site yielded the most significant archaeological find ever made in Israel: the Dead Sea Scrolls. (These are not on display at the site.) They were found under extraordinary circumstances in

The dryness of Qumran helped preserve the Dead Sea Scrolls stored in caves in the sculpted rock.

1947 when a young Bedouin goatherd stumbled on a cave containing parchment scrolls in earthen jars. Because the scrolls were made from animal hide, he first went to a shoemaker to turn them into sandals. The shoemaker alerted a local antiquities dealer, who brought them to the attention of Professor Eliezer Sukenik of the Hebrew University of Jerusalem. Six other major scrolls and hundreds of fragments have since been discovered.

Most scholars believe that the scrolls were written by the Essenes, a Jewish sect which set up a monastic community here in the late 2nd century BC. During the Great (Jewish) Revolt against Rome (AD 66–73), they apparently hid their precious scrolls in the caves in the cliffs before the site was destroyed in AD 68.

Almost all books of the Hebrew Bible were discovered here, many of them virtually identical to the texts still used in Jewish communities. Sectarian texts were also found, including the constitution or "Community Rule;" a description of an end-of-days battle ("The War of the Sons of Light Against the Sons of Darkness"); and the "Thanksgiving Scroll," containing hymns reminiscent of biblical psalms.

The scrolls are tremendously significant for Bible scholars and students of ancient Hebrew, and give researchers rare insights into this previously shadowy Jewish sect. Christian scholars have long been intrigued by the suggestion that John the Baptist, whose lifestyle seems to have paralleled that of the Essenes, may have been a member of this community. Several scrolls are on display at the Shrine of the Book in Jerusalem's Israel Museum.

A short film at the entrance introduces the mysterious sect that once lived here. Climb the tower for a good view, and note the elaborate system of channels and cisterns that gathered floodwater from the cliffs. Just below the tower (looking toward the Dead Sea) is a long room some scholars have identified as the **scriptorium.** A plaster writing table and bronze and ceramic inkwells found here suggest that this may have been where the scrolls were written. Other archaeologists dispute this interpretation, arguing that before Qumran was taken over by rebels during the Great Revolt against Rome in 66 to 73, the site was a plantation for the now-extinct balsam tree. Like frankincense and myrrh, the expensive balsam perfume was greatly prized in Rome. Thus the scriptorium was, in this view, a business office.

A good air-conditioned cafeteria and gift store serve the site. ⊠ *Rte. 90, 13 km (8 mi) south of Almog Junction* ☎ *02/994–2235* ⊕ *www.parks. org.il* ⊠ *NIS 18* ⊙ *Apr.–Sept., daily 8–5; Oct.–Mar., daily 8–4.*

BEACHES AND POOLS

Qumran is also near some beaches on the Dead Sea. You cannot actually swim in the briny water; you simply float in its incredible salinity, about 10 times that of the ocean. Anyone can enjoy the benefits of the mineral concentration in the Dead Sea water and mud, and the oxygen-rich atmosphere at the lowest point on Earth. Beach shoes, rubber sandals, or sneakers are a must, as the salt in the hyper-saturated water builds up into sharp ridges that are hard to walk on. Any open cuts on your body will sting when they encounter the briny water.

Beautiful **Biankini Beach** has a spa offering mineral treatments and massages, and a Moroccan restaurant. There are restrooms, showers, changing rooms, and a freshwater wading pool for kids. If you want to stay overnight, there are 21 bed-and-breakfast huts (NIS 650). Backpackers can pitch their own tents for NIS 85 per person per night. ⊠ *Off Rte. 90, 3 km (2 mi) north of Qumran* ☎ *02/940–0266* ⊕ *www.biankini. co.il* ⊠ *NIS 30* ⊙ *Oct.–Mar., daily 8–5; Apr.–Sept., daily 8–6.*

Known for its freshwater springs, **Einot Zukim** (also called Ain Fashkha), is a nature reserve with many species of trees and reeds not often found in the arid Judean Desert. You can swim in two spring-fed pools. Picnic and changing facilities are also available. ⊠ *Rte. 90, 3 km (2 mi) south of Qumran* ☎ *02/994–2355* ⊕ *www.parks.org.il* ⊠ *NIS 23* ⊙ *Oct.– Mar., daily 8–4; Apr.–Sept., daily 8–5.*

On the Dead Sea, **Kalia Beach** is the place to go for a free mud bath. Slather your whole body with the mineral-rich mud and let it dry before showering; you'll enjoy the rejuvenating properties of this spa-like experience. The beach also has chair and towel rentals, a gift shop, and a snack bar. ⊠ *3 km (2 mi) north of Qumran off Rte. 90* ☎ *02/994–2391* ⊠ *NIS 35* ⊙ *Oct.–Mar., daily 8–5; Apr.–Sept., daily 8–6:30.*

Less touristy than some of the other beaches, **Mineral Beach** is a good place to mix and mingle with Israelis. There are restrooms, showers, a freshwater wading pool for kids, and a snack shop. It also offers massages (reserve in advance). ⊠ *20 km (12½ mi) south of Qumran on Rte. 90* ☎ *02/994–4888* ⊕ *www.dead-sea.co.il* ⊠ *Sun.–Thurs. NIS 42; Fri. and Sat. NIS 50* ⊙ *Sun.–Thurs. 9–6, Fri. and Sat. 8–6.*

Neve Midbar Beach, south of Biankini Beach, has restrooms, showers, changing rooms, and a restaurant. The beach here is popular with boisterous Israeli young people, especially at night. There are 14 straw huts you can rent for NIS 190. Backpackers can pitch their own tents for NIS 50 per night. ✉ *Off Rte. 90, 3 km (2 mi) north of Qumran* ☎ *02/994–2781* ⊕ *www.nevemidbar-beach.com* ⛁ *NIS 35* ⊙ *Oct.– Mar., daily 8–5; Apr.–Sept., daily 8–7.*

EN ROUTE

Kibbutz Mitzpe Shalem (✉ *20 km, or 12½ mi, south of Qumran on Rte. 90* ☎ *02/994–5117*) manufactures the excellent Ahava skin- and hair-care products based on (but not smelling like) the Dead Sea minerals. The factory outlet here is open Sunday–Thursday 8–5, Friday 8–4, and Saturday 8:30–5. The prices here are very good, but it's worth the trip only if you're buying a lot. Otherwise, you can get individual products at stores in larger cities.

EIN GEDI

★ *33 km (21 mi) south of Qumran, 20 km (12½ mi) north of Masada, 83 km (52 mi) southeast of Jerusalem.*

After miles of burnt brown and beige desert rock, the green lushness of the Ein Gedi oasis provides a vivid and welcome contrast. This nature reserve is one of the most beautiful places in Israel—with everything from hiking trails to ancient ruins. Settled for thousands of years, it inspired the writer of the *Song of Songs* to describe his beloved "as a cluster of henna in the vineyards of Ein-Gedi."

GETTING HERE AND AROUND

Follow Route 1 east from Jerusalem for 50 km (31 mi), turning south on Route 90. Ein Gedi is on the right. Egged bus drivers will drop you off at the side of Route 90. From there it's a short hike to the gate of the national park.

SAFETY AND PRECAUTIONS

Check the weather forecast before hiking in the winter. Flash floods are a danger.

EXPLORING

A major attraction of the Ein Gedi Nature Reserve, **Nahal David** *(David's Stream)* is believed to be the place where David hid from the wrath of Saul (I Samuel 24:1–22) 3,000 years ago, cutting the edge of the king's robe rather than killing his monarch. The clearly marked trail goes past several pools and small waterfalls to the beautiful upper waterfall. There are many steps, but it's not too daunting. Allow at least 1¼ hours to include a refreshing dip under one of the lower waterfalls. Look out for ibex (wild goat), especially in the afternoon, and for the small, furry hyrax, often seen on tree branches. Leopards here face extinction because of breeding problems; they're seldom seen nowadays.

If you're a more serious hiker who is interested in further adventure, don't miss the trail that breaks off to the right 50 yards down the return path from the top waterfall. It passes the remains of Byzantine irrigation systems and offers breathtaking views of the Dead Sea. The trail doubles back on itself toward the source of Nahal David. Near

Waterfalls, pools, and desert landscapes are among the pleasures awaiting hikers in Ein Gedi's nature reserve.

the top, a short side path climbs to the remains of a 4th-millennium BC temple. The main path leads on to the streambed, again turns east, and reaches **Dudim (Lovers') Cave**, formed by boulders and filled with crystal-clear spring water. Swimming here is one of the most refreshing and romantic experiences in Israel. You are directly above the waterfall of Nahal David (don't throw stones—there are people below). Since this trail involves a considerable climb (and hikers invariably take time to bathe in the "cave"), access to the trail is permitted only up to 3½ hours before closing time. Reaching Ein Gedi from the north, the first turnoff to the right is the parking lot at the entrance to Nahal David. ⊠ *Ein Gedi* ☎ *08/658–4285* ⊕ *www.parks.org.il* ⊠ *NIS 23, includes admission to Nahal Arugot and the ancient synagogue* ⊗ *Sat.–Thurs. 8–4, Fri. 8–3; last admission 1 hr before closing.*

Although not quite as green as Nahal David, the deep canyon of **Nahal Arugot** is perhaps more spectacular. Enormous boulders and slabs of stone on the opposite cliff face seem poised in mid-cataclysm. The hour-long hike to the **Hidden Waterfall** (many steps, but not too steep) goes by beautiful spots where the stream bubbles over rock shelves and shallow pools offer relief from the heat. If you're adventurous and have water shoes, you can return through the greenery of the stream-bed, leaping the boulders and wading the pools. ⊠ *From Nahal David parking lot, continue south through the date orchards of the kibbutz, follow signs to Nahal Arugot (no entrance from Rte. 90), Ein Gedi* ☎ *08/658–4285* ⊕ *www.parks.org.il* ⊠ *NIS 23, includes admission to Nahal David and the ancient synagogue* ⊗ *Sat.–Thurs. 8–4, Fri. 8–3; last admission 2 hrs before closing.*

Continued on page 186

DID YOU KNOW?

King Herod built a dam in the valley so that reservoir water could be carried to cisterns atop Masada. His engineers also created channels, visible today, that guided water from streams into cisterns hewn into the mountainside.

MASADA: DESERT FORTRESS

The isolated flattop rock of Masada commands the surrounding desert, its ancient remains bearing witness to long-ago power and conflict. One of Israel's most stunning archaeological sites, Masada earned fame and a place in history first as one of King Herod's opulent palace-fortresses and later as the site of the last stand of Jewish rebels against the legions of Rome, almost 2,000 years ago.

A KING'S PALACE

Surrounded by steep cliffs and with spectacular views of the Dead Sea and the desert, the Masada plateau offers nearly impregnable natural protection.

Herod the Great, the brilliant builder and paranoid leader who reigned over Israel as king of the Jews by the grace of the Roman Empire in the 1st century BC, developed the 18-acre site. Both for his relaxation and as a possible refuge from his enemies (including Cleopatra) and hostile subjects, Herod built atop Masada a fantastic, state-of-the-art complex of palaces, storehouses, and water systems.

THE REVOLT OF THE JEWS

Herod died around 4 BC, and the Jews rebelled against Rome in AD 66. By AD 70, the Roman Empire had destroyed Jerusalem and crushed the Jewish revolt there. Around AD 72, the last Jewish rebels took refuge at Masada. For at least a year, 960 Israelite men, women, and children lived here, protected from thousands of Roman soldiers by cliffs more than 1,400 feet high.

The Roman general and governor Flavius Silva, determined to end the rebellion, built eight legionnaire camps around the mountain. Silva's forces gradually erected an assault ramp on Masada's western side.

THE REBELS' "TERRIBLE RESOLVE"

According to a few survivors who related the story to the 1st-century historian Flavius Josephus, the night before the Romans reached Masada's walls, the rebel leader Elazar Ben-Yair gave a rallying speech. He reminded his community that they had resolved "neither to serve the Romans nor any other save God." After discussion, the Jews agreed to commit suicide rather than be taken captive.

The men drew lots to choose the ten who would kill the others. Those ten, having carried out "their terrible resolve," Josephus wrote, drew additional lots to select the one who would kill the other nine and then himself. When the Romans breached the walls the next morning, they found hundreds of corpses. The zealots' final action made the Roman victory at Masada a hollow one.

Although Josephus' physical description of Masada is accurate, some historians doubt his narrative. Several artifacts, including pottery shards bearing names (the lots, perhaps?), support the accuracy of Josephus' text, but no one can be sure what happened at the end. Masada continues to inspire debate.

by Sarah Bronson

TOURING MASADA'S TOP SIGHTS

Ride the cable car up Masada, or walk the Snake Path or easier
Ramp Path. Take in these highlights of Herod's buildings and the Jewish
rebels' presence—and awesome desert views.

Museum

TO
← DEAD SEA, EIN GEDI,
AND EIN BOKEK

13 Mikveh

Casemate Wall

12

11 Church

1 **2**

4 Snake Path

Cable Car **3**

5 Commandant's Residence and Storerooms

Synagogue **8**

7

Bathhouse

Northern Palace

6

Path

❶ **Museum.** The fine museum, near the cable car, interprets the history of Masada and has archaeological artifacts.

❷ **Roman Camps.** The eight military camps around Masada are the most complete Roman siege works in the world. Museum visitors may also enter a restored Roman camp. From Masada's top, note the square camps and the remnants of the siege wall connecting them.

❸ **Cable Car.** The fastest way to ascend is also near the Masada Museum and a Roman siege camp on the east side.

❹ **Snake Path.** You can still climb the steep path on the eastern side of Masada used by Herod's workers and the Jewish rebels.

KEY	
🛈	Tourist information
🚶	Trail
🚠	Cable car
💧	Drinking water
🚻	Restroom
♿	Wheelchair access
🔭	Observation Point

Frescoed walls

❺ **Commandant's Residence and Storerooms.** With its frescoed walls, this area may have housed Herod's commanders. Simple ovens here indicate that the Jews, too, used the complex as living quarters. The undecorated rooms stored grain, dry fruit, and wine.

Inauguration of the synagogue: blowing the shofar (2005)

Bathhouse

7 Bathhouse. This spa on a desert cliff demonstrates Herod's grandiosity, his dedication to Roman culture, and the success of Masada's water systems. The building has cold and lukewarm baths, a sauna, frescoes, and tile work. Jewish rebels incorporated a ritual bath.

8 Synagogue. Built into the casemate wall, the synagogue is oddly shaped, but its benches and geniza (space for damaged scrolls) indicate its function. Here, perhaps, the rebels agreed to die at their own hands. Today the synagogue is used for bar and bat mitzvahs.

9 Roman Ramp. You can stand on the western edge where Romans breached Masada's defenses. The original ramp is below, as well as a modern path for walkers.

10 Western Palace. Believed to have been an administrative base and a guest house, this palace retains frescoed walls and mosaics in Greek style; unusual for Herodian mosaics, one has a fruit motif.

11 Church. During the 5th to 7th centuries, monks lived at Masada, choosing it for its isolation. This 5th-century chapel is Byzantine in design, with mosaic floors.

12 Casemate Wall. Despite Masada's strategic advantages, Herod built a casemate (double-layered) wall around the oblong flattop rock, including offices

Roman Ramp on the western slopes of Masada

and storerooms. The Jewish rebels used these rooms as dwellings.

13 Mikveh. In Jewish culture, the mikveh, or ritual bath, is a symbol of life and hope. Two found on Masada were built in accordance with Jewish laws still followed today. The presence of mikvehs indicates the rebels' religious piety.

14 Water Cistern. Like other cisterns at Masada, the southern cistern—into which you may descend—was built underground to prevent evaporation. Also make your way to see the spectacular canyon view to the south, and test the echoes.

14 Water Cistern

12 Casemate Wall

Western Palace 10

Western gate ♦

Ramp path

9 Roman Ramp

12 Casemate Wall

TO ARAD →

6 Northern Palace. Herod's personal living quarters is an extraordinary three-tiered structure that seems to hang from the cliffs. The amazing, terraced buildings feature colorful frescoes, Greek-inspired architecture, and Herod's personal bathhouse.

Northern Palace

Mikveh

MASADA FROM JERUSALEM

Masada lookout

BY CAR

For Masada's **eastern side**, take Route 1 east to Route 90 south along the Dead Sea. Masada is off Route 90, about 15 minutes south of **Ein Gedi** (it's also near **Ein Bokek**). One-way driving time is about 80 minutes; add time to get out of Jerusalem.

For Masada's **western side** and the Roman Path entrance, head to Route 6 south, which merges with Route 40; continue on Route 31 to Arad and Route 3199/Masada. It takes about 2.5 hours one way from southern Jerusalem. Avoid Route 60 and Hebron, and take a good map.

Note: There is no direct car access from the west side of Masada to the east. Those wishing to ascend on one side and descend on the other must arrange for their car to meet them on the other side; the drive is about 30 minutes.

BY GUIDED TOUR OR BUS

Your hotel can help you join a group tour to Masada, or contact **United Tours** (☎ 02/625–2187, ⊕ www.unitedtours.co.il) for daily, English-language trips from

Jerusalem to Masada and other sites in the Judean Desert and the Dead Sea.

Egged Bus Lines (☎ 03/694–8888) runs buses for the two-hour trip from Jerusalem's Central Bus Station to Masada approximately every hour Sunday through Thursday between 8:45 AM and 1 PM; return buses leave 8:30 AM to 7:50 PM. Friday service is limited.

THREE WAYS TO GET UP AND DOWN MASADA

On Masada's east side, the cable car takes only three minutes. The quickest way up, the **cable car** is convenient to the Masada Museum and a restored Roman siege camp. The long, steep **Snake Path** up the east side is an arduous but rewarding one-hour hike, recommended for visitors who are fit or determined to ascend Masada the same way the Jewish rebels did. Accessible from Arad on the west side, the **Ramp Path** is less grueling and takes fifteen to thirty minutes to ascend; it's equivalent to climbing about twenty flights of stairs.

MAKING THE MOST OF YOUR VISIT

WHEN TO VISIT
The weather at Masada is fairly consistent year-round; it's hot during the day. Visit in the early morning or late afternoon, when the sun is weakest. ■**TIP**→ It's popular to hike up before dawn via the Snake or Ramp Path, and watch the sun rise from behind Jordan and the Dead Sea. After 9 or 10 AM, extreme heat may dictate that you use the cable car.

WHAT TO WEAR AND BRING
Layered clothing is recommended, as cool early-morning temperatures rise to uncomfortable heat. Good walking shoes and hats or bandanas are musts. Free drinking water is available at Masada, but bring plenty to start with. Food is not sold atop the site. The museum cafeteria sells lunch after 11 AM. Sunscreen and a camera are essential.

TIMING AND HIGHLIGHTS
Visiting Masada, a UNESCO World Heritage Site, can take three to seven hours, depending on your interest. The museum takes about an hour. Going up can take from three minutes (cable car) to sixty minutes (Snake Path). Your tour at the top might take ninety minutes or up to three hours.

The **Masada Museum**, near the cable car, offers an excellent combination of life-size scenes depicting the history of Masada; archaeological artifacts; and audio guide (available in English). Watch the short English-language film near the cable-car entrance. Atop Masada, many highlights such as Herod's **Northern Palace** and the **bathhouse** are toward the site's northern

Cable car heading down from Masada

end. On the sparser southern side, the views and echo point near the southern **water cistern** are notable.

OTHER THINGS TO DO
If you're traveling or staying overnight on the Dead Sea side, combine your excursion with a hike in **Ein Gedi** or a visit to a spa in **Ein Bokek**. If you're staying in Arad, check out the Masada **Sound-and-Light Show** (☎ 08/995–9333) Tuesday and Thursday evenings at 8:30 PM from March through October. To arrange a bar mitzvah at Masada, contact the **Israel Parks Service** at ✉ info@parks.org.il.

VISITOR INFORMATION
Masada National Park: Off Rte. 90 (east) or Rte 3199 (west), ☎ 08/658–4207, ⊕ http://parks.org.il/ParksENG. **Note:** Most of Masada is wheelchair accessible.

🕑 **Park and cable car hours:** Apr.–Sept., Sun.–Fri. 8–5; Oct.–Mar., Sun.–Fri. 8–4; closes 1 hour earlier on Fri. and Jewish holiday eves. Closed Yom Kippur.

🕑 **Pre-dawn entrance for walkers:** Snake Path opens 1 hour before sunrise; Ramp Path opens 45 minutes before sunrise.

💳 **Admission:** NIS 25 park, via Snake or Roman paths; NIS 49 park plus cable car one-way; NIS 67 park plus round-trip cable car; NIS 20 museum (includes audio guides for museum and site); NIS 20 audio guide to park (includes museum entrance).

Cooking pots at Masada

Nestled between Nahal David and Nahal Arugot are the remains of a Jewish settlement from the late Roman and Byzantine periods (3rd to 6th centuries AD), including an **ancient synagogue** and ritual purification bath. The mosaic floor of the synagogue includes an inscription in Hebrew and Aramaic invoking the wrath of heaven on various troublemakers, including "whoever reveals the secret of the town." The secret is believed to refer to a method of cultivating a now-extinct balsam tree, which was used to make the prized perfume for which Ein Gedi

was once famous. ⊠ *From Nahal David parking lot, continue south a few hundred yards through the date orchards, Ein Gedi* ☎ *08/658–4285* ⊕ *www.parks.org.il* ⊠ *NIS 12; NIS 23 for combined ticket including Nahal Arugot and Nahal David* ⊙ *Sat.–Thurs. 8–4, Fri. 8–3.*

BEACHES AND POOLS

With access to the Dead Sea, **Ein Gedi Spa** lets you soak in an outdoor freshwater pool (in summer), slather yourself in mud, and relax in warm indoor sulfur pools. The place has good facilities, including indoor showers, lockers, and changing rooms. Massages (NIS 200 for 50 minutes) and treatments are available; advance reservation recommended. A snack bar and restaurant are here, too. ⊠ *3 km (2 mi) south of Ein Gedi gas station* ☎ *08/659–4813* ⊕ *www.ein-gedi.co.il* ⊠ *Sun.–Fri. NIS 65, Sat. NIS 70, NIS 40 if accompanied by licensed guide* ⊙ *Oct.– Mar., daily 8–5; Apr.–Sept., daily 8–6.*

The somewhat rocky **Ein Gedi Public Beach** gives you free access to the Dead Sea. Freshwater showers (absolutely essential) by the water's edge and basic changing facilities are NIS 8. There is also an air-conditioned restaurant and a gift shop. Don't leave valuables unguarded. ⊠ *200 yds south of Nahal David parking lot, behind the Paz Gas station on Rte. 90* ☎ *08/659–4761* ⊠ *Free* ⊙ *Oct.–Mar., daily 8–5; Apr.–Sept., daily 8–6.*

SPORTS AND THE OUTDOORS

There is no problem hiking the area alone, on well-marked trails. The map you receive with admission to the national park is perfectly adequate, but all the better ones are in Hebrew.

WHERE TO EAT AND STAY

$$ ✕ **Pundak Ein Gedi.** The nondescript entrance to the restaurant can be
FAST FOOD   somewhat misleading. In addition to offering a blissfully air-conditioned respite from the blistering desert sun, this self-service restaurant has a large salad bar, as well as assorted cooked entrées. It's nothing fancy, but the food is wholesome. The outdoor kiosk is open 24 hours a day and serves sandwiches, ice cream, and espresso. ⊠ *Rte. 90, 200 yds south*

A DRIVE TO THE DEAD SEA

From Arad, you can make the steep, 24-km (15-mi) descent to the Dead Sea and on to Ein Bokek via Route 31. With one sharp curve after another, the drive is an experience in itself. Watch for the sign on the right indicating that you've reached sea level.

The stunning canyons and clefts that unfold on every side enhance the drama of this drive. Two observation points soon appear on the left. You can't cross to the first—Metsad Zohar—from your side of the road. The second—Nahal Zohar—looks down on an ancient, dry riverbed, the last vestige of an eons-old body of water that once covered this area. The Dead

Sea lies directly east, with the Edom Mountains of Jordan on the other side. To the right (south) is Mt. Sodom.

You'll soon see, from above, the southern end of the Dead Sea, sectioned off into the huge evaporation pools of the Dead Sea Works, where potash and salts such as bromine and magnesium are extracted. On land are row after row of plastic "tunnels," which act as hothouses for fruit (often tomatoes and melons) that is sold to Europe in winter.

Two roads lead from Route 90 to the Ein Bokek hotel area; once there, you are at *the bottom of the world*: 1,292 feet below sea level.

of Nahal David parking lot, behind the Paz gas station ☎08/659–4761 ⊟*AE, MC, V* ⊘*No dinner.*

¢ ☂**Ein Gedi Youth Hostel.** Popular with backpackers, this hostel has beds in either dormitories or in guesthouse rooms with private baths. ✉*From Ein Gedi turnoff on Rte. 90, take an immediate right up the hill* ☎08/658–4165 ⊕*www.youth-hostels.org.il* ⇌*65 rooms* △*In-room: no phone* ⊟*AE, DC, MC, V* ⏆*BP.*

¢–$ ☂**Kibbutz Ein Gedi.** Surrounded by a spectacular tropical garden, this inn is nestled between 1,600-foot-high cliffs and the Dead Sea. Accommodations range from simple rooms to deluxe suites with terraces overlooking Nahal David. Rates for most include breakfast, another full meal, and unlimited entry to the nearby Ein Gedi Spa, to which there's a free shuttle throughout the day. Sitting by the swimming pool in the adjoining kibbutz, you're likely to meet some gregarious members or volunteers who have come from all over the world. ✉*Rte. 90, 5 km (3 mi) south of the kibbutz* ☎08/659–4220 or 08/659–4221 ⊕*www.ein-gedi.co.il* ⇌*175 rooms* △*In-room: no phone (some), kitchen. In-hotel: tennis courts, pool* ⊟*AE, DC, MC, V* ⏆*MAP.*

ARAD

20 km (12½ mi) west of Masada, 25 km (15½ mi) west of Ein Bokek and the Dead Sea.

Breathe deeply: Arad sits 2,000 feet above sea level and is famous for its dry, pollution-free air and mild climate, ideal for asthma sufferers. The modern town was established as a planned community in 1962. Its population of nearly 25,000 now includes immigrants from Russia and Ethiopia, as well as the acclaimed Israeli writer Amos Oz.

Arad is often used as a base for excursions to sites in the Dead Sea area, notably to Masada, and is the only approach (via Route 31) to Masada's sound-and-light show. It has an archaeological site and is also near Yatir, one of the country's desert wineries.

GETTING HERE AND AROUND

Arad is acessible by Route 31; the city is 46 km (28.5 mi) east of Beersheva. Driving from Jerusalem by Route 40 will take about 2½ hours; avoid Route 60 and Hebron in the West Bank. The tourist office is behind the Paz gas station opposite the entrance to Arad; you'll see a yellow sign with the "i" for Information on it. A small supply of maps, brochures, and hiking information is available; a simple 24/7 café called Yellow is next to the gas pumps.

ESSENTIALS

Visitor Information Arad Tourist Information Center (☎ *08/995–1622*).

EXPLORING

The **Glass Museum Gallery** displays the exciting creations of artist Gideon Fridman, who uses recycled glass in his personally developed fusing methods to create "talking glass" sculptures in ovens he built himself. Works by other artists working in glass are also on display. The gallery is on the road to the tourist information center. Pass the gas station on your left, turn right at the roundabout, take the second right, go to the end of the street, and it's on the left. A trip here is worth the effort. ✉ *11 Sadan St.* ☎ *08/995–3388* ⊕ *www.warmglassil.com* ⊙ *Sun.–Wed. 10–1, Thurs. and Sat. 10–5, Fri. 10–2.*

Approaching **Tel Arad,** the 250-acre site of the biblical city of Arad, from the west takes you through flat fields of the low shrub called *rotem* (white broom). At the entrance, pick up the National Parks Authority's pamphlet, which explains the ongoing excavations, and purchase (for NIS 8) the plan of the Canaanite city of Arad, with a map, recommended walking tour, and diagrams of a typical Arad house.

Arad was first settled during the Chalcolithic period (4000–3000 BC) by seminomadic pastoralists who lived and traveled together, herding and farming. It was they who first developed bronze. Arad was continually occupied until the end of the Early Bronze Age (3500–3200 BC), but the city you see most clearly is from the Early Bronze Age II (2950–2650 BC). Here you can walk around a walled urban community and enter the carefully reconstructed one-room "Arad houses."

After the Early Bronze Age II, Arad was abandoned and hidden beneath the light loess soil for nearly 2,000 years, until the 10th century BC, when a fortress—one of many in the Negev (the first may have been built by Solomon)—was built on the site's highest point. It's worth the trek up the somewhat steep path. Take a moment to appreciate the view as you take your leave of the Early Bronze Age; at the top, you step into the Iron Age (10th–6th centuries BC). The small, square fortress served the area intermittently until Roman times; most of the visible remains date from the end of the First Temple period (935–586 BC). Note the small Israelite temple sanctuary, with its two standing stones (these are replicas—the originals are in the Israel Museum in Jerusalem) and sacrificial altar of unhewn stone. In the 7th century BC, the southern part of the Israelite kingdom of Judah reached as far as today's Eilat.

Tel Arad is 8 km (5 mi) west of Arad. At the Tel Arad Junction on Route 31, turn north on Route 2808 for 3 km (2 mi.) ✉ *Off Rte. 31* ☎ *057/776–2170* ⊕ *www.parks.org.il* 🗝 *NIS 12* ☉ *Apr.–Sept., Sun.– Thurs. 8–5, Fri. and Jewish holiday eves 8–2; Oct.–Mar., Sun.–Thurs. 8–4, Fri. and Jewish holidays eves 8–2.*

At the foot of the ancient Tel Arad, you might stop to check out the modern **Yatir Winery** (☎ *08/995–9090* ⊕ *www.yatir.net*), an up-and-coming boutique vineyard established in 2000. The first wines were launched in 2004. Yatir Forest (Cabernet Sauvignon blend) is the premier label. The adjacent Yatir Forest, after which the winery is named, is the largest planted forest in Israel. Call ahead for a visit and tasting.

3

WHERE TO EAT AND STAY

$ ✕ **Muza.** With chunky wood furniture, a ceiling crammed with bar mats, soccer scarves draped along one wall, and a bar lined with beer bottles, this is a classic pub. It's on Route 31, at the entrance to Arad, next to the Alon gas station. The place is warm and cozy, staffed by smiling servers and filled with locals and travelers enjoying meat on skewers, hummus, hearty salads, and *malawach* (a flaky Yemenite pastry eaten with tomato sauce). Here you can also indulge your yen for an American-style tuna melt: request "toast," the Israeli term for a grilled cheese sandwich, with tuna salad, accompanied by Muza's home-cut, crunchy "chips" (french fries). A big-screen TV shows soccer matches, and the covered terrace with a billiard table at one end allows for alfresco dining. ✉ *Rte. 31* ☎ *08/997–5555* ⊕ *www.muza-arad.co.il* 🖉 *Reservations not accepted* ▭ *AE, DC, MC, V.*

MIDDLE EASTERN

★

$$ 🛏 **Inbar.** At the entrance to Arad, 50 meters from Route 31 toward the Dead Sea, is the only lodging option in town, the five-story Inbar hotel, built of white stone with orange trim. The upstairs lobby is inviting with its blue and yellow ceiling lamps; there's a sculpted-metal divider with birds on it at the entrance to the dining room, which overlooks the street. Rooms are petite, done in beige and olive. Minibars are available on request. **Pros:** welcoming staff; nice Dead Sea–style saltwater pool. **Cons:** nothing luxurious about the hotel; nothing interesting within walking distance. ✉ *38 Yehuda St.* ☎ *08/997–3303* 🖷 *08/997–3322* ⊕ *www.hotel-inbar.com* ➥ *103 rooms, 7 suites* 🛇 *In-room: safe. In-hotel: restaurant, pools* ▭ *AE, DC, MC, V* ⊙| *CP.*

EIN BOKEK

Fodor's Choice *40 km (25 mi) east of Arad, 8 km (5 mi) north of Zohar–Arad Junction on Rte. 90.*
★

The sudden and startling sight, in this bare landscape, of gleaming, ultramodern hotels surrounded by waving palm trees signals your arrival at the spa-resort area of Ein Bokek, near the southern tip of the Dead Sea. According to the Bible, it was along these shores that the Lord rained fire and brimstone on the people of Sodom and Gomorrah (Genesis 19:24) and turned Lot's wife into a pillar of salt (Genesis 26). Here, at the lowest point on Earth, the hot, sulfur-pungent air hangs heavy, and a haze often shimmers over the water. You can float, but you cannot sink, in the warm, salty water.

Once upon a time, Ein Bokek comprised a handful of hotels, each with a small "spa," with a pebbly beach out front. Today, it's a collection of large and luxurious hotels with curvy pools and grassy outdoor areas; each has a rooftop solarium and a state-of-the-art spa equipped to provide beauty and health treatments, and some have private beaches. Each hotel has a decent restaurant. There are no full-service restaurants outside the hotels, although a few casual eating places are set along the beach and in the two shopping centers. The central cluster of hotels is linked by a promenade to two hotels at the very southern end of the area.

GETTING HERE AND AROUND

To drive to Ein Bokek from Jerusalem, stay left, on Route 1, which is marked JERICHO–DEAD SEA. Continue 30 km (18 mi) to Route 90; at the Dead Sea, bear right (due south) and follow Route 90 along the coast, passing Qumran, Ein Gedi, and Masada, until you reach Ein Bokek. (Eilat is another 177 km, or 111 mi, south on Route 90, Arava Road.) The trip to Ein Bokek takes about an hour and a half.

EXPLORING

Going to the beach and the spas occupies time here, but you may want to explore other places nearby. Ein Bokek is a 30-minute drive south from **Masada,** a spectacular archaeological site in the desert that should not be missed, and a 45-minute drive from the nature reserve at **Ein Gedi**. You also can enjoy Jeep trips through the lunarlike landscape east of the hotel area and explore interesting local sights, such as the nearby **Flour Cave** (from which you emerge dusted with white powder) with a driver-guide arranged through your hotel concierge or through a tour company.

In Ein Bokek, **Yoel Tours** (⊠*Irit 13, Arad* ☎*08/995–4791* ✐*yoeltours@ walla.co.il*) offers tours to Masada (NIS 160), to Ein Gedi (NIS 140), and to the Bedouin market in Beersheva, followed by a cup of coffee with a Bedouin family (NIS 210). Yoel also offers a one-day trip (on Tuesday, priced NIS 290) to Eilat, which includes the Underwater Observatory and a swim in the Red Sea; a yacht trip and snorkeling are optional. If you'd like to see the famed Mountain of Sodom, where Lot's wife looked back, Yoel's half-day trip there includes a stop at the Flour Cave, for NIS 110. Desert agriculture tours are also available.

WHERE TO EAT

$$
AMERICAN

✕**Tapuah Sodom.** The name means "apple of Sodom," and the sign outside is only in Hebrew, but this place can't be missed as it's beside a shopping center and is usually quite crowded. Glass-enclosed, with a view of the public beach outside, it's a favorite wayfarer's stop, not a place for intimate, quiet conversation. You can stoke up on large portions of braised chicken, steak, pasta, fish, fresh salads, and sandwiches, plus beer and wine. It's open daily 7 AM to 10 PM, and if you're going to the beach, you can change into your bathing suit downstairs. ⊠*Next to shopping center* ☎*08/995–6128* ✐*Reservations not accepted* ▭*AE, DC, MC.*

WHERE TO STAY

Some of Ein Bokek's hotels are more lavish than others, but you can always check out the restaurants and spas at different establishments. If you want to make the pre-sunrise climb up the Snake Path at Masada, the budget Masada Guest House is an option.

3

$$ **Crowne Plaza.** Built in 1997, this 12-floor hotel is not as lavish as many of its neighbors, though its spa facilities are first-rate and it's right on the beach. The Sato Bistro ($$$$), a restaurant serving Asian fusion cuisine, is a treat in an area with a dearth of good eateries, and there's also a sushi bar. A third of the rooms have direct panoramic views of the Dead Sea, while the others have balconies from which you can view the sea (balcony furniture is available on request). Carpets, curtains, and bedspreads please the eye with their taupe-and-navy color scheme. The pool has a central island reached by a bridge, and one section is marked off for swimming laps. **Pros:** private beach; children's pool, activities, and entertainment. **Cons:** sometimes overrun by conventions; main dining room can be crowded and noisy, especially on weekends. *M. P. Dead Sea, 86930* *08/659–1919* *www.crowneplaza.com* *304 rooms, 15 suites* *In-room: safe. In-hotel: 2 restaurants, room service, bar, pools, gym, spa, beachfront, children's programs (ages 3–10), laundry service, no-smoking rooms, Wi-Fi* *AE, DC, MC, V* *CP.*

$$$ **Daniel Dead Sea.** The Daniel, formerly the Golden Tulip Privilege and now owned by the Tamares Hotel group, features two terraced wings, arched windows, a tower, and an undulating front wall that swirls around a huge flower-shape pool. The public rooms are on the plain side, but the guest accommodations are well appointed, most with a sofa that opens into an additional bed. The dining room serves several styles of cuisine each evening. There's a shuttle to the beach. Stay on the new Club Floor if you can. **Pros:** 8-lane bowling alley; excellent Shizen spa with 20 treatment rooms. **Cons:** some of the decor is drab; pool deck isn't as clean as it could be. *M. P. Dead Sea, 86930* *08/668–9999* *08/668–9900* *www.tamareshotels.co.il/e/daniel_dead_sea* *302 rooms, 12 suites* *In-room: safe. In-hotel: restaurant, room service, bar, tennis court, pool, gym, spa, children's programs (ages 3–10), Internet terminal, no-smoking rooms* *AE, DC, MC, V* *CP.*

$$ **Golden Tulip Club.** You might consider bringing the whole family to this all-inclusive property, formerly the Nirvana, where guests enjoy four meals daily (the last one being a midnight supper), and kids can have popsicles 24/7. The hotel is at the southern end of the promenade, and its nicest "deluxe" section was added in 1999. Huge windows in the reception lobby look out on the dolphin-shaped pool and the Lagoon with umbrellas in the water. Hues of soft green, sunny yellow, and tobacco decorate the rooms—request one with a balcony. Suites have hot tubs on the balcony. **Pros:** the only all-inclusive hotel at the

Dead Sea; good kids' programming. **Cons:** rooms not well appointed; the beach doesn't have its own natural black mud vats, like some other hotels. ⌂ *M. P. Dead Sea, 84960* ☎ *08/668–9444* 📠 *08/668–9400* ⊕ *www.fattal.co.il* ↪ *388 rooms, 12 suites* ☖ *In-room: safe, refrigerator, Internet. In-hotel: restaurant, bar, pool, spa, beachfront, children's programs, no-smoking rooms* ☰ *AE, DC, MC, V* ⎟○⎟ *FAP.*

$ ⎕ **Hod Hamidbar.** A distinctive feature of this homey, 13-floor hotel is
★ the private beach, reached via a short walkway lined with 10-foot-high Roman-style pillars. Guest rooms are not especially large, but they are handsomely furnished in blond wood with taupe and gray carpets and curtains; request a sea view. The contemporary lobby, in shades of sand with red stone, gives way to a pillared terrace. The dining room has a view of the Dead Sea. **Pros:** close and convenient beach access; consistently cheaper than other Ein Bokek hotels. **Cons:** pools and spa close early in the evening; breakfast not as extensive as at other hotels here. ⌂ *M. P. Dead Sea, 86930* ☎ *08/668–8222* 📠 *08/658–4606* ⊕ *www. hodhotel.co.il* ↪ *203 rooms* ☖ *In-room: safe, refrigerator. In-hotel: restaurant, room service, bar, pools, spa, beachfront, laundry service, Internet terminal, no-smoking rooms* ☰ *AE, DC, MC, V* ⎟○⎟ *CP.*

$$$ ⎕ **Isrotel Dead Sea.** Bright white both inside and out, the recently refurbished, terraced, nine-story Isrotel is across the road from the beach. Two 6-foot-high silver urns furnish the lofty lobby, and glass elevators add to the airy feel. Each room has a balcony; suites have balconies with whirlpool baths. The wooden wall at the entrance to the dining room is carved in a distinctive bas-relief with date palms, fish, flowers, and fruit. The gracious, ultra-equipped spa (small fee for guests) features hydrotherapy for two with an underwater aromatic-oil massage, and two sulfur pools. The Dead Sea–water pool starts inside the hotel and ends outside. A motorized trolley transports guests to the private beach. **Pros:** indoor and outdoor Dead Sea–water pool; convenient desert tourism information center. **Cons:** one Internet kiosk, for which you pre-pay; in summer overrun with kids. ⌂ *M. P. Dead Sea, 86980* ☎ *08/668–9666* 📠 *08/652–0301* ⊕ *www.isrotel.co.il* ↪ *298 rooms, 18 suites* ☖ *In-room: safe, refrigerator. In-hotel: restaurant, room service, bar, pools, spa, children's programs (ages 3–10), Internet terminal, no-smoking rooms* ☰ *AE, DC, MC, V* ⎟○⎟ *CP.*

$ ⎕ **Le Meridien.** Managed by the Fattal local hotel chain, Le Meridien
★ stands out for its stunning parquet-floor lobby and other inviting public spaces filled with paintings and sculptures by Israeli artists. The hotel is set against a backdrop of small palm trees and gurgling waterfalls. Treatments in the sparkling-white spa include the use of therapeutic mud; the medical center offers services such as sports medicine, post-surgery recovery, and alternative medical treatments. The comfortable rooms, all of which face the water, are decorated in shades of calm brown. Puffy white bedcovers are a pleasant touch. A shuttle zips guests to the hotel's private beach. **Pros:** the largest outdoor freshwater pools in Ein Bokek; the only squash court in the area. **Cons:** very crowded Fridays and Saturdays; occasional rude service at the front desk. ⌂ *M. P. Dead Sea, 86980* ☎ *08/659–1234* 📠 *08/659–1235* ⊕ *www.fattal.co.il* ↪ *509 rooms, 68 suites* ☖ *In-room: Internet, Wi-Fi (some). In-hotel:*

A DRIVE ON THE ARAVA ROAD

The Arava Road (Route 90) traverses the Arava Valley south from Ein Bokek to Eilat 177 km (111 mi) and parallels the Jordanian border, almost touching it at some points. To the east you'll see the spiky, red-brown mountains of Moab, in Jordan. The road follows an ancient route mentioned in biblical descriptions of the journeys of the Children of Israel.

The Arava (meaning "wilderness") is part of the Great Rift Valley, the deep fissure in the earth stretching from Turkey to East Africa, the result of an ancient shift of land masses. Just south of Ein Bokek, you'll pass signs for the settlements **Neot HaKikar** and **Ein Tamar** (home to many craftspeople), whose date palms draw water from underground springs rather than irrigation.

With the Edom Mountains rising in the east, the road continues along the southern Dead Sea Valley. You'll cross one of the largest dry riverbeds in the Negev, Nahal Zin.

A delicious place to break the monotony of the Arava Road is **Café Cartouche**, on Kibbutz Yahel, 60 km (37 mi) north of Eilat. ☎08/635–7019 ☉ Wed. and Thurs. 5–11, Fri. 9–2, Sat. 10–3.

restaurant, room service, bar, tennis courts, pool, gym, spa, children's programs (ages 3–10), laundry service, Internet terminal, no-smoking rooms ▭AE, DC, MC, V ⏐⃝⏐CP.

$ ⬚**Lot.** The exterior of this smaller, unpretentious property does not impress, but inside, the welcome is warm. Europeans are drawn to the cheerful and friendly atmosphere of this seven-story hotel where each of the rooms—in sprightly combinations of marine blue, bright yellow, and dark red—has a balcony with views either of the mountains or the sea. Unwinding is easy at the private beach, in the rooftop solarium, or on the terrace overlooking a colorful garden. The fancy hotels up the road are all about glitz—the Lot offers a rewarding stay that won't break the bank. It tends to attract an older, more European crowd than its neighbors. **Pros:** attractive beach with gazebo peninsula; 2 sulfur pools. **Cons:** rooms are small and a little faded; expensive Internet access. ⬚*M. P. Dead Sea, 86930* ☎08/668–9200 🖷08/658–4623 ⊕*www.lothotel.co.il* ⟿*199 rooms* ⬚*In-room: safe, refrigerator, Internet. In-hotel: restaurant, room service, bar, pool, gym, spa, beachfront, laundry facilities* ▭AE, DC, MC, V ⏐⃝⏐CP.

¢ ⬚**Masada Guest House.** Here's an option for those combining a trip to Ein Bokek with Masada, 15 km (9 mi) to the north. This moderately priced guesthouse at the foot of Masada is the most convenient lodging for those intent on watching the spectacular sunrise over the Dead Sea and mountains of Moab. It has single, double, and family rooms, each with private bath. **Pros:** convenient to Masada; swimming pool; air-conditioning. **Cons:** can be noisy with rowdy teenage groups; no evening entertainment. ⊠*Off Rte. 90 at the entrance to Masada* ☎08/995–3222 ⊕*www.youth-hostels.org.il* ⟿*88 rooms* ⬚*In-room: no phone, refrigerator. In-hotel: pool* ▭AE, DC, MC, V ⏐⃝⏐BP.

$$$$ ⬚**Royal.** A crown topped with the letter R sits perched atop this 18-story tower, the largest and newest (2001) of the Dead Sea hotels. The hotel

Continued on page 199

DID YOU KNOW?

The Dead Sea's salt and concentration of thick, black mud enriched with organic elements are sought after for their curative properties and beautifying elements.

THE DEAD SEA
A NATURAL WONDER

The Dead Sea at Ein Bokek

Taking a dip in the Dead Sea is a must-do experience in Israel. This unique body of water—the shores of which are the lowest point of dry land on Earth—was a resort for King Herod in the 1st century BC and the site of Queen Cleopatra's cosmetics empire.

It remains to be seen if the Dead Sea will be around centuries from now. A combination of less rainfall in the region and human interaction has caused its waters to recede at a rapid rate, threatening the area's ecology.

Israel started developing the Dead Sea as a tourist destination in the 1950s. Today, more than a dozen hotels in the area take advantage of the Dead Sea's mineral-rich mud and waters, known for nourishing, cleansing, and stimulating the skin, as well as for therapeutic benefits for treating medical conditions.

Spas offer an array of services: body wraps, mud massages, facial peels, and the like, in addition to general amenities such as Jacuzzis and saunas.

It's an easy day-trip from Jerusalem, but spending the night allows you to watch the sun rise over Jordan. After a day on the beach, you can head back to your hotel for lunch and a spa treatment, followed by a Turkish bath or a dip in a warm sulfur pool.

by Sarah Bronson

THE DEAD SEA: PAST AND PRESENT

The stark, beautiful shores of the Dead Sea are literally the lowest point of dry land on Earth, at 1,373 feet below sea level. It's called the Dead Sea because virtually nothing can live in it; with a salt concentration of about 32%, the water is almost 9 times saltier than the ocean.

WHY IS THE DEAD SEA SALTY?

The Dead Sea is salty because water flows in from the Jordan River and other sources, but has no way of flowing out. Evaporation leaves a massive amount of salt behind. Beaches here aren't sandy—they're caked with hardened crystals of salt. The consistently dry air surrounding the Dead Sea has a high oxygen content, low pollution and allergen levels, and weakened ultraviolet radiation.

HOW DID THE DEAD SEA FORM?

The high mesas of the Judean desert nearby, also below sea level, bear testimony to the millions of years of geological changes that created this unique place. The Dead Sea was formed by fault lines shifting in the Earth's crust, a process that began about 15 million years ago and created the basin where the Dead Sea is now located.

WHY IS THE DEAD SEA IN DANGER?

Since it receives a maximum of 2 to 4 inches of rain per year, the Dead Sea's main source of water is the Jordan River, and by extension, the Sea of Galilee to the north.

The Dead Sea's water levels have fluctuated greatly over the last 10,000 years. However, its shores have significantly receded in the past few decades—about one meter per year—due to the lack of rainfall in Israel's north and human activity. Israel, Jordan, and Syria all divert water away from the Jordan River for drinking and irrigation. Less than 7% of the river's original flow reaches the Dead Sea.

WHAT'S BEING DONE TO STOP IT?

Israel and Jordan have been in talks for years to seek a solution to this pressing environmental problem. Currently the countries hope to build a canal to pump water into the Dead Sea from the Red Sea. Environmentalists are concerned about the possible negative impacts of such a canal both on the Dead Sea and on the Arava region. In any case, no firm plans to move forward have been announced.

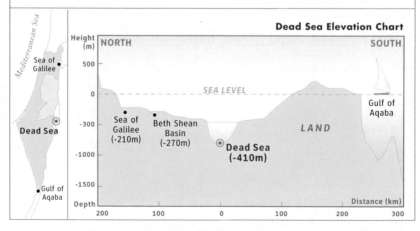

EXPERIENCING THE SPAS AND BEACHES

Before booking at a hotel or spa, carefully check what services it offers and whether any particular areas are closed for the season or for repairs. Quality of treatments at the spas can vary widely.

ENJOYING THE WATER

When entering the Dead Sea, wear flip flops or waterproof sandals, as the sea's floor has a rough, rock salt surface. Before getting in the water, check for the nearest source of fresh water, in case you get painful salt water in your eyes. (Note: The Ein Gedi spa provides freshwater spigots in the Dead Sea itself, floating on buoys). Lean back slowly and rise gently, and be careful not to splash water toward yourself or others.

Small wounds such as scratches will burn for a few moments, but avoid getting salt water in any deep or open wounds. Don't stay in the Dead Sea (or in the spas' warmed mineral pools) for more than 15 minutes at a time, and drink plenty of water afterward.

GETTING MUDDY

It can be surprisingly difficult to find free Dead Sea mud. Some hotels pump the mud to their grounds, or provide vats of it at their beach. You can also purchase

(top) People sunbathing on the shores of the Dead Sea. (bottom) Covered in Dead Sea mud

more refined mud in packets and apply it at the beach for your photos.

Bring a friend to the mudbaths so that you can help each other slather the dark goo on every inch of exposed skin. Cake it on evenly but thinly, so that it will dry within 15-20 minutes in the sun. You might need a third person to take pictures, unless you want mud on your camera!

Dead Sea products, including salts and mud, make great gifts and are available at all the spas, but note that similar items may be available at your local health food store at home.

PLANNING YOUR VISIT

(left) Dead Sea. (right) Artist creating salt sculptures in the Dead Sea

GETTING HERE FROM JERUSALEM

By car: Take Route 1 east past Jericho to Route 90 south along the Dead Sea shore. Continue about an hour to reach Ein Gedi or Ein Bokek. Total driving time is about 90 minutes.

By public transportation: Egged Bus Lines run buses from Jerusalem's Central Bus Station along the Dead Sea shore every hour or so Sun.–Thurs. from 8:45 AM to 1 PM, and return buses from 8:30 AM – 7:50 PM. Just tell your driver which hotel or spa you're visiting. On Fridays bus service is more limited. To check schedule updates, call Egged at 03/694-8888.

By guided tour: Hotel staff can help you join a group tour to the Dead Sea. Or contact United Tours (02/625-2187 www.unitedtours.co.il) for daily, English-language trips from Jerusalem.

WHEN TO GO

In fall (Oct.-Nov.) and spring (Mar.–May) it's almost always sunny and pleasant. In winter temperatures are 68°–74°, and there's consistent sun. In summer it's usually an uncomfortable 90°–102° and scorching.

BEACH AND SPA TIPS

■ The Dead Sea has several public beaches, sometimes with a token fee for use of the showers or for lawn chair rental. "Private" hotel beaches are, by law, open to anyone, though only hotel guests will receive amenities.

■ Inquire carefully when booking your hotel if the cost of meals is included. There are few restaurants in the area.

■ For non-guests, most hotels offer day rates of about NIS 80 to use their spas, pools, saunas, and fitness rooms. Extra charges apply for meals, facials, and massages.

WHAT ELSE IS NEARBY

■ Combine a visit to Ein Bokek with visits to Ein Gedi and Qumran, which also have Dead Sea beaches and nature reserves.

■ To arrange a Dead Sea cruise, desert hike, overnight camping trip, or group event, call the Dead Sea Tourist Information Center at 08/997-5010.

■ Ask your concierge about visiting the tiny town of Ein Tamar, just south of Ein Bokek, home to many artists and craftspeople.

has a spare, minimalist entrance, unlike the stunning indoor pool area where striped lounge chairs face windows that soar two floors high and overlook the sand-colored mountains. The pool, with hot tub, is immense. At the lavish spa with 52 treatment rooms, you can enjoy the fitness room and soak in individual sulfur and therapeutic baths. Peach walls in the guest rooms are set off by rust-colored curtains and bedcovers. Twenty-five rooms are wheelchair accessible. The beach is across the street. **Pros:** large and luxurious spa facilities; excellent buffet. **Cons:** because the hotel is perched on a steep hill, not ideal for senior citizens; some guests have complained that the plumbing is not sufficiently well maintained. ⌖ *M. P. Dead Sea, 86930* ☎*08/668–8555* 📠*08/668–8520* ➥*394 rooms, 26 suites* ♿*In-room: safe, refrigerator. In-hotel: 2 restaurants, room service, bar, pool, spa, children's programs (ages 3–10), laundry service, no-smoking rooms* ▭*AE, DC, MC, V* ⊠❙*CP.*

OUTDOOR ACTIVITIES AND SPAS

BEACHES

The Tamar Local Council has beautified the beaches of Ein Bokek. They're free to the public and are usually fairly crowded. Regrettably, there are no facilities for changing; the only option is to have a bite at the Tapuah Sodom restaurant and use its restrooms to change. A lifeguard is on duty year-round, and there's ample parking alongside the promenade. The only water sport in the Dead Sea is floating!

SPAS

★ Luxurious **spas** are a famous feature of Ein Bokek's hotels, but note that you must reserve treatments in advance and there's an extra charge. Make arrangements with your hotel upon arrival. You can certainly sample the sybaritic delights if you're in Ein Bokek only for a day; again, reserve treatments in advance. Many spas are operated under medical supervision; each has an indoor Dead Sea–water pool, a sauna, and a hot tub, and offers beauty and health treatments using curative substances from the Dead Sea. The mineral-rich mud works wonders on skin ailments. Sample prices for treatments are as follows: NIS 150 for a half-hour massage; NIS 50 for a sulfur bath; and NIS 200 for a 50-minute mud treatment. Hotel guests pay lower fees. Other facilities and services include fitness rooms, private solariums, and cosmetic treatments. Some hotels offer spa packages.

SHOPPING

★ Several companies manufacture excellent **Dead Sea bath and beauty products** made from mud, salts, and minerals; the actual mud is sold in squishy, leak-proof packages. Ahava and Jericho are popular brands whose products are sold at Tapuah Sodom restaurant, next door at the shopping center, and at the shops in most hotels.

Diamonds and jewelery are sold at the **Dead Sea Diamond Center** (☎*08/ 995–8777 or 057/755–4004*). Call for a shuttle to pick you up. The center is closed Thursday and Sunday.

Miri (⊠*Le Meridien* ☎*08/995–6543* ⊕*www.artists2.com*) creates unusual, handmade, soft-body dolls, about 2 feet high, as well as droll-face puppets.

Petra Kanion shopping center (⊠*near Le Meridien*) contains a mini-market that sells wine and liquor, a currency exchange kiosk, and two swimwear and resort wear boutiques.

WEST OF JERUSALEM

The rugged Judean Hills tumble down to the west, eventually easing into the gentler terrain of the Shefelah lowlands. This is a region of forests, springs, monasteries, battlefields, national parks, and archaeological treasures. It's the fastest-growing wine-producing area in the country, encompassing more than two dozen vineyards. A number of local farmers also produce goat and sheep cheese. For Jerusalemites, the Judean Hills are a place to hike and picnic. For visitors, this sparsely populated region with its ancient terraced hills evokes the landscape of the Bible with none of the distractions of a big city.

LATRUN

25 km (16 mi) west of Jerusalem on Rte. 1.

Latrun is the ridge that projects into and dominates the western side of the Ayalon Valley. A natural passage between the coastal plain and the Judean Hills, the valley has been a battleground throughout history, from the conquests of the biblical Israelite leader Joshua in the 13th century BC, through the Hasmonean campaigns of the 2nd century BC, to the bloody defeat of the newly-established Israel Defense Force by Jordan's Arab Legion in 1948. Today, the Trappist monastery is known for its olive oil and wine, and Mini-Israel is a favorite for children of all ages.

GETTING HERE AND AROUND

Coming from Jerusalem on Route 1, exit onto Route 3 (the Modi'in and Ashkelon–Beersheba road), about 5 km (3 mi) west of the Sha'ar Hagai gas station. At the T-junction, turn left for the Trappist Abbey of Latrun, the Latrun Armored Corps Museum, and Mini Israel.

EXPLORING

The 19th-century **Trappist Abbey of Latrun** belongs to the Trappist Order; the monks have also been producing wine here since the 1890s. The interior of the church is an odd mix of round neo-Byzantine arches and apses and the soaring ceiling that seems Gothic in inspiration. Survivors of the Cistercian Order suppressed in the French Revolution, the Trappists keep a vow of silence. But you needn't worry about making a faux pas by talking; the staff selling Domaine de Latroun wines and olive oil in the shop will address you—in English, French, Hebrew, or Arabic. You can explore the gardens here; the setting in the foothills is lovely. ⊠*Rte. 3 south, 2 km (1.5 mi) off Rte. 1* ☎*08/922–0065* ⛲*Free* ⊙ *Church: Apr.–Sept., Mon.–Sat. 8:30–noon and 3:30–5; Oct.–Mar., Mon.–Sat. 8:30–11 and 2:30–4. Wine shop: Apr.–Sept., Mon.–Sat. 8:30–6; Oct.–Mar., Mon.–Sat. 8:30–5:30.*

Ⓒ While the **Latrun Armored Corps Museum** is a memorial for many Israelis who have fought in the country's tanks, Latrun has a much longer history. The name "Latrun" is thought to derive from "La Toron

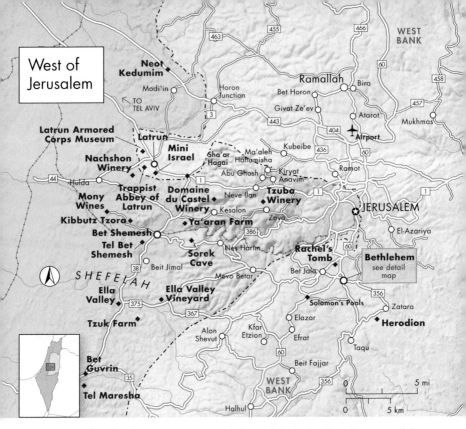

West of
Jerusalem

de Chevaliers" (the Tower of the Knights), the French name of the
Crusader castle that occupied the crest of the hill in the 12th century.
Eight centuries later, the British erected the concrete fortress that today
holds the museum. There are more than 100 assorted antique tanks
on which children love to climb. The museum has a decent restaurant,
offering salads and hot meals. ⊠*Rte. 3, 1 km (½ mi) south of Rte. 1*
☎*08/925–5268* ⊕*www.arcm-latrun.org.il* ✉*NIS 30* ☉*Sun.–Thurs.
8:30–4:30, Fri. 8:30 AM–12:30 PM, Sat. 9–4.*

☺ **Mini Israel,** one of the most popular attractions in Israel, is designed
in the shape of the Star of David. The world's largest miniature city
spreads over 13 acres and contains over 350 scale models of the most
important historical, national, religious, and natural sites in the country. Worth an hour's visit, the site is especially fun for children. The
thousands of miniature "residents" have been meticulously created to
present not just the physical, but also the cultural, religious, and social
aspects of contemporary Israel. A walk through the park allows visitors
to see and hear the people of different faiths and cultures that make
up the country's human landscape. ⊠*Rte. 424, 1 km (½ mi) south of
Latrun* ☎*08/922–2444* ⊕*www.minisrael.co.il* ✉*NIS 69, audio guide
NIS 10* ☉*Nov.–Mar., Sun.–Thurs. and Sat. 10–6, Fri. 10–2; Apr.–Oct.,
Sun.–Thurs. and Sat. 10–8, Fri. 10–2.*

OFF THE
BEATEN
PATH

Neot Kedumim *(Oasis of Antiquity).* About 20 km (12 mi) north of Latrun is this 625-acre "Biblical landscape reserve," where the ancient landscape has been re-created. The goal is to help you understand and visualize how the Bible uses the imagery of the native flora to convey its messages and values. Ancient terraces and wine and oil presses were excavated and restored, thousands of trees and shrubs were planted, and pools and cisterns were dug. A network of roads and walking paths (most of them paved and wheelchair accessible) allows for a leisurely exploration of the site. Take one of the self-guided tours (brochures and maps in English provided) or inquire ahead of time about guided tours in English. Allow two hours minimum for the visit. ✉ *Rte. 443, 40 km (25 mi) west of Jerusalem* ☎ 08/977–0777 💲 *NIS 25* ☼ *Sun.–Thurs. 8:30–4, Fri. 8:30–1.*

WHERE TO EAT

On the way to Latrun and its sights, you might stop at the Arab village of Abu Ghosh; Route 425, off Route 1, takes you there. A number of excellent, popular Middle Eastern restaurants are on its main street.

$$

AMERICAN

✕**Elvis Inn.** At the far western end of the village of Abu Ghosh (11 km [7 mi] east of Latrun and 21 km [13 mi] west of Jerusalem, off Route 1) is this American-style diner and gas station with the largest collection of Elvis memorabilia this side of Graceland. This is probably the only Elvis souvenir shop in the world where you can get shawarma. Don't worry, there's also traditional roadhouse fare that the King would love. Serious fans should come on his birthday (August 16) or his yahrzeit (anniversary of his death, January 8), when Israel's Elvis impersonators come to get all shook up. ✉ *Abu Ghosh village* ☎ 02/534–1275 ▭ *No credit cards.*

$$

FAST FOOD

✕**Nof Latrun.** At this self-service cafeteria with indoor seating and out-door picnic tables, indulge in one of the fish or meat dishes or par-take of the cold salad bar. It's a good place to try the staple Israeli food, "schnitzel and chips" (breaded and fried chicken or turkey breast served with french fries). Sandwiches and ice cream are available at the take-out window. The cafeteria is across the parking lot from the Latrun Armored Corps Museum. ✉ *Rte. 3, 1 km (½ mi) south of Rte. 1* ☎ 08/920–1670 ▭ *AE, MC, V* ☼ *No dinner Fri. Closed Sat.*

SOREK CAVE

25 km (17 mi) southwest of Jerusalem on Rtes. 386 and 3866, 12 km (7½ mi) east of Bet Shemesh on Rte. 3855.

GETTING HERE AND AROUND

Follow Route 1 west from Jerusalem, then head south on Route 38 towards Bet Shemesh, east on Route 3855, and northwest on Route 3866. The Sorek Cave is on your left. It's an 8-km (5-mi) hike in the mountains from the Bet Shemesh train station.

EXPLORING

★ The **Sorek Cave,** within the Avshalom Nature Reserve, is unique in that it contains every known type of stalactite and stalagmite formation. It was discovered in 1968 when a routine blast in the nearby Har-Tuv quarry tore away the rock face, revealing a subterranean wonderland.

Colored lights are used to highlight the natural whites and honey browns of the stones. Local guides have given the stalactite forms nicknames like "macaroni," "curtains," and "sombreros." In a series of "interfaith" images, some find rocky evocations of Moses, the Madonna and Child, Buddha, and the Ayatollah Khomeini. Photography is allowed only on Friday morning, when there are no guided tours. Despite the almost 100% humidity, the temperature in the cave is comfortable year-round.

A set of steps winds down to the cave entrance—visitors with mobility concerns should bear in mind the climb back to the parking lot. Local guides take groups as they arrive into the cave every 15 minutes for a 30-minute tour (English tours on request). An English-language video explains how the cave was formed. ✉*Rte. 3866* ☎*02/991–1117* ⊕*www.parks.org.il* 💰*NIS 23* ◷*Apr.–Sept., Sat.–Thurs. 8–5, Fri. 8–3; Oct.–Mar., Sat.–Thurs. 8–4, Fri. 8–1; last entry 1¼ hr before closing.*

WHERE TO STAY

There are some very good kibbutz guesthouses in wooded enclaves of the Judean Hills, a 15- to 20-minute drive west of Jerusalem. All have commanding hilltop views, quiet surroundings, very comfortable if not luxurious accommodations, and good swimming pools.

$ 🏨**Hotel Tzuba.** Fun family activities are the specialty of this kibbutz
🐣 hotel. On the premises are a children's entertainment park called Keftziba (one of the country's most popular), tennis courts, a swimming pool, and a sports center. Hikes to historical sites such as the Cave of John the Baptist, which he and his followers may have used for their ritual water immersions, are popular. Suites can accommodate up to five people and include a separate bedroom, a kitchen, and a porch with a magnificent view of the Judean Hills. Arrive on Friday to sample cheeses, fish, and salads as part of the hotel's unique Friday brunch. **Pros:** great place for young children; interesting tours of the area, panoramic views. **Cons:** no evening entertainment; meals eaten in the kibbutz dining hall. ✉*Rte. 39, 12 km (7½ mi) west of Jerusalem* ☎*02/534–7090* ⊕*www. belmont.co.il* 🛏*64 suites* ⚒*In-hotel: tennis courts, pool, gym* ⊟*AE, DC, MC, V* 🍴*BP.*

$ 🏨**Ma'aleh Hahamisha.** This large guesthouse, spread over beautiful landscaped gardens, has a health club, including an indoor heated pool, gym, saunas, and whirlpool baths. Some rooms lead to a garden patio. **Pros:** panoramic views; indoor pool; park-like setting. **Cons:** no evening entertainment; mountaintop location gets chilly. ✉*Rte. 1, 14 km (9 mi) west of Jerusalem* ☎*02/533–1331* ⊕*www.inisrael.com/maale5* 🛏*239 rooms* ⚒*In-hotel: pool, gym* ⊟*AE, DC, MC, V* 🍴*BP.*

¢ 🏨**Neve Ilan.** A cut above its neighbors, this hotel has larger and better-furnished rooms. Suites with their own whirlpool baths are available. The pool is covered year-round and heated in winter, and there is a well-equipped exercise room. **Pros:** panoramic views; beautiful swimming pool. **Cons:** no evening entertainment, nearby construction. ✉ *North of Rte. 1, 15 km (10 mi) west of Jerusalem* ☎ *02/533–9339* ⊕ *www. shalomplaza.co.il* ⤶ *160 rooms* ♿ *In-hotel: pool, gym* ⊟ *AE, DC, MC, V* ⏝◎*IBP.*

SHOPPING

The small but popular **Ya'aran Farm,** run by Yavshi and Bar Ya'aran, produces more than 10 types of hard and soft goat cheese. It's best to come on a Saturday, when the couple also bake their own bread. If Bar isn't too busy, she'll explain to you her vision of living off the land, using only rainwater, and solar power and windmills for energy. The couple was hired in 1995 by the Jewish National Fund as firewatchers for the newly replanted forest. Since grazing animals keep down the brush, the Bars began herding goats. ✉ *On Rte. 3866, near Sorek Cave* ☎ *02/999–7811* ⊙ *Call for hrs.*

BET SHEMESH

12 km (7½ mi) west of Sorek Cave on Rtes. 3855 and 38, 35 km (22 mi) west of Jerusalem.

The modern town of Bet Shemesh, a thriving bedroom suburb serving both Jerusalem and Tel Aviv, takes its name from its ancient predecessor, now entombed by the tell on a rise on Route 38, 2 km (1 mi) south of the main entrance.

This is Samson country. Samson, one of the judges of Old Testament Israel, is better known for his physical prowess and lust for Philistine women than for his shining spiritual qualities, but it was here, "between Zorah and Eshta'ol," that "the Spirit of the Lord began to stir him" (Judges 13). Today, Eshta'ol is a *moshav* (a cooperative settlement composed of individual farms) a few minutes' drive north, and Tzora (Zorah) is the wine-producing kibbutz immediately to the west.

GETTING HERE AND AROUND

Follow Route 1 west from Jerusalem, then head south on Route 38 to Bet Shemesh. Israel Railways provides regular train service between Jerusalem and Tel Aviv via Bet Shemesh on an hourly basis from 6 AM to 8 PM.

EXPLORING

The low-profile **Tel Bet Shemesh** has fine views of the fields of Nahal Sorek, where Samson dallied with Delilah (Judges 16). When the Philistines captured the Israelite Ark of the Covenant in battle (11th century BC), they found that their prize brought divine retribution with it, destroying their idol Dagon and afflicting their bodies with tumors and their cities with rats (I Samuel 5). In consternation and awe, the Philistines rid themselves of the jinxed ark by sending it back to the Israelites at Bet Shemesh. This is a nice spot to pull out the Bible, but the stone ruins of the tell are hard to interpret without an archaeologist on hand. ✉ *Rte. 38, 2 km (1 mi) from Tzora turnoff.*

WINERIES IN THE JUDEAN HILLS

For years good Israeli wine was an oxymoron, but in the past few decades a viniculture revolution has greatly improved the quality of wines. The Judean Hills has been a relatively undeveloped wine region, but interest in it has grown. The area is now home to more than two dozen vineyards, the majority of them close to Route 38, north and south of Bet Shemesh.

Since most vineyards are "boutique"—producing fewer than 100,000 bottles per year—few have visitor centers that encourage drop-in visits and offer regularly scheduled tours. Call ahead. The wineries are convenient to Tel Aviv (40 minutes away) as well as Jerusalem.

Domaine du Castel, one of Israel's best wineries, produces French-style vintages. The smaller winery is open by appointment to groups no larger than six people. ⊠ *Moshav Ramat Raziel* ☎ *02/534-2249* ⊕ *www.castel.co.il.*

The largest wine producer in the area is **Ella Valley Vineyards**, a "stone's throw" away from where David slew Goliath with his lethal sling (I Samuel 17). Although this young winery produced its first harvest in 2002, ancient winepresses from the Byzantine Period attest to the region's historical importance for the production of wine. It offers a number of outstanding, top-quality wines including Cabernet, Merlot, Chardonnay, and Muscat. ⊠ *Rte. 38, 10 km (6½ mi) south of Bet Shemesh* ☎ *02/999-4885* ⊕ *www.ellavalley.com* ☉ *Sun.–Thurs. 8:30–4:30, Fri. 8:30–12:30; by appointment only.*

One of the first vineyards in the area, **Kibbutz Tzora** produces some excellent red wines. Be sure to taste some of the homemade olive oil, honey, and goat and sheep cheeses. Breakfast and a light lunch are served in the garden. You can also buy a picnic basket—complete with tablecloth, plates, wine, cheeses, and salad—and explore picnic spots in the area. ⊠ *Rte. 38, 300 yds south of Bet Shemesh* ☎ *02/990-8261* ⊕ *www.tzorawines.com* ☉ *Sun.–Thurs. 10–5, Fri. 10–2.*

Next to the Deir Raffat monastery is **Mony Wines**. The Arab Christian Artul family moved here to cultivate land leased from the adjacent Catholic monastery. Still a family-run business, the vineyard became kosher in 2004. The shop sells their wines, mostly reds, but also Chardonnay and Muscat, as well as olives and olive oil. ⊠ *Rte. 3856, 4 km (2½ mi) west of Kibbutz Tzora* ☎ *02/991-6629* ☉ *Daily 9:30–5:30.*

Close to Latrun, **Nachshon Winery** is run by a kibbutz that also produces very tasty hard and soft sheep's cheese. The shop sells red wine and close to a dozen different cheeses, including feta, haloumi, brie, and camembert. Drop in to the shop or call in advance to arrange a tour of the winery, vineyard, and ancient winepress. ⊠ *Kibbutz Nachshon, 2 km (1¼ mi) south of Latrun, off Rte. 3* ☎ *08/927-8641* ☉ *Sun.–Thurs. 9–4, Fri. 9–3, Sat. 10–5.*

Tzuba Vineyard, belongs to the kibbutz of the same name. In early 2008 the winery released its first wines from the 2005 vintage. The winery produces an excellent red dessert wine. ⊠ *Rte. 39, 12 km (7½ mi) west of Jerusalem* ☎ *02/534-7090* ☉ *Daily 9–4:30.*

Bet Guvrin and Tel Maresha national park preserves ancient caves used for storage, industry, and tombs.

ELLA VALLEY

10 km (6 mi) south of Bet Shemesh, 42 km (26 mi) west of Jerusalem.

The Ella Valley is one of those delightful places—not uncommon in Israel—where you can relate the scenery to a specific biblical text and confirm the maxim that once you've visited this country, you'll never read the Bible the same way again. Beyond the junction of Route 38 with Route 383, and up to the right above the pine-wood slopes, is a distinctively bald flattop hill, **Tel Azekah,** the site of an ancient Israelite town. The hills are especially delightful in March and April when the wildflowers are out.

In the Ella Valley, the road crosses a usually dry streambed; 200 yards beyond it is a place to pull off and park. If you have a Bible, open it to I Samuel 17 and read about the dramatic duel between Israelite shepherd David and the Philistine champion Goliath. The battle probably took place close to where you're standing. Skeptical? Review the following passage:

Now the Philistines gathered their armies for battle; and they were gathered at Socoh, which belongs to Judah [identified by a mound 800 yards east of the junction ahead of you], *and encamped between Socoh and Azekah* [your location] . . . *And Saul and the men of Israel were gathered, and encamped in the valley of Ella, and drew up in line of battle against the Philistines. And the Philistines stood on the mountain on the one side, and Israel stood on the mountain on the other side, with a valley between them.*

Look east up the valley (across the road) to the mountains of Judah in the distance and the road from Bethlehem—the same road by which David reached the battlefield. The white northern ridge, a spur of the mountains of Judah, may have been the camp of the Israelite army. The southern ridge (where the gas station is today)—including Tel Socoh, where the Philistines gathered—ascends from the Philistine territory to the west. The creek is the only one in the valley: "And David . . . chose five smooth stones from the brook . . . ; his sling was in his hand, and he drew near to the Philistine." The rest, as they say, is history: Goliath was slain, the Philistines were routed, and David went on to become the darling of the nation and eventually its king.

EXPLORING

★ The **Tzuk Farm,** nestled in the hills south of the Ella Valley, offers a rich culinary experience. Two brothers have created a tranquil farm that produces fabulous goat cheese, wine, olives, olive oil, and pomegranates. Reservations are essential for meals, which include a platter of cheeses, fresh bread, and seasonal salads. Be sure to try the fennel root salad sprinkled with pomegranates, the beetroot in sour *labaneh,* and the spicy roasted eggplant. Picnic baskets with wine, tablecloth, cheese, and salads are also available. ✉ *Take eastern turn off south of Ella Valley Junction (Rtes. 38 and 375), 2 km (1 mi) down dirt road* ☎ *054/523–9117* ⊘ *Call for hrs.*

BET GUVRIN

21 km (13 mi) south of Bet Shemesh, 52 km (33 mi) southwest of Jerusalem.

GETTING HERE AND AROUND

Follow Route 1 west from Jerusalem, then head south on Route 38 through Bet Shemesh until the end of the road. At Nehushga Junction turn west on Route 35.

EXPLORING

★ In the Second Temple Period millions of pilgrims ascended to Jerusalem to offer animal sacrifices—including cattle and birds. It was here, at **Bet Guvrin,** that doves were raised on a vast scale to supply the pilgrims' need. Unlike many ruins, this national park allows you to readily envision life 2,000 years ago.

Bet Guvrin is a wonderland, both under the ground and above it. The antiquities sprawl around the kibbutz of Bet Guvrin, just beyond the junction of Routes 38 and 35. These are bits and pieces of the 2nd- to 3rd-century AD Bet Guvrin, renamed (around the year 200) Eleuthropolis, "the city of free men." The amphitheater—an arena for Roman blood sports and even mock sea battles—is one of only a few discovered in Israel, and the only one visitors can enter (via the parking lot of the gas station). The ruins of a 12th-century church are virtually the only evidence of the Crusader town of Bethgibelin.

After entering the park, drive toward the flattop mound of ancient Maresha, known today as **Tel Maresha.** This was already an important city in the Israelite period (early 1st millennium BC), but it was during the Hellenistic period (4th–2nd centuries BC) that the endless complexes of chalk caves were excavated. Maresha was finally destroyed by the Parthians in 40 BC, and replaced by the nearby Roman city of Bet Guvrin. The view from the tell is worth the short climb.

Ancient Mareshans excavated thousands of underground chambers around the tell to extract soft chalk bricks, with which they built their homes aboveground. Residents then turned their "basement" quarries into industrial complexes, including water cisterns, olive oil presses, and **columbaria** (derived from the Latin word *columba,* meaning dove or pigeon). The birds were used in ritual sacrifice, and as food, producers of fertilizer, and message carriers. Visit here on a hot summer day and you'll appreciate the relatively cool temperature of the caves.

The most interesting and extensive cave system is just off the road on the opposite side of the tell (at a parking lot, the trail begins through the posts, and down to the left). It includes water cisterns, storerooms, and a restored ancient olive press. The excitement of exploration makes this site a must for kids (with close parental supervision, though the safety features are good), but the many steps are physically demanding.

The great "bell caves" of **Bet Guvrin** date from the Late Roman, Byzantine, and even Early Arab periods (2nd–7th century AD), when the locals created a quarry to extract lime for cement. At the top of each bell-shaped space is a hole through the 4-foot-thick stone crust of the ground. When the ancient diggers reached the soft chalk below, they began reaming out their quarry in the structurally secure bell shape, each bell eventually cutting into the one adjacent to it. Although not built to be inhabited, the caves may have been used as refuges by early Christians. In the North Cave, a cross high on the wall, at the same level as an Arabic inscription, suggests a degree of coexistence even after the Arab conquest of the area in AD 636.

After leaving this system, make sure to continue walking down the hill to visit the **Sidonian Burial Caves.** These magnificent 3rd- to 2nd-century BC tombs—adorned with colorful, restored frescoes and inscriptions—offer important archaeological evidence as to the nature of the town's ancient Phoenician colonists.

On a ridge to the north of Tel Maresha, look for a large **apse** standing in splendid isolation. Known as Santahanna in Arabic, it has been identified by scholars as a remnant of the Crusader Church of St. Anne. Other fascinating but undeveloped complexes of caves near the tell have dangerous pits and are off-limits to visitors. Keep to the marked sites only. The brochure at the entrance has a good map of the site. ✉ *Off Rte. 35, 21 km (13 mi) south of Bet Shemesh* ☎ *08/681–1020* ⊕ *www. parks.org.il* ✉ *NIS 23, includes entrance to Bet Guvrin* ☉ *Apr.–Sept., Sat.–Thurs. 8–5, Fri. 8–4; Oct.–Mar., Sat.–Thurs. 8–4, Fri. 8–3.*

EN
ROUTE
Instead of the Tel Aviv–Jerusalem expressway, an attractive alternative route back to Jerusalem is Route 375 through the Ella Valley, past Israel's main satellite communications receiver, and up through wooded hill country to Tzur Hadassah (look out for the rock-hewn Roman road on the right). Route 386 heads off to the left and runs north to

DIG AT BET GUVRIN

Archaeological Seminars, in Jerusalem, runs a program at Bet Guvrin called **Dig for a Day** (☎ 02/586–2011 ⊕ www.archesem.com ✉ US$30).

The three-hour activity includes supervised digging in a real excavation inside a cave, into which local inhabitants dumped earth and artifacts 21 centuries ago. Participants then sift the buckets of dirt they have hauled out of the cave, looking for finds. Some museum-quality artifacts of the 3rd–2nd centuries BC (Hellenistic Period)

have been uncovered here. (No, you can't take home what you find!)

The participants are then led on a fun 30-minute exploration through caves not yet open to the public. This involves some crawling, because some spaces are too tight or too low for walking upright. Those who prefer to pass on that experience can just wait for the last component—a short talk in the pottery shed about how clay vessels are reconstructed.

Jerusalem through rugged mountain scenery, emerging in the Ein Kerem neighborhood on the city's western edge.

BETHLEHEM

Fodor's Choice

★ *8 km (5 mi) south of Jerusalem.*

Even from a distance, it's easy to identify the minarets and church steeples that symbolically struggle for control of the skyline of Bethlehem. Today the great majority of Bethlehem's residents, as elsewhere in the West Bank, are Muslim. But for Christians the world over, the city is synonymous with the birth of Jesus, and the many shrines that celebrate that event. As well, Bethlehem is the site of the Tomb of Rachel, the only one of the biblical patriarchs and matriarchs not buried in Hebron. Rachel's Tomb today lies in Israeli-controlled territory, immediately to the north of the looming separation wall that divides the area.

GETTING HERE AND AROUND

The birthplace of Jesus is 10 minutes south of Jerusalem. Although Bethlehem is part of the Palestinian Authority, tourists with a foreign passport will have no difficulty visiting here. While security may seem daunting at the heavily fortified border post, you show the cover of your passport to be whisked through. Israeli guides are not allowed to take you to the sights, but can help arrange for Palestinian guides to meet you at the border. If you're a more independent traveler, you can take one of the Palestinian taxis at the border. If taking a taxi, *sherut* (shared taxi), or bus from East Jerusalem, you must take a local bus or taxi from the Bethlehem side of the terminal to Manger Square. Driving is not recommended.

TIMING

Allow at least two hours for a visit to the Church of the Nativity and Manger Square.

SAFETY AND PRECAUTIONS

Tourists can travel to Bethlehem as political and security conditions permit. At press time, Israeli citizens are prohibited from entering areas under full Palestinian Authority control. Tourists are unlikely to be bothered in Bethlehem, but ask your hotel concierge if there have been any recent issues.

ESSENTIALS

Visitor Information Tourist Information Office (⊠ *Peace Center, Manger Sq., Bethlehem* ☎ *02/276–6677* ⊕ *www.visit-palestine.com*).

EXPLORING

❸ **Church of the Nativity.** The stone exterior of this church is crowned by the
★ crosses of the three denominations sharing it: the Greek Orthodox, the Latins (Roman Catholic, represented by the Franciscan order), and the Armenian Orthodox. The blocked square entranceway dates from the time of the Byzantine emperor Justinian (6th century AD), the arched entrance (also blocked) within the Byzantine one is 12th-century Crusader, and the current low entrance was designed in the 16th century to protect the worshippers from attack by hostile Muslim neighbors.

The church interior is vast and gloomy. In the central nave, a wooden trapdoor reveals a remnant of a mosaic floor from the original church, built in the 4th century by Helena, mother of Constantine the Great, the Roman emperor who first embraced Christianity. Emperor Justinian's rebuilding two centuries later enlarged the church, creating its present-day plan and structure, including the high columns that run the length of the nave in two paired lines.

This is the oldest standing church in the country. When the Persians invaded in AD 614, they destroyed every Christian church and monastery in the land except this one. Legend holds that the church was adorned with a wall-painting depicting the Nativity tale, including the visit to the infant Jesus by the Three Wise Men of the East. For the local artist, "east" meant Persia, and he dressed his wise men in Persian garb. The Persian conquerors did not understand the picture's significance, but "recognized" themselves in the painting and so spared the church. In the eighth century the church was pillaged by the Muslims, and was later renovated by the Crusaders. Patches of 12th-century mosaics high on the walls, the medieval oak ceiling beams, and the figures of saints on the Corinthian pillars hint at its medieval splendor.

The elaborately ornamented front of the church serves as the parish church of Bethlehem's Greek Orthodox community. The right transept is theirs, too, but the left transept belongs to the Armenian Orthodox. For centuries, all three "shareholders" in the church have vied for control of the holiest Christian sites in the Holy Land. The 19th-century Status Quo Agreement that froze their respective rights and privileges in Jerusalem's Church of the Holy Sepulcher and the Tomb of the Virgin pertains here, too: ownership, the timing of ceremonies, the number of oil lamps, and so on are all clearly defined.

Christmas in Bethlehem includes a colorful Greek Orthodox procession in Manger Square.

From the right transept at the front of the church, descend to the **Grotto of the Nativity.** Long lines can form at the entrance to the grotto, making the suggestion of spending just an hour to see the church an impossibility. Once a cave—precisely the kind of place that might have been used as a barn—the grotto has been reamed, plastered, and decorated beyond recognition. Immediately on the right is a small altar, and on the floor below it is the focal point of the entire site: a 14-point **silver star** with the Latin inscription HIC DE VIRGINE MARIA JESUS CHRISTUS NATUS EST (Here of the Virgin Mary, Jesus Christ was born). The original star was placed here in 1717 by the Latins, who lost control of the altar 40 years later to the more influential Greek Orthodox. In 1847 the star mysteriously disappeared, and pressure from the Turkish sultan compelled the Greeks to allow the present Latin replacement to be installed in 1853. The Franciscan guardians do have possession, however, of the little alcove a few steps down on the left at the entrance to the grotto, said to be the manger where the infant Jesus was laid. ✉ *Manger Sq.* ☎ *02/274–1020* ✉ *Free* ⊙ *Church: Apr.–Sept., daily 6:30 AM–7:30 PM; Oct.–Mar., daily 5:30–5:30. Grotto: Apr.–Sept., Mon.–Sat. 9–7:30, Sun. noon–7:30; Oct.–Mar., Mon.–Sat. 9–5:30, Sun. noon–5:30.*

❹ **Church of St. Catherine.** Adjacent to the Church of the Nativity, and accessible by a passage from its Armenian chapel, is Bethlehem's Roman Catholic parish church. Completed in 1882, and renovated in 1999, the church incorporates remnants of its 12th-century Crusader predecessor. It has fine acoustics but is otherwise unexceptional. From this church the midnight Catholic Christmas mass is broadcast around the world. Steps descend from within the church to a series of dim grottoes, clearly

CLOSE UP

The West Bank

The West Bank is that part of the one-time British Mandate of Palestine, west of the Jordan River, that was occupied by the Kingdom of Transjordan in its war with the nascent State of Israel in 1948 and annexed shortly afterward. That country then changed its name to the Hashemite Kingdom of Jordan to reflect its new geo-political reality. The territory was lost to Israel in the Six-Day War of 1967. Jordan's King Hussein subsequently abandoned his claim to the biblical heartland.

Following the Oslo Accords in 1993, much of the West Bank has been turned over to the Palestinian Authority. In Israel itself, the region is often referred to as "the territories," "over the Green Line" (a term denoting the 1949 armistice line between the West Bank and Israel), or by its biblical names Yehuda (or Judea, the area south of Jerusalem), and Shomron (or Samaria, the much larger area north of Jerusalem).

The West Bank is a kidney-shape area, a bit larger than the U.S. state of Delaware and almost half the size of Northern Ireland. The large majority of the approximately 2 million Arabs is Muslim, with the Christian minority living mostly in the greater Bethlehem area and Ramallah, and a tiny community of Samaritans living in Nablus and on Mount Gerizim.

While the Oslo Accords promised peace and final status discussions, a comprehensive agreement has proven elusive due to seemingly irreconcilable differences on the thorny issues of land, refugees, and Jerusalem. In 2000 the simmering crisis exploded with lethal ferocity as young Palestinians took to the streets in riots known as the Second Intifada. In 2005, Israel unilaterally withdrew from the Gaza Strip and four remote settlements in northern Samaria. Although violence has subsided significantly, many visitors still avoid the West Bank. Others, while exercising caution, visit such worthwhile West Bank sites as Bethlehem and Jericho.

In addition to the 2 million Arabs in the West Bank, half a million Israelis also live there in hundreds of small settlements and a number of major cities. Although the cities and bigger towns are really suburbs of Jerusalem and Tel Aviv, other settlements were set up by nationalist Israelis who see the region as an integral and inalienable part of their biblical homeland.

With its prime location within 14 km (9 mi) of the Mediterranean Sea, and its mountain heights—dominating Israel's main population centers—the West Bank has a strategic value that has convinced even many Israelis that it would be folly to relinquish it to potentially hostile Arab control. Other Israelis will consider some kind of two-state solution.

A person's attitude toward the questions of continuing settlement in the West Bank and the ultimate status of the region is an important touchstone of political affiliation in Israel. The country remains completely divided on these issues.

Tourists can travel to Bethlehem and Jericho as security conditions permit; they need to take passports with them. At this writing Israeli citizens are prohibited from entering areas under full Palestinian control. Please check your government's travel advisory before visiting these areas.

Church of the
Nativity **3**
Chuch of St.
Catherine **4**
Manger Square ...**2**
Rachel's Tomb **1**

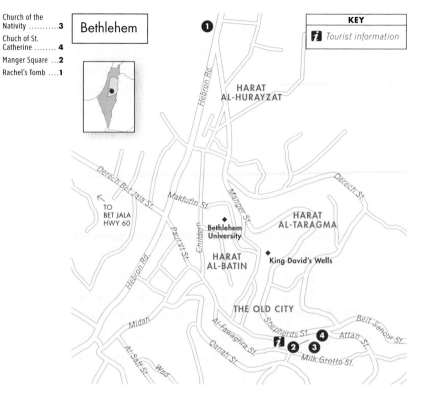

once used as living quarters. Chapels here are dedicated to Joseph; to the Innocents killed by Herod; and to the 4th-century St. Jerome, who wrote the Vulgate, the Latin translation of the Bible, supposedly right here. A small wooden door (kept locked) connects the complex with the Grotto of the Nativity. ⊠ *Manger Sq.* ☎ *02/274–2425* ⊙ *Apr.–Sept., daily 6–noon and 2–7; Oct.–Mar., daily 5:30–5:30.*

② **Manger Square.** Bethlehem's central plaza and the site of the Church of the Nativity, Manger Square is built over the grotto thought to be the birthplace of Jesus. The square has a tourist-information office, a few restaurants, and some shops.

① **Rachel's Tomb.** This Israeli enclave in a Palestinian area is on the right shortly after passing through the border. The historic white dome is now hidden behind the ugly renovations. Despite the security wall, the area is safe for travel and was opened to private cars in 2008. The Bible relates that the matriarch Rachel, second and favorite wife of Jacob, died in childbirth on the outskirts of Bethlehem, "and Jacob set up a pillar upon her grave" (Genesis 35:19–20). There is no vestige of Jacob's original pillar, but the velvet-draped cenotaph inside the building has been hallowed by observant Jews for centuries as the site of Rachel's tomb. People come to pray here for good health, fertility, and a safe birth. Some pilgrims wind a red thread seven times around the tomb,

DID YOU KNOW?

Bethlehem is a magnet for Christian pilgrims, but it's also a center of Palestinian culture. The city is known for handicrafts such as olive-wood carvings, embroidery, and mother-of-pearl items.

and give away snippets of it as talismans to cure all ills. Note that men and women are segregated here and have different entrances.

Rachel is venerated by Islam as well. Next to the tomb is a Muslim cemetery, reflecting the Middle Eastern tradition that it is a special privilege to be buried near a great personage. ⊠*Rte. 60* 🗐*Free* 🕙*Sun.–Thurs. 8–5, Fri. 8–1.*

Shepherds' Fields. As you approach Bethlehem, you'll see the fields of the adjacent town of Beit Sahour, traditionally identified with the biblical story of Ruth the Moabite, daughter-in-law of Naomi, who "gleaned in the field" of Boaz, Naomi's kinsman. The same fields are identified by Christian tradition as those where shepherds "keeping watch over their flock by night"

> **CHRISTMAS IN BETHLEHEM**
>
> In Bethlehem, Christmas is celebrated three times: December 25 by the Roman Catholics; January 6 by the Greek and Russian Orthodox; and January 19 by the Armenian Orthodox. For nearly a month Manger Square is brilliantly illuminated and bursting with life. On December 24, choirs from around the world perform carols and sacred music in the square between 8:30 PM and 11:30 PM, and at midnight at the Franciscan Church of St. Catherine. That mass is relayed on closed-circuit television onto a large screen in Manger Square and, via satellite, to all parts of the globe.

received word of the birth of Jesus in Bethlehem (Luke 2). Several denominations maintain sites in the valley, which they venerate as the authentic Shepherds' Fields.

WHERE TO EAT AND STAY

$ ✕**Ka'bar.** In the village just west of Bethlehem, this is the proverbial hole MIDDLE EASTERN   in the wall where the cognoscenti come to enjoy scrumptious grilled chicken. There's no menu; the restaurant only serves chicken grilled on charcoal on the outdoor grill. The set menu includes five side dishes, among them an excellent house-made hummus. Make sure to sample the hot chili sauce, and the restaurant's signature condiment, garlic and olive oil whipped into a mayonnaise-like dip for your chicken. End your meal with refreshing mint tea. Taxi drivers can take you here from Manger Square. ⊠*Near Municipality Bldg., Bet Jala* ☎*02/274–1419* ⊟*No credit cards* 🕙*Closed Sun.*

$ 🏨**Intercontinental Bethlehem.** Known to locals as Jacir Palace, this luxurious lodging is like something out of the *Thousand and One Nights.* In 1910 Mayor Suleiman Jacir built the mansion, intending that his entire extended family would live here. The main building, an arabesque fantasy, is now home to restaurants including Baidar, with international buffets and garden views, to the Rozana Terrace, set against the view of the Judean Hills. Two new wings hold the guest rooms, which are some of the most comfortable in the area. **Pros:** amazing architectural atmosphere; convenient to Bethlehem; relatively inexpensive. **Cons:** difficult to reach by taxi from Jerusalem. ⊠*Jerusalem-Hebron Rd.* ☎*02/276–6777* ⊕*www.ichotelsgroup.com* ⇄*250 rooms* ⚑*In-room:*

refrigerator. In-hotel: 4 restaurants, bars, room service, tennis courts, pool, gym, spa, laundry service $\equiv$*AE, DC, MC.*

SHOPPING

Bethlehem craftspeople make carved olive-wood and mother-of-pearl objects, mostly of a religious nature, but the many stores along the tourist route in town sell jewelry and trinkets. For quality and reliability, most of the large establishments on Manger Street are worth investigating, but some of the merchants near the Church of the Nativity, on Manger Square, have good-quality items as well.

4

Tel Aviv

WORD OF MOUTH

"Tel Aviv is wonderful—"I call it "New York light"—many of the same wonderful cultural and leisure venues, but much more laid back, better weather and beaches!!!"

—Ohdonnaoh

WELCOME TO TEL AVIV

TOP REASONS TO GO

★ **Exploring the neighborhoods:** Tel Aviv is a city of neighborhoods, each quite different in flavor. Check out Neveh Tzedek, Jaffa, the north end's Tel Aviv Port, and emerging Florentine in the south.

★ **Mediterranean beaches:** Hit the sand, walk along the promenade, or watch the sun dip into the Mediterranean with the locals in the evening.

★ **Bauhaus architecture:** Tel Aviv is nicknamed the "White City" because there is more Bauhaus architecture here than anyplace else in the world.

★ **Nahalat Binyamin Pedestrian Mall:** Stalls of this twice-weekly street fair show off a wealth of handmade jewelry and other crafts at very reasonable prices.

★ **Israel's best modern cuisine:** Tel Aviv has long been the country's best example of "café culture" and with the variety and quality of the city's restaurants, it's clearly the capital of culinary delights.

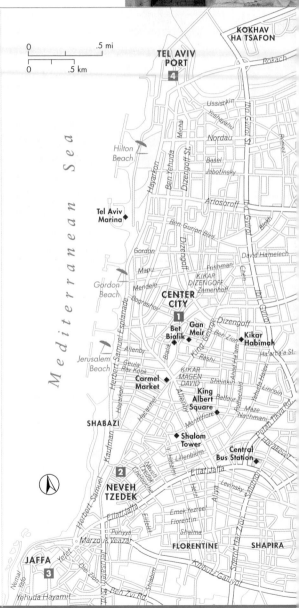

Azrieli Center

1 Center City. Most of Tel Aviv's major sites can be found here, including the Nahalat Binyamin Pedestrian Mall, Carmel Market, and the Bauhaus buildings of the White City.

2 Neveh Tzedek. Restoration has meant a renaissance for this neighborhood, with shops, museums, restaurants, and the Suzanne Dellal Center, graced by its orange-tree-studded square. A must-see destination day or night.

3 Jaffa. The port here—mentioned in the Bible and connected with a number of important events—is one of the oldest in the world. Today, Jaffa is home to the city's most diverse mix of people, as well as low-key restaurants and wine bars.

4 The Tel Aviv Port and Northern Tel Aviv. The abandoned old warehouses of the Tel Aviv Port have been transformed into the city's toniest place to see and be seen. Nearby is the expansive Hayarkon Park.

GETTING ORIENTED

Tel Aviv was carefully planned a century ago on a grid system that makes it easy to navigate on foot. The city's main north–south thoroughfares of Hayarkon, Ben Yehuda (which becomes Allenby), Dizengoff, and Ibn Gvirol streets run more or less parallel to the Mediterranean shoreline. Closest to the water is Hayarkon and the beachfront Tayelet (promenade). At the northern end of Hayarkon is the Tel Aviv Port. Most hotels are on the beachfront along Hayarkon.

Sheinkin Street

4

TEL AVIV
PLANNER

Getting Here

From the airport, the fastest and easiest way into the city is by taxi, and costs NIS 140 ($35). During rush hour, allow 45 minutes for a trip that would otherwise be 20 minutes.

The train is a money-saver for NIS 13 ($3.50), and takes about 25 minutes.

Driving in Tel Aviv is not for the fainthearted. Major highways lead in and out of Tel Aviv, road 1 from Jerusalem, 4 from the northern coast, and 5 from the east. Take advantage of Tel Aviv's belt road, the Ayalon Freeway, to access various parts of the city.

When to Go

Tel Aviv's mild Mediterranean climate means that any time is a good time to visit. However, midday summer temperatures in the 90s may mean choosing museums and other air-conditioned sites until the sun dips and the sea breeze stirs.

Weekends (in Israel this means Thursday nights, Fridays and Saturdays) are the busiest times, but also the most fun in terms of people watching and special events.

Getting Around

Bus Travel: Buses are run primarily by Dan, and also by Egged. The fare is a fixed NIS 5.30 within the city center, and you buy your tickets on the bus. There is a small discount for a 10-ride card. Combined train-and-bus tickets are also available. Two of the major lines, Bus 4 (Ben Yehuda and Allenby streets) and Bus 5 (Dizengoff Street and Rothschild Boulevard), are also serviced by privately run minibuses. You can flag these down and ask to get off at any point along their routes; the fare is the same as on regular buses. Minibuses also run on Saturday, when regular buses do not. Buses leave for Jerusalem every 15 minutes throughout most of the day.

Taxi Travel: Taxis here can be any car model or color and have lighted signs on top. They're plentiful, even in bad weather; drivers honk to catch your attention, even if you're not trying to catch theirs. If traveling within the metropolitan area, make sure the driver turns the meter on when you get in. Rates are NIS 10.40 for the first 18 seconds and 30 agorot in increments thereafter. *Sherut* taxis consist mainly of a fleet of vans at the Central Bus Station that run the same routes as the buses, at comparable one-way prices, and do run on Saturday at a higher charge.

Train Travel: The train is an excellent way to travel between Tel Aviv and cities and towns to the north, such as Netanya, Hadera, Haifa, and Nahariya. The northbound train leaves from the Central Railway Station and the Azrieli station. The information office is open Sunday to Thursday 6 AM–11 PM and Friday 6–3. Trains run roughly every hour on weekdays from 5–6 AM to 10–11 PM depending on destination; there are fewer trains on Friday and Jewish holiday eves and no service on Saturday or on holidays. There is also a line to and from Beersheva. The Tel Aviv–Jerusalem train runs to the new station in south Jerusalem near the Malkha Mall.

Contacts Dan Bus Services (☎03/639–4444). **Egged** (☎03/694–8888). **Central Railway Station** (✉Arlosoroff St. ☎03/611–7000 or *5700)

⇨ For more information on getting here and around, see Travel Smart Israel.

Planning Your Time

With two to four days in Tel Aviv you can explore neighborhoods, museums, sites and still have time for the beach—where it's easy to spend a few hours in between sightseeing. Although it's not a huge area to cover, see the city in geographical order. Start with old Jaffa in the south, and amble through the art galleries, flea market, and fishing port. Jaffa's a good choice in the evening for strolling, low-key restaurants, and wine bars. From here, it's a quick walk north to see Neveh Tzedek. Check out the well-restored buildings, and catch a performance at the Suzanne Dellal Center at night. In the center of town, don't miss the Bauhaus buildings of The White City or Nahalat Benyamin market (on Tuesday or Friday). With more time, explore the north, and see the Diaspora, the Palmach, and the Eretz Israel museums, as well as Yarkon Park for rock-climbing, pedal-boating, or cycling. The Tel Aviv Port is the best place in town for trendy dining and nightlife.

Dining and Lodging

The city's cosmopolitan character is well-represented in its restaurants, and still occupying many street corners are stands selling the Middle Eastern fast food—such as falafel and *shawarma* (spit-grilled meat)—for which this part of the world is famous. Tel Aviv is also very much a café society. There isn't the selection of kosher restaurants you'll find in Jerusalem, but the number of eateries outside hotels has grown in recent years.

The major hotels along Hayarkon Street are right on the Tayelet next to the beach. Staying at a boutique hotel in restored historic buildings adds a wonderful accent to the Tel Aviv experience. Most of the city's hotels are only a short distance from most major attractions.

WHAT IT COSTS					
	¢	$	$$	$$$	$$$$
Restaurants	Under NIS 32	NIS 32–49	NIS 50–75	NIS 76–100	Over NIS 100
Hotels		Under $120	$120–$200	$201–$300	$301–$400	Over $400

Restaurant prices are per person for a main course at dinner in NIS (Israeli shekels). Hotel prices are in US dollars, for two people in a standard double room in high season. Non-Israeli citizens paying in foreign currency are exempt from the 15.5% VAT tax on hotel rooms.

Visitor Information

The Israel Government Tourist Office operates a 24-hour information desk in the Arrivals hall at Ben Gurion Airport (☎ 03/975–4260) and will make reservations at Tourism Ministry approved hotels (for the same day only). The **Tel Aviv Tourist Information Office** is located at (✉ 46 Herbert Samuel St. ☎ 03/516–6188 ☉ Sun.–Thurs. 9:30–5:30, Fri. 9:30–1:00 ⊕ www. visit-tlv.com).

Walking Tours

The Tel Aviv–Jaffa municipality has laid out four self-guided tours of the city called the Tapuz (Orange) Routes; these take in both historic and current cultural sites. Maps are available from the Tel Aviv Tourist Information Office.

Free, city-sponsored walking tours with an English-speaking guide are available as follows: Old Jaffa, beginning at the clock tower on Wednesday at 9 AM; neighborhood evening historical tour beginning at the corner of Rothschild Blvd. and Herzl St., Tuesday 8 PM; the Bauhaus White City, Saturday 11 AM beginning at 46 Rothschild Blvd. No prior registration is required.

Updated by
Miriam Fein-
berg Vamosh

Tel Aviv doesn't have the aura that antiquity and sanctity have bestowed on Israel's other famous cities. But for visitors and residents who fall in love with Tel Aviv, that's precisely where its charm lies.

The founders, who broke new ground—literally and figuratively—would not have known the phrase "cutting edge," but they would certainly have recognized the concept. These founders are being paid special honor in 2009, as the city celebrates its 100th anniversary with a number of special events and the opening or reopening of historic sites that connect past, present, and future in new and interesting ways for visitors and locals alike.

Granted, in the city's name, the founders tipped their European hats to the ancients who left behind millennia-old remains at Jaffa in the south and Tel Qasileh in the north: they called it "Tel Aviv," which is a poetic rendering of "old-new", and comes from the Hebrew translation of the work by Zionist visionary Theodore Herzl's "Altneuland". But they gave the city its edgy-urban vibe that it enjoys to this day.

The first impression Tel Aviv makes depends on the direction from which visitors enter. Glass office towers along the Ayalon Freeway, the city's ring road, showcase the latest trends in high-rise architecture. A dose of Israeli urban sprawl circa 1960 awaits those who come in via the neighborhoods northeast of Old Jaffa along Kibbutz Galuyot Street, eventually easing into the area's Bauhaus and Art Deco masterpieces, the pride of Center City. Whatever the route, one thing is clear: Tel Aviv is the heart of Israeli commerce and culture, and its restaurants, art galleries, museums, and beaches are unmatched anywhere in the country.

The city's beginning as a string of separate neighborhoods helps to explain its eclectic appearance, with towering skyscrapers casting shadows over some of the restored masterpieces of the 1920s and '30s. Tel Aviv poet Natan Alterman dubbed it "the White city," and it is still the world's only city dominated by the International Style of Le Corbusier and Mies van der Rohe—an aesthetic of functional forms, flat roofs, and whitewashed exteriors that became known as Bauhaus. By the 1950s, many of these buildings were crumbling and cracked, or were demolished. Thankfully, city bylaws now mandate their preservation, and Tel Aviv's cluster of Bauhaus buildings, the largest in the world, has won it a place on UNESCO's World Heritage List.

Tel Aviv has come a long way in its short life. Today, many homes in the early neighborhoods and the White City have reemerged from their renovations as gentrified residences, museums, restaurants, and boutique hotels. The charming Neveh Tzedek—a neighborhood that had long been forgotten as the city spread north and west—has recently been reborn as the city's cultural center thanks to the Suzanne Dellal Center for Dance and Theater, with its surrounding area a wonderful place to wander among galleries, boutiques, and eateries. The working-class neighborhood of Florentine comes alive after dark with its pubs and dance clubs that are favorites with the young crowd. It's hard to imagine that just 90 years ago, this teeming metropolis was nothing but sand.

CENTER CITY

Think of downtown Tel Aviv as the center of a cat's cradle of boulevards and side streets leading to all the great sights the city has to offer. Swirling around you might be surfers heading up from the beach crossing paths with ladies doing lunch, or thirtysomethings after work huddled around a tiny table at a café on Sheinkin, or families enjoying play areas and paths along Rothschild or Yarkon Park.

TOP ATTRACTIONS

The Bauhaus Foundation Museum. Those who love architecture won't want to miss this new, one-room museum on historic Bialik Street. It occupies the ground floor of an original Bauhaus building, built in 1934 and home to the Bauhaus Foundation. Visitors discover that the pristine lines and basic geometric forms typical of the Bauhaus school extend to everyday objects as well, from furniture to light fixtures to glazed stoneware. There's even a door handle designed by Walter Gropius (1883–1969), founder and first director of the Bauhaus. ⊠*21 Bialik St., Jaffa* ☏*03/620–4664* ☞*Free* ⊙*Mon. 11–5, Fri. 10–4.*

Carmel Market. The first section of Carmel Market (commonly referred to as the *shuk*) consists of cheap clothing, but a little farther down, in the fruit and vegetable section, is where the real local color begins. Vendors loudly hawk their fresh produce, and crowded aisles reveal Israel's incredible ethnic mix. It's a great sight to see particularly on Tuesdays or Fridays, when it can be combined with a visit to the Nahalat Binyamin Pedestrian Mall's crafts fair. ⊠*Along Hacarmel St., Center City.*

NEED A BREAK? The Carmel Market borders the Yemenite Quarter, which hides several cheap and satisfying little eateries (closed Friday night and Saturday) offering *shawarma* and barbecued skewered meats, all kosher. Visitors can dig into any that catch their fancy, and wash them down with a cold beer.

Independence Hall Museum. This impressive building was originally the home of the city's first mayor, Meir Dizengoff; he donated it to the city in 1930 to be used as Tel Aviv's first art museum. More significantly, the country's leaders assembled here on May 14, 1948, to announce

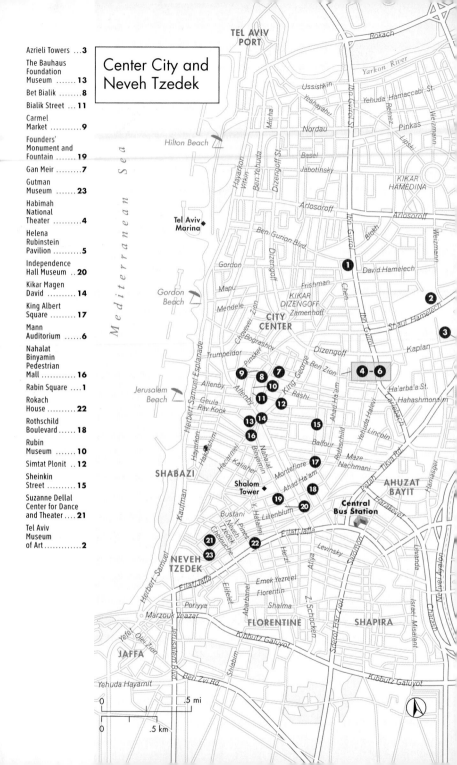

Azrieli Towers ...**3**

The Bauhaus
Foundation
Museum **13**

Bet Bialik **8**

Bialik Street ...**11**

Carmel
Market **9**

Founders'
Monument and
Fountain **19**

Gan Meir **7**

Gutman
Museum **23**

Habimah
National
Theater **4**

Helena
Rubinstein
Pavilion **5**

Independence
Hall Museum ..**20**

Kikar Magen
David **14**

King Albert
Square **17**

Mann
Auditorium **6**

Nahalat
Binyamin
Pedestrian
Mall **16**

Rabin Square **1**

Rokach
House **22**

Rothschild
Boulevard **18**

Rubin
Museum **10**

Sheinkin
Street **15**

Simtat Plonit ..**12**

Suzanne Dellal
Center for Dance
and Theater **21**

Tel Aviv
Museum
of Art **2**

Center City and
Neveh Tzedek

to the world the establishment of the State of Israel. Today the museum's **Hall of Declaration** stands as it did on that dramatic day, with the original microphones on the long table where the dignitaries sat. Behind the table is a portrait of the Zionist leader Theodor Herzl. ✉ *16 Rothschild Blvd., Center City* ☎ *03/517–3942* 💲 *NIS 20* ⏰ *Sun.–Fri. 9–2.*

⑯ Nahalat Binyamin Pedestrian Mall. The selection at this street market, open Tuesday and Friday, is broad—ranging from plastic trinkets to sophisticated crafts such as hand-carved wooden boxes, attractive glassware, and handmade silver jewelry. Nahalat Binyamin is further enlivened by a profusion of buskers. For a finishing touch of local color, cafés serving cakes and light meals line the street. At the end of the fair is a large Bedouin tent, where you can treat yourself to a *laffa* with *labaneh* and *za'atar* (large pita bread with tangy sour cream, sprinkled with hyssop, a mintlike herb). ✉ *Nahalat Binyamin St., off Allenby St., Center City* ⏰ *Tues. and Fri. until sundown.*

⑱ Rothschild Boulevard. Half a century ago, this magnificent tree-lined boulevard was one of the most exclusive streets in the city. Today, this is quintessential urban Tel Aviv, and the central stretch of the boulevard is once again what its designers at the beginning of the 20th century meant it to be—a place for people to meet, stroll, and relax. Along it are some of the best restaurants and pubs in the city, and some of the White City and Art Deco gems are also here and on the side streets off it.

⑩ Rubin Museum. Recognized as one of Israel's major painters, Reuven Rubin (1893–1974) bequeathed his house to Tel Aviv along with 45 of his works, which make up the permanent collection here. The house, built in 1930, is now an art gallery, with changing exhibits by Israeli artists in addition to the great Rubin's work. Upstairs is a small but well-stocked art library where you can pore over press clippings and browse through art books. A moving audiovisual presentation tells the story of Rubin's life, with many fascinating segments in his own voice. His original studio can still be seen on the third floor. ✉ *14 Bialik St., Jaffa* ☎ *03/525–5961* ⊕ *www.rubinmuseum.org.il* 💲 *NIS 20* ⏰ *Mon., Wed., and Thurs. 10–3, Tues. 10–8, Sat. 11–2.*

❷ Tel Aviv Museum of Art. The TAM houses a fine collection of Israeli and international art, including works by Israeli artist Reuven Rubin and a Roy Lichtenstein mural commissioned for the museum in 1989. There's also an impressive French Impressionist collection and many sculptures by Aleksandr Archipenko. In December 2009, in honor of Tel Aviv's Centenary, the museum will hold the first exhibition ever in Israel of the installations, or "stabiles," of the American sculptor Alexander Calder. ✉ *27 Shaul Hamelech Blvd., Center City* ☎ *03/607–7020* ⊕ *www.tamuseum.com* 💲 *NIS 42* ⏰ *Mon., Wed., and Sat. 10–4, Tues. and Thurs. 10–10, Fri. 10–2.*

Fodor'sChoice ★

4

WORTH NOTING

③ Azrieli Towers. A spectacular 360-degree view of Tel Aviv and beyond awaits on the 49th-floor observatory of this office building and mall complex, which consists of three buildings—one triangular, one circular, and one square. The observatory is sometimes closed for private events and hours change daily, so calling ahead to check availability is essential. ⊠ *Hashalom exit west, Ayalon Fwy., Center City* ☎ *03/608–1179* ☞ *NIS 22 for observatory entrance and audio-guide.*

⑧ Bet Bialik (Bialik House). Set to reopen in 2009 in time for the city's centen-
★ nial, Bialik House is the charmingly restored two-story home of Chaim Nachman Bialik (1873–1934), who is considered the father of Hebrew poetry. Bialik was already a respected poet and publisher by the time he moved to Tel Aviv from Russia in 1924; in the remaining 10 years of his life, his house, built in 1927, became the intellectual center of Tel Aviv. The house is still a cultural center, hosting evenings of readings and lectures by writers and artists, and it houses an archive of Bialik's work. In honor of the Centenary, a special exhibit entitled "100 Years of Tel Aviv-Yafo Art" is slated to open in June 2009, showcasing the city's famous artistic sons, including Menashe Kadishman amd Igael Tumarkin. ⊠ *22 Bialik St., Center City* ☎ *03/525–3403.*

⑪ Bialik Street. This area has been more successful than many other Tel Aviv neighborhoods in maintaining its charming older buildings. Bialik has long been a popular address with many of the city's artists and literati, so it's not surprising that some of the houses have been converted into small museums. Next to the Bialik House is a **mosaic,** designed by artist Nahum Gutman, which depicts the history of the city from the ancient days of Jaffa to the rise of Tel Aviv. Gutman was among the elite group of Tel Aviv's first artists. The mosaic stands in front of Tel Aviv's original city hall, set to reopen in June 2009 as the city's historical museum in honor of the Tel Aviv centennial events.

⑲ Founders' Monument and Fountain. Dedicated in 1949, the Founders' Monument names those who founded Tel Aviv. This large slab of stone also encapsulates the city's past in three copper bas-relief panels representing the earliest pioneer days of planting and building as well as modern architecture. ⊠ *Rothschild Blvd., on the traffic divider at Nahalat Binyamin St., Center City.*

⑦ Gan Meir. You're virtually guaranteed a traffic jam on this section of King George Street not far from Dizengoff Center, but you can get a respite by sitting on one of Gan Meir's benches, shaded by beautiful old trees. The first trees were planted in 1936 when the city offered to name the park after its first mayor, Meir Dizengoff, in honor of his 70th birthday. The feisty Dizengoff objected, so the park only got its official name in 1944, years after he passed away.

④ Habimah National Theater. The origins of Israel's national theater are rooted in the Russian Revolution, when a group of young Jewish actors and artists in Russia established a theater company that performed in Hebrew—this at a time when Hebrew was barely a living language. Subsequent tours through Europe and the United States in the 1920s won wide acclaim. In the late 1920s and '30s, many of the group's

TEL AVIV: 100 YEARS OF HISTORY

Having risen from desolate sand dunes less than a century ago, Tel Aviv lacks the ancient aura of Jerusalem (which some say is part of its attraction). Still, the city's southern border, the port of Jaffa, is as old as they come: Jonah set sail from here for what turned out to be his journey to the belly of a whale. The cedars of Lebanon used to build Solomon's Temple arrived in Jaffa before being transported to Jerusalem.

Jaffa was founded in the Middle Canaanite period, around 1600 BC. For the next 1,000 years it was dominated by one ancient people after another: Egyptians, Philistines, Israelites, Phoenicians, and Greeks. After being taken by Crusaders twice, in the 11th and 12th centuries, it was recaptured by the Muslims and remained largely under Arab control until the 20th century.

In the second half of the 19th century, Jewish pioneers began immigrating here in numbers that strained the small port's capacity. By the late 1880s, a group of Jewish families moved from the overcrowded city to the empty sands north of Jaffa to found Neveh Tzedek, now a beautifully restored shopping, cultural, and residential area. The next move was to Ahuzat Bayit (literally, "housing estate"), an area to the north of Neveh Tzedek that became the precursor of Tel Aviv. The city was named Tel Aviv in 1909; Arab riots in Jaffa in the 1920s then drove more Jews to Ahuzat Bayit, spurring further growth. These Jews were joined by immigrants from Europe, mostly Poland, and a decade later by an influx of German Jews fleeing the Nazis. These new, urban arrivals—unlike the pioneers from earlier immigrant waves—brought with them an appreciation for the arts and a penchant for sidewalk cafés, and left a strong social and cultural mark on Tel Aviv. The wave of immigration included some of the world's leading architects of the time, who saw their new home as virtually a blank slate on which they could realize their innovative and exciting ideas about urban planning. The movement that started with the functionalist, humanistic Garden City initiated by Scottish architect Patrick Geddes, became the Bauhaus School, and its monuments, now protected, are a major attraction for architecture lovers.

members moved to Israel and helped to establish the theater. The cornerstone was laid in 1935; the current large, rounded glass-front building, now undergoing extensive renovation and slated to reopen during Tel Aviv's centennial year, dates from 1970. ⊠ *Kikar Habimah, Center City* ☎ *03/526–6666* ⊕ *www.habima.co.il.*

 Helena Rubinstein Pavilion. This annex of the Tel Aviv Museum of Art houses changing contemporary art exhibitions of contemporary Israeli art in an intimate space that is a particularly effective venue for one-person exhibitions. There's no entry fee, so you can drop in for a little visual culture and an escape from the midday sun. ⊠ *6 Tarsat St., Center City* ☎ *03/528–7196* ⊕ *www.tamuseum.com* ⌨ *Free* ⊙ *Mon., Wed., and Sat. 10–4, Tues. and Thurs. 10–10, Fri. 10–2.*

 Kikar Magen David. This meeting point of six streets is named for the six-point Magen David, or Star of David. It's also an intersection of

Aside from colorful buildings, Sheinkin Street is packed with buskers, restaurants, and cafes.

cultures, surrounded by some of old Tel Aviv's historic buildings on one side and Sheinkin, the ultimate in trendiness, on the other. The intersection gives you an all-too-close look at the Israelis' hair-raising driving style; if you need to cross the street here, use the underpass.

⑰ King Albert Square. Named after the Belgian monarch who was a personal friend of Mayor Dizengoff, the square, reached from Rothschild Boulevard past the restored buildings on Nahmani Street, is in the heart of Tel Aviv's restored architectural area and has some interesting monuments of its own. Pagoda House, now made over as a gated luxury apartment building, was built in 1924 at the height of the Bauhaus period as a private home. It's very ornamental, topped with the Japanese element that gave it its name. Its architect, Alexander Levy, came to Palestine in the '20s, and designed a number of buildings, although he never felt at home here and eventually returned to Germany, where he was killed in Auschwitz. Inside the elegant stairwell of the Shifrin House, at 2 Melchett Street, off the square, are crumbling remnants of frescoes of the Western Wall and Rachel's Tomb.

⑥ Mann Auditorium. One of the several cultural centers on Kikar Habimah, Mann Auditorium is Israel's premier concert hall and the home of the Israel Philharmonic Orchestra, led by maestro Zubin Mehta. The low-slung gray building, among the most architecturally sophisticated cultural buildings in the country when it was completed in 1957, has excellent acoustics and a seating capacity of 3,000. It also hosts pop and rock concerts. ⊠*Habima Sq., Center City* ⊕*www.hatarbut.co.il.*

❶ Rabin Square. The square fronting the nondescript Tel Aviv municipality building was renamed for prime minister Yitzhak Rabin after he

If you're looking for a "birds'-eye" view of the city, it doesn't get better than from the top of the Azrieli Towers.

was assassinated here on November 4, 1995. Passersby often stop at the small monument of black stones, rippled and uneven as if after an earthquake, the work of Israeli artist Danny Karavan. On April 4, 2009, it is set to be the scene of the kickoff for the Tel Aviv Centenary with a huge audiovisual display projected against the surrounding apartment houses, and a concert by the Israel Philharmonic Orchestra. In September 2009, another Centenary event will be celebrated here: The Centennial Flower Carpet—where a carpet made entirely of flowers will be spread over nearly one square mile and will reveal a "secret message." ⊠ *Ibn Gvirol St., Center City.*

15 **Sheinkin Street.** This street, off Allenby across from Nahalat Binyamin, has plenty of cafés and restaurants and is fun for clothes shopping, especially for teens and young adults. Sizes tend to the tiny, the favored color is black, and some of the boutiques are so small you'll think you walked straight into the dressing room. Street performances in good weather and cute pedigree—or pedigree-look-alike—puppies for sale on Friday afternoons add to the boisterous fun (though it's hard to see much through the crowds).

12 **Simtat Plonit.** It's worth a wander down this alley to see old Tel Aviv decorative architecture at its best. Two gray-plastered obelisks at the entrance to the alley mark the city's first "gated" community. Note the stucco lion in front of **Number 7,** which used to have glowing eyes fitted with lightbulbs. The original apartment house is painted pale yellow with a garish orange trim. The tract of land that incorporates Simtat Plonit was bought in the 1920s by an outspoken builder from Detroit named Meir Getzel Shapira. (He established what is still known as the

A Focus on the Arts

For a tiny nation, Israel has a thriving and abundant arts scene. The country is home to thousands of classical musicians—many of whom immigrated from the former Soviet states—and the Israel Philharmonic Orchestra has a world-class reputation.

A number of music festivals are held annually, drawing international crowds—from the Red Sea Jazz Festival, in the south, to the Voice of Music chamber music event and Jacob's Ladder folk festival, in the north.

Israeli theater, too, enjoys a significant following. There are six professional repertory theaters—including the Habmiah and the Cameri in Tel Aviv—and dozens of regional and amateur companies performing throughout the country. They perform almost exclusively in Hebrew.

Professional dance companies are also abounding in Israel today. The Suzanne Dellal Center for Dance and Theater in Tel Aviv is the primary venue.

Folk dancing has always been unusually popular in Israel, where it is, in fact, an evolving art form. As well as "Israeli" folk dancing (really a blend of Jewish and non-Jewish folk dance forms from around the world), some of Israel's different ethnic groups have preserved their traditional dances.

Enthusiasm for the visual arts can be seen in all walks of Israeli life. A wide range of Israeli art can be seen at both the Israel Museum (in Jerusalem), the Tel Aviv Museum, and for modern Israeli art, the Ramat Gan Art Museum.

Shapira Quarter, just south of the Central Bus Station and now one of the city's seedier neighborhoods.) After buying the land, Shapira insisted that this pint-size street be named after him, and, as the story goes, he fought furiously with Tel Aviv's first mayor, Meir Dizengoff, to get his way. (Dizengoff had already planned to name another street Shapira, after a different Shapira.) The mayor emerged victorious and named the alley Plonit, meaning "What's-His-Name."

NEVEH TZEDEK

Neveh Tzedek is a prime tourist destination because of its restaurants, cafés, cultural life, and historic buildings. Not surprisingly, it's where you'll find the fantastic dance and arts complex, the Suzanne Dellal Center, as well as a growing number of small trendy galleries and gift shops. Though bordered on three sides by major thoroughfares (Eilat Road to the south, Herzl Street to the west, and Kaufman Street along the sea), this little quarter is very tranquil. Made up of about a dozen tiny streets stuffed with one- and two-story dwellings in various stages of renovation, Neveh Tzedek is rich with tales of 100 years ago.

This is where the saga of Tel Aviv began, when a small group of Jewish families from Jaffa laid the cornerstone for their new neighborhood, naming it Neveh Tzedek (Dwellings of Justice). Then, when Tel Aviv was busy expanding to the north and the east in the early days of the state, Neveh Tzedek became an unfashionable address and was allowed

A crowd enjoys the folk music and the sunshine on the Promenade Tayelet.

to deteriorate. But the beautiful old buildings here were too remarkable to be long neglected by the real estate market, and the restored homes here are now among the most prestigious addresses in the city.

TOP ATTRACTIONS

㉑ ★ Suzanne Dellal Center for Dance and Theater. The two large whitewashed buildings that make up this attractive complex started out as schools, one built in 1892 and the other in 1908. Both were used for education until the 1970s, though they also served as headquarters for the political force Etzel and the underground military group Haganah, which marched on Arab Jaffa in the 1940s. The square, designed by foremost landscape designer Shlomo Aronson, has hints of a medieval Middle Eastern courtyard in its scattering of orange trees connected by water channels. One side of the square is decorated with a tile triptych, which illustrates the neighborhood's history and famous people who lived here in the early years, including S.Y. Agnon who went on to win the Nobel prize for literature. The halls are open only for performances, but there's a café–bar on the premises. Just off the square on Cheloushe Street is a fun ice-cream shop with outdoor seating called Glidat Savta ("Grandma's ice-cream"). ✉6 *Yehieli St., Neveh Tzedek* ☎*03/510–5656* ⊕*www.suzannedellal.org.il.*

WORTH NOTING

㉓ Gutman Museum. A number of Tel Aviv's most famous writers lived in this building during the 1920s, but extensive renovation has somewhat obscured its original look. One of the first houses in Neveh Tzedek, the building now displays the art of Nahum Gutman, colorful chronicler of early Tel Aviv. Tours in English are available by prearrangement. ✉*21*

Rokach St., Neveh Tzedek ☎*03/510–8554* ⊕*www.gutmanmuseum. co.il* ▣*NIS 20* ☉*Sun. 10–4, Thurs. 10–10, Fri. and Jewish holiday eves 10–2, Sat. 10–3.*

㉒ Rokach House. This mansion was built by the founder of Neveh Tzedek, Shimon Rokach and his wife Hannah to be their home. Like several other homes in the quarter it fell into disrepair, and its restoration is the "baby" of the Rokachs' daughter, the artist Leah Majaro-Mintz. It now houses Majaro-Mintz's art and an exhibit of items from the quarter's early days. Guided tours in English are available by calling ahead. A dramatization (in Hebrew) of Neveh Tzedek's history, preceded by tastings of the period's cuisine, is offered most weekend evenings at 9:30. ⊠*36 Rokach St., Neveh Tzedek* ☎*03/516–8042* ⊕*www.rokach-house. co.il* ▣*NIS 10* ☉*Sun.–Thurs. 10–4, Fri. and Sat. 10–2.*

JAFFA

Exploring Jaffa is a wonderful reason to visit this ancient city, as it's ideal for strolling and a dinner at one of the no-frills fish restaurants that line the quay. High above is the restored part of town, where art galleries and shops now occupy the centuries-old beach-rock buildings along the narrow roads. At the Jaffa flea market, you can be part of the trading and bargaining for treasures—real and perceived—that are a hallmark of the Middle East.

History buffs will be at home here, too: some claim the town was named after its founder, Japhet, son of Noah, others think its name is from the Hebrew *yafeh* (beautiful). What is certain is its status as one of the oldest ports in the world—perhaps the oldest. The Bible says the cedars used in the construction of the Temple passed through Jaffa on their way to Jerusalem; the prophet Jonah set off from Jaffa before being swallowed by the whale; and St. Peter raised Tabitha from the dead here. Napoléon was but one of a succession of invaders who brought the city walls down; these walls were rebuilt for the last time in the early 19th century by the Turks and torn down yet again as recently as 1888.

Now part of the municipality of Tel Aviv, Jaffa is a mosaic of Jews, Christians, and Muslims, accented by communities of foreign guest-workers mainly from Asia and Africa.

South of Jaffa is the newly-hip Florentine. In a city where housing is painfully unaffordable, this neighborhood is popular with students. You'll find pubs popular with the twenties- to thirties-crowd, so the best time to go is late at night, especially on weekends.

TOP ATTRACTIONS

❿ ★ Flea Market. The flea market actually began as one of many small bazaars surrounding the clock tower in the mid-19th century, and it's now the only survivor of that era. The market's main street is **Olei Zion,** but there are a number of smaller streets and arcades to explore at your leisure, so take your time. While you're probably not going to lug a 19th-century sideboard home, you can watch the locals shop and bargain, and do what they do: never agree to the first price a seller demands. In

Andromeda's Rock **1**

Clock Tower Square **7**

El-Mahmoudiye Mosque **6**

Flea Market **10**

Ilana Goor Museum **8**

Jaffa Port **2**

Kedumim Square **3**

St. Peter's Monastery **4**

San Antonio Roman Catholic Church **11**

Summit Park **5**

Yefet Street **9**

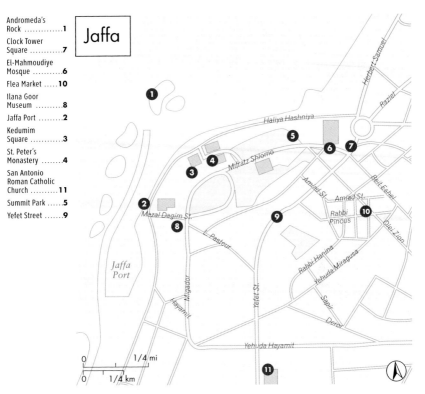

a former warehouse at 12 Amiad Street the city has housed a gallery that hosts changing contemporary-art exhibits.

2 **Jaffa Port.** A great many fishing boats line this small marina, as well as ★ a handful of houseboats. Along the waterfront are a number of restaurants whose main attraction is their view.

3 **Kedumim Square.** This is Old Jaffa's central plaza, filled with archaeological remains, restaurants, expensive gift and souvenir shops, and galleries. The artists who live here complain that there's too much noise on summer nights, and some visitors say it's too touristy. But beyond the square, Old Jaffa is indisputably charming and should not be missed. A labyrinthine network of tiny alleys snakes in all directions from Kedumim Square down to the fishing port; a good selection of galleries and jewelry stores can be found along Mazal Dagim Street and its offshoots, south of the square. The focus of Kedumim Square is an archaeological site that exposes 3rd-century BC catacombs; the site has been converted into an underground visitor center with large, vivid, illustrated descriptions of Jaffa's history. Admission is free.

4 **St. Peter's Monastery.** Jaffa is famous for being a true meeting point of East and West, and as soon as you step into this church established by Franciscans more than a century ago, you'll find yourself steeped in a European atmosphere. St. Peter's was built over the ruins of a

Old Town Jaffa.

citadel that dates from the Seventh Crusade, which was led by King Louis IX of France. A monument to King Louis stands today at the entrance to the friary. Napoléon is rumored to have stayed here during his Jaffa campaign of 1799. To enter, ring the bell by pulling the string on the right side of the door; you will probably be greeted by one of the custodians, most of whom speak Spanish and some English. Mass is celebrated every morning at 7 AM. On Saturday evenings at 8 and Sunday mornings at 9 the service is in English. ⊠ *Kedumim Sq., Jaffa* ☎ *03/682–2871.*

⑤ Summit Park. It's fun to watch the newlyweds who come here to be photographed in their wedding garb at sunset against the backdrop of the sea and the ancient buildings. Seven archaeological layers have been unearthed in a part of the park called Ramses II Garden. The oldest sections of wall (20 feet thick) have been identified as part of a 17th-century BC Hyksos city. Other remains include part of a 13th-century BC city gate inscribed with the name of Ramses II; a Canaanite city; a Jewish city from the time of Ezra and Nehemiah; Hasmonean ruins from the 2nd century BC; and traces of Roman occupation. At the summit is a stone sculpture called "Faith," in the shape of a gateway, which depicts biblical stories.

WORTH NOTING

① Andromeda's Rock. From Kedumim Square, a number of large boulders can be seen out at sea not far from shore. Greek mythology says one of these (pick your own, everyone does) is where the people of Jaffa tied the virgin Andromeda to sacrifice her to a sea monster to appease Poseidon, god of the sea. But Perseus, riding the winged horse Pegasus, soared down from the sky to behead the monster, rescue Andromeda, and promptly marry her.

7 **Clock Tower Square.** The clock tower is the focus of Jaffa's newly renovated central square with restored Old Jaffa to the west and the Jaffa flea market to the east. The centuries-old buildings have been carefully restored, preserving their ornate old facades. With Jaffa a major port in Turkish times, it's not surprising to

4

see the Turkish Cultural Center, sponsored by the Turkish Embassy, in one of the buildings. A fashion outlet, a music store, and other odd counterpoints have also taken up residence in some of the restored houses. The clock tower was completed in 1906, in time to mark the 30th anniversary of the reign of Sultan Abdul Hamid II; similar clock towers were built for the same occasion in Akko and in Jerusalem. The new stained-glass windows in the old tower depict events in Jaffa's history. ⊠*Clock Tower Square, Yefet St., Jaffa.*

 NEED A BREAK?

There's always a line outside **Abulafia Bakery** (⊠ *7 Yefet St., Jaffa*), south of the clock tower. The Middle East's answer to pizza goes like hot cakes here—literally. For a simple snack with an exquisite flavor, order a pita topped with the herb *za'atar* (hyssop), or stuffed with salty cheese, calzone-style. In the winter, Abulafia is a good place to try *sachlab*, a warm drink sprinkled with coconut and cinnamon. Making the most of their good name, the Abulafia family also has a Middle Eastern restaurant across the street from their bakery.

6 **El-Mahmoudiye Mosque.** When the fountain here was built by Turkish governor Mohammed Abu Najat Aja in the early 19th century, it had six pillars and an arched roof, providing shade as well as water. The fountain's foundation is still visible in the parking lot west of the minaret. It's closed to the general public, as is the rest of the mosque, but if its ornate carved doors on the western side are open, you can peek into the spacious restored courtyard surrounded by arches. The archway on the south side formed the entrance to the *hamam*, or old Turkish baths. In the late 19th century a separate entrance was built into the east wall to save the governor and other dignitaries the bother of having to push through the market-square crowds at the main entrance, on the south wall. The mosque managed to escape the fate of other sites in Jaffa that were destroyed during the War of Independence. ⊠ *Yefet St., Jaffa.*

8 **Ilana Goor Museum.** The veteran Israeli artist Ilana Goor works and resides in this restored 18th-century house with its romantic stone arches and high ceilings. She's turned part of it into a museum of her sculptures in wood, stone, and metal, some reminiscent of the "found-art" genre, and of local crafts. A gift shop also occupies part of the complex. ⊠*4 Mazal Dagim St., Jaffa* ☎*03/683–7676* ⊠*NIS 24* ⊙*Sun.–Fri. 10–4, Sat. and Jewish holidays 10–6.*

⑪ **San Antonio Roman Catholic Church.** Although it looks quite new with its clean white-stone bricks, this church actually dates from 1932, when it was built to accommodate the growing needs of Jaffa's Roman Catholic community. (St. Peter's was in a heavily populated Muslim area and was unable to expand due to lack of land.) The church is named for St. Antonius of Padua, friend and disciple of St. Francis of Assisi. Mass is celebrated daily at 6:30 AM. ✉ *51 Yefet St., Jaffa* ☎ *03/513–3800.*

⑨ **Yefet Street.** Think of Yefet as a sort of thread between eras: beneath it is the old market area, while all around you stand the Christian and Western schools and churches of the 19th and 20th centuries. Numbers 21, 23, and 25 deserve mention. The first is the **Tabitha School,** established by the Presbyterian Church of Scotland in 1863. Behind the school is a small cemetery where some fairly prominent figures are buried, including Dr. Thomas Hodgkin, the personal physician to Sir Moses Montefiore and the first to define Hodgkin's disease; he died in Jaffa in 1866. **Number 23** was a French Catholic school (it still carries the sign COLLÈGE DES FRÈRES) from 1882 but has long since been used by the French Embassy for administrative purposes. And next door, the neo-Tudor, fortresslike **Urim School,** with its round tower, was set up as a girls' school in 1882 by nuns of the same order that built the St. Louis French Hospital. It's now a local school. Farther down Yefet, Jaffa's working-class neighborhood begins, where you'll find a few fish restaurants and coffee shops the locals love.

TEL AVIV TOURS

PERSONAL GUIDES

Twelve Tribes provides personal guides, usually with a car, who will take you anywhere in the city and even around the country. Personal guides can also be arranged through most hotels.

BOAT TOURS

Kefland runs a half-hour boat tour on Saturdays year-round, from the Jaffa Port along the Tel Aviv waterfront and back. The fare is NIS 20.

Contacts Kefland (✉ *Jaffa Port* ☎ *03/682–9070).* **Twelve Tribes** (✉ *29 Hamered St.* ☎ *03/510–1911* ⊕ *www.twelve-tribes.co.il).*

THE TEL AVIV PORT AND NORTHERN TEL AVIV

While still considered center-city, from the east–west cross street of Arlozoroff north, Tel Aviv flows into blocks of tranquil residential streets of small apartment houses, up to the banks of the Yarkon River and its beautiful park. The Tel Aviv Port is the city's hottest place to eat, shop, and stroll. Just north of the river are three important museums. The Eretz Israel Museum is close to Tel Aviv University; the Palmach Museum is next door to it; and the Diaspora Museum is farther north. The museums are about 8 km (5 mi) from the downtown hotels; Dan buses 7, 25, and 45 will take you to the area, as will the Kavim company's buses 94, 95, and 137. Allow at least two hours to visit each. The train's University station will bring you within a short distance of all three, as well.

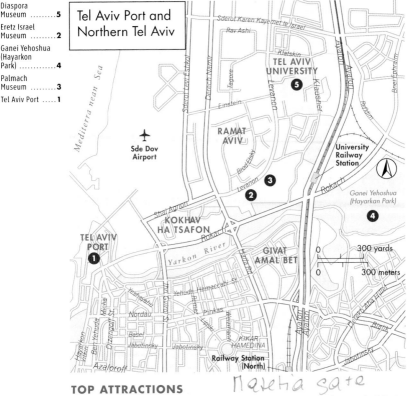

Diaspora
Museum **5**

Eretz Israel
Museum **2**

Ganei Yehoshua
(Hayarkon
Park) **4**

Palmach
Museum **3**

Tel Aviv Port **1**

TOP ATTRACTIONS

5 **Diaspora Museum.** Presented here are 2,500 years of Jewish life in
★ the Diaspora (the settling of Jews outside Israel), beginning with the
destruction of the First Temple in Jerusalem and chronicling such major
events as the exile to Babylon and the expulsion from Spain in 1492.
Also covered is Eastern Europe before the Holocaust. Photographs and
text labels provide the narrative, and films and music enhance the experience. One highlight is a replica collection of miniature synagogues
throughout the world, both those destroyed and those still functioning.
Another is the computerized genealogy section, where it's possible to
look up Jewish family names to determine their origins. In addition,
there's a music center containing a large listening library of Jewish
music from around the world. ⊠ *Tel Aviv University Campus (Gate 2),
Klausner St., Ramat Aviv* ☎ *03/640–8000* ⊕ *www.bh.org.il* ⊠ *NIS 35*
⊙ *Sun.–Tues. and Thurs. 9–4, Wed. 10–6, Fri. 9–1.*

2 **Eretz Israel Museum.** This national museum comprises eight pavilions
★ that present such facets of Israeli life as ethnography and folklore,
ceramics and other handicrafts, and coinage; the displays span 3,000
years of history. In the center of the complex is the ancient site of Tel
Kassile, where archaeological digs have so far uncovered 12 layers of
settlements. There is also a daily sound-and-light show in the adjacent

planetarium with Hebrew narration (call to verify hours). Castles in the Sand, displaying unique photographs and stories about the Tel Aviv beach, is a special exhibit in honor of the Centenary, set to open in June 2009. ⊠*2 Levanon (University) St., Northern Tel Aviv* ☎*03/641–5244* ⊕*www.eretzmuseum.org.il* ⊠*Museum NIS 35, planetarium NIS 58* ☉*Sun.–Thurs. 9–3, Fri. and Sat. 10–2.*

❹ **Ganei Yehoshua (Hayarkon Park).** This park is a strip of emerald tranquility in the midst of the hustle and bustle of the city. Located in the northern part of town, it's the place where Tel Avivians go to stretch out on the grass for a picnic or a nap in the shade. For those seeking more activity, a long walk on one of its paths can be combined with a visit to the tropical garden and the rock garden (open Sunday–Thursday 10–2:30, Friday 10–1:30, Saturday 10–3:30). Or you can rent a pedal boat, rowboat (NIS 80 per hour), or motorboat (NIS 110 per half-hour) to ply the Yarkon Stream or the park's artificial lake. There's even a pleasure boat, which take up to 80 people for 20-minute rides (NIS 15 per person). To really break a sweat, try the park's climbing wall, roller-skating rink, or basketball court, with equipment for rent. In addition, there's a booth (☎050/454–5444, 10–dusk Sun.-Sat.) that rents bicycles or four-wheelers that take up to six people (with two or four people pedaling depending on the size) and are great for family fun (NIS 30 per half-hour for the bikes, NIS 70 per half-hour for the 4-person 4-wheelers, NIS 80 per half hour for the 6-person 4-wheelers). In honor of the Tel Aviv Centenary, it is one of the sites where the works of local street artists will be displayed, including posters, comics, and even graffiti. In July–August 2009, the park will host the Tel Aviv-Yafo Children's Festival, a Tel Aviv Centenary event showing children the history of the first Hebrew city in music, stories, and pictures. ⊠*Rokach Blvd., Northern Tel Aviv* ☎*03/642–2828* ⊕*www.park.co.il.*

❶ **Tel Aviv Port.** The port, which a little over a decade ago was a cluster of hulking ruined warehouses, has reinvented itself with fish restaurants and cafés in its southern and northern sections. It ends where the pavement gives way to a wooden platform designed with moderate dips and curves, pleasing to the eye and fun for roller-skaters. Also here is Bayit Banamal, a small mall with eclectic boutiques. It's one of Tel Aviv's most popular attractions for locals. On weekends, when restaurants are all packed by 1 PM, there's a farmer's market and a small swap meet good for finding hand-made jewelry, old books, and circa-1950s Israeli crafts and memorabilia.

WORTH NOTING

❸ Palmach Museum. This museum makes you feel as if you were back in the days of the Palmach, the pre-state underground, with a group of young defenders. Visitors are led through rooms, each of which encompasses one part of the Palmach experience. There's the "forest," which has real-looking trees; a room with a falling bridge and faux-explosions; and a chilling mock-up of an illegal immigrants' ship. ⊠ *10 Haim Levanon St., Ramat Aviv* ☎ *03/923–4235* ⊕ *www.palmach.org.il* ☎ *25 NIS* ☾ *Sun., Mon., Wed .9–5, Tues. 9–8, Thurs. 9–2, Fri. 9–1; by reservation only.*

WHERE TO EAT

The city's cosmopolitan character is now happily represented in its food, although stands selling Middle Eastern fast food for which this part of the world is famous—such as falafel and *shawarma* (spit-grilled meat)—still occupy countless street corners. You'll find restaurants serving everything from American-style burgers to sushi and chili con carne. In contrast to Jerusalem, diners who keep kosher really have to search long and hard for a kosher restaurant, aside from those in the hotels. A spate of new kosher establishments seems to have started catering to a significant slice of the discerning dining market, but with the fairly rapid turnover of some Tel Aviv eateries, the concierge is still the best person to ask about the latest in kosher restaurants.

Most Tel Aviv restaurants, except those that keep kosher, are open seven days a week. Many serve business lunches at reasonable prices, making them less-expensive options than the price categories suggest. Like elsewhere in the Mediterranean, Israelis dine late; chances are there will be no trouble getting a table at 7 PM, whereas past 10, diners may face a long line. Casual attire is always acceptable in Tel Aviv, even in the poshest restaurants.

Tel Aviv's restaurants are concentrated in a few areas: Sheinkin and Rothschild streets, Basel, Ibn Gvirol Street, and the Tel Aviv Port. Herzliya Pituach, a seaside suburb north of Tel Aviv, has a cluster of good restaurants in the upscale Arena Mall at the Marina, with a picturesque view of the yachts at anchor.

WHAT IT COSTS IN ISRAELI SHEKELS					
	¢	$	$$	$$$	$$$$
Restaurants	under NIS 32	NIS 32–NIS 49	NIS 50–NIS 75	NIS 76–NIS 100	over NIS 100

Prices are for a main course at dinner.

BEST BETS FOR
TEL AVIV DINING

With hundreds of restaurants to choose from, how will you decide where to eat? Fodor's writers and editors have selected their favorite restaurants by price, cuisine, and experience in the lists below. In the first column, Fodor's Choice properties represent the "best of the best" across price categories. You can also search by area for excellent eats—just check out our complete reviews in the following pages.

Fodor's Choice ★

Messa, $$$$, p. 247
Orna and Ella, $$, p. 248
Mul-Yam, $$$$, p. 253

Best By Price

¢

Ilan's Coffee Shop, p. 246
Sabich, p. 249

$

Yaffo Caffé, p. 252
Shalvata, p. 253
Le Petit Prince, p. 246
Giraffe Noodle Bar, p. 245

$$

Orna and Ella, p. 248
Moses, p. 248
Abdu Hadayag, p. 250

$$$

Belini's, p. 249
NG, p. 250
Raphael, p. 248

$$$$

Messa, p. 247
Mul-Yam, p. 253
Montefiori, p. 247

Best By Cuisine

ITALIAN

Belini's, $$$, p. 249
Pronto, $$, p. 248
Allora, $$, p. 244

MEDITERRANEAN

Dallal, $$, p. 249
Suzanna, $$, p. 250

MIDDLE EASTERN

Petrozilia, $$, p. 248
Shupedei Hatikva, $$$, p. 253
Sabich, ¢, p. 249

Best By Experience

BRUNCH

Brasserie, $$, p. 244
Yaffo Café, $, p. 252
Puah, $, p. 250

HOT SPOTS

Raphael, $$$, p. 248
Messa, $$$$, p. 247
Orna and Ella, $$, p. 248

CHILD FRIENDLY

Shalvata, $, p. 253
Yaffo Caffe, $, p. 252
Manta Ray, $$$, p. 250
Dallal, $$, p. 249

OUTSIDE DINING

Café Metzada, $$, p. 245
Ashtor, $. p. 244
Shalvata, $, p. 253
Manta Ray, $$$$, p. 250
Sus Etz, $$, p. 249

MOST ROMANTIC

NG, $$$, p. 250
Mul-Yam, $$$$, p. 253
Montefiori, $$$$, p. 247

SEAFOOD

Mul-Yam, $$$$, p. 253
Abdo Hadayag, $$, p. 250
Shtsupak, $$, p. 249

VIEWS

Manta Ray, $$$$, p. 250
Raphael, $$$, p. 248
comme il faut, $$, p. 252
Allora, $$, 244

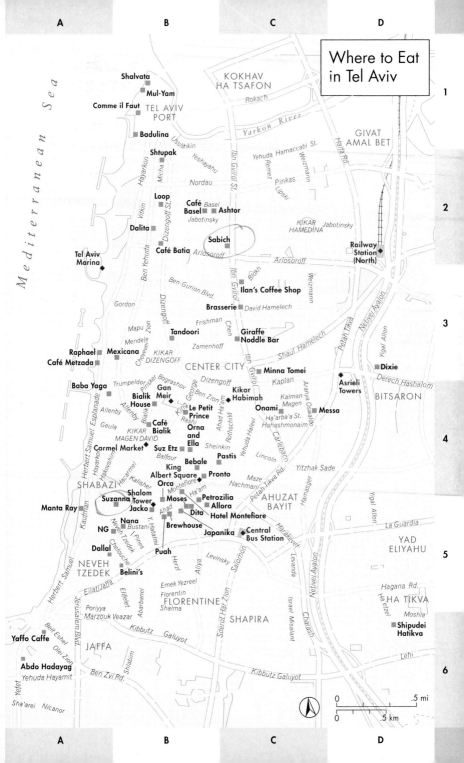

STREET FOOD IN ISRAEL

Fast, faster, fastest! If you're hungry right now, the streets of the Holy Land await your eating pleasure. Israel has a refined culture of noshing on the run, since everyone is always in a hurry and apparently hungry most of the time. Put food and drink in hand and join the locals.

To find the goods from falafel to fresh papayas, look for the food stalls and kiosks that line Israel's main city streets and shopping areas. Fruit and vegetable markets, notably Carmel Market in Tel Aviv and Machaneh Yehuda in Jerusalem, offer snack opportunities. In Tel Aviv, Rothschild Boulevard's central section has upscale food kiosks open daily. In Jerusalem, try the Old City's hummus spots or home-style restaurants with sidewalk tables; order at the counter—say "takeaway." Most fast-food stalls serve lunch only, though in touristed areas some stay open to early evening. The outdoor markets in Tel Aviv and Jerusalem close in late afternoon and on Shabbat. In Jerusalem, no food stalls open on Shabbat, but in the Old City (except the Jewish Quarter) hummus and falafel joints do business.

GRAB IT & GO

Some street fare is substantial, whether it's falafel or the sandwiches on five-nut artisanal breads that are edging out traditional favorites in Tel Aviv. Other choices are lighter. Sold in markets, in bakeries, and on street stands are sweet pastries called *rugelach*: these two-bite-size twists are rolled up with cinnamon or oozing with chocolate. Just-roasted nuts or sunflower seeds are a quick pick-me-up; or sip fresh-squeezed fruit juices such as pomegranate or carrot. Frosty frozen yogurt and rich ice creams are perfect on hot days. A frothy cappuccino is always good; in winter, try a cup of hot custard-like *sahlab*, perhaps sprinkled with cinnamon.

FALAFEL

The region's ultimate fast-food snack consists of deep-fried chickpea balls—the best are crispy outside with soft centers. Falafel also refers to the whole production of the balls served in pita pockets with an array of chopped vegetable salads plus hummus, tahini, and pickles that you add yourself and then eat (watch for drips!) with a waxed paper napkin for further refinement. Vendors compete with extra touches such as free salads. It's filling, nutritious, and cheap.

HUMMUS

Ubiquitous in the Middle East, hummus is a creamy paste made from mashed chickpeas, olive oil, garlic, and tahini (a sesame sauce). You eat it in a pita or scoop it up from a plate with the same. In Hebrew, there's a verb for this action specifically related to hummus: *lenagev*, meaning "to wipe." Heartfelt arguments prevail among Israelis over where to find the best hummus, but eat it at a Middle Eastern specialty place; some of the best are on market alleys and side streets—even at gas stations.

SHAWARMA

For this fast-food favorite, marinated lamb or turkey slices are stacked and grilled on a vertical spit, then sliced off and stuffed into a pita. Accompaniments are usually the same choice as for falafel, though onion rings and French

fries are other extras. Jerusalem mixed grill (me'oorav Yerushalmi) is unique to the Holy City; look for it on Agrippas Street, alongside the outdoor fruit and vegetable market. It's a well-seasoned meal of grilled chicken hearts and other organ meats eaten in a pita with grilled onions.

TAHINI

Silky in texture, this sauce with a nutty, slightly sweet taste is made from ground sesame seeds, fresh lemon juice, and sometimes garlic. The tasty green variety has parsley chopped in. Tahini is used as a sauce and is the main ingredient in halva, the famous Middle Eastern sweet. A popular dessert—among non-dieters—is a dish of vanilla ice cream topped with tahini and crumbled halva and flooded with date syrup.

BOUREKAS

From the Balkans comes Israel's favorite snack: flaky, crispy, golden-brown bourekas. Best eaten warm, they're pastry triangles, squares, or crescents deliciously filled with tangy cheese or mashed potato or creamy spinach and sometimes mushrooms. Small (two bites) or large (four bites), they can be made of several kinds of dough: puff pastry, phyllo, and short pastry. Bourekas are especially fine when topped with toasted sesame seeds.

—*By Judy Stacey Goldman*

CENTER CITY

$$
ITALIAN
✕**Allora.** The well-stocked wooden bar is the centerpiece of this tiny, 10-table eatery, where the roaring brick oven and pizza-dough kneaders are in full view. The pizza makes a great starter, served with a variety of dips including clemente olive spread, garlic confit, and, for Middle Eastern good measure, labaneh goat cheese. The narrow porch is your perch to watch the people strolling and cycling along the tree-lined center of Rothschild Boulevard. Come here for happy hour, weekdays from 3 to 8. ⊠*60 Rothschild Blvd., Center City* ☎*03/566–5655* ⊟*AE, DC, MC, V.* ✛*5B*

$
CAFÉ
✕**Ashtor.** This small corner café is where you can catch a glimpse of the beauty of European café culture. Coffee is the main event, over which you can linger for hours along with your newspaper, computer, and best of all, friends from the neighborhood. Because it's in the heart of the upscale Basel area, the patrons include the entertainment celebrities that live nearby. The sandwich and salad menu is solid, and the service is helpful. ⊠*37 Basel St., 62744 Center City* ☎*03/546–5318* ⊟*AE, DC, MC, V.* ✛*2B*

$$$$
EASTERN
EUROPEAN
✕**Baba Yaga.** A pleasant lawn and wooden deck front this small restaurant at the slightly shabbier end of Hayarkon Street. Black tablecloths, high-backed chairs, old-fashioned light fixtures, and beige-and-white wallpaper give Baba Yaga a touch of elegance to complement its high-end prices. Baba Yaga is a notorious witch in Russian folk tales, and there's a collection of witch dolls behind the bar. Small but delicious portions showcase mainly Russian classics (the Stroganoff is made with sweet cream rather than sour). There's a good selection of Israeli boutique wines, along with an interesting mix of foreign beers. Baba Yaga takes Tel Aviv's eclectic dining scene to new heights: the menu notes that diners can order "traditional Jewish dishes" a few days ahead of time. ⊠*12 Hayarkon St., Center City* ☎*03/516–7305* ⊟*AE, DC, MC, V.* ✛*5A*

$$
FRENCH
✕**Brasserie.** The dark upholstery, mustard-color walls, and menu in French (in addition to Hebrew and English) are all meant to recall Paris, and the wide selection of excellently prepared food is a credit to French cuisine. The families and groups of friends from the neighborhood and beyond that pack the place on the weekends come for the brunch, where eggs Creole and eggs Norwegian style (poached, on toast, with salmon and spinach), as well as pancakes and club sandwiches are served. For lunch or dinner, there's grilled fish, pasta, and even Asian steamed vegetables, among many other dishes, but that brasserie staple—steak-frites—is the talk of the town. ⊠*70 Ibn Gvirol, Center City* ☎*03/696–7111* ⊟*AE, DC, MC, V.* ✛*3C*

$$
AMERICAN
✕**Brewhouse.** One of Rothschild Boulevard's original mansions, the Brewhouse has been restored to house a working boutique brewery. Copper vats and pipes add a gleaming accent to the interior and beer is a highlight of the menu. The focus is grilled meat, but lunchtime specials sometimes include an Asian buffet. Service is excellent and prices are moderate for this area. ⊠*11 Rothschild Blvd., Center City 66881* ☎*03/516–8666* ⊟*AE, DC, MC, V.* ✛*5B*

$ ✕**Café Batia.** The plain decor of this Dizengoff Street institution hasn't
EASTERN been changed in years, and the menu is filled with old-fashioned Eastern
EUROPEAN European favorites. Try a bowl of matzoh-ball soup or stuffed cabbage
for a nostalgic reminder of the kind of meal Grandma used to prepare,
as well as some less well-known dishes such as pupiks, which is Yiddish
for gizzards. You can also eat outside. ✉*197 Dizengoff St., Center City*
☎*03/522–1335* ▭*AE, DC, MC, V.* ✛*2B*

$$ ✕**Café Bialik.** This veteran of Tel Aviv café culture is the perfect comple-
CAFÉ ment to a stroll down this historic street. Plenty of other Tel Aviv res-
taurants serve more or less the same menu as Café Bialik—an "Israeli
Breakfast," which is a wide selection of chopped salads with eggs done
in a variety of ways, toast, coffee and juice, and sometimes smoked
salmon and small sandwiches. But it's the old-fashioned chrome bar
stools, wooden tables, and Lenong-style wooden chairs that make this
place stand out. ✉*2 Bialik St., Center City* ☎*03/620–0832* ▭*AE,*
DC, MC, V. ✛*4B*

$$ ✕**Café Metzada.** A varied menu—including steak, generous salads, sand-
CAFÉ wiches, and pasta—makes this a great place for supper after a day at
the beach, or a nice spot to relax with a glass of wine at sunset. There's
a fabulous Mediterranean view and the option of indoor or outdoor
seating. ✉*83 Hayarkon St., Center City* ☎*03/510–3353* ▭*AE, DC,*
MC, V. ✛*3A*

$$ ✕**Dalita.** Located on the non-touristy section of Ben-Yehuda Street,
BAKERY midway between Ben-Gurion and Arlozoroff streets, you might miss
Dalita if you didn't know about it. It's a lovely place to stop and rest
your tired feet while on your way to or from the Dizengoff area. The
Hungarian pastries in this sweetshop filled with wrought-iron white
tables and chairs are prepared on-site by the owner Dalit Golan. It will
definitely spoil your dinner, but try the dumplings filled with apricots
that Hungarians call gumbotz, as well as biennenstich ("bee sting"),
a yeast cake with vanilla cream topped with almonds. Everything is
served on old-style porcelain dishes. ✉*146 Ben Yehuda St., Center*
City ☎*03/529–2649* ▭*AE, MC, V.* ✛*2B*

$$$ ✕**Dita.** This bistro-esque fixture of Rothschild Street eateries, with a
MIDDLE EASTERN bar and outdoor seating, is off a small square behind the main drag
where you can listen to street musicians performing on weekends. It's
famous locally for its grilled meat dishes, but has a varied menu with
savory Middle Eastern touches as well. ✉*45 Rothschild, Center City*
☎*03/560–4222* ▭*AE, DC, MC, V.* ✛*5B*

$$$ ✕**Dixie.** This bar and grill is west of central Tel Aviv, and mostly serves
AMERICAN the surrounding offices and commercial centers. But it's open 24 hours a
day, and there's no place like Dixie for a hearty American-style breakfast
of eggs Benedict or a stack of pancakes. The dinner menu includes prime
ribs, Cajun chicken, Norwegian salmon, and a selection of burgers.
There is a minimum charge to dine at the comfortable leather couches in
the main dining area, but feel free to sit at the bar with an order of spicy
chicken wings, the house specialty. ✉*120 Yigal Allon, corner of Tozeret*
Haaretz St., Center City ☎*03/696–6123* ▭*AE, DC, MC, V.* ✛*3D*

$ ✕**Giraffe Noodle Bar.** Generous portions of noodles in a variety of
PAN-ASIAN Japanese, Thai, and other Asian styles attract a loyal clientele to this

Most Israeli food is kid-friendly. This little one is trying pita and hummus. —photo by rooneyroo, Fodors.com member

often-crowded restaurant. There's a selection of soups and sushi for starters. Save room for the meringue-based, berry-topped pavlova. Lunch is a particularly good bargain. ⊠49 Ibn Gvirol St., Center City ☎03/691–6294 ⊟AE, DC, MC, V. ✛3C.

¢ ✕**Ilan's Coffee Shop.** The blends of over 20 types of coffee, including
CAFÉ those from Brazil, Papua New Guinea, Colombia, and Ethiopia, are not the only attraction at Ilan's, which has three other central Tel Aviv locations. The coffee shop is also a pioneer in Israel in importing products that adhere to the international Fairtrade standard, which ensures a fair price to the farmers in the countries producing the product. A selection of teas and tea blends, specialty sandwiches, and luscious desserts are also on hand. Especially recommended is the sugarless cheesecake, on one end of the calorie scale, and *jocolada*—a doughy cake that oozes melted white chocolate—at the other. ⊠90 Ibn Gvirol St., Center City ☎03/523–5334 ⊟AE, DC, MC, V. ✛3C

$$ ✕**Jacko.** This branch of the Jacko chain is opposite the Shalom Tower,
SEAFOOD and even though there's no view to speak of, it's located in one of the most successfully restored houses on the edge of the White City. The menu features a selection of Mediterranean seafood, grilled trout, and St. Peter's fish (tilapia). It's a good place to try sea bream, a mild-tasting fish that's a staple of sea-food and other restaurants in Tel Aviv. A filling array of appetizers is included in the price. ⊠2 Herzl St., Center City ☎03/516–9325 ⊲Reservations essential ⊟AE, DC, MC, V. ✛5B

$ ✕**Le Petit Prince.** You'll think you've walked into someone's circa-1920s
VEGETARIAN fixer-upper when you see this "living room," lined floor to ceiling with books. In addition to serving light vegetarian meals, coffee, and tea, Le Petit Prince, near the end of the cul-de-sac of Simtat Plonit, sells

everything on its shelves. ⊠*3 Simtat Plonit, Center City* ☎*03/629–9387* ☽*Sun.–Thurs. 10* AM*–8* PM*, Fri. 10* AM*–4* PM ☽*Closed Sat.* ✛*4B*

$$$$ ✕**Messa.** Chef Aviv Moshe's haute cuisine offers the flavors of the
Fodor'sChoice Middle East, like the shredded-wheat type of pastry, kadaif, but it's
★ in a class of its own that can be described as high-end "Israeli": Med-
MODERN ISRAELI iterranean–Middle Eastern, with French and Italian touches. And the
interior design is generating as much of a buzz as the cuisine. White
is the dominant color in the dining room, with tented ceiling lamps
on which video art is projected. A long, central table with stylish high
chairs is the room's centerpiece, perfect for mingling with co-diners
while the attentive waitstaff serves dishes such as goat cheese and eggplant accented with shrimp and citrus butter for a starter, and truffle
ravioli with lemon cream and Tassos olives for a main. Adjacent to the
restaurant is Messa's bar, its interior as starkly black as the dining room
is white. ⊠*19 Ha'arbaa St., Center City* ☎*03/685–8001* ✑*Reservations essential* ⊟*AE, DC, MC, V.* ✛*4C*

$$ ✕**Mexicana.** It's almost small enough to miss it as you head up Bogrash-
MEXICAN ov Street toward the main drag on Ben-Yehuda, but it's worth watch-
ing for if you're hankering after Mexican food. Spices are toned down
for the Israeli palate, but tell the kitchen if you prefer some kick and
they'll ratchet up the jalapenos for you. A specialty is *Sombrella*, strips
of chicken or entrecote stir-fried with vegetables and served in a confit
of red peppers and chipotle. Pizza is also on the menu, with a tortilla-
like crust. Business lunch at Mexicana means a 20% discount (Sunday–
Thursday from noon to 5) on the whole menu. ⊠*7 Bograshov St. at
Allenby, Center City* ☎*03/527–9911* ⊟*AE, MC, V.* ✛*3A*

$$ ✕**Minna Tomei.** This place fills up in typical Tel Aviv style after 9 PM,
ASIAN serving food that's prepared in front of salivating guests. Everything
on the menu is Asian-influenced with Indian accents thrown into the
mix. Try the butter chicken, served on skewers in a spicy yogurt, lemongrass, and garam masala sauce that you wrap in the *lafa* (a sweet,
fluffy flatbread). The quality of the food far surpasses the minimalist
decor, which falls short of elegant. It's a popular choice for families
with small children, so the noise level is pretty high. ⊠*30 Ibn Gavirol,
Center City* ☎*03/696–6363.* ✛*3C*

$$$$ ✕ **Montefiore.** The restaurant at Hotel Montefiore (which most Tel
FRENCH Avivians know just as "Montefiori's") serves modern brasserie fare, a
beautiful selection of fish, and even dares a few Vietnamese touches.
Mains include dishes such as baked sea fish with tomatoes and olive oil,
grilled lamb chops, and sirloin steak with wild mushrooms. The restaurant (and the 12 rooms of the boutique hotel above it) is in a lovingly
restored original home on Montefiori Street in the heart of historic Tel
Aviv. The white walls, potted plants, and slatted dark wooden Vene-
tian blinds—even the silver-plated sugar servers selected by co-owner
Ruthie Brouda from markets in England—evoke Old-World colonial
days. The impeccable service, well-prepared food, and interesting wine
list compare very favorably with the city's more expensive restaurants
that do not have the fabulous atmosphere. ⊠*36 Montefiori St., Center
City* ☎*03/564–6100* ⊟*AE, DC, MC, V.* ✛*4B*

$$ ✕**Moses.** This bar and grill, at the western end of tony Rothschild Bou-
AMERICAN levard, has an extensive menu. It's good for the whole family, with kids'
dishes like the Moses hamburger and, for the adults, an interesting selec-
tion of cocktails. The ribs in molasses are a real treat. ⊠*35 Rothschild
Blvd., Center City* ☎*03/566–4949* ▭*AE, DC, MC, V.* ✛*4B*

$$ ✕**Onami.** Located along the row of Tel Aviv's trendiest restaurants, Ona-
JAPANESE mi's chefs prepare a large variety of tastefully presented Japanese dishes
at the large bar that is the restaurant's centerpiece, while the tables are
filled with all sorts of locals, from three-generational families to groups
of thirtysomethings, who arrive mostly in clusters (it makes for a fun
people-watching, if noisy, dining experience). A choice of five different
kinds of *zosui* (rice-based soup) can be a whole meal, combined with
sushi or sashimi as a first course, making this a relatively economical
option among Tel Aviv's better restaurants. ⊠*18 Ha'arba'a, Center
City* ☎*03/562–1172* ▭*AE, DC, MC.* ✛*4C*

$$ ✕**Orna and Ella.** As the loyal clientele from the greater Tel Aviv area will
CONTEMPORARY attest, Orna and Ella is worth several trips a week because of its varied
Fodor's Choice menu. The comfort-food-with-a-twist entrées might be anything from
★ moussaka to pasta in butternut-squash sauce, but the house specialty
is sweet-potato pancakes. Desserts include a scrumptious *tarte tatin*
(apple tart) and pear pie. There's often a long wait, especially Friday
afternoon and after 8 PM on weekdays. ⊠*33 Sheinkin St., Center City*
☎*03/620–4753* ▭*AE, DC, MC, V.* ✛*4B*

$$ ✕**Petrozilia.** One of the few kosher restaurants on Rothschild Boulevard,
MIDDLE EASTERN this eatery, in one of the boulevard's original old brick buildings, has
a good selection of Israeli favorites, including the ubiquitous schnitzel
(breaded chicken breast), and a typical array of Middle Eastern salads.
Food is prepared by the garrulous chefs at a front-and-center counter.
⊠*47 Rothschild Blvd., Center City* ☎*03/516–2468* ▭*AE, DC, MC,
V* ⊘*No dinner Fri. No lunch Sat.* ⌁*Kosher.* ✛*5B*

$$ ✕**Pronto.** Pronto's owner was made a "knight of the Italian republic"
ITALIAN for his contribution to Italian culture outside Italy with this small oasis
of Roman cuisine tucked away on a side street in the historic district.
Dishes are imaginative, and although quality may vary, the grilled pul-
lets cento erbe ("one hundred herbs") are a treat. There's a NIS 5 cover
charge for "bread, parmesan and the tablecloth" (as the waitstaff put
it), which is unusual for a Tel Aviv restaurant. ⊠*26 Nahmani St., Cen-
ter City* ☎*03/566–0915* ▭*AE, DC, MC, V.* ✛*4B*

$$$ ✕**Raphael.** This place bills itself as a bistro (to be exact, a "resto-bis-
MEDITERRANEAN tro"), and diners can expect an exceptional meal, albeit not in the inti-
mate surroundings the term bistro might conjure up. Raphael's elegant
setting has touches of the Far East, and the Mediterranean framed by
its picture windows is also present in the seasonings used in the dishes
on its generously varied menu. From a sophisticated first course such
as asparagus with chestnuts and comté, you can move on to sword-
fish accented with white Madagascar pepper and tomato confit, or
saffron couscous with lamb ossobuco, or smoked sirloin and Golan
Heights lamb chops. Service is particularly attentive and pleasant.
⊠*87 Hayarkon, Center City* ☎*03/522–6464* ⌁*Reservations essential* ▭*AE, DC, MC, V.* ✛*3A*

¢ **✗Sabich.** This hole-in-the-wall eatery off the beaten tourist track on
MIDDLE EASTERN Ibn Gvirol Street specializes in *sabich*, a Middle Eastern meal-in-a-pita
considered a breakfast (the word comes from the Arabic for "morning")
because it's got a hard-boiled egg in it in addition to hummus, tomatoes,
peppers, and spices. It's a filling snack any time of day. The indoor dining area has three or four stools at a counter, and there are a few tables
outside as well. ⊠*99 Ibn Gvirol, Center City* ☎*03/523–1810* ⊟*No
credit cards.* ✛*2C*

$$ **✗Shtsupak.** Diners crowd the tables inside and out at this unadorned
SEAFOOD fish restaurant. The fact that they've been doing so for years in spite
of the fact that the much more trendy and scenic Tel Aviv Port, with
several fish places of its own, is a few steps away, shows you the locals
agree the food is good, reasonably priced, and always fresh. For the
main course, there's a daily selection of fresh "catches of the day,"
which may include whole trout, fried calamari, or oysters in cream
sauce. Fish entrées come with an assortment of salads and spreads for
starters. ⊠*256 Ben Yehuda St., Center City* ☎*03/544–1973* ⊟*AE,
DC, MC, V.* ✛*2B*

$$ **✗Sus Etz.** If you're hungry after shopping on Sheinkin, keep an eye out
CAFÉ for this eatery's landmark (there's no sign in English)—an old-fashioned
wooden horse. The menu is extensive, from a tempting array of sandwiches served alongside a generous salad, to pastas and desserts. Average folks as well as lunching ladies come here, and the people-watching
inside and from streetside tables is part of the fun. ⊠*20 Sheinkin St.,
Center City* ☎*03/528–7955* ⊟*AE, DC, MC, V.*

$ **✗Tandoori.** This veteran restaurant—the oldest of the Tandoori chain,
INDIAN which introduced Israelis to fine Indian cuisine—has maintained the
high quality of its food and service over the years. There are all the
standard curries, but tandoori chicken is the specialty: it comes to the
table sizzling hot, and finger bowls of rose water mean you can dig
in with abandon. A luncheon buffet offers a good selection from the
menu. ⊠*2 Zamenhoff St., Center City* ☎*03/629–6185* ⊟*AE, DC,
MC, V.* ✛*3B*

NEVEH TZEDEK

$$$ **✗Belini's.** With indoor and outdoor seating, this Tuscan-style establish-
ITALIAN ment facing the open square across from the Suzanne Dellal Center is
perfect for a before-theater dinner. The fine wide pasta with hunter's
sauce—a brown sauce with mushrooms and white wine—offers an
unusual blend of flavors. The service is friendly and helpful, and the
Italian house wine is a break from the usual. ⊠*6 Yechieli St., Neveh
Tzedek* ☎*03/517–8486* ⊟*AE, DC, MC, V.* ✛*5B*

$$ **✗Dallal.** The main reason to come to this bistro-inspired restaurant
MEDITERRANEAN inside a beautiful restored historic building is the atmosphere and the
on-premises bakery that turns out a luscious array of mainly French-
style pastries. The enclosed patio, with its wrought-iron tables and
chairs, is a lovely place to sit and enjoy a late afternoon coffee or
sweet. The setting fully compensates for a somewhat unexciting if wide
selection of meat, fish, poultry, and pasta dishes. ⊠*10 Shabazi, Neveh
Tzedek* ☎*03/510–9292* ⊟*AE, DC, MC, V.* ✛*5B*

$$$
CONTEMPORARY

✕**NG.** Tucked away in a quiet corner of the city, where downtown Tel Aviv becomes Neveh Tzedek, this small, elegant bistro specializes in fine cuts of meat expertly prepared. It's purported to be the only place in Israel where you can enjoy a real porterhouse steak. And for dessert? That depends on the time of year. Tangy strawberry-vanilla pie is a winter specialty, and fig-vanilla pie is a summer favorite. For a sugar infusion that will keep up your touring energy, there's luscious chestnut-and-chocolate pie year-round. The building is historic, but the interior is contemporary, complementing the Mediterranean tile floors with geometric patterns. ⊠*6 Ahad Ha'am St., Neveh Tzedek* ☎*03/516–7888* ▭*AE, MC, V* ⊗*No lunch Sun., Mon., Wed., and Thurs.* ⊹*5B*

$$
MEDITERRANEAN

✕**Suzanna.** This restaurant, which occupies a century-old building, bustles day and night. There's something for everyone: from Iraqi *kibbeh* (meat-filled semolina dumplings) and pumpkin soup, to a thick Moroccan soup, *Kharira*, with chickpeas, veal, and coriander, to seafood such as a spicy gray mullet in tomato sauce. The dessert menu is equally expansive, with home-style sorbet, pear-and-apple tart, and chocolate fudge cake. It's especially nice to sit on the leafy terrace. ⊠*9 Shabazi St., Neveh Tzedek* ☎*03/517–7580* ▭*AE, DC, MC, V.* ⊹*4B*

JAFFA

$$
SEAFOOD

✕**Abdu Hadayag.** According to neighborhood lore, Abdu, who will be on hand to greet you more often than not, was indeed a fisherman in his early years. His simple establishment has been a fixture of Jaffa's main street among the local businesses and apartments south of the tourist drag. The fishnets, lanterns, and other marine accoutrements are refreshingly down-to-earth in a city where the interior design of restaurants has sometimes become as important as the flavors and seasonings. The day's catch varies; the menu includes grouper, red snapper, gray mullet, and mackerel, as well as melita, an Israeli breed from the barracuda family. ⊠*37 Yefet, Jaffa* ☎*03/518–2595* ▭*AE, MC, DC, V.* ⊹*6A*

$$$
SEAFOOD

✕**Manta Ray.** This large restaurant has a relaxed atmosphere, with a great beach view, and indoor and outdoor dining, but tends to get noisy. It appeals to a cross-section of diners from families to couples looking for romance, and attracts a loyal clientele from as far away as Jerusalem. The filling, imaginative appetizers are perhaps Manta Ray's finest feature. These vary from day to day; some standards include the shrimp with spinach, mango, and cracked wheat, and the goat cheese and beets. The whole seabream baked in rosemary and olive oil is simple Mediterranean fare at its best, with a more exotic spicy rice dish in chili and pepper sauce on the side. ⊠*Alma Beach, near the Dolphinarium, Jaffa* ☎*03/517–4773* ⚔*Reservations essential* ▭*AE, DC, MC, V.* ⊹*5A*

$
BISTRO

✕**Puah.** In the heart of the Jaffa Flea Market, Puah's fresh flowers, lumpy sofa, and bargain-basement-style tables and chairs make for a kick-your-shoes-off atmosphere—and some patrons oblige. It's a popular gathering place for thirtysomething Tel Avivians as well as young families. Some Tel Aviv restaurants make do by ordering their baked goods elsewhere; at Puah, all the cakes, cookies, and croissants are baked fresh on the premises. There's a good selection of vegetarian

DID YOU KNOW?

The bountiful spread that is the traditional Israeli breakfast can include everything from salads to omelets to baked goods. But not all are served al fresco!

If you visit Jaffa, sit at the old port and watch the sun dip down into the Mediterranean.

dishes, alongside meat and fish. Among the veggie dishes is the Middle Eastern favorite *majadarah* (rice with lentils), served with a side salad and yogurt. One of their prize meat dishes is sautéed chicken breast with mushrooms, onions, garlic, shatta pepper, and pieces of apple, served on a bed of whole-grain rice. ⊠ *8 Rabbi Yohanan St., Jaffa* ☎ *03/682–3821.* ✛ *5B*

$ ✗ **Yaffo Caffe.** The Italian-style ice creams and sorbets prepared daily by
CAFÉ chef Ronnie Rivlin are the highlight of this light, airy corner café in the midst of the Jaffa Flea Market. Apple pie and berry frozen yogurt are among the most popular choices. The menu also includes an extensive list of pastas and pizzas, making it a good choice for families when the little ones begin to clamor for lunch or a break. ⊠ *11 Olei Tzion St., Jaffa* ☎ *03/518–1988* ═ *AE, DC, MC, V.* ✛ *6A*

TEL AVIV PORT AND NORTHERN TEL AVIV

$$ ✗ **Badulina.** This unassuming establishment in the Tel Aviv Port is
CAFÉ squeezed in along a row of splashier neon-lit restaurants. The main dishes (fish is their specialty) come with a choice of two sides, including salad and home-fried potatoes. This is a good stop for coffee and dessert, prepared on-site by the expert pastry chef and appetizingly displayed in a refrigerator up front. ⊠ *2 Yordei Hasira St., Tel Aviv Port* ☎ *03/544–9449* ═ *AE, DC, MC, V.* ✛ *1B*

$$ ✗ **comme il faut.** This trendy eatery opens onto the Tel Aviv Port board-
CAFÉ walk on one side and the high-end Bayit Banamal shopping center on the other. Striped sailor-style black, white, and red shirts are pulled over some of the wooden chair backs, which is a cute decorating touch.

Linger over coffee (soy milk is available) or wine, or enjoy entrées from the lunch or dinner menus, divided into two sections: "health" and "no pangs of conscience." Top choices are fusion specialties such as calamari mesabakha (with warm chickpeas and tahini sauce). ⊠ *1 Bayit Banamal, Tel Aviv Port* ☎ *03/681–8820 Ext. 7* ⊟ *AE, DC, MC, V.* ⊹ *1B*

$$$$
SEAFOOD
Fodor'sChoice
★

× **Mul-Yam.** This high-end seafood bar flies in its main attractions fresh from abroad—including Nova Scotia lobsters, purple-hued Forbidden Black Rice from China, red snapper from New Zealand, turbot from the North Sea, clams from Brittany, and wild berries from Provence. An extensive list of fine wines the owners have personally selected from Israel and around the world complement dishes whose complex seasonings and presentation put Mul-Yam in a class of its own. Diners can watch a slice of life at the trendy Tel Aviv Port through a glass wall. Summer lunchtimes are a chance to sample some of its gastronomic delights at business-price levels. ⊠ *Hangar 24, Tel Aviv Port* ☎ *03/546–9920* ⊟ *AE, DC, MC, V.* ⊹ *1B*

$
MIDDLE EASTERN

× **Shalvata.** In a shady outdoor spot, Shalvata does unusual double-duty: by day it's where trendy Tel Aviv parents take their kids to run around while they eat. By night Shalvata is one of the city's better-known watering holes, with live performances. Choices that are a real treat include the Greek salad with fresh vegetables and squares of smooth tangy feta drizzled with olive oil and fresh herbs. ⊠ *Near Hangar 25, Tel Aviv Port* ☎ *03/544–1279 or 03/546–8536* ⊟ *AE, DC, MC, V.* ⊹ *1B*

$$$
MIDDLE EASTERN

× **Shipudei Hatikva.** This family-owned restaurant chain is the best known of the many grills along Ha'etzel Street, the busy main drag of the working-class Hatikva Quarter. Pictures of famous patrons adorn the walls, showing where the "who's who" of Israel's entertainment and political world go when they're in the mood for good Middle Eastern fare. There's a selection of salads and spreads to begin, including eggplant in mayonnaise and hot Turkish salad, as well as hummus and pita. For the main course, diners can pick from a range of sumptuous skewered meats grilled over hot coals. The specialty is barbecued goose liver. ⊠ *37 Ha'etzel St., Tel Aviv Port* ☎ *03/688–5243* ⊟ *AE, DC, MC, V* ⊗ *No dinner Fri. Closed Sat.* ⊹ *6D*

WHERE TO STAY

Nothing stands between Tel Aviv's luxury hotels and the Mediterranean Sea except the golden beach and the Tayelet (promenade), outfitted with chairs and gazebos. Even the small hotels are only a short walk from the water. Tel Aviv's hotel row is on Hayarkon Street, which becomes Herbert Samuel Esplanade (known as the Tayelet) as you proceed south between the Tel Aviv Port area and Jaffa. Across the street from the luxury hotels are a number of more economical ones, and two new boutique hotels are also centrally located, gracing the historic districts of the White City and Neveh Tzedek, respectively. This means that no matter where you stay, you're never far from the main thoroughfares of Ben Yehuda and Dizengoff streets, with their shops and outdoor cafés, or the city's major concert hall, museums, art galleries, and open-air Carmel Market.

BEST BETS FOR TEL AVIV LODGING

Fodor's writers and editors have selected their favorite hotels and other lodgings by price and experience. Fodor's Choice properties represent the "best of the best" across price categories. You can also search by area for excellent places to stay—just check out our complete reviews on the following pages.

Fodor's Choice ★

Hotel Montefiore, $$$$, p. 259

David Intercontinental, $$$, p. 263

Sheraton Tel Aviv Hotel and Towers, $$$$, p. 262

Best By Price

$

Maxim, p. 259

Gordon Inn, p. 258

$$

Cinema, p. 257

Center, p. 257

Sea.Net, p. 260

$$$

Carlton, p. 256

Renaissance Tel Aviv, p. 260

Basel, p. 256

$$$$

Hotel Montefiore, p. 259

Sheraton Tel Aviv Hotel and Towers, p. 262

Daniel, p. 264

Best By Experience

BEST CONCIERGE

David Intercontinental, $$$, p. 263

Carlton, $$$, p. 256

Hilton Tel Aviv, $$$, p. 259

BEST ISRAELI BREAKFAST

Hilton Tel Aviv, $$$, p. 259

David Intercontinental, $$$, p. 263

BEST HOTEL BAR

Sheraton Tel Aviv Hotel and Towers, $$$$, p. 262

Hilton Tel Aviv, $$$, p. 259

Maxim, $, p. 259

BEST ROOF DECK

Grand Beach, $$, p. 258

Carlton, $$$, p. 256

Hotel de la Mer, $$, p. 259

BEST HOTEL SPA

Dan Accadia, $$$$, p. 263

Sheraton Tel Aviv Hotel and Towers, $$$$, p. 262

Hilton Tel Aviv, $$$, p. 259

BEST FOR KIDS

Sharon, $$$, p. 264

Regency Suites, $$, p. 260

Dan Accadia, $$$$, p. 263

BEST FOR ROMANCE

Hotel Montefiore, $$$$, p. 259

David Intercontinental, $$$, p. 263

Neve Tzedek Hotel, $$$$, p. 263

BEST VIEWS

David Intercontinental, $$$, p. 263

Sheraton Tel Aviv Hotel and Towers, $$$$, p. 262

Dan Panorama, $$, p. 262

BEST BEACH

Hilton Tel Aviv, $$$, p. 259

Dan Tel Aviv, $$$, p. 257

Renaissance Tel Aviv, $$$, p. 260

BEST HISTORICAL BUILDING

Cinema, $$, p. 257

Hotel Montefiore, $$$$, p. 259

Neve Tzedek Hotel, $$$$, p. 263

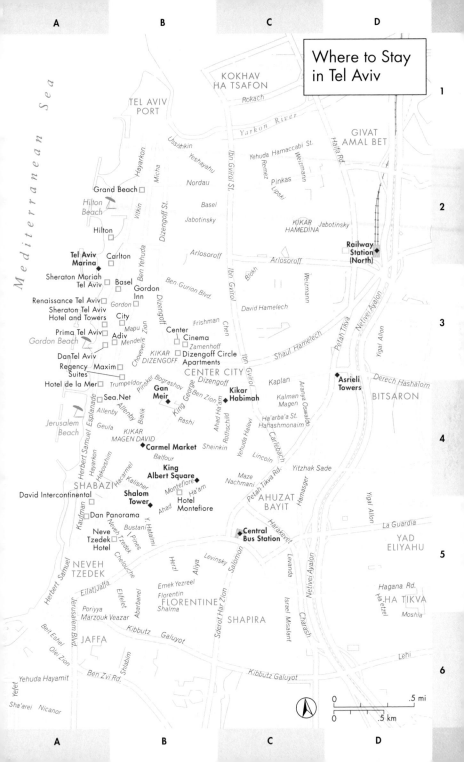

Where to Stay
in Tel Aviv

A   B   C   D

Mediterranean Sea

KOKHAV
HA TSAFON

TEL AVIV
PORT

Rokach

Yarkon River

GIVAT
AMAL BET

1

Ussishkin

Yehuda Hamaccabi St.
Remez
Pinkas
Lipski

Weizmann
Halfa Rd.

Yeshayahu

Nordau

Ibn Gvirol St.

Grand Beach

*Hilton
Beach*

Basel

Jabotinsky

KIKAR
HAMEDINA

Jabotinsky

Railway
Station
(North)

2

Hilton

Arlosoroff

Arlosoroff

Arlosoroff

**Tel Aviv
Marina**

Carlton

Ben Yehuda

Ben-Gurion Blvd.

Blokh

Weizmann

Sheraton Moriah
Tel Aviv

Basel

Renaissance Tel Aviv

Gordon
Inn

Dizengoff

David Hamelech

Netivei Avalon

Petah Tikva

Yigal Allon

3

Sheraton Tel Aviv
Hotel and Towers

Gordon

City

Frishman

Chen

Ibn Gvirol

Mapu

Prima Tel Aviv

Adiv

Gordon Beach

Mendele

Choevey Zion

Center

Cinema

Zamenhoff

Shaul Hamelech

DanTel Aviv

KIKAR
DIZENGOFF

Dizengoff Circle
Apartments

Regency Maxim
Suites

Hotel de la Mer

Trumpeldor

Dizengoff

CENTER CITY

Kaplan

**Asrieli
Towers**

Derech Hashalom

BITSARON

Sea.Net

**Gan
Meir**

Pinsker

Bograshov

**Kikar
Habimah**

Kalman
Magen

Aranya Oswald

Esplanade

Bialik

King

George

Ben Zion

Ahad Ha'am

Rothschild

Ha'arba'a St.
Hahashmonaim

4

*Jerusalem
Beach*

Herbert Samuel

Hayarkon

Hakovshim

Allenby

Allenby

Geula

KIKAR
MAGEN DAVID

Carmel Market

Rashi

Balfour

Sheinkin

Yehuda Halevi

Carlebach

Lincoln

Yitzhak Sade

**King
Albert Square**

Montefiore

Ha'am

Maze
Nachmani

Petah Tikva Rd.

Hamasger

Yigal Allon

La Guardia

YAD
ELIYAHU

SHABAZI

Kalisher

Hacarmel

**Shalom
Tower**

Ahad

Hotel
Montefiore

AHUZAT
BAYIT

David Intercontinental

Kaufman

Neveh Tzedek

Bustani

Y. Hatalmi

pines

Harakevet

Levanda

Israel Misalant

5

Dan Panorama

Neve
Tzedek
Hotel

Herbert Samuel

Jerusalem Blvd.

Chelouche

NEVEH
TZEDEK

Herzl

Aliya

Levinsky

Salomon

Netivei Avalon

Charash

**Central
Bus Station**

Hagana Rd.

Ha'etzel

HA TIKVA

Moshia

JAFFA

Beit Eshel

Olei Zion

Poriyya
Marzouk Veazar

Eilat/Jaffa

Elifelet

Abarbanel

Emek Yezreel
Florentin
Shalma

FLORENTINE

Sderot Har Zion

SHAPIRA

Lehi

Yefet

Sha'arei *Nicanor*

Yehuda Hayamit

Ben Zvi Rd.

Shibim

Kibbutz Galuyot

Kibbutz Galuyot

6

0   .5 mi

0   .5 km

A   B   C   D

Hotel reservations are essential during all Jewish holidays and are advised throughout the year. In winter, Tel Aviv hotels close their outdoor pools, and the lifeguards at the public beaches take a break as well. Hotel health clubs are open to anyone over age 18 but often charge an entrance fee for non-guests. Keep in mind that most hotels include breakfast in the price: fresh vegetables, salads, and fruit; cereals and pastries; and eggs and cheeses are usually among the options. If your rental car also needs a place to sleep, enquire about the nearest parking lot. Some hotels have them, but a few rely on public lots which can be at least a short walk away.

WHAT IT COSTS IN U.S. DOLLARS				
¢	$	$$	$$$	$$$$
Hotels	Under $120	$120–$200	$201–$300	$301–$400	over $400

Prices are for two people in a standard double room in high season. Non- Israeli citizens paying in foreign currency are exempt from the 15.5% V.A.T tax on hotel rooms.

CENTER CITY

$ **Adiv.** This amiable five-story hotel is on a side street between Hayarkon Street and Ben-Yehuda, which means it's a short walk from the eateries on Ben-Yehuda and its Judaica shops, as well as the beach. Rooms have pleasing modern furnishings and pastel-print bedspreads and curtains. Most rooms have no sea view. The fifth-floor four suites, all with kitchen facilities, are a good solution for traveling families. **Pros:** one of the few lower-priced Tel Aviv hotels with suites. **Cons:** minimum seven-night stay during high season; no Internet connection in rooms; limited parking. ⊠5 Mendele St., Center City ☎03/522–9141 ⊕www.adivhotel. com ⇨79 rooms ⌂In-room: safe, kitchen (some). In-hotel: restaurant, Internet terminal, parking (paid) ▭AE, DC, MC, V. ⊹3B

$$$ **Basel.** Several rooms on each floor of this seven-story hotel have either sea views or views of the small swimming pool, available at no extra charge, and are spacious and airy. A pleasant corner bar and coffee shop are open all day long in the lobby, and look out onto a sunny deck by the pool. **Pros:** a good deal for the price. **Cons:** not on the beach side of Hayarkon. ⊠156 Hayarkon St., Center City ☎03/520–7711 ⊕www.atlashotels.co.il ⇨120 rooms ⌂In-room: safe, refrigerator, Wi-Fi. In-hotel: restaurant, bar, Internet terminal, Wi-Fi, parking (paid), pool, some pets allowed. ▭AE, DC, MC, V. ⊹3B

$$$ **Carlton.** The lobby of the nearly 300-room Carlton has intimate sitting areas, each of which features the work of a different artist. The hotel's friendly service and casual atmosphere make it a favorite with tour groups, while business travelers enjoy its "i-rooms," with a computer workstation at a separate desk in the room. Fresh flowers and bowls of fruit can be found on every floor as well as in the rooms. Wake-up calls are accompanied by fresh juice and newspapers, and complimentary milk and cookies are delivered in the evening upon request. The rooms, with double-glazed windows that help muffle traffic noise, are designed in pleasant muted colors. The hotel also has a rooftop

pool, a glass-enclosed gym, and gives guests the option of breakfast on a deck facing the beach. **Pros:** homey feeling despite size; close to public beach. **Cons:** location near Atarim Square, which is rather shabby. ⊠ *10 Eliezer Peri St., Center City* 🕾 *03/520–1818* ⊕ *www.carlton.co.il* ↘ *300 rooms* ⌂ *In-room: Wi-Fi. In-hotel: restaurant, room service, bar, pool, gym, children's programs (ages 5–12), laundry service, Wi-Fi, parking (paid), some pets allowed* ➦ *AE, DC, MC, V.* ✛ *2B*

$$ 🏨 **Center.** This budget hotel has a cozy lobby (which has a library of books and albums about Tel Aviv) and rooms decorated by different contemporary Tel Aviv artists. Many balconies look out over some interesting slices of life on historic Dizengoff Circle. You'll recognize the building from the outside by its larger-than-life colorful statues of two people astride the balcony wall "talking" by means of empty vintage cottage-cheese containers connected by a string—a favorite pastime among Israeli kids in the 1950s. A lounge area screens vintage black-and-white films about Tel Aviv. Breakfast is served across the street at the fascinating Cinema Hotel, worth a visit in its own right. The hotel also has bicycles complimentary to guests, which are a great way to sightsee. **Pros:** free bicycles for guests; trendy Bauhaus design. **Cons:** Dizengoff Circle location not in the main tourist area. ⊠ *2 Zamenhoff St., Center City* 🕾 *03/526–6100* 🕾 *03/526–6101* ⊕ *www.atlashotels. co.il* ↘ *56 rooms* ⌂ *In-room: refrigerator, Wi-Fi. In-hotel: bicycles, Wi-Fi* ➦ *AE, DC, MC, V.* ✛ *3B*

$$ 🏨 **Cinema.** Hotel Cinema began life in the 1930s as the Esther Cinema, one of the first movie theaters in Tel Aviv. Skip the elevator and take the original, elegant winding staircase from the lobby to the various floors at least once: when restoring it, the architect left the depressions made by thousands of movie-goers over the decades. Vintage projection equipment, tickets, showbills, and other paraphernalia give the feel of a truly charming museum, while the comfortable guest rooms also recall the movies, with black decor and reading lamps that look like tiny stage spotlights. The hotel has designated business floors and a sunroof terrace with a wonderful view of Dizengoff Circle. **Pros:** theme hotel with a sense of history and style; complimentary afternoon coffee hour on the roof. **Cons:** Dizengoff Circle location not considered a main tourist area. ⊠ *1 Zamenhoff St., Center City* 🕾 *03/526–7100* ⊕ *www. atlashotels.co.il* ↘ *82 rooms* ⌂ *In-hotel: restaurant, bar, Wi-Fi* ➦ *AE, DC, MC, V* ⦿ *BP.* ✛ *3B*

$$ 🏨 **City.** On a street of small apartment houses a block from the beach, this six-story hotel has a light, airy lobby with a small sitting area on one side and a cozy restaurant on the other. Rooms are plain, but some have balconies that offer a glimpse of the sea. **Pros:** northern location close to Tel Aviv Port and Hayarkon Park. **Cons:** rooms are small for the price; only some have Wi-Fi access. ⊠ *9 Mapu St., Center City* 🕾 *03/524–6253* ⊕ *www.atlashotels.co.il* ↘ *96 rooms* ⌂ *In-room: Wi-Fi (some). In-hotel: restaurant, Wi-Fi* ➦ *AE, DC, MC, V.* ✛ *3B*

$$$ 🏨 **Dan Tel Aviv.** Return visitors say they love the sense of history surrounding them at the Dan, built in 1953 and billed as Tel Aviv's very first hotel. The rainbow-painted back side of the hotel, facing the Mediterranean, contributes to the landmark status—it was designed

by famed Israeli artist Ya'akov Agam. Rooms in the luxurious King David wing have panoramic sea views and double-glazed windows to muffle city noise. One of the hotel's two restaurants, the Gandan, has both a dairy and a meat section; the other, La Regeance, is gourmet Mediterranean style (and is kosher). Most of the Dan's rooms are at the higher-end executive or deluxe level. Color schemes range from sand-and-sea to rich burgundy. The leisure complex includes a gym and an indoor and outdoor (salt-water) pool. A popular stretch of public beach is right across the street. **Pros:** historic premises; deluxe suites have CD stereo systems and DVDs. **Cons:** guest lounge is off-limits to children under 18. ⊠*99 Hayarkon St., Center City* ☎*03/520–2525* ⊕*www. danhotels.com/Deluxe-Hotel-Tel-Aviv* ⤳*49 rooms, 37 suites* ⌂*In-room: safe, DVD (some), Wi-Fi. In-hotel: 2 restaurants, room service, bar, pools, gym, spa, children's programs (ages 6–12), laundry service, Wi-Fi, parking (paid), some pets allowed.* ▭*AE, DC, MC, V.* ✛*3A*

$ ⛌**Dizengoff Circle Apartments.** This apartment complex in the heart of Dizengoff Square provides a comfortable and reasonably priced alternative to Tel Aviv's more expensive hotels. The homey studios, rooms, and suites all have kitchenettes equipped with microwave and dishes, and come in a variety of sizes and prices. The larger suites can take up to four guests, which makes it a good choice for a small family or friends traveling together. **Pros:** large rooms. **Cons:** Dizengoff Circle is not the main tourist area. ⊠*4 Dizengoff Circle, Center City* ☎*03/524–1151* 🖷*03/523–5614* ⊕*www.hotel-apt.com/dsa* ⤳*32 studios, 3 suites* ⌂*In-room: kitchen, refrigerator, Wi-Fi. In-hotel: Internet terminal, Wi-Fi, some pets allowed* ▭*AE, DC, MC, V.* ✛*3B*

$ ⛌**Gordon Inn.** You'll find basic, hostel-style accommodations at a good location here, a block or so from the beach, with lots of art galleries in the vicinity, and midway between the attractions in north and south Tel Aviv. The price of the more expensive ($20 more than the standard rooms at this writing) includes a free voucher for a daily meal at La Mer, a beachside restaurant that's a short walk away. Guests in standard rooms are served a light breakfast in the small lobby, which is dominated by a pool table. **Pros:** no charge for Wi-Fi; location close to the beach. **Cons:** no restaurant in hotel at this writing; standard rooms don't have in-suite showers or toilets. ⊠*17 Gordon St. at Ben-Yehuda St., Center City* ☎*03/523–8239* ⊕*www.hosteltelaviv.com* ⤳*30 rooms* ⌂*In-room: Wi-Fi* ▭*AE, DC, MC, V.* ✛*3B*

$$ ⛌**Grand Beach.** This basic hotel near the northern entance to the city is 10 minutes from the beach and from the Tel Aviv Port. Slated for refurbishing in 2009, it caters mainly to business travelers but also sees a good deal of tourist traffic, mainly tour groups from South America, Europe, and Russia. The buffet restaurant's food is unremarkable meat-and-potatoes fare, but it does have an interesting view of life bustling along Nordau and Hayarkon streets. There's a small but inviting roof-top pool and sundeck. **Pros:** comfortable lobby bar and business center with complimentary coffee corner. **Cons:** hustle-bustle of tour groups makes for a noisy morning and evening lobby. ⊠*250 Hayarkon St., Center City* ☎*03/543–3333* 🖷*03/546–6589* ⊕*www.grandbeach.co.il* ⤳*212 rooms* ⌂*In-room: safe, Wi-Fi. In-hotel: restaurant, room service, bar, Wi-Fi* ▭*AE, DC, MC, V.* ✛*2B*

$$$ 🏨 **Hilton Tel Aviv.** The northernmost luxury hotel on the Yarkon Street strip, the Hilton is perched on a cliff and buffered on three sides from urban life by the green spaces of Independence Park. It has direct access to the beach, and for lovers of salt water but not sand, the large seawater pool is another option. Together with the spa and the guest rooms, it has recently been fully renovated. In addition to enjoying the excellent, eclectic cuisine at the intimate King Solomon Restaurant, serving everything from pan-fried duck breast on steamed Chinese cabbage and five-spice rice to sea bream with Kalamata olive tapenade and remoulade sauce, you can grab a bite at the Café Med or at the sushi bar that has a seaside view. Business travelers will find a particularly good array of services, especially its two lounges, which have a beautiful, uninterrupted view of the Mediterranean that will make you think you're on a cruise ship. **Pros:** separate shower stalls in many rooms; the lap of luxury with all that guests would expect of the chain. **Cons:** at the end of the hotel strip, somewhat detached from the city on the edge of Independence Park, parts of which are seedy though now undergoing renovation. ⊠*Hayarkon St., Center City* ☎*03/520–2222* ⊕*www.hilton.com* ⤵*582 rooms* △*In-room: safe, DVD (some), Wi-Fi. In-hotel: 5 restaurants, room service, bars, gym, spa, beachfront, children's programs (ages 5–12), laundry service, Internet terminal, Wi-Fi, parking, no fee* ▭*AE, DC, MC, V.* ✛*2B*

$$ 🏨 **Hotel de la Mer.** This boutique hotel is in a historic 1930s Bauhaus building a block from the beach. The establishment prides itself on its personalized service and adherence to the design principles of Feng Shui—both in color scheme and furnishings. Its lobby is graced with works by Israeli artist Amos Aricha. The rooftop terrace, overlooking the beach, has two massage rooms. **Pros:** 24-hour-a-day tea and coffee corner in the dining room. **Cons:** located on an unlovely side street; small lobby. ⊠*62 Hayarkon, off Nes Tziona St., Center City* ☎*03/510–0011* 🖷*03/516–7575* ⊕*www.delamer.co.il* ⤵*26 rooms* △*In-room* ▭*AE, DC, MC, V.* ✛*4B*

$$$$ 🏨 **Hotel Montefiore.** This boutique hotel shows off the best about what
Fodor's Choice restoration can bring to Tel Aviv. The two-story building stands out
★ among others that line the street due to its salmon-hued plaster exterior. The hotel's light-colored walls, hardwood floors, and arabesqued wrought-iron banisters evoke times gone by. Each of the 12 beautifully appointed rooms has the nice touch of a library filled with classics, cook-books, and art books. Interiors are accented by Ziegler Persian rugs. **Pros:** historical area; fine restaurant on property. **Cons:** location in a sometimes congested traffic area of downtown Tel Aviv. ⊠*36 Montefiore St., Center City* ☎*03/564–6100* ⊕*www.hotelmontefiore.co.il* ⤵*12 rooms* △*In-room: Wi-Fi. In-hotel: restaurant, bar, Wi-Fi, parking (paid)* ▭*AE, DC, MC, V.* ✛*4B*

$ 🏨 **Maxim.** This hotel is a good value, especially considering the location: just across the street from the luxury hotel strip and the beach. Most rooms have sea views. Europeans like to stay here, and there is a Continental feel about the place, owing in part to the many languages heard in the lobby when the guests come down from their afternoon rest or after a day at the beach. **Pros:** complimentary coffee and cake in lobby café. **Cons:** rooms are on the drab side. ✉ *86 Hayarkon St., Center City* ☎ *03/517–3721* ⊕ *www.maxim-htl-ta.co.il* ⤴ *71 rooms* ⅏ *In-room: Wi-Fi. In-hotel: restaurant, room service, bar, Internet terminal, Wi-Fi, parking (free), some pets allowed.* ▭ *AE, DC, MC, V.* ✛ *3B*

$$ ⊡ **Prima Tel Aviv.** Built on a rise on the corner of Frishman and Hayarkon streets, the Prima has an excellent view of the sea, and many of its rooms face the Mediterranean. Table lamps and soft lighting make the tiny lobby homey. The hallways and rooms display artwork highlighting Tel Aviv vintage cityscapes. The independently owned restaurant, the Prime Grill, has a beautiful canopied terrace that faces seaward. There's also a coffee bar. **Pros:** Glatt Kosher restaurant on the premises. **Cons:** not all rooms have Wi-Fi access. ✉ *105 Hayarkon St., Center City* ☎ *03/520–6666* ⊕ *www.prima.co.il* ⤴ *56 rooms* ⅏ *In-room: Wi-Fi (some). In-hotel: 2 restaurants, room service, bars, laundry service, Wi-Fi* ▭ *AE, DC, MC, V.* ✛ *3A*

$$ ⊡ **Regency Suites.** This Best Western hotel is made up entirely of well-equipped one-bedroom suites, each of which comes with a small living area and kitchenette. The decor is tasteful and the atmosphere cozy, and rooms have two televisions. There's also a lovely breakfast room, although breakfast isn't included. Daily cleaning services are provided. **Pros:** suites are good for a traveling family or friends; no charge for parking. **Cons:** a buzz-in policy to an otherwise locked lobby. ✉ *80 Hayarkon St., Center City* ☎ *03/517–3939* ⊕ *www.bestwestern.co.il* ⤴ *30 suites* ⅏ *In-room: safe, kitchen, Wi-Fi. In-hotel: restaurant, Wi-Fi, parking (free)* ▭ *AE, DC, MC, V.* ✛ *4B*

$$$ ⊡ **Renaissance Tel Aviv.** All rooms have balconies at this comfortably informal luxury hotel, which is part of the Marriott chain. Slices of sea views either face Jaffa to the south or the nearby Marina Club. Restaurants include the Jaffa Terrace, which serves a selection of dairy dishes and pastas, as well as sandwiches and beverages, and the Sabres Brasserie, with buffet and à la carte menus, open for lunch and dinner. The hotel has direct access to the beach (from 8:30 AM to 5 PM only) and one of the few indoor heated swimming pools in Tel Aviv. **Pros:** amenities; Marriott awards plan applies. **Cons:** dingy swimming-pool and changing-room floors give sports center a run-down look. ✉ *121 Hayarkon St., Center City* ☎ *03/521–5555* 🖷 *03/521–5588* ⊕ *www.marriott.com* ⤴ *342 rooms, 4 suites* ⅏ *In-room: safe, Wi-Fi. In-hotel: 2 restaurants, room service, bars, pool, gym, spa, laundry service, Internet terminal, Wi-Fi, parking (paid)* ▭ *AE, DC, MC, V.* ✛ *3B*

$$ ⊡ **Sea.Net.** Offering well-appointed rooms, this hotel has the informal atmosphere of a smaller establishment, and seems to cater to European travelers—French and German are frequently heard in the small lobby. Upper rooms have sea views (the hotel is a block from the real thing), and so does the rooftop terrace. Location at the southern end of the city offers good access to the Carmel Market, Jaffa, and Neveh Tzedek. **Pros:** the warm service. **Cons:** rooms are small; roof terrace can be noisy. ✉ *6 Nes Tsiona St., Center City* ☎ *03/517–1655* 🖷 *03/517–1656* ⊕ *www.seanethotel.co.il* ⤴ *70 rooms* ⅏ *In-room: safe, refrigerator (some), Internet. In-hotel: restaurant, bar, parking (paid), some pets allowed.* ▭ *AE, DC, MC, V.* ✛ *4B*

David Tel Aviv

Hotel Montefiore

Sheraton

See art that reflects aspects of Jewish life, past and present, at the Diaspora Museum at the Tel Aviv University campus.

$$$$
Fodor's Choice
★

🏨 **Sheraton Tel Aviv Hotel and Towers.** Combining a personal touch with the efficiency and experience of an international chain, this hotel is one of the most attractive lodging options in Tel Aviv. The newly redecorated lobby is exquisite; it's contemporary, marble-tiled, and elegant, with amazing flower arrangements by the in-house florist, and huge glass windows that draw your eyes toward the sea. The Sheraton Towers is also home to Cielo, an independently owned spa with 14 treatment rooms, a Turkish bath, mud wraps, salt peels, and more. **Pros:** spa and fine restaurant on the premises. **Cons:** located on a very busy and rather drab section of Hayarkon Street. ⊠ *115 Hayarkon St., Center City* 🕾 *03/521–1111* ⊕ *www.starwoodhotels.com* ↪ *345 rooms* ⚲ *In-room: Wi-Fi (some). In-hotel: 2 restaurants, room service, bar, pool, gym, spa, children's programs (ages 5–12), laundry facilities, laundry service, Internet terminal, Wi-Fi, parking (paid), some pets allowed* ▭ *AE, DC, MC, V.* ⊕ *3B*

NEVEH TZEDEK

$$

🏨 **Dan Panorama.** This high-rise hotel, located at the southern end of the Tel Aviv beachfront, is adjacent to a large office complex, a short walk to Jaffa and Neveh Tzedek and across the main road from Dolphinarium beach. Each room has a balcony; many have sea views, others overlook Neveh Tzedek. Poolside barbecues in the summer are a plus. ⊠ *10 Y. Kaufman St., Neveh Tzedek* 🕾 *03/519–0190* 🖷 *03/517–1777* ⊕ *www. danhotels.com* ↪ *500 rooms* ⚲ *In-room: Wi-Fi. In-hotel: restaurant, bar, pool, gym, parking (paid)* ▭ *AE, DC, MC, V* ꙴ *BP.* ⊕ *5A*

$$$

Fodor's Choice

★

David Intercontinental. At the southern end of the Tel Aviv coastline, this luxurious hotel is a top choice for celebrities. The atrium lobby is massive and elegant, with soaring ceilings, marble floors, and a high-end shopping arcade. Most rooms overlook the sea, but some have views of trendy Neveh Tzedek. The rooms have a hint of Spanish style, with warm colors accented by brick-hued pillows that complement the red-tile roofs of Neveh Tzedek's original buildings right below. Top floors are reserved for club-room guests, who have use of a private lounge. The hotel's restaurant, Aubergine, specializes in French and Italian cuisine with Middle Eastern accents, such as the sea bass in lemon and Galilee extra-virgin olive oil, and Golan Heights veal with a porcini mushroom risotto. An extensive menu of Israeli wines from the major wineries is another attraction. **Pros:** location adjacent to Neveh Tzedek. **Cons:** a busy avenue separates the hotel from the beach. ⊠ *12 Kaufman St., Neveh Tzedek* ☎ *03/795–1111* ⊕ *www.ichotelsgroup.com/* ⤷ *516 rooms, 39 suites* ⚇ *In-room: safe, Wi-Fi. In-hotel: restaurant, room service, bar, gym, spa, children's programs (ages 3–12), laundry service, Internet terminal, Wi-Fi, parking (paid)* ⊟ *AE, DC, MC, V.* ⊕ *5A*

$$$$

Neve Tzedek Hotel. The chef-owner of the quarter's popular bistro Nana, Golan Dor, and his brother, Tomi Ben-David (who owns the hotel), came up with the plan to restore the elegance of a historic building and turn it into this five-studio boutique hotel. Wooden doors and cabinets are among some of the appointments that were hunted down in flea markets, and the sinks are constructed out of halved old wine barrels. The lacy finishing on sheets and pillowcases adds a sense of luxurious comfort. **Pros:** innovative design elements; free Wi-Fi. **Cons:** located in a shabbier part of Neveh Tzedek still undergoing restoration as of this writing; urban views from balconies and terraces are not all very inspiring; no lobby. ⊠ *4 Degania St., Neveh Tzedek* ☎ *054/207–0706* ⊕ *www.nevetzedekhotel. com* ⤷ *5 rooms* ⚇ *In-room: kitchen, DVD, Wi-Fi. In-hotel: restaurant, room service, Wi-Fi* ⊟ *AE, DC, MC, V.* ⊕ *5B*

HERZLIYA PITUACH

Herzliya Pituach is a resort area 12 km (7½ mi) up the coast from Tel Aviv. It has a number of beachfront hotels, a public square with outdoor cafés that is a short walk from the beach, and a marina and adjacent Arena Mall with a selection of high-end shops, restaurants, and pubs. The area has a cosmopolitan air, as affluent suburbanites live here, as do diplomats and foreign journalists. At the northern end is Apollonia National Park, a beautiful Crusader-era fortress overlooking the sea. It's a good place to stay if you want resort-style accommodations relatively close to Tel Aviv, or if you have business in the Herzliya's hi-tech zone and want a great place to unwind at the end of the day or on the weekend.

$$$$

Dan Accadia. The two buildings of this seaside hotel are surrounded by plant-filled lawns, which in turn surround a pool overlooking the sea. The standard rooms in the four-story older part of the hotel are tastefully decorated in gold and aquamarine and have balconies with sea views. The newer two-story section has rooms facing either the pool, with its direct access to the beach, or the marina. Garden rooms on the

4

ground floor have their own outdoor Jacuzzis. Organized activities help keep children and teenagers amused on Friday and Saturday, with mid-week activities for the kids during the summer. Guests have access to the adjacent tennis courts. **Pros:** in-house tennis courts. **Cons:** insulated feel with little local atmosphere. ⊠ *22 Ramat Yam St., Herzliya Pituach* ☎ *09/959–7070* ⊕ *www.danhotels.com* ⤵ *209 rooms* ⚐ *In-room: DVD (some), Wi-Fi. In-hotel: 2 restaurants, room service, bar, tennis courts, pool, gym, beachfront, children's programs (ages 5–12), Wi-Fi, parking (free), some pets allowed* ▭ *AE, DC, MC, V.*

$$$$ 🏨 **Daniel.** The Daniel's high-ceilinged lobby has a glass wall that allows guests to gaze out at the Mediterranean, and all of the hotel's rooms have views. The decor is a tasteful mix of sea-blue and mustard hues. Business-club floors offer office services and access to a plush lounge that serves a light buffet breakfast, lunch, and dinner. There is a movie theater adjacent to the hotel. **Pros:** in-house boutique spa and spa-hotel. **Cons:** one of the hotel's two towers has plainer, smaller rooms that according to management are not necessarily lower-priced than the more recently refurbished ones; public parking is first-come, first-serve. ⊠ *60 Ramot Yam, Herzliya Pituach,* ☎ *09/952–8282* ⊕ *www.danielhotel.com* ⤵ *200 rooms* ⚐ *In-room: safe, Wi-Fi. In-hotel: 2 restaurants, room service, bar, tennis courts, pools, gym, spa, beachfront, diving, water sports, bicycles, children's programs (ages 5–12), laundry service, Wi-Fi, parking (free)* ▭ *AE, DC, MC, V.*

$$$ 🏨 **Sharon.** The Sharon is the northernmost hotel on the strip overlooking the water and close to a town square locals frequent for shopping and a bite to eat. Rooms here are cozy and decorated in earth tones, and several face the garden near the outdoor seawater pool. The hotel caters to a wide variety of guests, including tour groups. For families traveling with children, there's an activities club that runs during the summer months, on holidays, and on weekends. **Pros:** homey atmosphere with a sense of local color. **Cons:** most rooms do not have sea views; tourist-group traffic can make for noisy lobby hours morning and evening. ⊠ *5 Ramat Yam, Herzliya Pituach* ☎ *09/957–5777* ⊕ *www.sharon.co.il* ⤵ *170 rooms* ⚐ *In-hotel: restaurant, room service, bar, gym, children's programs (ages 5–12), Internet terminal, Wi-Fi, parking (paid)* ▭ *AE, DC, MC, V.*

NIGHTLIFE AND THE ARTS

When do they sleep? That's what visitors tend to ask about Tel Avivians because they always seem to be out and about, coming or going from a bar, restaurant, or a performance. Tel Aviv's reputation for having the country's best nightlife is well-deserved, and the city is also Israel's cultural center.

NIGHTLIFE

On Lilianblum and Allenby streets, and in Florentine, where many of the pubs and bars are clustered, things don't really get started until at least 10 PM, especially on Friday night. Most places stay open "until the last customer," which means at least 3 A.M. when things finally begin to wind down, although on Allenby and in Florentine, clubs are still crowded at 5 A.M. Note that some bars and clubs are 25-and-up.

For those who want to start and finish the evening early, some night-spots open before the night owls descend; typically, they offer either full dinners, beer and fries, or at the very least the coffee and cake they've been serving throughout the afternoon.

BARS AND CLUBS

Abraksas (✉ *40 Lilenblum St.* ☎*03/510–4435*) is considered very "in" because it's supposedly frequented by local celebrities. There's live music by local artists every Sunday, and on weekends it gets a little wild when it becomes a dance bar popular with students. Walls are adorned with changing exhibits of photographs by young artists.

Apartment98 (✉ *98 Dizengoff St., 2nd fl.* ☎*052/608–5552*) may be a bit hard to find, as it's in a nondescript tenement in the mid-section of Dizengoff Street, but inside it's a swanky lounge-bar with windows and a balcony overlooking the city streets. Closed during the day to host private and corporate events, Apartment98 opens at 9 PM weekdays and 6 PM Saturdays, and features mainstream music and a menu based on a variety of carpaccio dishes.

Armadillo (✉ *51 Ahad Ha'am St.* ☎*03/620–5573* ☉ *Sat.–Thurs. 6:30 PM–last customer, Fri. 7 PM–last customer*), billed as one of Tel Aviv's first neighborhood bars, has cold beer, a nice ambience, and isn't as dark as some bars tend to be. Regulars and staff tend to be in their 30s, making this a good choice if you're over the party scene.

With its three floors, **Artemis** (✉ *52 Nahalat Binyamin St.* ☎*03/510–0663* ☉ *Sun.–Sat. from 9:30*) can attract a crowd literally in the hundreds, and many are college students. The music is very loud, mainly mainstream Israeli rock. A huge Y-shaped bar on the first floor seats 40; there's a smaller bar on the third floor as well as couches around low tables, where you should grab a seat if you want to have a conversation.

Local journalist Ronit Vered pegged **Barbunia** (✉ *192 Ben-Yehudah St.* ☎*03/524–0961* ☉ *Sun.–Thurs.; Sat. noon to the last customer; Fri. 12 noon–6 PM*) one of the 10 best bars in the country. Aptly named for a small fish that's a staple of the city's old-time restaurants, Barbunia's restaurant and bar draw an unusual crowd, from fishermen to financial planners. It's a happy place, and has a private room for events. Music tends toward '70s oldies.

Betty Ford (✉ *48 Nahalat Binyamin St.* ☎*03/510–0650* ☉ *Sun.–Thurs. noon to the last customers, Fri. from 7 PM*), a restaurant as well as a pub, serves miniature hamburgers spicy enough to coax you into a second beer. This place prides itself on its American vibe, which involves country music, in addition to DJs on the weekends and live jazz on Tuesday nights. Brunch on Saturdays includes free refills on coffee—a virtual unknown in other Israeli restaurants. A small inner courtyard adds to the comfortable atmosphere.

Cafe Noga (✉ *4 Pinsker St.* ☎*03/629–6457* ☉ *Sun.–Sa.t from 11:30 AM*) is a bar that doubles as a pool hall, with 19 pool tables. And if darts is your sport, make sure to stop in on Wednesday nights for the contest. Music runs from oldies to hip-hop, depending on which waitress or bartender is working.

Eliezer (✉ *186 Ben-Yehuda St.* ☎ *050/748–4890* ⊗ *8 PM–wee hours.*) is a neighborhood establishment known for its friendly staff and its bar, designed like a grand piano and black-and-white chairs to match. Music is mainly rock, Israeli, and foreign. On the weekends, there's no room to move as it's popular with students, but it's quieter at the start of the week. Drinks are buy-one-get-one-free every night from 8 to 10. The food is solid; try the toasts with pesto and cheese or sun-dried tomatoes.

Evita (✉ *31 Yavne St.* ☎ *03/566–9559*), one of Tel Aviv's best gay bars, is a small, classy place with good food. It's often marked by the long line outside in the later hours, attesting to its popularity.

Friends (✉ *186 Ben-Yehuda St.* ☎ *054/803–5757* ⊗ *Sun.–Thurs; Sat. 8 PM– 5 AM; Fri. 9:30 PM–5 AM*) prides itself on its local Israeli atmosphere. One of the best nights to come is Thursday during the Macabbi Tel Aviv basketball game. Tuesday is "Triple B night," meaning half-pints of beer are NIS 20, and free Bamba, the ubiquitous Israeli peanut form of Cheez-Its. It has a convenient location, a block from the northern end of the Hayarkon hotel strip.

Haminzar (✉ *60 Alenby St.* ☎ *03/517–3015* ⊗ *24 hrs*) is the place to come—especially on Fridays—if you're looking to hang out with young, off-duty soldiers. It's popular with the after-work crowd, which arrives early-afternoon, as well as night owls and students. Take advantage of generous food-and-alcohol happy hour, which lasts from 10 AM to 8 PM The bar serves brunch and lunch, featuring chili con carne and a variety of hand-made sausages, and has a nice atmosphere, as the building it's in is slated for preservation for its Art Deco decor

Hashoftim (✉ *39 Ibn Gvirol at Hashoftim St.* ☎ *03/695–1153* ⊗ *Sun.– Thurs.; Sat. 6 PM–last customer; Fri. 9 PM–last customer*) offers an alternative to loud and trendy Tel Aviv bars, and is one of the city's veteran watering holes. Lots of places call themselves "neighborhood bars," but this one really is, with a loyal cadre of locals whose camaraderie with the staff is obvious. The crowd here tends to be older and mellow. Groups of friends can settle in at a table or the small bar, or at one of the large wooden tables for a drink or even a meal, while enjoying jazz or blues.

Hudna (✉ *13 Abarbanel St.* ☎ *03/518–4558*) plays to students and the young professional crowd that leans toward the political left. The bar is actually split in two with an alley in the middle ideal for kicking back and enjoying a pint of Goldstar beer for NIS 20—the only place in town it's still that cheap. Gobble up a burger and fries, or try some of their excellent home-made hummus. This place is known for its rave parties on Purim and Independence Day.

Jaffa Bar (✉ *Yeffet 30,* ☎ *03/518–4668*) is good choice if you're looking for a solid cocktail, space to breathe, and an easy time hearing conversation. The bar, which tends to attract an older, more sophisticated clientele, is spacious with a sleek bar and an eclectic decor.

Jajo (✉ *Shabazi 47.* seats only twenty people or so, but this dimly-lit jewel of a place, Neveh Tzedek's original neighborhood bar is as chic as it is tiny. The elegant chandelier drooping from the high ceiling, the stone walls, the candle-lit tables, the arched windows facing Shabazi

Continued on page 271

The Bat Sheva Dance Company from Tel Aviv is well known for exceptional modern dance.

TEL AVIV AFTER DARK

Settling in at your hotel after dinner isn't an option if you want to truly experience Tel Aviv like a local. In this city famous for its nightlife, dusk is the catalyst that propels the day's steady buzz of activity into high gear. Restaurants fill to max capacity, bars become packed with noisy crowds, and people rush to make the opening curtain at dance and musical performances. Generally speaking, southern Tel Aviv—where you'll find Jaffa—has a mellow, low-key vibe with a bohemian flavor. The northern neighborhoods, including the Tel Aviv Port, tend to have pricier places frequented by movers and shakers. In the middle is well-established Neveh Tzedek, where everyone mixes.

JAFFA

Jaffa at night

A winding, cobblestone street in Jaffa

An ancient part of the city, mentioned in the Bible, this is one of the best models of Jews and Muslims living side-by-side. Like the Old City in Jerusalem, this area of winding stone alleyways has kept its ancient atmosphere intact, and is today a serene spot perched on a hill in the southern end of Tel Aviv with promenades that afford alluring nighttime views of the twinkling coastline.

THE SCENE
With its tranquil vibe, Jaffa is the city's least fast-paced night spot. It's preeminently a romantic place to spend the evening to stroll, eat, and shop, where you'll find a relatively mature crowd of tourists and locals alike.

LOCATION LOWDOWN
Amble along the streets of the artist's quarter to Kedumim Plaza, and you'll find yourself at the top of the hill in the heart of Jaffa. There's live music offered here on Saturday evenings. Or catch a classical quartet at the Franciscan Church of St. Peter, a 17th-century building where Napoleon stayed after capturing the city.

NEIGHBORHOOD KNOW-HOW
If you're in the mood to learn something before going out, the Association for Tourism–Tel-Aviv–Jaffa (03/516–6188) offers free evening walking tours every Tuesday at 8 PM.

TOP PICKS

Try the candlelit **Yoezer Wine Bar** (2 Yoezer Ish Ha-Bira St., ☎ 03/683–9115), in a beautiful arched Ottoman building next to Jaffa's landmark Clock Tower.

Jaffa Bar (Yeffet 30, ☎ 03/518–4668) draws an older, sophisticated clientele.

Saloona (Tirza 17, in the Noga Compound, ☎ 03/518–1719) is Jaffa's sexiest lounge-bar with a hip, artistic feel.

NEVEH TZEDEK

The Mann Auditorium

Eating shellfish at Manta Ray in Neveh Tzedek

After many years of neglect, Neveh Tzedek recaptured its former prestige, becoming Tel Aviv's most popular neighborhood day or night. It brims with laid-back wine bars, galleries, boutiques, and restored two-storey stucco houses painted in bright pastels.

THE SCENE
Tel Aviv's first neighborhood was once home to Israeli artists and writers, and still attracts a trendy, avant-garde crowd mixed with nouveau-riche locals.

LOCATION LOWDOWN
The most scenic way to reach Neveh Tzedek is to walk from Jaffa, past the Valhalla neighborhood, across the Shlush Bridge. Neveh Tzedek centers around the Suzanne Dellal Center, Tel Aviv's modern dance hub and headquarters of internationally acclaimed dance companies such as Bat-Sheva, Inbal, and Vertigo.

NEIGHBORHOOD KNOW-HOW
After watching a contemporary dance performance, walk through the Dellal Center's beautiful piazza, with its burbling fountains and orange trees, to the neighborhood's main thoroughfare, Shabazi Street, which intersects Neveh Tzedek's charming smaller lanes.

TOP PICKS

Chill at one of the neighborhood's tiny but classy wine bars, like **Jajo** (Shabazi 47), or on the terrace at **Suzanna** (Shabazi 9).

Neveh Tzedek also happens to be a short walk from **Manta Ray** (☎ 03/517–4773, ⊕ www.mantaray.co.il), the quintessential Tel Aviv restaurant, and the perfect place to sip an aperitif on the curving terrace overlooking Alma Beach.

TEL AVIV PORT

The Tel Aviv Port

Whisky-A-Go-Go

Tel Aviv's hottest, loudest, most throbbing nightlife spot is the Tel Aviv Port (in Hebrew, the *Namal*) in the city's northern reaches (www.namal.co.il). With its cutting edge music, DJ-spun grooves, and raucous crowds, the Port has contributed in no small measure to Tel Aviv's newly-acquired fame as a major player in the clubbing world.

THE SCENE

Luckily for some, clubs here come alive only on weekends, when they house churning thickets of stylish club crawlers. During the week, it's all about trying the latest trendy restaurant.

LOCATION LOWDOWN

Restaurants and clubs here were built above a small, artificial harbor which stands beside the Yarkon River's estuary. Over the last decade, the port was transformed into a chic waterfront area that includes a 150-square-foot wooden deck, the largest in Israel, its wave-like shape inspired by the sand dunes of Tel Aviv's early days.

NEIGHBORHOOD KNOW-HOW

Long, disorganized lines form at club entrances, so do your best to catch the doorman's eye. Speaking English sometimes helps. The Port's clubs only warm up at 2 AM, so fortify yourself with a disco nap. And most clubs won't take plastic for cover charges or drinks.

TOP PICKS

Two of the Port's most flamboyant clubs are the **TLV**, (☎ 03/541–0222) with a state of the art speaker system, and the split-level **Whisky A-Go-Go**, (☎ 03/544–0633) where willowy women dance on the bar.

If clubs aren't your scene, satisfy your musical appetite and catch a trio at the first-rate **Shablul Jazz Club** (⊕ www.shabluljazz.com), housed in spacious quarters at the Port's Hangar 13.

street, and the oh-so-hip clientele all give Jajo its classy and alluring air, and make it an ideal place for a lingering, romantic drink.

Lansky (✉ *6 Montefiori St.* ☎ *03/517–0043*), located on the ground floor of the Shalom Meir Tower, lays claim to the longest bar in the country, staffed by a veritable army of bartenders. Age limitations apply (under 27 not encouraged), which makes it a good choice for a more settled crowd.

M.A.S.H. (✉ *275 Dizengoff St.* ☎ *03/605–1007*) is a sports bar trying for a British-pub ambience, but with the focus squarely on the big screen rather than on the alcohol. To watch football, American Israelis (a preponderance of guys) and visitors might head to Mike's Place (see below). But for soccer and rugby (that is, for the Brits and Aussies), M.A.S.H. is the place to go, showing events that are hardly seen elsewhere, thanks to an all-included satellite-TV package, no doubt.

Mike's Place (✉ *81 Hayarkon* ☎ *03/516–8619* ⊙ *11 AM–last customer*) is small and has a well-stocked bar, with a variety of music that would appeal to an over-30 crowd (unlike many other Tel Aviv nightspots). Its location on the Promenade at the southern end of the hotel strip makes it a popular tourist watering hole. Mike's Place sometimes organizes parties, especially around sporting events, which patrons can watch on a big-screen TV and rejoice or cry into their beer over the fate of their team until the wee hours.

Mishmish (✉ *17 Lilienblum St.* ☎ *03/516–8178* ⊙ *Sun.–Sat. 8–last customer*) is a classy and retro cocktail lounge with great service that's a favorite with locals for birthday and bachelorette parties. A wide-ranging menu has a wide selection of finger foods that go well with the good drinks, like potato croquettes laced with parmesan cheese, and sirloin pieces on a skewer.

Molly Bloom (✉ *32 Mendele St.* ☎ *03/522–1558* ⊙ *Sun.–Thurs. 4 PM–last customer; Fri. 2 PM–last customer*) might very well be the most authentic Irish pub in Israel because it's owned by an Irishman—Robert Segal. Live music is on Mondays, Wednesdays, and Friday afternoons (open session). There's a full menu including Emerald Isle favorites such as shepherd's pie and beef stew in Guinness. The location is convenient, in the mid-section of the Hayarkon hotel strip (across the street from the Dan Hotel).

Norma Jean (✉ *23 Elipelet St.* ☎ *03/683–7383* ⊙ *Sun.–Fri. 7 PM–last customer; Sat. 1 PM–last customer*) is a bistro-bar with an attractive red-brick front and red-trimmed windows on the edge of the Florentine quarter. Behind the 14-seat bar are more than 130 kinds of whisky, which Norma Jean brags is the biggest collection in the country, and there are 15 kinds of beer on tap. The kitchen also serves full meals, with a focus on pleasing the carnivorous.

Norman (✉ *8 Hillel Hazaken St.* ☎ *03/517–1030* ⊙ *Sun.–Thurs. and Sat. 7 PM–last customer; Fri. 9 PM–last customer*), located in the old Yemenite Quarter of South Tel Aviv near the Nahalat Benyamin pedestrian mall and Carmel Market, is a charming small bar with a cozy vibe. The age range of the regulars is pretty wide—people from their twenties to fifties come to hear blues and jazz and enjoy the beer. The owners say they were the first in the country to import some of the Belgian beers like the Trappist-made Chimay and Duvel. They also serve the Tel Aviv microbrewery's Dancing Camel.

Bistro-bars, such as Nanutchka, are all the rage in Tel Aviv. Many have DJs and dancing nightly.

Nanutchka (✉ *28 Lilienblum St.* ☎ *03/516–2254* 🕑 *Sun.–Sat. 10 PM to last customer*) is a bistro-bar with an ornate Georgian (of the former Soviet Union) design occupying a number of rooms in an old building adorned with authentic Georgian wall tapestries and paintings. Drinks include specialties of the house—a selection of sweet but light Georgian wines. The menu, to match the decor, features among its selections *tinakali*, cheese dumplings with yogurt, and sea bass stuffed with cheese. Good to know, one way or another, that there's smoking allowed at the bar. There's a DJ and dancing every night.

Saloona (✉ *17 Tirza St., Jaffa* ☎ *03/518–1719*) is the place to go if you're in Jaffa and feel the urge to sit someplace sexy to sip a cocktail. Although this place is swank, it retains the hip, artistic feel that this neighborhood is known for.

At **Tassa D'oro,** (✉ *6 Ahad Ha'am St.* ☎ *03/516–6329* 🕑 *Sun.Sat. 7:30 AM– 12:30 AM*) serves nine kinds of whisky and five of vodka, along with a selection of aperitifs that make you wonder why the place is better known as a restaurant and café. It's actually one of only a few spots in this city outside of a hotel bar where a couple or small group of friends can sit for a quiet drink, either indoors or on the attractive patio. And for visitors, the location can't be beat: it's in the heart of the trendy Neveh Tzedek.

TLV (✉ *Tel Aviv Port,* ☎ *03/561–1022*) One of the Port's two late-night hotspots (the other is Whisky-A Go-Go), doesn't start jumping until around 2 AM, and has a state-of-the-art speaker system that really gets the crowds moving.

Whisky A-Go-Go (⊠*3 Hataarucha Street, Tel Aviv Port* ☎*03/544–0633*) can only be described as flamboyant, with its split-level set-up and the willowy women dancing on the bar.

Yoezer Wine Bar (⊠*2 Yoezar Ish Habira, near clock tower, Jaffa* ☎*03/ 683–9115* ⊗*Sun.–Sat. 1* PM*–1* AM) is a posh wine bar set under the evocative stone arches of an old Jaffa house. Maintaining the same location for 13 years is almost unheard-of in Tel Aviv, and certainly has everything to do with its romantic atmosphere and fine Provençal French menu created by one Israel's best-known gourmets, Shaul Evron. The wine list is said to be one of the largest in the country, and includes a selection from Burgundy imported especially for Yoezer.

Zimmerman, (⊠*2 Brenner St., Center City* ☎*03/528–0218* ⊗*Sun.– Thurs., Sat. 7*PM*–last customer; Fri. 8:30–last customer*) off of Allenby not far from the Sheinken area, is named after the nice Jewish boy whose portraits are a centerpiece of this small bar—Bob Dylan. Patrons range from young off-duty soldiers to the 40-to-50s crowd who stop in after work or on the weekends. Seating is indoors or in the courtyard. If bourbon is your drink of choice, you're in luck, as there's a wide selection. The music, of course, is of the good old American folk variety that's Zimmerman's trademark.

THE ARTS

Tel Aviv is Israel's cultural capital, and it fulfills this role with relish. The Tel Aviv Art Museum, the city's major artistic venue (for concerts and lectures as well as the fine arts) is complemented by a host of galleries, especially along Gordon Street. The Israeli Opera has the finest local and foreign talents in classical and modern works. Tel Aviv is also home to the Israeli Philharmonic and a dynamic dance scene, including the iconic Bat Sheva Dance Company for modern dance, the Israel Ballet Company for classical, and two percussion troupes—Mayumana and Sheketek.

For the city's 100th birthday, several projects and events are being planned in terms of public art, such as veteran Tel Avivians' family photographs displayed around and billboards covered with locals' paintings, drawings, and even graffiti.

The Friday editions of the English-language *Jerusalem Post* and *Ha'aretz* contain extensive entertainment listings for the entire country.

There are three main ticket agencies for performances in Tel Aviv. All accept major credit cards. You must pick up your tickets in person and have your credit card with you: **Hadran** (⊠*90 Ibn Gvirol St.* ☎*03/521–5200*), **Castel** (⊠*153 Ibn Gvirol St.* ☎*03/604–5000*), and **Le'an** (⊠*101 Dizengoff St.* ☎*03/524–7373*).

DANCE

Most of Israel's dance groups, including the contemporary Bat Sheva Dance Company, perform in the **Suzanne Dellal Center for Dance and Theater** (⊠*5 Yehieli St.* ☎*03/510–5656*) and Neveh Tzedek itself is home to artists and a growing number of tony galleries and gift shops. The complex itself is an example of new Israeli architectural styles used to restore some of the oldest buildings in Tel Aviv.

MUSIC

The **Enav Cultural Center** (⊠*Gan Ha'Ir [roof level], 71 Ibn Gvirol St.* ☎*03/521–7766 or 03/521–7763)* is a 300-seat, city-run venue offering an eclectic fare of music and theater.

Ganei Yehoshua (Hayarkon Park) (☎*03/642–2828)* is where large outdoor concerts are held at the Wohl Amphitheater.

Gold Star Zappa Club (⊠*24 Raoul Wallenberg St.* ☎*03/649–9550)* is Tel Aviv's best pop music venue, located in the Ziv Towers just a short cab ride away from downtown.

The **Mann Auditorium** (⊠*1 Huberman St.* ☎*03/528–9163)*, Israel's largest concert hall, is home to the Israel Philharmonic Orchestra. It's also possible to catch an occasional rock, pop, or jazz concert here.

Mayumana (⊠*15 Louis Pasteur St., Jaffa* ☎*03/681–1787)* is Israel's answer to *Stomp,* an exciting troupe of drummers who bang in perfect synchronicity on anything from garbage pails to the floor to actual drums from cultures all over the world.

Shablul Jazz Club (⊠*Hangar 13, Tel Aviv Port* ☎*03/546–1891)* is an intimate jazz club, playing everything from hip-hop to bee-bop to Latin and ethno-jazz Monday through Saturday nights. Performers include veteran jazz artists and up-and-coming young talents; there's an open stage every Monday.

OPERA

The **Tel Aviv Performing Arts Center** (⊠*19 Shaul Hamelech St.* ☎*03/692–7777 for box office)* is home to the Israeli Opera as well as the Israel Ballet Company and the Cameri Theater. Tickets are available at the box office, through agencies, or by emailing the box office at kupa@tapac.org.il.

THEATER

While there are a few exceptions, theater performances are almost always in Hebrew, so inquire before booking.

Most of the plays at **Bet Leissin** (⊠*101 Dizengoff St. at Frishman* ☎*03/725–5333)* are by Israeli playwrights and are in Hebrew.

The **Cameri Theater** (⊠*19 Shaul Hamelech St.* ☎*03/606–1900)* sometimes offers screened English translations.

Habimah (⊠*Habimah Sq.* ☎*03/629–5555)* is the national theater; plays here are all in Hebrew, but some have simultaneous translation.

Hasimta Theater (⊠*8 Mazal Dagim St.* ☎*03/681–2126)*, in Old Jaffa, features avant-garde and fringe performances, in Hebrew only (or sometimes without words).

SPORTS AND THE OUTDOORS

Almost all outdoorsy activity in Tel Aviv centers around its gorgeous beaches, from boating to scuba diving to spreading out a towel in the sand to get some sun.

Surfers line the beach in Herzliya, a resort area less than ten miles up the coast from downtown Tel Aviv.

BEACHES

Going to one of the city's beaches—by day and for sunset— is a must-do Tel Aviv experience. **Tel Baruch Beach** at Namir Road and Propes Street is popular for families with young children because it has a breakwater that creates a quiet stretch of surf. Because it's the furthest from the downtown stretch, you need a car or taxi to get there, so it's less popular with younger beach-goers and can be less crowded for the same reason. Unfortunately, the beauty of the beach is compromised by the adjacent promenade, which has an unsavory reputation after nightfall, and is somewhat poorly kept-up. Visitors who chose this beach try to avoid the promenade by driving straight to the parking lot or arriving by taxi.

One beach that does attract a younger crowd is **Hametzizim Beach**, near the outlet of the Yarkon River, where some people like to buy a beer at a nearby pub and watch the sunset.

Speaking of sunsets, **Dolphinarum Beach**, at the southern end of Hayarkon Street within view of Jaffa, has a special atmosphere on Fridays as the day ends, with lots of young people and musicians who gather and form drumming circles. Another good Sabbath-eve beach is **Jerusalem Beach**, at the bottom of Allenby Road.

Beaches are generally named after something nearby—a street or a hotel, for example. Thus, you have **Hilton Beach** in front of the hotel of that name, **Gordon Beach** at the end of Gordon Street (another beach popular with local families), and likewise **Bograshov Beach**.

South of Hametzizim Beach the city has set up a special beach for Orthodox Jews who prefer gender-separated swimming. It's surrounded by a stone wall. The days alternate for men and for women, beginning with women's day on Sunday.

South of the Orthodox beach and north of the Hilton Beach is a strip of waterfront known locally as "**Dogs Beach**" because no lifeguards means people let their dogs off-leash.

And what about swimming? When choosing a beach, look for one with wooden lifeguard huts, where first aid is available. Lifeguards are on duty from roughly May to October, from 7 AM until between 4 PM and 7 PM, depending on the month (check with your hotel's concierge). Be forewarned: Tel Aviv's lifeguards are fond of yelling commands over the loudspeakers if they think swimmers are misbehaving.

Most beaches have public amenities, including bathrooms and changing rooms. If you sit in a chaise lounge or under an umbrella, a municipal worker will come by to charge you a small fee and give you a receipt.

PARTICIPANT SPORTS

BOATING

Ganei Yehoshua (Hayarkon Park) (☎03/642–0541), along Rokach Boulevard in the northern part of the city, rents out pedal boats and rowboats (NIS 60 per hour) and motorboats (NIS 80 per half hour). You can also opt for pleasure boats, which take up to 100 people for 20-minute rides (NIS 12 per person); bicycles; or tandems that take up to six people (NIS 45 per half hour).

HEALTH CLUBS

Most of the city's luxury hotels have health clubs, normally free for guests.

The Cybex Spa at the **Hilton** (✉*Hayarkon St.* ☎03/520–2222) has the largest gym, but it and the sauna are open only to guests and members. The club is open Sunday–Thursday 6 AM–10 PM, Friday 6–6, Saturday 9–7.

The Cielo Spa at the **Sheraton Tel Aviv Hotel and Tower** (✉*115 Hayarkon St.* ☎03/521–1111) has 14 treatment rooms and is open Sunday–Thursday 9:30–9:30, Friday and Saturday 9:30–6.

SAILING

All sailboats require an Israeli license. However, you can charter a sailboat or a yacht with a skipper at **Ofek Yachts** at the Tel Aviv Marina (✉*Hayarkon St., next to Carlton Hotel* ☎03/529–9988) and at the Herzliyah Marina at **Derech Hayam** (✉*1 Yordei Hasira* ☎09/957–8811).

SCUBA DIVING

The **Dugit Diving Center** (✉*250 Ben-Yehuda St.* ☎03/604–5034) serves as a popular meeting place for veteran divers. Although the view beneath the surface of the Mediterranean Sea doesn't offer as breathtaking an array of fish and coral as the Red Sea, it's a good place to start. Diving and fishing equipment is available for sale and for rent on a daily basis to licensed divers. Dugit can also make arrangements for visitors to attend a diving course in Herzilyah.

SWIMMING

Memadiyon (⊠*Ganei Yehoshua [Yarkon Park]* ☎*03/642–2777*), open from May to October, is Tel Aviv's 25-acre water park featuring a half-size Olympic swimming pool, water slides (including a pool with challenging "slalom" slides), a wave-pool, a toddlers pool (from age 3), and lawns with plastic easy chairs and sun-shades, all on the grounds of Yarkon Park on the northern edge of the city. Opening days vary even within the season due to private events; call ahead to make sure it's open to the public the day you want to go, and to check closing time on that day. Hours on public days are 9–5.

WATERSKIING

Menachem Begin Park (☎*03/739–1168*), in southern Tel Aviv, near the Halitkvah neighborhood, runs cable waterskiing in an artificial lake, a system that holds no appeal for some but is particularly good for beginners. Costs are around NIS 82 per hour, including instruction. It's open daily from April through October, and on Friday and Saturday from November to end-March. Hours vary, so call in advance.

SPECTATOR SPORTS

Bloomfield Stadium (⊠*1 Hatehiya St., Jaffa* ☎*03/682–1237*) hosts soccer matches.

Nokia Stadium (⊠*51 Yigal Alon St.* ☎*03/537–6376*) is the place to go for basketball games.

The **Ramat Gan Football Stadium** (⊠*Abba Hillel Rd., Ramat Gan* ☎*03/617–1500*) is another venue for soccer.

SHOPPING

The Tel Aviv shopping scene is the most varied in the country. It's Israel's fashion capital, with boutiques galore, and you'll find styles quite different from what you might see back home in terms of design and color.

The real pleasure of shopping in Tel Aviv is access to the exciting creations of its cadre of young designers that have made waves around the world. The historic Dizengoff Street, in the 1930s so famous a place to see-and-be-seen that it gave rise to its own Hebrew word for a stroll down the boulevard (which roughly translated, would be "Dizengoffing"), is once again being resurrected after several down-at-the-heels years. The part of Dizengoff north of its intersection with Arlozoroff Street is where you'll find the shops of many of Israel's best-known designers.

Israel is also famous for its footwear, most notably Naot sandals, to be found in many shoe stores throughout the country, but also beautiful and unusual leather designs with a European flair.

If it's crafts and jewelry you're shopping for, Neveh Tzedek is the place to go, especially along the main drag of Shabazi Street. Crafts and jewelry also star in the Tuesday and Friday Nahalat Benyamin Pedestrian Mall, where prices can be lower than at regular stores and you can almost always meet the artist who made them. As for Judaica, Jerusalem and Safed are of course much more famous than Tel Aviv, but there

Jaffa is the place to browse in shops and galleries, as the neighborhood has a slow-paced, mellow vibe.

are still a number of stores here that are fun to browse on Ben-Yehuda, and Dizengoff streets.

DEPARTMENT STORES

Hamashbir (⊠*Dizengoff Center, Dizengoff and King George Sts.* ☎*03/ 528–5136*) carries, for the most part, a rather banal selection of goods, often at prices a little higher than those in smaller stores. On the second floor, however, its Designer Avenue has women's clothing by local designers, who also have boutiques at the northern end of Dizengoff Street or in the surrounding area—sample the range here, and then ask for the address if you'd like to see more of a particular designer's line. It's open 10 AM–9:30 PM Monday–Thursday; Friday until 2 PM.

SHOPPING DISTRICTS AND MALLS

Shopping malls are generally open from 9:30 AM to 9:30 PM Monday–Thursday, and Friday 9:30 AM to 2 PM.

The **Azrieli Center** (⊠*Hashalom Rd., above the railway station*) is a sparkling new mall with the added attraction of the view from the top floor.

Gan Ha'Ir (⊠*71 Ibn Gvirol St., Northern Tel Aviv*) is a small, quiet, upscale mall centrally located off Rabin Square.

The **Dizengoff Center** (⊠*Dizengoff and King George Sts.*) is Israel's first shopping mall and is definitely not its most lustrous. It's multileveled and somewhat confusing to navigate. Stores sell everything from air conditioners to camping equipment, with many fashion boutiques in between.

Kikar Hamedina, in northern Tel Aviv, is arguably the most expensive real estate in the country; this is where the wealthy shop. Hit the shops on this circular street for, say, your favorite international designer (less so for the Israeli ones, though), a Kenzo creation, or a pound of Godiva chocolates.

The **Opera Tower** (⊠ *1 Allenby St.*) is near the sea and has a small but eclectic range of stores. It's particularly good for jewelry. The Tower Records on the ground floor is a great place to find local music.

The **Ramat Aviv Mall** (⊠ *40 Einstein St.,Ramat Aviv*) is a good place to shop and have lunch if you're visiting the Ramat Aviv museums.

SPECIALTY STORES

JEWELRY, JUDAICA AND ETHNIC CRAFTS

Ayala Bar (⊠ *36 Shabazi St.* ☎ *03/510–0082* ⊗ *Sun.–Thurs. 10:15–7, Fri. 10:15–4*) is the sparkling multicolored creation of Israeli designer Ayala Bar. Her bracelets, earrings, and necklaces, now famous around the world, can be seen from time to time in shops throughout the country, but the best selection is here at the flagship store.

The Bauhaus Center (⊠ *99 Dizengoff St.* ☎ *03/522–2049* ⊗ *Sun.–Thurs. 10–7:30, Fri. 10–2:30*) with its display of books, maps, posters, furnishings, dishes, and even Judaica, all inspired by Bauhaus design, reminds visitors that this school of design embraced more than buildings. At the center, you can book a two-hour tour Friday morning at 10:00 (in English) of Tel Aviv's Bauhaus buildings, which are on the prestigious UNESCO World Heritage List. Self-guided audio-tours are also available for rent.

Nahalat Binyamin Pedestrian Mall has a street fair on Tuesday and Friday. Shop for sophisticated gems and jewels at **H. Stern**, with branches in the David InterContinental, Daniel, Sheraton Tel Aviv, Hilton, and Dan hotels.

One of the most pleasant memento-shopping experiences in Tel Aviv, and in a good location—two long blocks east of the main hotels on Yarkon Street—is at **Raphael** (⊠ *96 Ben Yehuda St., Center City* ☎ *03/527–3619* ⊗ *Sun.–Thurs. 10–2 and 4–7, Fri. 10–2*), which carries a large selection of Judaica, jewelry, and colorful ethnically inspired textiles. Also specializing in Judaica, and with a particularly wide selection of silver items, is **Miller** (⊠ *157 Dizengoff St., Center City* ☎ *03/524–9383* ⊗ *Sun.–Thurs. 9:30–7:30, Fri. 9:30–2:30*).

Visitors wandering Neveh Tzedek shouldn't miss the **Shlushshloshim Ceramics Gallery** (⊠ *30 Shlush St., Neveh Tzedek* ☎ *03/510–6067* ⊗ *Sun.–Thurs. 10–7, Fri. 10–2:30, Sat. 11–6*), a cooperative of 11 ceramicists who display a pleasingly eclectic mix of both decorative and practical items in a variety of colors, shapes, and textures at a range of price points. Many of them travel well, and make great gifts. One of the outside walls is covered with colorful ceramic pieces stuck in by the artists, and has become a city landmark of sorts.

Homer Tov Ceramics Gallery (✉ *27 Shabazi St., Neveh Tzedek* ☎ *03/516–6229* 🕐 *Sun.–Thurs. 10–8, Fri. 10–5*) is another great ceramics gallery, on Neveh Tzedek's main drag, where many of the items are country-kitch.

Bait Banamal (✉ *Hangar 26, Tel Aviv Port* ☎ *03/681–8820* 🕐 *Sun.–Thurs. 9–9, Sat. 10 AM–11 PM, Fri. 10–4*) is a cluster of high-end clothes and housewares shops connected with the popular comme il faut.

Galilee's (✉ *Bait Banamal, Hangar 26, Tel Aviv Port* ☎ *03/544–2834* 🕐 *Sun.–Thurs., Sat. 10 AM–11 PM, Fri. 10–4*), located in the Bait Banamal retail space, features agricultural and artistic products made in the north, among them wines, olives, herbs and spices, health and beauty products, and pottery.

Dar-Fez (✉ *23 Raziel St., Clock Tower Sq., Jaffa* ☎ *03/518–1417* 🕐 *Sun.–Thurs. 9–5, Fri. 9–2:30*) has an extensive and colorful selection of ceramics, fabrics, silver and copper repoussé-adorned and mother-of-pearl inlayed Judaica, and furnishings.

CLOTHING

Bingo specializes in high-end, high-fashion foreign brands such as Manas, Anna Sui, and Hispanitas (✉ *24 Hey B'Iyar St., Kimar Hamedina, Center City* ☎ *03/695–3933* 🕐 *Sun.–Thurs. 10–7:30, Fri. 10–2:30*).

CoupleOf is known for making beautiful and comfortable shoes for hard-to-fit narrow feet. (✉ *144 Dizengoff St., Center City* ☎ *03/529–1098* 🕐 *Sun.–Thurs. 10–3, Fri. 10–2*).

Orly Golan (✉ *154 Dizengoff St., Center City* ☎ *03/560–0905* 🕐 *Sun.–Thurs. 10–6, Fri. 10–2:30*) is a fresh young designer offering eye-catching accessories and textures, such as sequined-pocket jeans perfect for wearing out at night.

Rina Zin (✉ *216 Dizengoff St., Center City* ☎ *03/523–5476150* 🕐 *Sun.–Thurs. 10–7:30, Fri. 10–3*) is another trendy designer whose chic styles with a European cut appeal to women of all ages.

SWIMWEAR

For a bargain, visit two of Tel Aviv's bathing-suit factory outlets, in Yad Eliyahu near the Cinerama arena: **Gottex** (✉ *62 Anilvich St.* ☎ *03/537–3879* 🕐 *Mon.–Thurs. 9–5:45, Fri. 9–1:30*), and **Oberson** (✉ *8 Nirim St.* ☎ *03/639–6151* 🕐 *Mon.–Thurs. 9:15–6:30, Fri. 9:15–1:30 PM*).

STREET MARKETS

At the **Nahalat Binyamin** street fair, held Tuesday and Friday, local crafts ranging from handmade puppets to olive-wood sculptures and silver jewelry attract throngs of shoppers and browsers. The **Carmel Market** begining at Allentoy Road , is the city's primary poduce market and also has stalls with clothes and housewares. The **flea market** in Jaffa is mostly full of junk these days, but you can still find a bargain, even if it's not an authentic antique. The flea market has a wide selection of reasonably priced Middle Eastern–style jewelry that uses chains of small silver coins and imitation stones.

Haifa and the Northern Coast

WITH CAESAREA, AKKO, AND ROSH HANIKRA

WORD OF MOUTH

"Then we headed south to Ein Hod, an artists' colony that people had recommended. We really loved the town. Very pleasant, beautiful gardens and homes, lots of public (and private) art. Next trip we're determined to stay a night or two at one of the bed-and-breakfasts there."

—zooey91

WELCOME TO HAIFA AND THE NORTHERN COAST

TOP REASONS TO GO

★ **Caesarea:** Originally built by King Herod, these 2,000-year-old ruins occupy a strategic spot on the sea. They include Byzantine bathhouses and Crusader moats.

★ **Baha'i Gardens:** In the middle of Haifa, this unforgettable series of gardens tumbles down from the mountaintop. The 18 jewellike terraces enclose a shimmering gold-domed shrine.

★ **Underground Akko:** At this fascinating archaeological site, see how the Crusaders built numerous halls lined with huge pillars. There's a secret tunnel and a Turkish bathhouse.

★ **Glorious beaches:** The coast means beaches, and this is Israel's finest stretch of golden sand. Haifa's beaches are particulary beautiful. Whether you're into scuba diving or paragliding, there's plenty to keep you busy.

★ **Great wine:** Taste and toast internationally known wines at the Shomron wineries, in the hillsides of the northern coast. Tishbi and Carmel are worth visiting.

Rosh Hanikra

LEBANON

Baha'i Gardens, Haifa

GALILEE

Nazareth

2 **The Northern Coast.**
The Mediterranean is especially lovely at this string
of beach resorts south of
Haifa. Besides the stretches
of sand, you'll find wonderfully preserved archaeo-
logical sites at Caesarea and
Nahsholim-Dor.

3 **The Wine Country and
Mt. Carmel.** The quality of
Israeli wines has risen to
heady heights on the international scene. One of the
country's very first wineries
is here, along with two others of equal stature. They're
in or near the main towns
such as Zichron Ya'akov,
making access as easy as
saying "l'chaim."

4 **Akko to Rosh Hanikra.**
The northern coast is known
for its fine-sand beaches
and nature reserves. You'll
also find upscale B&B lodgings tucked away in long-
established rural agricultural
settlements. The sea-bat-
tered caves at Rosh Hanikra
are worth the trip north.

1 **Haifa.** This is a city of
fairly steep slopes, which
reward you not only with
sights to see amid pine
trees and blossoming foliage but also with vistas of
the Mediterranean at every
turn, all accompanied by
hillside breezes. At the base
of the hill are the beaches,
some of the area's best.

GETTING
ORIENTED

Two seaside cities anchor
this stretch of coastline.
Haifa, a hilltop city on a
peninsula jutting into the
Mediterranean, offers the
magnificent Baha'i Shrine
and Gardens, the bustling
German Colony, fine restaurants, the Carmelite Monastery, and more. The ancient
port city of Akko has underground ruins dating from
the era of the Crusaders.
Many people come to this
area for the beaches, but
the coastal Route 2 and the
slightly more inland Route
4 can whisk you to such
sites as King Herod's port
city of Caesarea, the 19th-
century town of Zichron
Ya'akov, and the artists'
colony of Ein Hod. Far to
the north are the cliffs and
grottoes of Rosh Hanikra.

5

Crusader halls, Akko

HAIFA AND THE NORTHERN COAST PLANNER

When To Go

There's really no bad time to visit this region. Spring (April and May) and fall (October and November) are balmy and crisp, making them the most pleasant seasons for travelers. Summer (June to September) is hot, but there's no humidity, and soft sea and mountain breezes cool things down. Winter (from late December and into March) brings cold weather (sun interspersed with rain), while the sea makes the wind chilly.

As in the rest of Israel, hotels and other lodgings are often booked solid on the weekends. On Saturdays and national holidays, Israelis themselves hit the road, so it's best to avoid north-to-south travel out of Tel Aviv or Jerusalem altogether. If you're taking a few days to explore the region, traveling Sunday to Thursday will guarantee you plenty of peace and quiet. If you can only go on Friday and Saturday, make reservations well in advance. Prepare for big crowds at the beaches and tourist sights.

Getting Here and Around

Air Travel: Ben Gurion International Airport, near Tel Aviv, is 105 km (65 mi) south of Haifa, about a 90-minute drive. A convenient *sherut* (shared taxi) to Haifa costs NIS 30. You can also catch Haifa-bound Bus 945 or 947.

Bus Travel: Egged serves the coastal area from Jerusalem Central Bus Station to Tel Aviv Central (also called Arlozoroff Station and Tzafon). There's service to Netanya, Hadera, Zichron Ya'akov, and Haifa from both cities. A direct bus leaves from Jerusalem and takes one hour 40 minutes. Getting to Caesarea requires a change at Hadera. To get to Akko or Nahariya, change at Haifa. Crowds are heavy at bus stations on Sunday morning and Thursday night. Buses usually do not operate from Friday evening to Saturday evening; in Haifa, some buses run on Saturday.

Car Travel: You can take Route 2 (the coastal road) or Route 4 (parallel to Route 2, but slightly inland) north along the coast from Tel Aviv to Haifa, continuing on Route 4 up to the Lebanese border. From Jerusalem follow Route 1 to Tel Aviv; connect via the Ayalon Highway to Herzliya and Route 2. Driving can be the most comfortable and convenient way to tour this region.

Taxi Travel: In towns, taxis can be hailed on the street day or night. Ask the driver to turn on the meter (*moneh*).

Train Travel: The Northern Coast is one part of Israel where train travel is fairly practical. As always, remember that service is interrupted Friday evening to Saturday evening. Israel Railways trains from Jerusalem and Tel Aviv travel at least twice a day to Netanya, Binyamina, Caesarea, Haifa, Atlit, Akko, and Nahariya. You might have to change trains in Tel Aviv when coming from Jerusalem.

The train line from Ben Gurion Airport travels to Tel Aviv, Binyamina, Atlit, Haifa, Akko, and Nahariya. The trip from Tel Aviv to Haifa takes about one hour. Sunday to Thursday, trains depart every 20 minutes from 6:20 AM until 9:30 PM; on Friday they run from 6 AM until 3:20 PM. On Saturday there are four departures after 7:30 PM. Train travel from Jerusalem to Haifa is feasible only if you have plenty of time, as you have to change in Tel Aviv.

⇨ For more information on getting here and around, see *Travel Smart Israel*.

Dining

You won't have to look hard for a restaurant, whether simple or fancy, with a striking view of the Mediterranean or excellent fish, or both. Fish is served grilled or baked, with a variety of sauces: most common are *locus* (grouper), *mulit* (red mullet), *churi* (red snapper), and *farida* (sea bream). Also fresh, but from commercial fishponds and the Sea of Galilee, are *buri* (gray mullet), the ubiquitous tilapia, and the hybrid *iltit* (salmon-trout). Fresh seafood, such as shrimp and calamari, is also found along the coast. Many casual restaurants serve schnitzel (breaded and fried chicken cutlets) with french fries, which kids often love.

Until recently, coastal restaurants weren't as refined as those in Tel Aviv. No longer. Hilly Haifa has several interesting restaurants with creative chefs. The artists' village of Ein Hod has sumptuous Argentinian dining, and there's locally famous falafel in the Druze village of Daliyat el Carmel. Netanya has the region's highest concentration of kosher establishments. Dress is always informal.

Lodging

Options range from small inns to luxury hotels, though the selection and quality of accommodations doesn't equal that of, say, Tel Aviv. Gracious B&Bs (known in Israel as *zimmers*) are tucked into coastal rural settlements, mostly north of Nahariya. The splendid spa hotel in the Carmel Forest near Haifa deserves its reputation. In some places, such as Zichron Ya'ackov, pickings are slim; but because this region is so compact, you can cover many coastal sights from one base, such as Haifa.

The chart below lists peak-season prices—July, August, and the main Jewish holidays. Many hotels are less expensive—sometimes 40% less—from November through February.

Planning Your Time

Haifa, the country's third-largest city, can be a useful base for seeing top sights to the south (Caesarea and the wine country) and north (the Crusader city in historic Akko and the coast up to Rosh Hanikra). Ein Hod, an artists' colony, and the Carmel Caves are also nearby. Haifa itself is notable for the Baha'i Gardens and Germany Colony. However, the coast's southern sights can also be seen easily if you're staying in Tel Aviv. Both United and Egged tours have day tours to Caesarea and Akko from Jerusalem, Tel Aviv, and Netanya; this may be a useful option.

Not counting time in Haifa, you could see the area's highlights in a couple of days, starting with King Herod's port city, Caesarea, and the wine country in the Carmel Hills. Check tour information for the wineries in Binyamina and Zichron Ya'akov. The Druze villages of Daliyat el Carmel and Isfiya are worth a visit, too. You can also explore Akko, to the north; the grottoes at Rosh Hanikra are lovely, but far north. Plan time for swimming or hiking; the Mediterranean coast has great beaches and scenic trails.

WHAT IT COSTS					
	¢	$	$$	$$$	$$$$
Restaurants	under NIS 32	NIS 32–NIS 49	NIS 50–NIS 75	NIS 76–NIS 100	over NIS 100
Hotels		under $120	$120–$200	$201–$300	$301–$400	over $400

Restaurant prices are per person for a main course at dinner in NIS (Israeli shekels). Hotel prices are in US dollars, for two people in a standard double room in high season. Non-Israeli citizens paying in foreign currency are exempt from the 15.5% VAT tax on hotel rooms.

By Judy Stacey Goldman

Stretched taut on a narrow coastal strip between Tel Aviv and the Lebanese border, this region offers more than balmy beaches. Historical sights line the shore along with the dunes, fertile fields, and citrus groves of the Sharon Plain. The ancient port of Caesarea has spectacular restored Roman, Byzantine, and Crusader ruins, and vast Crusader halls beckon from underground in seaside Akko. In Haifa, the sea surrounds a modern city on a promontory.

It was in the softly contoured foothills and valleys at the base of Mt. Carmel that the philanthropic Baron Edmond de Rothschild came to the Jews' aid in helping Israel create a wine industry, now one of the region's most successful enterprises. The Carmel range rises dramatically to its pine-covered heights over the coast of Haifa, a friendly, hardworking, and thoroughly modern port city. Just across the sweeping arc of Haifa Bay lies Akko, a jewel of a Crusader city that combines Romanesque ruins, Muslim domes and minarets, and swaying palms. To the north, the resort town of Nahariya draws droves of vacationing Israelis. And south of the Lebanese border, don't miss the amazing seaside caves at Rosh Hanikra, which have been scooped from the cliffs by the pounding surf.

As the scenery changes, so does the ethnic mix of the residents and their ancestors: Druze, Carmelite monks, Ottomans, Baha'is, Christian and Muslim Arabs, and Jews. Paleontologists continue to study on-site the artifacts of the most ancient natives of all, the prehistoric people of the caves of Nahal Me'arot, on Mt. Carmel. The Baha'is, whose universalist religion embraces the teachings of many others, dominate Haifa's mountainside. Their golden-domed shrine gleams, and the terraced gardens spill down the slope like bright jewels. Robed Carmelite monks preside quietly over their monasteries in Haifa and in Mukhraka, on Mt. Carmel, next door to the Druze villages. Although the north-coast Druze consider themselves an integral part of Israeli society, they maintain a unique cultural and religious enclave on Mt. Carmel, with the secret rites and rituals of their faith and the distinctive handlebar moustaches and white head scarves favored by the older men. Akko's vast subterranean Crusader vaults and halls, Ottoman skyline of domes and minarets, and outdoor *shuk* (market) are enchanting.

As you drive north, you'll enjoy long stretches of unimpeded views of the sparkling blue Mediterranean. Beautiful beaches lie beside Netanya, Haifa, and Achziv (and in between), with soft sand, no-frills hummus joints, and seaside restaurants. You can learn to scuba dive or explore underwater shipwrecks, and then visit ancient Caesarea and Akko, listening to the crash of the surf all the while. Other great pleasures of the region include hiking the slopes of pine-scented Mt. Carmel, treading the winding lanes of Ein Hod artists' village, and tasting local wines and tangy cheeses at some excellent wineries.

HAIFA

Spilling down from the pine-covered heights of Mt. Carmel, Haifa is a city with a vertiginous setting that has led to comparisons with San Francisco. Israel's largest port and third-largest city, Haifa was ruled for four centuries by the Ottomans and gradually grew up the mountainside into a cosmopolitan city whose port served the entire Middle East. In 1902, Theodor Herzl enthusiastically dubbed it "the city of the future."

The most striking landmark on the mountainside is the gleaming golden dome of the Baha'i Shrine, set amid utterly beautiful circular grass terraces that fill the slope from top to bottom. The city is the world center for the Baha'i faith, and its members provide charming walking tours of the flower-edged terraces. At the top of the hill you'll find some small but interesting museums, while at the bottom is the lovingly restored German Colony.

GETTING HERE AND AROUND

A direct bus operated by Egged leaves Tel Aviv for Haifa every 20 minutes between 5:20 AM and 11 PM; travel time is one hour. Trains from Tel Aviv to Haifa also take one hour and cost NIS 25. Trains depart every half hour from 6 AM until 10:30 PM; on Friday from 6 AM until 3:20. During the day on Saturdays trains do not run, but there are four departures after 7:30 PM.

A car is a must for getting to, and around, the city of Haifa, mostly because it's built on a steep hill. There are plenty of nice walks in the city, but to see the sites, a car or a taxi is required; another option is the local buses.

Haifa has the six-station Carmelit subway—actually a funicular railway—which runs from Gan Ha'em Park on Hanassi Boulevard (opposite the Dan Panorama) in Central Carmel down to Kikar Paris in the port area in six minutes. The fare is NIS 6, and the train operates Sunday–Thursday 6 AM–10 PM, Friday 6–3, and Saturday 7 PM–midnight. Though the Carmelit doesn't serve the tourist sites, children enjoy this ride (it's so short you just travel both ways). At this writing it was said that the funicular might close, so check.

TOURS   The Haifa Tourist Board conducts a free Saturday morning 1½-hour walking tour that departs at 10 AM from 89 Yefe Nof (Panorama Road), behind the Nof hotel and near the Mane Katz museum. On this tour you take a leisurely stroll along the Promenade, see entrancing views, step into one of the Baha'i terraces, and visit the Sculpture Garden.

Carmelit offers boat tours of Haifa Bay from Magan Hadayag, beside the airport. The ride lasts one hour and costs NIS 30. Call ahead for departure times.

ESSENTIALS

Banks and Exchange Service First International Bank (⊠ *1 Elchanan St., Haifa* ☎ *04/835–0200*). **Super Change** (⊠ *113 Hanassi Blvd., Haifa* ☎ *04/810–7141*).

Boat Contact Carmelit (☎ *04/841–8765*).

Bus Contact Egged Information Center (☎ *03/624–8888* ⊕ *www.egged.co.il*).

Internet NorEm Internet Cafe (⊠ *27–29 Nordeau St., Hadar, Haifa* ☎ *04/866–5656*).

Medical Assistance Rambam Medical Center (☎ *04/854–3111* ⊕ *www.rambam.org.il*).

Taxi Contacts Carmel-Ahuza (☎ *04/838–2727 Haifa*). **Mercaz Mitzpe** (☎ *04/866–2525 Haifa*).

Train Contact Israel Railways Information Centre (☎ *03/577–4000* ⊕ *www.israrail.org.il*).

Visitor Information Haifa Tourist Board (⊠ *48 Ben Gurion Blvd., German Colony* ☎ *04/853–5606* ⊕ *www.tour-haifa.co.il*).

EXPLORING HAIFA

The metropolis is divided into three main levels, each crisscrossed by parks and gardens: the port down below; Hadar HaCarmel, a rather unappealing commercial shopping area in the middle; and Merkaz HaCarmel, with the posher hotels and many restaurants, on top.

Thanks to the beneficence of the Baha'is, you can enjoy two different walks that take you through the stunning terraces that lie like multicolored jewels from the crest of the city at Mt. Carmel to the German Colony below.

TOP ATTRACTIONS

❶ Fodor's Choice ★

Baha'i Shrine and Gardens. The most striking feature of the stunning gardens that form the centerpiece of Haifa is the Shrine of the Bab, whose brilliantly gilded dome dominates—and illuminates—the city's skyline. You must book a free tour of the gardens in advance, but it's well worthwhile. Note that the shrine is being restored and will be covered with scaffolding for two years, beginning in 2009. Access will continue, however.

Haifa is the world center for the Baha'i faith, founded in Iran in the 19th century. It holds as its central belief the unity of mankind. Religious truth for Baha'is is not doctrinaire; rather, it consists of progressive revelations of a universal faith. Thus the Baha'is teach that great

WORD OF MOUTH

"Shrine of the Bab is one of many holy sites in Israel. Perched on the slopes of Mt. Carmel, the Baha'i Gardens pay homage to Baha'i's founders."

—photo by GeneZ, Fodors.com member

Haifa

EIN HAYAM

Elijah's Cave

KIRYAT ELIEZER

BAT GALIM

Train Station

Bus Station

KIRYAT ELIAHU

FRENCH CARMEL

NEVE DAVID

RAMAT HATISHBI

WESTERN CARMEL

KABABIR

MERKAZ CARMEL (THE TOP OF THE MOUNTAIN)

Hashalom
Ha'atiya
Hashnia
Sderot Hahagana
Sderot Hahagana
Sderot Hahagana
Haforen St.
Zahal St.
Tel Aviv St.
Yitzhak Sadeh
Sderot Hameginim
Derekh Zorfat
Stella Maris Rd.
Allenby Road
Sderot James de Rothschild
Hageten Blvd.
Allenby Rd.
Devol
Sha'ar Ha'aliya St.
Shaul Tshernichovski
Yeshayahu
Ezel St.
Hayam
Shomron
Yefe Nof St.
Sderot Hatziyonut
HaNassi Blvd.
Hacarmel St.
Hayam
Kabirim St.
Eliyahu Golomb St.
Hahashmonaim St.
Kadima St.
Sderot Wedgewood
Ha'asif St.

6
7
5
2
1
8
9
10
11
12

KEY
↦ Rail Lines

Baha'i Shrine
and Gardens 1

Carmelite Monastery
and Stella Maris Church 5

Clandestine Immigration
and Naval Museum 6

German Colony 3

Haifa Museum of Art 4

Haifa Zoo 9

Hecht Museum 12

Mané Katz
Museum 10

National Maritime
Museum 7

National Museum of
Science and Technology 13

Technion 14

Tikotin Museum
of Japanese Art 11

Vista of Peace
Sculpture Garden 2

Yefe Nof Street 8

prophets have appeared throughout history to reveal divine truths, among them Moses, Zoroaster, Buddha, Jesus, Mohammed, and most recently, the founder of the Baha'i faith, Mirza Husayn Ali, known as Baha'u'llah—the Glory of God. Baha'u'llah (1817–92) was exiled from his native Persia by the Shah and then by the Ottomans to Akko, where he lived as a prisoner for almost 25 years. The Baha'is' holiest shrine is on the grounds of Baha'u'llah's home, where he lived after his release from prison and where he is now buried, just north of Akko.

Here in Haifa, at the center of the shrine's pristinely manicured garden terraces, is the mausoleum built for the Bab (literally, the "Gate"), the forerunner of this religion, who heralded the coming of a new faith to be revealed by Baha'u'llah. The Bab was martyred by the Persian authorities in 1850. The gardens and shrine were built by Baha'u'llah's son and successor, who had the Bab's remains reburied here in 1909. The building, made of Italian stone and rising 128 feet, gracefully combines the canons of classical European architecture with elements of Eastern design and also houses the remains of Baha'u'llah's son. The dome glistens with some 12,000 gilded tiles imported from the Netherlands. Inside, the floor is covered with rich Oriental carpets, and a filigree veil divides the public area from the inner shrine.

The magnificent gardens are a sight to behold: 19 stunningly landscaped circular terraces extend from Yefe Nof Street for 1 km (½ mi) down the hillside to Ben Gurion Boulevard, at the German Colony. The terraces are a harmony of color and form—pale-pink and gray-stone flights of stairs and carved urns overflowing with red geraniums set off the perfect cutouts of emerald-green grass and floral borders, dark-green trees, and wildflowers, with not a leaf out of place anywhere. The gardens are one of Israel's 11 UNESCO World Heritage sites.

Three areas are open to the public year-round (except on Baha'i holidays): the Shrine and surrounding gardens (from Hatziyonut Avenue); the upper terrace and observation point (Yefe Nof Street); and the entry at the lower terrace (Hagefen Square, at the end of Ben Gurion Boulevard). You can visit the gardens only by guided tour; these take place daily and must be reserved at least three days in advance by phone, Sunday–Thursday 9–5. The Shrine of the Bab (along with the Shrine of Baha'u'llah, north of Akko) is a pilgrimage site for the worldwide Baha'i community; visitors to the shrine are asked to dress modestly (no shorts). ⊠ *65 Sderot Hatziyonut, Merkaz Carmel* ☎ *04/835–8358, 04/831–3131 for garden tour* ⊕ *www.bahai.org* ✉ *Free* ⊗ *Shrine daily 9–noon; gardens daily 9–5.*

❸ **German Colony.** It is only one street—actually a broad boulevard—but Fodor'sChoice "The Colony" packs in history (with explanatory placards), interest-
★ ing architecture, great restaurants, and wonderful spots for people-

CLOSE UP

Haifa's History

First mentioned in the Talmud, the area around Haifa had two settlements in ancient times. To the east, in what is today a congested industrial zone in the port, lay Zalmona, and 5 km (3 mi) west around the cape was Shiqmona.

The Crusaders conquered Haifa when it was an important Arab town and maintained it as a fortress along the coastal road to Akko for 200 years; it was lost and repeatedly regained by the Christians. During this period, in 1154, the Order of Our Lady of Mount Carmel (the Carmelite order) was founded on the slopes of Mt. Carmel by a group of hermits following the principles of the prophet Elijah and the rules of poverty, vegetarianism, and solitude.

After Akko and Haifa succumbed to the Mamluk Sultan Baybars in 1265, Haifa was destroyed and left derelict. It was a sleepy fishing village for centuries.

The city reawakened under the rule of Bedouin sheikh Dahr el-Omar, who had rebelled against direct Ottoman rule in the mid-18th century and independently governed Akko and the Galilee. In 1761 Dahr ordered the city to be demolished and moved about 3 km (2 mi) to the south. The new town was fortified by walls and protected by a castle, and its port began to compete with that of Akko across the bay.

Napoléon, too, came to Haifa, though only briefly, and en route to ignominious defeat at Akko during his Eastern Campaign. Napoléon left his wounded at the Carmelite Monastery when he beat a retreat in 1799, but the French soldiers there were killed and the monks driven out by Ahmed el-Jazzar, the victorious pasha of Akko.

With the creation of a deep-water port in 1929, Haifa's development as a modern city began. By the time the state of Israel was declared in 1948, its population was already more than 100,000. Today Haifa is the country's third-largest city, home to Arabs and Jews and the world center for the Baha'i faith.

5

watching. Ruler-straight Ben Gurion Boulevard was the heart of a late-19th-century colony established by the German Templer religious reform movement. Along either side are robust one- and two-story stone houses with pointed red-tile roofs. Many bear German names, dates from the 1800s, biblical inscriptions above the doors, and old wooden shutters framing narrow windows.

Neglected for years, the German Colony is now one of the city's loveliest (and flattest) strolls. It's best to start your exploration around Yaffo (Jaffa) Street so that you're walking toward the stunning Baha'i Gardens. At dusk, you can watch the lights flicker on one by one. Along the way you can have a meal or a cup of coffee, explore the shops in the City Centre Mall, and learn about the history of the German Templers. Any time of day is pleasant, but evening, when the cafés and restaurants are brimming with people, is best.

The Templers' colony in Haifa was one of five in the Holy Land. The early settlers formed a self-sufficient community; by 1883 they had built nearly 100 houses and filled them with as many families. Industrious workers, they introduced the horse-drawn wagon—unknown before their arrival—to Haifa. They also built with their own funds a pilgrimage road from Haifa to Nazareth. The Germans' labors gave rise to modern workshops and warehouses, and it was under their influence that Haifa began to resemble a modern city, with well-laid-out streets, gardens, and attractive homes.

Haifa's importance to Germany was highlighted in 1898, when Kaiser Wilhelm II sailed into the bay, on the first official visit to the Holy Land by a German emperor in more than 600 years. During World War II the Germans who lived in the colony were expelled, suspected of being Nazis. ⊠ *German Colony.*

⓫ **Tikotin Museum of Japanese Art.** Established in 1957 by Felix Tikotin, this
★ graceful venue adheres to the Japanese tradition of displaying beautiful objects that are in harmony with the season, so exhibits change frequently. The Japanese atmosphere, created in part by sliding doors and partitions made of wood and paper, enhances a display of scrolls, screens, pottery and porcelain, lacquer and metalwork, paintings from several schools, and fresh-flower arrangements. ⊠ *88 Hanassi Blvd., Merkaz Carmel* 🕾 *04/838–3554* ⊕ *www.hms.org.il* 🎫 *NIS 24* ⊗ *Mon., Wed., Thurs. 10–4, Tues. 4–8, Fri. 10–1, Sat. and Jewish holidays 10–3.*

❽ **Yefe Nof Street.** Also known as Panorama Road, this curving street high
★ above the city skirts the backs of Haifa's biggest hotels, providing superlative views. Part of the walk (through the black iron gate) takes you past two magnificent terraces of the Baha'i Gardens. Enjoy the beauty of the lushly planted Louis Promenade, with shaded benches along the way, beginning behind the Dan Carmel Hotel. On a clear day, from any of several lookouts you can see the port below, Akko across the bay, and the cliffs of Rosh Hanikra, with Lebanon in the distance. Panorama Road is beautiful during the day and at night. ⊠ *Merkaz Carmel.*

WORTH NOTING

❺ **Carmelite Monastery and Stella Maris Church.** Perched high up on the hillside is this imposing church. The wall paintings bring to life the dramatic story of the prophet Elijah, the patron of the Carmelite order. During the Crusader period, certain hermits emulating the ascetic life of the prophet Elijah lived in caves on this steep mountain slope. In the early 13th century they united under the leadership of Saint Berthold, who petitioned the patriarch of Jerusalem for a charter. Thus was born the Carmelite order, which spread across Europe. The Carmelite monks were forced to leave their settlements on Mt. Carmel at the end of the 13th century, and they did not return until nearly four centuries later. When they found Elijah's cave inhabited by Muslim dervishes, they set up a monastery nearby.

The church of the present monastery dates from 1836 and was built with the munificence of the French monarchy, hence the name of the surrounding neighborhood: French Carmel. The French connection is explained by a small pyramid, topped with an iron cross, that stands outside. The monument commemorates those French who were slaughtered here by the Turks in 1799 after the retreating Napoléon left his ailing troops behind at the monastery. Inside, the academic paintings in the dome depict Elijah in the chariot of fire in which he ascended to

Haifa's restored, 19th-century German Colony is a relaxing place to dine or spend an evening.

heaven, and other biblical prophets. The small cave a few steps down at the end of the nave is traditionally associated with Elijah and his pupil, Elisha. ⊠ *Carmelite Monastery, Stella Maris Rd., French Carmel* ☎ *04/833–7758* 🖅 *Free* 🕑 *Daily 8–12:30 and 3–6; Sun. 10–6.*

❻ Clandestine Immigration and Naval Museum. The rather dull name of this museum belies the dramatic nature of what's inside. The museum tells the story of the often heroic efforts to bring Jewish immigrants to Palestine from war-torn Europe in defiance of British policy.

Emigration to Palestine was well nigh impossible after the British imposed a naval blockade, bowing to pressure by Arabs opposed to Jewish immigration. In 1939, on the eve of World War II, the British issued the so-called White Paper, which effectively strangled Jewish immigration to Palestine. Small boats sometimes managed to elude British warships and unload their human cargoes at secret landing beaches, but for bigger ships the odds were daunting. Out of 63 clandestine ships that tried to run the blockade after the war's end, all but five were intercepted, and their passengers were deported to Cyprus.

The museum is full of moving stories of courage, tenacity, and disaster. A photomural of the celebrated ship the *Exodus* recalls the story of the 4,530 refugees aboard who were forcibly transferred back to Germany in 1947, but not before the British forces opened fire on the ship.

One of the blockade runners was an old American tank-landing craft renamed *Af-al-pi-chen* ("Nevertheless," in Hebrew), which serves as the museum's centerpiece. This ship left Italy in 1947 for Palestine and was intercepted by the British, at which point its 434 passengers, all survivors of the Holocaust, were sent to internment camps in Cyprus.

The blue Mediterranean, Haifa's hills, and the rolling green of the Baha'i Gardens make irresistible photos.

✉ *204 Allenby Rd., Kiryat Eliezer* ☎ *04/853–6249* ⊕ *www.amutayam. org.il* 🎫 *NIS 10* 🕐 *Sun.–Thurs. 8:30–4.*

Elijah's Cave. This site is considered sacred by Jews, Christians, and Muslims; an early Byzantine tradition identified it as the cave in which Elijah found refuge from the wrath of Ahab, king of Israel from 871 to 853 BC. Graffiti from pilgrims of various faiths and different centuries are scrawled on the right wall, and written prayers are often stuffed into crevices. Modest dress is requested. The cave is a 20-minute walk down the fairly steep path across from the entrance to the Carmelite Monastery and church. ✉ *Allenby Rd., Ein Hayam* 🎫 *Free* 🕐 *Sun.– Thurs. 8–5, Fri. and Jewish holiday eves 8–1.*

❹ **Haifa Museum of Art** *(Museum of Modern Art)*. Displayed here are works from all over the world, dating from the mid-18th century to the present. It's an excellent venue to learn about contemporary Israeli art: included are 20th-century graphics and contemporary paintings, sculptures, and photographs. The print collection is of special note. ✉ *26 Shabbtai Levy St., Hadar* ☎ *04/852–3255* ⊕ *www.hms.org.il* 🎫 *NIS 29* 🕐 *Sun.–Tues., Wed. and Sat. 10–4; Thurs. 4–7; Fri. 10–1.*

NEED A BREAK? In a city known for its falafel, check out the falafel joints called Michel and Haskenim at 18 and 21 Wadi Street, the circular street in the Wadi Nisnas market. You'll get plenty of fresh steaming chickpea balls, warm pita bread and toppings, and a choice of cold drinks.

❾ **Haifa Zoo.** Down past the play equipment in the Gan Ha'Em park, amid masses of trees and foliage, is a seemingly happy collection of roaring lions, two tigers, big brown bears, chattering monkeys, stripe-tailed lemurs, a placid camel, lots of snakes, one croc, and fierce-eyed eagles and owls—plus a bat cave and a water-bird pond. It's a hilly place, but there's a tram to take visitors up the steepest terrain. ⊠*Hanassi Blvd., Merkaz Carmel* ☎*04/837–2886* ⬛*NIS 30* ◷*Apr.–June, Sun.–Thurs. 8–5; July–Aug., Sun.–Thurs. 8–6; Sept.–Mar., Sun.–Thurs. 8–4.*

⓬ **Hecht Museum.** It's worth the trip to Haifa University to see this museum's archaeological treasures. At the summit of Mt. Carmel, in the main campus tower, the collection spans the millennia from the Chalcolithic era to the Roman and Byzantine periods, concentrating on "The People of Israel in Eretz Israel." The artifacts range from religious altars and lamps to two coffins and figurines from the Early Bronze Age. Featured prominently are finds from the excavations of Jerusalem's Temple Mount. A separate wing displays a small collection of paintings, mostly Impressionist works by Monet, Soutine, and Pissarro, among others. The roof observation deck, on the 27th floor, affords spectacular views. To get here, take Bus 37 from the Nof Hotel. ⊠*Abu Hushi St., Mt. Carmel, Har Carmel* ☎*04/824–0577* ⊕*www.mushect.haifa.ac.il* ⬛*Free* ◷*Sun., Mon., Wed., and Thurs. 10–4; Tues. 10–7; Fri. and holiday eves 10–1; Sat. 10–2.*

⓾ **Mané Katz Museum.** This is the house and studio where the Expressionist painter Emmanuel Katz (1894–1962) lived and worked for the last four years of his life. Katz spent the 1920s in Paris, where he exhibited with a group of Jewish artists from the École de Paris. As in the canvases of fellow members Marc Chagall and Chaim Soutine, a recurring theme in his work is the village life of Jews in Eastern Europe. A whitewashed building, it contains Katz's paintings, drawings, and sculptures. You'll also find the Ukrainian-born artist's legacy to the city plus his collection of rugs, 17th-century antiques from Spain and Germany, and Judaica. ⊠*89 Yefe Nof St., Merkaz Carmel* ☎*04/838–3482* ⬛*Free* ◷*Sun., Mon., Wed., and Thurs. 10–4, Tues. 2–6, Fri. 10–1, Sat. 10–2.*

❼ **National Maritime Museum.** About 5,000 years of maritime history are told (and made more interesting than you might imagine) with model ships, archaeological finds, coins minted with nautical symbols, navigational instruments, and other artifacts. There are also intriguing underwater finds from nearby excavations and shipwrecks. The ancient-art collection is one of the finest in the country; it comprises mostly Greek and Roman stone and marble sculpture, Egyptian textiles, Greek pottery, and encaustic grave portraits from Fayyum, in Lower Egypt. Particularly rare are the figures of fishermen from the Hellenistic period. Among numerous terra-cotta figurines from Syria and Egypt are several curious animal-shape vessels—once used as playthings, incense burners, or funerary gifts—from Haifa's nearby Shiqmona excavation. ⊠*198 Allenby Rd., Kiryat Eliezer* ☎*04/853–6622* ⊕*www.hms.org.il* ⬛*NIS 29* ◷*Mon.–Wed. 10–4, Thurs. 4–9, Fri. 10–1, Sat. 10–3.*

⓭ **National Museum of Science and Technology (Technoda).** Both children and ☺ adults are captivated by the hands-on chemistry and physics exhibits in this beautifully designed building, the original home of the Technion. ⊠*12 Balfour St., Hadar* ☎*04/861–4444* ⊕*www.mustsee.org.il* ⬛*NIS 29* ◷*Mon.–Wed. 10–4, Thurs. 4–9, Fri. 10–1, Sat. 10–3.*

5

⑭ Technion. Israel's top institute for science and technology, the 300-acre Israeli Institute of Technology is highly fertile ground for research in such fields as engineering, medicine, architecture, and city planning. Visitors can get an insight into the institute's history, its research achievements, and its future goals. There's a virtual tour of the institute and an interactive film about the 2004 Nobel prize in chemistry. To get here, take Bus 31 from the Nof Hotel or the Dan Panorama Hotel. ⊠*Kiryat Ha-Technion, Neve Sha'anan* ☎*04/829–3863* ⊕*www.technion.ac.il* 🖃*Free* ☉*Sun.–Thurs. 8:30–3.*

② Vista of Peace Sculpture Garden. You can contemplate the life-size bronzes of people and animals from a bench on the winding path through this garden, which has views of Haifa Bay beyond. Sculptor Ursula Malbin, who came to Israel as a refugee from Nazi Germany, created this oasis. The garden opens at sunrise and closes at 6. ⊠*Just west of Baha'i Shrine, Bahai* ⊕*www.malbin-sculpture.com.*

WHERE TO EAT

There are plenty of restaurants at the top of the city in Merkaz Carmel. A popular place to eat is along Ben Gurion Boulevard in the German Colony. The port area is being gentrified, so there are always new restaurants opening up. Dress is casual, Israeli style.

$$ ✕**Douzan.** Inside this old German Templer building with a pleasant out-
MEDITERRANEAN door terrace, a huge metal lamp studded with colored glass casts lacy designs on the walls. The food, much of it prepared by the owner's mother, is an intriguing combination of French and local Arabic cuisines. Her specialty is *kibbeh,* deep-fried torpedoes of cracked wheat kneaded with minced beef, pine nuts, onions, and exotic spices. A variation on it is *sfeeha,* puff pastry topped with delicately spiced beef, onions, and pine nuts. Among the French dishes are chicken cordon bleu with mustard cream sauce, and an onion, bacon, and thyme quiche. ⊠*35 Ben Gurion Blvd., German Colony* ☎*04/852–5444* ⊟*AE, DC, MC, V.* ✛*4C*

$$ ✕**Fattoush.** Olive trees hung with blue and olive lights and a patterned
MIDDLE EASTERN rug on the sidewalk set the tone for the elaborate interior, which contains several intimate rooms. One is a "cave" with Arabic script on the walls, low banquettes, wooden stools, and filigree lamps; another is modern with leather seats, embroidered cushions, and a changing art exhibit set against burnt-orange walls. And now for the food: Fattoush salad is a favorite, consisting of chopped tomato, cucumber, onion, and mint and sprinkled with crisp toasted pita pieces. You might follow it with *emsakhan,* roast chicken topped with pieces of sumac and served on oven-baked pita. For a daring dessert, try Arabic *knaffe,* consisting of crispy noodles with soft cheese and honey. ⊠*40 Ben Gurion Blvd., German Colony* ☎*04/852–4930* ⊟*AE, DC, MC, V.* ✛*4B*

$$ ✕**Giraffe.** Here's a welcome combination of jolly atmosphere and tasty
ASIAN food—and there's some culinary combining going on here, too: Asian cuisine is followed by French desserts. It's sort of a New York lounge–style hangout: stainless-steel open kitchen, black tables and chairs, black bar and stools, silver photography-studio ceiling lights, and a wait-staff in bright white T's, jeans, and long black aprons. Noodles are the

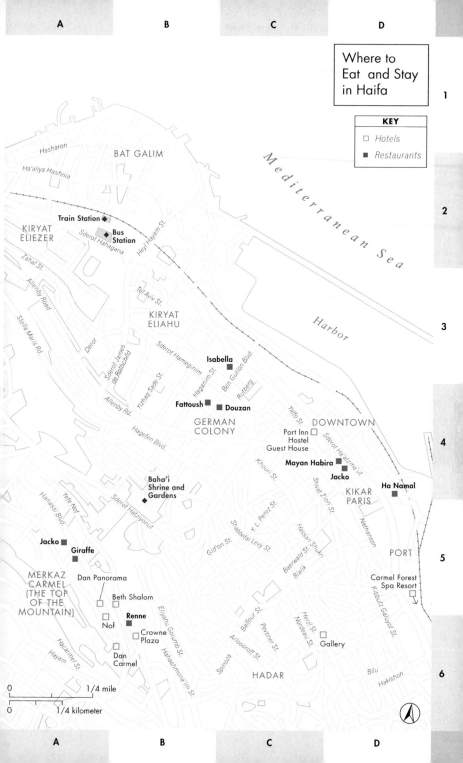

Where to
Eat and Stay
in Haifa

KEY
□ Hotels
■ Restaurants

Mediterranean Sea

BAT GALIM

Hasharon

Ha'aliya Hashnia

◆ Train Station

KIRYAT
ELIEZER

Sderot Hahagana

◆ Bus Station

Hey! Hayam St.

Zahal St.

Allenby Road

Stella Maris Rd.

Deror

Tel Aviv St.

KIRYAT
ELIAHU

Sderot Hameginim

Sderot James de Rothschild

Yizhaq Sade St.

Allenby Rd.

Hagefen Blvd.

Haganim St.

Ben Gurion Blvd.

Rutberg

■ Isabella

■ Fattoush   ■ Douzan

GERMAN
COLONY

Harbor

Yaffo St.

DOWNTOWN

Port Inn □
Hostel
Guest House

Sderot Ha'atzma'ut

■ Mayan Habira

■ Jacko

Khouri St.

Shivat Zion St.

KIKAR
PARIS

■ Ha Namal

Baha'i Shrine and
Gardens ◆

Sderot Hatziyonut

Hanassi Blvd.

Yefe Nof

■ Jacko

■ Giraffe

MERKAZ
CARMEL
(THE TOP
OF THE
MOUNTAIN)

Dan Panorama
□

Beth Shalom
□

Nof □

Dan
Carmel □

Hacarmel St.

Hayam

Eliyahu Golumb St.

Hahashmona Inn St.

Shabbetai Levy St.

Gid'on St.

Y. L. Perez St.

Baerwald St.

Bialik

Spinoza

Arlosoroff St.

Balfour St.

Pevsner St.

HADAR

Hassan Shukri

Renne ■

□ Crowne
Plaza

Herzl St.

Nordau St.

□ Gallery

Natharson

PORT

Carmel Forest
Spa Resort
□

Kibbutz Galuyot St.

Bilu

Hakishon

0   1/4 mile

0   1/4 kilometer

A   B   C   D

1

2

3

4

5

6

specialty, and most dishes are prepared in a wok. You might start with a crispy Thai salad in peanut sauce; then feast on spicy Philippine egg noodles with chicken, roast goose, and chopped shrimp in a hot chili sauce. ⊠ *131 Hanassi Blvd., Merkaz Carmel* ☎ *04/810–4012* ⊟ *AE, DC, MC, V.* ✛ *5A*

$$$ ✕ **Ha Namal.** Careful renovations have transformed this old wheat and
MODERN ISRAELI   corn warehouse in Haifa's rather rundown port into a Tuscan country inn. Climbing the stairs you arrive at five different rooms (one's the bar, with leather sofas) with original stone floors, brick walls, and lofty ceilings. The inventive chef offers starters such as salmon fillet covered in herbs and coriander seeds and entrées such as lamb sirloin in a cashew-pesto crust, smoked shrimp in a pastry shell, and Swiss chard and ricotta tortellini with white-truffle cream. There's a fixed-price lunch and a children's menu. ⊠ *24 Hanamal St., off Sha'ar Palmer St., the Port* ☎ *04/862–8899* ⊟ *AE, MC, V* ⊘ *Closed Sun.* ✛ *4D*

$$ ✕ **Isabella.** With tiny lights in the ceiling, walls in muted gray tones,
ITALIAN   dark-wood tables with sleek leather chairs, and a brushed-cement floor, Isabella is a suitable setting for modern Italian cuisine. Among the appetizers try the eggplant carpaccio in garlic-lemon tahini sauce or the excellent "stuffed" pizza (filled with, among other choices, ham, mozzarella cheese, grilled eggplant, and tomatoes). Streetside on the patio, or inside with the crowd, you can enjoy hearty dishes such as veal scaloppine, seafood in a champagne and saffron sauce, or veal with rosemary and lemon sauce. An extensive wine list rounds out the offerings. ⊠ *6 Ben Gurion Blvd., City Center Mall, German Colony* ☎ *04/855–2201* ⌂ *Reservations essential* ⊟ *AE, DC, MC, V.* ✛ *3C*

$$ ✕ **Jacko.** If ever there was a beloved eating place in Haifa, Jacko is it.
SEAFOOD   Give the name to your taxi driver, he'll nod approvingly, gun the motor, and drop you at a nondescript building with a Hebrew sign. Since 1976, this family-run restaurant has been serving up delicious food in a rowdy, informal setting with shared tables. The specialties here are fish and seafood served grilled or fried. There are piles of crab, mussels, and calamari served with a variety of sauces, large shrimp grilled in their shells, and Mediterranean lobster (in summer). For dessert try the Turkish cookies or semolina and coconut cake. Wine and draft beer are available. If it's Tuesday night, there'll be a jazz performance to liven up the night. ⊠ *12 Hadekalim St., Downtown* ☎ *04/866–8813* ⊠ *11 Moriah St., Merkaz Carmel* ☎ *04/810–2355* ⌂ *Reservations essential* ⊟ *AE, DC, MC, V* ⊘ *No dinner Sat.* ✛ *5A, 4D*

$$ ✕ **Mayan Habira.** If you're looking for meat with a capital "M," you've
EASTERN   found the place. This well-known restaurant is in the traffic-ridden
EUROPEAN   downtown area, with a sign in Hebrew. The decor is informal: beer kegs are piled up in a corner; the walls are covered with photos of glowing restaurant reviews and a mural of the customers painted by an art student in 1989. The family-run business has been around since 1962; today Reuven and his son do the excellent cooking. To start, savor chopped liver, jellied calf's foot, gefilte fish, or oxtail soup. Then go to work on delectable spareribs or goose or beef pastrami, which they smoke themselves. Grilled rabbit is also a good choice (order in advance). There's a huge selection of draft beer. In the summer diners sit outside and enjoy

live music. ⊠*4 Nathanson St., Downtown* ☎*04/862–3193* ▭*AE, DC, MC, V* ⊘*Closed Sat. No dinner.* ✛*4D*

$$$
MODERN ISRAELI
Fodor'sChoice
★

✕**Renne.** A wall of windows opens out onto a startling and stunning view of the sea from the very top of Haifa. Pale-wood floors, tobacco-colored tables, and leather banquettes scattered here and there are set beneath a chandelier dripping with crystals. All in all, it's a winning setting for the wonderful modern Israeli cuisine. You might start with mussels in almond butter, then try spring mullet fillet cooked in olive oil and served with gnocchi in a sauce of sun-dried tomatoes, garlic-touched broad beans, and pine nuts. If you prefer pasta, there's hunter's penne—strips of veal fillet, tomatoes, mushrooms, and onion in a veal stock flavored with a touch of cream. For dessert, let's hear it for the Peanut Bar, a glunky confection of chocolate, peanuts, and caramel. ⊠*99 Yefe Nof St., Merkaz Carmel* ☎*04/837–5602* ✍*Reservations essential* ▭*AE, DC, MC, V.* ✛*6B*

WHERE TO STAY

Haifa's best-known hotels are at the top of the city in the Merkaz Carmel area. The Colony Hotel, one of the city's newest lodgings, is in the downtown area, as is the Port Inn hostel-guesthouse; both offer more affordable stays. Within easy reach of the city, the Carmel Forest Resort Spa is quiet and pampering.

¢

🏨**Beth Shalom.** Plain but pleasant, this Christian-run lodging has three floors of small rooms. Each has wicker furniture, beds with fluffy duvets, and good reading lights. A healthy breakfast is served cafeteria-style, and you can enjoy it on the patio. Beth Shalom is on a busy street, but the front rooms are quiet thanks to the double-glazed windows. **Pros:** central location; modest price. **Cons:** no restaurant; basic decor. ⊠*110 Hanassi Blvd., Merkaz Carmel* ☎*04/837–7481* ⊕*www.beth-shalom. co.il* ⌕*30 rooms* ⚐*In-room: Wi-Fi. In-hotel: bar, parking (free), no-smoking rooms* ▭*AE, DC, MC, V* ⦿*CP.* ✛*5B*

$$$$
Fodor'sChoice
★

🏨**Carmel Forest Spa Resort.** Set off by itself in the Carmel Forest, this spa-resort lies 25 km (15 mi) from Haifa. It's the ultimate escape: a handsome, top-of-the-line spa with a tastefully appointed lodging designed to pamper guests in a calm and healthful setting (no cell phones or children under 16). The hotel is on a hillside, with stunning views of pine trees and the Mediterranean. Treatment rooms offer a variety of massages, including aromatherapy, body peels, and seaweed wraps. Green wicker chaises let you relax with a cup of herbal tea as you contemplate nature through the solarium windows. A sample day? Consult the nutritionist, strike out on a forest walk, have a sesame-oil massage, and then sit down to a meal prepared with all-natural ingredients. Day guests are welcome. **Pros:** peaceful setting; lovely forest walks. **Cons:** no public transportation; rather pricey. ⊠*Carmel Forest* ☎*04/830–7888* ⊕*www.isrotel.co.il* ⌕*126 rooms* ⚐*In-room: safe, Wi-Fi. In-hotel: restaurant, bar, tennis court, pools, gym, spa, bicycles, parking (free), no kids under 16, Internet terminal* ▭*AE, DC, MC, V* ⦿*FAP.* ✛*5D*

$$

🏨**Crowne Plaza.** This well-designed hotel is built into a pine-shaded slope, so the main entrance is actually on the ninth floor. The glass-domed

lobby has mauve and silver couches set off by floral arrangements in clay pots. The executive floor has a fully equipped business center and rooms with fax machines, Internet connections, and trouser presses to keep you looking spiffy. Views from the guest rooms are gorgeous, especially the ones on the sixth floor with balconies. **Pros:** pleasant atmosphere; quiet setting. **Cons:** dark dining room. ✉ *111 Yefe Nof St., Merkaz Carmel* ☎ *04/835–0835* 📠 *04/835–0836* ⊕ *www.holiday-inn.com/haifaisrael* 🛏 *100 rooms* ♿ *In-room: safe, refrigerator. In-hotel: restaurant, room service, bar, pool, gym, Internet terminal, Wi-Fi, parking (paid), no-smoking rooms* ☐ *AE, DC, MC, V* 🍴 *BP.* ✛ *6B*

$$$ 🏨 **Dan Carmel.** The Dan is beautifully situated on the heights of Merkaz Carmel. One of Haifa's first hotels, this longtime favorite has a stately charm and a devoted staff. The premises could use a renovator's touch, but the deluxe rooms on the upper floors are nicely furnished, with wooden bureaus and satin bedspreads. Other rooms are less luxurious, but they're cheerfully decorated in pastels. All guest rooms have balconies with stunning views over the city or the bay below. The large garden around the pool, with potted geraniums and many trees, is always breezy and pleasant. **Pros:** great views; doting staff. **Cons:** outdated decor; pricey for what you get. ✉ *87 Hanassi Blvd., Merkaz Carmel* ☎ *04/830–6211* ⊕ *www.danhotels.co.il* 🛏 *204 rooms, 18 suites* ♿ *In-room: safe (some), refrigerator. In-hotel: restaurant, room service, bar, pool, gym, parking (paid), no-smoking rooms, Internet terminal, Wi-Fi* ☐ *AE, DC, MC, V* 🍴 *BP.* ✛ *6B*

$$ 🏨 **Dan Panorama.** Another member of the Dan hotel chain, this one is somewhat glitzier than its sister up the road. Popular with business executives, the hotel has an efficient staff and a clubby feel. The rooms are spacious with blue-and-yellow color schemes and light-wood furnishings; some look out onto the gold-topped Baha'i Shrine and the bay; the rest have lovely city views, though none have balconies. The hotel is connected to the Panorama Center mall, with casual eateries and boutiques. **Pros:** helpful staff; good reading lights. **Cons:** no balconies, dated decor. ✉ *107 Hanassi Blvd., Merkaz Carmel* ☎ *04/835–2222* ⊕ *www.danhotels.co.il* 🛏 *266 rooms* ♿ *In-room: safe, refrigerator, Wi-Fi. In-hotel: restaurant, room service, bar, pool, gym, Internet terminal, parking (paid), no-smoking rooms* ☐ *AE, DC, MC, V* 🍴 *BP.* ✛ *5A*

$ 🏨 **Gallery.** A quiet retreat, this homey hotel offers peace amid the clamor of the city's downtown area. Its location north of the city center means you have easy access to Akko and other points north without having to travel through the city's heavy traffic. In a creatively renovated 1938 building, the hotel feels modern and you can see works by local artists displayed in several tiny gallery areas. The wood-floored rooms are pleasingly decorated in warm shades of gold and beige. Heavy drapes and triple-glazed windows ensure quiet nights, and bright reading lights are a plus. The two suites have pull-out sofas to accommodate up to four guests. **Pros:** homey; good for single travelers. **Cons:** far from tourist sites. ✉ *61 Herzl St., Downtown* ☎ *04/861–6161* ⊕ *www.haifa.hotelgallery.co.il* 🛏 *40 rooms* ♿ *In-room: safe, Wi-Fi. In-hotel: restaurant, spa, gym, Internet terminal* ☐ *AE, DC, MC, V* 🍴 *BP.* ✛ *6D*

$ ☆**Nof.** On Merkaz Carmel, this smaller lodging holds its own with the fancier hotels nearby. The modest guest rooms take full advantage of the setting, with large windows facing the sea. Ask for a room on the fourth, sixth, and seventh floors; they've all been nicely renovated. The lobby lounge, which opens onto the Promenade, also has superb views; a pianist plays in the evening. The friendly front-desk staff is welcoming; the on-site kosher Chinese restaurant makes for a convenient and rewarding dining experience. **Pros:** central location; modest prices. **Cons:** basic rooms; lobby can be noisy. ⊠ *101 Hanassi Blvd., Merkaz Carmel* ☎*04/835–4311* ⊕*www.inisrael.com/nof* ↳*80 rooms, 6 suites* ♿*In-room: refrigerator, Wi-Fi (some). In-hotel: restaurant, room service, bar, Internet terminal, parking (free)* ⊟*AE, DC, MC, V* ⊗ *BP.* ✛*6B*

¢   ☆**Port Inn Hostel Guest House.** A haven for budget travelers is in a neighborhood that buzzes with interesting shops. The inn occupies a beautifully renovated house painted quiet shades of pale yellow. The dormitories mainly interest backpackers (one is for women, one for men, and two are co-ed), but there are 10 double rooms with private bath, and one that has a shared bath. **Pros:** cheerful; good for single travelers. **Cons:** far from tourist sites; not a lot of privacy. ⊠ *34 Yaffo St., Downtown* ☎*04/852–4401* ⊕*www.portinn.co.il* ↳*10 rooms, 9 with bath* ♿*In-room: Wi-Fi. In-hotel: bar, laundry service, Internet terminal* ⊟*AE, DC, MC, V* ⊗*CP.* ✛*4C*

NIGHTLIFE AND THE ARTS

Haifa isn't Tel Aviv, but it does have interesting things to do after dark. For information on performances and other special events in and around Haifa, check Friday's *Jerusalem Post* or the *Ha Aretz* newspaper; both publish separate weekend entertainment guides. In balmy weather, a stroll along the Louis Promenade and then along Panorama Road, with lovely views of nighttime Haifa, is a relaxing way to end the day. For a guided hour-long evening walk, which ends with wine and cheese, call **G.U.Y. Tours** (☎*04/810–0999 or 050/532–1169*).

NIGHTLIFE

For a festive evening, try the restaurants and cafés-cum-pubs in the German Colony. Nightspots in Haifa come and go, and some open only on certain evenings, so call ahead if possible.

BARS

The bar at **Barbarossa** (⊠ *8 Pica St., Merkaz Carmel* ☎*04/811–4010*) is on the balcony, where you can enjoy happy hour while soaking up the great view from 6:30 to 9.

In the warm and cheery space at **Brown** (⊠ *131 Moriah Blvd., Merkaz Carmel* ☎*04/811–2391*), you can choose from 15 kinds of beer and nibble on Italian food.

The lovely **Duke** (⊠ *107 Moriah Blvd., Merkaz Carmel* ☎*04/834–7282*) is old-world European and offers entertainment from noon on.

In the Haifa tradition, **Mydlar's** (✉ *126 Moriah Blvd., Merkaz Carmel* ☎ *04/824–8754*) serves food at the bar, and it's particularly tasty fare. This is a warm and inviting place for a drink, too.

★ One of Haifa's oldest and most reliable bars, **Pundak Ha Dov** (✉ *135 Hanassi Blvd., Merkaz Carmel* ☎ *04/838–1703*) has live music weekly and tends to fill with enthusiastic revelers.

THE ARTS
FILM
Around the Sukkot holiday (end of September, start of October), Haifa hosts an international film festival. Contact the **Haifa Cinemateque** (☎ *04/835–3521*) for schedules and venues.

MUSIC
The **Israel Philharmonic Orchestra** (✉ *138 Hanassi Blvd., Merkaz Carmel* ☎ *04/810–1558*) gives approximately 20 concerts at the Haifa Auditorium from October through July. Concerts start at 8:30 PM or 9 PM, and the box office opens one hour before performances.

The **New Haifa Symphony Orchestra** (✉ *6 Eliyahu Hakim St., French Carmel* ☎ *04/859–9499*) performs at the Haifa Auditorium three times a month from October through July. For ticket and performance information, contact the box office.

SPORTS AND THE OUTDOORS

BEACHES
Haifa's coastline is one fine, sandy public beach after another. From south to north, **Dado, Zamir, Carmel, and Bat Galim beaches** (☎ *04/ 852–4231*) cover 5 km (3 mi) of coast, with many lifeguard stations among them. To be on the safe side, never swim when a lifeguard is not on duty. The beaches have sports areas, changing rooms, showers, toilets, refreshment stands, restaurants, and a winding stone promenade. On Saturday afternoon (morning in winter) at Dado Beach (near the Hof HaCarmel bus and train station at the city's entrance), Israelis of all ages come and folk dance, to the delight of onlookers.

BEACH BASICS
Between Tel Aviv and the Lebanese border are miles of beautiful sandy beaches, most of them public and attended by lifeguards from early May to mid-October. Many Israeli beaches are left untended off-season and get pretty grubby, but they're generally cleaned up and well maintained once warm weather returns. Beachside restaurants can make for rough-and-tumble eating because of loud music, but it's fun to eat fresh food by the beach. *Never swim in the absence of a lifeguard*, as the currents and undertows can be dangerous.

Hof HaShaket, just north of Aliya Street, offers separate gender days: Sunday, Tuesday, and Thursday for women; Monday, Wednesday, and Friday for men; Saturday for whoever.

DIVING
Learn to dive at the **Val Tal Diving Club** (✉ *2 Hubert Humphrey St., Bat Galim* ☎ *04/851–1523*), or—if you already know how and would like to explore 20th-century wrecks, reefs, and an Italian submarine sunk

by the British—look for Val Tal at the bottom station of the cable car, near the Yotvata restaurant. Rental equipment is available, and it's open daily 9 to 5.

SHOPPING

Haifa is studded with modern shopping malls with boutiques, eateries, and movie theaters plus drugstores, photography stores, and money-exchange desks. Near the railway station, a popular mall called **Castra** sells local art and is filled with jewelry and clothing stores. Ceramic wall art decorates the mall. Convenient to the hotels on the Carmel is the **Panorama Center,** next to the Dan Panorama hotel. Travelers will find everything from a pharmacy and newspaper stand to a wine outlet and clothing shops.

Amira's IOS Gallery (⊠*55 Ben Gurion Blvd., opposite the tourism office, German Colony* ☎*04/850–7504*) has lovely glass art, jewelry, and souvenirs; Amira's workshop is behind the shop.

★ **Sara's Gift Shop** (⊠*Dan Carmel hotel, 85–87 Hanassi Blvd., Merkaz Carmel* ☎*04/830–6238*) is crammed with jewelry made exclusively for this boutique; the silver and Roman glass pieces are unique. Other choices are Judaica and gifts for Baha'i visitors.

THE NORTHERN COAST

Beaches abound, the sea sparkles, and it's sunny most of the year along the Northern Coast. Archaeological sites, such as the oustanding Roman, Byzantine, and Crusader ruins at Caesarea, are not just dusty old ruins but rather beautiful restored treasures, and historical museums are fun and not fusty. Netanya and Nahsholim-Dor have plenty for the sun and fun seeker, including paragliding and other adventures. Fresh fish, seafood, and good local wine please every palate.

NAHSHOLIM-DOR

29 km (19 mi) south of Haifa.

Today the beautiful beach at Dor is fit for a king, but it has a long history with other royal associations. Founded 3,500 years ago, biblical Dor was once the maritime capital of the Carmel coast. Its small bay made it the best harbor between Jaffa and Akko and thus a target for many imperial ambitions, from the ancient Egyptians and the "Sea Peoples" through to King Solomon and on down. It was renowned in antiquity for its precious purple dye; reserved for royalty, this hue was extracted from a mollusk that was abundant along the coast.

GETTING HERE AND AROUND

Take Route 2, taking the Zichron Ya'akov exit. At the Fureidis Junction, travel north about 1 km (½ mi) until you reach the small sign for Nahsholim-Dor. There is no public transportation to this place.

EXPLORING

☾ Well worth a visit is the **Nahsholim-Dor Museum**, a rich trove of finds from
★ both local nautical digs and excavations at nearby Tel Dor. It's in the
partly restored former glass factory opened by Baron Rothschild in 1891
to serve the wineries of nearby Zichron Ya'akov. The sequence of peoples
who settled, conquered, or passed through Dor—from the Canaanites to
Napoléon—can be traced through these artifacts. Of particular interest
is the bronze cannon that Napoléon's vanquished troops dumped into
the sea during their retreat from Akko to Egypt in May 1799. An interesting film in English illuminates the history of the ancient city of Dor.
⊠*Kibbutz Nahsholim, Rd. 7011 off Rd. 4* ☎*04/639–0950* ☎*NIS 20*
☉*Sun.–Thurs. 8:30–2, Fri. 8:30–1, Sat. 10:30–3.*

WHERE TO EAT AND STAY

$ ✕**Pikalily–Sahara.** Grab a table on the deck at this raucous beach bar
ISRAELI and you'll soon be enjoying cool ocean breezes. Israeli beach fare is on
offer here, so order a tasty melted cheese on a seeded roll (called "cheese
toast"), fresh fillet of salmon, or a meaty kebab. Polish off your meal
with a glass of wine or knock back a beer at the bar. ⊠*Dor Beach*
☎*No phone* ⊟*AE, DC, MC, V.*

$$ 🛏**Nahsholim Hotel.** You'd have to travel a great distance to find a pret-
☾ tier beach than the one you'll find here. Low-slung buildings contain
standard rooms (many with sea views) and apartments with room for
up to five people. Breakfast is included in the rate; for other meals you
can enjoy seaside eating at the restaurant at nearby Dor Beach. Small
islets just off the coast attract nesting birds and give nature watchers
plenty to see in spring and fall. **Pros:** fabulous beach; family-friendly
vibe. **Cons:** expensive for what you get. ⊠*Kibbutz Nahsholim, Rd.
7011* ☎*04/639–9533* ⊕*www.nahsholim.co.il* ☎*41 rooms, 48 apart-
ments* ♨*In-room: refrigerator, Wi-Fi (some). In-hotel: restaurant, ten-
nis court, Internet terminal* ⊟*AE, DC, MC, V* ⊖*BP.*

SPORTS AND THE OUTDOORS

★ **Dor Beach** (☎*04/630–7180*), also known as Tantura Beach, is a dreamy
stretch of beige sand. Rocky islets form breakwaters that provide calm
seas for happy bathers. Amenities are ample: lifeguards in season, chair
and umbrella rentals, a first-aid station, a restaurant, parking, and
changing rooms and showers. The beach, beside Kibbutz Nahsholim,
gets crowded on summer weekends and holidays.

Paradive (⊠*Habonim Beach* ☎*04/639–1068* ⊕*www.paradive.co.il*) offers
you thrills and chills with tandem skydives over the Mediterranean.

★ Kurt Raveh, a diver-archaeologist and resident of Kibbutz Nahsholim,
runs the **Underwater Archaeological Center** (☎*052/279–6695*). Raveh
conducts underwater expeditions and "dives into history" where divers
(even those without experience) get to tour ancient shipwrecks under
his experienced eye.

**EN
ROUTE** Atlit is a peninsula with the jagged remains of an important Crusader
castle. Of more recent vintage, to the west (about 1,500 feet from the
highway), is the **Atlit detention camp.** It was used by the British to house
refugees smuggled in during and after World War II. The reconstructed

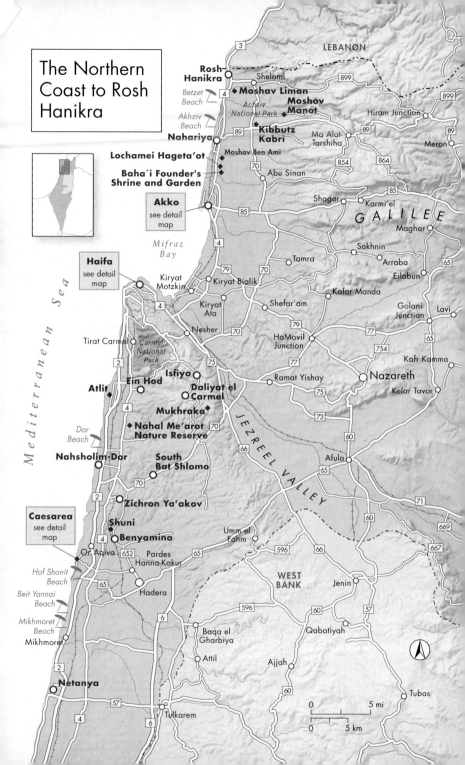

The Northern Coast to Rosh Hanikra

LEBANON

3

Rosh-Hanikra

Shelomi

899

899

Betzet Beach

◆ **Moshav Liman** 4

Achziv National Park

Moshov Manot

Hiram Junction

89

89

Akhziv Beach

Nahariya 89

◆ **Kibbutz Kabri**

Ma Alot-Tarshiha

89

Meron

Lochamei Hageta'ot

Moshav Ben Ami

854

864

85

Baha'i Founder's Shrine and Garden

70

Abu Sinan

Shagor

Karmi'el

GALILEE

Akko
see detail map

85

Maghar

4

Sakhnin

Arraba

65

Eilabun

Mifraz Bay

Tamra

Kafar Manda

Golani Junction

Lavi

Haifa
see detail map

Kiryat Motzkin

Kiryat Bialik

70

79

Shefar'am

77

HaMovil Junction

754

65

Kiryat Ata

4

Nesher

70

Kafr Kamma

Carmel National Park

Tirat Carmel

75

77

Ramat Yishay

Nazareth

Isfiya

Ein Hod

Atlit

Daliyat el Carmel

75

Kelar Tavor

2

Mukhraka ◆

73

Nahal Me'arot Nature Reserve 70

60

Dor Beach

JEZREEL VALLEY

Nahsholim-Dor

South Bat Shlomo

66

Afula

4

65

Zichron Ya'akov

70

71

2

60

Caesarea
see detail map

Shuni

Benyamina

Umm el Fahm

669

Or Aqiva

652

Pardes Hanna-Karur

65

596

66

667

Hof Shonit Beach

65

WEST BANK

Jenin

Beit Yannai Beach

Hadera

6

Mikhmoret Beach

596

60

57

Mikhmoret

Baqa el Gharbiya

Qabatiyah

2

Attil

Ajjah

Netanya

57

60

Tubas

4

6

Tulkarem

| 0 | | 5 mi |
| 0 | | 5 km |

Mediterranean Sea

barracks, fences, and watchtowers stand as reminders of how Jewish immigration was practically outlawed under the British Mandate after the publication of the infamous White Paper in 1939. More than a third of the 120,000 illegal immigrants to Palestine passed through the camp from 1934 to 1948. The authenticity of the exhibit is striking: it was re-created from accounts of actual detainees and their contemporaries; you'll see the living quarters, complete with laundry hanging from the rafters. The camp is 15 km (9 mi) south of Haifa. ☒ *Rte. 2* ☎ *04/984–1980* ☜ *NIS 17* ☉ *Sun.–Thurs. 9–4, Fri. 9–12:30.*

CAESAREA

49 km (29½ mi) south of Haifa.

GETTING HERE AND AROUND

A car is your best option for reaching Caesarea. It's on Route 2, about one hour by car from Tel Aviv or Haifa. You can also opt for a guided tour. Egged Tours and United Tours are two well-regarded companies.

ESSENTIALS

Tour Contacts Egged Tours (☎ *03/920–3919* ⊕ *www.eggedtours.co.il*). **United Tours** (☎ *03/693–3412, 03/522–2008* ⊕ *www.inisrael.com/united/index.html*).

EXPLORING

Fodor'sChoice
★

By turns an ancient Roman port city, a Byzantine capital, and a Crusader stronghold, **Caesarea** is one of the country's major archaeological sites. There's no need to think of this as a "dusty piles of stones." It is a delightful place to spend up to a day of leisurely sightseeing among the fascinating ruins. You can browse in souvenir shops and art galleries, swim at the beach, snorkel or dive around a submerged port, or enjoy a seaside meal. There's a modern town as well. Caesarea is an easy day trip from Tel Aviv and Haifa, or even Jerusalem.

There are two entrances to this intriguing site. A good strategy is to start at the Roman Theater, at the southern entrance. After exploring, you can then leave through the northern entrance. If you're short on time, enter through the northern entrance and take a quicker tour of the site. At either entrance, pick up the free brochure and map.

Entry to the **Roman Theater** is through one of the vomitoria (arched tunnels that served as entrances for the public). Herod's theaters—here and elsewhere in Israel—were the first of their kind in the ancient Near East. The theater today seats 3,600 and is a spectacular venue for summer concerts and performances. What you see today is predominantly a reconstruction. Only a few of the seats of the *cavea* (where the audience sat) near the orchestra are original, in addition to some of the stairs and the decorative wall at the front of the stage.

The huge **Herodian Amphitheater** is a horseshoe-shape stadium with sloping sides filled with rows of stone seats. It's most likely the one mentioned by 1st-century AD historian Josephus Flavius in *The Jewish War.* A crowd of 10,000 watched horse and chariot races and various sporting events here some 2,000 years ago. Up the wooden steps, you'll see the the street's beautiful and imaginative mosaic floors in the bathhouse complex of the Roman-Byzantine administrative area.

The walls that surround the **Crusader City** were built by King Louis IX of France. The bulk of what you see today—the moat, escarpment, citadel, and walls, which once contained 16 towers—dates from 1251, when the French king actually spent a year pitching in with his own two hands to help restore the existing fortifications. The Crusaders first besieged and conquered Caesarea in 1101 after it had been ruled for nearly five centuries by Arabs, who had allowed the port to silt up.

As you enter the southern wall gate of the Crusader city, note the shooting niches and the groined vaults of the gatehouse. Once inside, you'll see the remains of an unfinished cathedral; the three graceful curves of its apses stand out. At the observation point looking seaward, there's a lookout over the ancient port, now underwater. An earthquake devastated the harbor in AD 130, which is why the Crusaders utilized only a small section of it when they conquered the city in 1101.

Even today, **Herod's port** can be regarded as an awesome achievement. Josephus Flavius described the wonders of the port in glowing terms, comparing it to Athens's port of Piraeus. Once archaeologists explored the underwater ruins, it became clear that what had been long dismissed by many historians as hyperbole was exactly as Josephus described it.

♺ When you're exploring the harbor area, don't miss the **Time Trek.** Inside, you'll meet Caesarea's fascinating historic personages—among them King Herod, Rabbi Akiva, and St. Paul. These realistic-looking, larger-than-life figures can answer all kinds of questions you might have about their long-ago lives in Caesarea. Now climb the stairs of the nearby squarish stone tower with glass windows, on the pier sticking out into the harbor. Here you can view an intriguing three-dimensional animation on giant screens that explains the amazing construction of Herod's port.

East of the northern entrance to the site, a fenced-in area encloses Caesarea's **Byzantine street.** It was during the Byzantine period and in late Roman times that Caesarea thrived as a center of Christian scholarship. In the 7th century, Caesarea had a famous library of some 30,000 volumes that originated with the collection of the Christian philosopher Origen (185–254), who lived in Caesarea for two decades. Towering over the street are two headless marble statues, both probably carted here from nearby Roman temples. The provenance of the milky white statue is unknown; the reddish figure facing it might have been commissioned by the Emperor Hadrian when he visited Caesarea. ☎04/636–1010 ⊕*www.parks.org.il* ✉*NIS 23 without the Time Tower; NIS 40 with the Time Tower* ☉*Oct.–Mar., daily 8–4; Apr.–Sept., daily 8–5.*

Outside Ceasarea, the excellent **Caesarea Museum of Antiquities** houses many of the artifacts found by kibbutz members as they plowed their fields in the 1940s. The small museum has arguably the best collection of late-Roman sculpture in Israel; impressive holdings of rare Roman and Byzantine gemstones; and a large variety of coins minted in Caesarea over the ages, as well as oil lamps, urns excavated from the sea

CLOSE UP

Herod's Amazing Port at Caesarea

The port's construction at Caesarea was an unprecedented challenge—there was no artificial harbor of this size anywhere in the world. During preliminary underwater digs in 1978, archaeologists were stunned to discover concrete blocks near the breakwater offshore, indicating the sophisticated use of hydraulic concrete (which hardens underwater).

Historians knew that the Romans had developed such techniques, but before the discoveries at Caesarea, they never knew hydraulic concrete to have been used on such a massive scale. The main ingredient in the concrete, volcanic ash, was probably imported from Mt. Vesuvius, in Italy, as were the wooden forms. Teams of professional divers actually did much of the trickiest work, laying the foundations hundreds of yards offshore.

Once finished, two massive breakwaters—one stretching west and then north from the Citadel restaurant some 1,800 feet and the other 600 feet long, both now submerged—sheltered an area of about 3½ acres from the waves and tides.

Two towers, each mounted by three colossal statues, marked the entrance to the port; and although neither the towers nor the statues have been found, a tiny medal bearing their image was discovered in the first underwater excavations here, in 1960. The finished harbor also contained the dominating temple to Emperor Augustus and cavernous storage facilities along the shore.

5

floor, and fragments of jewelry. ⊠ *On grounds of Kibbutz Sdot Yam, about 600 feet south of southern entrance to the site.* ☎ *04/636–4367* ⊕ *www.parks.org.il* ⊠ *NIS 13* ☿ *Tues.–Thurs. 10–4, Fri. 10–1.*

Once you've entered Caesarea's villa area you can't miss the two Spanish-style buildings of the **Ralli Museum,** with their red-tiled roofs and expansive terraces. One of these dazzlingly white buildings houses an exhibit on the ancient city's history. The second building examines Spanish Jewry in the Middle Ages. It's a pleasure to wander along the walls of the courtyard and gaze at the sculptures of various dignitaries such as Maimonides and Nostradamus. Inside are paintings with biblical themes by European artists of the 16th to 18th centuries. ⊠ *Rothschild Blvd.* ☎ *04/626–1013* ⊠ *Free* ☿ *Mar.–Dec., Mon., Tues., Thurs., and Fri. 10:30–3; Jan. and Feb., Fri. and Sat. 10:30–3.*

A wonderful finale to your trip to Caesarea, especially at sunset, is the beachfront **Roman aqueduct.** The chain of arches tumbling northward until they disappear beneath the sand is a captivating sight. During Roman times, the demand for a steady water supply was considerable, but the source was a spring about 13 km (8 mi) away in the foothills of Mt. Carmel. Workers had to cut a channel approximately 6½ km (4 mi) long through solid rock before the water was piped into the aqueduct. In the 2nd century, Hadrian doubled its capacity by adding a new channel. Today you can walk along the aqueduct and see marble plaques dedicated to the support troops of various legions who toiled here. ⊠ *Villa area, north of Caesarea.*

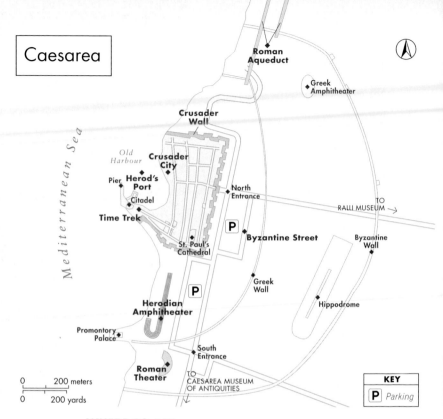

Caesarea

Mediterranean Sea

Roman
Aqueduct

Greek
Amphitheater

Crusader
Wall

Old
Harbour

Crusader
City

Pier

Herod's
Port

Citadel

North
Entrance

TO
RALLI MUSEUM →

Time Trek

P

Byzantine Street

Byzantine
Wall

St. Paul's
Cathedral

P

Greek
Wall

Hippodrome

Herodian
Amphitheater

Promontory
Palace

South
Entrance

Roman
Theater

TO
CAESAREA MUSEUM
OF ANTIQUITIES

0   200 meters
0   200 yards

KEY
P Parking

WHERE TO EAT

$
AMERICAN

✕**Agenda.** In the same building as the Japanese restaurant Minato, Agenda serves great breakfasts 24 hours a day. Try "shakshuka," which is eggs poached in a sharp tomato sauce. For lunch and dinner there are also sandwiches, salads, pizzas, and other light fare, plus cocktails and wine. The staff is friendly, the ambience casual. ⊠ *At the entrance to Caesarea* ☎ *04/626–2092* ▤ *AE, DC, MC, V* ☉ *No dinner Fri. No lunch Sat.*

$$$
SEAFOOD

✕**Crusaders' Restaurant.** You can depend on satisfying, tasty fare at this cavernous restaurant named for the nearby Crusader City. Expect the menu to include plenty of fresh seafood, caught right from the sea below the restaurant. An excellent starter salad is grilled eggplant, hummus, and fried cauliflower—crunchy pita rounds toasted with olive oil and local spices are served alongside. House specialties include baked red snapper topped with chopped vegetables, or black mussels sautéed in garlic, butter, and wine. Still hungry? Creamy cheesecake or warm apple pie with ice cream does the trick. ⊠ *Northern end of the port* ☎ *04/636–1679* ▤ *AE, DC, MC, V.*

$$$
MEDITERRANEAN
Fodor's Choice
★

✕**Helena.** Two of Israel's best-known culinary personalities opened this restaurant, aiming to create a first-rate yet affordable dining experience. It occupies a beautifully restored stone building near the ancient port, and large windows everywhere maximize the view. The chef specializes

Caesarea: Roman City

Herod the Great gave Caesarea its name, dedicating the magnificent Roman city he built to his patron, Augustus Caesar. It was the Roman emperor who had crowned Herod—born to an Idumean family that had converted to Judaism—King of the Jews around 30 BC.

Construction began in 22 BC; Herod spared nothing in his elaborate designs for the port and the city itself, which included palaces, temples, a theater, a marketplace, a hippodrome, and water and sewage systems. When Caesarea was completed 12 years later, only Jerusalem outshined it. Its population under Herod grew to around 100,000, and the city covered some 164 acres.

In AD 6, a decade after Herod died, Caesarea became the seat of the Roman procurators, one of whom was Pontius Pilate, governor of Judea when Jesus was crucified. With Jerusalem predominantly Jewish, the Romans preferred the Hellenistic Caesarea, with its Jewish minority, as the seat of their administration.

Religious harmony did not prevail. The mixed population of Jews and Gentiles (mainly Greeks and Syrians) repeatedly clashed, with hostilities exploding during the Jewish revolt of AD 66. The first Jewish rebellion was squelched by Vespasian, proclaimed emperor by his legions in AD 69. A year later, his son and co-ruler, Titus, captured and razed Jerusalem and celebrated his suppression of the Jewish revolt.

Henceforth Caesarea was a Roman colony and the local Roman capital of Palestine for nearly 600 years. It was here that Peter converted the Roman centurion Cornelius to Christianity—a milestone in the spread of the new faith—and Paul preached and was imprisoned for two years. In the 2nd century, Rabbi Akiva, the spiritual mentor of the Bar Kochba revolt, was tortured to death here.

in Mediterranean-style cooking, turning out such tantalizing appetizers as calamari with lemon and hyssop leaves on sheep's milk yogurt and sliced sirloin in aged balsamic vinegar with Cambozola cheese and pistachios. Main dishes include an aromatic fish stew made of red mullet, spinach, and Swiss chard, and *barbuni* (tiny, grilled sardinelike fish). The wine room holds a selection of mainly Israeli wines. A children's menu is available. ⊠*Southern end of the port* ☎*04/610–1018* ▭*AE, DC, MC, V.*

$$
JAPANESE ✕**Minato.** With a name that means "port" in Japanese, Minato is perfect for beachgoers craving sushi. The Japanese restaurant does a brisk takeout business, serving sashimi and nigiri as well as a variety of tempura dishes. You can also eat in at the long sushi bar and watch the knives flash in front of you. ⊠*At the entrance to Caesarea* ☎*04/636–0812* ▭*AE, DC, MC, V* ⊘*No dinner Fri. No lunch Sat.*

WHERE TO STAY

$$ 🖭**Dan Caesarea.** Equidistant from Tel Aviv and Haifa, this chain hotel ❂ suits businesspeople and holiday makers alike. The 15 acres of rolling green lawns filled with trees and flowers (and an attractive swimming pool) make it great for families. All the guest rooms in this four-story hotel have balconies with a view towards the sea or the

Caesarea. "We stumbled upon this field of flowers by the ruins." —photo by mgplessner, Fodors.com member

open countryside. Especially recommended are the comfortable deluxe doubles, with marble bathrooms and modern decor in cheerful hues. The hotel is a short drive to the beach and the archaeological site of Caesarea. Bikes are on hand for riding around in the conveniently flat countryside. **Pros:** family-friendly vibe; helpful staff. **Cons:** no public transportation. ⊠ *North of Caesarea site, Caesarea* ☎ *04/626–9111* ⊕ *www.danhotels.com* ☎ *111 rooms, 3 suites* ☺ *In-room: safe, refrigerator, Wi-Fi. In-hotel: restaurant, room service, bar, tennis courts, pool, gym, spa, Internet terminal, parking (free)* ⊟ *AE, DC, MC.*

NIGHTLIFE AND THE ARTS

At Caesarea's **Roman Theater** you can watch occasional evening performances by local and international artists and troupes between May and mid-October. Check the Friday editions of major newspapers for schedule information.

SPORTS AND THE OUTDOORS

BEACHES

Bathers have two choices here. In a calm, sandy cove in Caesarea's ancient harbor is the **Caesarea Beach Club**, where the admission charge of NIS 25 includes chairs, umbrellas, and showers. A lifeguard is on duty in season, and the restaurant sells sandwiches and other light fare. The largest and most popular beach in the area is **Hof Shonit**, just south of the Caesarea site. There are lifeguards in season, a refreshment stand, and a restaurant, as well as restrooms and cold showers. Parking is NIS 15.

At the **Roman Aqueduct,** just north of the Caesarea site, is a spacious beach with the dramatic backdrop of Roman arches disappearing into the sand. The amenities, however, are few: restrooms and a lifeguard in season. There is no entrance fee, and there's plenty of parking. The beach and swimming area have been cleared of rocks and debris, but swimming outside the designated area is prohibited. Never swim unless the lifeguard is on duty.

GOLF

At the 9-hole **Ga'ash Golf Club** (✉ *Off Rte. 2* ☎ *09/951–5111*), you can play a second time from alternative tees to make for an 18-hole experience. Greens fees are NIS 300 for 9 holes on weekdays and NIS 400 on weekends. There's a shop and a restaurant here, too.

The country's only 18-hole golf course is the **Caesarea Golf Club.** Adjacent to the Dan Caesarea, it is being completely remodeled by legendary designer Pete Dye, and is expected to reopen in 2010.

SCUBA DIVING

★ The **Old Caesarea Diving Center** (✉ *Ceasarea harbor, behind the Time Tower* ☎ *04/626–5898* ⊕ *www.caesarea-diving.com*) runs a full range of diving courses for novices, experts, and everyone in between. Snorkelers are welcome, and divers can use a plastic map to follow a route of numbered artifacts in the submerged port built by King Herod 2,000 years ago.

NETANYA

65 km (43 mi) south of Haifa, 30 km (18 mi) north of Tel Aviv.

Netanya has a pretty seaside promenade along the cliffs, endless sandy beaches, a pleasant town square, and plenty of cafés and restaurants. Once a sleepy place surrounded by orange groves, the town—named after Jewish philanthropist Nathan Strauss—has steadily grown from a few settlers in 1929 to some 200,000 residents today.

Though citrus farming is still evident on Netanya's outskirts, there are few traces of small-town charm. Tracts of residential development during the past five years or so can be seen all along the southern approach to the city following the shoreline, with high-rise towers dotting the landscape, many of the apartment units bought up by vacationers from abroad.

GETTING HERE AND AROUND

To get here from Tel Aviv or Haifa, take coastal Route 2.

ESSENTIALS

Medical Assistance Laniado Hospital (☎ *09/860–4666*).

Vistor Information Netanya Tourist Information Office (✉ *12 Ha'atzmaut Sq.* ☎ *09/882–7286*).

EXPLORING

Lively **Ha'atzmaut Square,** near the beach, is the heart of the city. Benches set among the palm trees surround a large fountain. Its open-air cafés and restaurants are crowded from the morning until late into the evening. Netanya attracts droves of French visitors, and in summer their lilting tones float above the café au lait and croissants. Saturday night is enlivened by folk dancing, and the amphitheater hosts free concerts in summer and an arts-and-crafts fair on Friday morning.

NEED A BREAK? Cool off at Tony's Ice Café (⊠ *Ha'atzmaut Sq. near Dizengoff St.*) with divine authentic Italian ice cream (*gelati*) in a huge array of flavors, all made by hand by a family of immigrants from Italy. Tony's also has a wide selection of coffees, milkshakes, and pastries.

♺ ★ Netanya's **Seaside Promenade** (also known as the "Boulevard") extends north and south of the city for a total of about 6 km (4 mi). This beautifully landscaped walkway winds around the contours of the cliffs overlooking the sea; at every angle there's a different gorgeous view. It's dotted with pergola-shaded benches, colorful playground areas on soft groundcover, and waving palm trees. An elevator at the center of the promenade eases the climb up and down the seaside cliff, and numerous paths running off the promenade provide access to the sea.

In February and March, detour a few kilometers south of the city to see **fields of flowers**: a rare, exotic variety of deep-indigo wild iris, indigenous to this area, carpets the fields. Marked paths lead the way, and there's a parking lot on Ben Gurion Boulevard.

WHERE TO EAT

$$ MIDDLE EASTERN ★ ♺ ✕ **Bat Ha'ikar.** The locally beloved "Farmer's Daughter" is worth a visit despite its setting amid workshops, garages, and warehouses in an industrial zone. Spacious, busy, noisy, and informal, it's a venue for bustling family celebrations. The cooking is strictly Middle Eastern, including an endless array of fresh salads and skewers of grilled lamb and chicken. It's fun to roll the various foods into piping-hot *laffas* (large, thin pitas), which are baked in full view of the dining area inside massive ovens. ⊠ *8 Pinkas St., Old Industrial Zone* ☎ *09/884–4474* ▭ *AE, DC, MC, V* ⊘ *No dinner Fri. No lunch Sat.*

$$$ STEAK ✕ **El Gaucho.** Tucked into the Carmel Hotel, El Gaucho is one of Israel's best kosher steak houses. Decorated in a rustic style, the restaurant is dominated by a dramatic view of the sea. Come at sunset for a memorable meal. South American–style meat specialties, among them various cuts of beef, are cooked over embers on a giant grill. Juicy steaks, grilled fish, and chicken (often done on a spit) are highlights, and the wine list is extensive. ⊠ *Carmel Hotel, Jabotinsky St.* ☎ *09/884–1264* ⌦ *Reservations essential* ▭ *AE, DC, MC, V* ⊘ *No dinner Fri. No lunch Sat.*

$$ MEDITERRANEAN ✕ **Myriam's Grill.** A stone's throw from the main approach to the beach, this eatery is on Ha'atzmaut Square facing a bubbly fountain. Moroccan-style grilled fish and lamb dishes are served both indoors and outdoors. Appetites sharpened by sea breezes and splashes in the surf will be rewarded with appetizers like creamy hummus, tasty couscous, or shakshuka (eggs poached in spicy tomato sauce). Main dishes are served up with crispy fries or green salads. Wine and beer are served. ⊠ *7 Ha'atzmaut Sq.* ☎ *09/834–1376* ▭ *AE, DC, MC, V* ⊘ *No dinner Fri. No lunch Sat.*

$$ SEAFOOD ✕ **Rosemarine.** At this unpretentious heaven for fish lovers, you can enjoy fresh and tasty fare as you sit indoors or on the terrace overlooking the famous promenade. The kitchen serves a wide range of fish dishes, such as tilapia and gray mullet, which are grilled, baked, or sautéed. Entrées come with salad or roasted potatoes. ⊠ *8 Nice St.* ☎ *09/832–3322* ▭ *AE, DC, MC, V* ⊘ *No dinner Fri. No lunch Sat.*

During the Jewish holiday of Purim, revelers in Netanya and around the country dress up in costume.

WHERE TO STAY

$ 🏨 **Mizpeh Yam.** Don't expect luxury at this family-owned hotel. What you can count on is good value and a warm welcome. This is a fine option if you're passing through and need a clean and basic lodging for a night or two. The rooms are compact but have modern furnishings; the entrance has limited but pleasant sitting areas on an attractive front veranda. There's no pool, though the beach is a few minutes away. There's a sundeck on the roof, and self-service coffee machines are in the hallways. **Pros:** five-minute walk to the promenade; near the beach. **Cons:** no sea views; basic decor. ✉ *1 Jabotinsky St.* ☎ *09/862–3730* ⊕ *www.mizpe-yam.co.il* ⬅ *30 rooms* ♿ *In-room: safe, refrigerator. In-hotel: restaurant, Wi-Fi* ▭ *AE, DC, MC, V* ⍾*BP.*

$ 🏨 **Seasons Netanya.** Consistently good service is one of the hallmarks of this hotel. Guest rooms are spacious, with private terraces and sea views; the bathrooms are luxurious. Eight garden rooms surround the pool, and suites are big enough to accommodate couples with three or four children. The pool (open all year, but not heated in winter) overlooks the sea and is surrounded by colorful gardens and yellow chaise longues. A nicely furnished lobby features live piano music in the evening. **Pros:** good for families; plenty for kids to do; all rooms have sea views. **Cons:** not for those seeking peace and quiet. ✉ *1 Nice Blvd.* ☎ *09/860–1555* ⊕ *www.seasons.co.il* ⬅ *103 rooms, 45 suites* ♿ *In-room: safe, refrigerator. In-hotel: 2 restaurants, room service, bar, tennis court, pool, gym, children's programs (ages 3–11), laundry service, Internet terminal, Wi-Fi* ▭ *AE, DC, MC, V.*

SPORTS AND THE OUTDOORS
BEACHES

Standard facilities, including lifeguards, first-aid station, showers, toilets, and changing rooms, are available free at all of Netanya's beaches, which cover 14 km (8½ mi) of soft, sandy coastline. Most beaches also rent beach chairs and umbrellas.

★ The main section of beach, **Sironit,** is open year-round. The parking lot is on the beach, just south of Ha'atzmaut Square. It costs NIS 15 per car. An elevator at Gad Machness Street, just south of Ha'atzmaut Square, takes pedestrians down the seaside cliff to this beach. There are volleyball nets and snack bars along the sand. North of town is the Orthodox beach **Kiryat Sanz,** where men and women have different bathing days and hours. **Herzl,** near Ha'atzmaut Square, has a restaurant and refreshment stand.

About 5 km (3 mi) north of Netanya is lovely **Beit Yannai** beach. Amenities include barbecue grills, picnic tables, restrooms with showers, chair and umbrella rentals, and seasonal lifeguards. There's a seafood restaurant right on the beach. Parking is NIS 20 on weekdays and NIS 28 on Saturday.

The beach at **Mikhmoret,** 7½ km (4½ mi) north of Netanya, is popular with swimmers as well as those who laze away the day under an umbrella. The huge dirt parking lot, which charges NIS 30 per car, is 1 km (½ mi) after the turnoff from Route 2. There are three lifeguard stations, a restaurant, a café, and chair and umbrella rentals.

HORSEBACK RIDING

The **Ranch** (✉ *HaMelachim St.* ☎ *09/866–3525*) is in northern Netanya, 2 km (1 mi) up the road from the Blue Bay Hotel. It's wise to reserve well ahead for weekend trips or for sunset rides along the beach. The stables are open daily 9 to 6; the cost is NIS 120 per hour.

PARAGLIDING

Netanya's cliffs can provide exciting paragliding. Under the guidance of experienced instructors, you take off from a specially designed field near the Promenade. **Dvir Paragliding** (☎ *09/899–0277*) is an established company that offers thrilling adventures. **Sky Paragliding School** (☎ *09/884–1981 or 052/222–3221*) offers a one-time guided experience plus equipment rental. **Udi Paragliding** (☎ *052/803–3824*) offers paragliding instruction as well as a video of you soaring through the air.

SHOPPING

Inbal Jewelry (✉ *1 Ussishkin St.* ☎ *09/882–2233*) is worth visiting for its special in-house designs and competitive prices.

THE WINE COUNTRY AND MT. CARMEL

This route south of Haifa wanders through the foothills and up the spine of Mt. Carmel. It's a major wine region, and three of the country's most famous vineyards are here: Carmel, Binyamina, and Tishbi. Druze villages are another attraction. The Druze are known for their hospitable ways; a meal in one of the towns will not only be a tasty experience, but also a warmly welcoming one.

Though wine has been produced in Israel for thousands of years, and the Rothschilds updated viniculture around Zichron Ya'akov some 120 years ago, truly high-quality wines have appeared on the market only in the last decade or so. This is one of the country's prime wine-growing areas (its classification is Shomron). After a tour of the winery it's delightful to sit under the grapevines and sample the vintages along with fresh salad, warm bread, and good local cheese.

Route 4 is smooth sailing, with Mt. Carmel looming to the east beyond cultivated fields and banana plantations (though you may not see the bananas, as they're usually bagged in blue or gray plastic to protect them from bugs). The road leads through undulating countryside dotted with cypresses, palms, and vineyards.

EIN HOD

★ *15 km (10 mi) south of Haifa, 5 km (3 mi) west of Isfiya.*

A charming little village, Ein Hod is home to around 135 families of sculptors, painters, and other artists. The setting is an idyllic one, with rough-hewn stone houses built on the hillside and sweeping views down to the Mediterranean. The Dadaist painter Marcel Janco (1895–1984) wrote upon his first visit in 1950: "The beauty of the place was staggering."

Parking is across the road, opposite the entrance to the village. Climbing up the hill, you soon come to a winding street on the left that starts a lovely walk through the small village. Signs along the way indicate studios and workshops where artists paint, sculpt, and make jewelry, pottery, silkscreen prints, and clothing. You can continue straight to the town square, bordered by a restaurant and a large gallery where works by Ein Hod artists are exhibited.

GETTING HERE AND AROUND

Your best option is to get here by car via Route 4, since buses are few and far between. The village itself is small and very walkable.

EXPLORING

On the village square is the **Janco-Dada Museum,** dedicated to one of the founders of the Dada movement. The Romanian-born Marcel Janco had already established a considerable professional reputation by the time he emigrated to Israel (then Palestine) in 1941. The museum houses a permanent collection of the artist's works in various media, reflecting Janco's 70-year output both in Europe and Israel. A 20-minute slide show chronicles the life of the artist and the Dada movement. Also exhibited are works by other Israeli modern artists. Don't miss the view from the rooftop before leaving. ☎*04/984–2350* 💲*NIS 35* 🕙*Sun.– Thurs. 9:30–5, Fri. 9:30–2, Sat. 10–4.*

WHERE TO EAT

💲 ✕**Abu Yakov.** You reach Abu's by climbing the stone seats of Ein Hod's
ISRAELI amphitheater, or you can walk through nearby Café Ein Hod. There are a few seats inside—most people head outside to the blue plastic chairs beneath a ragged plastic cover. It feels a bit makeshift, but the fresh food counts for everything. Dine on what's often called "Oriental" (meaning

Middle Eastern) food in Israel: hummus, fluffy pita bread, chopped vegetable salad, and grilled meat on skewers. On Saturdays when there's a crowd, they make french fries. ⊠*At the top of the amphitheater, near village square* ☎*04/984–3377* ▭*No credit cards.*

$ ✕**Café Ein Hod.** As you climb up the stone steps to the right of Dona
CAFE   Rosa restaurant, keep an eye out on your left for a two-level collection of mismatched chairs and odd tables surrounded by small trees and potted plants—there's often a cat sunning himself on a stool. Inside the old stone building, handmade handbags and clothes are for sale. Guests sit outside to drink coffee; eat delectable carrot cake, apple pie, and other seasonal fruit tarts; or nosh on grilled cheese sandwiches with salad. You can stop for a beer or glass of wine, too. ⊠*Near village square* ☎*077/324–1052* ▭*No credit cards* ☉*Closed Mon.*

$$$ ✕**Dona Rosa.** If you can't read the restaurant's sign in Hebrew, just
ARGENTINE   follow the tantalizing aroma up the steps of this wooden building on the town square. Dona Rosa's grandsons, Uri and Doron, import meat and special charcoal from Argentina and slow grill the food in the true Argentinian style. The bar is decorated with a drawing of a hefty cow that illustrates each cut of meat. Highlights include pork spareribs marinated all night, then grilled the next day; seafood simmered with fragrant yellow rice; and *assado*, delicious, chunky ribs (available only on Saturday). There's beer and Chilean and Argentinian wine, too. ⊠*On the village square* ☎*04/954–3777* ▭*AE, DC, MC, V* ☉*Closed Sun.*

WHERE TO STAY

$ ⌂ **Jancourt B&B.** Batia and Claude's bed-and-breakfast is quiet and private, hidden behind masses of hot-pink bougainvillea. There are two units to choose from: the "Provence" is a ground-level 2-room apartment with a little garden and patio. Furnished in antique French provincial style, you'll find armchairs, a pullout sofa and dining nook in the large living area, plus a good-size bedroom and kitchenette. The "Green Room" is a studio on two levels (one for sleeping, one for living) furnished with art deco chairs (green), a French bed (green), and various pretty green touches. A covered patio with table and chairs is just outside. Olives from the yard, local cheeses, and homemade bread and jam make breakfast special. **Pros:** pretty, private building; fun shop. **Cons:** views not featured; often gets booked in advance. ⊠*Second part of Ein Hod* ☎*04/984–1648* ⊕*www.eisenwasser-jancourt.co.il* ↪*2 rooms* ⌂*In-room: DVD, kitchen, Wi-Fi* ▭*No credit cards* ⍰*BP.*

$ ⌂ **Yakir Ein Hod.** Care for a dip in a pool ringed by olive trees while you gaze at the blue Mediterranean? That's what you can do at this delightful lodging. Host Yakir offers two delightful suites, one with a large wooden deck, the other with a deck and a hot tub. Each unit has a sitting area for reading or watching television and a kitchenette. A brunch-like breakfast for two costs NIS 70. Finding the place can be tricky. From the main entrance to Ein Hod, drive up the hill, turn right, then left, and look for the third house on the right. (There's no sign in English). **Pros:** quiet location; lovely views. **Cons:** breakfast is extra; hard to find. ⊠*Ein Hod* ☎*050/554–3982* ⊕*www.yakireinhod.co.il* ↪*2 rooms* ⌂*In-room: kitchen. In-hotel: pool* ▭*AE, DC, MC,V.*

NIGHTLIFE AND THE ARTS

Just off the main square, **Gertrud Kraus House** (☎ *04/984–2018*) features chamber music on occasional Saturday evenings at 6:30. Admission is NIS 40, which includes complimentary coffee and cakes.

SHOPPING

Many of the artists who live in the winding lanes of Ein Hod throw open their workshops to visitors, who are welcome to browse and buy. Between the olive trees and behind painted gates, look for signs on homes that indicate the sale of jewelry, gold metalwork, sculptures, paintings, ceramics, stained glass, hand-painted clothing, and artistic photography. Start either at the entrance to the village where signs point to the left, or head for the village square straight ahead.

★ **The Gallery** (☎ *04/984–2548*) carries a selection of handicrafts and art at its space on Ein Hod's main square. Displayed in the front room are ceramics, enamel, and silver and gold jewelry. Three other rooms are devoted to paintings, sculptures, and graphic works by resident artists, some of them internationally known. The gallery is open Sunday–Thursday and Saturday 11–4, Friday 10–2.

Silver Print (☎ *04/954–1673*) is a lovely little studio holding Vivienne Silver-Brody's collection of works by Israel's best photographers. The emphasis is on the building of the state of Israel. There's also a wide range of 19th-century photos of the Holy Land. A digital print costs NIS 150. Vivienne also offers "How to Look" workshops (fun for families) in the village. It's best to call ahead for an appointment.

NAHAL ME'AROT NATURE RESERVE

3 km (2 mi) south of Ein Hod, 1 km (½ mi) east of Rte. 4.

The prehistoric **Carmel Caves** are a highlight of the Nahal Me'arot Nature
★ Reserve. The three excavated caves are up a steep flight of stairs, on a fossil reef that was covered by the sea 100 million years ago. The first discoveries of prehistoric remains were made when this area was being scoured for stones to build the Haifa port. In the late 1920s, the first archaeological expedition was headed by Dorothy Garrod of England, who received assistance from a British feminist group on condition that the dig be carried out exclusively by women.

In the Tannur cave, the first on the tour, the strata Garrod's team excavated are clearly marked, spanning about 150,000 years in the life of early humans. The most exciting discovery made in the area was that of both Homo sapiens and Neanderthal skeletons; evidence that both lived here has raised fascinating questions about the relationship between the two and whether they lived side by side. A display on the daily life of early man as hunter and food gatherer occupies the Gamal cave. The last cave you'll visit, called the Nahal, is the largest—it cuts deep into the mountain—and was actually the first discovered. A burial place with 84 skeletons was found outside the mouth of the cave.

The bone artifacts and stone tools discovered in the Nahal cave suggest that people who settled here, about 12,000 years ago, were the forebears of early farmers, with a social structure more developed than that of hunters and gatherers. There is also evidence that the Crusaders once used the cave to guard the coastal road. Inside, an audiovisual show sheds light on how early man lived here. There's a snack bar and parking lot at this site. ☎*04/984–1750* ⊕*www.parks.org.il* ✉*NIS 23* ☉*Oct.–Mar., Sat.–Thurs. and holidays 8–4, Fri. and Jewish holiday eves 8–1; Apr.–Sept., Sat.–Thurs. 8–5, Fri. 8–2.*

SPORTS AND THE OUTDOORS

At the entrance to the Carmel Caves is the stone office of the **Nature Reserves Authority** (☎*04/984–1750*), where trained staff provide maps and information about two well-marked nature walks that leave from this point. The route of the Botanical Path takes two hours, while the Geological Path takes 40 minutes; both include lookout points.

ISFIYA

15 km (10 mi) south of Haifa.

Very similar to neighboring Daliyat el Carmel, Isfiya is a village of flat-roof homes built closely together into the hillside, many of them raised on pillars and cut with arched windows. Hospitality is second nature to the Druze who live here; you may be able to visit a village home and eat pita bread with yogurt cheese and spices while hearing about Druze life.

As you leave the village, at the top of the hill note the vista of the Jezreel Valley opening suddenly on your right. The approach to Haifa also affords a magnificent view of the coast stretching up to Akko, across the bay.

GETTING HERE AND AROUND

Coming from Haifa, drive south on Route 672.

To really get to know Isfiya, arrange a tour through Druze Hospitality. Your guide will take you to visit their place of prayer, to an olive oil press, and then to a private home where the matriarch bakes pita bread in a taboon oven. You will hear about the distinctive Druze way of life. It's best to call a few days ahead. The price is NIS 120 per person.

ESSENTIALS

Tour Information Druze Hospitality (☎*04/839-0125*).

WHERE TO EAT

$$

MIDDLE EASTERN

✕**Nof Carmel.** To find this very good Druze restaurant, drive to the northern edge of the village. The eatery is on your left; look for a few tables outside under the trees. People come from all over for the fine Middle Eastern fare, especially the homemade hummus with pine nuts, olive oil, garlic, and lemon juice, and the well-seasoned kebab on skewers. Those with a sweet tooth should sample the *sahlab* (a warm, custardlike pudding of crushed orchid bulb with thickened milk and sugar), or the scale-bending baklava. ✉*Rte. 672* ☎*04/839–1718* ⚡*Reservations not accepted* ▤*AE, MC, V.*

DALIYAT EL CARMEL

16 km (11 mi) south of Haifa, 1 km (½ mi) south of Isfiya.

Daliyat el Carmel is Israel's largest Druze village, and well worth exploring. You can do a little shopping here, too.

GETTING HERE AND AROUND

Coming from Haifa, drive south on Route 672.

WORD OF MOUTH

"When you go to the Carmel, there are some Druze villages. Daliyat el Carmel is the most accessible that you pass as you drive along the spine of the Carmel mountains. The views are beautiful, and you should make sure to have a falafel."—SandyMerm

EXPLORING

The attraction here is the chance to walk along the main street and mingle with the people of this fascinating community. Though most of the younger generation wears jeans and T-shirts, most older people wear traditional garb. Head coverings indicate the degree of religious belief, from the high white turban resembling a fez to the white kerchief covering the head and shoulders. Many men sport a bushy moustache, a hallmark of the Druze, and some older ones wear dark robes and black pantaloons. A tour offered by a local member of the community takes you to see their place of prayer and then to hear about local customs. At the House of Heritage you can experience a traditional meal in a home.

About 1 km (½ mi) inside town, take a right turn into the **marketplace,** a colorful jumble of shops lining the street. You can be assured of eating excellent falafel at any of the roadside stands or restaurants.

WHERE TO EAT

$$ ✕**House of Druze Heritage.** The Druze are famous for their hospitality.
MIDDLE EASTERN Here you get not only a warm welcome and a delicious meal, but an up-close look at the Druze way of life. The traditional meal begins with appetizers such as hot-pepper salad, pickles, sesame paste, and hummus with big, flat pita bread. The main course consists of skewers of grilled lamb or steak; baklava and Turkish coffee provide the finishing touch. The museum in the back displays Druze clothing and farm implements, household objects, handicrafts, and photos. ⊠*4 Ahat St.* ☎*04/839–3242* ▭*AE, DC, MC, V.*

SHOPPING

Along a brief stretch of the main road that winds through Daliyat el Carmel are shops selling lightweight throw rugs, handwoven baskets, brightly colored pottery, brass dishes, characteristic woven wall hangings, and embroidered skullcaps worn by men. Bargaining is expected. Some shops close on Friday; the strip is crowded on Saturday.

MUKHRAKA

18 km (12 mi) south of Haifa, 2 km (1⅓ mi) west of Daliyat el Carmel.

★ Past open, uncultivated fields and a goatherd's rickety shack, the **Carmelite Monastery** at Mukhraka stands on the spur of the Carmel range, at

CLOSE UP

The Druze

The Druze are an Arabic-speaking people who practice a secret religion; they form one of the most intriguing entities in the mosaic of Israel's population, of which they number about 118,000, or 2%. They live in areas from Mt. Carmel to the Upper Galilee and the Golan Heights. Larger kindred communities exist in Syria and Lebanon.

So exclusive is this sect that only a fraction of the community is initiated into its religious doctrine, one tenet of which is a belief in continuous reincarnation.

The Druze broke away from Islam about 1,000 years ago, incorporating other traditions and also believing in the divinity of their founder, al Hakim bi Amir Allah, the Caliph of the Egyptian Fatimid dynasty from AD 996 to 1021. They do not permit gambling or the use of alcohol.

The Druze who live in the two existing villages on Mt. Carmel (Daliyat el Carmel and Isfiya) serve in the Israeli Army, a sign of their loyalty to Israel.

---

an altitude of 1,580 feet, on or near the site where the struggle between Elijah and the priests of Ba'al is believed to have taken place. *Mukhraka* is the Arabic word for a place of burning, referring to the fire that consumed the offering on Elijah's altar. The conflict developed because the people of Israel had been seduced by the pagan cults introduced by King Ahab's wife, Jezebel. Elijah demanded a contest with the priests of Ba'al in which each would erect an altar with a butchered ox as an offering and see which divinity sent down fire. Elijah drenched his altar with water, yet it burst into flames. On his orders, the priests were taken down to the Brook of Kishon and executed.

The stark stone monastery was built in 1883 over Byzantine ruins. Records show that the site was revered as early as the 6th century, when hermits dwelled here. The Carmelites, a Roman Catholic monastic order established in the 13th century, look to Elijah as their role model. The courtyard contains a statue of a fearless Elijah brandishing a knife. The monks who live here have no telephones and only a generator for power. Climb to the roof for an unforgettable panorama: to the east stretches the Jezreel Valley and the hills of Nazareth, Moreh, and Gilboa. On a clear day you can even see Jordan's Gilead Mountains beyond the Jordan River and Mt. Hermon. ☎*No phone* ✉*NIS 4* ☉*Mon.–Sat. 8–1:30 and 2:30–5.*

ZICHRON YA'AKOV

★ *61 km (40 mi) north of Tel Aviv.*

A planted roundabout marks the main entrance to Zichron Ya'akov, a town named by its original settlers in honor of Baron Edmond de Rothschild's father, James, in 1882. Pick up a town map in the tourist office just opposite, next to the Founders' Monument and near the old cemetery. Good restaurants, interesting shops, and a couple of small museums line the 19th-century streets. The well-known Carmel Winery is one of the main draws.

GETTING HERE AND AROUND
If you're driving from Haifa or Tel Aviv, take Route 2 to the Zichron Ya'akov exit. Buses run from Haifa and Tel Aviv.

ESSENTIALS
Vistor Information Zichron Ya'akov Tourist Office (⊠ *southern entrance to town, opposite the cemetery* ☎ *04/639–8811*).

EXPLORING

A visit to this old-world town starts at the white stone arch with the red-tile roof, just past the Founders' Monument, and continues along the main street, **Hameyasdim.** Residents have made every effort to maintain the original appearance of this short thoroughfare, and the cobblestone street is lined, for the most part, with small, restored, red-roof 19th-century homes. In those days, people needed courtyards behind their homes to house animals, carts, and farm equipment. These days, upscale restaurants and shops are more common.

About halfway down Hameyasdim is **Bet Aaronson** *(Aaronson's House)*, whose late-19th-century architecture successfully combines Art Nouveau and Middle Eastern traditions. This museum was once the home of the agronomist Aaron Aaronson (1876–1919), who gained international fame for his discovery of an ancestor of modern wheat. The house remains as it looked after World War I, with family photographs and French and Turkish furniture, as well as Aaronson's library, diaries, and letters.

Aaronson and his sisters became local heroes as leaders of the spy ring called the NILI (an acronym for a quotation from the Book of Samuel: "The Eternal One of Israel will not prove false")—a militant group dedicated to ousting the Turks from Palestine by collaborating with the British during World War I. Both sisters, Sarah and Rebecca, were in love with Aaron's assistant, Absalom Feinberg. A double agent was disrupting NILI's communications with the British, so Feinberg set off to cross the Sinai desert to make contact. He was killed in an ambush in the Gaza Strip. His remains were recovered some 50 years later from a grave marked simply by a date tree, the tree having sprouted from some dates in Feinberg's pockets. A tour in English is provided; the last one takes place at 1:30 PM. ⊠ *40 Hameyasdim St.* ☎ *04/639–0120* 🖃 *NIS 15* ☉ *Sun., Mon., Wed., and Thurs. 8:30–2:15, Tues. 8:30–3, Fri. 8:30–noon.*

On Hameyasdim, near Bet Aaronson, is **Binyamin Pool,** a misnomer because it's actually the town's original water tower, built in 1891. Zichron was the first village in Israel to have water piped to its houses; Meir Dizengoff, the first mayor of Tel Aviv, came here to see how it was done. The facade resembles that of an ancient synagogue.

At the corner of Hanadiv and Hameyasdim streets stands the old synagogue, **Ohel Ya'akov,** built by Rothschild in 1886 to satisfy the settlers' needs.

At the end of Hanadiv Street, off Hameyasdim, stands the **First Aliya Museum,** in the former Administration House. Commissioned by Baron de Rothschild, it is a fine example of late-19th-century Ottoman-style

Continued on page 333

In a land where grapes have been grown and enjoyed since biblical times, a modern winemaking revolution has taken hold. Whether the vintage is from big producers or boutique up-and-comers, the improved quality of Israeli wine has catapulted all things oenological into the spotlight. This tiny country is now home to over 200 wineries large and small. It was Baron Edmond de Rothschild—the proprietor of France's prestigious Château Lafite winery and an early Zionist—who jumpstarted the modern Israeli wine industry by providing money to found wineries in the 1880s. After a few false starts, Carmel Mizrachi, which his funds helped support, flourished; to this day it is Israel's most prolific wine producer.

by Adeena Sussman

(top) Ancient floor mosaic depicting wine vase at Eretz Israel Museum, Tel Aviv. (right) Golan Heights Winery

The
Wines
of
Israel

WINEMAKING IN ISRAEL

(top left) Winemaking barrel shop in Zichron Ya'akov, 1890s. (bottom left) Golan Heights Winery. (right) Wine fair in Tel Aviv.

Israel manufactured mostly mediocre wines until the late 1970s, when the first *moshavim* and *kibbutzim* (living cooperatives) planted vines in the Golan Heights on the advice of scientists from California, who saw a grape-growing diamond in the rough amid the mountain ranges of this northern region. Soon thereafter Golan Heights Winery was born, and awards and accolades were uncorked almost immediately.

GROWTH AND CHALLENGE

Besides two dozen or so larger operations, more than 150 smaller wineries now operate, many less than 15 years old and some producing just a few thousand bottles per year. Five large wineries account for 80 percent of production. Winemaking is a relatively young industry, sparked by a new crop of winemakers with experience at outstanding wineries. Though top wine writers have given some Israeli wines high marks, confirming internationally that these are vintages worth seeking out, there is still room for improvement in the ongoing, so-called "quality revolution."

Per capita wine consumption in Israel has nearly doubled since the late 1990s but remains low. A culture of wine appreciation is gradually fomenting, although the lion's share of bottles are exported to the United States and Europe. Despite challenges, winemakers continue to experiment: up-and-coming regions include the Judean Hills outside Jerusalem and even the Negev desert.

KOSHER & MEVUSHAL: MESSAGE ON A BOTTLE

For a wine to be certified kosher, as many Israeli wines are, a religious supervisor must oversee the process to ensure that no nonkosher tools or ingredients are used. Only rigorously observant Jews can handle equipment. Critics agree that these regulations don't affect the quality of wine. *Mevushal* wines, with more stringent kosher requirements, are flash-pasteurized, and then rapidly chilled; this can affect quality. However, many top-tier Israeli wines today are non-Mevushal, or are unsupervised altogether.

WINE REGIONS AND GRAPES

Sea Horse winery

GRAPE EXPECTATIONS

After commercial vines were first planted in the 19th century, Israeli winemakers focused on a small group of grape varietals that seemed to take well to Israeli terrain. The country has no indigenous grapes. With the help of technology, experience, and trial and error, a wide range of grapes are now raised with success.

Some of Israel's red wines are world-class, notably those that blend Cabernet Sauvignon grapes with Merlot, Cabernet Franc, and Petit Verdot. Chardonnays also do well here— the warm days and cool nights of the northern region seem particularly advantageous for this varietal.

Winemakers consistently push the envelope, introducing exciting new wines into the market. Two recent examples? Viognier, which has been one of the darlings of the current Israeli wine market, and Syrah, a grape that flourishes amid the country's hot days and cool, breezy nights.

Israel's wine-growing areas are typically divided into five regions, although no official, European-style government-regulated classification system exists. Since the country is so small—about the size of New Jersey—grapes are often shared among the regions. This is especially true of the northern plains, which provide grapes to many of the country's best wineries. Still, each area is geographically unique.

GALILEE Actually two regions, this area covers a lot of geographical ground in the north. The Galilee is a rocky area, and the Golan Heights, which borders Syria, sees winter snowfall at its highest altitudes. With cool climes and rich soil, the Galilee and Golan still claim bragging rights as home to many of the country's premier grapes.

SHOMRON/CARMEL The advantageous growing conditions of the lush Carmel Mountains make this coastal plain south of Haifa the most prolific grape-growing region in Israel, if not the most prestigious. The climate and soil variety make it the most traditionally Mediterranean of the regions.

SAMSON/CENTRAL COAST Situated west of Jerusalem and stretching north toward Tel Aviv and south toward Ashkelon, this region has hot, humid summers and mellow winters that make for good growing conditions. If you're in Tel Aviv, this is an easy region for accessing great wineries.

JUDEAN HILLS Ten years ago, barely a winery or tasting room existed here, though ancient winemaking equipment has been unearthed. Thin limey or rocky soil, sunny days, and breezy nights have helped this region's wines shine. With its winding roads, and lush, shallow mountainsides, the region west and south of Jerusalem is day-trip perfect from Jerusalem and Tel Aviv.

THE NEGEV Thanks to drip-irrigation technology, grapes are thriving in the desert. Since there are relatively few wineries in the southern part of the Negev, they're best included in a trip to Eilat or Mitzpe Ramon; call to schedule a visit.

Clos de Gat Winery in the Judean Hills

WINE TOURING AND TASTING

Visiting wineries in Israel can require a different approach from touring vineyards in California, and your touring strategy may depend on the size of the winery.

Most of the **bigger players**, including Golan Heights, Carmel, and Barkan/Segal, offer tasting rooms. You can simply stop by and visit to sample and purchase wines, though generally it's good to call in advance if you want to include a winery tour. Many **medium- and smaller-sized wineries** are often happy to accommodate visitors, but always call ahead to ensure that English-speaking staff will be on hand and to confirm hours.

A few **boutique** wineries welcome tourists, but many of the best aren't equipped for a regular onslaught of visitors. While you can call yourself, this is where private tour guides come in handy. Often, these individuals have the connections to get you inside wineries you'd otherwise never see—not to mention the knowledge of the back roads in some of the harder-to-find locales.

Israel Wine Experience (☎ 02/990–8422, ✉ israel.wine.exp@gmail.com) offers customized half- and full-day tours. Fees vary, but a half-day tour of three wineries is about $400 for a group of up to 5 people.

PICK OF THE VINEYARDS

These wineries either have open tasting rooms, or visits can be arranged with an advance phone call. Note: most kosher wineries are open only a half-day on Friday, and are closed on Saturdays and Jewish holidays. Small tastes are usually free, but at most wineries a guided tasting costs between $10 and $18 per person for three to five wines.

Carmel Winery

GALILEE

❶ Golan Heights Winery Still the standard bearer for Israeli wines, this large producer has a welcoming visitor center and tours. Wines are made under the Yarden, Gamla, and Golan labels. Kosher. *Try: Single-vineyard Odem Organic Chardonnay; Yarden Syrah.* ✉ Rte. 87, Industrial Zone, Katzrin ☎ 04/696–8420 ⊕ www.golanwines.com.

❷ Chateau Golan A French-style chateau houses an art-filled tasting room. It's open daily; call in advance. Not kosher. *Try: Plummy, balanced-tannin Eliad Cabernet blends.* ✉ Moshav Eliad, Ramat Hagolan ☎ 04/660–0026 ⊕ www.chateaugolan.com.

❸ Galil Mountain Winery A sleek, modern low-lying stone-and-wood building offers views of the

---

WINES IN RESTAURANTS AND SHOPS

Clos de Gat

Even if you don't visit these wineries, look for vintages from these superior regional producers in restaurants or shops in Israel.

Galilee: Golan Heights and Chateau Golan in the Golan; Dalton and Galil Mountain in the Galilee

Shomron/Carmel: Recanati, Margalit, Amphorae

Samson/Central Coast: Carmel, Barkan, Soreq

Judean Hills: Sea Horse, Domaine du Castel, Clos de Gat

The Negev: Yatir, La Terra Promessa

Galil Mountain

vineyards and the wine-making facilities. These are great-value wines for the money. Kosher. *Try: Fruity, mineral-tinged Sauvignon Blanc.* ✉ Kibbutz Merom, Yiron ☎04/686–8740 ⊕www.galilmountain. co.il.

④ Tabor Winery Set amid almond groves near Mt. Tabor in the Galilee, this intimate visitor center offers tastings and tours, plus a restaurant called Bordeaux. Kosher. *Try: Full-bodied, oaky Mas'ha 2003, a Cabernet-Shiraz-Merlot blend that is the winery's calling card.* ✉Kfar Tavor, ☎04/676–0444 ⊕www.taborwinery. com.

SHOMRON/ CARMEL
⑤ Tishbi Winery
The vistor center at this fourth-generation winery offers harvest activities August–October. Kosher. *Try: Woodsy, berry-rich Pinot Noir.* ✉ 33 Hameyasdim St., Zichron Ya'akov ☎ 04/638–0435 ⊕ www.tishbi.com.

⑥ Amphorae Winery This boutique winery is set in

a series of rustic, Tuscan-style stone buildings. Call in advance to arrange a visit. Not kosher. *Try: Balanced, full-bodied Cabernet Sauvignon.* ✉ Makura Farm, Kerem Maharal ☎09/970–4301 ⊕www.amphorae-v. com.

SAMSON/ CENTRAL COAST
⑦ Carmel Winery
One of two visitor centers for Carmel (the other is in Zichron Ya'akov near Haifa), this facility at the country's largest winery offers tours of the original underground cellars built by Baron Edmond de Rothschild, as well as the facility's original barrel room. Kosher. ✉ 25 Hacarmel St. Rishon LeZion ☎ 03/948–8851 ⊕ www.carmel wines.com.

JUDEAN HILLS
⑧ Ella Valley For about $16 you can tour the winery and sample four vintages in a wood-bar tasting room. Kosher. *Try: Fruity Sauvignon Blanc.* ✉ Rte. 475, off Rte. 38, Netiv Halamed Heh ☎ 02/999–4885 ⊕ www.ellavalley.com.

⑨ Flam Winery
Two dynamic brothers, the sons of a former chief winemaker for Carmel Mizrachi, run this well-regarded producer. Call to arrange a cheese and wine tasting. Not kosher.

Try: Woodsy, berry-rich Flam Reserve Merlot. ✉ Eshtal Junction, Ya'ar Ha'kodshim ☎ 02/992–9923 ⊕ www.flamwinery. com.

THE NEGEV
⑩ Yatir Winery Generating great excitement, Yatir is a desert gem with promise.

Haifa

Tel Aviv

Jerusalem

Beersheva

Mediterranean Sea

③ GOLAN HEIGHTS
①
②
GALILEE
④
⑥
⑤
SHOMRON/ CARMEL
⑦
SAMSON/ CENTRAL COAST
⑨
⑧
JUDEAN HILLS
GAZA
⑩
THE NEGEV

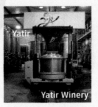
Yatir
Yatir Winery

Call in advance. Kosher. *Try: Yatir Forest, whose grape blend varies from year to year; fruity, light Viognier.* ✉ Off Rte. 80, Tel Arad ☎ 08/995–9090 ⊕ www.yatir. net.

5

IN FOCUS THE WINES OF ISRAEL

MORE ISRAELI WINE RESOURCES

Pina BaRosh Wine Bar

WINE FESTIVALS

Annual wine festivals offer the opportunity to meet winemakers and taste their products, often in beautiful surroundings. Every July, Jerusalem's **Israel Museum** (☎ 02/670–8811 ✉ info@imj.org.il for dates) turns over its outdoor space at night for a weeklong wine festival featuring more than 150 wineries, food from local restaurants, and various other vendors. This Jerusalem tradition is highly recommended.

Up north, the **Golan Heights Winery** stages harvest festivals in September or October at their Katzrin headquarters (☎04/696–8420 ✉ghwinery@golanwines.co.il).

The **Yoav Yehuda Wine Festival** (☎ 08/850–2240 ✉ tour@yoav.org.il) occurs every year during wine season (fall) and celebrates the more than two dozen wineries operating near Jerusalem in the Judean Hills and the surrounding area.

TASTING IN SHOPS AND BARS

Avi Ben, Jerusalem. This chain of retail wine shops offers free wine tastings every Friday from 11 to 2:30. On Thursday evenings look for winemaker-hosted tastings (NIS 20—NIS 50 per glass). ✉ 22 Rivlin St. ☎02/625–9073 ✉3 Harmonim St. ☎02/625–2339 ⊕www.avibenwine.com.

Pri Hagefen, Tel Aviv. Charming and lounge-like, this wine bar and store in Neveh Tzedek hosts free wine tastings on Fridays from 12 to 4, featuring boutique pours. Themed Thursday-evening tastings typically occur twice monthly, and prices vary. 4 Ahad Ha'Am St. ☎03/516–9168 ⊕www.pri-hagefen.co.il.

Pina BaRosh Wine Bar, Rosh Pina. A recent addition to the most famous B&B in funky Rosh Pina, near Tzfat, features more than 100 northern Israeli wines. Wines by the glass are available every day from 8:30 AM to midnight, as are tastings, which range from NIS 74 to NIS 134. ✉8 Ha Chalutzim St. ☎03/693–7208 ⊕www.pinabarosh.com.

BRINGING IT HOME

Although you can ship wines home for personal enjoyment, the prices are prohibitively high, and your wines may get held up in U.S. Customs. A better bet is to save suitcase space for a few boutique bottles. Then, at the larger wineries, take notes on favorites and purchase them back home. **Skyview Wines & Spirits** in New York has the largest selection (⊕www.skyviewwine.com ☎888/759–8466) from conventional wineries.

Wine clubs like **Israeli Wine Direct** (⊕www.israeliwinedirect.com) are a good source for hard-to-find smaller producers like Margalit, Pelter, Flam, and Clos de Gat. Wines are shipped direct to your home.

READING & PLANNING

An increasing number of resources are available for vino-tourists in Israel. The Web site **Wines Israel** (⊕www.wines-israel.co.il), a great place to start, has an easy-to-read English-language section including information about the industry, winemaking history, wine routes, places to visit, and more.

Rogov's Guide to Israeli Wines (Toby Press, $19.95) is updated annually by Daniel Rogov, Israel's preeminent wine writer. It's a great resource for tasting wines.

architecture, built of white stone with a central pediment capped by a tile roof. The museum is dedicated to the lives of immigrants who came to Israel with the First Aliya (a period of settlement from 1882 until 1904). Life-size model displays of local immigrants (like Zachariya, the seed vendor, and Izer, the cobbler) help illustrate how life was lived at that time. One film, among others, traces the struggles of a family who came from Europe in this difficult period of Israel's modern history. ✉ *2 Hanadiv St.* ☎ *04/629–4777* 🎫 *NIS 15* ⊘ *Mon. and Wed.–Fri., 9–2, Tues. 9–3.*

NEED A BREAK? An inviting place to relax and watch the action in this still-rural town is the sweet little park on Hanadiv Street, opposite the old synagogue and the First Aliya Museum. In the spring it's filled with multicolored roses and year-round flowers blossom vibrantly.

★ The well-regarded **Carmel Wine Cellars** is Israel's largest winery, producing more than 160 different wines and spirits. The old wooden buildings house a wine shop and a homey restaurant where local cheeses and pasta are served on weekdays. The original storage vats and oak barrels are still on view in caves dug out of the hillside, although the wine is now stored mostly in stainless-steel vats and concrete tanks. A guided one-hour tour outlines the stages of local wine production. Included in the tour are a tasting of some four varieties, and a seven-minute audiovisual presentation screened in a 100-year-old wine cellar. Tours leave between 9 AM and 4 PM; it's a good idea to reserve ahead. The finest Carmel wines are the Rothschild vintages: Merlot, Chardonnay, Cabernet Sauvignon, Sauvignon Blanc, and the single-vineyard series. An autumn wine festival takes place around the time of the Sukkoth holiday. ☎ *04/629–0977* ⊕ *www.carmelwines.co.il* 🎫 *NIS 22* ⊘ *Sun.– Thurs. 9–6, Fri. 9–1.*

WHERE TO EAT

$$$
MEDITERRANEAN
✗ **Haneshika.** The restaurant's huge courtyard with dark-orange umbrellas is usually packed with diners. Inside, the place is small and cozy. For country-style eating, you might start with mozzarella gnocchi with sautéed mushrooms, or a zucchini and feta cheese terrine. Main courses include baked crabs in a sweet-and-hot chili sauce, lamb casserole with eggplant and pine nuts, and seafood and fennel salad. Apple crumble with a cinnamon-flavored sauce is a delightful dessert. A hearty breakfast is served most days. ✉ *37 Hameyasdim St.* ☎ *04/639–0133* ⚠ *Reservations essential* 🖃 *AE, DC, MC, V* ⊘ *No dinner Fri. Closed Sun.*

$
MIDDLE EASTERN
✗ **Hatemaniya shel Santo.** Grab a table in the courtyard well off the main street if you want a tasty and authentic Yemenite meal. There's no menu—the waiter brings you soft pita bread, country black bread, a fresh vegetable salad, and a rugged hummus dripped with olive oil. You can order stuffed vegetables or chicken, but make sure you also try the potato cakes and a plate of the small meat patties flavored with cilantro. It's all delicious, and nicely washed down by Yemenite coffee or cold water with lemon and mint. ✉ *52 Hameyasdim St.* ☎ *04/639–8762* 🖃 *AE, DC, MC, V* ⊘ *Closed Sat.*

$$
MEDITERRANEAN
✗ **Kashtunyo Wine Cellar.** An old underground wine cellar is a happy place to learn about wines from owner Amos Meroz, whose Australian hat is

always rakishly tilted to one side. Eight tables covered with checkered cloths fill a small space defined by curving stone walls. Dishes of olives glisten on a tiny wooden bar in the dimly-lighted room. Scores of wine bottles line the back wall, where you'll find vintages from Israel, Italy, Australia, California, France, and South Africa. Meroz's knowledge of wine is far-ranging, and you can enjoy cheese and stuffed grape leaves while learning from an expert. Or just sit quietly with your glass while French songs fill the air. ⊠ *56 Hameyasdim St.* ☎ *04/629–1244* ⚲ *Reservations essential* ▭ *AE, MC, V.*

$$$
ECLECTIC

✕ **Picciotto.** Pots of geraniums and rosemary and lavender bushes are at the entrance of this charming, eclectic eatery. The ceiling of this historic building is the original wood, and the original settlers peer out sternly from photos on the vanilla-colored walls. A woodburning stove in the middle keeps everything cozy. The chef's lemon-cured salmon with cucumber dressing merits mention, as does the roasted eggplant with tomatoes and mint leaves. Each makes a fine introduction to main courses such as seafood pasta in white wine and wild herbs and lemony chicken breast with capers. For dessert, try the phyllo leaves filled with crème anglaise and seasonal fresh fruit. ⊠ *41 Hameyasdim St.* ☎ *04/629–0646* ⚲ *Reservations essential* ▭ *AE, DC, MC, V.*

WHERE TO STAY

¢ ☖ **Bet Maimon.** On the western slopes of Zichron Ya'akov, this family-run hotel has a spectacular view of the coastal valley and the sea. The terrace restaurant serves both Middle Eastern and Eastern European lunches. The rooms are done up in blues and yellows. There's a pretty garden and an above-ground pool. Guests who are less than fit will feel the climb to the sundeck on the roof; the three-story building has no elevator. **Pros:** city's best lodging; nice views. **Cons:** lots of steps to climb; old-fashioned feel. ⊠ *4 Zahal St.* ☎ *04/639–0212* ⊕ *www.maimon. com* ⇆ *25 rooms* ☖ *In-room: Wi-Fi. In-hotel: restaurant, pool, parking (free)* ▭ *AE, DC, MC, V.*

SOUTH BAT SHLOMO

5 km (3 mi) northeast of Zichron Ya'akov.

The oldest part of South Bat Shlomo has just one street; it's a charming stroll past small, square houses with red-tile roofs, the spaces between each of them leaving just enough room for a farmer's horse and wagon. The old synagogue is in the middle of the block. A few of the owners still cultivate the land and sell cheese, olive oil, and honey, much like their forebears. The short walk ends with a dramatic view of vineyards below and, opposite, the lushly forested hill of a nature reserve established by the British in 1941.

GETTING HERE AND AROUND

Look for the sign for South Bat Shlomo as you drive on Route 70.

EXPLORING

Along the main street, behind a giant ficus tree, you'll find **Gallerina** (☎ *04/639–9735*), an art gallery with café that's open on Thursday, Friday, and Saturday. The owners change the exhibition according to the season and the food suits the show; for instance, in winter they'll have ceramic soup bowls on sale and soup in the café. Other art objects for sale are photographs, paintings, and jaunty papier-mâché figures; on the menu are cheese plates, quiches, cake, and good hot coffee, served from 9:30 to 5.

BENYAMINA

5 km (3 mi) south of Zichron Ya'akov, 55 km (34 mi) north of Tel Aviv.

Picturesque Benyamina, the youngest settlement in the area, was founded in 1922. It was named after Baron Edmond de Rothschild (1845–1934), the head of the French branch of the famous family, who took a keen interest in the welfare of his fellow Jews in Palestine. (His Hebrew name was Benyamin.) With his prestige, vision, and financial contributions, Rothschild laid the foundations in the late 19th century for Zichron Ya'akov and Bat Shlomo, as well as other towns along the coastal plain and in the Upper Galilee.

The advice of the viniculture experts Rothschild hired in the 1880s paid off handsomely, at least in this region—the fruit of the vines flourished in the 1890s. Rothschild's paternalistic system was not without its pitfalls, however; some of his administrators ruled his colonies like petty despots, trying, for instance, to impose use of the French language on the local settlers, who wished to speak Hebrew. Language notwithstanding, the Binyamina Winery was founded in 1952; you can find it at the end of the village by following the Hebrew signs that show a bunch of grapes.

GETTING HERE AND AROUND

You can easily reach Benyamina by train. If you're driving, take Route 4. Either option makes for a very pretty ride. Once you're here, you'll need a car to get around because public transport is uneven at best.

EXPLORING

The large visitor center at **Binyamina Winery,** the country's fourth-largest winery, was once a perfume factory. It hasn't changed as much as you'd think, as cosmetics made from grape seeds are some of the products for sale here. You can also find olive oil, vinegar, and yes, even wine. The production facilities are next door in buildings surrounded by towering palm trees. Reservations are required for the 45-minute tour of winery and barrel rooms, including a sampling of four or five wines. You can also do your tasting while having lunch or dinner in the restaurant that was once an orange packing facility. Or, you can simply drop in for coffee and cake. ✉ *Hanassi St.* ☎ *04/638–8643* ⊕ *www.binyaminawines. com* 🎫 *Free* 🕙 *Sun.–Fri. 9–noon.*

Among the hills and valleys of this pastoral area is the **Tishbi Estate Winery,** one of the country's most esteemed wineries. The first vines were planted almost 120 years ago. Estate is the premier label (the Sauvignon Blanc and Chardonnay are among the best in Israel). At the country-style visitor center, it's a treat to eat brunch or lunch under the grape-vines in the courtyard. Apart from wine, you'll also find local cheeses, olive oil, honey, and wine jellies at the shop. Call ahead to reserve the one-hour tour, which includes tastings and a visit to the old alembic distillery where their prized brandy is made. It's about 3 km (1½ mi) north of Benyamina. ⊠ *Rte. 652* ☎ *04/628–8195* ⊕ *www.tishbi.com* ⌨ *Free* ☉ *Sun.–Thurs. 8–5, Fri. 8–3.*

The stone fortress of **Shuni** was built in the 18th and 19th centuries, on the site of existing ruins, because of its sweeping command over the surrounding lands, some planted with grain (*shuni* is Arabic for granary). The Ottoman fort is now part of the beautifully landscaped Jabotinsky Park. The spring at present-day Shuni was also the source of the spring water that was tapped for the aqueducts of ancient Caesarea. In the 1930s and '40s, the site was chosen for its remote location as a training ground for members of self-organized units inspired by Ze'ev Jabotinsky (1880–1940), the right-wing Zionist leader who was the spiritual head of the Jewish underground organization Irgun Zvai Leumi. Armed Irgun units later launched attacks from here.

Jabotinsky Park also has a well-preserved **Roman Theater.** Excavations of the structure have revealed the remains of bathing pools lined with 2nd-century Roman mosaics and a marble statue of the Greek god of medicine, Aesculapius. Both are now in storage at the Rockefeller Museum in Jerusalem. These finds support the theory that this was once a sacred spa whose waters had healing powers—indeed, an early-4th-century pilgrim wrote that women who bathed here always became pregnant, like it or not. The theater also contains an ancient olive press, carved lintels, and fragments of columns. The site is 1 km (½ mi) north of Benyamina. ⊠ *Rte. 652* ☎ *04/638–9730* ⊕ *www.shuni.co.il* ⌨ *NIS 12* ☉ *Sun.–Thurs. 9–4, Fri. 9–12:30, Sat. 9–4.*

AKKO TO ROSH HANIKRA

One of the oldest port cities in the world, Akko has an Old City ringed by ancient ramparts. Inside are an 18th-century domed mosque, underground Crusader halls, and winding lanes leading past a marketplace and restaurants at the water's edge. Wide beaches, two of them within nature reserves, follow one after the other up the coast. The moshavim and kibbutzim (rural agricultural settlements) are often unusual settings for gourmet restaurants and upscale B&Bs. Rosh Hanikra, at the top of the northern coast, has a cable car that carries you down to caves hollowed out by wildly crashing waves.

AKKO

Fodor's Choice *22 km (13½ mi) north of Haifa.*

★ The Old City of Akko is an enchanting mix of mosques, markets, and vaulted Crusader ruins (many of them underground). A walk through the cobbled alleys and outdoor market stalls brings you to a small port filled with fishing boats. When viewed from the surrounding ramparts, it's one of the country's prettiest views.

Akko's History

History clings to the stones of old Akko, with each twist and turn along its streets telling another tale. The city's history begins 4,000 years ago, when Akko was first mentioned in Egyptian writings that refer to the mound northeast of its walls. The Old Testament describes in Judges 1 that after the death of Joshua the tribe of Asher was unable to drive the Canaanites from Akko, so they lived among them. Akko has always been worth fighting for. It had a well-protected harbor, fertile hinterland, and a strategic position that linked Egypt and Phoenicia. Alexander the Great had such regard for Akko that he set up a mint here. Akko was Phoenician for long periods, but when the Hellenistic king Ptolemy II gained control in the 2nd century BC, he renamed it Ptolemais.

The Crusaders who conquered Akko in 1104 were led by King Baldwin I. The port city, which the victorious French Hospitallers renamed for their patron saint—Jeanne d'Arc—was the Crusaders' principal link to home. Commerce thrived, and the European maritime powers Genoa, Pisa, Venice, and Marseilles developed separate quarters here. After the disastrous defeat of the Crusader armies in 1187, Akko surrendered to Saladin, but Richard the Lionheart soon recaptured the European stronghold. In its Crusader heyday, Akko had about 40 churches and monasteries and a population of 50,000. In the 13th century, after the conquest of Jerusalem by the Muslims, Akko became the effective capital of a shrunken Latin kingdom. Dahr el-Omar, the Bedouin sheikh, moved his capital from Tiberias to Akko in 1749 and rebuilt the walls of the city.

Napoléon couldn't conquer the city in 1799, but the British captured it in 1918. With the founding of the state of Israel in 1948, many Arab inhabitants left Akko, though a good number remain. Akko's population now numbers about 46,000, with people living inside the Old City itself and in new developments pushing the city limits to the north.

GETTING HERE AND AROUND

From Haifa, you can get here via Route 4. A much slower but far prettier inland route takes you north on Route 70, passing through rolling hills and avoiding the drab satellite towns north of Haifa. There are direct buses from Haifa, and trains from Jerusalem and Tel Aviv (you may have to change trains). Once you are here, a car is the best way to get around.

From Akko's port, the *Queen of Akko* ferry makes a 40-minute jaunt around the bay. The cost is NIS 25. Two well-known companies, Egged Tours and United Tours, offer one-day trips to Akko from Haifa.

TIMING AND PRECAUTIONS

Plan on spending the better part of a day if you want to see everything, including the excellent presentation in the Turkish Bath House. Women on their own should exercise caution walking around at night.

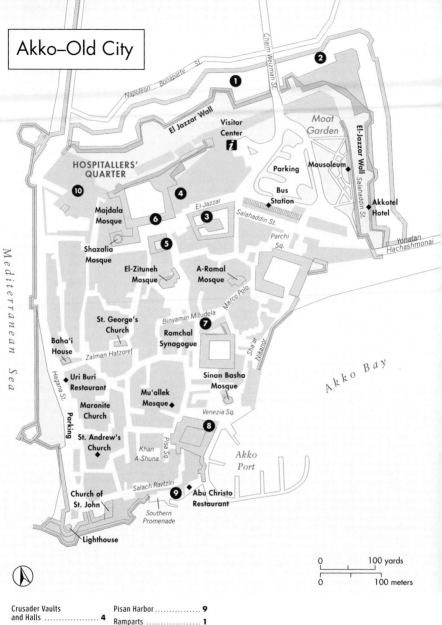

Akko–Old City

❷

❶

Napoleon Bonaparte St.

Chaim Weizman St.

El Jazzar Wall

Visitor Center

ℹ️

Moat Garden

El-Jazzar Wall

HOSPITALLERS' QUARTER

Parking

Mausoleum

❿

❹

Majdala Mosque

❻

El-Jazzar

❸

Bus Station

Salahaddin St.

Salahaddin St.

Akkotel Hotel

Yonatan Hachashmonai

❺

Shazalia Mosque

El-Zituneh Mosque

A-Ramal Mosque

Parchi Sq.

Marco Polo

M e d i t e r r a n e a n   S e a

St. George's Church

Ramchal Synagogue

Binyamin Mitudela

❼

Sha'ar Nikanor

A k k o   B a y

Baha'i House

Zalman Hatzoref

Sinan Basha Mosque

Hagana St.

Uri Buri Restaurant

Mu'allek Mosque ◆

Maronite Church

Venezia Sq.

Parking

St. Andrew's Church ◆

❽

Khan A-Shuna

Pisa Sq.

Akko Port

Church of St. John

Salach Ravtziri

❾ ◆ **Abu Christo Restaurant**

Lighthouse

Southern Promenade

🧭

0 —— 100 yards

0 —— 100 meters

Crusader Vaults and Halls **4**

El-Jazzar Mosque **3**

Ethnography Center of Acre **2**

Khan el-Umdan **8**

Museum of the Underground Prisoners .. **10**

Pisan Harbor **9**

Ramparts **1**

Refectory **6**

Souk **7**

Turkish bathhouse **5**

ESSENTIALS

Vistor and Tour Information Akko Tourist Information Office (✉*at the town entrance* ☎*04/995-6727* ⊕*www.akko.org.il*). **Egged Tours** (☎*03/920-3919* ⊕*www.eggedtours.co.il*). **Queen of Akko** (☎*050/555-1136*). **United Tours** (☎*03/693-3412 or 03/522-2008* ⊕*www.inisrael.com/united/index.html*).

EXPLORING AKKO

The walled city of Old Akko is relatively small and the sights are close to one another, making it easy to tour. You approach the Old City on Weizman Street (watch for signs that say OLD AKKO), proceeding through a breach in the surrounding walls. If you're driving, park in the large lot.

OLD CITY

One good place to part exploring is at the Ramparts in the northern part of the Old City; nearby is the Ethnography Center. Deeper in the Old City are the El-Jazaar Mosque and the fascinating Crusader Vaults and Halls, among other sights. After exploring this area, you can walk south to the souk and the Pisan Harbor.

❹ ★ **Crusader Vaults and Halls.** Here you'll find a series of barrel-vaulted rooms known as the Crusader Vaults and Knights Halls (one of which is sometimes used for chamber-music concerts). Six such halls have been discovered thus far. Arrows point the way through dimly lit vast rooms filled with ongoing reconstruction work, huge marble columns, and myriad archaeological pieces from the past. Above this part of the Crusader city stands the Ottoman citadel, which you can glimpse from the courtyard. Raised by Dahr el-Omar in the 18th century on the rubble-filled Crusader ruins, the citadel was the highest structure in Akko. It was later converted by the British into a prison (now a museum), and in order to unearth the Crusader Halls, the former prison courtyard was completely dug out. Archaeologists are always busy delving into the mysteries of Akko, but signs keep you on a safe path.

The seeds of the Crusaders' downfall in Akko were probably sown by the different factions within its walls. The French Hospitallers and Templars, the so-called fighting monks, had separate quarters (the Templars lived near the lighthouse by the western Crusader sea wall), and by the mid-13th century, open fighting had broken out between the Venetians and Genoese. When the Mamluks attacked with a vengeance in 1291, the Crusaders' resistance quickly crumbled, and the city's devastation was complete. It remained a subdued place for centuries, and even today Akko retains a medieval cast. ✉*1 Weizman St.* ☎*04/991-1764* ⊕*www.akko.org.il* ✉*Refectory with Crusader Vaults and Halls, NIS 27; Bathhouse with Crusader Vaults and Halls, NIS 46* ⊙*Nov.–Mar., Sat.–Thurs. 9–4:15, Fri. 9–1:15; Apr.–Oct., Sat.–Thurs. 9–5, Fri. 9–2:15.*

❸ ★ **El-Jazzar Mosque.** This house of worship is considered one of the most magnificent in Israel. Ahmed el-Jazzar, who succeeded Dahr el-Omar after having him assassinated, ruled Akko from 1775 to 1804. During his reign he built this mosque along with other public structures. His cruelty was so legendary that he earned the epithet "the Butcher." (He is buried next to his adopted son in a small white building to the right of the mosque.)

Just beyond the entrance is a pedestal engraved with graceful calligraphy; it re-creates the seal of a 19th-century Ottoman sultan. Some of the marble and granite columns that adorn the mosque and courtyard were plundered from the ruins of Caesarea. In front of the mosque is an ornate fountain used by the faithful for ritual washings of hands and feet. Inside the mosque, enshrined in the gallery reserved for women, is a reliquary containing a hair believed to be from the beard of the prophet Muhammad; it is removed only once a year, on the 27th day of Ramadan.

The mosque closes five times a day for prayers, so you might have a short wait. Dress modestly. ⊠ *Off El-Jazzar St., on the left of the square* 🖃*NIS 6* ⊗ *Sat.–Thurs. 8–5, Fri. 8–11 and 1–5.*

NEED A BREAK? In the plaza outside the El-Jazzar Mosque are outdoor restaurants where you can enjoy a falafel, fresh-squeezed orange juice (or pomegranate in season), or coffee while watching the world go by.

➋ **Ethnography Center of Acre.** There are two sections to this small museum: one re-creates a 19th-century marketplace, including craftsmen's workshops such as a hatmaker and blacksmith's, filled with every last tool they'd need to make hats and horseshoes; the other room displays a traditional Damascene living room, complete with an astounding collection of furniture and accoutrements. To get here once you're up the steps to the Ramparts, keep an eye out for the flight of stairs heading down to the left. ⊠ *On the ramparts* ☎*04/991–1004* 🖃*15 NIS* ⊗*Daily 10–4.*

➑ **Khan el-Umdan.** In Venezia Square, in front of the port, is the Inn of the Pillars. Before you visit this Ottoman *khan*—the largest of the four in Akko—and the Pisan Quarter beyond, take a stroll around the port, with its small flotilla of fishing boats, yachts, and sailboats. Then walk through the khan's gate beneath a square clock tower, built at the turn of the 20th century. The khan served vast numbers of merchants and travelers during Akko's golden age of commerce, in the 18th century. The 32 pink-and-gray granite pillars that give it its name are compliments of Ahmed el-Jazzar's raids on Roman Caesarea. There was once a market at the center of the colonnaded courtyard. ⊠ *Venezia Sq.*

➓ **Museum of the Underground Prisoners.** Located at the sea's edge, this museum is in several wings of the citadel built by Dahr el-Omar and then modified by Ahmed el-Jazzar in 1785. It became a prison during the British Mandate. On the way in, you pass the citadel's outer wall; the difference between the large Crusader building stones and the smaller Turkish ones above is easy to spot. Prison life is illustrated by the original cells and their meager contents, supplemented by photographs and documents that reconstruct the history of the Jewish resistance to British rule in the '30s and '40s. During the Mandate, the citadel became a high-security prison whose inmates included top members of Jewish resistance organizations, among them Ze'ev Jabotinsky. In 1947 a dramatic prison breakout by leaders of the Irgun captured headlines

Now a museum, the 18th-century Turkish bathhouse in Akko receives light through a dome with glass bubbles.

around the world and provided Leon Uris's novel *Exodus* with one of its most dramatic moments. ✉ *Hahagana St.* ☎ *04/991–8264* ✉ *NIS 10* ⏱ *Sun.–Thurs. 9–3, Fri. 9–1.*

❾ Pisan Harbor. Climbing the stone steps at the water's edge, you can walk along the sea walls at the Pisan Harbor. Start at the café perched on high—a great lookout—and head west in the direction of the 18th-century Church of St. John. You'll end up at the southwestern extremity of Akko, next to the lighthouse. Head north along Haganah Street, which runs parallel to the crenellated western sea wall. After five minutes you'll reach the whitewashed, blue-trimmed Baha'i house (not open to the public), where the prophet of the Baha'i religion, Baha'u'llah, spent 12 years of his exile. His burial site is just north of Akko at the Baha'i Founder's Shrine and Gardens. ✉ *Southern tip of Akko.*

❶ The Ramparts. As you enter the Old City, climb the signposted blue-railing stairway on your right for a stroll along the city walls. Walking to the right, you can see the stunted remains of the 12th-century walls built by the Crusaders, under whose brief rule—just under two centuries—Akko flourished as never before or since. The indelible signs of the Crusaders, who made Akko the main port of their Christian empire, are much more evident inside the Old City itself.

The wall girding the northern part of the town was built by Ahmed el-Jazzar, the Pasha of Akko, who added these fortifications following his victory over Napoléon's army in 1799. With the help of the British fleet, el-Jazzar turned Napoléon's attempted conquest into a humiliating rout. Napoléon had dreamed of founding a new Eastern empire, thrusting northward from Akko to Turkey and then seizing India from Great

Britain. His defeat at Akko hastened his retreat to France, thus changing the course of history. Walk around to the guard towers and up an incline just opposite; there's a view of the moat below and Haifa across the bay. Turn around and let your gaze settle on the exotic skyline of Old Akko, the sea-green dome of the great mosque its dominating feature. Walk down the ramp, crossing the rather messy Moat Garden at the base of the walls; straight ahead is the El-Jazzar Mosque.

6 Refectory. The Refectory was once known as the Crypt of St. John—before excavation it was erroneously thought to have been an underground chamber. The dimensions of the colossal pillars that support the roof (they're girded with metal bands for extra support) make this one of Israel's most monumental examples of Crusader architecture. It's also one of the oldest Gothic structures in the world. In the right-hand corner opposite the entrance is a fleur-de-lis carved in stone—the crest of the French house of Bourbon—which has led some scholars to suggest that this was the chamber in which Louis VII convened the knights of the realm.

Just outside this room is an entrance to an extremely narrow subterranean passageway. Cut from stone, this was a secret tunnel that the Crusaders probably used to reach the harbor when besieged by Muslim forces. (Those who are claustrophobic can take an alternate route, which goes back to the entrance of the Turkish Bathhouse and continues from there.) You'll emerge to find yourself in the cavernous vaulted halls of the fortress guardpost, with a 13th-century marble Crusader tombstone at the exit. Go up the stairs to the left and turn right into the covered market, where artisans beat pieces of copper into bas-relief plates and bowls and sell other handcrafted items. Exit to the left. ⊠*Parking lot at 1 Weizman St.* ☎*04/991–1764* ⊕*www.akko.org.il* ⊠*Refectory with Crusader Vaults and Halls, NIS 25; Bathhouse with Crusader Vaults and Halls, NIS 46* ☉*Nov.–Mar., Sat.–Thurs. 9–4:15, Fri. 9–1:15; Apr.–Oct., Sat.–Thurs. 9–5, Fri. 9–2:15.*

7 Souk. At this market, stalls heaped with fresh produce alternate with specialty stores: a pastry shop with an astonishing variety of exotic Middle Eastern delicacies; a spice shop filled with the aromas of the East; a bakery with steaming-fresh pita. You'll often see fishermen sitting on doorsteps, intently repairing their lines and nets to the sounds of Arabic music blaring from the open windows above.

NEED A BREAK?

In the souk, duck into the Oudah Brothers Cafe (⊠*Khan ha Frankim St.* ☎**04/991–2013) and enjoy a coffee, hummus, or kebab in the courtyard of the 16th-century Khan el-Faranj, or Franks' Inn. Note the 18th-century Franciscan monastery and tower to your left.**

5 Turkish Bathhouse. Built for Pasha el-Jazzar in 1781, Akko's remarkable Turkish Bathhouse was in use until 1947. Don't miss the sound-and-light show called "The Story of the Last Bath Attendant," set in the beautiful bathhouse itself. You follow the story, with visual and audio effects, from the dressing room decorated with Turkish tiles and topped with a cupola, through the rooms with colored-glass bubbles protruding from the roof domes, sending a filtered green light to the steam rooms below. ✉ *1 Weizman St.* ☎ *04/991–1764* 🌐 *www.akko.org.il* 🎫 *Bathhouse with Crusader Vaults and Halls, NIS 46* ⏲ *Nov.–Mar., Sat.–Thurs. 9–4:15, Fri. and Jewish holiday eves 9–1:15; Apr.–Oct., Sat.–Thurs. 9–5, Fri. and Jewish holiday eves 9–2:15.*

NEAR THE CITY

★ **Baha'i Founder's Shrine and Gardens.** For the Baha'is, this is the holiest place on earth, the site of the tomb of the faith's prophet and founder, Baha'u'llah. First you'll pass the gardens' west gate, open only to Baha'is. Take the first right (no sign) and continue to the unobtrusive turn, 500 yards up, to the north (main) gate. Baha'u'llah lived in the red-tile mansion here after he was released from jail in Akko, and was buried in the small building next door, now the Shrine of Baha'u'llah. Going through the black iron gate, you follow a white gravel path in the exquisitely landscaped gardens, with a fern-covered fountain and an observation point along the way, until you reach the shrine. Visitors are asked to dress modestly. The shrine is on Route 4, about 1 km (½ mi) north of the gas station at Akko's northern edge. ✉ *Rte. 4* 🎫 *Free* ⏲ *Gardens daily 9–4; Shrine Fri.–Mon. 9–noon.*

5

Lochamei Hageta'ot. Kibbutz Lochamei Hageta'ot was founded in 1949 by survivors of the German, Polish, and Lithuanian Jewish ghettos and veterans of the ghetto uprisings against the Nazis. To commemorate their compatriots who perished in the Holocaust, the kibbutz members set up a **Ghetto Fighters Museum,** which you enter to the right of the main gate. Exhibits include photographs documenting the Warsaw Ghetto and the famous uprising, and halls devoted to different themes, among them that of the Jewish communities before their destruction in the Holocaust; the death camps; and deportations at the hands of the Nazis. You can also see the booth in which Adolf Eichmann, architect of the "Final Solution," sat during his Jerusalem trial.

In a cone-shaped building, the adjacent **Yad Layeled** (Children's Memorial) is dedicated to the memory of the 1½ million children who perished in the Holocaust. It's designed for young visitors, who can begin to comprehend the events of the Holocaust through a series of tableaux and images accompanied by recorded voices, allowing them to identify with individual victims without seeing shocking details. There is a small cafeteria on the premises. The site is 2 km (1 mi) north of Akko on Route 4. ✉ *Kibbutz Lochamei Hageta'ot, Rte. 4* ☎ *04/995–8080* 🎫 *Free* ⏲ *Sun.–Thurs. 9–4.*

WHERE TO EAT

$$ SEAFOOD ✕ **Abu Christo.** In the Old City, this popular waterfront fish restaurant stands at one of the original 18th-century gates built by Pasha Ahmed el-Jazzar when he fortified the city after his victory over Napoléon. It's a family business that's been passed from father to son since 1948. The covered patio is an idyllic place to dig into earthy hummus with pine nuts, eggplant salad spiced up with sumac, and other salads. Abu

Christo serves up the daily catch—often grouper, red snapper, or sea bass—prepared simply, either grilled or deep fried. Shellfish such as jumbo shrimp and crabs, and grilled meats are also available. ⊠ *Crusader Port* ☎ *04/991–0065* △ *Reservations essential* ⊟ *AE, DC, MC, V.*

$$$
SEAFOOD
Fodor's Choice
★

✕ **Uri Buri.** Known far and wide for its excellent fish and seafood, Uri's restaurant is housed in an old Turkish building. One room is furnished with sofas, copper dishes, and *nargillas* (water pipes). Everything on the menu is seasonal, and the fresh fish is steamed, baked, or grilled. Allow time to linger here—it's not your everyday fish fry. Two house specialties are gravlax and Thai-style fish; delicious seafood soup is another fixture. Or have a go at baby calamari with kumquats and pink grapefruit, or Creole shrimp with five spices. Uri Buri is near the lighthouse, on one edge of the waterside parking lot. ⊠ *93 Haganah St.* ☎ *04/955–2212* △ *Reservations essential* ⊟ *AE, DC, MC, V* ⊘ *Closed Tues.*

WHERE TO STAY

$
🏨 **Akkotel.** A welcome addition to the city's lodgings is this three-story hostelry, a former Turkish police station built into the rampart wall. Original wood doors lead into the small lobby where a painted plaster rosette decorates the gold ceiling. (Painted plaster architectural details are a trademark of 19th-century buildings in Israel). The lavish old-world Turkish decor has been updated: original bathrooms have been beautifully modernized and surprising touches of original stonework remain in the windows and walls. Double rooms are decorated in brown, caramel, and beige, and net curtains embroidered with flowers frame the windows. Each of the five family rooms has a loft with two beds so four people can settle in comfortably. The rooftop café showcases the lovely skyline of Old Akko. Family run, the welcome is warm as can be. **Pros:** unusual lodging; warm service. **Cons:** no pool, no parking. ⊠ *Salahaddin St.* ☎ *04/987–7100* ⊕ *www.akkotel.com* ⤳ *16 rooms, 2 suites* ⌂ *In-room: safe, refrigerator. In-hotel: restaurant, Internet terminal, Wi-Fi* ⊟ *AE, DC, MC, V.*

$
🏨 **Nes Ammim Guest House.** Founded in 1964, Nes Ammim is an ecumenical Christian settlement focusing on mutual respect and tolerance. Guests are invited to chat with members of the community, who can take you around the grounds. Lodging options are either standard rooms or family apartments with fully-equipped kitchens. The setting, 10 km (6 mi) north of Akko, is picturesque and rural, once you get past the dismal approach road. A friendly and welcoming staff is a nice plus. In summer, classical music is performed in the serene chapel, or near the large pool, often after a barbecue meal. To get here, drive north from Akko on Route 4. **Pros:** good for families; modest price. **Cons:** basic rooms, few activities. ⊠ *D. N. Western Galilee* ☎ *04/995–0000* ⤳ *48 rooms, 13 apartments* ⌂ *In-room: safe, refrigerator. In-hotel: restaurant, bar, pool, Internet terminal, Wi-Fi* ⊟ *AE, DC, MC, V.*

$$
🏨 **Palm Beach.** On Route 4 just south of Akko, the Palm Beach is right on the beach, with fine views of Haifa Bay and the rooftops of the Old City. Rooms are outfitted with blond-wood furniture with gold-and-brick curtains, bedspreads, and carpets; all face the sea. The comprehensive relaxation and entertainment facilities are in the country club adjacent to the hotel, a few steps away. **Pros:** beach access; lots of activities. **Cons:**

Despite modern boats, the old harbor in Akko retains echoes of past eras.

outside the Old City; dated decor. ⊠*Rte. 4* ☎*04/987–7777* ⊕*www.*
palmbeach.co.il ↘*98 rooms, 27 suites* ♿*In-room: safe, refrigerator*
(some). In-hotel: 2 restaurants, room service, tennis courts, pools, gym,
spa, parking (free), no-smoking rooms, Wi-Fi ▭*AE, DC, MC, V.*

SPORTS AND THE OUTDOORS

Just south of the Old City on the Haifa–Akko road is a sandy stretch of
municipal beach in **Akko Bay,** with parking, showers, toilets, and chair
rentals. Admission is NIS 10.

SHOPPING

David Miro (⊠*1 Weitzman St., at the entrance to Old Akko, at the park-*
ing lot ☎*04/955–3439*) sells a whole range of Israeli-made products.
The jewelry that combines silver and gold is especially interesting; some
incorporates Roman glass, some uses turquoise Eilat stone, and there's
also hand-worked copperware and silver pieces.

⌐ EN
  ROUTE

To the west of Route 4, as you travel north from Akko, stands a segment
of the multitiered **aqueduct** built by Ahmed el-Jazzar in the late 18th
century to carry the sweet waters of the Kabri springs to Akko.

NAHARIYA

8 km (5 mi) north of Akko.

One of the region's most beautiful beaches is just at the end of the main
street of Nahariya. Two others sit just north of town. The popular
seaside town was built along the banks of a river, now dried up, lined
with shady eucalyptus trees. The town's name comes from *nahar,* the
Hebrew word for "river."

Although German was once the main language here, you're now just as likely to hear Russian or Amharic (spoken by Ethiopians), and blue-bereted U.N. soldiers from bases to the north are frequent visitors. In July and August, there's dancing in the amphitheater at the mouth of the river, and Israeli stars perform on the beach and in the town square.

GETTING HERE AND AROUND

There are direct buses from Haifa. Trains from Jerusalem and Tel Aviv travel at least twice a day to Nahariya. You might have to change trains along the way. By car, take Route 4 north of Akko. From a location 5 km (3 mi) north of Nahariya, Trek Yam takes you on an exciting 30-minute ride up the coast in a high-speed motorboat. The cost is NIS 70 per person.

ESSENTIALS

Medical Assistance Western Galilee Regional Hospital (⊠ *Opposite Moshav Ben Ami* ☏ *04/910–7107*).

Vistor and Tour Information Nahariya Tourist Information Office (⊠ *19 Ga'aton Blvd.* ☏ *04/987–9830* ⊕ *www.nahariya.muni.il*). **Trek Yam** (☏ *04/982–3671*).

EXPLORING

The **Byzantine church** has an elaborate, 17-color mosaic floor, discovered in 1964, that depicts peacocks, other birds, hunting scenes, and plants. It was part of what experts consider one of the largest and most beautiful Byzantine churches in the Western Galilee, where Christianity rapidly spread from the 4th to the 7th century. To get here, head east on Haga'aton to Route 4, making a left at the stoplight and then the first right onto Yechi'am Street. From here take the third left and then an immediate right onto Bielefeld Street. The church is next to the Katzenelson school. ⊠ *Bielefeld St.* ☏ *NIS 2.*

WHERE TO EAT

$$$

MEDITERRANEAN

Fodor's Choice

★

✕**Adelina.** When dining at this stellar restaurant, you may wonder how you got so lucky. There's the knockout view of the Mediterranean from the stone terrace, the olive tree-shaded setting, and the wonderful Spanish-accented dishes prepared by Adelina. Cooking is done in the huge silver *taboon* (oven) as Spanish music drifts across the dark wooden tables. Try the paella marinara packed with shellfish, roast sirloin with bacon and tarragon, or broccoli cannelloni in a creamy pepper sauce. Onward to *knafe* (a local pastry) with pistachio ice cream. Cocktails, beer, and wine are served. ⊠ *Off Rte. 4, turn into Kibbutz Kabri on Rte. 89 and follow the signs* ☏ *04/952–3707* ☐ *AE, DC, MC, V* ⊙ *Closed Sun.*

$$

MEDITERRANEAN

✕**Estousha.** The exotic name means Esther in Polish, and an enterprising woman of this name created this country restaurant with mostly Mediterranean fare. She still makes the desserts; the white chocolate mousse is proof of her continuing expertise. You can dine inside the wood-raftered building or outside on the large vine-covered terrace in the middle of an agricultural settlement. The latter is a fine place for family meals. Chicken-liver pâté makes a tasty starter, as does crab ravioli with saffron-flavored cream sauce. For the main course, choose from beef bourguignon with root vegetables, Viennese-style veal schnitzel, or seafood fettuccine. ⊠*Moshav Liman* ☎*04/982–1250* ⚓*Reservations essential* ▤*AE, DC, MC, V.*

$$ **✕Ida.** On the main street, you'll recognize Ida's by the curvy white
MODERN ISRAELI wrought-iron lamppost and the white stucco building topped by a sign in big blue letters. Ida was the wife of the town's first mayor, and the couple lived here in the 1950s. The mood is friendly and relaxed. Gold roses are stenciled on several walls, and wood screens divide the interior into cozy areas. It's an impressive modern Israeli dining experience in a town not as yet known for culinary greatness. Consider starting off with duck confit with cranberry sauce, then moving on to shellfish risotto with a creamy shrimp sauce or the pan-fried trout with a coconut and carrot sauce. It'll be hard to say no to chocolate cheesecake as a finale. ⊠*48 Haga'aton Blvd.* ☎*04/951–3444* ▤*AE, DC, MC, V.*

$$ **✕La Crepe Jacob.** This popular place is in a small cottage with blue
FRENCH window frames and a flower-filled garden. A wood-burning stove keeps
★ things cozy inside. Locally made goat cheeses cram the counter as you walk in. The hefty crepes, lovingly prepared by Betty and Jacob, come with fillings such as feta cheese, ham, and mushrooms; smoked salmon and cheese; and tomato, onion, olives, cheese, and mushrooms. The banana and chocolate crepe is a delicious wrap-up. In addition, the menu includes heartier dishes like veal filet with shrimp. ⊠*Moshav Ben Ami* ☎*04/952–0299* ▤*AE, DC, MC, V* ☾*Closed Sun.*

$$ **✕Penguin.** This casual, main-street institution opened its doors in
ECLECTIC 1940—it's probably the oldest restaurant in the country. Three generations of the same family work here, and the walls carry enlarged photographs of how the place looked when it was just a hut. Stop off for coffee and cake, or make a meal of spinach blintzes with melted cheese, hamburger platters, or Chinese dishes. The management swears that the schnitzel gets accolades from Viennese visitors. All main dishes come with salad, rice, french fries, and vegetables. Kids will enjoy the enclosed playground. ⊠*31 Haga'aton Blvd.* ☎*04/992–8855* ▤*AE, DC, MC, V.*

WHERE TO STAY

$$$$ 🛏**Aromantica.** In the rural farming settlement of Moshav Ben Ami, these
★ comfortable country cottages are run by Varda, who makes every effort to provide a relaxing stay for guests. Her touches include chocolates left bedside, and complimentary wine, lemonade, and ice cream. A tiny rock fountain burbles outside the door of each tile-roofed cabin, and wind chimes provide soothing sounds. Inside, each room has clay-hued sofas, bright white pillows and coverlets, woodburning stoves, and hot tubs. **Pros:** personal service; pretty location. **Cons:** not for families; a bit hard to find. ⊠*Off Rte. 4, turn into Moshav Ben Ami on Rte. 89* ☎*054/498–2302 or 04/982–0484* ⊕*www.aromantica.co.il* ⌂*3 cabins* ⚙*In-room: kitchen* ▤*AE, DC, MC, V* ⎟⊙*BP.*

$$ 🛏**Carlton.** This six-story hotel is popular with Israeli travelers. The common spaces are rather drab, but the pool is in good shape. You can walk down the street to a wonderful beach, soaking up the flavor of a bustling town as you go. The guest rooms are tasteful, with taupe curtains, white duvets, and black-and-taupe carpets. Some rooms have balconies facing the pool. On the seventh floor is a business center with

At Rosh Hanikra, take a cable car down the cliffs for an up-close look at the sea grottoes.

wireless Internet connections. La Scala dance club attracts revelers with live music. **Pros:** helpful staff; nice pool. **Cons:** noisy lobby; crowded on weekends. ✉ *23 Haga'aton* ☎ *04/900–5555* 🖶 *04/982–3771* 🛏 *192 rooms, 8 suites* ⚿ *In-room: refrigerator. In-hotel: restaurant, room service, bar, pool, parking (free)* ═ *AE, DC, MC, V* ⦿*IBP.*

$$$$ 🏨 **Pinhas & Gaston.** Called a "holiday estate," Pinhas & Gaston has a wonderful entrance through a fairytale garden, densely shaded in every color of green and crammed with flowers and plants. Accommodations have carved-wood beds, white down quilts, and plasma TVs that swivel so you can see from around the room. The espresso machine in the well-equipped kitchen is a thoughtful touch. Outside on the wooden decks are private pools and hot tubs. Wicker chaises under huge umbrellas face a tangerine orchard. **Pros:** beautiful setting; romantic getaway. **Cons:** expensive rates; no Internet. ✉ *Off Rte. 4, turn into Moshav Liman and make an immediate left* ☎ *057/728–2828 or 04/952–6000* 🛏 *4 rooms* ⚿ *In-room: kitchen, DVD. In-hotel: pools, bicycles* ═ *AE, DC, MC, V* ⦿*IBP.*

$ 🏨 **Pivko Village.** Nestled among the trees on the grounds of a kibbutz,
★ these cabins hold up to five people, making them good for families. The amazing view from the wide windows and patios (each with a hot tub) sweeps from Haifa across the sea to the cliffs of Rosh Hanikra. The interiors are warm and comfortable, with separate living and sleeping areas. There are plenty of activities, such as horseback riding, hiking, swimming, and tennis. You can enjoy lunch in the kibbutz dining room, and the excellent restaurant Adelina is right on the grounds. **Pros:** lots of activities; good restaurant nearby. **Cons:** a bit hard to find. ✉ *Kibbutz Kabri, Rte. 89* ☎ *04/995–2711* 🌐 *www.pivko-village.co.il* 🛏 *6*

cabins ⟆*In-room: kitchen, Internet. In-hotel: restaurant* ☰*AE, DC, MC, V* ⓞ*BP.*

$$$$ 🔂**Villa Provence.** Hidden away in a rural settlement, this out-of-the-
★ ordinary lodging looks as though it was plucked from an Italian hillside
and gently set down here among the trees. Inside the main building are
six individually decorated suites named for French flowers (the Lilac
Suite is sweet as can be). Every piece of furniture and all the decorative
accessories, from armoires to picture frames, have been hand-painted
and decorated in Provençal style by owner Katrine. The soft, thick towels and robes come from Morocco, as do the fine bed linens. Outside
are a pool and a hot tub surrounded by chaise longues. The breakfast,
served in a dining room overlooking the pool or outside on the terrace,
is organic. A fish dinner is served on Friday. **Pros:** gorgeous setting;
pretty pool. **Cons:** very expensive; no restaurants nearby. ⊠*Moshav
Manot* ☎*04/980–6246* ⊕*www.villaprovence.co.il* ⇌*6 rooms* ⟆*In-
room: refrigerator. In-hotel: Wi-Fi.* ☰*AE, MC, V* ⓞ*BP.*

NIGHTLIFE AND THE ARTS

La Scala (☎*04/900–5555*), Nahariya's flashiest disco, draws the over-30
crowd for standard dance tunes with a throbbing beat. It's in the passageway just west of the Carlton. The cover charge on Friday is NIS 50;
doors open at 10 PM.

SPORTS AND THE OUTDOORS

BEACHES

Nahariya's public bathing facilities at **Galei Galil Beach,** just north of
Haga'aton Boulevard, are ideal for families. Apart from the lovely
beach, facilities include an Olympic-size pool, a wading pool, a play-
ground for children, changing rooms and showers, plus a snack bar.
In peak season, the beach offers exercise classes early in the morning.
The entrance fee is NIS 12.

Beautifully maintained because it's in the Achziv National Park, gor-
★ geous **Akhziv Beach** is great for kids because of its shallow seawater
pool. (Don't worry, there's a larger one for adults.) There are protected lagoons, watchful lifeguards, and playground facilities. In July and
August, female turtles lay their eggs on the beach. You can picnic on
the grassy slopes or make use of the restaurant. Enter at the second sign
for Akhziv Beach, not the first. Admission, which is NIS 25, includes
the use of showers and toilets.

Betzet Beach, a bit farther north of Akhziv Beach, is part of a nature
reserve and offers abundant vegetation, trees, and the ruins of an ancient
olive press. There's a lifeguard on duty in season. Admission is free.

SCUBA DIVING

★ **Trek Yam** (☎*04/982–3671*) takes scuba divers to explore the caves at
Rosh Hanikra along the northern coast. The price of each trip is NIS
190, and includes all equipment. Reserve several days in advance.

ROSH HANIKRA

☃   *7 km (4½ mi) north of Nahariya.*

★   The dramatic white cliffs on the coast signal both Israel's border with Lebanon and the sea **grottoes** of Rosh Hanikra. Even before you get in line for the two-minute cable-car ride down to the grottoes, take a moment to absorb the stunning view back down the coast. Still clearly visible is the route of the railway line, now mostly a dirt road, built by the British through the hillside in 1943 to extend the Cairo–Tel Aviv–Haifa line to Beirut. After the descent, you can see the 12-minute audiovisual presentation called *The Sea and the Cliff.*

The incredible caves beneath the cliff have been carved out by relentless waves pounding away at the white chalky rock for countless years. Footpaths inside the cliff itself lead from one huge cave to another, while the sound of waves echoes among the water-sprayed rocky walls. Huge bursts of seawater plunge into pools at your feet (behind protective rails). It's slippery, so hang on to the children. ☎*04/985–7109 or 1800/229–494* ☀*www.rosh-hanikra.com* ✉*NIS 42* ☀*Nov.–Mar., Sat.–Thurs. 8:30–4, Fri. 9–4; Apr.–June, Sat.–Thurs. 9–6, Fri. 9–4; July–Aug., Sat.–Thurs. 8:30 AM–11 PM, Fri. 8:30–4. Call to verify hrs.*

WHERE TO EAT

$$ ✕**Brew House.** This bright and breezy spot for Israeli fare has an unexpected name, especially since Israel is better known for orange juice than

ISRAELI   for beer. There's a fabulous view of the sea swirling and crashing below. The selection of beers on tap—all produced in the Golan Heights—range from pale ale to a tangy red lager. Starters include a bagel with corned beef and a baked potato with garlic sauce and fried onions. As a main course, the appealing casserole of beef and root vegetables simmered in beer is a sure hit, as are franks and sauerkraut, steaks, and burgers. ✉*Top of the Rosh Hanikra cliff* ☎*04/952–0159* ═*AE, DC, MC, V* ☀*Closed Sat.*

Lower Galilee

WITH NAZARETH, TIBERIAS, AND THE SEA OF GALILEE

WORD OF MOUTH

"We enjoyed Nazareth (walking through the old city and imagining where the carpenter's workshop would be), and we traveled north through the Sea of Galilee. Don't miss the museum at Ginosar with the recovered 2,000-year-old boat. We drove from Jerusalem, and it was easy. But I would say skip Tiberias itself."

—laurie_ann

WELCOME TO LOWER GALILEE

National park at Beit She'an

TOP REASONS TO GO

★ **Sunset on the Sea of Galilee:** The lake at sundown is always evocative, often beautiful, and occasionally spectacular. Walk a beach, sip a drink, or take a sail as dusk slowly settles.

★ **Zippori:** The distant past is palpable at this archaeological site, once a worldly Jewish and Hellenistic city. Set amid woods, it has the loveliest ancient mosaics in the land.

★ **Nazareth:** Tradition and modernity collide in the town where Jesus grew up. Today it is a city of baklava and BMWs, new politics and ancient passions. Talk to a local as you sample Middle Eastern delicacies.

★ **Mt. Gilboa:** This little-visited region offers local beauty and grand views for the independent traveler who has a bit of time and no checklist of must-see famous sites.

★ **A spiritual source:** Tune your ear to the Galilee's spiritual reverberations. Listen as pilgrims chant a mass at the Mount of Beatitudes or sit meditatively on Tabgha's shore.

1 Jezreel and Jordan Valleys. Crisscrossed by ancient highways that once linked Egypt and Mesopotamia, the scenic Jezreel and Jordan valleys are studded with major archaeological and historical sites. Megiddo, corrupted in Greek as Armageddon, is known for a biblical battle and is prophesied to be the site of a future one. Zippori, also called Sepphoris, is a site with Jewish and Christian links. The Roman ruins at Beit She'an evoke the glory of one the richest cities in the eastern Mediterranean.

2 Nazareth and the Galilee Hills. The once-sleepy town of Nazareth, the site of Jesus's boyhood, has boomed in recent decades to become a regional center. The nearby hills, such as Mount Tabor and Mount Gilboa, are both biblical byways and part of the reforested landscape many find so entrancing.

GETTING ORIENTED

The Hebrew word *gal* means "wave," and the Lower Galilee is indeed a hilly country, with deep valleys framed by mountain ridges. The Jordan River, not much more than a creek, cuts through the topography on the eastern border, first draining into the freshwater Sea of Galilee and then flowing south toward the Dead Sea. The Galilee is the storied land where King Saul lost his life fighting the Philistines; where the Romans built cities such as Beit She'an; where Jesus, who grew up in Nazareth, carried out much of his ministry; and where the Crusaders built and lost a kingdom. The lakeside resort city of Tiberias beckons with its hot springs and history.

3 Tiberias and the Sea of Galilee. The tranquil Sea of Galilee was the site for much of Jesus's ministry. But you don't have to be a Christian to fall in love with the mystic charm of this harp-shaped lake. A number of historic hotels, inns, ranches, and private villas ring the lake. The hot springs at Tiberias and Hammat Gader have been attracting guests since the time of Augustus Caesar.

Olive grove

Basilica of the Annunciation, Nazareth

6

LOWER GALILEE PLANNER

When To Go

The Galilee is prettiest in the spring months of March and April when it is covered with wild flowers, and its hills are draped in green. Summer can be torrid. Avoid the Sea of Galilee during Passover (March–April) and the High Holidays and Sukkot (September–October). Although the weather is great at these times, half the country vacations here; rates soar.

Some hotels charge high-season rates during July and August; this is also true the week of Christmas. Weekends in general (Thursday night through Saturday night) are more crowded; some hotels hike rates substantially.

Special Walks

Two annual *Tza'adot* (Big Walks) take place in March or April, one along the shore of the Sea of Galilee (2½ km [1½ mi] and 9 km [5½ mi]), the other along the trails of Mt. Gilboa (routes range from 6 km [4 mi] to 40 km [25 mi] over two days). These mass rambles attract folks from all over the country and abroad.

A promenade suitable for jogging follows the lakeshore for 5 km (3 mi) from Tiberias south; the views are lovely.

Getting Here and Around

Bus Travel: The Egged bus cooperative provides regular service from Jerusalem, Tel Aviv, and Haifa to Nazareth, Beit She'an, Afula, and Tiberias. There is no direct service from Ben Gurion International Airport; change in Tel Aviv or Haifa. There are several buses an hour from Tel Aviv to Afula (1½ hours). Bus 842 (*yashir,* or "direct") is quickest; Buses 829, 830, and 835 are express, stopping at major stations en route. Bus 823 from Afula to Nazareth (20 minutes) is infrequent. The 830 and 835 continue from Afula to Tiberias (about an hour). The 829 and 843 link Afula to Beit She'an (20 minutes) three times a day.

To get from Haifa to Tiberias, take the slow Bus 430 (about an hour), which leaves hourly from Merkazit Hamifratz. From the same Haifa station, the slow Bus 301 leaves two or three times an hour for Afula. Buses from Jerusalem to Beit She'an and Tiberias (Buses 961, 963, 966, and the slower 948) depart roughly hourly; change in Beit She'an for Afula, where you change again for Nazareth. Buses 961 and 963 continue to Tiberias. The ride to Beit She'an is about two hours, to Tiberias another 25 minutes. Bus 431 connects Nazareth and Tiberias once every two hours.

Car Travel: Driving is the best way to explore the Lower Galilee. Driving time from Tel Aviv or Jerusalem to Tiberias is two hours. Some newer four-lane highways are excellent, but some secondary roads may be in need of repair.

Signposting is clear (and usually in English), with route numbers clearly marked. Most sights are indicated by brown signs. The Lower Galilee is served by a number of highways. Route 90, going up the Jordan Valley to Tiberias and on to Metulla on the Lebanese border, is the most convenient road from Jerusalem. Routes 2 and 4, both multilane expressways, lead north from Tel Aviv. Turn east onto Route 65, then north onto Route 60 to get to Nazareth. Stay on Route 65 and turn east on Route 77 to reach Tiberias. While Route 6 is a modern superhighway, it is also an electronic toll road. If you're driving a rental car, you'll be charged for using it.

⇨ *For more information on getting here and around, see Travel Smart Israel.*

Dining

Tiberias in particular and the Sea of Galilee are a far live-lier culinary proposition than other parts of Lower Galilee. Some places in the countryside are worth going out of your way for, and there are satisfying if unmemorable local eat-eries. Restaurant attire is casual.

The local specialty is the native St. Peter's fish (tilapia), though most restaurants serve the (still excellent) pond-bred variety. Meat dishes tend to be Middle Eastern: shashlik and kebabs (ground meat grilled on skewers) accompanied by hummus, pickles, and french fries. Most economical are *shawarma* (slices of spit-grilled turkey meat served in pita bread) and falafel. The cheapest eats are always at the stands at a town's central bus station.

Lodging

Tiberias, the region's tourist center, has hotels for budgets from deluxe to economy. Within a 20- to 30-minute drive are excellent guesthouses, some run by kibbutz residents and some on the Sea of Galilee. Nazareth has a couple of deluxe hotels and several older inexpensive ones that cater primarily to Christian pilgrim groups but also attract individual travelers and Israelis. Also in Nazareth, and to a lesser extent around Tiberias, are hospices run by Christian orders.

Bed-and-breakfasts have sprung up in profusion. Many are in or adjacent to private homes in rural farming communities; others are within kibbutzim. These are a good value, especially for families.

Many "guesthouses," as upgraded youth hostels are now called, are suitable for families; these are generally the cheapest deals.

WHAT IT COSTS

	¢	$	$$	$$$	$$$$
Restaurants	Under NIS 32	NIS 32–NIS 49	NIS 50–NIS 75	NIS 76–NIS 100	over NIS 100
Hotels	Under $120	$120–$200	$201–$300	$301–$400	over $400

Restaurant prices are per person for a main course at dinner in NIS (Israeli shekels). Hotel prices are in US dollars, for two people in a standard double room in high season. Non-Israeli citizens paying in foreign currency are exempt from the 15.5% VAT tax on hotel rooms.

Planning Your Time

It's possible to get a feeling for this region in a few days, but you can expand your trip to include some highlights of the Upper Galilee and the Golan including Tzfat (Safed). Tiberias, with its many accommodations, or the Sea of Galilee region is a good base for exploring archaeological sites—Beit She'an is impressive—as well as sites associated with the ministry of Jesus. Nazareth is worth a trip, either from Tiberias or en route to it from other areas. The Galilee is is a low-key area with some lovely national parks and natural sites, including Mt. Tabor, if you choose to linger.

Both Egged Tours and United Tours have one-day tours around the region from Jerusalem and Tel Aviv that take in Nazareth, the Sea of Galilee, and other highlights.

Top Festivals

Ein Gev, on the eastern shore of the Sea of Galilee, has an Israeli-music festival in the spring. Beit She'an revives its ancient Roman theater for a short series of events in October, and in May and December, Jacob's Ladder—the twice-annual folk festival—fills the air above Nof Ginosar, on the Sea of Galilee, with traditional folk and country music of the British Isles and North America.

By Mike Rogoff
Updated by Gil Zohar

The Lower Galilee is a history-soaked region where scores of events in the Hebrew Bible and the New Testament took place. Blessed with forested hills, fertile valleys, gushing springs, and the mystical lake called the Sea of Galilee, it has strong appeal for many people. The graves of Jewish, Christian, Muslim, and Druze holy men attract those seeking spiritual solace. However, this region is also the scene of earthly delights, including fine restaurants and spas.

To most Israelis, the Galilee is synonymous with "the North", a land of nature reserves and national parks. In short, they would claim, it's a great place to visit, but they wouldn't want to live there: it's provincial and remote. Still, the Lower Galilee has its own quiet beauty and varied landscape. Whatever your agenda—spiritual, historical, recreational, or restful—take time to savor the region. Follow a hiking trail above the Sea of Galilee. Wade through fields of rare irises in the spring. Bathe in a warm mineral spa. Buy some good goat cheese.

Farming and tourism form the economic base. The region's *kibbutzim* and a smaller number of *moshavim* (Jewish family-farm villages) are concentrated in the Jezreel and Jordan valleys and around the Sea of Galilee. The rockier hill country is predominantly Arab (*Israeli* Arab; this is not disputed territory), and for the last half-century it has been a challenge for the two communities—Jewish and Arab—to cultivate neighborly relations despite the ethnic tensions that swirl around them. By and large, they have succeeded.

Culture and entertainment are not this region's strong suits. A number of annual festivals and other events are the highlights. Tiberias's pubs and restaurants probably come closest to providing lively nightlife, but there are worse ways to spend an evening than sitting by a moonlit lake washing down a good St. Peter's fish or a lamb shashlik with an excellent Israeli wine.

About 50 km (31 mi) square, the Lower Galilee embraces three distinct regions: the Jezreel and Jordan valleys, traversing the southern part of the region from west to east; Nazareth and the rugged hill country just to the north; and the Sea of Galilee. The fertile Jezreel Valley, known in Hebrew simply as Ha'emek—the Valley—is sentimentally, if not scientifically, perceived by many Israelis as distinct from the rest of the Lower Galilee. The valley towns of Afula, Migdal Ha'emek, and Beit She'an (despite the wonderful antiquities) have little to recommend them. The larger hill town of Nazareth, the region's administrative center, has more character and deserves some time. To the north, the steep hillsides above the Sea of Galilee merge into the Upper Galilee, while Route 85 west follows the Beit Hakerem Valley, the natural division between the two regions. Toward the Mediterranean Sea, the hills flatten out as you reach the coastal plain; Route 70 follows the region's western edge.

Most travelers come up Route 65 (the Wadi Ara Pass) from the Mediterranean coast, or up the Jordan Valley (Route 90) from Jerusalem. While some stop at the national parks of Megiddo or Beit She'an, most visitors zip through the Jezreel Valley on their way to the recreation grounds farther north. Slow down: there are no fewer than 11 national parks in this region.

JEZREEL AND JORDAN VALLEYS

"Highways of the world cross Galilee in all directions," wrote the eminent Victorian scholar George Adam Smith in 1898. The great international highway of antiquity, the Via Maris (Way of the Sea), swept up the Mediterranean coast from Egypt and broke inland along three separate passes through the hills to emerge in the Jezreel Valley before continuing northeast to Damascus and Mesopotamia. It made the Jezreel Valley a convenient and frequent battleground. In fact, the Jezreel Valley heard the clash of arms so often that the very name of its most commanding tell—Har Megiddo (Mt. Megiddo), or Armageddon—became a New Testament synonym for the final apocalyptic battle of all time. Today, this and other ancient sites such as Beit She'an remain highlights here.

On a topographical map, the Jezreel Valley appears as an equilateral triangle with sides about 40 km (25 mi) long, edged by low mountains and with a narrow extension east to Beit She'an, in the Jordan Rift. From there, the Jordan Valley stretches like a ribbon north to the Sea of Galilee. Your first impression will be one of lush farmland as far as the eye can see. But as recently as 50 years ago, malarial swamps still blighted the area; some pioneering settlements had cemeteries before their first buildings were completed.

With a few exceptions, restaurants in this rustic area are confined to roadside cafeterias, lunchtime diners at or near parks, and small restaurants and snack bars in the towns of Afula and Beit She'an.

BEIT SHE'ARIM

20 km (12½ mi) southeast of Haifa, 25 km (15½ mi) west of Nazareth.

GETTING HERE AND AROUND

Driving from Tel Aviv, take Route 4 (the old Tel Aviv–Haifa Highway) to Furadis Junction, then turn east on Route 70. Continue to Yokneam Junction, then take Route 722 to Hashomrim Junction. Take the first left, and continue until you reach the national park.

EXPLORING

Chalk slopes are honeycombed with catacombs around the attractively landscaped site of ancient **Beit She'arim**—today Beit She'arim National Park. Orthodox Jews come on pilgrimage here to the Tomb of Judah ha-Nasi. But you don't need to be religious to appreciate the role this vast necropolis has played for centuries in the development of rabbinic Judaism. Only a few of the catacombs are open to the public. Equipped with a flashlight and free park brochure and map, you'll discover ornately carved sarcophagi that attest to the complex intercultural relations in the Roman world.

A Jewish town flourished here after (and to some extent because of) the eclipse of Jerusalem brought about by Titus's legions in AD 70 and its reconstruction as a pagan town by Hadrian in AD 135. For generations Jews were denied access to their holy city and its venerated burial ground on the Mount of Olives. The center of Jewish life and religious authority shifted first to Yavne, in the southern coastal plain, and then northward to the Lower Galilee for several centuries.

By around AD 200 Beit She'arim had become the unofficial Jewish capital, owing its brief preeminence to the enormous stature of a native son. Rabbi Yehuda "ha-Nasi" (the Patriarch: a title conferred on the nominal leader of the Jewish community) was responsible both for the city's inner workings and for its relations with its Roman masters. Alone among his contemporaries, Yehuda ha-Nasi combined worldly diplomatic skills with scholarly authority and spiritual leadership.

The rabbi eventually moved east to Zippori because of its more salubrious climate, and there he gathered the great Jewish sages of his day and compiled the Mishnah, which remains the definitive interpretation of biblical precepts for religious Jews. Nonetheless, it was in his hometown of Beit She'arim that Yehuda ha-Nasi was finally laid to rest. If Beit She'arim was a magnet for scholars and petitioners in his lifetime, it became a virtual shrine after his death. With Jerusalem still off-limits, the town became the most prestigious burial site in the Jewish world for almost 150 years.

Two major expeditions in the 1930s and '50s uncovered a vast series of 20 **catacombs**. The largest of these is open to the public, with 24 chambers containing more than 200 sarcophagi. A wide range of carved Jewish and Roman symbols and more than 250 funerary inscriptions in Greek, Hebrew, Aramaic, and Palmyrene throughout the site testify to the great distances some people traveled—from Yemen and Mesopotamia, for instance—to be buried here. Without exception, the sarcophagi

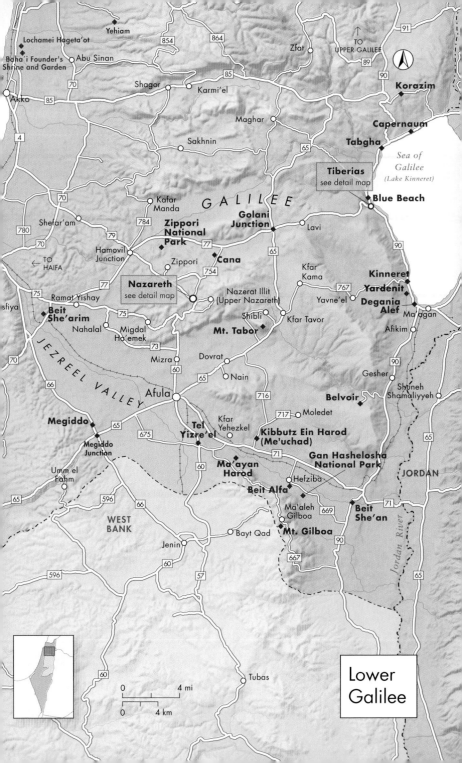

Lower Galilee

were plundered over the centuries by grave robbers seeking the posses-sions with which the dead were often interred. ✉ *Follow the signs in Kiryat Tivon, off Rte. 75 or 722* 🕾 *04/984–1643* ⊕ *www.parks.org.il/ ParksENG* ✑ *NIS 18* ⊘ *Apr.–Sept., Sat.–Thurs. 8–5, Fri. 8–4; Oct.–Mar., Sat.–Thurs. 8–4, Fri. 8–3.*

MEGIDDO

★ *20 km (12½ mi) southeast of Beit She'arim, 2 km (1¼ mi) north of the Megiddo Junction, 12 km (7½ mi) west of Afula.*

GETTING HERE AND AROUND

A car is the best way to get here, as the site is poorly served by public transportation. You can reach the site by taxi from Afula.

ESSENTIALS

Taxi Contact Yizre'el (✉ *Afula* 🕾 *04/652-3111).*

EXPLORING

Recognized by UNESCO as a World Heritage Site in 2005, Megiddo is an ancient city built on even older foundations dating back to the bib-lical era. Today called **Tel Megiddo National Park,** it's one of the region's most impressive ruins. Allocate about 90 minutes to see the park.

Most people are fascinated by the ancient water system. In a masterful stroke, King Ahab's engineers dug a deep shaft and a horizontal tunnel through solid rock to reach the vital subterranean spring outside the city walls. With access secure, the spring's original opening was per-manently blocked. There is nothing more than a trickle today, the flow perhaps choked by subsequent earthquakes. As you descend 180 steps through the shaft, traverse the 65-yard-long tunnel under the ancient city wall, and climb up 83 steps at the other end, look for the ancient chisel marks and hewn steps. A visit to the water system at noon offers a reprieve from the summer heat.

Apart from the ancient water system, don't miss the partially restored Late Bronze Age gate, perhaps the very one stormed by Egyptian troops circa 1468 BC, as described in the victory stela of Pharaoh Thutmose III. A larger gate farther up the mound was long identified with King Solomon (10th century BC)—Megiddo was one of his regional military centers—but has been redated by some scholars to the time of Ahab, a half-century later. There is consensus, however, on the ruined stables at the summit of the tell: they were certainly built by Ahab, whose large chariot army is recorded in an Assyrian inscription.

Evidence indicates prehistoric habitation here as well, but among the earliest remains of the *city* of Megiddo are a round altar dating from the Early Bronze Age and the outlines of several Early Bronze Age temples, almost 5,000 years old, visible in the trench between the two fine lookout points.

A tiny museum at the site's entrance offers good visual aids, including maps, a video, and a model of the tell. A small gift shop alongside the museum sells handsome silver and gold jewelry, some incorporating pieces of ancient Roman glass. There is also a cafeteria. ✉ *National Park, Rte. 66* 🕾 *04/659–0316* ⊕ *www.parks.org.il/ParksENG* ✑ *NIS*

The archaeological layers at Megiddo include prehistoric remains and an ingenious biblical-era water system.

23 ⏱ *Apr.–Sept., Sat.–Thurs. 8–5, Fri. and Jewish holiday eves 8–4; Oct.–Mar., Sat.–Thurs. 8–4, Fri. and Jewish holiday eves 8–3.*

EN
ROUTE

From the Afula road (Route 60), Route 675 heads southeast through a small farming region called the Ta'anach. Just 500 yards past the intersection with Route 60, at the location of the Kibbutz Yizre'el, turn left and then immediately right to the low-rise **Tel Yizre'el.** This is the site of the Old Testament city of Jezreel, King Ahab's winter capital. Here he coveted Naboth's vineyard (I Kings 21), and his Phoenician wife, Jezebel, met the gruesome death predicted by the prophet Elijah. The excavated ruins are indecipherable, but the site provides a magnificent view of the valley.

MT. GILBOA AND ENVIRONS

Fodor's Choice
★

24 km (15 mi) southeast of Megiddo via Rtes. 675 and 667, 10 km (7 mi) east of Afula.

Visit Mt. Gilboa in February or March and you'll find yourself surrounded by people enraptured with the delicate purple iris native to these slopes. The views of the valley below and the hills of Galilee beyond are great year-round, but on a clear winter or spring day they're amazing, reaching as far as the snowcapped Mt. Hermon, far to the north. Afternoon is the best time to come.

Mt. Gilboa—actually a steep mountain range rather than a single peak—is geographically a spur of the far greater Samaria Range (the biblical Mt. Ephraim, today the West Bank) to the southwest. Half the mountain has been reforested with evergreens, while the other half has been left in pristine rockiness. Environmentalists prefer the latter, as it protects the wildflowers that splatter the slopes with color every spring. From the gravel parking area off Route 667, easy and well-marked trails wind through the natural habitat of the rare black (actually deep purple) iris, which draws hordes of Israelis every spring.

Three thousand years ago, the Israelites were routed by the Philistines on Mt. Gilboa. Saul, the nation's first king, was wounded and took his own life on the battlefield. The next day, the Bible relates, when the Philistines came to plunder their fallen foes, they discovered the bodies of Saul and his sons. Seeking trophies, "they cut off his head, and stripped off his armor, and they fastened his body to the wall of [Beit She'an]" (I Samuel 31). In his eulogy for Saul and his son Jonathan, king-to-be David cursed the battlefield where "thy glory, O Israel" was slain: "Let there be no dew or rain upon you" (II Samuel 1).

GETTING HERE AND AROUND

Driving from Afula, follow Route 71 east, turn right on Route 67, then left on Route 667. There is no reliable public transportation.

EXPLORING

Ma'ayan Harod *(Spring of Harod)* , at the foot of Mt. Gilboa, is a small national park with huge eucalyptus trees and a big swimming pool fed by a spring. Today it's a bucolic picnic spot, but almost 3,200 years ago, Gideon, the reluctant hero of the biblical Book of Judges, organized his troops to fight a Midianite army that had invaded from the desert. At God's command—in order to emphasize the miraculous nature of the coming victory—Gideon dismissed more than two-thirds of the warriors and then, to reduce the force still more, selected only those who lapped water from the spring. Equipped with swords, ram's horns, and flaming torches concealed in clay jars, this tiny army of 300 divided into three companies and surrounded the Midianite camp across the valley in the middle of the night. At a prearranged signal, the attackers shouted, blew their horns, and smashed the jars, revealing the flaming torches, whereupon the Midianites panicked and fled, securing an Israelite victory.

The spring has seen other armies in other ages. It was here in 1260 that the Egypt-based Mamluks stopped the invasion of the hitherto invincible Mongols. And in the 1930s, the woods above the spring hid Jewish self-defense squads training in defiance of British military law. ⊠*Off Rte. 71* ☎*04/653–2211* ⊕*www.parks.org.il/ParksENG* ☎*NIS 33* ☉*Apr.–Sept., Sat.–Thurs. 8–5, Fri. and Jewish holiday eves 8–4; Oct.–Mar., Sat.–Thurs. 8–4, Fri. and Jewish holiday eves 8–2.*

NEED A BREAK?   At Michal and Avi Barkin's goat farm (⊠*1 km [½ mi] east of Navot Junction [Rtes. 71 and 675], Kfar Yehezkel* ☎*054/649-2799*), you can sample their excellent cheeses over a glass of wine or coffee in the wooden reception room or enjoy a light meal of salads, toasted sandwiches, or hot stuffed pastries. The farm is open Thursday from 7 PM, Friday 10 AM–2 PM and again at 7 PM, and Saturday from 10 AM. It doesn't close until well into the evening.

CLOSE UP

Kibbutz Life Now & Then

The founding fathers and mothers would probably be bewildered by life on a 21st-century kibbutz (meaning a collective settlement, but literally translated as "a gathering"). Many of Israel's founders came from Russia in the early 20th century, inspired by Zionist ideals of returning to their ancestral homeland and a work ethic that regarded manual labor as an almost spiritual value. They were socialists who believed "from each according to his ability, to each according to his need."

EARLY DAYS

Degania, the first kibbutz, was founded in 1909 on the shores of the Sea of Galilee, where ten men and two women began to work the land. The utopian ideology, in which individual desires were subordinated to the needs of the community, was wedded to the need for a close-knit communal structure, in order to cope with forbidding terrain and a hostile neighborhood. Life was arduous, but their numbers grew.

Kibbutzim played a considerable role in molding the fledgling state, absorbing immigrants and developing agriculture. By 1950, two years after Israel's independence, there were more than 200 kibbutzim. Their egalitarian ethos meant that chores and responsibility—but also ownership of the means of production—was shared by all. The kibbutz movement became the world's largest communitarian movement.

GROWTH AND CHALLENGE

With time, many kibbutzim introduced light industry or tourism enterprises, and some became successful businesses. The standard of living improved, and kibbutzim took advantage of easy bank loans. When Israel's hyperinflation reached 454% during the mid-1980s, many communities found themselves

bankrupt. Change became inevitable, and the movement peaked around 1990, when the almost 270 kibbutzim across the country reached 130,000 members. (An individual kibbutz can range from fewer than 100 to more than 1,000 members.)

THE KIBBUTZ TODAY

In today's Israel, many young "kibbutzniks," after compulsory military service or university studies, have found the kibbutz ethos stifling and have opted for the individualism and material attractions of city life. Despite the changes, city folk, volunteers, and tourists are still drawn to this rural environment, which offers a slower pace.

Only some 15% of kibbutz members now work in agriculture, though they account for a significant proportion of the national production. Industry, services, and tourism—including kibbutz guesthouses and hotels—are the real sources of income. Differential wage systems have been introduced, unemployment is growing, and foreign laborers often provide menial labor in fields and factories. All kibbutzim have abandoned children's dormitories, instead allowing parents to raise their children in a family home.

Many members of the older generation have become distressed by what they see as the contamination of pioneering principles. But reality bites hard, and ironically, only those kibbutzim that succeed economically can afford to remain socialist.

6

Panoramic views of the Galilee draw hikers to explore Mt. Gilboa.

Across Route 71 from Mt. Gilboa, **Kibbutz Ein Harod (Me'uchad)**, not to be confused with its neighbor to the west, Kibbutz Ein Harod (Ichud), has two interesting reasons to visit. Its **Museum of Art Ein Harod** (⊠ *Rte. 71, opposite gas station* ☎ *04/653–1670* ⊕ *www.museumein harod.org.il* ⊠ *NIS 16* ☉ *Sun.–Thurs. 9–4:30, Fri. and Jewish holiday eves 9–1:30, Sat. and Jewish holidays 10–4:30*) is housed in an early example of modernist architecture. (The building, which uses diffused natural lighting, attracts architecture buffs.) It houses a permanent collection of Jewish art spanning cultures and genres. An English-speaking guide can sometimes be arranged in advance. **Bet Sturman** (⊠ *Rte. 71* ☎ *04/653–3284* ⊠ *NIS 15* ☉ *Sun.–Thurs. 8–3, Fri. 8–1, Sat. and Jewish holidays 11–3*) is a museum of the region's natural history and human settlement. There is a video in English.

☾ **Gan Hashelosha National Park,** commonly known as Sachne, was developed around a warm spring (28°C, or 82°F, most of the year) and a wide, still stream deep enough to dive into at spots, with artificial cascades in others. Lifeguards are on duty. Facilities include changing rooms for bathers, two snack bars, and a restaurant. Apart from swimming, this is also a very popular picnic spot. ⊠ *Off Rte. 669* ☎ *04/658–1017* ⊕ *www.parks.org.il/ParksENG* ⊠ *NIS 33* ☉ *Apr.–Sept., Sat.–Thurs. 8–5, Fri. and Jewish holiday eves 8–4; Oct.–Mar., Sat.–Thurs. 8–4, Fri. and Jewish holiday eves 8–3.*

☾ **Gan-Garoo,** a 4-acre zoo of exclusively Australian wildlife, has different kinds of kangaroo and wallabies, koala bears, and kookaburras, emus, and other exotic birds. An enclosure of snakes, lizards, and other reptiles opened in 2008. English-speaking guides are on hand for groups.

✉ *Rte. 669, at entrance to Gan Hashelosha* ☎ *04/648–8060* 💲 *NIS 39* 🕐 *Sun.–Thurs. 9–4, Fri. 9–3, Sat. 9–5; usually July and Aug., Sun.–Thurs. to 8, Fri. to 4, Sat. 9–5.*

Now part of Beit Alfa Synagogue National Park, the ancient synagogue of **Beit Alfa** was discovered in 1928 by members of Kibbutz Hefziba who were digging an irrigation trench. Their tools hit a hard surface, and excavation uncovered a multicolored mosaic floor, almost entirely preserved. The art is somewhat childlike, but that, too, is part of its charm. An Aramaic inscription dates the building to the reign of Byzantine emperor Justinian in the second quarter of the 6th century AD; a Greek inscription credits the workmanship to one Marianos and his son, Aninas. In keeping with Jewish tradition, the synagogue faces Jerusalem, with an apse at the far end to hold the ark. The building faithfully copies the architecture of the Byzantine basilicas of the day, with a nave and two side aisles, and the doors lead to a small narthex and a onetime outdoor atrium. Stairs indicate there was once an upper story.

Classic Jewish symbols in the top mosaic panel leave no doubt that the building was a synagogue: a holy ark flanked by lions, a menorah, and a shofar (ram's horn). The middle panel, however, is the most intriguing: it is filled with human figures depicting the seasons, the zodiac, and—even more incredible for a Jewish house of worship—the Greek sun god, Helios, driving his chariot across the sky. These images indicate more liberal times theologically, when the prohibition against making graven images was perhaps not applied to two-dimensional art. The last panel tells the story of Abraham's near-sacrifice of his son Isaac, captioned in Hebrew. Take time to watch the lighthearted but informative film. Allocate 45 minutes for a visit here. ✉ *Kibbutz Hefziba, Rte. 669* ☎ *04/653–2004* ⊕ *www.parks.org.il/ParksENG* 💲 *NIS 18* 🕐 *Apr.–Sept., Sat.–Thurs. 8–5, Fri. and Jewish holiday eves 8–4; Oct.–Mar., Sat.–Thurs. 8–4, Fri. and Jewish holiday eves 8–3.*

WHERE TO EAT AND STAY

$$ ✕ **Herb Farm on Mount Gilboa.** The sweeping panorama from the wooden
MODERN ISRAELI deck and picture windows is attraction enough, but this family restau-
Fodor'sChoice rant—operated by Yossi Mass, his wife Penina, and their son Oren—
★ is also known for its fresh herbs. The menu is partly seasonal, partly weekly inspiration. Homemade bread and a "salad basket" of antipasti are fine starters, but try one of the imaginative salads. Tempting entrées might include a tart of shallots, forest mushrooms, and goat cheese, or a colorful pie of beef, lamb, goose breast, tomatoes, pine nuts, and basil. Desserts make for an agonizing decision, so share. ✉ *Rte. 667, 3 km (2 mi) off Rte. 675* ☎ *04/653–1093* ✍ *Reservations essential* ▤ *AE, DC, MC, V* 🕐 *Closed Sun.*

$$$ ✕ **Mizra Grill.** A short drive from the Gilboa region, Mizra is best known
ISRAELI as a superior cafeteria with an excellent salad bar. In the late afternoon it becomes a good sit-down dinner restaurant, serving a variety of grilled meats. Kibbutz Mizra produces high-quality pork products, making its restaurant a magnet for those indifferent to kosher prohibitions. There is an adjacent high-end deli-supermarket. ✉ *Rte. 60, entrance to Mizra* ☎ *04/642–9214* ✍ *Reservations essential* ▤ *AE, DC, MC, V.*

$ ⌷ **Ma'ayan Harod Guest House.** An example of how the facilities have been improved at many Israel Youth Hostel Association lodgings, rooms here are a cut above the usual hostel offerings, with TVs, refrigerators, and coffeemakers. The somewhat spartan bungalows have two single beds rather than a double bed. **Pros:** convenient to national parks; air-conditioned rooms. **Cons:** rowdy teenage crowd; no evening activities. ⌧*Gidona* ☎*04/653–1669* ✉*mayanh@iyha.org.il* ⌁*28 rooms* ♿*In-room: refrigerator* ⊟*AE, DC, MC, V* ⍾*BP.*

SPORTS AND THE OUTDOORS

On the international calendar, the annual **Gilboa Big Walk** *(Tza'adat Hagilboa)* takes place over a Friday and Saturday in March, when the famous black irises are in bloom. For the intrepid, there are two one-day hikes of 20 km (12½ mi) each; for the more casual walker—or families—there are 6-km (4-mi) walks on both Friday and Saturday and an additional 11-km (7-mi) route on Saturday. All routes end at Ma'ayan Harod; leave your car there and take the transportation provided to the starting point. It's best to register in advance. For details, contact **Hagilboa Community Centers** (⌂*M. P. Gilboa 18120* ☎*04/653–3361*).

BEIT SHE'AN

23 km (14 mi) southeast of Afula, 39 km (24 mi) south of Tiberias.

The modern town of Beit She'an has little to offer visitors, but the past beckons. Unlike some archaeological sites that appear to be just piles of rocks, ancient Beit She'an is a gloriously rich ruin, complete with bathhouses, pagan temples, and public theaters. It's one of the country's most notable sites.

GETTING HERE AND AROUND

The national park is northeast of modern Beit She'an. From Route 90, turn west on Sha'ul Hamelech Street, and right after Bank Leumi.

EXPLORING

★ At the intersection of the Jordan and Jezreel valleys, this town has one spectacular site, **Beit She'an National Park.** A Roman theater was excavated in the 1960s, but the rest of Scythopolis, as this great Late Roman and Byzantine (2nd–6th centuries AD) city was known, came to light only in more recent excavations. The enormous haul of marble statuary and friezes says much about the opulence of Scythopolis in its heyday—especially when you remember that there are no marble quarries in Israel, and all that stone was imported from what is today Turkey, Greece, or even Italy.

A free site map available at the visitor center gives a good layout. In summer it's best to arrive early in the morning, as the heat quickly becomes insufferable. Better yet, consider returning in the evening for the **sound-and-light spectacle,** inaugurated in 2008 and presented Monday, Wednesday, and Thursday from 7 PM to 9:30 PM and Saturday from 7:30 PM to 9:30 PM. Tickets cost NIS 40; reserve in advance and check times. Scythopolis's **downtown area,** now exposed, has masterfully engineered colonnaded main streets converging on a central plaza that once boasted a pagan temple, a decorative fountain, and a monument. An

The remains of the wealthy late Roman and Byzantine city of Beit She'an include a large public bathhouse.

elaborate Byzantine bathhouse covered more than 1¼ acres. On the main thoroughfare are the remains of Scythopolis's amphitheater, where gladiatorial combats were once the order of the day.

The high tell dominating the site to the north was the location of Old Testament **Canaanite/Israelite Beit She'an** 2,500–3,500 years ago. Don't climb to the top for the meager archaeological remains, but the fine panoramic view of the surrounding valleys and the superb bird's-eye view of the main excavations are worth every gasp.

The semicircular **Roman theater** was built of contrasting black basalt and white limestone blocks around AD 200, when Scythopolis was at its height. Although the upper *cavea*, or tier, has not survived, the theater is the largest and best preserved in Israel, with an estimated original capacity of 7,000–10,000 people. The large stage and part of the *scaena frons* (backdrop) behind it have been restored, and Beit She'an hosts autumn performances as in days of yore.

✉ *Off Sha'ul Hamelech St.* ☎ *04/658–7189* ⊕ *www.parks.org.il/Park-sENG* 💲 *NIS 23* ⏱ *Apr.–Sept., Sat.–Thurs. 8–5, Fri. and Jewish holiday eves 8–4; Oct.–Mar., Sat.–Thurs. 8–4, Fri. and Jewish holiday eves 8–3.*

NEED A BREAK?

Bis Le'chol Kis (✉ *24 Merkaz Rasco* ☎ *04/658–7278*) translates loosely as "a bite for every budget." Falafel and shawarma are their thing, and they do it well. Instead of pita bread, you can opt to have your turkey-meat shawarma in a fresh, home-baked baguette. Air-conditioning in summer is a welcome relief. Look for this place in a small commercial center right next to the Egged Central Bus Station.

WHERE TO STAY

¢   ⚅ **Beit She'an Guest House.** This modern limestone and basalt building is wrapped around a courtyard shaded by palm trees. Many rooms, including suites with private balconies, have great views east over the Jordan Valley. All are simply but agreeably furnished. The lobby café has comfortable cane chairs in which to enjoy pizzas and sandwiches. Breakfast is included; other meals are available on request. Make sure to see the memorable mural humorously depicting life in ancient Beit She'an. **Pros:** convenient to the national park; pretty pool area. **Cons:** sometimes noisy with teenage groups; no evening entertainment. ⊠ *126 Menachem Begin Blvd. [Rte. 90]* ☎04/606–0760 ⊕ *www.youth-hostels.org.il/english.html* ⬎*60 rooms, 2 suites* ⬥*In-room: no phone, refrigerator. In-hotel: pool, Internet terminal, parking (free)* ▭*AE, DC, MC, V* ⎮❂⎮*BP.*

NIGHTLIFE AND THE ARTS

The marvelous **Roman theater** (☎*04/658–7189*) hosts concerts, mostly by Israeli artists, every October.

BELVOIR

Rte. 717; turnoff 12 km (7½ mi) north of Beit She'an; continue 5 km (3 mi) to site.

GETTING HERE AND AROUND

Driving north on Route 90 from Beit She'an, turn west on Route 717. While any bus traversing Route 90 will let off at the road, the fortress is high above the valley. It's a long hike, and don't count on getting a ride. The road from Ein Harod via Moledet is passable in dry weather but in very bad condition in places.

EXPLORING

The Crusaders chose their site well: **Belvoir,** they called it—"beautiful view"—and it was the most invincible fortress in the land. The Hebrew name "Kochav Hayarden" (the Star of the Jordan) and the Arabic "Kaukab el Hauwa" (the Star of the Wind) underscore its splendid isolation. Today it's part of **Kochav Hayarden National Park.** The breathtaking view of the Jordan River valley and southern Sea of Galilee, some 1,800 feet below, is best in the afternoon. You don't need to be a military historian to marvel at the never-breached concentric walls.

The mighty castle was completed by the Hospitallers (the Knights of St. John) in 1173. In the summer of 1187 the Crusader armies were crushed by the Arabs under Saladin at the Horns of Hittin, west of Tiberias, bringing to an end the Latin Kingdom of Jerusalem in one decisive battle. Their remnants struggled on to Tyre (in modern Lebanon), but Belvoir alone refused to yield; 18 months of siege got the Muslims no further than undermining the outer eastern rampart. The Crusaders, for their part, even sallied out from time to time to battle the enemy, but their lone resistance had become pointless. They struck a deal with Saladin and surrendered the stronghold in exchange for free passage, flags flying, to Tyre.

Don't follow the arrows from the parking lot; instead, take the wide gravel path to the right of the fortress. This brings you right to the panoramic view and the best spot from which to appreciate the strength of the stronghold, with its deep, dry moat; massive rock and cut-stone ramparts; and gates. Once inside the main courtyard, you're unexpectedly faced with a fortress within a fortress, a scaled-down replica of the outer defenses. Not much remains of the upper stories; in 1220, the Muslims systematically dismantled Belvoir, fearing another Crusade. Once you've explored the modest buildings, exit over the western bridge (once a drawbridge) and spy on the postern gates, the protected and sometimes secret back doors of medieval castles. ⊠*National Park, Rte. 717, 5 km (3 mi) west of Rte. 90* ☎*04/658–1766* ⊕*www.parks.org.il/ParksENG* ⊠*NIS 23* ☉*Apr.–Sept., Sat.–Thurs. 8–5, Fri. and Jewish holiday eves 8–4; Oct.–Mar., Sat.–Thurs. 8–4, Fri. and Jewish holiday eves 8–3.*

NAZARETH AND THE GALILEE HILLS

Remove the modern roads and power lines, and the landscape of this region becomes a biblical illustration. Villages are scattered haphazardly on the hillsides, and small farm-holdings crowd the valleys. Olive groves, the region's ancient resource, are everywhere. Visually arresting moments are provided by hilltop views and modern pine forests, white-and-red houses, and decorative trees that dab the countryside.

There are several New Testament settings here—Nazareth, where Jesus grew up; the Cana wedding feast; and Mt. Tabor, identified with the Transfiguration—but Jewish history resonates strongly, too. Tabor and Yodefat were fortifications in the Great Revolt against the Romans; Shefar'am, Beit She'arim (in a nearby valley), and Zippori were in turn the national centers of Jewish life (2nd–4th centuries AD); and latter-day Jewish pioneers, attracted to the region's untamed scenery, put down roots where their ancestors had farmed.

NAZARETH

Fodor'sChoice
★
25 km (15½ mi) east of Beit She'arim, 56 km (35 mi) east of Haifa, 15 km (9½ mi) north of Afula.

The Nazareth where Jesus grew up was an insignificant village nestled in a hollow in the Galilean hills. Today's city of 65,000 is pulsing with energy. Apart from the occasional donkey plying traffic-clogged Paulus VI Street, there's little that evokes the Bible in contemporary Nazareth. The scene is hardly quieter on Friday, the holy day for Muslims, who make up two-thirds of the city's population. It calms down somewhat on Wednesday afternoon, however, when many businesses close for a midweek sabbatical; and on Sunday, the day of rest for the Christians who make up the other third of the town, it's positively placid.

If you're out for local color (and traffic jams), come on Saturday, when Arab villagers come to the big city to sell produce and buy goods, and Jewish families from the surrounding area come looking for bargains in the souk.

GETTING HERE AND AROUND

If you're driving from Beit She'arim or Haifa on Route 75, Route 77 breaks off to the north—to Zippori, the Golani Junction, and Tiberias. Route 75 continues to skirt the north side of the picturesque Jezreel Valley as it climbs into the hills toward Nazareth; at the crest of the hill, it's joined by Route 60 from Afula. A turn to the left takes you down to Paulus VI, Nazareth's main drag. If you pick up Route 77 from the opposite side, from Tiberias and points north, a left turn onto Route 764 takes you into Nazareth's Paulus VI Street. Nazareth's Central Bus Station is downtown on Paulus VI Street, not far from the Basilica of the Annunciation.

Route 60 was blasted through the mountains as a bypass road in 2008, but Nazareth itself remains mired in traffic. The historic and religious sites are all close together, so it's best to park and walk.

While fine for a local trip in Nazareth, a taxi is generally an uninspiring and expensive way to travel around the Galilee. Theoretically, cab drivers are supposed to operate their meters outside cities as well, but it is quite acceptable to negotiate a fare beforehand.

Both Egged Tours and United Tours run one-day tours three times a week that take in Nazareth, Capernaum, Tabgha, the Sea of Galilee, Tiberias, and the Jordan River. Current prices are US$60 from Tel Aviv, $64 from Jerusalem.

ESSENTIALS

Hospital English Hospital (✉ 5112 St., next to YMCA, Nazareth ☎ 04/602–8888).

Taxi Contacts Abu el-Assal (✉ Nazareth ☎ 04/655–4745). Diana (✉ Nazareth ☎ 04/655–5554).

Visitor and Tour Information Egged Tours (☎ 03/694–8888 or *2800 ⊕ www.egged.co.il/Eng). Tourist Information Office (✉ Casa Nova St., Nazareth ☎ 04/657–3003 or 04/657–0555). United Tours (☎ 03/616–2656 or 03/693–3412 ⊕ www.inisrael.com/united).

EXPLORING

❸ **Baptist Church.** Christianity speaks with many voices in Nazareth. The Baptist Church, a few hundred yards north of the Church of St. Gabriel, is affiliated with the Southern Baptist Convention of the United States. Call to arrange a visit. ✉ Paulus VI St. ☎ 04/657–6946 or 04/657–4370.

❶ **Basilica of the Annunciation.** Casa Nova Street climbs steeply to the ★ entrance of the Roman Catholic Basilica of the Annunciation, the largest church in the Middle East, consecrated in 1969. It enshrines a small ancient cave dwelling or grotto, identified by many Catholics as the home of Mary. Here, they believe, the angel Gabriel appeared to her and announced (hence "Annunciation") that she would conceive "and bear a son" and "call his name Jesus" (Luke 1). Pilgrim devotions suffuse the site throughout the day. Crusader-era walls and some restored Byzantine mosaics near the grotto bear witness to the antiquity of the tradition. The grotto is in the so-called "lower church." Look up through the "well" or opening over the grotto that connects with the "upper church" to the grand cupola, soaring 195 feet above you.

Baptist Church ...**3**

Basilica of the
Annunciation **1**

Church of St.
Gabriel **2**

Nazareth Village .**4**

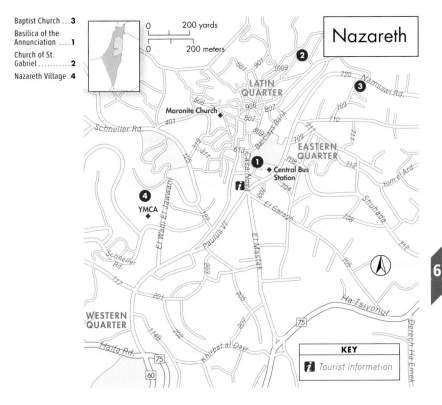

A spiral staircase leads to the vast upper church (some 70 yards long and 30 yards wide), the parish church of Nazareth's Roman Catholic community. Beautiful Italian ceramic reliefs on the huge concrete pillars represent the Stations of the Cross, captioned in the Arabic vernacular. You now have a closer view of the cupola, its ribs representing the petals of an upside-down lily—a symbol of Mary's purity—rooted in heaven. It is repeatedly inscribed with the letter *M* for her name. The huge mosaic behind the altar shows Jesus and Peter at the center and an enthroned Mary behind them, flanked by figures of the hierarchical church (to your right) and the charismatic church (to your left).

The artwork of the site, donated by Catholic communities around the world, is eclectic in the extreme but the more interesting for it. The portico around the courtyard just inside the main gate is decorated with striking contemporary mosaics, many depicting the Madonna and Child in styles and with facial features reflecting the donor nation. The massive main doors leading to the lower church relate in bronze relief the central events of Jesus' life. The dim lighting of the lower church is the central events of Jesus' life. The dim lighting of the lower church is brilliantly counterpointed by abstract stained-glass windows. The large panels on the walls of the upper church, again on the theme of mother and child, include a vivid offering from the United States, a fine Canadian terra-cotta, and mosaics from England and Australia. Particularly interesting are the gifts from Japan (with gold leaf and real pearls), Venezuela (a carved-wood statue), and Cameroon (a stylized painting in black, white, and brick red).

In the exit courtyard, a glass-enclosed baptistery is built over what is thought to have been an ancient mikvah, a Jewish ritual immersion bath. The adjacent small Church of St. Joseph, just past Terra Sancta College, is built over a complex of rock-hewn chambers traditionally identified as the workshop of Joseph the Carpenter. Be warned that parking is hard to find; try Paulus VI Street or the side streets below it. ⊠ *Casa Nova St.* ☎ *04/657–2501* ✉ *Free* ⊙ *Apr.–Sept., Mon.–Sat. 8–6, Sun. 2–6; Oct.–Mar., Mon.–Sat. 8–6, Sun. 2–5.*

| NEED A BREAK? | **Try the unbeatable Arab pastries at the Mahroum** (⊠ *Casa Nova and Paulus VI Sts.* ☎ *04/656–0214*) **confectionery. It's clean, has bathrooms, and serves wonderful** *bourma* **(cylindrical pastry filled with whole pistachio nuts), cashew baklava, and great halvah. Don't confuse this place with another one nearby: look for the Arab pastries, not the gooey Western cakes.** |

❷ **Church of St. Gabriel.** The Greek Orthodox Church of St. Gabriel, about 1 km (¾ mi) north of the junction of Paulus VI and Casa Nova streets, is built over Nazareth's only natural water source, a spring dubbed Mary's Well. The Greek Orthodox, citing the noncanonical Gospel of St. James, believe it to be the place where the angel Gabriel appeared to Mary to announce the coming birth of Jesus. (On Paulus VI Street, at the bottom of the short approach to the church, is a round, white, stone structure marked MARY'S WELL, but this is merely a modern outlet.)

The ornate church was built in 1750 and contains a carved-wood pulpit and iconostasis (chancel screen), with painted New Testament scenes and silver-haloed saints. The walls are adorned with frescoes of figures from the Bible and the Greek Orthodox hagiography. A tiny "well" stands over the running water, and a modern aluminum cup gives a satisfying plop as it drops in. (The water is clean; the cup is more suspect.) ⊠ *Off Paulus VI St.* ☎ *04/657–6437* ✉ *Donation expected* ⊙ *Mon.–Sat. 8–5, Sun. after services–5.*

❹ **Nazareth Village.** Using information gained from archaeological work done in the area, this attraction aims to reconstruct Jewish rural community life as Jesus would have known it more than 2,000 years ago. Workshops, farms, and houses have been created with techniques that would have been used at the time. Interpreters in period costume cook, weave, and work at wine presses, giving a sense of daily life. The village is geared toward Christian travelers but may also be of interest to others; there is a re-created synagogue and mikveh (ritual bath). Guided tours with different themes are offered; check in advance about these. ⊠ *5105 St., by the Nazareth YMCA downtown* ☎ *04/645–6042* ⊕ *www.nazarethvillage.com* ✉ *NIS 50* ⊙ *Mon.–Sat. 9–5.*

Shopping in Nazareth's popular market is a good introduction to this growing, largely Arab city.

Souk. Nazareth's market, in the old city, may have something for everyone, from coffee sets to pastries to T-shirts; antiques can also be found. The old lanes are narrow and shops are tiny, with goods spilling into the street. If it gets overwhelming, take a break and have some coffee. ⊠ *Casa Nova St. and vicinity.*

WHERE TO EAT

After a full day of visiting Nazareth's shrines, quench your thirst at the little Arab restaurants along Paulus VI Street, frequented mostly by locals. Dinner here means hummus, shish kebab, baklava, and the like. Decor is incidental, atmosphere a function of the clientele of the moment, and dinnertime early. Needless to say, reservations are not necessary, and dress is casual.

$$$
MIDDLE EASTERN
✕ **Al-Reda.** In a magnificent 19th-century mansion with a *Thousand and One Nights* atmosphere, Al-Reda matches its magical setting with excellent Arab cuisine, from interesting salads (eggplant with cheese) and roasted lamb neck to kebabs and shishlik, as well as some French and Italian dishes. Pesto and grilled vegetables stuffed in a chicken breast is another choice. Don't pass up the good deserts. Above the restaurant is a guesthouse with large windows overlooking the dome of the Basilica of the Annunciation. ⊠ *23 Al Bishara St.* ☎ 04/608–4404 ▭ AE, DC, MC, V ⊘ *Closed Mon.*

$$$
MIDDLE EASTERN
✕ **Diana.** Ranked among the region's best Arab restaurants, Diana doesn't fail to impress. Owner Duhul Safadi is most famous for his kebabs and lamb chops, but the fish and seafood dishes are all equally wonderful. There's a plant-filled terrace and a sophisticated dining room that would not be out of place in Tel Aviv. ⊠ *Grand New Hotel, 51 Paul VI St.* ☎ 04/657–2919 ▭ AE, DC, MC, V ⊘ *Closed Mon.*

Nazareth's Basilica of the Annunciation has a venerable cave many Catholics believe was the home of Mary.

WHERE TO STAY

$ 🏨 **Fauzi Azar Inn.** In a gloriously restored 200-year-old mansion in the heart of the Old City, Fauzi Azar offers everything from dorm-style accommodations for backpackers to private rooms for individuals and families. Rooms have soaring ceilings, expansive windows, and traditional furnishings. A traditional Arab breakfast and a daily tour of the Old City are available. The hotel is extremely difficult to find. Call when you arrive in the city and the staff will pick you up. **Pros:** picturesque building; quaint courtyard; reasonable rates. **Cons:** little parking; hard to find the hotel. ⊠ *Old City* 🕿 *04/602–0469* ⊕ *www.fauziazarinn. com* 🛏 *10 rooms* 🔥 *In-hotel: room service, Internet terminal, Wi-Fi* 🚬 *V* 🍴*BP.*

$ 🏨 **Plaza.** The white–and–soft-pink stone of this building is the first hint that Nazareth has at last acquired an upscale hotel. The guest rooms have dark wood furnishings that lend a touch of class. Since the hotel is on a hill, many rooms enjoy a view of Old Nazareth. A huge gym is another of the draws. In a town where dining options are limited for those seeking more than just kebabs, the restaurant is a good choice. The hotel offers guests a free tour of the Old City on Saturdays. **Pros:** pretty swimming pool; air-conditioning. **Cons:** no evening entertainment; far from Nazareth's shrines. ⊠ *2 Hermon St., Upper Nazareth* 🕿 *04/602–8200* 🛏 *177 rooms, 7 suites* 🔥 *In-room: safe, Internet. In-hotel: room service, bar, pool, gym, laundry service, Internet terminal, parking (free), no-smoking rooms* 🚬 *AE, DC, MC, V* 🍴*BP.*

$$ 🏨 **Rimonim Nazareth.** As you walk through the doors, your first impression is likely to be that the place is rather staid. That's because the action is underground, where the adjoining bar, lounge, and dining room add a

bit of buzz. Rooms are comfortable and well appointed; ask for one on the fourth floor so you'll have a balcony. The location—on Nazareth's main street, very close to Mary's Well—is a limited blessing; this is not a town that comes alive at night. **Pros:** convenient to the sights; air-conditioning. **Cons:** street noise; no evening entertainment. ✉ *Paulus VI St., 1* ☎ *04/650–0000* ⊕ *www.rimonim.com* ⏎ *226 rooms* ⟁ *In-room: safe, refrigerator, Internet. In-hotel: room service, bar, laundry service, Internet terminal, parking (free)* ⊟ *AE, DC, MC, V* ⦿ *BP.*

¢ 🏨 **St. Gabriel.** Sitting high on the ridge that overlooks Nazareth from the west, this hotel began life as a convent—hence the charming neo-Gothic church still in use today. Renovations extended the nuns' old cells, and half the rooms enjoy some of the city's greatest views. The reception area is furnished with inlaid tables, chairs, and mirrors in the old Damascene style, and the dining room prides itself on its local dishes. The garden and the view are perfect for unwinding at sundown. **Pros:** near the shrines; memorable views. **Cons:** no evening entertainment. ✉ *2 Salesian St. 16000* ☎ *04/657–2133 or 04/656–7349* ⏎ *60 rooms* ⟁ *In-room: no a/c, Wi-Fi. In-hotel: restaurant, laundry service, Internet terminal, parking (free)* ⊟ *AE, DC, MC, V* ⦿ *BP.*

ZIPPORI

Village 5 km (3 mi) northwest of Nazareth off Rte. 79; site 3 km (2 mi) from village via bypass; 47 km (29 mi) east of Haifa.

GETTING HERE AND AROUND

Driving to this national park from Nazareth, follow Route 79 west and turn north at the signs. No buses service this route. The easiest way to get here without a car is by taxi from Nazareth. Make sure you agree on the price in advance, and consider asking the driver to wait for you.

EXPLORING

Fodor's Choice ★ Like many places during the Roman era, **Zippori**—known by Latin and Greek speakers in the classical world as Sepphoris—was a prosperous city where Jews and gentiles co-existed fairly peaceably. The extensive ruins at the much-visited Zippori National Park include Israel's finest Roman-era mosaics. The ancient city, situated on a high ridge with commanding views, can be visited in two hours. The key sites are all in relatively close proximity.

Zippori's multiple narratives begin with a Jewish town that stood here from at least the 1st century BC. Christian tradition reveres the town as the birthplace of the Virgin Mary. Zippori's refusal to join the Great Revolt of the Jews against the Romans (AD 66–73) left a serious gap in the rebel defenses in the Galilee, angering its compatriots but sparing the town the usual Roman vengeance when the uprising failed. The real significance of Zippori for Jewish tradition, however, is that in the late 2nd or early 3rd century AD, the legendary sage Rabbi Yehuda ha-Nasi, head of the country's Jewish community at the time, moved here from Beit She'arim, whereupon the Sanhedrin (the Jewish high court) soon followed. Rabbi Yehuda summoned the greatest rabbis in the land to Zippori to pool their experience. The result was the encyclopedic work known as the Mishnah. Further commentary was added in later centuries to produce the Talmud, the primary guide to Orthodox Jewish practice to this day.

But Zippori also had a cosmopolitan soul. By the 3rd century AD, it had acquired a mixed population of Jews, pagans, and Christians. The most celebrated find on the site is the mosaic floor of a Roman villa, perhaps the governor's residence, depicting a series of Dionysian drinking scenes. Its most stunning detail is the exquisite face of a woman, by far the finest mosaic ever discovered in Israel, which the media at once dubbed "the Mona Lisa of the Galilee." The restored mosaics are housed in an air-conditioned structure with helpful explanations. In other parts of the park, the so-called Nile Mosaic displays Egyptian motifs, and a mosaic synagogue floor (below the parking lot) is decorated with the signs of the zodiac, just like those found in Beit Alfa and Hammat Tiberias.

If the mosaic floors bespeak the opulence of Roman Sepphoris, the relatively small Roman theater is mute evidence of the cultural life the wealth could support. Take a few minutes to climb the watchtower of Dahr al-Omar's 18th-century castle for the panoramic view and the museum of archaeological artifacts. About 1 km (½ mi) east of the main site—close to the entrance of the park—is a huge section of ancient Zippori's water system, once fed by springs just north of Nazareth. The ancient aqueduct-reservoir is in fact a deep, man-made, plastered canyon, and the effect is extraordinary. ⊠ *Off Rte. 79* ☎ *04/656–8272* ⊕ *www.parks.org. il* 🎫 *NIS 23* ⊙ *Apr.–Sept., Sat.–Thurs. 8–5, Fri. and Jewish holiday eves 8–4; Oct.–Mar., Sat.–Thurs. 8–4, Fri. and Jewish holiday eves 8–3.*

CANA

8 km (5 mi) north of Nazareth on Rte. 754, 1 km (½ mi) south of junction of Rtes. 77 and 754; 50 km (31 mi) east of Haifa.

Many scholars identify the large, modern Arab village of Kfar Kanna as the site of the ancient Jewish village of Cana, mentioned in the New Testament. Here Jesus performed his first miracle, turning water into wine at a wedding feast, thereby emerging from his "hidden years" to begin a three-year ministry in the Galilee.

From Nazareth the road winds down through typical Galilean countryside. The profusion of olive groves, pomegranates, grapevines, fig trees, and even the occasional date palm (unusual at this altitude) is a reminder of how much local scenery is described in the Bible. Even the clutter of modern buildings, power lines, and industrial debris cannot entirely ruin the impression.

PLANT A TREE IN ISRAEL

Around the Golani Junction are groves of evergreens planted by visitors as part of the Plant a Tree with Your Own Hands project of the Jewish National Fund. Since the early 1900s more than 230 million trees have been restored to barren hillsides across Israel. At the **Planting Center**, a few hundred yards from the junction, you can choose a sapling, dedicate it to someone, and plant it yourself; cost is NIS 50. ⊠ *Take Rte. 7707 off Rte. 77 east of Golani Junction at Lavi, then immediate left on secondary road* ☎ *02/670-7433* ⊙ *Sun.-Thurs. 8-3, Fri. 8-noon.*

GETTING HERE AND AROUND

Part of the sprawling suburbs of Nazareth, Kfar Kanna sits astride Route 754, linking Route 77 to the north and Route 79 to the south.

EXPLORING

Within the village, red signs lead to rival churches—one Roman Catholic, the other Greek Orthodox—that enshrine the scriptural tradition. (The alley to these churches is just wide enough for cars, and you can sometimes park in the courtyard of a souvenir store. If the street is blocked, park on the main road.)

The present Catholic **Cana Wedding Church** was built in 1881 on what the Franciscans believe to be the very spot where the wedding at which Jesus performed this first miracle (John 2:1-11) took place. It's worth a short visit. ⊠ *Churches St.* ☎ *04/651–7011* ✉ *Free* ☉ *Apr.–Sept., Mon.–Sat. 8–noon and 2–6, Sun. 8–noon; Oct.–Mar., Mon.–Sat. 8–noon and 2–5, Sun. 8–noon.*

EN ROUTE One of the region's most strategic crossroads, **Golani Junction** is about 6 km (4 mi) east of Cana. It is named for the Israeli brigade that captured it in the War of Independence in 1948. A monument, a museum, and a McDonald's share the northeast corner of the intersection.

MT. TABOR

★ *16 km (10 mi) south of the Golani Junction off Rtes. 65 and 7266, 17 km (10½ mi) northeast of Afula.*

The dome-like Mt. Tabor, the region's highest mountain, looms over one of the prettiest stretches of the Lower Galilee. Quilts of farmland kaleidoscope through the seasons as different crops grow, ripen, and are harvested. Modern woods of evergreens cover the hillsides.

Apart from the natural beauty, Mt. Tabor and its immediate surroundings have considerable biblical history. About 32 centuries ago, Israelite warriors of the prophetess-judge Deborah and her general, Barak, routed a Canaanite chariot army that had gotten bogged down in the mud. The modern kibbutz of Ein Dor, south of the mountain, is the site of ancient Endor, where King Saul unsuccessfully beseeched the spirit of the prophet Samuel for help before his fateful (and fatal) battle against the Philistines (I Samuel 28:3-25).

GETTING HERE AND AROUND

If you're driving, take Route 7266 through Shibli, a village of Bedouin who abandoned their nomadic life a few generations ago. A narrow switchback road starts in a clearing between Shibli and the next village, Dabouriya. Nazareth-based taxis often wait at the bottom of the mountain to provide shuttle service to the top. Watch out for them if you're driving your own car up; they come down in overdrive like the lords of the mountain they almost are.

EXPLORING

As far back as the Byzantine period, Christian tradition identified Mt. Tabor as the "high mountain apart" that Jesus ascended with his disciples Peter, James, and John. There, report the Gospels, "he was transfigured before them" (Matthew 17:2) as a radiant white figure, flanked by Moses

Continued on page 385

Jesus *in the* Galilee

Galilee beckons shyly. As in days of old, there is little of the frenetic pace and charged emotions of Jerusalem. For many Christians, the evocative, soft landscapes breathe new life into old familiar stories, and brush black-and-white scriptures with color. But curious visitors with less religious motivation will be drawn into Galilee's gentle charm. This tour of selected sights will speak to both.

"And passing along by the **Sea of Galilee,** he saw Simon and Andrew the brother of Simon casting a net into the sea, for they were fishermen. And Jesus said to them,

'Follow me and I will make you become fishers of men.'"

(Mark 1: 16–17)

Hills ring the Sea of Galilee, a freshwater lake.

Jesus was born in Bethlehem and died in Jerusalem, but it was in the Galilee that his ministry was forged. Over time, archaeologists and historians have unearthed many sites referred to in the Bible. Today you can walk the hillsides, sail the Sea of Galilee, explore the ruins, and touch the churches of this beautiful region. Or you can sit under a tree and read the Bible in the place where its narrative unfolded. If you have an eye for the contours of the land and an ear for echoes of the past, the experience can be unforgettable.

The activity and teachings of Jesus gain meaning and resonance from the landscape and social setting in which they emerged. Understand their context, and you will enhance your understanding of the events that have so shaped Western civilization.

By Mike Rogoff

RESTLESS SOCIETY, TURBULENT TIMES

Christ in the Storm on the Sea of Galilee by Jan Brueghel the Elder

The Romans came for the weekend in 63 BC and stayed for four centuries. Herod (later "the Great"), scion of a powerful political family, began his brutal reign as King of the Jews, courtesy of Rome, in 37 BC. He died in 4 BC, only a short time after the birth of Jesus (Matt. 2:1).

Herod's kingdom was divided among his three surviving sons: Archelaeus, Herod Antipas (who got Galilee, and Perea beyond the Jordan River), and Philip. This was the Herod who executed John the Baptist (Matt. 14:10), and was in Jerusalem at the time of the crucifixion (Luke 23:7).

RIVAL THEOLOGIES

Jewish society in the land of Israel was anything but unified and placid 2,000 years ago. Two ideological streams dominated: the Sadducees were the establishment, many of them wealthy, led by the priestly class that controlled the Temple-based cult of Yahweh, the One God, in Jerusalem. They took religious texts literally, and rejected the idea of resurrection and an afterlife (Acts 23:6-9).

The Pharisees, on the other hand, drew their strength from the common people, offering a comforting belief in resurrection and an afterlife in a better world. Their rabbis, or teachers, would interpret biblical law, a practice that laid the groundwork for post-Temple Judaism as practiced until today.

Jesus himself came from the Pharisaic tradition, and "taught in their synagogues" (Luke 4:15). He was critical of the Pharisees' behavior, but not of their theology: They "sit on Moses' seat," he told his followers, "so practice and observe whatever they tell you" (Matt. 23:2).

SECTS AND CATACLYSM

Theological differences and domestic politics gave rise to numerous Jewish sects with strong religious agendas: the followers of Jesus, and of John the Baptist before him, were just two. One of the best known at the time were the Essenes, widely identified today as the monastic Jewish community that wrote the Dead Sea Scrolls.

There were other, less spiritual types like the Zealots—extreme nationalists who spearheaded the Great Revolt against Rome in AD 66. The cataclysm was not long in coming: Jerusalem and the Temple were razed in AD 70, four decades after Jesus's prediction that "there will not be left here one stone upon another" (Matt. 24:2).

Marriage Feast at Cana by Hieronymus Bosch

FACT, FAITH, AND TRADITION

The church on the Mount of Beatitudes has sweeping views of the Sea of Galilee.

Finding evidence of events or personalities in the distant past, the New Testament era included, is a kind of treasure hunt; and there is rarely an "X" to mark the spot. But when you do strike gold through archaeological discoveries or ancient writings, for example, it thrills scholars and laypeople alike.

POPULATING ANCIENT MAPS

There are Galilean towns, like Nazareth and Tiberias, that have survived the centuries and are obviously genuine. Others, like Cana, are still debated. A lot of rocks have been turned over in the last three-quarters of a century, however, and archaeologists have exposed and identified Capernaum, Bethsaida, Chorazin (Korazim), Caesarea Philippi (Banias) in the Upper Galilee, and, to the satisfaction of many, Gennasaret (Ginosar) and Nain as well.

"TRADITIONAL" SITES: WHERE MEMORIES ENDURE

Other sites have been linked to events over time, though no evidence exists. Scriptural descriptions don't exactly offer geographical coordinates, and some locations that are still much visited by pilgrims are conjecture that has jelled into tradition. Visitors in the distant past often took local hearsay for hard fact when tour guides and other opportunists pointed out the very rock or glade or spring where this or that happened. It's not surprising that many traditional holy places are found so close to each other. Guides were often paid by the site—why should they journey unnecessary distances?

Events like the Sermon on the Mount, the Transfiguration, the feeding of the multitudes, the "feed my sheep" encounter of John 21, and the swine of the Gadarenes are all in this category. But for the faithful, the personal spiritual experience is more than a search for solid stones. It hardly depends on proof of where (or even whether) a particular event actually took place. Centuries of prayers and tears will sanctify a site, making it a remembrance place in the region where it all began.

TOURING THE CRADLE OF CHRISTIANITY

An astonishing three-quarters of the activity of Jesus recorded in the New Testament took place on, around, or within sight of the "Sea" of Galilee. The lake provided the largely Jewish towns and villages on its shores with a source of fresh water, a fishing industry, and a means of transportation.

Base yourself in Tiberias and head north, or clockwise, around the lake. The sights are close enough to see in a day. To visit Nazareth, Cana, and Mt. Tabor, 25 miles west of Tiberias, allot another day or be selective. Below are key places associated with Jesus and biblical references to them.

① TIBERIAS *"... boats from Tiberias came near the place ..." (John 6:23).* Herod Antipas, son of Herod the Great, built the city as capital of the Galilee in AD 20. The town never lost its importance, and is today the region's urban center.

② GINOSAR/GENNESARET Eight kms (5 mi) north of Tiberias, modern Ginosar is a kibbutz, with a museum that houses the extraordinary 1st-century-AD wooden boat found nearby. *"... they came to land at Gennesaret ... immediately the people recognized him... and as many as touched [the fringe of his garment] were made well" (Mark 6:53–56).*

③ MT. OF BEATITUDES *"Seeing the crowds, he went up on the mountain, and when he sat down his disciples came to him ... 'Blessed are the poor in spirit ...'" (Matt. 5–7).* The traditional site of Jesus's Sermon on the Mount is set in hilltop gardens, with a church and a superb view of the lake.

④ TABGHA Two events in the life of Jesus are recalled in two churches here. The Multiplication was one: a famous 5th-century mosaic records the event. Crowds followed Jesus and evening came. What about food? *"You give them something to eat' ... 'We have only five*

loaves here and two fish' ... 'Bring them...' He looked up to heaven, and blessed ... And they all ate and were satisfied ... about 5,000 men, besides women and children" (Matt. 14: 15–21).

The primacy of Peter is another. The beach and an attractively simple chapel recall the appearance of Jesus on the shore: *"'Have you any fish?' ... 'No' ... 'Cast the net'... 'It is the Lord!' ... 'Simon [Peter] ... Do you love me? ... Feed my sheep' " (John 21:1–19).*

⑤ CAPERNAUM Jesus made this thriving Jewish town, now an archaeological site, the center of his ministry: *"He went and dwelt in Capernaum ..." (Matt. 4:13).* Here he preached— *"... and immediately on the sabbath he entered the synagogue and taught" (Mark 1:21).*

Greek Orthodox church, Cana

Basilica of the Annunciation, Nazareth

Mt. Tabor

Golani Junction

Lavi

⑨ Cana

65

Zippori

754

79

Kfar Kamma

Nazerat Illit (Upper Nazareth)

Nazareth ⑩

Kfar Tavor

Migdal Ha'emek

Shibli

Mt. Tabor ⑪

716

6 BETHSAIDA This was the hometown of the disciples Philip, Andrew, and Peter (John 1:44); the place where Jesus cured a blind man (Mark 8:22–25). The town was left stranded when its lagoon dried out, and eluded identification until recently.

7 KURSI Jesus cured two madmen on the Golan Heights slopes, *"the country of the Gadarenes": "... a herd of swine was feeding ... [the demons] came out [of the demoniacs] and went into the swine ..."* (Matt. 8:28–34).

8 JORDAN RIVER Today people come to be baptized in the Jordan in this northern region, but the New Testament story almost certainly refers to the river's southern reaches, near Jericho: *"Then Jesus came from the Galilee to the Jordan to John, to be baptized by him"* (Matt. 3:13).

9 CANA When the wine ran out at a wedding feast, Jesus (after some persuasion) turned six stone jars-full of water into superior wine. *"This, the first of his signs, Jesus did in Cana of Galilee ..."* (John 2:1–11).

Mosaic at Church of the Multiplication, Tabgha

Synagogue at Capernaum

Byzantine church at Kursi

87
6 Bethsaida
5 Capernaum
3 Mount of Beatitudes **92**
4 Tabgha
2 Ginosar
Kursi 7
Sea of Galilee (Lake Kinneret)
1 Tiberias
Ein Gev
90
Ancient boat at Ginosar
O Kinneret
767
Yavne'el
Jordan River
8
Degania Alef
Baptism in the Jordan River
90
0 ___ 4 mi
0 ___ 4 km

10 NAZARETH Here, the New Testament relates, an angel appeared to Mary to announce the coming birth of Jesus (Luke 1:26–38). It was here he grew up (his so-called "hidden years") and to Nazareth he returned as a teacher: *"... he went to the synagogue ... on the sabbath ... he stood up to read... the prophet Isaiah..."* (Luke 4:16–30).

11 MT. TABOR In the event called "the Transfiguration," Jesus took three of his disciples *"up a high mountain apart,"* where they had a vision of him as a radiant white figure flanked by Moses and Elijah (Mark 9:2–8). Mt. Tabor has long been identified as the place, though some prefer Mt. Hermon in the far north.

6

IN FOCUS JESUS IN THE GALILEE

TIPS FOR EXPLORING THE GALILEE

Greek Orthodox church at Capernaum

GETTING AROUND

Buses may be the cheapest way to see Israel, but they are not time-effective in the Galilee. Nazareth and Tiberias are easy to get to (and are 35 minutes apart), and a few less-frequent lines stop at Cana, Ginosar, and near Tabgha. Other Christian sites in the area are a fair hike from the highway or only doable by car.

HOLIDAYS, SERVICES, AND MORE

The Christmas and Easter celebrations that are so much part of the culture in many places are absent in Israel, where only 1.5% of its citizens are Christian. In the Galilee, the exception is Nazareth, with its lights and Christmas trees, and a traditional procession downtown at 3 PM on Christmas Eve. Many denominations are represented here, but Nazareth has no scheduled services in English.

In Tiberias, English-speakers can attend Catholic mass in St. Peter's Church (daily at 6:30 PM, Sundays at 8:30 AM) and occasional Protestant services at YMCA Penuel (just north of town) and St. Andrew's (opposite the Scots Hotel). A good source of information is the Web site of the Christian Information Center: ⊕ http://198.62.75.1/www1/ofm/cic/CICxmasothers.htm.

■ TIP➔ For information about Nazareth Village, which re-creates the town as it was 2,000 years ago, and Yardenit, a group baptismal site, see the listings elsewhere in this chapter.

VISITING SUGGESTIONS

Christian sites demand respectful behavior and a conservative dress code (no shorts, short skirts, or sleeveless tops). Photography is usually permitted, but professionals may require prior permission. Pay attention to advertised opening times—most sites are strict about this—and allow time for unexpected delays in getting there.

HIKING THE LANDSCAPE

Hikers can consider the Jesus Trail. Its primary route is 65 kms (40 mi) long, but you can select individual sections for a shorter hike, or spread the experience over several days. See it as a multisensory way of appreciating where scripture unfolded. Visit ⊕ www.jesustrail.com.

CREATING SPECIAL MOMENTS IN THE GALILEE

■ Carry a Bible and a good map.

■ In fine weather, the Mount of Beatitudes is best in the afternoon, when the light is gentler on the lake and the hills.

■ If you are unencumbered by luggage, and don't have a car to retrieve, stroll the easy trail from Mount of Beatitudes down to Tabgha (cross the highway with care), visit the two sites there, and then walk the 2-mi promenade that follows the highway east to Capernaum.

■ The little beach of volcanic pebbles at Tabgha (the Primacy site) can be magical.

■ Bethsaida is evocative—pure 1st century: no Byzantine, Crusader, or modern structures. It's never crowded, and offers a great place to sit with a view of the lake and read your favorite verses.

and Elijah. The altar of the present imposing **Church of the Transfiguration,** which was consecrated in 1924, represents the tabernacle of Jesus that Peter suggested they build; those of Moses and Elijah appear as small chapels at the back of the church. Step up to the terrace to the right of the church doors for a great view of the Jezreel Valley to the west and south. From a platform on the Byzantine and Crusader ruins to the left of the modern church (watch your step), there is a panorama east and north over the Galilean hills. Fifty yards from the church, a Franciscan pilgrim rest stop has refreshments and bathrooms. ☎*04/673–2283* 🎫*Free* ⊙*Daily 8–noon and 2–5.*

The veteran farming village of **Kfar Tavor** was founded by Jewish pioneers in 1901 in the shadow of the domed mountain from which it took its name. Not everyone farms today, and the village side streets, with single-family homes and well-tended gardens, feel like a nice piece of suburbia anywhere.

An excellent time-out from regular touring, the **Tabor Winery** was founded in 1997. The quality of its wines has risen steeply in the last decade. They aren't the cheapest wines, but after tasting a few you might not be able to resist taking a couple of bottles home. A 12-minute film and tasting are free. From late July through September, you can pay to stomp grapes the traditional way—a great family activity. ⊠*Visitors Center, Kfar Tavor* ☎*04/676–0444* ⊕*www.taborwinery.co.il* 🎫*Free* ⊙*Sun.–Thurs. 10–5, Fri. 10–3.*

☺ In the same compound as the Tabor Winery, the charming **Marzipan Museum** contains explanations and delectable products made from locally grown almonds. If you have kids in tow, don't think twice about signing up for the fun, marzipan-making workshop. (There's also a chocolate workshop.) Best of all, you get to take your creations home. ⊠*Visitors Center, Kfar Tavor* ☎*04/677–2111 or 050/570–1677* 🎫*NIS 15* ⊙*Sun.–Fri. 9–6, Sat. 10–6.*

WHERE TO EAT

$$$
ISRAELI
✗**Bordeaux.** The name hints at the restaurant's location, adjacent to the Tabor Winery. The style is "country," with warm wood decor inside and a great scenic deck for outside dining. With special effort made to use excellent local farm produce, the wide-ranging menu stretches from modestly priced pastas, salads, and sandwiches to more sophisticated steaks, fish, and chicken dishes. A children's menu and good desserts contribute to the family-friendliness. ⊠*Visitors Center, Kfar Tavor* ☎*04/676–7673* ⚒*Reservations essential* ▭*AE, DC, MC, V.*

$$$
MIDDLE EASTERN
✗**Sahara.** The menu of this Middle Eastern restaurant is a bit more sophisticated than that of its neighbors. Within the stone building with a landmark round tower is a spacious interior with stone floors and arches, wooden tables, and a centerpiece water cascade. Follow the excellent *mezze* (local salads) with traditional skewers of grilled meat, baked lamb, or one of the fish or chicken dishes. The Jordanian *mansaf* (a mix of rice, pine nuts, and pieces of lamb cooked with aromatic herbs) is an interesting discovery. ⊠*Rte. 65, next to gas station* ☎*04/642–5959* ⚒*Reservations essential* ▭*AE, DC, MC, V.*

EN
ROUTE

If you're heading to the Sea of Galilee, take Route 767, which breaks off Route 65 at Kfar Tavor. It's a beautiful drive of about 25 minutes. The first village, **Kfar Kama**, is one of two in Israel of the Circassian (*Cherkessi*) community, Sunni Muslim non-Arabs from Russia's Caucasus Mountains who settled here in 1876. The unusually decorative minaret of the mosque is just one element of the tradition the community vigorously continues to preserve. On the descent to the lake, there is a **parking area** precisely at sea level. The Sea of Galilee is still more than 700 feet below, and the view is superb, especially in the afternoon. You meet Route 90 at the bottom of the road.

TIBERIAS AND THE SEA OF GALILEE

The Sea of Galilee is, in fact, a freshwater lake, measuring 21 km (13 mi) long from north to south and 11 km (7 mi) wide from east to west. Almost completely ringed by cliffs and steep hills, the lake lies in a hollow about 700 feet below sea level, which accounts for its warm climate and subtropical vegetation. This is Israel's Riviera-on-a-lake, filled with beaches and outdoor recreation facilities. Its shores are also dotted with sites hallowed by Christian tradition (note that several of these sites demand modest dress) as well as some important ancient synagogues. Tiberias itself is one of Judaism's four holy cities, along with Jerusalem, Hebron, and Tzfat.

The city of Tiberias is the logical starting base for exploration. One sightseeing strategy is to circle the Sea of Galilee clockwise from Tiberias (via Routes 90, 87, 92, and 98).

TIBERIAS

★ *38 km (23½ mi) north of Beit She'an, 36 km (23 mi) east of Nazareth, 70 km (43 mi) east of Haifa.*

As the only city on the Sea of Galilee, Tiberias, with a population of 40,000, has become the region's hub. The city spreads up a steep hillside, from 700 feet below sea level at the lake, to about 80 feet above sea level in its highest neighborhoods—a differential big enough to create significant variations in comfort levels during midsummer.

The splendid panoramic views of both the lake and the Golan Heights on the far shore deserved a better sort of development. Tiberias has little beauty and less class, and although almost 2,000 years old, it still has the atmosphere of a place neglected for decades, if not centuries. It is at once brash and sleepy, with a reputation as a resort town based more on its location than its attractions. Travelers tend to see little of the town itself, sticking to the restaurants and hotels along the lake. Those traveling by car often skip the town altogether, opting for the numerous B&Bs that dot the region.

GETTING HERE AND AROUND

The city sits astride the junction of Routes 90 and 77. Egged buses regularly serve Tiberias from Haifa, Nazareth, Tel Aviv, and Jerusalem. Haifa is one hour away, while Tel Aviv and Jerusalem are both

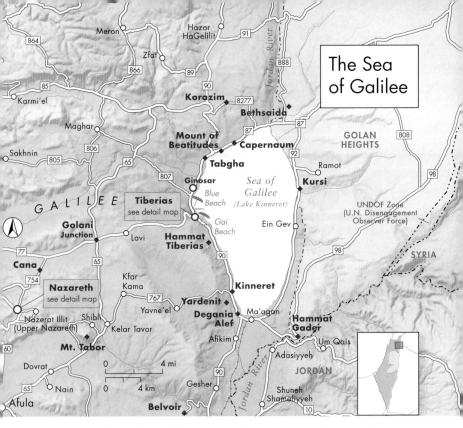

two hours distant. Tiberias is small enough to walk to most locations, though given the punishing summer heat you may wish to have a taxi take you for even short jaunts.

Both Egged Tours and United Tours run one-day tours three times a week that take in Nazareth, Capernaum, Tabgha, the Sea of Galilee, Tiberias, and the Jordan River. Current prices are US$60 from Tel Aviv, $64 from Jerusalem. Matan Tours, based in Tiberias, operates a guide-driven limo-van for a day tour of some Sea of Galilee sites and the Golan Heights. The cost is $45 per person.

ESSENTIALS

Bus Contact Egged (☎ 03/694–8888 or *2800 ⊕ www.egged.co.il/Eng).

Medical Contacts Emergency Medical Service (✉ Habanim St., at Kishon St., Tiberias ☎ 04/671–7611). **Superpharm** (✉ 1 Hayarden St., Tiberias ☎ 04/671–6663).

Taxi Contacts Ha'emek (✉ Tiberias ☎ 04/672–0131). **Hagalil** (✉ Tiberias ☎ 04/672–0353).

Visitor and Tour Information Egged Tours (☎ 03/694–8888 or *2800 ⊕ www.egged.co.il/Eng). **Matan Tours** (✉ Aviv Hotel, 66 Hagalil St., Tiberias ☎ 04/672–3510 or 054/461–6148). **Tiberias Tourist Information Office** (✉ Habanim St. ☎ 04/672–5666). **United Tours** (☎ 03/616–2656 or 03/693–3412 ⊕ www.inisrael.com/united).

Tiberias Through Time

Tiberias was founded in AD 18 by Herod Antipas, son of Herod the Great, and dedicated to Tiberius, then emperor of Rome. The Tiberians had little stomach for the Jewish war against Rome that broke out in AD 66. They soon surrendered, preventing the vengeful destruction visited on other Galilean towns.

With Jerusalem laid waste in AD 70, the center of Jewish life gravitated to the Galilee. By the 4th century, the Sanhedrin had settled in Tiberias. Here Jewish Oral Law was compiled into what became known as the Jerusalem Talmud, and Tiberias's status as one of Judaism's holy cities was assured.

Tiberias knew hard times under the Byzantines, and further declined under the hostile Crusaders. Starting in the 1700s, newcomers from Turkey and Eastern Europe swelled the Jewish population, but an 1837 earthquake left Tiberias in ruins.

Relations between Jews and Arabs were generally cordial until the Arab riots of 1936, when some 30 Jews were massacred. During the 1948 War of Independence, an attack by local Arabs brought a counterattack from Jewish forces, and the Arabs abandoned the town. Today the citizenry is entirely Jewish, and abandoned mosques stand as silent monuments.

EXPLORING

Foremost among Tiberias's many venerated resting places is the **tomb of Moses Maimonides** (1135–1204). Born in Córdoba, Spain, Maimonides—widely known by his Hebrew acronym, the "Rambam" (for Rabbi Moshe Ben Maimon)—won international renown as a philosopher, as physician to the royal court of Saladin in Egypt, and in the Jewish world, as the greatest religious scholar and spiritual authority of the Middle Ages. To his profound knowledge of the Talmud, Maimonides brought an incisive intellect honed by his study of Aristotelian philosophy and the physical sciences. The result was a rationalism unusual in Jewish scholarship and a lucidity of analysis and style admired by Jewish and non-Jewish scholars alike.

Maimonides never lived in Tiberias, but after his death in Egypt, his remains were brought to this Jewish holy city for interment. His whitewashed tomb has become a shrine, dripping with candle wax and tears. To get here, walk two blocks up ha-Yarden Street, and turn right onto Ben Zakkai Street. The tomb is on your right, topped by a soaring spire of red steel girders. ⊠*Ben Zakkai St.* 🕾*No phone* ⊕*www.maimonidesheritage.org/Tomb.asp* 🎫*Free* ☉*Sun.–Thurs. dawn–dusk, Fri. and Jewish holiday eves until 2* PM.

WHERE TO EAT

At a right angle to the waterside promenade, the *midrachov* (pedestrian mall), between the Sheraton Moriah and Caesar hotels, has a wide range of affordable dining options. There are also a couple of budget places on Habanim Street. If you're into local color, look for the tiny, modest restaurants (where English really *is* a foreign language) on Hagalil

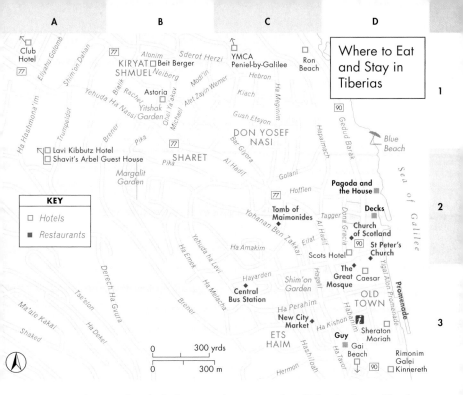

Street and in the little streets that connect it to Habanim Street, like the pedestrian-only Kishon Street.

$$$$
MODERN ISRAELI

✕ Decks. Built on a pier, this place is something of an institution. Try to catch the eye of manager Vered Gross or her octogenarian father Eitan—they'll regale you with stories of Tiberias. The family-run restaurant keeps locals coming back because of the great food. The kitchen specializes in delicious meats—steak, goose liver, or long skewers of veal and vegetables—grilled slowly over hickory wood. The blue-fin tuna carpaccio, caught by Vered's brother Ido, makes for a rare delicacy. An apple tart pan-baked at your table is the house dessert. ⊠ *Lido complex, Rte. 90, at the exit from Tiberias north* ☎ *04/672–1538* ⊟ *AE, DC, MC, V* ⊗ *No dinner Fri. No lunch Sat.* ⊕2D

$$
MIDDLE EASTERN

✕ Guy. Stuffed vegetables are the calling card of this family-run restaurant, whose name means "ravine" in Hebrew. The cook-matriarch Geula comes from a Tiberias family, but her Moroccan ancestry shows through in delicious dishes like eggplant stuffed with seasoned ground beef. There are good, if more conventional, Middle Eastern meat and salad options, but go for the excellent soups, and try some *kibbeh* (a Kurdish-Iraqi specialty of seasoned ground meat and bulgur). The restaurant faces the lake slightly set back from the sidewalk and opposite a small traffic circle. ⊠ *63 hagalil St.* ☎ *04/672–3036* ⊟ *No credit cards* ⊗ *Closed Sat. No dinner Fri.* ⊕3D

$$$
ASIAN

✕ Pagoda and the House. This faux-Chinese temple has tables on an outdoor patio overlooking the lake. Across the road there's a maze

To escape the heat or just have fun, take a ride on the Sea of Galilee.

of more intimate rooms entered through a garden. These are essentially the same restaurant, with identical kosher menus, but Pagoda is closed on the Sabbath, while the House is open. Apart from the Chinese standards, try the Thai soups (such as the tasty hot-and-sour soup), the goose spareribs, or strips of beef with peanut sauce. There's a sushi bar as well. ⊠*Gedud Barak St. (Rte. 90)* ☎*04/672–5513 or 04/672–5514* ⌕*Reservations essential* ☰*AE, DC, MC, V* ☉*Pagoda: no dinner Fri. No lunch Sat. The House: no dinner Sat.–Thurs. No lunch Sun.–Fri.* ✢*2D*

WHERE TO STAY

$ ⊞ **Astoria.** One of Tiberias's better moderately priced hotels, the Astoria is set away from the lake. Don't worry; there are still views from guest rooms. What it lacks in location, however, it makes up for in quality. It's comfortable, clean, and family-run, with furnishings in attractive pastels. Large family rooms are available. **Pros:** good value; great views of the water. **Cons:** too far to walk downtown; basic decor. ⊠*13 Ohel Ya'akov St.,* ☎*04/672–2351* ⊕*www.astoria.co.il* ⌕*88 rooms* ⌕*In-hotel: bar, pool, spa, laundry service, Internet terminal, parking (free), no-smoking rooms* ☰*AE, MC, V* ☉*BP.* ✢*1B*

¢ ⊞ **Beit Berger.** This family-run hotel has spacious rooms, most with balconies. A car is an advantage here, but there is frequent public transportation downtown (except on the Sabbath). The hotel is self-catering, so the supermarket across the street is very convenient. Recent additions such as satellite TV have made this place quite a bargain. **Pros:** reasonable rates; hillside views, kitchens. **Cons:** too far to walk downtown; no swimming pool. ⊠*27 Neiberg St.* ☎*04/671–5151* ⌕*45 rooms,*

2 apartments ☺In-room: kitchen, refrigerator. In-hotel: bar, laundry service, Internet terminal, parking (free) ☐*AE, DC, MC, V.* ✛*1B*

$$ ☎**Caesar.** Part of a small national chain, the lakefront Caesar offers views from all rooms. Public areas—with much marble, brass, and leather—are nicely decorated, providing islands of intimacy inside and out. The spacious guest rooms have tasteful, if unexceptional, furnishings, and every suite has a whirlpool bath. The outside pool area is entirely concrete, while the warm indoor pool uses natural thermal spring water from Hammat Gader. A large gym and wide range of treatments make the spa a definite attraction. **Pros:** convenient location; spring-fed pool. **Cons:** crowded on weekends. ✉*The Promenade* ☎*04/672–7272* ⊕*www.caesarhotels.co.il* ⤵*229 rooms, 7 suites, 2 penthouses* ☺*In-room: refrigerator, Wi-Fi. In-hotel: bar, pools, gym, spa, laundry service, Internet terminal, parking (free)* ☐*AE, DC, MC, V* ⭐*BP.* ✛*3D*

$$ ☎**Club Hotel.** Cascading down a hillside, this all-suites hotel offers an unimpeded view of the lake. Units sleep at least four, and the rate is the same up to that number. This classic vacation property has cheerful decor and an upbeat style, an all-season team to engage the kids, and a good health club to relax their parents. Downtown is less than 10 minutes away by car or cab. **Pros:** spectacular views; spacious rooms. **Cons:** crowded on weekends; away from downtown. ✉*Ahad Ha'am St.* ☎*04/672–8000* ⤵*307 suites* ☺*In-room: safe, refrigerator, kitchen. In-hotel: bar, tennis court, pool, gym, laundry service, parking (free)* ☐*AE, DC, MC, V* ⭐*BP.* ✛*1A*

$$ ☎**Gai Beach.** The rare lakeshore location is a big plus, and for some, so is the distance from the noisy downtown promenade. A marble lobby lounge is large and airy, yet clusters of comfortable armchairs create some intimacy. Guest rooms are well designed and tastefully furnished, if a bit small; about half face the lake. On two floors the rooms have private balconies. The hotel gives you free access to the adjacent water park, with seven slides, a wave pool, and a children's pool, making it arguably the most family-friendly hotel in town. The guests-only spa has a very private feel. **Pros:** on the lake; gorgeous spa; far from the hubbub. **Cons:** a bit isolated; crowded on weekends. ✉*Rte. 90* ☎*04/670–0700* ⊕*www.gaibeachhotel.com* ⤵*198 rooms, 2 suites* ☺*In-room: safe, Wi-Fi. In-hotel: restaurant, room service, bar, pools, gym, spa, beachfront, laundry service, parking (free)* ☐*AE, DC, MC, V* ⭐*BP.* ✛*3D*

$ ☎**Lavi Kibbutz Hotel.** With a new wing built in 2008, this guesthouse is keeping up with the times. Rooms are spacious, and many have good views. The religious community here allows no checking in or out and no use of cars between Friday and Saturday evening. That said, the atmosphere is welcoming for all, and waking up in peaceful rural surroundings has much to recommend it. The hospitality of kibbutz members offers a window on life at one of the country's 17 religious kibbutzim. Ask to see the synagogue furniture factory and the unique apparatus set up in the cowsheds to milk the cows on Saturday without violating the Sabbath. **Pros:** opportunity to experience kibbutz life; central location. **Cons:** no evening entertainment; sabbath restrictions. ✉*Rte. 77, Lavi, 11 km (7 mi) west of Tiberias* ☎*04/679–9450* ⊕*hotel.lavi.co.il* ⤵*188 rooms, 4 suites* ☺*In-hotel: bar, tennis court, pool, gym,*

6

children's programs (ages 3–13), laundry service, Internet terminal, parking (free), no-smoking rooms ⊟*AE, DC, MC, V* ⦿⏐*BP.* ⊹*1A*

$$$$ ⚏ **Rimonim Galei Kinnereth.** It's easy to understand why this grand dame was a personal favorite of Israel's founding prime minister, David Ben-Gurion. Its location right on the lake is unbeatable. The spa is a soothing complex suffused with incense and candles; a large whirlpool gurgles away in its own glassed-in gazebo. Guest rooms are nicely decorated, but they are neither extraordinary enough nor large enough to justify the rack rate. Breakfast and either lunch or dinner are included. **Pros:** convenient to Tiberias; lakeside swimming pool; sense of history. **Cons:** can be crowded on weekends. ⊠*1 Eliezer Kaplan St.* ☎*04/672–8888* ⦿*www.rimonim.com* ⤢*113 rooms, 7 suites* ⟁*In-room: safe, refrigerator, Wi-Fi. In-hotel: bar, pool, gym, spa, beachfront, water sports, laundry service, Internet terminal, parking (free), no-smoking rooms* ⊟*AE, DC, MC, V* ⦿⏐*MAP.* ⊹*3D*

$$ ⚏ **Ron Beach.** The northernmost hotel in Tiberias, the family-run Ron Beach has rare private lake frontage, though no beach. Most guest rooms, in well-chosen shades of gold and light blue, are in a two-story building facing the water. The upper floor is made up of suites; the lower floor opens out to lawns and the pool area. In addition, there are several very large family rooms. All in all, it's a great value. **Pros:** lakeside location; pretty pool. **Cons:** too far to walk to downtown; no beach. ⊠*Gedud Barak St.* ☎*04/679–1350* ⦿*www.ronbeachhotel.com* ⤢*70 rooms, 4 suites* ⟁*In-room: refrigerator. In-hotel: room service, bar, pool, laundry service, Internet terminal, parking (free)* ⊟*AE, DC, MC, V* ⦿⏐*BP.* ⊹*1C*

$$$ ⚏ **Scots Hotel.** Formerly a hospital, this place has been successfully rein-
Fodor's Choice vented as an interesting upscale hotel. Two renovated older structures and
★ one entirely new one produce a pleasingly asymmetrical complex filled with pleasant surprises, such as a roof terrace where you can have a drink or light meal, and an inviting courtyard with a waterfall. Everywhere are unexpected views of the lake. The aesthetics are wonderful, with nicely decorated rooms and well-appointed bathrooms. **Pros:** boutique-hotel feel; historic setting; central location. **Cons:** no nightly entertainment. ⊠ *1 Gedud Barak St., at Hayarden St.* ☎*04/671–0710* ⦿*www.scotshotels.co.il* ⤢*69 rooms* ⟁*In-room: safe, refrigerator, Wi-Fi. In-hotel: room service, bar, pool, beachfront, laundry service, Internet terminal, parking (free), no-smoking rooms* ⊟*AE, DC, MC, V* ⦿⏐*BP.* ⊹*2D*

$ ⚏ **Shavit's Arbel Guest House.** Israel and Sarah Shavit make congenial hosts: he's a licensed tour guide, and she's a chef. Their inn, containing whirlpools and wooden balconies, is surrounded by a riot of greenery, including an inviting *bustan* (a local-style garden redolent with fragrant herbs). Four apartments have a living room and a bedroom (one is wheelchair accessible); the fifth has two bedrooms. The rustic environment, 10 minutes from Tiberias and the Sea of Galilee, is pleasing, and the dining room transforms into a good-value à la carte restaurant in the evening. **Pros:** warm hospitality; delicious food. **Cons:** far from downtown Tiberias; no swimming pool. ⊠*Rte. 7717, off Rte. 77, Arbel Village* ☎*04/679–4919* ⦿*www.inisrael.com/shavit* ⤢*1 room, 5 apartments* ⟁*In-room: no phone, kitchen, refrigerator. In-hotel: restaurant,* *laundry service* ☰*AE, DC, MC, V* ❘◯❘*BP.* ✛*2A*

$$$$ ⊞ **Sheraton Moriah.** The lobby and bar are bright, comfortable places to relax, the service generally professional and accommodating. The spa makes it one of the most relaxing places in the area. The hotel overlooks the water, but does not have lake frontage. **Pros:** convenient to Tiberias; views from most rooms. **Cons:** no beach. ✉*Off Habanim St.* ☎*04/671–3333* ⊕*www.sheraton.com* ⮔*258 rooms, 23 suites* ⌂*In-room: safe, refrigerator. In-hotel: room service, bar, pool, gym, spa, laundry service, Internet terminal, parking (free)* ☰*AE, DC, MC, V* ❘◯❘*BP.* ✛*3D*

$ ⊞**YMCA Peniel-by-Galilee.** Archibald Harte, founder of Jerusalem's landmark YMCA, built a lakeside retreat here in the 1930s and later bequeathed his property to the Jerusalem YMCA. You can still feel his presence walking on the pebbly beach, and relaxing in the common areas decorated with antique Damascene wood panels. Spacious guest rooms, most with lake views, are furnished simply but comfortably; two have kitchenettes. The pool is fed by a natural spring, with little fish swimming in the clear water. A loyal clientele responds to the quiet charm of the place, making reservations essential. **Pros:** rustic apppeal; reasonable rates. **Cons:** too far to walk to town; no evening entertainment. ✉*Off Rte. 90, 3 km (2 mi) north of Tiberias* ☎*04/672–0685* ⊕*www.ymca-galilee.co.il* ⮔*12 rooms, 1 suite* ⌂*In-room: kitchen (some), refrigerator. In-hotel: restaurant, pool, beachfront* ☰*AE, DC, MC, V* ❘◯❘*BP.* ✛*1C*

NIGHTLIFE AND THE ARTS

Much of the entertainment, especially in the larger hotels in Tiberias, is of the live-lounge-music variety: piano bars, one-man dance bands, and crooners. Thursday and Friday are "nightclub" nights at some hotels, with dance music for the weekend crowds. The clientele tends to be a bit older. Generally speaking, the younger set wouldn't be caught dead here, preferring to hang out at one of the few pubs, where the recorded rock music is good and loud and the beer is on tap.

The cultural center **Bet Gabriel** (✉*650 feet east of Tzemach Junction, west of Ma'agan* ☎*04/675–1175* ✉*bg@betgabriel.co.il*) is located on the southern shores of the Sea of Galilee, only a 10-minute drive from Tiberias. Its fine architecture, beautiful garden setting, and concert facilities have established its popularity in the area. Tiberias's Tourist Information Office and major hotels carry information on the month's performances and art exhibits.

SPORTS AND THE OUTDOORS
BEACHES
The Sea of Galilee—a freshwater lake—is a refreshing but rocky place for a swim. You can recline on pleasant commercial beaches with amenities ranging from cafeterias to water parks, or on free beaches with minimal facilities. Note that the region has seen a drought over the past few years, so at this writing the water level is low. The numerous water parks with slides and pools remain popular.

September's **Kinneret Swim,** a tradition since 1953, has both amateur (3½ km [2 mi] and 1½ km [1 mi]) and competitive (1½ km [1 mi]) categories. At several locations around the Sea of Galilee you can hire pedal boats, rowboats, and motorboats and arrange to water-ski. Serious kayakers convene for an annual international competition in March.

Blue Beach (✉ *Rte. 90, at northern exit from Tiberias* ☎ *04/672–0105*) is one of the oldest establishments in the region. It's open May to October, and admission is NIS 40. Open May to October, **Gai Beach** (✉ *Rte. 90, at southern exit from Tiberias* ☎ *04/670–0713*) has a multi-slide water park in addition to swimming. Admission is NIS 70.

WALKING AND JOGGING
A **promenade** follows the lakeshore for about 5 km (3 mi) south of Tiberias, offering nice views of the lake and Golan Heights. As you leave the hotels behind, you appreciate the Sea of Galilee's mystic beauty. At this writing the promenade is being extended north of the city.

WATER SPORTS
Waterskiing and boat rentals are popular activities on the lake. You can ride in everything from large ferries to reproductions of the fishing boat St. Peter would have used. The recent drought has had an impact on ferries: ask your hotel or the tourist office about sailing opportunities.

Holyland Sailing (✉ *Tiberias Marina* ☎ *04/672–3006* ⊕ *www.jesusboats. com*) has five wooden boats that are replicas of those in use during the time of Jesus. The 45-minute cruises include historical commentary and concerts of traditional music. Sunset cruises are especially popular.

SHOPPING
Tiberias relies heavily on tourism, yet has little in the way of shopping. The exception is jewelry. There are a few jewelry stores near the intersection of Habanim and Hayarden streets and in some of the better hotels. **Caprice** (✉ *Tabor St.* ☎ *04/670–0600*), a large diamond factory, introduces you to the industry with a video and a short tour of its workshops and small museum.

HAMMAT TIBERIAS

★ *2 km (1 mi) south of Tiberias, 7 km (4 mi) north of Kinneret.*

GETTING HERE AND AROUND
Hammat Tiberias is on the southern edge of Tiberias on Route 90. While you can walk from the downtown hotels, the summer heat makes this unbearable. Best to take a taxi.

The god Helios occupies the center of a spectacular 4th-century mosaic of the zodiac at Hammat Tiberias.

EXPLORING

Not to be confused with the nearby Tiberias Hot Springs (a modern spa where you can bathe), **Hammat Tiberias** is a national park that includes a notable mosaic floor, and the remains of an ornate 4th-century synagogue and ancient therapeutic baths. The Hamam Suleiman (Turkish bath), which was in use from 1780 until 1944, is now a museum. It's located just to the right of the park entrance. Hammat Tiberias is worth a half-hour visit, though the experience parallels the more impressive ruins and hot springs in which you can soak at Hammat Gader.

The site has Israel's hottest spring, gushing out of the earth at 60°C (140°F) because of cracks in the earth's crust along the Syrian-African Rift. Alas, this is an archaeological site, so you don't get to try the waters here. The healing properties of its mineral-rich waters were already recognized in antiquity, as evidenced by the ruins of ancient towns—including an exquisite 4th-century AD mosaic floor of a synagogue.

Legend says that Solomon, the great king of Israel, wanted a hot bath and used his awesome authority to force some young devils below ground to heat the water. The fame of the salubrious springs spread far and wide, bringing the afflicted to seek relief. Seeing such gladness among his subjects, Solomon worried about what would happen when he died and the devils stopped their labors. In a flash of the wisdom for which he was renowned, Solomon made the hapless devils deaf. To this day, they have not heard of the king's demise and so continue to heat the water for fear of his wrath.

By the end of the Second Temple period (the 1st century AD), when settlement in the Sea of Galilee region was at its height, a Jewish town called Hammat (Hot Springs) stood here. With time, Hammat was overshadowed by its newer neighbor, Tiberias, and became known as Hammat Teverya (Tiberias Hot Springs). The benefits of the mineral hot springs were already legendary: a coin minted in Tiberias during the rule of Emperor Trajan, around AD 100, shows Hygeia, the goddess of health, sitting on a rock with a spring gushing out beneath it.

Parts of ancient Hammat have been uncovered near the road, bringing to light a number of ruined **synagogues.** The most dramatic dates from the 4th century AD, with an elaborate **mosaic floor** that uses motifs almost identical to those at Beit Alfa: classical Jewish symbols, human figures representing the four seasons and the signs of the zodiac, and the Greek god Helios at the center. The mosaics of Hammat Tiberias are among the finest ever found in Israel. Later cultures exploited the hot springs, too, as the small adjacent Turkish bath attests.

Behind Hammat Tiberias, a turquoise dome marks the **tomb of Rabbi Meir Ba'al Ha-Ness,** the "Miracle Worker," who supposedly took a vow that he would not lie down until the Messiah came—and was therefore buried in an upright position. His name has become an emblem for charitable organizations, and many a miracle has been attributed to the power of prayer at his tomb. ⊠*Rte. 90* 🕾*04/672–5287* ⊕*www.parks.org.il/ParksENG* 🖂*NIS 12* ☉*Apr.–Sept., Sat.–Thurs. 8–5, Fri. and Jewish holiday eves 8–4; Oct.–Mar., Sat.–Thurs. 8–4, Fri. and Jewish holiday eves 8–3.*

Tiberias Hot Springs, on the lake side of Route 90, is a modern spa fed by the mineral spring. In addition to sophisticated therapeutic services and facilities, it has a large, warm indoor mineral pool (35°C or 95°F) and a small outdoor one right near the lake's edge. A restaurant serves lunch. ⊠*Rte. 90* 🕾*04/672–8500* 🖂*Pools NIS 60, NIS 35 Sun.–Thurs. after 4 and Fri. after 2* ☉*Sun., Mon., and Wed. 8–8, Tues. and Thurs. 8 AM–11 PM, Fri. 8–4, Sat. 8:30–6.*

GINOSAR

10 km (6 mi) north of Tiberias.

Many Israelis know Ginosaur, a kibbutz founded in 1937, as the home of the late Yigal Allon (1918–80), commander of the crack Palmach battalions in the War of Independence and deputy prime minister of Israel in the 1970s under Golda Meir and Yitzhak Rabin. Travelers, however, come here to see an ancient fishing boat.

GETTING HERE AND AROUND

Egged buses frequently make the short trip here from the Tiberias Central Bus Station. Ask the driver to tell you where to get off.

EXPLORING

Kibbutz Ginosar's premier tourist attraction is a **wooden fishing boat** from the 1st century AD, found on the shore by two amateur archaeologists in 1986. Three years of drought had lowered the level of the lake, and bits of the ancient wood were suddenly exposed in the mud. Excavated in a frenetic 11 days, the 28-foot-long boat became an instant media sensation. Given the frequency of New Testament references to Jesus and his disciples boating on the Sea of Galilee—including coming ashore at Gennesaret, perhaps today's Ginosar—the press immediately dubbed it the "Jesus Boat." On the other hand, the startlingly vivid relic might have been a victim of the Roman naval victory over the rebellious Jewish townspeople of nearby Magdala in AD 67, as described by the historian Josephus Flavius. Whatever its unknown history, it is the most complete boat this old ever found in

an inland waterway anywhere in the world. Today it is exhibited dry in all its modest but remarkably evocative glory in a specially built pavilion. A short video tells the story. ⊠*Nof Ginosar, Off Rte. 90* ☎*04/672–7700* ⊕*www. jesusboat.com* ☜*NIS 20* ☉*Sat.–Thurs. 8–5, Fri. and Jewish holiday eves 8–1; last entry 1 hr before closing.*

WHERE TO STAY

$ 🏨 **Nof Ginosar.** Its grand location—with a private beach right on the Sea of Galilee—makes this kibbutz guesthouse especially popular. Renovated in 2008, the inn is warm and inviting, with spacious balconies looking out over the Sea of Galilee. There is a morning tour of the lovely grounds, and the nearby museum is free to guests. The dinner buffet includes both meat and vegetarian choices, the latter offering outstanding blintzes with sweetened cheese. **Pros:** convenient location; opportunity to experience kibbutz life; beautiful gardens. **Cons:** too far to walk to town; no evening entertainment. ⊠*Rte. 90* ☎*04/670–0300* ⊕*www. ginosar.co.il* ⇆*162 rooms* ⚐*In-room: refrigerator, Internet. In-hotel: bar, tennis court, pool, beachfront, laundry service, Internet terminal, parking (free), no-smoking rooms* ⊟*AE, DC, MC, V* ⦿*BP.*

EN ROUTE On Route 90, on your right a few miles north of Ginosar, is an electric substation that powers huge water pumps buried in the hill behind it. The Sea of Galilee is Israel's primary freshwater reservoir and the beginning of the **National Water Carrier**, a network of canals and pipelines that integrates the country's water sources and distribution lines. On the hill above is the small tell or mound of the Old Testament city of **Kinneret**, which dominated a branch of the Via Maris, the main highway of the ancient Near East. Scholars assume that the Hebrew name for the lake—Kinneret—comes from that of the most important city on its shores in antiquity. Romantics contend that the name derives from the lake's shape, which resembles the biblical *kinnor* (lyre).

TABGHA

★ *4 km (2 ½ mi) north of Ginosar, 14 km (8 mi) north of Tiberias, at Capernaum Junction (Rtes. 90 and 87).*

With a name that is an Arabic corruption of the Greek Heptaegon (Seven Springs), Tabgha is a cluster of serene holy places associated with Jesus' ministry in the Galilee. A promenade and hiking trails connect the shrines.

Churches are among the sights along the peaceful shores of the Sea of Galilee.

GETTING HERE AND AROUND

Tabgha is located off Route 87, a few hundred meters from the junction with Route 90. A promenade connects the Church of the Multiplication with the Church of the Primacy of St. Peter. A trail leads up to the Mount of Beatitudes, but the hike is best enjoyed going downhill, with the glorious views of the lake in front of you. Even without a car, Tabgha can be easily walked to from Route 90.

EXPLORING

The large, orange-roofed **Church of the Multiplication** was dedicated by the German Benedictines (Roman Catholic) in 1936 on the scanty remains of earlier shrines. The site has long been venerated as the "deserted place" of the Gospels, where Jesus miraculously multiplied two fish and five loaves of bread to feed the crowds that followed him. The present airy limestone building with the wooden truss ceiling was built in the style of a Byzantine basilica to give a fitting context to the beautifully wrought 5th-century mosaic floor depicting the loaves and fishes in front of the altar. The nave is covered with geometric designs, but the front of the aisles is filled with flora and birds and, curiously, a Nilometer, a graded column once used to measure the flood level of the Nile for the purpose of assessing that year's collectible taxes. ⊠ *Rte. 87* ☎ *04/670–0180* ✉ *Free* ⊙ *Daily 8–5:20.*

The austere, black basalt **Church of the Primacy of St. Peter,** 200 yards east of the Church of the Multiplication, is built on the water's edge, over a flat rock known as Mensa Christi (the Table of Christ). After his resurrection, the New Testament relates, Jesus appeared to his disciples by the Sea of Galilee and presented them a miraculous catch of fish. Three times

Jesus asked the disciple Peter if he loved him, and after his reply of "You know that I love you," Jesus commanded him to "Feed my sheep." Some scholars see this affirmation as Peter's atonement for having thrice denied Jesus in Jerusalem after Jesus' arrest. The episode is seen as establishing Peter's "primacy" (Matthew 16:18) and, in the Roman Catholic tradition, that of the popes, his spiritual successors. The site was included in the itineraries of both Pope Paul VI in 1964 and Pope John Paul II in 2000. ⊠*Rte. 87* ☎*04/672–4767* ✉*Free* ⊙*Daily 8–noon and 2–5.*

MOUNT OF BEATITUDES

★ *8 km (5 mi) north of Ginosar, 3 km (2 mi) north of Capernaum Junction.*

Tradition identifies this tranquil hillside as the site of Jesus' most comprehensive teaching, recorded in the New Testament as the Sermon on the Mount: "And seeing the multitudes, he went up into a mountain; and when he was set, his disciples came unto him. And he opened his mouth, and taught them, saying: 'Blessed are the poor in spirit, for theirs is the kingdom of Heaven . . .'" (Matthew 5:3). In 2000, Pope John Paul II celebrated mass with some 100,000 faithful a bit higher up the hill.

GETTING HERE AND AROUND
It's best to drive here. Lots of tourist buses make the journey, but there is no public transportation.

EXPLORING
The domed **Roman Catholic church**, run by the Franciscan Sisters (Italian), was designed by the famous architect Antonio Barluzzi and completed in 1937. Windows are inscribed with the opening words (in Latin) of the Beatitudes, the initial "Blessed are . . ." verses from the Sermon on the Mount. The terrace surrounding the church offers a superb view of the Sea of Galilee, best enjoyed in the afternoon, when the diffused western sun softens the light and heightens colors. Keep in mind this is a pilgrimage site, so dress modestly and respect the silence. Catholics and Protestants feel equally at home at this site, where the sisters also run a pilgrim hospice. ⊠*Rte. 8177, off Rte. 90* ☎*04/679–0978* ✉*NIS 5 per vehicle* ⊙*Apr.–Sept., daily 8–noon and 2:30–5; Oct.–Mar., daily 8–noon and 2:30–4.*

KORAZIM

Rte. 8277, at Rte. 90, 6 km (4 mi) north of Capernaum Junction.

GETTING HERE AND AROUND
Scenic Route 8277 offers some breathtaking views of the Sea of Galilee far below, but you'll need a car to enjoy them. There is no public transit here. Consider saddling up a horse from the stables at Vered Ha-Galil and riding here.

EXPLORING
The main attraction is the archaeological site of **Korazim**, a national park; there are also some special accommodations in the area. Built on a basalt bluff a few miles north of the Sea of Galilee, the ancient Jewish town of Korazim was renowned for its high-quality wheat. It also provided services and hospitality for travelers on the nearby high

road to Damascus and the east. Korazim (or Chorasin) is mentioned in the New Testament (Matthew 11:21) as one of the towns rebuked by Jesus, but almost nothing survives from that era. The extensive ruins exposed in modern excavations date to the 4th or 5th century AD. The dominant building is the monumental basalt **synagogue** adorned with the stone carvings of plants and animals. One remarkable artifact, a decorated and inscribed stone "armchair" dubbed the Throne of Moses, is thought to have been used by the worthies of the community during the reading of the Torah. The lake views from the site are impressive. ✉ *Rte. 8277* ☎ *04/693–4982* ⊕ *www.parks.org.il/ParksENG* 🔁 *NIS 18* ⊙ *Apr.–Sept., Sat.–Thurs. 8–5, Fri. and Jewish holiday eves 8–4; Oct.–Mar., Sat.–Thurs. 8–4, Fri. and Jewish holiday eves 8–3.*

WHERE TO STAY

$ 🛏 **Frenkels Bed and Breakfast.** Americans Etha and Irwin Frenkel retired to this rustic village on the border between the Lower and Upper Galilee, and have made gracious hospitality a second career. Each spacious unit, set amid lovingly tended gardens and with tantalizing views of the Sea of Galilee, has its own distinct character, courtesy of combinations of wood and stone, cane furniture, tiles, and throw rugs. The atmosphere is one of warmth and intimacy. **Pros:** convenient to national parks; charming rooms. **Cons:** no evening entertainment; no telephones in room. ✉ *Rte. 8277, Korazim* ☎ *04/680–1686* ⊕ *www.thefrenkels. com* 🔁 *3 suites* ⚿ *In-room: no phone, refrigerator. In-hotel: Internet terminal, no-smoking rooms* ⊟ *No credit cards* ⦿ *BP.*

$$ 🛏 **Vered Ha-Galil Guest Farm.** When former Chicagoan Yehuda Avni and
★ his Jerusalem-born wife Yonah came here in the 1960s, building this inn took a lot of imagination. While the stunning views of the Sea of Galilee were unbelievable, the site was barren hillside. The Avnis created something then unique in Israel: a ranch where guests can ride during the day and retire to luxurious rooms at night. The units, from cozy one-room cabins to larger, more luxurious cottages, combine wood and basalt rock. Some have wood-burning stoves and hot tubs overlooking the lake. The restaurant has a fine regional reputation for its hearty soups, salads, and steaks. **Pros:** best stable in the area; convenient to national parks; panoramic views. **Cons:** no evening entertainment. ✉ *Rtes. 8277 and 90, Korazim* ☎ *04/693–5785* ⊕ *www.veredhagalil.co.il* 🔁 *7 cabins, 14 cottages* ⚿ *In-room: kitchen (some), refrigerator. In-hotel: restaurant, bar, pool, laundry service, Internet terminal* ⊟ *AE, DC, MC, V.*

CAPERNAUM

3 km (2 mi) east of Tabgha and the Capernaum Junction, 17 km (10½ mi) northeast of Tiberias.

GETTING HERE AND AROUND

Capernaum is on Route 87, east of the intersection with Route 90. Since buses leave you a few miles from the site, it's best to drive.

EXPLORING

Two millennia ago, **Capernaum** (Kfar Nahum in Hebrew) was a thriving town of merchants, farmers, and fishermen; among them was St. Peter, with whom Jesus stayed. Today the archaeological site, which includes

Capernaum was the base of Jesus's Galilean ministry, but the synagogue remains date from a later era.

a beautifully manicured garden and two monasteries, is visited for its religious connections. The eastern monastery, distinguished by its red-domed church, is Greek Orthodox and is seldom visited. The western, Franciscan one, at the first turnoff after Tabgha, is what you come to see. For Christians, this is among the most moving sites in Israel, with a futuristic church built astride the ruins of Peter's house and the room where Jesus is believed to have slept.

Jesus established his base in Capernaum for the three years of his ministry in the Galilee, where, the New Testament relates, he recruited some of his disciples ("Follow me, and I will make you fishers of men" [Matthew 4:19]). He ultimately cursed the city for not heeding his message. Suspended from outer support pillars over the scanty remains of Capernaum's central Christian shrine, the **House of St. Peter** (where Jesus is believed to have lodged), an ultra-modern church follows the octagonal outline of the Byzantine basilica that once stood here.

The prosperity of this ancient Jewish community is immediately apparent from the remains of its **synagogue,** which dominates the complex. (It was excavated by the Franciscan friars in the early 20th century and partly restored.) The ancient Jewish community went to the expense of transporting white limestone blocks from afar to set the building off from the town's crudely built basalt houses. Stone benches line the inside walls, recalling the synagogue's original primary function as a place where the Torah was read. Once thought to date to the 2nd or 3rd century AD, the synagogue is now regarded by many scholars as belonging to the later Byzantine period (4th–5th centuries AD). It is certainly not the actual one in which Jesus taught, but since consecrated ground was often reused, the small earlier structure in the excavation pit in the present building's southeastern corner may have been.

Limestone reliefs that once graced the synagogue exterior represent a typical range of Jewish artistic motifs: the native fruits of the land, the biblical Ark of the Covenant, a seven-branched menorah, a shofar, and an incense shovel (to preserve the memory of the Temple in Jerusalem, where they were used prior to the city's destruction in AD 70). A small 1st-century mosaic from Magdala shows a contemporary boat, complete with oars and sails—a dramatic illustration of the many New Testament and Jewish references to fishing on the lake. ⊠ *Rte. 87* ☎ *04/672–1059* ✆ *NIS 3* ☉ *Daily 8–4:50.*

SPORTS AND THE OUTDOORS

Northeast of Capernaum, the so-called kayaks of **Abukayak** (⊠ *Jordan River Park, Rte. 888* ☎ *04/692–2245 or 04/692–1078*) are really inflated rubber canoes. Abukayak offers a serene one-hour paddle down the lower Jordan River, from March through November; a truck picks you up at the end. Life jackets are provided, and the trip is appropriate for young children.

EN ROUTE Route 87 continues east past Capernaum and crosses the **Jordan River**— somewhat muddy at this point—at the Arik Bridge. Those raised on spirituals extolling the Jordan's width and depth are often surprised to find how small a stream it really is: seldom wider than 30 feet. The Jordan enters the Sea of Galilee just a few hundred yards downstream.

In this wetland area (now the Jordan River Park, 1 km [½ mi] up Route 888), archaeologists have excavated the elusive site of the ancient Jewish town of **Bethsaida,** the home of Philip, Andrew, and Peter (according to John 1:44 and 12:21). Only a fraction of the extensive ruins here have been excavated; work is still in progress. However, this is a peaceful and evocative site, with great lake views, off the usual route. There's a charge per car.

KURSI AND THE EASTERN SHORE

Kursi: 17 km (10½ mi) southeast of Capernaum on Rte. 92, 5 km (3 mi) north of Ein Gev.

Kursi, where Jesus healed two men possessed by demons (Matthew 8:28-32), is today a park incorporating the ruins of a Byzantine monastery. The eastern shore of the Sea of Galilee is far less developed than the western and northern sides. That relatively rural character remains today, even as negotiations sputter along between Israel and Syria about returning this area to the control of Damascus.

GETTING HERE AND AROUND

Route 92 follows the eastern shore of the Sea of Galilee while Route 87 circles to the north of the lake. You can reach Kursi either by driving north or south from Tiberias. Whether you circle the lake clockwise or counterclockwise, the views are often breathtaking.

EXPLORING

Huddling under the imposing cliffs of the Golan Heights, where Route 789 climbs away from 92, the national park of **Kursi** is linked with the New Testament story of a man from Gadara (other gospels mention

Gerasa) who was possessed by demons. Jesus exorcised the evil spirits, causing them to enter a herd of swine grazing nearby, which then "rushed down the steep bank into the lake, and perished in the waters" (Matthew 8:32). Fifth-century Byzantine Christians identified the event with this spot and built a monastery. It was an era in which the holy places, true and new, were inundated with earnest pilgrims, and the monastery prospered from their gifts. The partly restored ruins of a fine Byzantine church are a classic example of the basilica style common at the time; the ruined monastery is perched higher up the hillside. ⌧*Rte. 92* ☎*04/673–1983* ⊕*www.parks.org.il/ParksENG* 🎟*NIS 12* ⊗*Apr.– Sept., Sat.–Thurs. 8–5, Fri. and Jewish holiday eves 8–4; Oct.–Mar., Sat.–Thurs. 8–4, Fri. and Jewish holiday eves 8–3.*

WHERE TO EAT AND STAY

$$ ✕**Ein Gev Fish Restaurant.** At lunchtime this popular establishment on
SEAFOOD the eastern shore bustles with tour groups, but it's a fine dinner option as well. Famous for St. Peter's fish (whole or filleted), it has added sea bream, trout, and gray mullet to the menu. Diners who want to avoid the baleful glare of a whole fish can opt instead for light entrées such as quiche, pizza, pasta, salads, and omelets. In fine weather, sit on the large outdoor terrace, and take in the view across the lake to Tiberias. Watch for the signs for Kibbutz Inn Ein Gev. ⌧*Kibbutz Ein Gev* ☎*04/665–8136* ⊕*www.eingev.com* ▭*AE, DC, MC, V.*

$ 🏨**Ein Gev Holiday Village.** Located on the palm-shaded eastern shore, this complex offers several options: spacious motel-style rooms, some with a view; waterfront units with sunset-watching patios; apartments designed for families; and older family cottages (called "kafriot"), some close to the water, others not. All have fully-equipped kitchenettes, and an on-site market means you can cook your own meals. About a mile north, Kibbutz Ein Gev, which runs the village, has a famous fish restaurant, small harbor, and wagon-train ride. **Pros:** convenient to national parks; beachfront setting. **Cons:** no evening entertainment. ⌧*Rte. 92, 12 km (7½ mi) north of Tzemach Junction, Ein Gev* ☎*04/665–9800* ⊕*www.eingev.com* ↩*184 rooms* ♿*In-room: kitchen. In-hotel: restaurant* ▭*AE, DC, MC, V* ⑩*BP.*

$$ 🏨**Ma'agan.** At the southern tip of the Sea of Galilee, this kibbutz has
☺ arguably the most enchanting view of all the properties around the lake. Furnishings are comfortable but not luxurious. Choose between a regular guest room and a spacious suite that includes a living room (with picture windows and fold-out sofas), a small bedroom, a kitchenette, and a patio. The food is unmemorable, but the facilities—sandy beach, swimming pool near the shore, extensive lawns—make it the best deal in the area. There is a smaller pool and a play area for kids. **Pros:** pretty beach; convenient location. **Cons:** no evening entertainment. ⌧*Rte. 92, 1 km (½ mi) east of Tzemach Junction* ☎*04/665–4411* ⊕*www. maagan.com* ↩*36 rooms, 112 suites* ♿*In-room: kitchen (some). In-hotel: bar, pool, beachfront, water sports, laundry facilities, Internet terminal, parking (free)* ▭*AE, DC, MC, V* ⑩*BP.*

$$ 🏨**Ramot Resort Hotel.** High up in the foothills of the Golan Heights, this hotel is only a few minutes from good beaches and a water park. Its main building has comfortable, well-appointed guest rooms with

private balconies and fabulous lake views. The deluxe wood chalets are in a different class, with whirlpool tubs, saunas, entertainment systems, and other perks. For a family on a more limited budget, the cabins are a cheaper option. Free guided tours of the area are available in summer. **Pros:** convenient to national parks; cooler temperatures than at the lake; beautiful vistas. **Cons:** no evening entertainment. ✉ *East of Rte. 92* ☎ *04/673–2636* ⊕ *www.ramot-nofesh.co.il* 📞 *80 rooms, 12 chalets, 17 cabins* ⚬ *In-room: Wi-Fi. In-hotel: bar, pool, laundry service, parking (free)* ☰ *AE, DC, MC, V* ⦿ *BP.*

NIGHTLIFE AND THE ARTS

The **Ein Gev Spring Festival** (✉ *gbg@betgabriel.co.il*), in business since the 1940s, once hosted the likes of Bernstein and Rampal, Dietrich and Sinatra, but its focus today is Israeli vocal music, from traditional to contemporary. It is held on Kibbutz Ein Gev during the Passover holiday (in April) but is organized by Bet Gabriel. E-mail ahead for dates and details, being sure to mention the festival in the subject line.

SPORTS AND THE OUTDOORS

Since the level of the Sea of Galilee is low, the shoreline has receded. With the coastal shelf exposed, the shrinking lake has become dangerous for poor swimmers since the bottom now drops precipitously. Keep a close eye on children.

BEACHES

Dugit Beach (✉ *Rte. 92, 8 km [5 mi] north of Ein Gev* ☎ *04/673–1750*) is a stone's throw north of Golan Beach. The neighbors are now under one management and provide similar recreational facilities, but Dugit has lifeguards.

Golan Beach (✉ *Rte. 92, 7 km [4½ mi] north of Ein Gev* ☎ *04/673–1750*) is the best-known beach on the northeastern shore of the lake. Its wide range of attractions include powerboat, rowboat, kayak, and pedalboat rentals; waterskiing; and the inflatable, boat-towed "bananas." There is no lifeguard, however.

WATER PARK

☺ **Lunagal,** a popular water park within Golan Beach, has pools, water slides, and other diversions for kids. ✉ *Rte. 92, 7 km (4½ mi) north of Ein Gev* ☎ *04/673–1750* 💲 *NIS 60 Apr.–June, Sept., and Oct.; NIS 80 July and Aug.* ⊙ *Call for hrs.*

HAMMAT GADER

10 km (6 mi) east of Tzemach Junction on Rte. 98, 22 km (14 mi) southeast of Tiberias, 36 km (22½ mi) northeast of Beit She'an.

GETTING HERE AND AROUND

Whether you are driving via Tiberias (Route 90) or the Golan Heights (Route 98), this highway is one of the most captivating in Israel with expansive views across the Yarmuk River into Jordan. Don't leave the roadway. The minefield signs mean exactly what they say.

EXPLORING

At **Hammat Gader,** you might feel like Caesar, bathing in hot springs that were popular in Roman times. In its heyday, Hammat Gader was the second-largest spa in the Roman Empire (after Baiae, near Naples). Built around three hot springs, Hammat Gader's impressive complex of baths and pools attests to the opulence that once attracted voluptuaries and invalids alike. In its time, the entrance corridor was kept dimly illuminated to dramatize the effect of the fine ornamental pool beyond. The large number of ancient clay oil lamps found in one small pool is proof of nighttime bathing and a hint that this area might have been set aside for lepers, to keep them out of sight of the regular patrons. Today, Hammat Gader is immensely popular among Israelis, who come for the freshwater pool, giant water slide, alligator farm, performing parrots, petting zoo, and restaurants. ⊠ *Rte. 98* ☎ *04/665–9999* ⊕ *www. hamat-gader.com* ✉ *NIS 50–69* ⊙ *Weekdays 7 AM–11 PM, Sat. 7 AM–10 PM, Sun. 7–5; last entry to park 1 hr before closing.*

WHERE TO STAY

$$$ 🏨 **Spa Village.** Though only a few yards away from the recreation park at Hammat Gader, this Thai-style complex is a world apart. Superbly outfitted wooden cabin-suites include hot tubs using thermal mineral water from the nearby springs; a few have their own saunas as well. Treatment rooms and exercise equipment are for hotel guests only. The warm mineral pool area, a serene oasis by day, feels almost mystical when you take the torch-lighted waters at night. The rest of the park is free for hotel guests. On weekends (Thursday and Friday nights), there is a minimum two-night stay. **Pros:** sybaritic experience; tropical gardens; pampering staff. **Cons:** no evening entertainment. ⊠ *Rte. 98, Hammat Gader* ☎ *04/665–5555* ⊕ *www.hamat-gader.com* ⤵ *29 suites* ⚘ *In-room: safe, refrigerator, Wi-Fi. In-hotel: restaurant, pool, spa, laundry service, Internet terminal, parking (free)* ⊟ *AE, DC, MC, V* ⓞ*BP.*

DEGANIA AND KINNERET

Degania Alef: 10 km (6 mi) south of Tiberias; Kinneret: 2 km (1 mi) northwest of Degania Alef.

Degania and Kinneret, two historic kibbutzim founded in the early 20th century, contain museums and historic graveyards worth a visit. Also nearby is Yardenit, a baptism site for Christians.

GETTING HERE AND AROUND

Both Degania Alef and Kinneret are south of Tiberias along Route 90. If you take a bus, ask the driver in advance about stopping.

EXPLORING

The first kibbutz, the collective village of **Degania Alef** was founded in 1909 by Jewish pioneers from Eastern Europe and established here at its permanent site on the banks of the Jordan River the following year. (Alef is the "A" of the Hebrew alphabet; don't confuse the kibbutz with its younger neighbor, Degania Bet.) Near the entrance is a small Syrian tank of World War II vintage. On May 15, 1948, the day after Israel declared its independence, it was invaded from all sides by Arab armies. Syrian forces came down the Yarmuk Valley from the east, overran two other kibbutzim en route, and were only stopped here, at the gates of Degania. The lead tank was set alight by a teenager with a Molotov cocktail.

Within restored stone buildings of the early kibbutz is the museum of **Beit Gordon** *(A. D. Gordon House)*, named for the spiritual mentor of the early pioneers. It houses two collections: one devoted to the region's natural history, the other examining the history and archaeology of human settlement in the surrounding valleys. Among the prehistoric sites represented is Ubeidiya, just south of the kibbutz and Israel's oldest human settlement, which scholars now date back to 1¼ million years ago. ✉*Near Rte. 90* ☎*04/675–0040* 🎫*Museum NIS 13* ⊙*Sun.– Thurs. 9–3, Fri. and Jewish holiday eves 10–1.*

Just across the Jordan from Degania, **Kinneret** was founded in 1911 as the country's second kibbutz, taking its name from the Hebrew word for the Sea of Galilee. Two places in the immediate vicinity are of interest to travelers.

The serene **Kibbutz Kinneret Cemetery** (✉*Off Rte. 90, 600 rds south of junction with Rte. 767* ☎*No phone*) includes the grave of Rachel *Hameshoreret* (Rachel the Poetess), a secular shrine for many Israelis. The cemetery offers a superb view of the lake, the Golan Heights, and majestic Mt. Hermon, to the north. Among the other distinguished denizens of this ground are pioneer leaders of the early Zionist movement. A few steps down from the clearing is Rachel's grave, identified by the low stone seat attached to it.

The pebbles left on her grave by visitors (a token of respect in the Jewish tradition) are a tribute to Rachel's renown and to the romantic hold she has on the national imagination. Born in Russia in 1890, she became a poet of national stature in Hebrew; she died in 1931. Rachel wrote with great sensitivity of the beauty of this region and with passion—knowing that her end was near—of her frustrated dream of raising a family. Her tombstone is eloquently devoid of biographical information; it carries only her name and four lines from one of her poems: "Spread out your hands, look yonder: / nothing comes. / Each man has his Nebo / in the great expanse." ✉*Rte. 90, 1 km (½ mi) north of the Jordan River.*

On a picturesque bend of the Jordan River where huge eucalyptus trees droop into the quiet water, is **Yardenit**, developed as a baptism site for Christian pilgrims. The baptism of Jesus by John the Baptist (John 1:28) is traditionally identified with the southern reaches of the Jordan River, near Jericho. However, that area was controlled by Jordan from 1949 to 1967 and then became a hostile frontier between Israel and Jordan following the Six-Day War. Pilgrims began to seek out accessible spots beyond the conflict zone. Here you will often see groups of white-robed pilgrims being immersed in the river amid prayers and hymns and expressions of joy. Snacks and souvenirs are available. ✉*Off Rte. 90* ☎*04/675–9111* ⊕*www.yardenit.com* 🎫*Free* ⊙*Sat.–Thurs. 8–5, Fri. 8–4, Jewish holiday eves 8–3.*

Upper Galilee and the Golan

WITH TZFAT (SAFED)

WORD OF MOUTH

"The tour of Golan Heights is optional, GO AT ANY COST!! With a good guide, you'll see the Syrian bunkers, mine fields, and the beauty of this area."

—FainaAgain

WELCOME TO UPPER GALILEE AND THE GOLAN

TOP REASONS TO GO

★ **The Old City of Tzfat:** Tiny historic synagogues offer a rare taste of Jewish houses of worship from bygone days. The many art galleries here are saturated with contemporary colors and shapes.

★ **Kayaking on the Jordan River:** A cool ride downriver can be a strenuous adventure or a tame family float; either way, it adds an interesting accent to a trip to the northern Galilee.

★ **The Hula Nature Reserve:** The Hula Reserve provides shelter for hundreds of species of birds, some 500 million of which fly over the Hula Valley twice a year on their migrations between Europe and Africa.

★ **Hermon River Nature Reserve:** Hike to the Banias waterfall and the Crusader ruins, and pick up a freshly baked pita from the Druze mill along the way.

★ **Gamla:** This is the site of Jews' heroic last stand following a siege by the Romans in AD 67. Aside from its history, it offers a challenging hike or an easy amble, with glimpses of wildlife.

1 Tzfat (Safed) and Environs. At 3,000 feet above sea level, Tzfat is Israel's highest city, known for being the center of Kabbalah, or Jewish mysticism. Although it's one of several holy sites in Israel, this city north of the Sea of Galilee has a spiritual dimension found nowhere else. Its twisting passageways, vestiges of the Ottomans and the Crusaders, caught the attention of artists, who make this one of the country's most enchanting destinations every spring and summer.

2 Upper Hula Valley. Situated between the Golan Heights, Naftali Ridge, and the Beqaa Valley, the Upper Hula Valley is best known for the Tel Dan Nature Reserve. Spread out over 800 acres, it's a prime spot for hiking, cycling, or picnicking. Bustling Kiryat Shmona and sleepy Metulla are the region's largest communities.

3 Golan Heights. This region's main geographic feature is the Sea of Galilee, the country's main water reservoir. This is the northernmost part of the country, and from Mount Hermon you can gaze out over Lebanon and Syria. The Golan Heights draws visitors throughout the year to its relaxing countryside, inventive restaurants, and leading wineries.

Katzrin

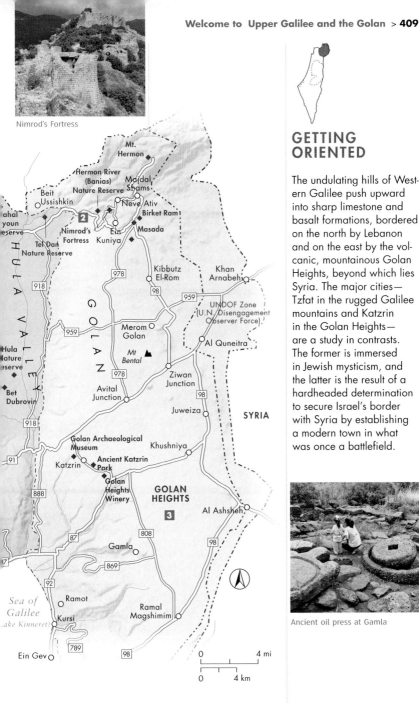

Nimrod's Fortress

GETTING ORIENTED

The undulating hills of Western Galilee push upward into sharp limestone and basalt formations, bordered on the north by Lebanon and on the east by the volcanic, mountainous Golan Heights, beyond which lies Syria. The major cities— Tzfat in the rugged Galilee mountains and Katzrin in the Golan Heights— are a study in contrasts. The former is immersed in Jewish mysticism, and the latter is the result of a hardheaded determination to secure Israel's border with Syria by establishing a modern town in what was once a battlefield.

7

Ancient oil press at Gamla

UPPER GALILEE AND THE GOLAN PLANNER

Getting Here

Only one airline flies from Tel Aviv to the small airport of Mahanayim, near Rosh Pina. Ayit operates a few 35-minute flights each day.

There is no transportation at the airport except for taxis. However, you can arrange for a rental car to be waiting at the airport. From the airport it's 10 km (6 mi) to Tzfat and 30 km (19 mi) to Kiryat Shmona.

When to Go

Unlike other parts of the country, there is no single time of the year to tour the Upper Galilee and the Golan.

The range of colors is wonderful in spring, when hillsides are covered with wildflowers. Summer brings families traveling with children, as well as music and culinary festivals; days can be hot, but the low humidity makes it manageable.

Wine fans appreciate the area in autumn during harvest time at the vineyards. Nights can be cold year-round. In winter, more precipitation means gushing streams and gray skies.

Getting Around

Bus Travel: Local Egged buses stop at all major sights in this region (there is always a kibbutz, a town, or some other small residential settlement nearby). Avoid buses if you're on a tight schedule, as they tend to be infrequent.

Car Travel: The Upper Galilee and the Golan are a three-hour, 180-km (112-mi) drive from Tel Aviv; a 1½-hour, 60-km (37-mi) drive from both Akko and Nahariya; and four hours from Jerusalem, which is 200 km (124 mi) to the south.

There are a few different ways to get here. From Tiberias and the Sea of Galilee, Route 90 runs north between the Hula Valley, on the east, and the hills of Naftali, on the west.

The more rugged Route 98 runs from the eastern side of the Sea of Galilee up through the Golan Heights to Mt. Hermon. Near the top of Route 98 you can pick up Route 91, which heads west into the Upper Galilee.

From the Mediterranean coast there are several options, but the main one is Route 85 from Akko. Route 89 runs parallel to Route 85 a little farther north, from Nahariya, and has some gorgeous scenery.

From Haifa take Route 75 to Route 77, turning onto Route 90 at Tiberias, or Route 70 north onto Route 85 east. If you're starting from Tel Aviv, drive north on Route 4 or 2 to Hadera; from there you'll head northwest on Route 65, exiting onto Route 85 east.

The state of Israel's roads is generally fair to good, but in the Upper Galilee in particular, some roads are still two-lane. Drive cautiously. Try to avoid driving during peak hours (usually late Thursday and Saturday afternoons), when city folk crowd the roads back to Jerusalem and Tel Aviv after a day out in the country.

There are plenty of gas stations along Route 90 and in the towns, such as Katzrin (Route 87) and Tzfat (Route 89). Most are open daily but close by 9 PM, so it's best to fill up during the day.

⇨ *For more information on getting here and around, see Travel Smart Israel.*

Planning Your Time

A day trip to the Golan Heights from Tiberias is doable but there's something about the lush foliage of the forests and the mountain air of the Golan Heights that slows the pace. Three or four days is ideal for a leisurely exploration of the region including wine-tasting, hiking a piece of wilderness, country meals, kayaking, or just kicking back in a room with a stunning view. The ideal way to see this area is by car, although local buses will get you almost anywhere you want to go if you have plenty of time. Note: touring in the Upper Galilee and the Golan is usually safe. If, however, security demands unusual caution, certain areas may be temporarily inaccessible to visitors.

Dining and Lodging

The Upper Galilee and the Golan's crisp, appetite-whetting air is an exquisite backdrop for some excellent restaurants. Fresh grilled Dan River trout, Middle Eastern fare prepared by Druze villagers, or home-style Jewish cooking in the heart of the holy city of Tzfat are all regional fare. Excellent local wines enhance any meal: try the Mt. Hermon red, Gamla cabernet sauvignon, and Yarden cabernet blanc and merlot. Note that in a few places (such as Tzfat) it can be hard to find a restaurant open on Shabbat (sundown Friday until sundown Saturday).

There are few grand hotels here, but the ample selection of guesthouses and inns ranges from ranch-style to home-style. As the local tourist industry has developed, many communities, especially kibbutzim and moshavim, have added hotels (or guest wings attached to homes); many will arrange tours, from rafting to Jeep excursions.

WHAT IT COSTS

	¢	$	$$	$$$	$$$$
Restaurants	under NIS 32	NIS 32–NIS 49	NIS 50–NIS 75	NIS 76–NIS 100	over NIS 100
Hotels		under $120	$120–$200	$201–$300	$301–$400	over $400

Restaurant prices are per person for a main course at dinner in NIS (Israeli shekels). Hotel prices are in US dollars, for two people in a standard double room in high season. Non-Israeli citizens paying in foreign currency are exempt from the 15.5% VAT tax on hotel rooms.

Visitor Information

Bet Ussishkin Museum has information about area nature reserves, natural history, and bird-watching. The Golan Tourist Association has a wealth of information about the Golan. The Israel Nature and Parks Authority staff are good resources for planning itineraries that include their sites in other parts of the region and the country. The visitor information service at Moshav Beit Hillel is especially helpful, with a wide selection of bed-and-breakfast accommodations in the moshav, which is in the heart of the Hula Valley tourist region. The Rosh Pina Information Center provides tips on touring Tzfat and Rosh Pina. The Tiberias Tourist Information Office can furnish information on the entire region. The Tourist Information Center–Upper Galilee can also provide information; it's open weekends and holidays only.

Contacts Bet Ussishkin Museum (✉ *Kibbutz Dan, M.P. Upper Galilee,* ☏ *04/694-1704*). **Golan Tourist Association** (🖃 *Box 175, Katzrin 12900* ☏ *04/696-2885* ⊕ *www.tour. golan.org.il*). **Israel Nature and Parks Authority Northern District** (✉ *Megiddo National Park* ☏ *04/659-0316* ⊕ *www.parks. org.il*). **Tiberias Tourist Information Office** (✉ *HaKishon St., Tiberias* ☏ *04/672-5666*). **Tourist Information Center–Upper Galilee** (✉ *Mahanayim Junction* ☏ *04/693-6945*).

Updated by
Shelly Paz

"Israel's Little Tuscany" has long been a nickname for the Upper Galilee. The green countryside, the growing numbers of both large-scale and boutique wineries, and the laid-back atmosphere have attracted urbanites for weekend jaunts (and sometimes for good).

The mountain air is redolent with the fragrance of spice plants; visitors can hike, cycle, or ride horses along trails that range from easy to challenging; and opportunities for kayaking, bird-watching, and other outdoor pursuits abound. These are the best vacation treats, all in a fascinating historical setting.

The main feature of this region is towering Mt. Hermon, known as Israel's "sponge." Huge volumes of water from winter snow and rainfall soak into its limestone, emerging at the base of the mountain in an abundance of springs that feed the Jordan River and its tributaries and provide half of Israel's water supply. The water also sustains lush vegetation that thrives year-round and is home to wildcats, hyraxes, gazelles, and hundreds of species of birds.

This water, and the strategic vantage points of the Galilee mountaintops and the Golan Heights, have made the region a source of political contention since time immemorial. Over the centuries, Egyptians, Canaanites, Israelites, Romans, Byzantines, Muslims, Crusaders, and Ottomans locked horns here; in the 20th century alone, the borders have been changed by Russia, Britain, France, and of course, Israel and Syria.

Borders are not the only things that have shifted here. A geological fault line, the Syrian-African Rift, cuts straight through the 30-km-long (19-mi-long) Hula Valley; in 1837 Tzfat and Tiberias were razed by an earthquake, though no significant rumbles have been heard since. Extinct volcanic cones give the Golan its unusual topographic profile.

With all this water and fertile soil, the region has long been an agricultural center and is today studded with apple orchards, kiwi plantations, fish ponds, sunflowers, and vineyards. The pastoral beauty and variety of outdoor activities attract people from elsewhere in Israel and the world, supplying the region's other main industry: tourism.

Proximity to Lebanon and Syria does not ordinarily deter people from visiting the Upper Galilee and the Golan. On the contrary, the combination of an exciting past with a gorgeous natural setting is precisely the draw here.

Since their arrival at the turn of the 20th century, the Jews have confronted a host of hardships and hurdles. Yet the tenacious Galileans will say there's no better place to live. Only four hours' drive from hectic Tel Aviv and visceral Jerusalem, visitors find this is truly another world.

TZFAT (SAFED) AND ENVIRONS

In the southern part of the Upper Galilee, attractions range from the narrow streets and historic synagogues of Tzfat's Old City to the wilderness of the Hula Nature Reserve. Other reserves, like Mt. Meron, have both scenic appeal and spiritual importance. At Rosh Pina you can shop and dine where the Galilee's first Zionist pioneers once labored. Or you can just relax at an inn or a kibbutz guesthouse and enjoy the wooded scenery.

TZFAT

33 km (20 mi) north of Tiberias, 72 km (45 mi) northeast of Haifa.

GETTING HERE AND AROUND

If you're driving to Tzfat from Jerusalem, take Route 6 north. If you're starting in Tel Aviv, head north on Route 2. Either way, you'll want to turn east on Route 65, then north on Route 90, then west on Route 89 to Tzfat. If your journey starts in Haifa, head north on Route 4, then east on Route 89 to Tzfat. Egged runs at least one bus daily to Tzfat from Tel Aviv, at least seven from Jerusalem, and at least 35 from Haifa.

In Tzfat the private company Nativ Express runs eight local bus lines. The Hamavreek taxi company in Tzfat will pick up incoming travelers at the Mahanayim Airport and take them to various destinations in the region. Buses from Tzfat central bus station, at the entrance to the city, head to most towns in the region.

Both of Israel's major bus companies, Egged Tours and United Tours, offer one- and two-day guided tours of the region, departing from Tel Aviv and Jerusalem.

ESSENTIALS

Bus Contacts Egged (☎ *2800 ⊕ www.egged.co.il). **Nativ Express** (☎ 1/599–599–599).

Taxi Contacts Hamavreek (☎ 04/697–4222).

Visitor and Tour Information Egged Tours (✉ 4 Bareket St., Petah Tikvah ☎ 1700/707–577). **Tzfat Visitor Center** (✉ Kikar Haatzmaut ☎ 04/692–7485). **United Tours** (✉ 113 Hayarkon St., Tel Aviv ☎ 03/522–2008 or 03/693–3412 ⊕ www.unitedtours.co.il).

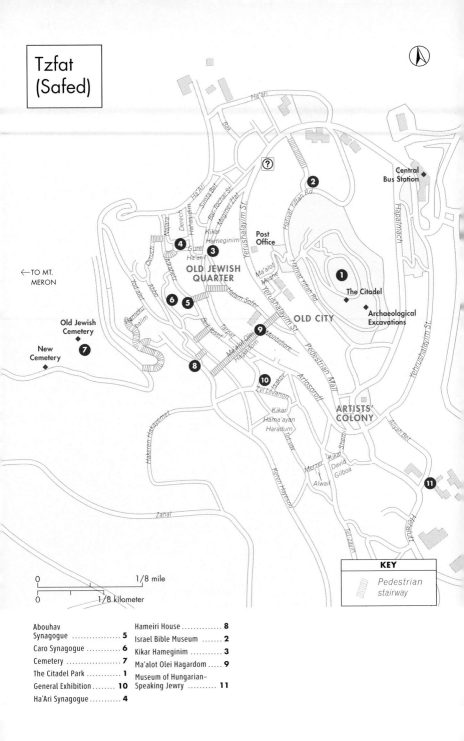

Tzfat
(Safed)

TO MT.
MERON →

Central
Bus Station

Ha'ari

Bat Yo'chai St.

Simta Bet

Margnet Zlat

Yerushalayim St.

Hativat Yiftah Rd.

Hapalmach

Kikar
Hameginim

Post
Office

Derech Hamasprim

Ha'ari

Mitzra

Natara

Arraher

Church

Abbo

Ma'alot
Moshe

Yerushalayim St.

Hativat Yiftah Rd.

The Citadel

Archaeological
Excavations

OLD JEWISH
QUARTER

OLD CITY

Pedestrian Mall

Yehrushalayim St.

Old Jewish
Cemetery

New
Cemetery

Tor Aslet

Hamaki

Jbalim

Beit Yosef

Talpat

Jatam Sofer

Ma'alot Olei
Hagardom

Montefiore

Artosoroff

Hameiri House

Kikar
Hama'ayan
Haradum

Zvi Levanon

Isator

Tavor

ARTISTS'
COLONY

Aliyah Bet

Hakeren Hakayemet

Keren Hayesod

Merzer

Alwail

Kikar
David
Gilboa

Tet Zayin

Hazati

Zahat

| 0 | | 1/8 mile |
| 0 | | 1/8 kilometer |

KEY

Pedestrian
stairway

Abouhav
Synagogue **5**

Caro Synagogue **6**

Cemetery **7**

The Citadel Park **1**

General Exhibition **10**

Ha'Ari Synagogue **4**

Hameiri House **8**

Israel Bible Museum **2**

Kikar Hameginim **3**

Ma'alot Olei Hagardom **9**

Museum of Hungarian-
Speaking Jewry **11**

CLOSE UP

What is Kabbalah?

The Kabbalah—which dates to ancient times but gained popularity starting in the 12th century, possibly as a reaction against formal rabbinical Judaism—is about reading between, behind, and all around the lines.

Each letter and accent of every word in the holy books has a numerical value with particular significance, offering added meaning to the literal word.

During the Middle Ages, the great mystic rabbis were the soul of this city. Under their tutelage, religious and mystical schools and meeting places mushroomed here.

Some of these leaders would leave their mark on the age, on the generations to follow, and of course, on Tzfat itself.

EXPLORING

Tzfat attracts artists who look for inspiration, travelers charmed by its cobbled alleys, and religious people in search of meaning—a rare example of harmony between the secular and the spiritual. The city is known for its spiritual, even sacred, air and its breathtaking views.

It doesn't take long to walk all of Tzfat's Old City. Visitors can poke around the little cobbled passages that seem to lead nowhere, or linger over some minute architectural detail on a building from another time. And it's almost impossible to get lost; Yerushalayim (Jerusalem) Street is a good orientation point—it runs through the heart of the Old City, encircles the Citadel, and from there, steps lead down to the two main areas of interest, the Old Jewish Quarter and the adjacent Artists' Colony. There is no way to avoid the hilly topography, though, so do wear comfortable walking shoes. As the town is largely Orthodox, modest dress is recommended when visiting synagogues. For women, this means a longish skirt or long pants and at least a half-sleeve top; for men, long pants are appropriate.

Tzfat hibernates from October through June, when the city's artists move to their galleries in warmer parts of the country. This does not mean you should leave Tzfat out of your itinerary during those months; there is enough to occupy the curious wanderer for at least a few hours, and much of it is free. In the summer, especially during July and August, Tzfat is abuzz with activity: galleries and shops stay open late, klezmer music (Eastern European Jewish "soul music") dances around corners, and the city extends a warm welcome to everyone.

TOP ATTRACTIONS

❺ Abouhav Synagogue. This large Sephardic synagogue is named in honor of a 14th-century Spanish scribe, one of whose Torah scrolls found its way here with the Spanish Jewish exiles 200 years later. A look around reveals a number of differences between this synagogue and its Ashkenazi counterparts, such as the Ha'Ari; for example, the walls are painted the lively blue typical of the Sephardic tradition, and the benches run along the walls instead of being placed in rows (so that no man turns his back on his neighbor).

Every detail is loaded with significance: there are three arks—for the three forefathers, Abraham, Isaac, and Jacob (the one on the right is said to be the Abouhav original)—and 10 windows in the dome, referring to the Commandments. The charmingly naive illustrations on the squinches include a depiction of the Dome of the Rock (referring to the destruction of the Second Temple) and pomegranate trees, whose 613 seeds are equal in number to the Torah's commandments. The original building was destroyed in the 1837 earthquake, but locals swear that the southern wall—in which the Abouhav Torah scroll is set—was spared. Call ahead, as there are no set visiting hours. ⊠ *Abouhav St.* ☎ *04/692–3885.*

Artists' Colony. The colony, set in Tzfat's old Arab Quarter, was established in 1951 by six Israeli artists who saw the promise hidden in Tzfat's war-torn and dilapidated condition; for them, the old buildings, the fertile landscape, and the cool mountain air fused into the magic ingredients of creativity. Others soon followed until, at its peak, the colony was home to more than 50 artists, some of whom are exhibited internationally. Most galleries are open only in the spring and summer, from about 10 AM to 6 PM. ⊠ *Old City of Tzfat* ☞ *Free.*

❻ Caro Synagogue. This is arguably the most charming synagogue in the Old City. It was named after Rabbi Yosef Caro, who arrived in Tzfat in 1535 and led its Jewish community for many years. He is the author of the Shulchan Aruch, the code of law that remains a foundation of Jewish religious interpretation to the present day, and this synagogue is said to have been Caro's study hall. It was destroyed in the great earthquake of 1837 and rebuilt in the mid-19th century. If you ask, the attendant might open the ark containing the Torah scrolls, one of which is at least 400 years old. A glass-faced cabinet at the back of the synagogue is the *geniza,* where damaged scrolls or prayer books are stored (because they carry the name of God, they cannot be destroyed). The turquoise paint here—considered the "color of heaven"—is believed to help keep away the evil eye. ⊠ *Alkabetz St.* ☎ *04/692–3284* ⊙ *Call for hrs.*

❿ General Exhibition. An important stop in a tour of the Artists' Colony, the works inside this large space are a representative sample of the work of Tzfat's artists, ranging from oils and watercolors to silk screens and sculptures, in traditional and avant-garde styles. The permission of the Muslim authorities was required to organize the Exhibition, as it is housed in the old mosque, easily identified from afar by its minaret. The Artists' Colony has recognized the growing presence of artists from the former Soviet Union, and the adjacent building holds the **Immigrant Artists' Exhibition.** In either facility, if any works catch your fancy, just ask directions to the artist's gallery for a more in-depth look at his or her work. ⊠ *Isakov and Zvi Levanon Sts.* ☎ *04/692–0087* ☞ *Free* ⊙ *Sun.–Thurs. 10–5, Fri., Sat., and Jewish holidays 10–2.*

❹ Ha'Ari Synagogue. This Ashkenazi synagogue has associations going back to the 16th century. It is named for a rabbi who left an indelible mark on Tzfat and on Judaism; his real name was Isaac Luria, but he was known to all as the Ari, Hebrew for "lion" and an acronym for

Adoneinu Rabbeinu Itzhak ("our master and teacher Isaac"). In his mere three years in Tzfat, he evolved his own system of the Kabbalah, which drew a huge following that would influence Jewish teaching and interpretation the world over, right up to the present day. Even more astounding is the fact that he died in his mid-thirties; it is generally said that one should not even consider study of the Kabbalah before the age of 40, when one reaches the requisite level of intellectual and emotional maturity.

The pale colors of this tiny Ashkenazi synagogue contrast sharply with its olive-wood Holy Ark, a dazzlingly carved tour de force with two tiers of spiral columns and vibrant plant reliefs. The synagogue was built after Luria's death, on the spot where he is said to have come with his disciples on Friday evenings to welcome the Sabbath. It was leveled by the 1837 earthquake and rebuilt in 1857. (The Sephardic Ari Synagogue, where the rabbi prayed, is farther down the quarter, by the cemetery. The oldest of Tzfat's synagogues, this 16th-century structure has especially fine carved wooden doors.) There are no set visiting hours. ⊠*Ha'Ari St.* ⊗*No set visiting hrs.*

❽ Hameiri House. This centuries-old stone building houses a museum documenting the life of the Jewish community of Tzfat over the past 200 years. ⊠*Keren Hayesod St.* ☎*04/697–1307 or 04/692–1939* ⊠*NIS 14* ⊗*Sun.–Thurs. 9–2:30, Fri. 9–1:30, Sat. by appointment only.*

WORTH NOTING

❼ Cemetery. An old and a new cemetery are set into the hillside below the Old Jewish Quarter. The old plots resonate with the names and fame of the Kabbalists of yore, and their graves are identifiable by sky-blue markers. It is said that if the legs of the devout suddenly get tired here, it is because they are walking over hidden graves. The new cemetery holds the graves of members of the pre-State underground Stern Gang and Irgun forces, who were executed by the British in Akko's prison (⇨*Chapter 5*). In a separate plot, bordered by cypresses, lie the 21 Tzfat teenagers killed by terrorists in 1974—they were taken hostage while they were on a field trip and sleeping overnight in a school in the northern Galilee town of Ma'alot. ⊠*Below Keren Hayesod St.* ⊠*Free.*

❶ Citadel Park. In Talmudic times, 1,600 years ago, hilltop bonfires here served as a beacon to surrounding communities heralding the beginning of the lunar month, the basis for the Jewish calendar. In the 12th century, the Crusaders grasped the strategic value of this setting and built the Citadel. It was conquered by the Muslim sultan Baybars in 1266, leaving only the scattered pieces you see today.

The Jewish settlement outside the Citadel's walls grew and prospered during and after the Crusader era, with the city becoming a center of Kabbalah studies. When the departing British Mandate forces left the town's key strategic positions to the Arab forces, the remains of the Citadel once again became a battleground between Jews and Arabs. ⊠*Old City.*

❷ Israel Bible Museum. This stone mansion was once the home of the Ottoman governor. Today it houses the somewhat dramatic paintings and sculptures of artist Phillip Ratner, all inspired by the Bible. ⊠*Hativat*

Tzfat is an artsy village in the northern Galilee known for being the birthplace of Kabbalah (Jewish mysticism).

Yiftah St., adjacent to Citadel Park ☎*04/699–9972* ✉*Free* ☉*May–Sept. Sun.–Thurs. 10–4, Fri. 10–1; Oct.–Dec. Sun.–Thurs. 10–2, Fri. 10–1.*

❸ Kikar Hameginim. "Defenders' Square" is the main square of the Old Jewish Quarter and was once its social and economic heart. A sign points to a two-story house that served as the command post of the neighborhood's defense in 1948—hence the plaza's name. ✉*Bar Yochai St.*

❾ Ma'alot Olei Hagardom. Part of Tzfat's charm is its setting, on the slope of a hill. This *ma'alot*, or stairway, which extends all the way down from Yerushalayim Street, forms the boundary between the Old Jewish Quarter and the Artists' Colony. It is named for Tzfat freedom fighters executed by the British during the Mandate. ✉*Off Yerushalayim St.*

⓫ Museum of Hungarian-Speaking Jewry. The founders and driving force of this museum are Tzfat residents and Holocaust survivors Hava and Yosef Lustig. The varied exhibits in the museum's few small rooms, including letters, children's books, drawings, items of clothing, and more, tell of the everyday life of communities and individuals in the Hungarian-speaking Jewish pre-Holocaust world. Visitors see a 20-minute video, and can search the computer database, which has information about 1,700 communities of Jews from Hungary, Transylvania, Slovakia, and other countries, including photographs of some 10,000 headstones. ✉*The old Ottoman government center (the Saraya), Kikar Haatzmaut* ☎*04/692–5881 or 04/692–3880* ⊕*www.hjm.org.il* ✉*NIS 15* ☉*Sun.–Fri. 9–1.*

WHERE TO EAT

$$$–$$$$ ✕ **Bat Ya'ar.** This timbered restau-
ISRALEI rant's delicious food is enhanced by
its wooded mountaintop setting. A
meaty bowl of bean stew, eaten by
the fireplace, is a pleasure on any
day. A kosher kitchen is available
for reserved groups. Outside the

restaurant is a playground for children. Hour-long family nature activity packages are offered, as well as horseback-riding excursions. Bat Ya'ar is 5 km (3 mi) north of Tzfat. It's best to call for directions. ✉*Birya Forest* 🕾*04/692–1788* ⚏*Reservations essential* ▭*AE, DC, MC, V.*

$$$ ✕ **Ein Camonim.** The Galilee Hills make perfect pastureland for live-
Fodor'sChoice stock—in this case, goats—and here you can taste the fresh output of
★ Ein Camonim's dairy. The all-you-can-eat menu includes a platter of
VEGETARIAN goat cheeses, a selection of home-baked bread, one bowl of fresh veg-
etable salad and another of French-style lettuce salad, a set of home-made salads, local wine, coffee, and dessert. There's a half-price menu for children 12 and under. The specialty shop next door sells the cheeses and other homemade products, including the dairy's own olives, vac-uum-packed rather than in glass jars—handy for travelers. ✉*Rte. 85, 20 km (12½ mi) southwest of Tzfat, 5 km (3 mi) west of Kadarim Junction (north of highway)* 🕾*04/698–9894* ⊕*www.ein-camonim. co.il* ▭*AE, DC, MC, V.*

$$ ✕ **Gan Eden.** The setting, an old stone house, lends great atmosphere
ECLECTIC to this family-run kosher eatery. Taking in the view of Mt. Meron (the restaurant's name means "paradise"), the place is best known for its fish, especially its fillet of sea bass. The "Calzones a Galil" (dumplings stuffed with salty Tzfat cheese) are served on lettuce leaves, cranber-ries, and walnuts. Gan Eden serves no meat or chicken. ✉*Mt. Canaan Promenade* 🕾*04/697–2434* ▭*AE, MC, V* ⊗*Closed Sat.*

$$$ ✕ **Habayit Bektze Hanof.** The "House at the View's Edge" is perched high
ISRAELI in the Birya Forest with a stunning vista of the surrounding hills. This restaurant serves a selection of dishes using local ingredients. The place's most popular meal includes several vegetarian dishes and a loaf of bread baked on the premises. There are private parties here sometimes, so call ahead. ✉*Birya Forest, 7 km (4 mi) from Tzfat* 🕾*04/692–3737* ▭*V* ⊗*Closed Sun. Oct.–Feb.*

¢ ✕ **Mifgash Rasko.** One of Tzfat's institutions, Mifgash (which means
ISRAELI "meeting place") is one of the city's most popular pizza parlors. Tzfat's youngsters pack the place, especially on Thursday and Saturday night. Though the decor is on the simple side, the dishes are generous, filling, and cheap. ✉*11 Weizmann St.* 🕾*04/692–1005* ▭*AE, DC, MC, V* ⊗*Closed Sat.*

WHERE TO STAY

$$$ 🖾 **Canaan Spa.** This elegant hotel on the outskirts of Tzfat knows how to pamper its guests. In addition to conventional Swedish massage, you can enjoy reflexology or aromatic massages or hot-stone treatments. Paintings and sculptures adorn public areas that are coordinated in tranquil colors for an effect of refined luxury. Facilities include tennis

and basketball courts and a 1½-acre private forest. The price includes brunch and dinner. **Pros:** truly relaxing atmosphere; great pool; fabulous brunch. **Cons:** remote location; not for families. ⊠ *Mt. Canaan Promenade, Tzfat* ☎ *04/699–3000* ⊕ *www.canaanspa.com* ⚲ *116 rooms, 8 suites* ⚘ *In-room: safe, refrigerator. In-hotel: restaurant, pools, spa, tennis court, no kids under 14* ☰ *AE, DC, MC, V* ⚭ *MAP.*

$ ⚹ **Joseph's Well.** At Kibbutz Amiad, 10 km (6 mi) south of Tzfat, this
⚙ lodging has rooms in clusters of three with a shared patio. Each room is like a cozy studio apartment, with pine furniture, coordinated table-cloths and sheets, and chintz curtains. They all have a coffee corner with an electric kettle, and tea and coffee. Breakfast is served in the kibbutz dining room. Unlike the bigger kibbutz hotels, Joseph's Well offers few activities, but is a good base for exploring both the Upper Galilee and the Panhandle. **Pros:** informal; terrific for children; a peek into kibbutz life. **Cons:** plain decor; don't expect sophisticated breakfast. ⚐ *M.P. Upper Galilee, 12335* ☎ *04/690–9829* ⊕ *www.amiad-inn.com* ⚲ *27 rooms* ⚘ *In-room: no phone. In-hotel: pool* ☰ *AE, DC, MC, V.*

$ ⚹ **Ron.** The rooms in this unassuming and somewhat old-fashioned hotel are spacious and light-filled; half have mountain views. The Ron is centrally located, making it a good choice for Orthodox travelers on the Sabbath. The pool is only open in the summer. **Pros:** Big pool, central location. **Cons:** Simple decor, men and women use pool at separate times. ⊠ *Near the Citadel Park, Hativat Yiftah, Box 22, Tzfat* ☎ *04/697–2590* ⚲ *50 rooms* ⚘ *In-hotel: restaurant, pool* ☰ *AE, MC, V.*

$$ ⚹ **Ruth Rimonim.** About 200 years ago, this gracious old building was
⚙ the local post office. Over the years, rooms were added and it became a *khan*, or inn. Since its transformation into a hotel in 1961, it has enjoyed a reputation for charm and excellence. The stone-walled rooms are both comfortable and rustic; the former stables serve as a dining room. Half the rooms have mountain views. Children's programs are offered in the summer. **Pros:** romantic; nice pool; central location. **Cons:** pool is open only in summer; menu is not inspiring; older kids can get bored. ⊠ *Artists' Quarter, Box 1011, Tzfat* ☎ *04/699–4666* ⊕ *www.rimonim.com* ⚲ *77 rooms* ⚘ *In room: refrigerator. In-hotel: 2 restaurants, bar, pool, gym, children's programs (ages 3–6)* ☰ *AE, DC, MC, V.*

$$$$ ⚹ **Sea View (Mizpe Hayamim).** This serene hotel, halfway between Tzfat
Fodor's Choice and Rosh Pina, has a splendid view of the Sea of Galilee. It specializes
★ in spa treatments that use local ingredients, such as the olive-branch massage and massages with oils distilled from wildflowers. If you're here for pampering, you hardly need to change out of your bathrobe. Half the rooms are suites and junior suites with whirlpools. The organic restaurant is known throughout the region, and the lobby has an herbal tea corner open around the clock. A gallery exhibits and sells Israeli artwork, and a gift shop offers homemade breads, cheeses, and other local products. **Pros:** great food; enchanting walking paths; pretty pool. **Cons:** need a car to get around; not a place for families. ⚐ *Box 27, Rosh Pina 12000* ☎ *04/699–4555* ⊕ *www.mizpe-hayamim.com* ⚲ *100 rooms* ⚘ *In-hotel: restaurant, pool, gym, spa, no-smoking rooms, no kids under 10* ☰ *AE, DC, MC, V* ⚭ *MAP.*

Getting on horseback is a popular activity in the Galilee, with its verdant hills, quiet forests, and gentle paths.

NIGHTLIFE AND THE ARTS

Every July or August Tzfat hosts a **klezmer festival** (☎04/692–7484), and there could be no better setting for three days of "Jewish soul music" than this mystical, cobbled-lane city. Some of klezmer's roots are Hasidic, making it plaintive and almost prayer-like in tone, especially with its emphasis on wind and string instruments. Many events are street performances and therefore free. Keep in mind, though, that Tzfat practically bursts at the seams at this time, with revelers both religious and secular.

SPORTS AND THE OUTDOORS

In the Birya Forest 5 km (3 mi) from Tzfat, **Bat Ya'ar** (☎04/692–1788) offers outdoor fun for the whole family including pony rides, a "rope park" with rope bridges between trees, and outdoor bowling with wooden lanes and balls. Admission is NIS 110 per person. Horseback riding is available for NIS 120 per person; children must be at least 10.

SHOPPING

Tzfat Candles (✉*Najara St., near the Ari Synagogue* ☎04/682–2068 🕙*Mon.–Thurs. 9–7, Fri. 9–12:30*) has grown from a one-room workshop to a huge store filled with the pleasant aroma of beeswax and the bright colors of Sabbath, Havdalah, and Hanukkah candles. Don't miss the museum of intricate wax sculptures.

MT. MERON

21 km (13 mi) west of Tzfat on Rte. 89.

GETTING HERE AND AROUND
From Tzfat, head west on Route 89.

EXPLORING

Mt. Meron. The spiritual importance of Tzfat extends beyond the city limits to Mt. Meron, a pilgrimage site both for ultra-Orthodox Jews and nature lovers.

The village of Meron has for centuries drawn thousands upon thousands of Orthodox Jews to pay homage to several of the great rabbis of the Roman era who are buried at the eastern foot of the mount. The most important site on Mt. Meron—and one of the holiest places in Israel—is the **Tomb of Rabbi Shimon Bar Yochai,** survivor of the Bar Kochba Revolt of almost 2,000 years ago. Bar Yochai is said to have fled from the Romans with his son Elazar after the fall of Jerusalem to a cave at Peki'in, not far from here, where he remained for 13 years. The faithful, beginning with the 16th-century mystics who settled in Tzfat, believe that from his cave-hideout Bar Yochai penned the Zohar (the Book of Splendor), his commentary on the first five books of the Hebrew Bible. Others claim that the Zohar dates from 13th-century Spain. Nevertheless, the constant flow of visitors is evidence of the pilgrims' devotion to the great rabbi and rebel.

The pilgrimage is still celebrated en masse on Lag Ba'Omer, the festive 33rd day of the seven solemn weeks that begin with Passover and end with Shavuot (Pentecost). At this time Mt. Meron comes alive as a grand procession arrives on foot from Tzfat, carrying Torah scrolls and singing fervently. Bonfires are lighted, with celebrations lasting days. Many ultra-Orthodox Jews still uphold the tradition of bringing their three-year-old sons here on Lag Ba'Omer for their first haircuts.

WHERE TO EAT AND STAY

$$$
VEGETARIAN

✗ **Dalia's.** The cheerful chef at this restaurant, the oldest dining establishment in Moshav Amirim, is a former nutritionist, so you know everything on the menu is wholesome as well as toothsome. The set menu includes, among other items, almond and peanut patties in onion sauce and tomatoes stuffed with wheat and barley, as well as a beautiful array of salads and soups. Dessert, consisting of yogurt with fresh fruit, is served with a big helping of fresh air and scenery. It's a bit hard to find, so call for directions. ⊠ *On the main road in Amirim* ☎ *04/698–9349* ⌂ *Reservations essential* ▤ *AE, DC, MC, V.*

$
VEGETARIAN

✗ **Stupp's.** Esther and Mordechai are not just biblical characters; they are also the Stupps, the Canadian couple who run this small kosher dairy establishment. The menu has something for everyone, from stir-fried vegetables to mushrooms filled with nuts, cheese, and pesto. Kosher. ⊠ *On the main road into Amirim* ☎ *04/698–0946* ▤ *AE, DC, MC, V* ⊗ *Closed Sat.*

$

🏨 **Al Jarmak 2000.** This family-owned bed-and-breakfast is in the Druze village of Beit Jann, about 25 km (17 mi) west of Tzfat. The rooms are basic but cozy—some have balconies—with lovely views of the wooded

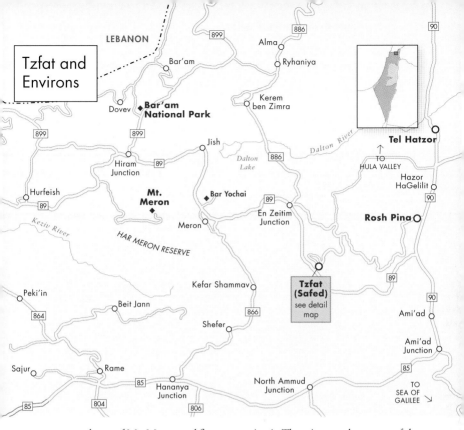

slopes of Mt. Meron and fine mountain air. There is a good measure of the famous Druze hospitality, which really makes the stay here unique. **Pros:** great food; warm hospitality. **Cons:** simple decor; need a car to get around. ⊠ *Beit Jann24990* ☎ *04/980–2962* ⊕ *www.al2000.com* ⊷ *8 rooms* ⟟ *In-room: no phone, kitchen. In-hotel: restaurant* ⊟ *No credit cards.*

$ **🏨 Amirim Holiday Village.** Moshav Amirim offers something quite differ-
Fodor'sChoice ent from the typical hotel. The accommodations are owned and oper-
★ ated by several different families, and they have clearly put their heart into the details. You can find everything from single rooms to suites, and from plain to luxurious. This is a real get-away-from-it-all kind of place where you can enjoy the country air and take in the incomparable view of the Sea of Galilee. You can choose from a range of health and beauty treatments, including those at "Spa in the Forest," where the treatment room and hot tub are built around the trunk of an old oak tree. There are a number of homey vegetarian restaurants and cafés within walking distance.The community is about 4 km (2½ mi) north of the junction of Route 89 and Route 886. **Pros:** homey accommodations; lovely spa. **Cons:** need a car to get around. ⊠ *Moshav Amirim* ☎ *04/698–9571* ✉ *alitamirim@hotmail.com* ⟟ *In-room: no phone (some), kitchen (some), no TV (some). In-hotel: spa* ⊟ *AE, DC, MC, V* ⦿ *BP.*

$$–$$$ 📷 **Hase'uda Ha'aharona.** This lodging's peculiar choice of name (it means "The Last Supper") shouldn't stop you from enjoying its magnificent views of the Golan Heights, the Sea of Galilee, and the Galilee mountains. The owners, Bella and Laurence, have outfitted each of the suites in classic style with furnishings they collected while traveling through Europe. They are happy to prepare gourmet breakfasts, lunches, and dinners, but many guests skip breakfast because each room has a kitchen stocked with a selection of cereal, yogurt, fruit, and other delicacies. **Pros:** pretty pool; cozy; tasty food. **Cons:** not much for non-vegetarians; need a car to get around. ⊠ *Near the entrance to Moshav Amirim* 📞 *04/698–9788* ⊕ *www.haseudah-haacharonah.com* ↪ *7 rooms* ⚐ *In-room: kitchen, DVD, Wi-Fi. In-hotel: pool, spa* ▭ *AE, DC, MC, V.*

SPORTS AND THE OUTDOORS

More than 1,000 acres of Mt. Meron is a nature reserve, and it's crisscrossed with hiking trails. One relatively easy loop, which takes about 1½ hours, winds around the 900-meter-high peak, revealing beautiful views in every direction. Depending on the time of year, wildflowers, including brilliant yellow meadow saffron, may grace the trail, and bright red anemones and delicate pink cyclamens might peep out from among several species of hardy oak.

At **Eretz Hagalil Jeeps** (⊠ *Moshav Amirim* 📞 *04/698–0434 or 050/531–6140* ⊕ *www.eretz-hagalil.co.il*), Yoram Zarchi takes off-road aficionados on two-hour excursions through the Galilee and the Golan, taking in sites of natural beauty and historical significance along the way. Trips cost NIS 590 to NIS 650 per person.

Malkiya Stables (⊠ *Kibbutz Malkiya* 📞 *052/281–6293*) offers spectacular mountain views on its rides. Ask about trail rides of one to four hours for ages 7 and up. The stables are on Route 899, about 29 km (18 mi) north of the Khiram junction.

OFF THE BEATEN PATH
Peki'in. High in the mountains north of the main Akko–Tzfat highway, Peki'in is truly an off-the-beaten-track destination. It's an ancient village whose 12,000 inhabitants—Druze, Christians, Muslims, and Jews—peacefully coexist. Pomegranate and carob trees grow in the yards of some of the old stone houses. Some have grape vines as thick as tree trunks wending their way around windows and doorways. The town's synagogue, open intermittently, has carvings the locals say were brought from the Jerusalem Temple after the Roman destruction, and a piece of ancient Torah scroll preserved in glass above the Holy Ark. The tiny candlelit cave where Rabbi Shimon Bar Yochai hid from the Romans is an attraction for Jewish pilgrims. On the main street is the factory and shop where the Druze Savta (Grandma) Jamila makes the "secret recipe" olive oil soap that has become famous in Israel and even has a following abroad.

BAR'AM NATIONAL PARK

15 km (9 mi) northwest of Meron, 40 km (25 mi) northwest of Tzfat.

GETTING HERE AND AROUND

From Tzfat, head west on Route 89, then north on Route 899. After 3 km (1½ mi), turn right onto a dirt road. There's no bus service to Bar'am.

EXPLORING

In an otherwise deserted spot lie the ruins of **Bar'am,** one of the best-preserved ancient synagogues anywhere. Like most other synagogues uncovered in this area, this structure dating from the 3rd century faces south, toward Jerusalem; unlike any other, however, this one has lavish architectural elements, such as an entrance with a segmental pediment, and freestanding giant columns in front. The interior, which resembles that of other Galilean synagogues of the Talmudic period (3rd–8th centuries AD), is less well preserved. Rows of pillars in the prayer hall apparently served as supports for the ceiling, and the building may have had a second story. A section of the facade's lintel, now in the Louvre in Paris, contains the Hebrew inscription "May there be peace in this place, and in all the places of Israel. This lintel was made by Jose the Levite. Blessings upon his works. Shalom." ⊠*Rte. 899* ☎*04/698–9301* ✆*NIS 12* ⊙*Apr.–Sept., Mon.–Thurs. 8–5; Oct.–Mar. Mon.–Thurs. 8–4, Fri. 8–3.*

WHERE TO EAT

$$ ✕**Jascala.** Departing from the usual Middle Eastern plate of hummus
MIDDLE EASTERN and pita bread, this Lebanese restaurant serves salads overflowing with greens like chard and mallow that grow wild in the hills, and melt-in-your-mouth pastries stuffed with mushrooms cooked in tangy yogurt sauce. The stuffed vine leaves made by the owner's mother come with or without meat; the fried *koubeh*, a small bulgur wheat pocket, is filled with either meat or hummus. The restaurant is in the village of Jish. ⊠*Jish, on the left when entering the village* ☎*04/698–7762* ▭*AE, DC, MC, V.*

ROSH PINA

Fodor'sChoice *10 km (6 mi) east of Tzfat, 25 km (15½ mi) north of Tiberias.*
★
GETTING HERE AND AROUND

From Tel Aviv, you can fly into the small airport of Mahanayim, near Rosh Pina. There are daily buses from Tzfat, Tiberias, and Haifa. If you're driving from Tzfat head east on Route 89, then north on Route 90.

ESSENTIALS

Taxi Contacts Meir Taxi (☎*04/693–5735*).

EXPLORING

The restored village of Rosh Pina is a gift-shop and gallery-browser's delight, and the dilapidated wooden doors and stonework of some still-abandoned premises are part of the charm.

Rosh Pina—literally "cornerstone"—gets its name from Psalm 118:22: "The stone that the builders rejected has become the chief cornerstone." This verse inspired the Galilee's first Zionist pioneers, who came from Romania in 1882, determined to build a village. They bought this land, 1,500 feet above sea level at the foot of the mountain ridge east of Tzfat, and arrived with all they needed for their new home, right down to the timber for construction.

The Romanians derived their main livelihood at Rosh Pina from the production of silk by silkworms; the philanthropist Baron Edmond de Rothschild donated the necessary mulberry trees. However, the rewards

Visit Rosh Pina for its charming streets, shops, and galleries.

of their efforts were elusive: residents walked around in silk scarves and socks but had nothing to eat. Eventually, the immigrants moved away to other settlements, and for decades the village was inhabited only by squatters.

The two-story **Schwartz Hotel,** on Ha'elyon Street, built in 1890, was the first rest house in the Galilee. Today it is a mere skeleton of the original, but try to imagine what it was like to check in here after a long, tiring journey on foot and enjoy the tranquil view of the Sea of Galilee below and white-capped Mt. Hermon to the north. ⊠*Ha'elyon St.* ☎*No phone.*

The **synagogue** is usually locked, but ask around and you might find someone to open it for you. The interior remains as it was when it was built in the mid-1880s; the dark pews and Ark made of the timber brought from Romania have aged gracefully. The ceiling has painted depictions of palm trees and biblical motifs. ⊠*Ha'elyon St.* ☎*No phone.*

The **Old Rosh Pina Office** occupies the house that belonged to Professor Gideon Mer, a leading expert on malaria in the 1930s. Legend has it that Mer used to inject his wife and children with experimental remedies in his efforts to combat malaria in this region. (All survived.) The British were so impressed with Mer's work that they sent him to Burma to fight malaria epidemics there. Implements and household items from the early days of Rosh Pina are on display. Next door, a colorful audiovisual presentation showcases the founding of this pioneering community. ⊠*Ha'elyon St.* ☎*04/693–6603* ✉*NIS 15* ◷*Sun.–Thurs. 8:30–5, Fri. and Sat. 8:30–1.*

WHERE TO EAT

$$$

Fodor's Choice

★

MODERN ISRAELI

✕**Auberge Shulamit.** This charming inn takes its name from the original Hotel Shulamit, where the 1948 Armistice Treaty was signed. Among the menu's delectables—along with the home-smoked meats—are chestnut soup (in season),

shrimp with wild rice, and an elegant array of desserts. If you can't bear to leave, the inn has three French country–style guest rooms where you can rest your weary head. ⊠*David Shub St., Rosh Pina* ☎*04/693–1485* ⊕*www.shulamit.co.il* ⌖*Reservations essential* ▭*AE, DC, MC, V.*

$$$–$$$$

ARGENTINE

✕**Babayit Shel Rafa.** The sizzling steaks of his native Argentina figure prominently on Rafa's menu. The best starters are the pickled tongue and the meat or corn empanadas. Entrées include roast beef and sausage and lamb casserole with rice, saffron, and green beans. Vegetarians shouldn't despair, as the rich vegetable, mozzarella, prune, and almond stew is delicious. Business lunches are served daily from noon to 5 and are both good and surprisingly economical. ⊠*Old Rosh Pina restoration site, next to the Rosh Pina office* ☎*04/693–6192* ⌖*Reservations essential* ▭*AE, DC, MC, V.*

$$$–$$$$

STEAK

✕**Black Steer.** This red-roof steak house specializes in spareribs. Outdoor dining is especially pleasant here, as the garden is leafy and surprisingly private. The location—right off the road—is handy for those on the move. Business lunches on weekdays from noon until 5 PM are a good deal. ⊠*West side of Rte. 90, at bottom of Rosh Pina* ☎*04/693–6250* ▭*AE, MC, V.*

$

ISRAELI

✕**Choclolata.** The original arched stone basement of the old synagogue is the setting of this romantic restaurant. In addition to the usual Israeli salads, pasta specialties, and sandwiches, try unusual dishes like artichokes filled with cheese. True to its name, the kitchen serves a host of chocolate delights, including 37 different kinds of pralines made by the house chocolatier. Kosher. ⊠*Old Rosh Pina, east lower entrance to the synagogue* ☎*04/686–0219* ⌖*Reservations essential* ▭*AE, DC, MC, V.*

$–$$

ECLECTIC

✕**Ja'uni.** The century-old structure that houses Ja'uni was once used as a post office, and later as an armory. The menu is seasonal and eclectic. The Spanish-style tapas change daily and may include roasted peppers, zucchini or fried cabbage in tahini, or eggplant in ginger, honey, and soy sauce. The outdoor seating is pleasant, especially in the evening and early morning. There is live music on summer evenings. ⊠*30 David Shub St.* ☎*04/693–1881* ▭*AE, DC, MC, V.*

WHERE TO STAY

Rosh Pina is a budding center of tourism for this region, and many residents are now opening their homes as bed-and-breakfasts.

$

☾

🏕**Kfar Hanassi Tourism.** These accommodations at Kfar Hanassi give you a real taste of communal life. The one- and two-room units overlook a garden, and each has a barbecue and full kitchenette. Boldly colored sheets and dhurrie rugs add a country touch. Meals are in the kibbutz's communal dining room. Several artists live and work at Kfar

Hanassi, and you're welcome to visit their studios. Guided hikes to the mountainous Jordan River area northeast of the kibbutz are available and there are plenty of other activities to keep kids occupied, too. **Pros:** great for families; friendly. **Cons:** basic rooms; no restaurant. ⊠*Kibbutz Kfar Hanassi, M.P. Upper Galilee* ☏*04/691–4870* ⊕*www.k-hanassi. co.il* ↰*20 units* △*In-room: no phone, kitchen, Wi-Fi. In-hotel: tennis court, pool* ▭*AE, DC, MC, V.*

SHOPPING

The Well. Sigal Eshet-Shafat and her husband Inbar used to sell typical handicrafts, but it turned out that their own jams, dressings, and liqueurs were what attracted their loyal clientele. The on-site coffee shop lets you sample the store's delights and sign up for the occasional cooking class. Our recommendation? Try the onion jam that adds a refreshing tang to both dairy and meat dishes. ⊠*Beit Wilkomitz* ☏*04/693–0340* ⊙*Sun.–Thurs. 10:30–1, Fri. 10:30–3.*

NIGHTLIFE AND THE ARTS

Blues Brothers Pub. The atmosphere in this small stone basement may best be described as "happy Gothic." Light and inexpensive meals are served to the mainly youthful clientele. ⊠*7 Hachalutzim St., Villa Tehila* ☏*04/693–7788.*

Julian. Although it's also a restaurant, this is probably the closest thing in the area to a trendy bar. It's in what used to be the region's custom house: over a hundred years ago it marked the boundary between British and French jurisdictions. The menu includes a selection of wines, draft beer, and more than 50 varieties of whisky and cocktails. ⊠*46 Derech HaGalilee* ☏*04/693–0207.*

TEL HATZOR

8 km (5 mi) north of Rosh Pina, 14 km (9 mi) east of Tzfat.

GETTING HERE AND AROUND
From Tzfat, head east on Route 89, then north on Route 90.

EXPLORING

Tel Hatzor is a good stop for archaeology buffs—its massive mound is made up of the remnants of 21 cities. The excavation and restoration of some of these antiquities have produced fascinating results.

Situated on the Via Maris—the major trade route linking Egypt and Mesopotamia—Hatzor is referred to several times in documents from ancient archives in both lands, and scholars believe a huge archive may someday be found here as well.

The Book of Joshua (11:13) notes that Joshua destroyed Canaanite Hatzor in the 13th century BC, and Israelites resettled it. Its next heyday came three centuries later, when King Solomon decided it would serve him well as a regional military and administrative center, like Megiddo and Gezer. In 732 BC, Hatzor met its end when invading Assyrian king Tiglath Pileser III conquered the Galilee and forced its Israelite inhabitants off the land in chains and into exile.

The huge site is divided into two areas: the **Upper City**, which comprised the most ancient settlements, and the **Lower City,** first settled in the 18th century BC. Only the Upper City, covering less than a fifth of the total excavation site, is open to the public. The **Hatzor Museum** (on the grounds of Kibbutz Ayelet Hashachar, across the highway) houses figurines, weapons, stone pots, and other artifacts unearthed in the two areas; others are at the Israel Museum in Jerusalem. It's open by appointment only. ⊠*Tel Hatzor National Park, off Rte. 90* ☎*04/693–7290* ⊠*NIS 18* ⊗*Park and museum Apr.–Sept., Sat.–Thurs. 8–5, Fri. 8–4; Oct.–Mar., Sat.–Thurs. 8–4, Fri. 8–3.*

WHERE TO STAY

$$ 🏨**Pausa–Gourmet Galilee Inn.** This beautiful boutique hotel is designed in a minimalist style that often calls to mind Japan. The carefully landscaped and tranquil setting includes a bocce court, herb and vegetable gardens, and orchards that produce the ingredients used in the inn's kitchen. Meals are served family style; guests get acquainted over pre-dinner cocktails, and the Spanish, Japanese, and Israeli food is served at a massive wooden table. **Pros:** unforgettable meals; lovely decor; outdoor hot tub. **Cons:** remote location; expensive for what you get. ⊠*Moshav She'ar Yashuv, Rt. 99, northeast of Kiryat Shmona 12240* ☎*054/690–4434* ⊕*www.pausa-inn.co.il* ⊠*8 rooms* ⊘*In-room: no phone, Wi-Fi. In-hotel: restaurant, no kids under 14* ⊟*AE, DC, MC, V* Ⓞ*MAP.*

HULA NATURE RESERVE

8 km (5 mi) north of Tel Hatzor, 24 km (15 mi) northeast of Tzfat.

GETTING HERE AND AROUND
From Tzfat, head east on Route 89, north on Route 90.

EXPLORING

★ The **Hula Nature Reserve** contains the last vestige of wetlands preserved after the rest were drained in the 1950s to create arable land. Over the years it became apparent that in addition to affecting water quality in the Sea of Galilee, draining the wetlands had destroyed the habitat of millions of birds that came to the Hula Valley on their migrations between Europe and Africa.

Pelicans, wild geese, storks, cranes, plovers, and raptors once again have a sanctuary here, and the swampy waters abound with carp, catfish, and perch. There are rare thickets of papyrus, and you might see a water buffalo or two. The visitor center has informative displays of the history of the valley and on the 800-acre reserve. There's an observation tower and a snack bar, and the main path is wheelchair accessible. Hunting and fishing are strictly forbidden. ⊠*East of Rte. 90* ☎*04/693–7069* ⊠*NIS 18 for park, additional NIS 15 for visitor center* ⊗*Park Sat.–Thurs. 8–4, Fri. 8–3; visitor center Sat.–Thurs. 10–4, Fri. 10–3.*

NEED A BREAK? For a rest stop with a bit of history, try **Bet Dubrovin** (⊠*Yesod Hama'ala* ☎*04/693–7371* ⊠*NIS 10* ⊗*Mon.–Thurs. 10:30–4, Fri. 10:30–2*), near the entrance to the Hula Nature Reserve. This reconstructed farmhouse was once owned by the Dubrovins, a family of Russian immigrants. The property was eventually donated to the Jewish National Fund and was opened to the public in 1986. An exhibit in the former family home highlights the old days. On the premises is a kosher restaurant specializing in smoked meat dishes.

UPPER HULA VALLEY

The sights that hug the border with Lebanon show contrasting sides of Israel. The bustling town of Kiryat Shmona and sleepy Metulla bear eloquent witness to the varying fortunes of Israel's relationships with its Arab neighbors. Tel Dan Nature Reserve, on the other hand, draws visitors with its antiquities, surging river, and lush, wild beauty.

KIRYAT SHMONA

45 km (28 mi) north of Tiberias, 39 km (24 mi) north of Tzfat.

GETTING HERE AND AROUND
From Tzfat, head east on Route 89, then north on Route 90.

There are at least 16 buses daily from Tel Aviv, at least 19 from Haifa, and 4 from Jerusalem.

ESSENTIALS
Taxi Contacts Hatzafon Taxi (☎ *04/694–2333*).

EXPLORING
The major urban center in the Upper Hula Valley, Kiryat Shmona offers fast food, a pharmacy, and other shopping in a mall on Route 90, but the Manara Cable Car is its major tourist attraction. For years, the instability in neighboring Lebanon profoundly affected life in the town, and by 1982 the spate of terrorist attacks had reached such proportions that Israel responded by invading Lebanon, the first stage of what would become the war with Lebanon. Kiryat Shmona was again in the news in 1996 when Hezbollah terrorists launched a focused and continued attack on the town and its environs using katyusha rockets. The Israel Defense Forces responded by targeting Hezbollah's bases in southern Lebanon in a campaign that became known as the Grapes of Wrath.

The Kiryat Shmona–Kibbutz Manara **Manara Cable Car** gives you a bird's-eye view of the Hula Valley. It has one station midway on the 1,890-yard trip, where the adventurous can step out and do some rappelling and dry-sliding (a roller-coaster-like activity), or try the climbing wall. One option is to take the cable car up and mountain bike down. There's also the thrill of a 600-foot zip line—a harnessed, partially free-fall jump down a cable to the ground. If you opt to remain in the cable car, the trip takes eight minutes each way, overlooking cliffs and green hills from a height of some 850 yards. There is wheelchair access to the cable car and upper station. (⊠ *Kibbutz Manara, Rte. 90* ☎ *04/690–4680* 💲*NIS 49 weekdays, NIS 59 weekends* ⊙ *Daily 9:30–5*)

Perched on the northern edge of Kiryat Shmona is **Tel Hai,** meaning "hill of life" in Hebrew. In a sense, the hill did become a monument to life after a memorable battle in 1920. In the aftermath of World War I,

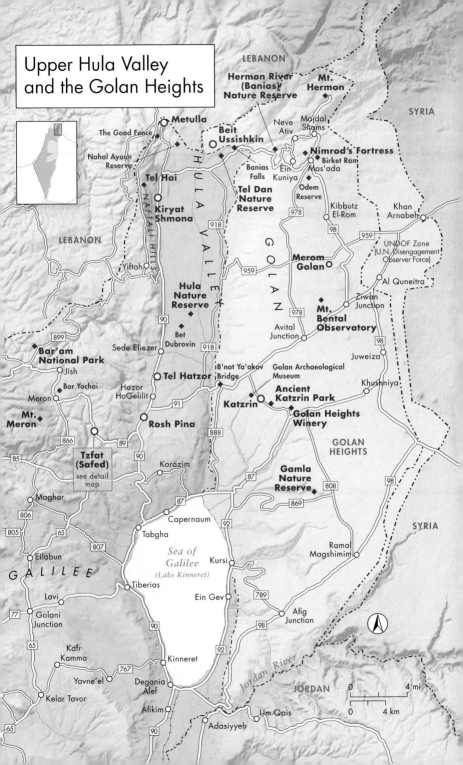

Upper Hula Valley
and the Golan Heights

LEBANON

Mt. Hermon

SYRIA

**Hermon River
(Banias)
Nature Reserve**

Metulla

The Good Fence

Neve Ativ

Majdal Shams

**Beit
Ussishkin**

Nahal Ayoun Reserve

Banias Falls

Ein Kuniya

Nimrod's Fortress

Birket Ram

Mas'ada

Tel Hai

**Tel Dan
Nature
Reserve**

Odem Reserve

**Kiryat
Shmona**

918

Kibbutz
El-Rom

978

98

Khan
Arnabeh

959

LEBANON

Yiftah

**Merom
Golan**

UNDOF Zone
(U.N. Disengagement
Observer Force)

959

Al Quneitra

**Hula
Nature
Reserve**

Ziwan
Junction

899

**Bar'am
National Park**

Jish

Bet
Dubrovin

918

Avital
Junction

978

**Mt.
Bental
Observatory**

98

Sede Eliezer

Juweiza

90

Tel Hatzor

B'not Ya'akov
Bridge

Golan Archaeological
Museum

Khushniya

Bar Yochai

Hazor
HaGelilit

91

**Ancient
Katzrin Park**

Meron

**Mt.
Meron**

Rosh Pina

Katzrin

**Golan Heights
Winery**

866

888

85

**Tzfat
(Safed)**
see detail
map

89

**GOLAN
HEIGHTS**

90

Korazim

87

**Gamla
Nature
Reserve**

808

Maghar

87

Capernaum

92

869

806

Tabgha

SYRIA

805

*Sea of
Galilee*
(Lake Kinneret)

Kursi

Ramat
Magshimim

Eilabun

807

Kfar

65

Tiberias

Lavi

Ein Gev

789

GALILEE

77

Golani
Junction

Afig
Junction

98

65

Kafr
Kamma

90

Kinneret

92

JORDAN

767

Yavne'el

Jordan River

Kelar Tavor

Degania
Alef

Um Qais

65

Afikim

0   4 mi

90

Adasiyyeh

0   4 km

while Britain and France bickered over who should have final control of the upper Hula Valley, bands of Arabs often harassed the tiny Jewish farming settlements. They overran Tel Hai, and caused the temporary abandonment of the old village of Metulla; only Kibbutz Kfar Giladi was successful in defending itself, and it has since gone on to become one of the largest and most prosperous kibbutzim.

Following the Tel Hai incident, in which two defenders were killed, Tel Hai resident Josef Trumpeldor and seven comrades were called on to protect the place. Trumpeldor already had a reputation as a leader in the czar's army in his native Russia, where he lost an arm fighting. Fired by Zionist ideals, he moved to Palestine in 1912 at the age of 32 with a group of followers in tow. During the final battle in 1920 Trumpeldor and his comrades were killed and it is for them that Kiryat Shmona— City of the Eight—is named. It is said that Trumpeldor's last words were: "It is good to die for our country." He is buried just up the road from the museum, beneath the stone statue of a lion.

The heroic last stand at Tel Hai was important not only because it was the first modern instance of Jewish armed self-defense, but also because the survival of at least two of the Jewish settlements meant that when the final borders were drawn by the League of Nations in 1922, these settlements were included in the British-mandated territory of Palestine and thus, after 1948, in the State of Israel. ⊠ *Off Rte. 886.*

The **Tel Hai Courtyard Museum** displays agricultural tools used in Trumpeldor's time. A moving audiovisual show highlights the history of the place. ⊠ *Off Rte. 886* ☏ *04/695–1333* ✉ *NIS 22* ⊙ *Sun.–Thurs. 9–4, Fri. and Sat. 10–3.*

WHERE TO EAT

$$$
SEAFOOD
✕ **Dag al Hadan.** Fresh trout and a glass of wine, in a shady copse by the gurgling Dan River—it's as good as it sounds, which is why Dag al Hadan draws crowds on weekends. This was the first restaurant in the region to specialize in the fish the Dan yields in abundance; you can see the trout ponds in a small installation on the grounds. The same management also runs a café next door where light vegetarian meals are served. The restaurant is tucked away behind the main road, but it's large and well signposted. ⊠ *Off Rte. 99 near Kiryat Shmona, opposite Kibbutz Hagoshrim* ☏ *04/695–0225* ✑ *Reservations essential* ⊟ *AE, DC, MC, V.*

$$
ECLECTIC
✕ **Focaccia Bar.** This family restaurant in the Alonim Mall serves a good selection of pastas and pizzas, as well as meat dishes with a Middle Eastern touch. ⊠ *Off Rte. 99 near Kiryat Shmona, opposite Kibbutz Ma'ayan Baruch* ☏ *04/690–04474* ⊟ *AE, DC, MC, V.*

$$$
ASIAN
✕ **Jordan Pagoda.** Unlikely as it seems, a pagoda stands on the banks of the Jordan River. It's the home of this Chinese, Thai, and Japanese restaurant. The Chinese menu includes the traditional rice, stir-fried vegetables, fried chicken or fish in sesame sauce, chicken in sweet and sour sauce, corn soup, egg rolls, and so on. The Thai cuisine has a respectable selection of noodle dishes, and you can watch the Japanese dishes being prepared before your eyes. The complex is on the grounds of Kibbutz Sde Nechemia, 8 km (5 mi) from Kiryat Shmona. ⊠ *Kibbutz Sde Nechemia, Rte. 918* ☏ *04/694–6010* ⊟ *AE, DC, MC, V.*

WHERE TO STAY

$$ 🏨 **Hagoshrim Kibbutz Hotel.** The waters of the Hermon River flow right through Hagoshrim—under a glass-topped channel set in the ceramic tile of the lobby and then through the property, creating a uniquely natural setting. While the rooms are simply decorated, the lobby is especially pleasant, with blond-wood furniture and colorful cushions and throw rugs. Gosh, the kosher restaurant, specializes in meat dishes. Kayaking and guided walking tours are available. **Pros:** wide selection of activities; nice common areas. **Cons:** basic decor; can get loud in summer. ✉*Rte. 99, east of Kiryat Shmona, Upper Galilee* ☎*04/681–6000* ⊕*www.hagoshrim-hotel.co.il* ⤵*164 rooms* ♿*In-room: refrigerator. In-hotel: restaurant, bar, pool, gym, Wi-Fi* ▭*AE, DC, MC, V.*

$$ 🏨 **Kfar Blum Guest House.** Tucked in the northern Hula Valley, Kfar Blum is known for its warm welcome. The spacious rooms in the new wing are a cut above the usual kibbutz accommodations. One of the kibbutz's major attractions is its kayaks—what better way to experience the Jordan River? Kfar Blum hosts an annual chamber-music festival in summer. **Pros:** music on weekends; terrific location; activities for the entire family. **Cons:** expensive spa treatments; room rates a bit pricey. ✉*North of Rte. 977, near Kiryat Shmona, Upper Galilee* ☎*04/683–6611* ⊕*www.kfarblum-hotel.co.il* ⤵*147 rooms* ♿*In-room: refrigerator, Wi-Fi. In-hotel: restaurant, bar, tennis courts, spa, pool* ▭*AE, DC, MC, V.*

$ 🏨 **Kibbutz Hotel Kfar Giladi.** Atop a hill behind Tel Hai is one of the country's oldest and largest kibbutz hotels. It's run very efficiently, but it still retains a homey atmosphere. As in most kibbutz hotels, the rooms are on the plain side, but some have lovely views of the Hula Valley and Mt. Hermon. The gift shop has some unusual handcrafted items, many made by members of the community. The Bet Hashomer Museum, which explores the pre-State history of the kibbutz and the vicinity, is on the grounds. **Pros:** good value; lovely indoor and outdoor swimming pools. **Cons:** basic decor; uninspired food. ✉*Rte. 886, Upper Galilee* ☎*04/690–0000* ⊕*www.kfar-giladi.co.il* ⤵*170 rooms* ♿*In-room: refrigerator. In-hotel: pools, gym, Wi-Fi* ▭*AE, DC, MC, V.*

THE ARTS

For the classically minded, **Upper Galilee Local Council** (✉*Upper Galilee 12100* ☎*04/681–6640*) hosts **Chamber Music Days** each year in late July and early August, a nationally renowned festival of chamber music in a pastoral setting.

SPORTS AND THE OUTDOORS

A plethora of outfits organize water-sports trips in this region, and almost all hotels can make reservations for you. The minimum age for kayaks and other water "vehicles" is usually six.

BOATING

Sde Nechemia (✉*Kibbutz Huliot, Rte. 99* ☎*04/694–6010*), near Kiryat Shmona, offers boating and tubing trips for NIS 70 per person.

In the Upper Hula Valley, you'll find the Tel Dan Nature Reserve and the Hermon River (Banais) Nature Reserve.

KAYAKING

Hagoshrim Kayaks (☎04/681–6034) has a 5-km (3-mi) "family" course that lasts 1½ hours and a 6-km (4-mi) "stormy" course that expands on the family course and lasts almost two hours. The family course costs NIS 75 per person, the stormy course NIS 95 per person.

Kibbutz Kfar Blum (☎04/690–2616) rents two-person rubber kayaks for 1½-hour or two-hour runs. The cost is NIS 75 per person for the short course and NIS 109 per person for the long course. Kayaks are available from March through October; call ahead to inquire at other times of the year. At the same site, they also have a climbing wall, a rope park, a zip line across the water, and archery, at NIS 100–159 per person for the full package.

Jordan Source (✉*On the grounds of Kibbutz Sde Nechemia* ☎04/694–6010 Ext. 3) runs a 3½-hour kayaking trip (this one can be rough) costing NIS 75 per person and a 1½-hour trip for NIS 50 per person.

OFF-ROAD VEHICLES

Easy Track (✉*Moshav She'ar Yashuv* ☎04/690–4440 ⊕*www.mbez.co.il*), a company based in the northern Hula Valley, offers wind-in-your-hair ways to explore the countryside, including self-drive dune buggies (driver's license required) or 1½-hour guided Jeep trips.

METULLA

7 km (4 mi) north of Kiryat Shmona, 46 km (28 mi) north of Tzfat.

GETTING HERE AND AROUND

From Tzfat, head east on Route 89, then north on Route 90.

EXPLORING

Israel's northernmost town, Metulla, is so picturesque that it's hard to believe this tranquil spot is just a stone's throw from its foes in Lebanon.

The tensions of the Middle East dissipate here in the charm of the European-style limestone buildings that line Metulla's main street, and the city itself seems to have changed little since its founding as a farming settlement in 1896. The Continental atmosphere is enhanced by the numerous signs offering ZIMMER (German for "room") for rent. Even the weather is decidedly un-Mediterranean, with refreshingly cool mountain breezes carrying whiffs of cypress and spice plants in summer, and snow in winter.

Nahal Ayoun Nature Reserve. In summer, the stream that gives this nature reserve its name slows to a trickle because the water is channeled away to irrigate agricultural fields. In winter, however, the water gushes, becoming a beautiful backdrop for hiking and picnicking. The towering Oven Fall is the most famous of the reserve's four waterfalls. Two trails meander through the reserve; the shorter one, taking about half an hour, begins and ends in the lower parking lot and goes to Oven Fall. The longer one, taking 1½ hours, begins in the upper parking lot and leads downstream. ⊠*East of Rte. 90* ☎*04/695–1519* 💲*NIS 23* 🕑*Apr.–Sept., Sat.–Thurs. 8–4, Fri. 8–3; Oct.–Mar., daily 8–3.*

SPORTS AND THE OUTDOORS

The multistory **Canada Centre** (⊠*1 Harishonim St.* ☎*04/695–0370*), at the top of the hill, has just about everything a sports complex can offer. For the price of admission (NIS 85) you can spend the whole day here, playing basketball, ice-skating, working out, bowling, swimming, zooming down the water slide, or taking aim on the shooting range. If it gets to be too much, the spa offers a sauna, hot tub, and massages. The complex is open Monday–Saturday 10–8 and has a restaurant, in case you've burned too many calories.

TEL DAN NATURE RESERVE

25 km (15½ mi) southeast of Metulla, 15 km (9 mi) northeast of Kiryat Shmona, 50 km (31 mi) northeast of Tzfat.

GETTING HERE AND AROUND

From Tzfat head east on Route 89, then turn north on Route 90. Once you pass Kiryat Shmona, turn right (east) on Route 99. The reserve is near Kibbutz Dan.

EXPLORING

Fodor'sChoice
★
The **Tel Dan Nature Reserve** is hard to beat for sheer natural beauty. A river surges through it, and luxuriant trees provide shade. A host of small mammals live here—many partial to water, such as the otter and the mongoose—as well as the biblical coney, also known as the hyrax. This is also the home of Israel's largest rodent, the nocturnal Indian crested porcupine, and its smallest predator, the marbled polecat. The reserve has several hiking trails; a short segment, on a raised wooden walkway, is wheelchair accessible.

Dan was a majestic city in biblical times. According to Genesis, Abraham came here to rescue his nephew Lot and, five centuries later, Joshua led the Israelites through the area to victory. Fine ruins from several epochs lie here. Among them are the 9th-century BC city gate and the cultic site where King Jeroboam set up a golden calf to rival the Jerusalem Temple. Just inside the city gate is the platform for a throne, where the city's king pronounced judgment. One of the site's most extraordinary finds is an arched gateway dating from the 18th-century BC Canaanite period, more than a millennium earlier than scholars had previously thought. ⊠*North of Rte. 99* ☎*04/695–1579* 💲*NIS 23* 🕓*Apr.–Sept., Sat.–Thurs. 8–5, Fri. 8–4; Oct.–Mar., Sat.–Thurs. 8–4, Fri. 8–3; last entrance 1 hr before closing.*

☪ Adjacent to the Tel Dan Nature Reserve, the **Bet Ussishkin Museum** has interesting exhibits about the flora, fauna, and geology of the Hula Valley, the Golan Heights, and the Jordan River. The audiovisual presentations are concise and informative. ⊠*Off Rte. 99* ☎*04/694–1704* 💲*NIS 18* 🕓*Sun.–Thurs. 8–4, Fri. and Jewish holiday eves 8–2, Sat. 10–3.*

THE GOLAN HEIGHTS

Considered the most fertile land in Israel, the Golan Heights is known for its many fine wineries. As you drive through these verdant hills, covered with wildflowers in the spring, you'll also see abundant olive groves and apple and cherry orchards.

The whole region was once volcanic, and many symmetrical volcanic cones and pronounced reliefs still dominate the landscape, particularly in the upper Golan. The gentle terrain and climate of the rest of the region have historically attracted far more settlement than the less hospitable northern Upper Galilee. Today it's home to Jewish, Druze, and Alawite communities.

You can explore the area's exceptional nature by joining a guided tour, whether galloping through on a horse or zipping by in a four-wheel-drive vehicle. There are lots of ways to spend the day, from skiing on Mt. Hermon to exploring ancient Nimrod's Fortress to visiting Druze villages.

HERMON RIVER (BANIAS) NATURE RESERVE

20 km (12½ mi) east of Kiryat Shmona, 50 km (31 mi) northeast of Tzfat.

GETTING HERE AND AROUND
From Tzfat, head east on Route 89, then turn north on Route 90. Once you pass Kiryat Shmona, go east on Route 99.

EXPLORING
★ **Hermon River (Banias) Nature Reserve.** One of the most stunning parts of Israel, this reserve contains gushing waterfalls, dense foliage along riverbanks, and the remains of a temple dedicated to the god Pan. There are two entrances, each with a parking lot: the sign for the first reads BANIAS WATERFALL; the other is 1 km (½ mi) farther along the same road and is marked BANIAS.

The City of Pan

The name Banias is an Arabic corruption of the Greek *Panias* (Arabic has no *p*), the original name given to the area that, in the early 4th century BC, was dedicated to the colorful Greek god Pan, the half-goat–half-human deity of herdsmen, music, and wild nature—and of homosexuals and nymphs. The Banias Reserve encompasses the ruins of this ancient city.

Herod the Great ruled the city in the 1st century AD; his son Philip inherited it and changed the city's name to to Caesarea Philippi, to distinguish it from the Caesarea his father had founded on the Mediterranean coast. Roman rule in this part of the kingdom did not last another generation past Philip, but Panias continued to flourish until after the Muslim conquest in the 7th century AD,

when it declined into no more than a village. In the 10th century AD Muslim immigration brought renewed settlement and Jews also came to Banias (as it became known sometime during the 7th century), and the town also became an important center for the Karaite sect (an offshoot of Judaism).

In the early 12th century, Banias was held by Crusaders, who saw it as a natural border between their kingdom and the neighboring Muslim realm, whose center was Damascus. The Muslims recaptured Banias in 1132, but the city declined in importance and was taken over by Bedouin chieftains. It became a small village, which it remained until the area was conquered by the IDF in the 1967 Six-Day War and was abandoned by its inhabitants.

7

The **Banias Spring** emerges at the foot of mostly limestone Mt. Hermon, just where it meets the basalt layers of the Golan Heights. The most popular short route in the reserve is up to the **Banias Cave,** via the path that crosses the spring. Excavations have revealed the five niches hewed out of the rock to the right of the cave; these are what remains of Hellenistic and Roman temples, depicted in interesting artist's renderings. Three of the niches bear inscriptions in Greek mentioning Pan, the lover of tunes; Echo, the mountain nymph; and Galerius, one of Pan's priests. All early references to the cave identify it as the source of the spring, but earthquakes over the years have changed the landscape, and the water now emerges at the foot of the cave rather than from within it.

The Banias Reserve offers three interconnected hiking trails—ask for the English-language trail map and advice at the cashier's booth. One, which passes a Crusader gate, walls, and moat, takes about 45 minutes. The second, also about 45 minutes, explores the magnificent 1,613-square-foot palace complex dating to the reign of Herod's grandson, Agrippa II, on top of which are the ruins of what is thought to have been the marketplace of the day: a string of single chambers along a well-preserved section of wall might well have been shops. The third is a 90-minute trail leading past the **Officers' Pool,** built by the Syrians,

WORD OF MOUTH

"We were in the Golan last week. There are many tours possible and you won't have to walk far to see many sites. We went on a jeep tour and saw wild boars, storks, beautiful views"　　—Orcas and a water-operated flour mill, to the thundering 33-meter-high **Banias Waterfall**. The trails are spiced with the pungent aroma of mint and figs, and studded with blackberry bushes. If time is short, you may prefer to take a brief walk to the falls, return to your car, then drive on to the second entrance to see the caves and the spring where the Hermon River originates. The cost of admission covers entry to both sites.

If you're ready for a real hiking challenge, and can have a car waiting at the other end, a long, very steep trail leads from the parking lot at the Banias Nature Reserve through the oak and thorny broom forest up to Nimrod's Fortress, a 40- to 60-minute climb. ✉ *Off Rte. 99* ☎ *04/695–0272* 🎫 *NIS 23* ☉ *Apr.–Sept., Sat.–Thurs. 8–5, Fri. 8–4; Oct.–Mar., Sat.–Thurs. 8–4, Fri. 8–3; last entrance 1 hr before closing.*

NEED A BREAK?	A few minutes' walk along the trail leading to the waterfall is the ancient flour mill and a stall where Druze villagers make their traditional pita (bigger and flatter than the commercial version), which is not only baked on the premises but also milled here. Pull up a rock, and for a few shekels you'll be served a large rolled-up pita with *labane* (white goat's cheese) and Turkish coffee.

NIMROD'S FORTRESS

5 km (3 mi) east of Hermon River (Banias) Nature Reserve, 58 km (36 mi) northeast Tzfat.

GETTING HERE AND AROUND

From Tzfat, head east on Route 89, then turn north on Route 90. Once you pass Kiryat Shmona, go east on Route 99. Once you pass the Hermon River Nature Reserve, turn north on Route 989. The fortress is on the left.

EXPLORING

☮ ★ **Nimrod's Fortress.** The dramatic views of this towering, burly fortress perched above Banias, appearing and disappearing behind each curve of the narrow road that leads to it, are part of the treat of a visit to Nimrod's Fortress (Kal'at Namrud). And once you're there, the fortress commands superb vistas, especially through the frames of its arched windows and the narrow archers' slits in its walls.

This fortress was built in 1218 by the Mameluke warlord al-Malik al-Aziz Othman to guard the vital route from Damascus via the Golan and Banias, to Lebanon and to the Mediterranean coast against a Crusader *reconquista* after their 1187 defeat. It changed hands between Muslims and Christians in the succeeding centuries as both vied for control of the region. During one of its more interesting periods, from 1126 to 1129, Nimrod's Fortress was occupied by a fanatic sect of Muslims infamous for their murderous violence. Before heading out to track down their enemies, the cutthroats are said to have indulged in hashish, thus earning the nickname *hashashin* (hashish users), from which the word *assassin* is derived.

Nimrod's Fortress is a highlight for kids, with a ladder down to a vaulted cistern, a shadowy spiral staircase, and unexpected nooks and

WORD OF MOUTH

"The road to Nimrod's Fortress was steep and winding. Surprises were everywhere—an underground cistern, a spiral stairway that descended into darkness, and underground passages. The ancient fortress gave spectacular views of the valleys below."

—photo by Keith_Marks,
a Fodors.com member

Israel's highest mountain—Mt. Hermon, at 9,230 feet—gets plenty of snow in winter and spring.

crannies. A path leads up to the fortress's central tower, or keep, where the feudal lord would have lived. ✉ *Nimrod's Fortress National Park, Rte. 989 (off Rte. 99)* ☎ *04/694–9277* 💳 *NIS 18* ⏱ *Apr.–Sept., Sat.–Thurs. 8–5, Fri. 8–4; Oct.–Mar., Sat.–Thurs. 8–4, Fri. 8–3; last entrance 1 hr before closing.*

MT. HERMON

12 km (7½ mi) northeast of Nimrod's Fortress, 25 km (15½ mi) northeast of Kiryat Shmona, 66 km (41 mi) northeast of Tzfat.

GETTING HERE AND AROUND

From Tzfat, head east on Route 89, then turn north on Route 90. Once you pass Kiryat Shmona, go east on Route 99. At Mahanayim Junction turn east on Route 91, then north on Route 98.

EXPLORING

The summit of **Mt. Hermon**—famous as Israel's highest mountain, at 9,230 feet above sea level—is actually in Syrian territory. Its lower slopes attract Israelis to the country's only ski resort. Summer is arguably the most interesting time on the Hermon, though: after the winter snows melt, hikers can discover chasms and hidden valleys here, the long-term result of extremes in temperature. Moreover, a powerful array of colors and scents emerges from the earth as cockscomb, chamomile, and scores of other flowers and wild herbs are drawn out by the summer sun. Approaching from Nimrod's Fortress, you'll pass **Moshav Neve Ativ,** designed to look like a little piece of the Alps in the Middle East, complete with A-frame chalet-style houses, a handful of which have guest rooms. A detour through the old Druze village of **Majdal Shams** offers a number of good eateries.

SKIING

The slopes of **Mt. Hermon** (☎04/698–1337 ⊕www.skihermon.co.il) have little to offer the serious, or even the novice, skier. There is a chair lift to the top, year-round—NIS 40 for entrance and the lift—the better to enjoy the place in summer, when it's bursting with wildflowers. A track sled that spirals down a 950-yard course is another attraction. To get to Mt. Hermon, take Route 99 east to Route 989 north to Neve Ativ.

EN ROUTE   **Ein Kiniya,** which appears across a valley on your left as you head east into the Golan on Route 99, is the most picturesque of the several Druze villages around here. The houses are built of the black basalt typical of the Golan.

MEROM GOLAN

20 km (12½ mi) south of Mt. Hermon, 46 km (28 mi) northeast of Tzfat.

GETTING HERE AND AROUND

From Tzfat, head east on Route 89, then north on Route 90. At Mahanayim Junction turn east on Route 91, then north on Route 98. Merom Golan is on the left.

EXPLORING

Kibbutz Merom Golan was the first settlement built in the Golan after the Six-Day War. Its fields and orchards are typical of local kibbutzim. Apples and cherries are especially good in these parts.

WHERE TO EAT

$$–$$$ ✕**Cowboys' Restaurant.** This is the best corral this side of the Israel-Syria
STEAK   Disengagement Zone. Saddle-shape stools at the bar and cattle hides on the walls contribute to the frontier atmosphere. But it's the grub—specifically the hearty steaks and the house specialty, chicken breast stuffed with smoked meat—that packs 'em in. ⊠*Kibbutz Merom Golan, off Rte. 959* ☎04/696–0206 ⊟*AE, DC, MC, V.*

MT. BENTAL OBSERVATORY

20 km (12½ mi) south of Mt. Hermon, 46 km (28 mi) northeast of Tzfat.

GETTING HERE AND AROUND

From Tzfat, head east on Route 89, then north on Route 90. At Mahanayim Junction turn east on Route 91, then north on Route 98. Mt. Bental is on the left.

EXPLORING

Mt. Bental Observatory. From the top of this volcanic cone, once a military outpost, Mt. Hermon rises majestically to the north and the Syrian side of the Golan stretches eastward like it's on the palm of your hand. Opposite is the ruined town of Kuneitra, captured by Israel in 1967, lost and regained in the 1973 Yom Kippur War, and returned to Syria in the subsequent Disengagement Agreement—it is now a demilitarized zone. Modern Kuneitra is in the distance. The cluster of white buildings south of old Kuneitra houses the United Nations Disengagement Observer Force. A pine-cabin shop serving delicious herb teas and snacks is the perfect place to get out of the wind that often sweeps this peak. ⊠ *Off Rte. 9981 near Kibbutz Merom Golan, north of the Avital junction with Rte. 91.*

KATZRIN

20 km (12½ mi) south of Merom Golan, 38 km (23½ mi) northeast of Tiberias, 35 km (22 mi) northeast of Tzfat.

GETTING HERE AND AROUND

From Tzfat, head east on Route 89, then north on Route 90. At Mahanayim Junction turn east on Route 91, then south on Route 9088.

ESSENTIALS

Visitor Information Kessem HaGolan Visitor Center (⊠ *Rte. 9088* ☎ *04/ 696–3625*).

EXPLORING

Katzrin, founded in 1977 near the site of a 3rd-century town of the same name, has a suburban feel, despite its strategic location and attendant sensitivity. The water here, which comes straight from the basalt bedrock, is delicious and makes your skin feel like silk.

The **Golan Archaeological Museum** has a fascinating collection of animal bones, stones, and artifacts that put the region into historical and geographical perspective. Among the exhibits is a Bronze Age dwelling reconstructed from materials excavated nearby. Don't miss the moving film on the history and last stand of Gamla, the "Masada of the North," during the Great Revolt against the Romans (AD 66) and its rediscovery by archaeologists 1,900 years later. The museum is run in conjunction with the Ancient Katzrin Park. ⊠ *Katzrin commercial center* ☎ *04/696–1350* ⊕ *www.museum.golan.org.il* ⊠ *NIS 24, includes Ancient Katzrin Park* ⊙ *Sept.–May, Sun.–Thurs. 9–4, Fri. 9–2; June–Aug., Sun.–Thurs. 9–6, Fri. 9–4.*

Ancient Katzrin Park, 2 km (1 mi) east of downtown Katzrin, is a partially restored 3rd-century Jewish village. The Katzrin synagogue has decorative architectural details, such as a wreath of pomegranates and amphorae in relief on the lintel above the entrance. The complexity of its ornamentation reflects the importance of the city. Built of basalt, the synagogue was used for 400 years until it was partly destroyed, possibly by an earthquake, in 749.

The park's two reconstructed buildings, the so-called House of Uzi and House of Rabbi Abun (presumably a Talmudic sage), are attractively

The ancient ruins of the synagogue at Gamla are surrounded by rolling green hills and rocky terrain.

decorated with rope baskets, weavings, baking vessels, and pottery (based on remnants of the originals), and lighted with little clay oil lamps. ⊠ *Rte. 87* ☎ *04/696–2412* ⊕ *www.museum.golan.org.il* 💲 *NIS 24, includes Golan Archaeological Museum* ☼ *Sept.–May, Sun.–Thurs. 9–4, Fri. 9–2; June–Aug., Sun.–Thurs. 9–6, Fri. 9–4, Sat. 10–4.*

The **Golan Heights Winery** caught the world's attention with its award-winning Yarden, Gamla, and Golan labels. The area's volcanic soil, cold winters, and cool summers, together with state-of-the-art wine-making, have proven a recipe for success. The shop sells the full line of wines, including the Katzrin Chardonnay, the Yarden Gewürztraminer, and the Yarden Cabernet Sauvignon, as well as sophisticated accessories for the oenophile. Call ahead for tour information. ⊠ *Rte. 87 (east of town center)* ☎ *04/696–8435* ⊕ *www.golanwines.co.il* 💲 *NIS 20* ☼ *Sun.–Thurs. 8–6:30, Fri. 8–2.*

WHERE TO EAT

The commercial center of Katzrin, the "capital" of the Golan Heights, has a number of falafel stands, a couple of restaurants, and a pizzeria, making it a perfect midday stop for travelers.

¢ ✗ **The Big Restaurant.** This tiny eatery in the old commercial center is not
ISRAELI as impressive as its name might imply, but the Yemenite flavors and aromas certainly are. Shalom, the owner, chief cook, and bottle washer, makes a hearty meat soup, served alongside fluffy pitas and tangy salsa. Middle Eastern salads, hamburgers, and other local favorites are also on offer. ⊠ *Katzrin old commercial center* ☎ *04/696–2120* ▬ *No credit cards* ☼ *Closed Sat.*

NIGHTLIFE

Within Katzrin Park, there's a **pub** (☎ *04/685–0449*) in a century-old Syrian dwelling, with a selection of 10 different beers on tap and a dairy menu. The experience of having a drink among the ancient ruins is reason enough to make a detour if you're lodging in this area. The pub is open Saturday to Thursday, from 9 PM until the last patrons leave.

OFF THE BEATEN PATH

Mitzpe Gadot. If you continue northwest on Route 87 from Katzrin and then west on Route 91, you'll pass this tall, triangular concrete monument to fallen Israeli soldiers of the Golani Brigade. Caution: The site is safe, but don't explore beyond any marked paths, because there may be undetonated Syrian minefields.

GAMLA NATURE RESERVE

20 km (12 mi) southeast of Katzrin.

GETTING HERE AND AROUND

From Tzfat, head east on Route 89, then south on Route 90. Turn east on Route 87, then south on Route 808. Watch for Gamla signpost.

EXPLORING

Gamla Nature Reserve. Aside from the inspiring history of "the Masada of the north," the beauty of Gamla's rugged terrain, softened in spring by greenery and wildflowers, is truly breathtaking. Griffon vultures soar above and gazelles can often be seen bounding through the grasses. The main story of the camel-shaped Gamla (the name *Gamla* comes from *gamal*, the Hebrew word for "camel") goes back to the year AD 67, when at the beginning of the Great Revolt, Vespasian launched a bloody attack here that ended seven months later, when the 9,000 surviving Jews flung themselves to their deaths in the abyss below the town. The vivid descriptions of the battle, as written by Flavius Josephus in *The Jewish War,* are engraved in stones along the trail site. "Built against the almost vertical flank, the town seemed to be hung in the air . . ."—exactly the impression visitors still have as they approach the site.

Because Gamla was never rebuilt, the relics of the battlefield still eerily match the ancient sources; among them the fortifications, 2,000 "missile stones," and a large number of arrowheads. From a much earlier period (probably the 2nd millennium BC) there are about 200 **dolmens** scattered in the area—strange basalt structures shaped like the Greek letter "pi," probably used for burial. There is an excellent film on the story of Gamla at the Golan Archaeological Museum in Katzrin. ⊠ *Off Rte. 808* ☎ *04/682–2282* ⌖ *NIS 23* ⊗ *Apr.–Sept., Sat.–Thurs. 8–5, Fri. 8–4; Oct.–Mar., Sat.–Thurs. 8–4, Fri. 8–3; last entrance 1 hr before closing.*

WHERE TO STAY

Rooms in kibbutz guesthouses can be reserved directly or through Kibbutz Hotels Chain, a central reservation service based in Tel Aviv, although not all the kibbutzim are represented. Moshav Beit Hillel also makes kibbutz and bed-and-breakfast reservations.

Contacts Kibbutz Hotels Chain (⊠ *90 Ben Yehuda St.* ☎ *03/560–8118* ▤ *03/527–8088* ⊕ *www.kibbutz.co.il*). **Moshav Beit Hillel** (⊡ *M.P. Upper Galilee, 12255* ☎ *04/690–4001 or 04/694–2728*).

8

Eilat and the Negev

WITH A SIDE TRIP TO PETRA

WORD OF MOUTH

"Sde Boker is a kibbutz in the Negev Desert. Most famously known for being the final resting place of David Ben-Gurion, Israel's first prime minister. Hiking trails leading into the desert begin here, and, sometimes, nature blesses you with a chance encounter."
—photo by Keith_Marks, a Fodors.com member

WELCOME TO EILAT AND THE NEGEV

TOP REASONS TO GO

★ **Coral Reserve, Eilat:** Put on your snorkel, and marvel at the brilliant-colored fish and entrancing corals at one of the finest protected coral reefs in the world.

★ **Hiking the desert:** Explore the splendid scenery, deep wadis, rugged heights, and steep cliff faces of the Negev. The mountains of Eilat and the desert craters offer spectacular hikes.

★ **Makhtesh Ramon:** This giant crater is a geological phenomenon, with hundreds of rock formations and multihued cliffs that offer knockout views.

★ **Side trip to Petra:** Located just over the border in Jordan, Petra's awe-inspiring Khazneh, carved into the side of a rose-red cliff, is one of many archeological treats found at this UNESCO World Heritage site.

★ **Timna Park:** Spend the day trekking across the lunarlike landscape, making sure to see this desert park's famous red-hued Solomon's Pillars and its 20-foot mushroom-shaped rock formation.

Solomon's Pillars, Timna Park

1 **The Heart of the Negev.** In the very center of the upside-down triangle that makes up the Negev, here you'll find several of the region's top sites, including Ben-Gurion's desert home and grave, as well as the ancient Nabatean city of Avdat.

2 **Beersheva and the Northern Negev.** The biblical city of Beersheva, a World Heritage Site, is Israel's fourth-largest city and makes a great jumping-off point for trips around the Negev.

3 **Eilat and Environs.** Sunny Eilat is a beach town on the shores of the Red Sea, with luxury hotels, restaurants, and the Negev's only nightlife. It's just south of Timna Park, which is not to be missed.

Bedouin men in the Negev

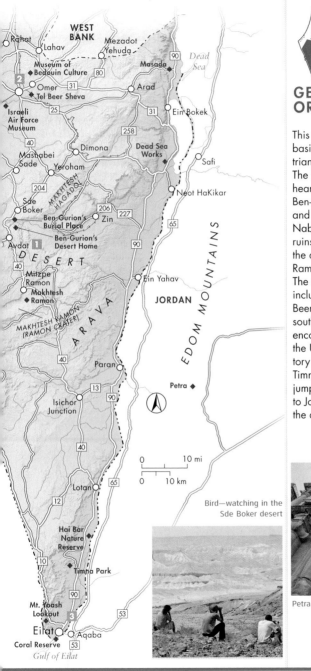

GETTING ORIENTED

This chapter covers three basic areas in the inverted triangle of the Negev. The first is the Negev's heart, with sites such as Ben-Gurion's desert home and grave, the ancient Nabatean-Roman-Byzantine ruins at Tel Avdat, and the amazing Makhtesh Ramon (Ramon Crater). The second, in the north, includes the capital city of Beersheva. The third, and southern, tip of the triangle encompasses carefree Eilat, the Underwater Observatory at Coral Beach, and Timna Park. Eilat is also the jumping-off point for a trip to Jordan and the ruins of the ancient city of Petra.

Bird—watching in the Sde Boker desert

Petra

EILAT AND THE NEGEV PLANNER

When to Go

October through May is the best time to explore the Negev. In January and February it's dry and cold, especially at night. Scorching-hot conditions prevail in the summer, from June through September (though it's very dry). In early March, scarlet, bright yellow, white, and hot pink desert flowers burst out against the brown desert earth; March is also when Eilat's International Bird-watchers' Festival takes place.

Desert Precautions

To remain comfortable and *safe*, respect certain rules of the desert. Drink two quarts of water a day in winter, and one quart per hour in summer. Keep a jerrican (which holds five gallons) of water in your car, plus extra bottles. Water fountains found along the way don't always work. Flash floods pose a very real danger from September through March, especially after rainfall farther north. If even a small amount of water is flowing across the road, wait for it to stop (it can take awhile); it can be a sign of imminent flooding. Driving at night is not recommended; plan to reach your destination by 5 PM in winter and by 8 PM in summer.

Getting Here and Around

Air Travel: Flights to Eilat take off from Ben Gurion Airport (about halfway between Jerusalem and Tel Aviv), Sde Dov Airport in north Tel Aviv, and Haifa Airport. In Eilat, the airport is actually in the middle of the city, and thus a five-minute cab ride from hotels and a five-minute walk to the center of town.

Bus Travel: The national bus company, Egged, provides frequent bus service to Beersheva from Tel Aviv and Jerusalem; each takes about 1½ hours. Buses run from Tel Aviv to Eilat at least four times a day and twice at night and takes 4½ to 5 hours. Service from Jerusalem to Eilat takes about 5½ hours. You can reserve Eilat bus tickets up to two weeks in advance, recommended for weekend travel. Within Eilat, the No. 15 bus starts at the Central Bus Station (entrance to town) and runs through the hotel area to pick up passengers and take them to points south.

Car Travel: The only way to see the Negev Desert comfortably and efficiently is to drive (air-conditioning in summer is a must). Beersheva is 113 km (70 mi) southeast of Tel Aviv and 83 km (52 mi) south of Jerusalem. To get to Eilat from Tel Aviv, the most direct way is Route 40 south to Beersheva, which takes about 5 hours.

Taxi Travel: In Eilat, the preferred way of hopping from one place to another is by taxi. Rides don't usually cost much more than NIS 35, and you can hail a cab on the street.

Train Travel: Israel Railways provides service only between Tel Aviv and Beersheva. There's frequent service (except on Saturday, when just two trains run, and both late in the evening) from the north to Beersheva all day; the trip takes 1½ hours.

Contacts Beersheva Central Bus Station (☎ *2800 ✉ *Eilat Rd. 15, next to Negev Mall and train station*). **Egged** (☎ *03/694–8888 or *2800 ⊕ www.egged.co.il*). **Eilat Central Bus Station** (✉ *Ha-Tmarim Blvd. 12, next to Shalom Mall*).

⇨ *For more information on getting here and around, see Travel Smart Israel.*

Planning Your Time

As you drive along the Negev's scenic roads, you'll pass stretches of flat, uninhabited countryside under hot, blue skies, punctuated by the odd acacia tree, twisting wadi, or craggy mountain. In winter delicate desert flowers decorate the landscape. If you want to skip the desert-driving experience, you might limit your trip to Eilat. In Eilat you can stay at a luxurious hotel, relax on the sunny shore, take a cruise on the bay, visit the underwater observatory, and dive or snorkel amid the coral reefs.

Most Negev sites open at 8:30 AM and close by 4 PM in winter and 5 PM in summer. Keep in mind that outside Eilat, restaurants close early on Friday for the Jewish sabbath, and since the main meal of the day is served at noon in the desert, lunch may be history if you arrive after 1:30; roadside diners close at around 1:30 PM.

Dining and Lodging

Although Eilat is at the southern tip of a desert, it has all the essentials—Italian, Indian, and French to Argentinian, Yemenite, and Thai. There's excellent sea fish here, including delicacies such as *denise* (sea bream). In the rest of the Negev, with the notable exception of the Mitzpe Ramon Inn, plan to dine in humble surroundings—typically a roadside diner—on meals that are apt to reflect the cook's ethnic background. Hotels in sunny Eilat run from family-style to huge, lush, and luxurious. Pleasure comes first: business facilities on a modest scale are available in larger hotels, whereas a beautiful and luxurious spa with a wide range of facilities is an important feature of each large hotel. Even many of the smaller hotels have installed spas. In Eilat, a few hotels operate on an all-inclusive basis. High season is Hanukkah/Christmas, Passover/Easter, and July and August.

Visitor Information

Hours vary greatly among the region's tourist information offices and visitor centers—it's best to phone ahead.

In Eilat, be sure to pick up the useful "Events in Eilat" brochure from the tourist information office.

Eilat Friendly Tours is a business that provides advice about hotels, tours, and activities; does booking; and offers guide service in and around Eilat.

Contacts Eilat Friendly Tours (⊕ *friendlytours-online.com*). **Beersheva Tourist Information Office** (✉ *1 Derech Hebron, near the Central Bus Station, Beersheva* ☎ *08/623–4613*). **Eilat Tourist Information Office** (✉ *Arava Road, corner of Yotam Blvd., across from Mull Yam shopping center* ☎ *08/637–2111*). **Mitzpe Ramon Visitor Center** (✉ *Top of the main street, Box 340, Mitzpe Ramon* ☎ *08/658–8691 or 08/658–8620*).

WHAT IT COSTS

	¢	$	$$	$$$	$$$$
Restaurants	under NIS 32	NIS 32–NIS 49	NIS 50–NIS 75	NIS 76–NIS 100	over NIS 100
Hotels	under $120	$120–$200	$201–$300	$301–$400	over $400

Restaurant prices are per person for a main course at dinner in NIS (Israeli shekels). Hotel prices are in US dollars, for two people in a standard double room in high season. Non-Israeli citizens paying in foreign currency are exempt from the 15.5% VAT tax on hotel rooms.

By Judy Stacey Goldman
Updated By Benjamin Balint

With its stark mountains, dramatic wadis, the Nabatean city of Avdat, colorful Bedouin encampments, and the spectacular Ramon Crater, the Negev—a word meaning "dry" in Hebrew—can definitely be described in more ways than simply "a desert."

The Negev contains Israel's most dramatic natural scenery, with its rugged highlands, as well as Eilat, a resort town set on the Red Sea, with luxury hotels, hot restaurants and nightclubs, and duty-free shopping.

The region also has notable sites and ruins. You can visit the kibbutz home and grave of Israel's first prime minister—David Ben-Gurion, the man who first dreamed of settling the desert—and on the same day you can tour the millennia-old ruins at Tel Beer Sheva, visited by the biblical patriarch Abraham. For those who love active adventures, the Negev is the place to take camel treks and Jeep tours, spend the afternoon hiking, or scuba dive in the Red Sea.

If all this isn't enough, the Negev is the idea base for taking a day trip or overnight visit to Petra in Jordan. The rose-red remains of this ancient city of the wealthy Nabateans, who controlled a spice route that stretched from Arabia to the Mediterranean, are carved into towering sandstone cliffs. Petra's gigantic monuments and royal tombs, 2,000 years old, are treasures even in a region filled with antiquities.

The Negev makes up about half the country's land mass, yet is home to only 8% of its population. The ancient Israelites had fortifications here, as did the Nabateans and the Romans after them. The region's first kibbutzim were established in the early 1940s, with new immigrants sent south after the War of Independence, in 1948. Two years later, people started trickling into Eilat, which was nothing but a few rickety huts. The desert itself was pushed back, and the semiarid areas between Tel Aviv and Beersheva became fertile farmland. Today, agricultural settlements throughout the Negev make use of advanced irrigation to raise tomatoes, melons, olives, and dates that are sent to winter markets in Europe.

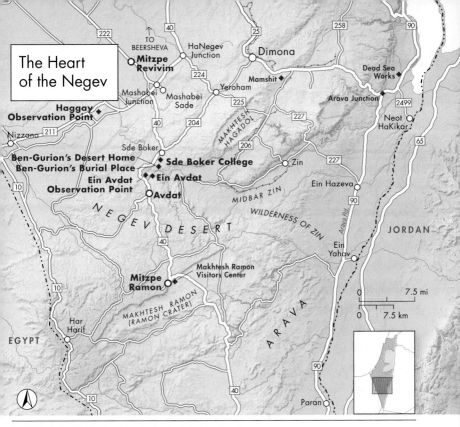

THE HEART OF THE NEGEV

The area extending from the Negev Highlands to Eilat offers a whole range of sights: Mitzpe Revivim, a reconstructed desert outpost; David Ben-Gurion's kibbutz home and grave site; an icy desert pool at Ein Avdat; the 2,000-year-old Nabatean hilltop stronghold of Avdat; and the immense Makhtesh Ramon (Ramon Crater). You'll also have the opportunity to be introduced to the Negev's indigenous people, the Bedouin.

MITZPE REVIVIM

36 km (22 mi) southeast of Beersheva. On Rte. 40 turn right onto Rte. 222 after Kibbutz Mashabei Sade, then drive 9 km (6 mi) to turnoff to Retamim, following signs to the Mitzpe.

Mitzpe Revivim is the site of an early desert outpost, and an interesting example of early Jewish settlement history. In 1943, in a desolate and empty Negev, three such outposts were set up to gauge the feasibility of Jewish settlement in the southernmost part of the country; one of these was Mitzpe Revivim (*mitzpe* means "lookout," and *revivim* means "rain showers"). Revivim's very presence, along with a handful of other Negev settlements, influenced the U.N.'s decision to include the Negev as part of the State of Israel in the 1947 partition plan. During the War of Independence, isolated Mitzpe Revivim was besieged by Egyptian soldiers, and a hard battle was won by a small band of pioneers and Palmach soldiers. The defenders' fort and living quarters have been preserved: the radio room (the radio crackles original messages), ammunition room, and kitchen contain original equipment. Outside are a cave where a medical clinic was set up, and two airplanes used to bring supplies and evacuate the wounded. A one-page "self guide" brings the rooms to life. Snacks, drinks, and Revivim's fine "Halutza" olive oil are available at the visitor center. ⊠ *Rte. 222* ☎ *08/656–2570* ⊆ *NIS 14* ☉ *Sun.–Thurs. 8–4, Fri. and Jewish holiday eves 8–noon.*

EN ROUTE

Proceed south along Route 40 and you'll come to the gas station at **Mashabim Junction**, which also serves as a roadside café (good for stocking up on bottled water). Continue on Route 40 for 2 km (1 mi) past the station and make a left at the sign for Mitzpe Ramon, at Telalim Junction. Heading southwest along this stretch of road, you'll pass through areas where signs announce FIRING ZONE. The signs indicate closed military areas, which you may not enter without proper authorization. It's perfectly safe to travel on the main roads; just don't wander off them.

Continuing along Route 40, you'll see a sign on the right for the **Haggay Observation Point.** The parking lot is on the opposite side of the highway at a curve in the road. After parking the car, carefully cross the road to the observation point for a glorious first view of the **Wilderness of Zin**—stark, flat, beige terrain—and **Kibbutz Sde Boker.** Except for the greenery of the kibbutz, the area looks just as it did to the wandering Children of Israel making their way from Egypt to the Land of Canaan more than 3,000 years ago, no doubt complaining all the while about the lack of figs, vines, and water.

BEN-GURION'S DESERT HOME

24 km (15 mi) south of Mitzpe Revivim. Sign for Ben-Gurion's Home is just after Kibbutz Sde Boker.

Thousands of people make their way to this pilgrimage site every year. David Ben-Gurion (1886–1973), Israel's first prime minister, was one of the 20th century's great statesmen. He regarded the Negev as Israel's frontier, and hoped that tens of thousands would settle there. When Ben-Gurion resigned from government in 1953 (later to return), he and his wife moved to the isolated, brand-new **Kibbutz Sde Boker** to provide an example for others. "Neither money nor propaganda builds a country," he announced. "Only the man who lives and creates in the country can build it." And so, the George Washington of Israel—whose interests were history, philosophy, and politics—took up his new role in the kibbutz

WORD OF MOUTH

"You have 2 weeks which is enough time to drive to Eilat. I would plan on driving one day and stopping on the interesting sights. You could go one way through Mizpe Ramon, see the Ramon Crater, Avdat, Sde Boker and visit Ben Gurion home (very interesting how the first prime minister of Israel lived). Visit his grave—one of the most beatiful sights in the desert."   —eri

Makhtesh Ramon (Ramon Crater), shown in the valley below, is one of the Negev's top sites.

sheepfold. In February 1955 he became prime minister once more, but he returned here to live when he retired in 1963. (He moved back to his Tel Aviv residence some months before his death, at the age of 87, in 1973.)

Amid the waving eucalyptus trees is Paula and David Ben-Gurion's simple dwelling. Ben-Gurion's small Negev home is commonly known as "the hut," owing to its humble appearance. It's a one-story wooden home with a small kitchen, an eating corner with a table and two chairs, and simple furniture throughout. Visitors such as United Nations Secretary-General Dag Hammarskjöld drank tea with Ben-Gurion in the modest living room. Ben-Gurion's library shelves contain 5,000 books (there are 20,000 more in his Tel Aviv home, on Ben-Gurion Boulevard). His bedroom, with its single picture of Mahatma Gandhi, holds the iron cot on which he slept (often only three hours a night) and his slippers on the floor beside it. The house is exactly as he left it.

Next door, in another painted-wood building, is an exhibition whose themes are the story of Ben-Gurion's extraordinary life, original documents that show the leader's strong ties to the Negev, and the Negev today in light of Ben-Gurion's dream. A film showing the footage of kibbutz members actually voting on his acceptance into their community is shown in the **visitor center**; the shop here sells gifts, jewelry, and books about the "Old Man," as he was known locally. ☎08/656–0457 ⊕bgarchives.bgu.ac.il/moreshet ⌨10 NIS ⊘ Sun.–Thurs. 8:30–4, Fri. and Jewish holiday eves 8:30–2, Sat. and Jewish holidays 9–3; last admission ½ hr before closing.

BEN-GURION'S BURIAL PLACE

Fodor's Choice *3 km (2 mi) southwest of Ben-Gurion's home, to the right of the main*
★ *gate for Sde Boker College.*

Ben-Gurion's grave is not far from his former home. Walk through the
beautiful garden until you reach the quiet, windswept plaza; in the center are the simple raised stone slabs marking the graves of David and
Paula Ben-Gurion (she died five years before her husband). The couple's
final resting place—selected by Ben-Gurion himself—commands a view
of Zin Valley's geological finery: a vast, undulating drape of stone that
changes hue as the daylight shifts. The cluster of greenery and palm trees
to the right on the valley floor indicates Ein Avdat (Avdat Spring).

SDE BOKER COLLEGE

Enter through the gate with the traffic arm, next to the BEN-GURION'S
MEMORIAL *sign.*

Ben-Gurion envisioned a place of learning in the desert. Sde Boker College, which specializes in environmental studies, became part of Ben-
Gurion University of the Negev, whose main campus is in Beersheva.
Although there isn't much to see here, the **National Solar Energy Center**
(☎ *08/659–6934*), where a research program investigates new ideas
for harnessing solar energy, is interesting. For the traveler, the college
is primarily a place to eat and possibly spend the night. The commercial center in the middle of the campus has a restaurant, a supermarket
open until 8 PM, a post office, and the field school of the **Society for the
Protection of Nature in Israel**. ☎ *08/653–2016* ⊕ *www.boker.org.il.*

**NEED A
BREAK?**   Looking for zinfandel (or cabernet sauvignon or merlot) in the desert? Call San
Francisco–born kibbutznik Zvi Remak (☎ *050/757–9212*), and he'll lead you
on his bicycle to his garage winery behind Ben-Gurion's home. Tasting is done
on a barrel by the front door of what was once a kibbutz shower room.

By the gas station just to the south of the entrance to Ben-Gurion's Desert
Home is a small café called Menta (☎ *08/657–9938*), which is open 24 hours,
and offers tasty cappuccino, espresso, muffins, and sandwiches.

WHERE TO EAT AND STAY

$ ✕ **Zin Inn.** This modest, air-conditioned spot with a shaded deck is where
AMERICAN   everyone hangs out—desert researchers from overseas, soldiers from
the nearby base, visiting schoolchildren, and field-school guides. The
menu is the usual desert-restaurant fare (plus croissants at breakfast):
soup, schnitzel, chicken, falafel, salad, ice cream, and coffee. It's open
weekdays 8 AM until 11 PM; Fridays 8 AM to 2 PM; Saturdays 10 AM to
6 PM. ⊠ *Sde Boker campus* ☎ *08/653–2800* ▭ *AE, MC, V.*

$ ⊡ **Sde Boker Field School Hostel and Hamburg Guest House.** Known locally
as "Midreshet Sde Boker," these two facilities have the same ownership
and both make especially good options for budget-minded families. At
the hostel, the octagonal units each contain a large room with a skylight,
two bunk beds, two twin beds, and a private bathroom. At Hamburg
House, the rooms are in a single building and, although modest, are

comfortable—each has a TV and a refrigerator. Lunch and dinner are available in the pleasant dining room. **Pros:** a short walk from the commercial center; large rooms. **Cons:** dining options limited; no more than basic service. ⊠*Sde Boker campus* ☎*08/653–2016* ⊕*www.boker.org. il* ⌐*47 rooms (6 beds each) in Field School, 20 rooms (2–4 beds each) in Hamburg House* ⊟*AE, MC, V* ⫪*BP.*

EIN AVDAT

🌤 *On Rte. 40, 3 km (2 mi) south of Ben-Gurion's grave and Sde Boker*
★ *College.*

Ein Avdat (Avdat Spring) lies at the foot of the narrow canyon dividing the plateau between the ancient Nabatean city of Avdat and Kibbutz Sde Boker, in **Ein Avdat National Park.** To get to the spring from Ben-Gurion's grave, head down the curving road to a clump of palm trees. Ask for the explanatory leaflet when you pay. Lock the car, taking valuables with you. Walk toward the thickets of rushes, and look for ibex tracks, made with pointed hoofs that enable these agile creatures to climb sheer rock faces. It's not easy to spot an ibex—their coats have striped markings that resemble the rock's strata. Rock pigeons, Egyptian vultures (black-and-white feathers, bright yellow beak, and long, pinkish legs), and sooty falcons nest in the natural holes in the soft rock and in cliff ledges.

The big surprise at Ein Avdat are the Ein Marof pools of ice-cold, spring-fed water, complete with splashing waterfall. To reach this cool oasis, shaded by the surrounding cliffs, walk carefully along the spring and across the dam toward the waterfall. Swimming and drinking the water are not allowed (you'll not be *sorely* tempted, though—the water is swarming with tadpoles), but enjoying the sight and sound of water in the arid Negev certainly is. The trail leads through stands of Euphrates poplars, and by caves inhabited by monks during Byzantine days, and then continues up the cliffside (using ladders and stone steps), but you can't follow it unless your party has two cars and leaves one at the destination, the Observation Point; the descent is considered too dangerous and is prohibited. ⊠*Ein Avdat National Park* ☎*08/655–5684* ⊕*www. parks.org.il* ⫧*NIS 23* ⏱*Apr.–Sept., Sun.–Thurs. 8–5, Fri. and Jewish holiday eves 8–4; Oct.–Mar., Sun.–Thurs. 8–4, Fri. and Jewish holiday eves 8–3; last admission 1 hr before closing.*

EN
ROUTE

For an eagle's-eye view of the waterfall and spring below, turn off Route 40 at the orange sign for Ein Avdat to get to the **Ein Avdat Observation Point.** Below you is the white canyon carved out by the Zin River, with its waterfall (most of the year) tumbling into a pool surrounded by greenery. From the lookout, a path leads around the top of the cliff (be very careful), enabling you to see the rope marks in the rock; these have been created over the years by Bedouin pulling up water buckets. For information on the hike from here to ancient Avdat, consult the SPNI Field School at Sde Boker College.

8

AVDAT

Fodor's Choice *Off Rte. 40, between Kibbutz Sde Boker and Mitzpe Ramon, about 20*
★ *km (12 mi) south of Ben-Gurion's desert home and grave.*

The Nabatean city of Avdat, a 12-acre acropolis, looms on a hilltop over
the spice route between Petra and Gaza. Here you can see the ancient
stronghold and urban ruins of three peoples who have left their mark
on the Negev: the Nabateans, the Romans, and the Byzantines.

The Nabateans were seminomadic pagans who came here from northern Arabia in the 3rd century BC. With their prosperous caravan routes
connecting the desert hinterland to the port city of Gaza, on the Mediterranean coast, they soon rose to glory with a vast kingdom whose
capital was Petra (in present-day Jordan). Strongholds to protect the
caravans—which carried gold, precious stones, and spices—were established along these routes, usually a day's journey apart.

The name "Avdat" is the Hebrew version of Oboda (30 BC–9 BC), a
deified Nabatean king who may have been buried here. Another king
of Avdat, Aretes, is mentioned in the New Testament. The prominent
local dynasty intermarried with the family of Herod the Great, and the
Nabatean kingdom was finally abolished by the Romans in AD 106.
Most of the remains on the acropolis date from the 3rd, 4th, and 5th
centuries—the Christian Byzantine period. The city was sacked by the
Persians in AD 620 and was rediscovered only in the 20th century.

Start at the **visitor center** (the Avdat Data Shop), where you can learn
about the Nabateans in a 10-minute video, see examples of what these
ancient traders actually transported across the desert, and examine
archaeological artifacts found in the excavations. Be sure to pick up the
Nature and National Parks Authority's excellent explanatory brochure
and map of the site. Drive up the road (save your energy for walking
around the site itself), stopping first at the sign for the **Roman burial
cave.** Park, and walk the 300 feet for a quick peek. The 21 double catacombs cut into the rock date from the 3rd century BC.

Back in your car, drive up to the lookout point at the restored Roman
building. The cultivated fields below were re-created in 1959 in order
to see if the ancient Nabatean and Byzantine methods of conserving the
meager rainfall (measured in millimeters) for desert farming would still
work. The proof is in the cultivated crops and orchards before you.

Using the Nature and National Parks Authority's map, you can trace
the lifestyle of these former locals at sites that include a reconstructed
three-story Roman tower; a rare Nabatean pottery workshop; a Byzantine winepress; cisterns; two Byzantine churches; and a large baptismal
font (to accommodate the converted). Near the baptismal font you can
walk down the steps to see 6th-century AD Byzantine dwellings, each
consisting of a cave (possibly used as a wine cellar) with a stone house
in front of it. At the bottom of the hill, north of the gas station, is a
Byzantine bathhouse. There is an eatery that serves light meals at the
visitor center. ⊠ *Rte. 40* ☏ *08/655–1511* ⊕ *www.parks.org.il* ☞ *NIS
23* ⊙ *Apr.–Sept., Sat.–Thurs. 8–5, Fri. and Jewish holiday eves 8–4;
Oct.–Mar., Sat.–Thurs. 8–4, Fri. and Jewish holiday eves 8–3.*

MAKHTESH RAMON AND MITZPE RAMON

Israel's most spectacular natural sight, the Ramon Crater in the heart of the Negev, is a place of unparalleled serenity and breathtaking views. The crater's walls are made from layers of different-color rock beds containing fossils of shells, plants, and trees. At one time under the sea, the makhtesh floor is today covered with heaps of black basalt, the peaks of ancient volcanoes, jagged chunks of quartzite, natural prism rock, and beds of multicolor clays.

Fodor's Choice ★ *On Rte. 40, between Beersheva and Eilat, 21 km (13 mi) south of Avdat, 80 km (50 mi) south of Beersheva.*

Makhtesh Ramon *(the Ramon Crater)* is an immense depression 40 km (25 mi) long, 10 km (6 mi) wide, and at its deepest, measuring 2,400 feet. Because it's a phenomenon known only in this country (there are two others in the Negev), the Hebrew term *makhtesh* is now accepted usage. By definition, a makhtesh is an erosion valley walled with steep cliffs on all sides and drained by a single watercourse.

Mitzpe Ramon is a town of 5,500 people on the northern edge of the crater, founded in 1951 by workers building the road to Eilat. Its raison d'être these days is to serve as an access point to the magnificent giant crater, and as a center of ecotourism and hiking. Visitors love the area because of its pure air and natural beauty. The local main road runs through the crater on its way to Eilat, a promenade winds along its edge, and a huge sculpture park sits on its rim. Outdoor enthusiasts will enjoy exploring the geology, nature (note the metal fences around the trees to keep the ibex from eating the leaves), and stunning scenery by foot, mountain bike, or Jeep. The weather here in November, December, and January is cool and pleasant.

If you're continuing south to Eilat, you can still see the crater, as Route 40 goes right through it; just try to plan your day so that you won't be driving to Eilat after dark. There are no gas stations between Mitzpe Ramon and Yotvata, a distance of more than 100 km (62 mi).

The impressive **visitor center,** at the very edge of the makhtesh, is built in the shape of an ammonite fossil (a spiral-shape sea creature that lived here when everything was underwater, millions of years ago). The helpful rangers with the Israel Nature and National Parks Protection Authority can suggest hiking routes in the makhtesh. ☎08/658–8691 ⊕*www. parks.org.il* ⊠*NIS 23* ⊙*Summer: Sat.–Thurs. 8–4, Fri. 8–3; Winter: Sat.–Thurs. 8–3, Fri. 8–2.* For a clear understanding of the makhtesh phenomenon, the center offers a full-color, sound-and-screen presentation with a walk-around model of the makhtesh—this definitely outshines the 12-minute film shown in the auditorium. On the way to the top-floor lookout there are informative, wall-size panels describing the makhtesh's geological makeup, ecology, vegetation, and settlement. As you stand behind the glass, you peer out at a world formed millions of years ago.

Just outside the center's front door, and included in its admission, is **Bio Ramon,** a zoological garden of ordinarily hidden small Negev animals, such as snakes, sand rats, beetles, turtles, and hedgehogs, who dwell in conditions that imitate their natural surroundings. Staff members are

These ruins in the ancient Nabatean city of Avdat are perched more than 2,000 feet above sea level.

happy to offer explanations of desert ecology, as well as educational children's activies. ✉ *On main road in Mitzpe Ramon* ☎ *08/658–8755* 💳 *NIS 12* 🕐 *Sat.–Thurs. 8–5, Fri. 8–4.*

★ You can take a walk (about 1 km, or ½ mi) along the **Albert Promenade**, which winds east to west along the edge of the crater from the visitor center to the cantilevered observation platform hanging over the rim. This is not the time to forget a camera—the view is overwhelming. The promenade is fashioned from local stone, as is the huge sculpture by Israel Hadani, the back of which faces town and represents the crater's geological layers.

With the crater as a magnificent backdrop, the **Desert Sculpture Park** exhibits a far-flung collection of 19 huge contemporary stone sculptures. The park took shape in 1962 with the work of a group of prominent Israeli and foreign sculptors under the direction of Negev artist Ezra Orion. Their idea was to add to the natural stone "sculptures" with geometrical rock formations of similar design. The sculptors brought their chosen rocks and formed their desert works of art with minimal hand shaping. Ibex often wander through. ✉ *Turn off near gas station on main road at sign marked* MA'ALE NOAH.

For a look at one of the crater's geological subphenomena, drive into the makhtesh to see the **Carpentry**, a hill of black prismatic rock. A path goes up to a wooden walkway, built to protect nature's artwork from travelers' feet. Long ago, the sandstone was probably hardened and slightly warmed by volcanic steam, and the rocks split into prisms, owing either to cooling joints or to another unknown process. The formations look like wooden chips piled up in a carpentry shop. ✉ *Along Rte. 40, going south.*

Another of nature's works is the **Ammonite Wall,** which is on the right as you drive through the crater (on its northeastern edge). A sign indicates a distance of 5 km (3 mi), which applies to the marked hike in the crater (for fit walkers only—take water). The rock face contains hundreds of ammonite fossils, which look like rams' horns and are indeed named for the Egyptian god Ammon, who had the head of a ram.

Just outside town is the **Alpaca Farm,** with its herd of 600 sweet-faced alpacas and llamas. Young and old get a kick out of feeding the animals, even if they receive the occasional spit in the face from these long-eyelashed creatures. Children weighing less than about 50 pounds can take a llama ride; horseback rides (some at night) and tours are available to all. You can also weave wool on a loom, and everyone loves to watch the shearing at Passover. ✉ *Turn off main road opposite gas station* ☎ *08/658–8047 or 052/897–7010* ⊕ *www.alpaca.co.il* ✉ *NIS 25* ⊙ *Daily 8:30–6:30 (8:30–4:30 in winter).*

EN
ROUTE

It's a **scenic drive** through the Ramon Crater on Route 40. The Negev wadis increase in size from their source in the Sinai, and cut through the Negev on their way to the Arava Valley, to the east. The sight of the Edom Mountains on the eastern horizon is beautiful, especially in the light of late afternoon.

South of the crater on Route 40, near the Shizafon Junction, stop at Kibbutz Neot Smadar, home both to an arts center with stained glass, ceramics, and textile workshops, and to a farm shop that sells dates, cheeses, almonds, olive oil, and herbal creams.

After the Tsichor Junction with Route 13 (which connects with the nearby north–south highway Route 90), you'll see limestone strata that have "folded" over the millennia. After the Ketura Junction (where Route 40 ends), there are breathtaking views of the Arava Valley (on your left), which marks the Israel–Jordan border and is part of the Great Syrian-African Rift, a fault line formed millions of years ago. From here, Route 90 leads straight to Eilat (52 km, or 33 mi). It's not advisable to take Route 12 to Eilat if you're finishing this tour after a long day's drive or toward dark; Route 90 is the better and safer road.

WHERE TO EAT AND STAY

CAFE
★

✗ **Cafeneto.** Ah, the taste of a flaky croissant and the enticing scent of cappuccino—in the desert! You can get a full Israeli breakfast here (including local cheese, omelets, and vegetables) as well as sandwiches such as the "Baghdadi" (hard-boiled egg, roasted eggplant, tomato, cucumbers, scallions, parsley, and tahini). Or you might try a salad of finely chopped vegetables with mint, coriander, lemon, and olive oil. Sip an iced chai, fresh juice, espresso, or a latte with shredded chocolate on the terrace. Open until 10 PM. ✉ *Nahal Tsiah 5* ☎ *08/658–7777* ⚠ *Reservations not accepted* ☐ *AE, DC, MC, V.*

ISRAELI

✗ **Havit.** If you're lucky enough to get a window table at Havit ("beer barrel"), you'll be sitting right on the edge of the crater, and the scenery may just overshadow whatever's on your plate. At this pub-restaurant, you can choose from fairly predictable fare including onion soup, pasta, meatballs, chicken, schnitzel, hummus, and stuffed mushrooms. You can raise a toast to the spectacular view with beer or wine. On Tuesday night, Havit morphs into a disco, and soldiers come to dance the night away. ⊠*Beside Mitzpe Ramon visitor center* ☎*08/658–8226* ⚒*Reservations not accepted* ⊟*DC, MC, V.*

$$ 🍽 **Desert Home.** Here's a little piece of heaven on the outskirts of Mitzpe
★ Ramon: a building with five lovely guest rooms, each with a covered terrace facing the surrounding desert hills. In this two-story, sand-colored, adult-oriented inn that's fenced with tree branches, each room has a bleached-wood floor, handmade wood furniture, and pale lime, mauve, or blue walls, a double bed with bright-white pillows and taupe spread, a white fan overhead (in addition to individual air-conditioning), and a blue sofa with Moroccan cushions. The wood kitchenette sparkles with shiny utensils, and there's a microwave. **Pros:** lots of privacy; breakfast of local delicacies delivered to your room each morning. **Cons:** remote location; not geared for children. ⊠*70 En Shaviv* ☎*052/322–9496* 🖷*08/658–6327* ⇌*5 rooms* ⚒*In-room: no phone. In-hotel: no kids under 16.* ⊟*No credit cards* ⫟*BP.*

$$$ 🍽 **Ramon Inn.** There's nothing rugged about a stay at this charming
★ desert hotel. The four-story building has no elevator, but the accommodations are entirely comfortable. Stay in a pastel-and-white studio apartment (for one or two) or a two- or three-room suite (for four to six people); suites have well-equipped kitchenettes. The lobby has an open fireplace for chilly winter nights. The 20-yard-long heated swimming pool would not be out of place at any luxury hotel. Even if you're not staying here, the restaurant is worth a visit; hearty buffet meals are enlivened by condiments made by local cooks. **Pros:** helpful staff; close to Ramon Crater. **Cons:** no views to speak of; other than the crater, which is a daytime activity, not much to do nearby at night. ⊠*Box 318, Mitzpe Ramon* ☎*08/658–8822* 🖷*08/658–8151* ⊕*www.isrotel.co.il* ⇌*96 rooms* ⚒*In-room: safe, kitchen, refrigerator. In-hotel: restaurant, room service, bar, pool, gym, bicycles, laundry facilities, no-smoking rooms.* ⊟*AE, DC, MC, V* ⫟*CP.*

$$ 🍽 **Succah in the Desert.** In the middle of nowhere (but accessible by road)
★ is this out-of-the-ordinary encampment of huts (like the portable dwellings used by the Children of Israel when they wandered in this desert). On a rocky hillside are eight isolated dwellings, 150 meters apart, each made of stone and wood, with a palm-frond roof. It's an appealing combination: the starkness and purity of the desert and some modern amenities. Each succah has a carpet on its earthen floor and a mattress with cozy blankets; household essentials include a tea corner, a clay water jar, and copper bowls for ablutions. The units are solar-powered, and there's an ecological-toilet cabin. Guests eat in the communal succah. You can ask a staff member to pick you up from outside the Ramon Inn. **Pros:** homemade vegetarian breakfasts and dinners included in the price; great for stargazing. **Cons:** can be cold during the desert nights; difficult to reach without a car. ⊠*On road to Alpaca Farm, 7 km (4½ mi) west of Mitzpe Ramon, Box 272* ☎*08/658–6280* ⊕*www.succah.co.il* ⇌*8 units that sleep 2, 1 unit that sleeps 10, all with shared bath* ⊟*AE, DC, MC, V* ⫟*MAP.*

$ 🛏Youth Hostel. Known in Israel for its high standards, at least as hostels go, this property must be booked well in advance (June and September are the busiest months). Fine for families, the place is done in bright colors and has a cheerfully decorated dining room. Several room sizes are available, from those with three bunk beds and one cot, to rooms with just one bunk bed (none have double beds). The decor is simple and functional. Food at the two dining rooms is inexpensive and plentiful, and you can order box lunches; nonguests must reserve for dinner. **Pros:** each room has its own bathroom; breakfast is included. **Cons:** not the softest linens; no televisions. ✉ *Opposite Mitzpe Ramon visitor center, Nahal Nikrot 4* ☎*08/658–8443* 📠*08/658–8074* 🌐*www.iyha. org.il* 🛏*47 rooms* ▤*DC, MC, V* ⎟⎷⎟*CP.*

SPORTS AND THE OUTDOORS
ARCHERY
Desert Archery (☎*050/534–4598* 🌐*www.desertarchery.co.il*) offers trips where you hike through a desert course while shooting arrows at targets. Suitable and safe for children.

JEEP AND HIKING TOURS
A hike, or a ride in a Jeep, is an unforgettable way to immerse yourself in the landscape. The staff at the **visitor center** (☎*08/658–8691*) in Mitzpe Ramon can help you plan local hikes, though the explanatory maps are in Hebrew.

Camel-supported hikes, and Jeep trips, are run by **Adam Sela Tours** (☎*050/ 530–8272* 🌐*www.adamsela.com*), which offers ecological tours and Bedouin visits as well. **Society for the Protection of Nature in Israel** (*SPNI* ☎*03/638–8666*) often includes the Negev heartland in its trips.

MOUNTAIN BIKING AND RAPPELLING
★ Treat yourself to a thrilling bike ride: **Negev Land (Siurei Midbar)** (☎*08/ 633–6660* 🌐*www.negevland.co.il*) rents mountain bikes for the day. It also offers Jeep tours, rappelling with instructors, and it rents climbing equipment. Closed on Saturday.

SWIMMING
You'll find a large indoor pool at **Mitzpe Ramon Inn** (☎*08/658–8151*).

SHOPPING
At the visitor center, the **Amonit Gallery** (☎*08/658–6166*) has a rather unusual selection: jewelry and batiks made by the owner, Bedouin drums, Armenian pottery, T-shirts with pictures of local animals, and desert stones and fossils.

☾ **Alpaca Farm** (☎*08/658–8047*) sells skeins of alpaca wool—light as a feather, soft as down, and warm as toast. There are cozy hats, too.

★ For all-natural, family-made, deliciously scented soaps and body-care products, visit **Naturescent** (☎*08/653–9333* 🌐*www.naturescent.co.il*) in the Industrial Area.

8

Continued on page 470

ADVENTURES

The Negev—a word that means "dry" in Hebrew—is a desert that covers more than half of Israel's land area, yet remains a wilderness waiting to be explored.

At first glance, the Negev appears to be a monolithically desolate landscape. But take a closer look and you'll find an impressive variety of sights: stark ridges, enormous erosion craters, serpentine wadis (dry riverbeds) and gorges, sun-scorched mesas, burnt cliffs, sculptured sandstone, treeless plains and sand dunes.

The Negev Desert

IN THE NEGEV

Since the days of the biblical patriarchs, the Negev has played host to ancient Egyptian miners, Bedouin herders, and Nabatean spice merchants who made the Negev the trade crossroads of Asia, Africa, and Europe.

With its sense of remoteness, the Negev is unusually—almost eerily—still and silent. But it's also an excellent activity base that invites fast-paced adventures. Whether you choose to explore it by jeep or camel, or experience its Bedouin culture, or take a stargazing or bird-watching trip, time spent in this giant desert wonderland won't disappoint.

by Benjamin Balint

ACTIVE ADVENTURES

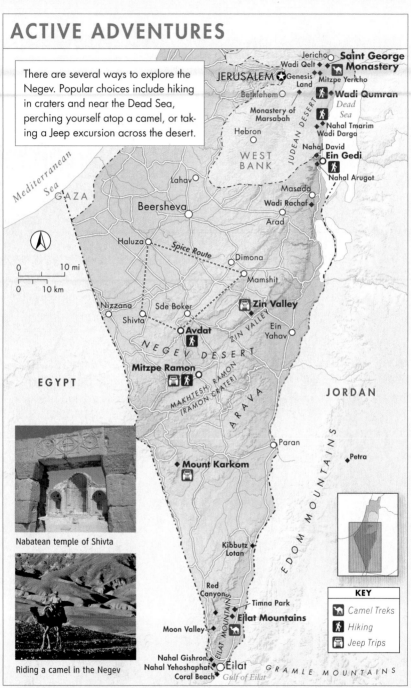

There are several ways to explore the Negev. Popular choices include hiking in craters and near the Dead Sea, perching yourself atop a camel, or taking a Jeep excursion across the desert.

Jericho
Wadi Qelt
Saint George Monastery
JERUSALEM Genesis Land Mitzpe Yericho
Bethlehem
Wadi Qumran
Monastery of Marsabah
Dead Sea
Hebron
Nahal Tmarim
Wadi Darga
Nahal David
Ein Gedi
WEST BANK
JUDEAN DESERT
Nahal Arugot

Mediterranean Sea
GAZA
Lahav
Masada
Wadi Rachaf
Arad
Beersheva
Haluza Spice Route
Dimona
Mamshit
0   10 mi
0   10 km
Nizzana
Sde Boker
Zin Valley
Shivta
Ein Yahav
Avdat
ZIN VALLEY
N E G E V   D E S E R T
EGYPT
Mitzpe Ramon
MAKHTESH RAMON (RAMON CRATER)
A R A V A
JORDAN
Paran
Petra
Mount Karkom
E D O M   M O U N T A I N S
Kibbutz Lotan
Red Canyons
Timna Park
Moon Valley
Eilat Mountains
EILAT MOUNTAINS
Nahal Gishron
Nahal Yehoshaphat
Coral Beach
Eilat
Gulf of Eilat
G R A M L E   M O U N T A I N S

KEY
🐫 Camel Treks
🚶 Hiking
🏛 Jeep Trips

Nabatean temple of Shivta

Riding a camel in the Negev

HIKING TRIPS

Hiking in the Negev

Israel's trails are excellently marked, and well signposted in both English and Hebrew. Although some guided one-day hikes are in English, don't dismiss hikes in Hebrew; English-speakers in the group are often glad to translate.

THE DEAD SEA

The labyrinth of rocky, brush-covered canyons and wadis found here are eminently hikable. Spend the day exploring one of several in the region, such as **Wadi Qumran**, where the Dead Sea Scrolls were discovered. The most accessible hikes are in **Ein Gedi**, a lush oasis with waterfalls, springs, and shade. The **Ein Gedi National Park** encompasses two wadis, Nahal David and Nahal Arugot, and has the area's best maintained trails.

THE SPICE ROUTE

Many of the ancient towns found in the heart of the Negev were once part of the Spice Route, which stretched from south Arabia to the Mediterranean, and flourished from the 3rd century BC to the 2nd century AD. One of the most spectacular of these towns, all of which are in complete ruin, is **Avdat**.

These cities, now in ruins, reflect the rich trade in frankincense and myrrh from south Arabia to the Mediterranean, which flourished from the 3rd century BC until the 2nd century AD. You'll see remains of the fortresses, irrigation systems, and caravanserai.

THE CRATERS

The Negev has three stunning craters: the Large Crater, the Small Crater, and Makhtesh Ramon (Ramon Crater), said to be the largest erosion crater on earth, at about 24 miles (40km) long, 5 miles (8 km) wide, and 1,600 feet (500 m) deep. Each has well-marked trails that lead past dizzying cliffs of multi-hued stratified rock.

HOW TO GO A **visitors' center** on the edge of Makhtesh has maps and helpful rangers. A safe, interesting, alternative is a guided, off-the-beaten-track hike. If you are planning a multi-day hike and prefer having gear and food provided, you can easily arrange a private tour. ■TIP➜ Summer temperatures can easily reach 100 degrees, so drink a liter of water every hour.

CAMEL TREKS

(left) A camel trip through the Negev. (right) Greek Orthodox Saint George Monastery

If you'd like to give your feet a rest, but still experience the desert up close, a camel ride is just the thing.

The local Bedouin name for camels is Ata Allah, or God's gift. The animal has traditionally provided both transport—a camel can go 5–7 days with little or no food and water—and milk. And meat from young male camels is a delicacy of the Arabian diet.

After you mount, the camel lurches forward rump first, which means you should lean back to avoid getting "camelpulted." Once you get going, however, riding is surprisingly comfortable. A walking camel moves both feet on one side of its body, then both feet on the other. This long-strided gait suggests the rolling motion of a boat, which explains the camel's other nickname in this part of the world:

"ship of the desert." The reins used to steer a camel, unlike a horse's reins, are attached to a bit inserted in the nose, so be gentle. Since camels travel in single-file, however, you won't have to worry too much about steering your beast.

Common routes, which can run up to half-day, take you through the **Eilat Mountains,** or to the lip of (known in Hebrew as Nahal Prat), home to the beautiful **Greek Orthodox Saint George Monastery,** often stopping at a shady oasis along the way.

HOW TO GO Eilat's Camel Ranch (enter just after the Texas Ranch opposite Coral Beach) is one place that offers tours for every taste: a daily tour at 4:30 ventures into the desert mountains and canyons (affording fabulous sunset views). Or try the two-hour tour on which you ride for an hour, then savor a desert meal including vegetables and goat cheese. Finally, you might try the family ride, which lasts 1½ hours. The ranch is closed Sunday.

A Nubian ibex, often seen in the Ramon Crater.

JEEP TRIPS

"Mushroom Rock," one of the many sandstone formations found in Timna Park.

After visiting the Negev, Mark Twain described it as "a desolation that not even imagination can grace with the pomp of life and action." Had he roared through the desert on the back of a 4x4, the American writer might have taken a different view.

Many jeep tours whisk you through the **Ramon Crater**, the **Zin Valley** (a desert moonscape punctuated by natural springs), or **Mount Karkom** (an ancient sacred mountain where you can see rock art, stone circles, geoglyphs, and cultic altars).

Other than the lurching off-road excitement, one of the advantages of jeep tours is the high standard of guiding. Licensed Israeli guides undergo rigorous training, and most have developed an amazing feel for the contours of the landscape. Guides will introduce you to the desert's geologic past and present habitat, and describe Israel's sophisticated water and soil conservation programs.

HOW TO GO From Eilat, the well-established **Red Sea Sports Club** leads jeep safaris through the **Granite Mountains** around Eilat to lookout points above **Moon Valley**, with a descent into the **Red Canyon** where you walk for an hour and take in the natural beauty. The cost is NIS 140 per person. Another experienced company, **Jeep See**, offers a 1½-hour "Desert Glimpse" tour, with a view of the hot-pink flamingos near Eilat; the cost is NIS 65. Jeep See also provides a four-hour trip to the Red Canyon (including hiking) for NIS 140 per person.

8

IN FOCUS ADVENTURES IN THE NEGEV

SPECIAL-INTEREST ACTIVITIES

Hiking, trekking, and zooming across the desert in a jeep aren't the only ways to experience the Negev. Try spending an overnight in a Bedouin tent, joining an archaeological dig, or bird-watching.

A Bedouin hospitality tent

THE BEDOUIN EXPERIENCE

Spending a day with Bedouins usually involves making a meal. You'll sit on beautiful woven mats and dine on *labane* (thick, tangy yogurt), *taboun* (Bedouin bread) with hummus, fresh-baked pita with zatar, goat cheese, and skewered meat. The feast is then washed down with sweet mint tea or black cardamom-spiced coffee. Sometimes there's belly dancing and music played on traditional instruments like the shabbaba, a kind of flute, and the rababa, a one-string violin. As you're soaking it in, smoke a *nargilla* (water pipe) with your host, and ask him about the herbal expertise and plant lore that are so intrinsic to Bedouin culture.

STAYING OVERNIGHT Staying overnight in a Bedouin tent is a worthwhile experience as part of your time in the Negev. The two best Bedouin outfitters are **Khan Shayarot** (☎ 08/653–5777), on route 40, about 20 minutes north of Mitzpe Ramon, and **Kashkhar** (☎ 050/668–9743), which is a family-run and organizes night-tracking tours, located a little more than a mile north of Avdat, also on route 40.

THE BIBLICAL EXPERIENCE

Visit **Genesis Land**, (Eretz Breishit) (☎ 02-9974477), where Israeli actors bring Biblical stories to life in the landscape in which they took place. You might be greeted by Eliezer, who'll lead you to Abraham's tent to enjoy meats, shepherd casseroles, and pita with zatar. Activities can include letter-writing with a quill on parchment, baking bread, or making pottery. Or, you can take a camel ride to the Monastery of Marsabah or the nearby Ein Mabua oasis.

STAYING OVERNIGHT Stay the night (Genesis Land offers accommodation either in Abraham's tent or a cabin), allows you to watch the sun set and the moon rise over the stark Judean hills, and put yourself into the rhythms of an ancient and simpler way of life.

The Wise Star Observatory

ASTRONOMY

If stargazing is your thing, the Negev offers an awesome nightly spectacle, completely free of light pollution.

HOW TO DO IT To peer at some constellations and nebulae, visit Tel Aviv University's world-class **Wise Observatory** (☎ 08/6588133), located on a high plateau in the central Negev, 5 km west of the town of Mitzpe Ramon. Astronomers here recently discovered a planetary system—a star and two giant planets. The best—most cloudless—season to visit is June through August.

ECOTOURISM

Over the past decade, the Negev has incubated the development of ecotourism for the naturalistically minded. For this experience, you can visit one of several kibbutzim, which have traditionally engaged in environmentally friendly practices. Visitors can learn how the kibbutz deals ecologically with waste disposal, grows organic agriculture, reuses solid waste for alternative building, composts, and recycles.

Sifting for artifacts on an archaeological dig

Working on a kibbutz

HOW TO DO IT A good place to start is **Kibbutz Lotan**, 55 km (33 mi) north of Eilat. The kibbutz, which was awarded a prize for ecological villages, also conducts tours to familiarize visitors with mud huts that do not use electricity. (Tours leave daily at 9 AM from the parking lot in front of the holiday village.) The kibbutz also offers tours that introduce visitors to birds' migratory paths and local agriculture like date harvesting. (These tours depart at 10 AM from the parking lot.)

Another recommended Negev company with expert guides is the ten-year-old **Beerotayim Ecotourism Center**, which offers everything from 3-hour donkey rides to 8-day combined camel and 4 x 4 excursions (bring your own sleeping bag). Wadi Beerotayim itself lies in the western Negev Highland, near the Sinai–Negev border, and offers an excellent base for exploring the Ramon Crater.

DESERT DIGS

In late 2008, a British tourist visiting Israel discovered almost 300 24-carat gold coins dating from the 7th century at a dig where she had been volunteering. If you fancy working in the dust under a blazing sun in the hopes of finding treasure, take part in one of several ongoing archaeological digs.

HOW TO DO IT The best resource to volunteer for digs that appeal to you is the **Israel Ministry of Foreign Affairs** Web site (⊕ www.israel-mfa.gov.il).

BIRD-WATCHING

Millions of birds fly over Eilat and the Negev on their journey between winter grounds in Africa and summer breeding grounds in Eurasia. Migration takes place between mid-February and the end of May, and between early September to late November (spring is the larger of the two migrations). Lanner falcons, imperial eagles, long-legged buzzards, oriental skylarks, white storks, Egyptian vultures, and desert eagle owls—all these and many more come to visit.

HOW TO DO IT The **International Birding and Research Center,** just north of Eilat, is aflutter year-round (except August, when it closes); it's open Sunday–Thursday 8:30–5. The center conducts half- and full-day trips with names like "Morning Birder," "Desert Birding Trip," and "The Grouser." Binoculars are provided. Prices range from NIS 15 to NIS 230 per person per trip.

Blackstart

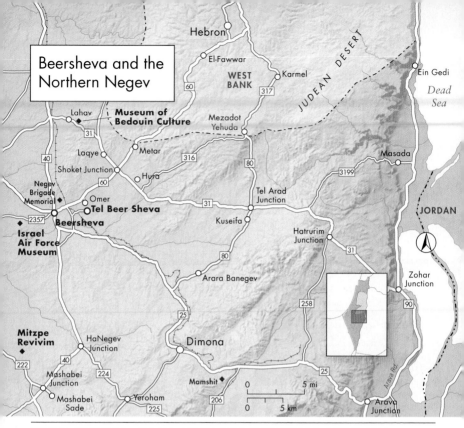

BEERSHEVA AND THE NORTHERN NEGEV

This area in the north of the region stretches east from Beersheva, known as the capital of the Negev. The Northern Negev is a mountainous region, and you'll encounter scenes that look strikingly biblical— black tents, Bedouin shepherds in robes, and sheep and goats bumbling around.

MUSEUM OF BEDOUIN CULTURE

⏰ 95 km (57 mi) south of Tel Aviv, 24 km (14 mi) north of Beersheva. At ★ the Lahavim Junction, turn east onto Rte. 31, and turn in at the sign for the Joe Alon Center.

Once off the main road, you'll drive through the Lahav pine forest to reach the Joe Alon Center, whose centerpiece is this one-of-a-kind museum focusing on the Bedouin people, who have long populated the Negev. The study center (marked with an orange sign) is named for the late Colonel Joe Alon, a pilot who took a great interest in this area and its people. Housed in a circular, tentlike building, the museum tells the story of the Bedouin's rapid change from a nomadic to a modern lifestyle through tableaux of life-size mannequins. The tableaux are grouped by subject: wool spinning and carpet weaving, bread baking, the Bedouin coffee ceremony, wedding finery (including a camel elaborately decorated for the event), donkeys and camels at work, and toys made from found objects such as pieces of wire and wood. The tools and artifacts—most handmade, and many already out of use in modern Bedouin life—form an outstanding collection. Admission includes a cup of thick coffee in a real Bedouin tent, where the sheikh performs the coffee ceremony over an open fire. ⊠*Rte. 325 off Rte. 31* ☎*08/991–3322* ⊕*www.joealon.org.il* ✉*NIS 20* ☉*Summer: Sun.–Thurs. 9–5, Fri. 9–2; Winter: Sun.–Thurs. 9–4, Fri. 9–2.*

BEERSHEVA

24 km (14 mi) south of Museum of Bedouin Culture, 113 km (70 mi) southeast of Tel Aviv.

Beersheva is one of the oldest cities in Israel. Its emblem consists of a tamarisk tree, representing the biblical past, and a pipe through which water flows, symbolizing the city's modern revival. Four thousand years ago, the patriarch Abraham dug wells (*be'er* in Hebrew) here and swore an oath (*shevua*) over seven (*sheva*) ewes with the king of Gerar, who vowed to prevent his men from seizing the well. And it was here that Abraham planted a grove of tamarisk trees. Isaac built an altar here, the prophet Elijah found refuge here from Jezebel, and King Saul constructed a fort here. It's easy to envision these scenes today thanks to the cloaked figures of Bedouin shepherds with their sheep and goats on the hillsides surrounding the city.

Tel Beer Sheva, just outside the city, is the site of biblical Beersheva and could easily be the site of Abraham's well. An expression from the Book of Judges, "from Dan to Beersheva," once indicated the northern and southern boundaries of the Land of Israel. It was declared a World Heritage site by UNESCO in July 2005.

Romans and Byzantines built garrisons in Beersheva, but in subsequent centuries the city was abandoned. In 1900 the Ottoman Turks, who had ruled Palestine since 1517, rebuilt Beersheva as their Negev district center (the present Old City). They set aside an area for a Bedouin market, which still takes place every Thursday. During World War I, when the British took Beersheva from the Turks, the city rapidly expanded; in October 1948 it was conquered by Israel.

Beersheva is now the the sixth-largest city in Israel, with a population of some 200,000. It houses a major university, named after David Ben-Gurion, an Israel Aircrafts Industries complex, a high-tech center, and a regional hospital serving Bedouin shepherds, kibbutzniks, and other desert dwellers. Largely blue-collar, the city is struggling to provide housing for thousands of recent immigrants, many from Ethiopia and the former Soviet Union.

The famed Bedouin Market, once a source of some of Israel's best ethnic handicrafts, has been hit hard by modern times (especially the competition of cheap imports from the Far East) and isn't what it used to be. But it now has a permanent location, and you might still find something authentic. Most intriguing are the Bedouin themselves, sitting cross-legged with their goods spread out on the ground.

8

Because it's quite close to Tel Aviv and Jerusalem, the city serves as a jumping-off point for Negev travel—main roads branch out from here; buses serving the Negev depart from here; and trains from the north end up in Beersheva. If your schedule permits, stay overnight in Beersheva for a glimpse of a growing desert city with an interesting citizenry.

GETTING HERE AND AROUND

Beersheva is 113 km (70 mi) southeast of Tel Aviv and 83 km (52 mi) south of Jerusalem. The drive from either Tel Aviv or Jerusalem takes about 1½ hours. To Beersheva from Tel Aviv, take Route 2 (the Ayalon Highway) south until the turnoff marked "scbeersheva—ashdod". After this you'll be on Route 41, which runs into Route 40 after 6 km (4 mi). Continue on Route 40 to Beersheva; there are clear signs all the way.

To reach Beersheva from Jerusalem, take Route 1 west to the Bet Shemesh turnoff (onto Route 38); traveling south, follow Route 38, then Route 32, which turns into Route 35, to Kiryat Gat. Here you'll pick up Route 40 south to Beersheva.

OFF THE BEATEN PATH

Neve Midbar. This health spa (for daytime visits) centers on a pool of natural thermo-mineral waters pumped up from deep underground, at a temperature of 39°C (around 102 °F). The spa also has two freshwater pools and a shallow pool for babies. A hot tub, sauna, various massages, and aromatherapy treatments make for an unusual desert experience. A gift shop, restaurant, and coffee shop share the premises. ⊠ *Rte. 40, 20 minutes' drive from Beersheva* ☎*08/657–9666* ☉*Sun., Mon., Wed., and Sat. 9–6, Tues. and Thurs. 9* AM*–10* PM*; Fri. 9–4.*

WHERE TO EAT AND STAY

$$$$
CONTINENTAL

✕**Ahuzat Smilansky.** On a tree-lined street with old-fashioned street lights, you'll find this perfect venue for a rarified dining experience. The rustic stone building has high ceilings, leafy potted plants, floors enhanced with arabesque tiles, and an inner courtyard. Candle boxes hang from the walls, and dark-wood padded chairs and beautifully set tables give serene elegance to the lovely setting. The creatively prepared dishes don't disappoint: start with furnace-baked camembert or smoked duck in aspic and move on to such main courses as saffron salmon, roasted eggplant ravioli, lamb osso buco, and fillet of beef. ⊠ *23 Smilansky, Old City* ☎*08/665–4854* ✍*Reservations essential* ▭*AE, DC, MC, V* ☉*Sun.–Thur. 12—11* PM*; Fri.–Sat. 6* PM*—11* PM.

$
CONTEMPORARY

✕**Pitput.** The name of this grilled-meat restaurant means "chattering" in Hebrew, and the young crowd definitely lives up to this moniker. The washed beige walls are hung with shadow boxes filled with wine corks and coins. The staff here is congenial and the food attractively presented. Sitting outside on the busy sidewalk or inside listening to recorded jazz or blues, diners have a range of selections besides the meat specialities like entrecote hamburgers: salads, omelets, blintzes from cheese to salmon, pasta, grilled fish with grilled vegetables, and pizza. Cheese sandwiches are made on sesame-seed rolls called *begeles*. Half bottles of Yarden wine are available. You can't go wrong by finishing with hot homemade pecan pie or cheesecake with fresh fruit. There's live music some evenings and the restaurant is wheelchair accessible. ⊠ *122 Herzl St.* ☎*08/628–9888* ✍*Reservations not accepted* ▭*AE, DC, MC, V.*

$$$ ⛨**Golden Tulip Negev.** It's the only real hotel in town, and it provides up-to-date lodgings. The building's beige-and-brown stone reflects its desert surroundings, and arched windows soften the city's square look. Guest rooms are comfortably outfitted with wicker chairs, and the curtains and bedspreads form a snappy color scheme of red, green, and butterscotch. Good reading lights are a welcome touch. Rooms on the business floor are equipped with safes and minibars. The breezy outdoor patio, with bubbling fountains, is a cool place to relax in the hot desert climate. **Pros:** good rates for what you get; for those using Beersheva as a base for a Negev road trip, easy location at the entrance to the city. **Cons:** dull, urban setting; Internet costs extra. ✉*Henrietta Szold St., near City Hall* ☎*08/640–5444* 🖷*08/640–5445* ⊕*www.fattal.co.il* 🛏*210 rooms, 48 suites* ⌂*In-room: kitchen (some), Wi-Fi (some). In-hotel: restaurant, room service, bar, pool, gym, spa, laundry service* ▭*AE, DC, MC, V* ⫪❙*BP.*

NIGHTLIFE AND THE ARTS

BARS
Join Ben-Gurion University students for a beer and delicious pub food at **Coca Bar and Restaurant** (☎*08/623–3303*), behind the student dorms.

★ Savor a long evening of wine and tapas at **Hatzer Hayayin Wine Bar** (✉*25 Smilansky St.* ☎*08/623–8135*), a popular romantic spot in the Artists' Quarter. Proprietor, wine expert, and congenial host Michael will guide you through the intricacies of Israeli and other wines from 7:30 PM 'til very late. It closes weekends.

MUSIC
Beer Sheva Sinfonietta (☎*08/623–1616*) is a well-regarded symphonic group.

THEATER
Once a year, in March or April, **Light Opera Group of the Negev** (☎*08/641–4081*), a non-profit group of amateur singers, presents performances of Gilbert and Sullivan and other modern musicals in English.

SHOPPING
The Negev is still the home of the Bedouin, but today's Bedouin women are less interested than yesterday's in staying home all day to weave and embroider. An eagle's eye and a saint's patience will guide your search through the bundles and stacks of rather ordinary stuff at the **Bedouin market,** where you can find goods made by elder generations. The market starts at daybreak each Thursday and lasts until early afternoon; it's on the eastern side of the huge outdoor market site near the bridge, at Derech Eilat and Derech Hebron streets. (A goat and sheep sale takes place once in a while.) The best time to visit is 6 AM, an hour or so later in winter. Walk to the back, passing coffee and tea sellers. For sale, if you can find them, are embroidered dresses, yokes, and side panels from dresses; woven camel bags; rugs; earrings, bracelets, amulets, and nose rings; coin headbands (used as dowry gifts); tassels; copperware; and *finjans* (Bedouin coffee pots).

An elegant desert wine shop? You may be surprised by the state-of-the-art design, stock of imported and local wines, and well-informed

8

CLOSE UP

Bedouin Culture

Bedu, the Arabic word from which the name Bedouin derives, simply means "inhabitant of the desert." Some 160,000 Bedouin, semi-nomadic Arab tribesmen and full citizens of Israel, live in the Negev. The present-day Bedouin of the Negev (and the Sinai) trace their origins to nomads of the Arabian peninsula who wandered west 400 to 600 years ago. The exceptions are members of the Jebeliya tribe, descendants of East European slaves sent by Emperor Justinian to serve Greek monks at St. Catherine's Monastery at Mt. Sinai. The slaves slowly adopted the Bedouin way of life, and they still serve the monks from their desert nearby.

Since Israel gained independence in 1948, the Bedouin's urbanization and integration into Israeli society has been difficult. The Negev's Bedouin men have loyally served in the Israeli army, and some have lost their lives doing so. Starting in the late 1960s, however, the Israeli government built seven Bedouin towns, the largest of which is Rahat, and encouraged resettlement. Their simple, nomadic way of life becomes more difficult to maintain each year as they resist these policies.

Earning a living. The Bedouin's main livelihood is the raising of livestock, camels and black goats in particular. The animals supply milk, meat, hair for weaving, and dung for burning as fuel. The wanderings of the Bedouin are driven by the unending search for grazing land and water for their flocks. Marriages are arranged, taking family interests into account. It is not uncommon today for a man to have two wives, the first wife and a younger one to help her. The Bedouin have one of the highest birth rates in the world.

The family is structured as a business. Men, who work as herders, make decisions about buying and selling livestock as well as finding new pastures. Women and children do the cooking, weaving, searching for firewood, and often caring for the flocks.

Hospitality and heritage. A Bedouin proverb says, "He who shares my bread and salt is not my enemy." Bedouin are known for their warm hospitality. It is not only a pleasure to extend hospitality but the Bedouin see it as a duty. A Bedouin host would never fail to invite a stranger into his tent. And refusing a Bedouin's invitation would be unthinkable because it would deny the host an opportunity to display his kindness. Having the honor of being invited by a Bedouin host to drink sweet tea or coffee, made over an open fire in his tent, is an unforgettable experience. A Bedouin tent is customarily divided into two sections by a woven curtain known as a ma'nad. Having been welcomed into a tent, guests are honored, respected, and nourished, frequently with cardamom-spiced coffee, and music played on a traditional instrument called the rababa, a one-string violin.

A rich heritage of poetry has been passed down through the generations by word of mouth. Only in the past few years have these words been recorded, written in their original Arabic, and preserved by scholars who recognize that the Bedouin way of life is rapidly slipping away.

staff at **Wine Aficionado (Aninei Ha-Yayin)** (✉*117 Trumpeldor St.* ☏*08/628–9444*).

On Route 40 northeast from Beersheva to Arad is the large and impressive **Negev Brigade Memorial,** designed by Israeli artist Danny Karavan, and built during the 1960s. The monument's 15 symbolic parts and Hebrew text tell the story of the battle of the Palmach's Negev Brigade against the Egyptians during the War of Independence after the birth of the State of Israel in 1948. The tower offers a great view of Beersheva and the surrounding desert.

Kafriat Shoket, a kibbutz-run way station, has a large cafeteria with two sections, one for grilled meat-dishes, the other serving dairy food: sandwiches, salads, and cakes. Eat inside or outside under the tamarisk trees. ✉*Near Shoket Junction, intersection of Rte. 31 and Rte. 60* ☏*08/646–9421* ⊘*Daily 6* AM*–9* PM.

ISRAEL AIR FORCE MUSEUM

⏱ *7 km (4½ mi) west of Beersheva.*

★ For plane lovers, this is a field of dreams. The open-air Israel Air Force Museum (also known as Hatzerim) is a gigantic concrete field with 90 airplanes parked in rows. The fighter, transport, and training (plus a few enemy) aircraft tell the story of Israel's aeronautic history, from the Messerschmitt—obtained in 1948 from Czechoslovakia, and one of four such planes to help halt the Egyptian advance in the War of Independence—to the *Kfir,* the first fighter plane built in Israel. The young air force personnel who staff the museum lead tours that take about 1½ hours and include a movie shown in an air-conditioned Boeing 707 used in the 1977 rescue of Israeli passengers held hostage in a hijacked Air France plane in Entebbe, Uganda. Another attention-getting display is a shiny, black Supermarine Spitfire with a red lightning bolt on its side, flown by Ezer Weizmann, the IAF's first pilot, and later President of Israel. Tours are available in English and French. ✉*Rte. 233* ☏*08/990–6855* ⊠*NIS 28* ⊘*Sun.–Thurs. 8–5, Fri. 8–1* PM.

TEL BEER SHEVA

★ *2 km (1¼ mi) east of Beersheva, on the road between Beersheva and Shoket Junction.*

Tel Beer Sheva, biblical Beersheva—traditionally associated with the patriarch Abraham—is an artificial tell (mound of ruins) created by nine successive settlements between 3500 BC and 600 BC. The tell is a recent addition to the Nature and National Parks Authority's roster; ask for the excellent explanatory leaflet.

At the top of the tell is the only planned Israelite city uncovered in its entirety, which includes sophisticated waterworks and a fascinating reconstructed horned altar. Most of the visible remains date from the 10th to 7th centuries BC. A fine example of a circular layout typical of the Iron Age, the city is believed to have been destroyed around 706 BC by Sennacherib of Assyria. At the northeastern end, outside the 3,000-year-old city gate, is a huge well (the deepest in Israel, and more

DID YOU KNOW?

Dromedary camels, such as this one, have been used in the Negev for thousands of years, and are particularly well-suited for transporting substantial amounts of goods.

than 6 feet in diameter) which apparently once reached groundwater 90 feet below. This ancient well served the city from its earliest times, and scholars speculate that it could be the well that is documented in the Bible as Abraham's Well (Genesis 21:22–32). The observation tower is rather ugly, but it does afford beautiful views. ⊠ *Rte. 60* ☎ *08/646–7286* ⊕ *www.parks.org.il* ⊠ *NIS 12* ⊘ *Apr.–Sept., Sun.– Thurs. 8–5, Fri. and Jewish holiday eves 8–3; Oct.–Mar., Sat.–Thurs. 8–4, Fri. and Jewish holiday eves 8–2.*

EILAT AND ENVIRONS

The Arava Plain comes to an abrupt end where it meets the Bay of Eilat, site of the country's southernmost town: the sun-drenched resort of Eilat. The Gulf of Eilat gives way to the Red Sea, which lies between the Sinai Mountains to the west and Jordan's Edom Mountains to the east. The Jordanian port of Aqaba is directly across the bay—Eilat residents will eagerly point out the Jordanian royals' yacht and vacation villa—and to the southeast is Saudi Arabia. The Sinai Desert is just over the Egyptian border.

Most travelers fly into or whiz down to Eilat to flop down on its beaches and snorkel or scuba dive among its tropical reefs. But if you have time, explore the vast desert landscape to the north of Eilat. You'll find cliffs, canyons, and unique geological formations at Timna Park, and indigenous animals at Hai Bar Nature Reserve. Both make good side trips from Eilat; just leave time for a sunset stop at Mt. Yoash. Another option is to explore ancient Petra, over the border in Jordan.

8

EILAT

307 km (190 mi) south of Jerusalem, 356 km (221 mi) south of Tel Aviv.

A legend says that after the Creation, the angels painted the earth. When they got tired, they spilled their paints: the blue became the waters of Eilat, and the other colors became its fish and coral. Whether or not this is true, add to this rainbow of colors Eilat's year-round warm weather, its superb natural surroundings of sculptural red-orange mountains, and its situation on the sparkling Red Sea—whose coral reefs attract divers from all over the world—and you've got a first-rate resort.

Eilat, a city of about 60,000, is now Israel's prototypical "sun-and-fun" destination, but its strategic location as a crossroads between Asia and Africa has given it a long place in history. According to the Bible, the Children of Israel stopped here as they fled from Egypt into the Promised Land, and King Solomon kept his fleet in the area between Aqaba and Eilat. Later, because of its position on a main trade and travel route, Eilat was conquered by every major power: the Romans, Byzantines, Arabs, Crusaders, Mamluks, Ottoman Turks, and, most recently, the British, whose isolated police station, called Umm Rash Rash (headquarters of their camel corps), was the first building in modern-day Eilat. When David Ben-Gurion visited in 1935, he envisioned an international port here, and in 1945 Shimon Peres, today President of

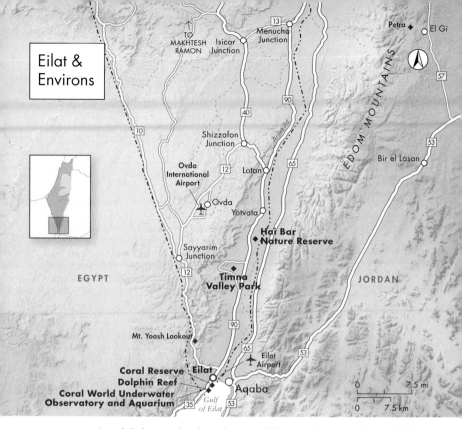

Israel, led a camel trek to the area. "Shards of coral and beautiful large seashells are scattered on the shore," he reported. "A lone boat, its sail bent to the wind, delivers foodstuff from Aqaba to Umm Rash Rash. White-winged kingfishers pounce on their prey. A gulf with a natural port pleads for life."

The area was taken by the Israelis in March 1949, the last action of the War of Independence. The modern town was founded in 1951 and developed as a port in 1956 after the Egyptian blockade of the Tiran Straits was lifted.

Most travelers have concluded that Eilat's natural assets more than make up for its undistinguished architecture and overdevelopment. For wherever you are in Eilat, a glance eastward presents you with the dramatic sight of the granite mountain range of Edom, whose shades of red intensify toward evening, culminating in a crimson sunset blaze over the Red Sea. This incongruous name for a body of water that's brilliantly turquoise along the shore is the result of a 17th-century typographical error by an English printer: in setting the type for an English translation of a Latin version of the Bible, the printer left out an "e" and thus "Reed Sea" became "Red Sea." The name was easily accepted because of the sea's red appearance at sunset.

GETTING HERE AND AROUND

The most direct way from Tel Aviv to Eilat is Route 40 south to Beersheva. Leave Beersheva via Route 25 (marked "dimona—eilat"), driving 69 km (43 mi) to the Arava Junction. Turn right (south) onto Route 90 (Arava Road), and travel straight to Eilat. The trip takes about five hours.

EXPLORING

Start exploring Eilat with a walk along the **promenade**, beginning at Herod's Hotel, near the Jordanian border. The 3-km (2-mi) promenade is also known as the Peace Walk, since it is hoped that one day it will continue to Aqaba, Jordan. Purple and pink bougainvillea pour down from the Royal Beach Hotel's terrace above; add to your enjoyment by stopping for an ice cream (say, mango) from one of the stands. If you're here at sunset, sit and savor the show-stopping view of the Red Sea turning red, with the dark, reddish-gray shapes of the Edom Mountains to the east and the rugged Eilat Mountains to the west. On a clear day, you can see as far as Saudi Arabia and Egypt.

A stroll past swanky hotels and loads of shops, coffee bars, and restaurants, with palmy beaches on the other side, brings you to the Dutch Bridge, which opens for tall-masted vessels. On one side is the Lagoon, or inner marina, where yachts are anchored and various small craft are for hire; on the other is the marina, where cruise boats of all types wait to sally forth. The promenade winds along beside more beaches, covered with folks reddening in the sun. The scene includes sophisticated strollers, the backpack crowd, artists doing quick portraits, vendors selling earrings, and tattoo artists, all accompanied by strolling street musicians. At the intersection of Durban and Arava streets (at the roundabout), you can continue along the waterfront, with the Sea Gate Mall on your right, until you reach a small palm-filled plaza with a tiny, cement block–shape building with a statue of four fighters raising a comrade aloft while a flag "flies" above. This is Umm Rash Rash, where the Israelis first took control of the Gulf of Eilat in March 1949, as determined by the U.N.'s Partition Plan. The small building—the only one that existed then—is a far cry from today's luxury resorts.

NEED A BREAK? At the western end of the promenade, at the Mul Yam (Mall Yam) shopping mall (identified by the seahorse over its entrance), is an outdoor café which feeds the crowd with ice cream, sweet drinks, and good coffee. Locals turn out in force here to sip, chat, and watch the tourists go by.

The **Coral World Underwater Observatory and Aquarium**, one of Eilat's star attractions, can be recognized by its tall space-needle structure floating offshore. This is the largest aquarium complex in the Middle East. Plan to spend several hours here (there's a cafeteria for lunch on the premises). The **Aquarium's** 12 windows provide views of rare fish so magnificent and so Day-Glo colorful that it's hard to believe they're real; there's an unlighted room where phosphorescent fish and other sea creatures glow in the dark. And there's the turtle and stingray pools, too. Don't miss feeding time (11 AM) in the **Shark Pool**. The anaconda snakes, poisonous frogs, and piranha are fed in the **Amazonas** at 3 PM. Captain Jaws takes you on a sea journey during an audiovisual show presented in a simulated-motion theater with moving seats at the **Oceanarium**.

The **Underwater Observatory** is reached by a 300-foot wooden bridge. Head down the spiral staircase and into the sea—you are now 15 feet underwater, where two round, glass-windowed halls, connected by a tunnel, offer stunning views of the surrounding coral reef, home to exotic tropical fish. The **Observatory Tower**—reached by stairs—gives coastal views of Israel's neighboring countries. There's a café up here. You can also take a ride on a glass-bottom boat, or on a 100-ton yellow submarine which dives to 60 meters. Bus no. 15 runs to and from downtown Eilat every half-hour. ✉ *Rte. 90 (Eilat–Taba Rd.)* ☎ *08/636–4200* ⊕ *www.coralworld.com/eilat* 🖙 *NIS 79, NIS 89 including Oceanarium* ⊙ *Sat.–Thurs. 8:30–5, Fri. and Jewish holiday eves 8:30–4.*

Ꮳ **Kings City.** This gigantic fairy-tale castle looms behind the hotels on the northern beach. Kings City, a biblical theme park on three levels, offers three distinct sections of sophisticated entertainment, and there's a high-flying water ride to boot. The **Cave of Illusions** has, among other interactive diversions, hands-on games that test your mental acuity, a jail to test your ability to escape, a huge maze, and a large, end-less kaleidoscope. Next, you reach the **Bible Cave** in an elevator that descends almost 200 feet underground to a gigantic cave where human-like robots reenact Bible stories about King Solomon and other tales. In the **Journey to the Past** you see 3-D films of pharaohs in ancient Egypt, and then there's the thrilling 10-minute waterfall ride that ends in a pool (you're in a boat). **David's Spiral** includes two slides, one of them 150 feet long, that end in the Cave of Illusions. There is a res-taurant (with kid stuff like pizza and burgers), a café, a bar, and a gift shop, too. You'll need three to four hours to do this park justice. It is located at the end of the promenade, next to the eastern lagoon. Note that children under 1 meter tall (about 3 feet) are not admitted, and the park is handicapped-accessible. ✉ *East Lagoon* ☎ *08/630–4444* ⊕ *www.kingscity.co.il* 🖙 *NIS 118* ⊙ *Sun.–Thurs. 9–10, Fri. 9–three hours before Shabbat.*

★ Less than 1 km (½ mi) south of Eilat, the **Coral Beach Reserve** is one of the finest such protected areas in the world. Close to the shoreline, its coral reef is 1¼ km (¾ mi) long and is zealously guarded by the Nature and National Parks Protection Authority. The most northern reef in the world, it contains over 100 types of coral and 650 species of fish. In the Lagoon, divers and snorklers take two bridges, or a trail marked by buoys, to get to the reef wall. Stunning multicolored fish and soft and hard corals are your rich reward. There are hot showers, snorkel rental, and a snack bar on the premises. Kids should be over 5 to snorkel—younger ones can fool around on the beach. ✉ *Rte. 90 (Eilat–Taba Rd.)* ☎ *08/637–6829* ⊕ *www.parks.org.il* 🖙 *NIS 23* ⊙ *Daily 9–5.*

The Red Sea, just off the coast of Eilat, offers spectacular snorkeling and scuba diving.

WHERE TO EAT

Eilat has so many restaurants that you can easily dine on a different cuisine each night over a long holiday. Savor the finest local seafood and fresh fish; charcoal-grilled meats of every kind; or Chinese, Indian, Thai, and Italian cuisine and other ethnic meals, reflecting Israel's many waves of immigration. Many restaurants have outdoor seating, often near the water or amid pots of pink bougainvillea. Outdoor cafés serve café *hafuch* (strong coffee with a frothy, hot-milk topping) and light food, such as cheese toast (grilled-cheese sandwiches) and salads, as well as rich cakes, ice cream, iced drinks, and various other coffee concoctions.

$$$ ✕**Eddie's Hideaway.** As the name suggests, Eddie's is slightly hard to find.
ECLECTIC The affable Eddie ("I consider each guest a visitor in my own home—a friend," he says) prepares straightforward but delicious food, which makes it easy to understand why his restaurant—one of the oldest in Eilat—is worth seeking out and earns such stellar reviews, especially for delicious steaks. Devotees also appreciate the shrimp and fish dishes. Try Filet Dijon (filet mignon graced with mustard and brown sugar) or Shanghai fish with hot soybean paste. If you can pack it in, try the pecan pie. Inquire if Eddie has prepared a "daily"—a dish he particularly likes to cook. Eddie does lunch only on Saturday. ⊠ *68 Almogim St. (enter from Elot St.)* ☎ *08/637–1137* ⚏ *Reservations essential* ▭ *AE, DC, MC, V* ☻ *Closed Sun. No lunch.* ✛ *2A*

$ ✕**Ginger Asian Kitchen and Bar.** A duo of Thai chefs presents an Asian
ASIAN fusion and sushi cuisine of delicate spiciness at this spiffy New York
★ look-alike. It's small, and the menu's huge. Recessed lighting contributes to the chic vibe, as do the off-white walls and black leather chairs. Start

with plump *kioza* dumplings stuffed with chicken, goose, and vegetables or shrimp tempura on avocado with miso sauce, then try the Jakarta (chicken or beef with eggplant and zucchini with an Indonesian sweet sauce) or Exotica (chicken or seafood dressed with coconut milk and chili paste and scattered with basil leaves). Finish off with an almond and butter pastry, topped with caramelized bananas and ginger parfait. A lighter bar menu is served from midnight until 3 AM Thursday–Sunday night. ⊠ *Yotam St. across from the Imax* ☎ *08/637–2517* ⊕ *www. gingereilat.com* ⌂ *Reservations essential* ▬ *AE, DC, MC, V.* ✚ *3A*

$$$　✕ **Josephine.** This is the best bistro in Eilat, with a posh, minimalist, but
FRENCH　calming all-white interior. After whetting your appetite with asparagus in a cream and truffle sauce, try the rack of lamb with crushed pistachio. ⊠ *3 Ayalot St.* ☎ *08/632–3787* ⌂ *Reservations essential* ▬ *AE, DC, MC, V.* ✚ *B1*

$$$　✕ **La Cucina.** Right here on the North Beach Promenade you'll find a little
ITALIAN　slice of Tuscany at this restaurant with arched wooden windows, paintings of Italian cities, a fireplace, and bougainvillea spilling over the outdoor terrace. If you love thin-crust pizza, try Cucina's, which is crunchy as a cracker and especially delicious when topped with seafood. Other good bets are fried spinach ravioli with ricotta cheese, and peppered fillet of beef medallions in a cream and Gorgonzola sauce. Passion-fruit and forest-berry sherbet flavored with lemongrass makes a cool ending. ⊠ *North Beach Promenade near the Royal Beach* ☎ *08/636–8932* ⌂ *Reservations essential* ▬ *AE, DC, MC, V.* ✚ *4D*

$$　✕ **Lalo.** This lunch restaurant, one of the most established in Eilat, is a
MOROCCAN　top-drawer example of Moroccan-Israeli ethnic cooking, by a mother-and-son team. Upon your arrival, five different salads (including cauliflower, tehina, eggplant, and hot peppers) are set quickly upon the table. The menu may confront you with foods you've never eaten before, but it rewards any adventuresome choices you make. Consider such delicacies as beef cooked with hummus (a house specialty); tongue; calves' brains served straight-up with Moroccan spices; succulent couscous with vegetables, chickpeas, and tender chicken; and spicy-hot fish. No fancy pitas are served here—just plain bread. Dessert is specially prepared fruit, such as oranges cooked until thick and soft, accompanied by tea with mint. You might also try the homemade jams. ⊠ *259 Horev St., Shkunat Alef* ☎ *08/633–0578* ▬ *AE, DC, MC, V* ⊙ *Closed Fri. and Sat. No dinner.* ✚ *4B*

$$$　✕ **Last Refuge.** Eilatis hold this fine restaurant in high regard and take
SEAFOOD　their guests from "up north" here as a real treat. The dining room,
Fodor's Choice　with dark wood paneling and nautical motifs, spills onto a spacious
★　balcony, where diners eat beside the water, looking at Jordan across the way. Presented with a flourish are fish or crab soups, freshly-caught charcoal-grilled Red Sea fish, lobster (order in advance), jumbo shrimp, and creamed seafood served in a seashell. A Refuge specialty is stir-fried, small, spicy sea crabs, prepared in olive oil and garlic. Start with the coquille of seafood. Friday night is extra busy, so it's smart to reserve several days ahead (and to ask for balcony seating). ⊠ *Coral (Almog) Beach, Rte. 90 near overhead bridge* ☎ *08/637–3627* ⌂ *Reservations essential* ▬ *AE, DC, MC, V.* ✚ *5A*

KEY
- ☐ Hotels
- ■ Restaurants

Where to Eat and Stay in Eilat

A   B   C   D

INDUSTRIAL AREA

Hativat Golani

90

Josephine

Ha Tmarim

Shderot Ayalot

Kampen

Arava Road

Agamim

Kamen

Astral Village

Hativat Ha Negev

Central Bus Station

Eddie's Hideaway

Eilat Airport

Crowne Plaza

Lagoon

New Marina

Central Park

Tarshish

King Solomon's Palace

Durban

Derech Yotam

Antib

Smolin

Ginger Asian Kitchen & Bar

Olla

Information

Hilton Queen of Sheba

Horev

Shderot Eilot

Spring Onion

Sheraton Moriah Eilat

Ha Yam

Royal Beach

Lalo

La Cucina

Promenade

90

Dan Eilat

Argaman

Mul Yam

Tourist Police

Eilat Youth Hostel & Guest House

North Beach

Herod's Palace

Le Meridien

Dekel Beach

Eilat-Taba Road

TO TABA BORDER CROSSING

Eilat Port

Gulf of Eilat

Texas Ranch

Coral Beach

Last Refuge

☐ The Orchid
☐ Princess
☐ Yam Suf

0   300 yrds

0   300 meters

$$$ ✕**Olla.** Far and away the best tapas bar in Eilat, this restaurant has
TAPAS   leather-backed booths and tastefully subdued lighting. The bar level,
extraordinarily lively on weekends, offers some of the best bartending
in the city. As for the tapas, try the goose-liver slices on caramelized
apple with figs, the cadaif-coated shrimp, and the mussels in cream with
Roquefort cheese. ⊠ *Tarshish 17, Bell Hotel* ☎08/632–5566 ⊕*www.
olla-tapas.co.il* ⍋*Reservations essential* ⊟*AE, DC, MC, V.* ⊹3C

$$ ✕**Spring Onion.** Vegetarians, front and center! Diners come to this two-
VEGETARIAN   story restaurant for the city's largest offering of garden-fresh salads with
interesting toppings, as well as delicately cooked vegetable quiches,
fresh fish, sushi, blintzes, and wonderfully authentic pizzas. Noodles
tossed with vegetables in ginger and soy sauce make an appetizing dish.
There's also a selection of "cheese toast" (grilled-cheese sandwiches)—
try the one with Bulgarian cheese, olive oil, and black olives. Portions
are large (it's acceptable to split a dish); if you have room, try a wedge
of cream cake. Beer and wine are available. Both floors are crowded and
sometimes claustrophobic, but there's plenty of outdoor seating. Service
can be brusque. ⊠*Bridge House, near the bridge on the promenade*
☎08/637–7434 ⊟*MC, V.* ⊹3C

WHERE TO STAY

$$ ⌂**Agamim.** With a name that means "lakes," this water-garden hotel,
★   also part of the Isrotel chain, was designed with pure relaxation in
mind. Built in 2002, the compound of four-floor buildings is set amid
palm trees, emerald grass, and tropical plants, around a lagoon-shaped
pool with hammocks and swing chairs. Pale-green wicker chairs invite
leisure time on the nearby terrace. Many rooms (all the same size) sit
right over the curving waterways that flow from the pool, and all have
balconies. Recessed lighting in the rooms casts a soft light on striped
sofas, bedspreads, and curtains of tobacco, blue, dark green, and dark
rose, along with dark turquoise rugs. **Pros:** one of Eilat's more laid-back
hotels; great pool area. **Cons:** it's a 10- to 15-minute walk to the beach;
not convenient for strollers or wheelchairs. ⊠*Kampan St., North Beach*
☎08/630–0300 ⊟08/630–0302 ⊕*www.isrotel.co.il* ⌂*In-room: safe,
refrigerator. In-hotel: 2 restaurants, bar, pools, gym, spa, children's
programs (ages 3–12), laundry service, Internet terminal, no-smoking
rooms* ⊟*AE, DC, MC, V* ⍉*CP.* ⊹2D

$ ⌂**Astral Village.** Not exactly otherwordly, but certainly fun for a family,
this relatively affordable compound opened in 2005 consists of small,
trim cottages in beige stucco, with wooden shutters and red-tile roofs.
White-frame windows with red-and-white flowers planted out front
look out onto the huge pool, where holiday activity is centered. Music
plays, palm trees sway. The cheerful turquoise-trimmed dining room
is off the lobby. **Pros:** clean; good value; staff is eager to please. **Cons:**
a 10-minute walk to the beach; mediocre food. ⊠*Kempen St. near
King Solomon's Palace hotel* ☎08/636–6888 ⊟08/638–8889 ⊕*www.
eilatinhotels.co.il* ⍉170 *rooms, 12 suites* ⌂*In-room: safe, refrigera-
tor. In-hotel: restaurant, bar, pool, gym, spa, children's programs (ages
3–10)* ⊟*AE, DC, MC, V* ⍉*CP.* ⊹2D

$ ⌂**Crowne Plaza.** Once you've admired this hotel's blue, yellow, and
green painted-glass entrance, and the glass-domed ceiling in the

CLOSE UP

Kids in the Negev

The Negev is a huge sandbox for kids. There's lots to do and enjoy: alpaca rides, camel trips, Jeep excursions, snorkeling, floating in the Dead Sea, smearing on mud. And children like the kind of food prevalent in the Negev, such as french fries and schnitzel (fried breaded chicken cutlets). Even fancy restaurants have these on their menus, to please the young ones. The hotels in Eilat go out of their way to cater to kids, trying to outdo one another with their children's sections, often called Kiddyland. These are separate facilities on the hotel grounds, filled with every imaginable distraction, from toys and crafts to Playstations, and there are trained attendants on hand. Many hotels employ staff trained to keep kids entertained. And even in upscale restaurants at night it's not unusual to see baby strollers parked beside the candlelit tables.

reception area, you'll encounter the lobby's fat artificial trees with huge snakes (also fake), bananas, and lotus flowers. You can count on competent service at this nine-floor hotel, which faces the Lagoon. You can splash around under a waterfall in the pool. The fifth floor and public areas are non-smoking. **Pros:** great kids' programs, including a clown at breakfast, crafts, poolside games, and baby-sitting, and for teenagers, swimming lessons. **Cons:** noisy at night; gym costs extra; not on the beachfront. ⊠ *Lagoon, North Beach* ☎ *08/636–7777* 🖷 *08/633–0821* ⊕ *www.crowneplaza.com* 🛏 *267 rooms; 24 suites* ♿ *In-room: Wi-Fi. In-hotel: restaurant, room service, bar, pool, gym, spa, children's programs (ages 3–10), laundry service, Internet terminal, no-smoking rooms* ▭ *AE, DC, MC, V* ¶❍¶ *CP.* ⊕ *3C*

\$\$\$\$
Fodor's Choice
★
🖭 **Dan Eilat.** The glitzy 14-floor, U-shape Dan is on the North Beach Promenade near the Jordanian border. Its design, by internationally acclaimed Israeli architect Adam Tihani, effectively combines snazzy high style with comfort. The two connecting two-story lobbies feature a winding glass stairway (as scary as it sounds), craggy rock walls with a water cascade, floating ceiling sculptures, a huge aviary, and a rock pool with iguanas. The spacious blue–and–terra-cotta rooms have blond-wood furnishings, and the dresser mirror can be adjusted to reflect the sea. A 20-meter pool for serious swimmers anchors the large, lush outdoor area. The 13th and 14th floors have been recently renovated. **Pros:** great location on the beach; excellent breakfasts and superb dinners prepared by chef Ofir Kedem. **Cons:** sometimes noisy; crowded dining room. ⊠ *Promenade, North Beach* ☎ *08/636–2222* 🖷 *08/636–2333* ⊕ *www.danhotels.co.il* 🛏 *373 rooms, 48 suites* ♿ *In-room: safe. In-hotel: 2 restaurants, bar, pools, gym, spa, children's programs (ages 3–10), laundry service, Internet terminal, no-smoking rooms* ▭ *AE, DC, MC, V* ¶❍¶ *CP.* ⊕ *4D*

¢
🖭 **Eilat Youth Hostel & Guest House.** The word *hostel* takes on new meaning here: each room is air-conditioned and has its own bathroom. The pleasant rooms are simply furnished and sleep two to six (in bunks); some rooms have coffee corners and/or refrigerators. Bed linens and

towels are provided. Two rooms are wheelchair-equipped. A mere 10-minute walk from the central bus station, this hostel is popular with the backpack crowd, so make reservations well ahead of time. The kosher dining room serves lunch and dinner if ordered ahead. **Pros:** right across the highway from the beach; a competent and helpful staff; breakfast included. **Cons:** loud hallways; mediocre food. ⊠*7 Arava Rd.* ☏*08/637–0088* ✆*08/637–5835* ⊕*www.iyha.org.il/eng* ⤢*106 rooms* ♿*In-room: no phone, refrigerator (some). In-hotel: bar, laundry service, Internet terminal* ⊟*AE, DC, MC, V* ⦵*BP.* ✛*4B*

$$$$
★ 🏨 **Herod's Palace.** Herod's—designed with the legendary king in mind— is all about over-the-top opulence and palatial pizzaz. Until late 2007 part of the Sheraton chain, it's really three hotels in one. The main build- ing, the Palace, is graced by the dramatic 12-story lobby, decorated with Italian wrought-iron chandeliers, carved marble planters, and mosaics. The Vitalis is a spa hotel with large public areas (no kids allowed). The Forum is designed to host conventions, and includes the largest ball- room in Eilat, with a seating capacity of 1,200. Luxury is everywhere, from the minaret towers that greet you outside to Romanesque domes, arches, bridges, and niches inside, all designed by well-known architect Yoav Igra (also one of the hotel's investors) to convey Israel's archaeo- logical flavor. Rooms are spacious, with warm, dark-wood furniture and lush curtains. Unlike the Dan, where you can't see the sea from the pool, the Herod's pool sits at the end of an avenue of palm trees— it looks as though it flows straight into the sea. **Pros:** widest, quietest beach in Eilat; no cell phones in public areas; measured by square meter per guest, the largest hotel in Eilat. **Cons:** furniture is worn in some rooms. ⊠*North Beach, Box 4201* ☏*08/638–0000* ⊕*www.herods. co.il* ⤢*Palace: 296 rooms, 33 suites. Vitalis: 52 rooms, 4 suites. Forum: 104 rooms, 20 suites* ♿*In-room: safe, DVD (some), Wi-Fi (some). In- hotel: 4 restaurants, room service, bar, pools, spa, beachfront, bicycles, children's programs (ages 2–12), laundry service, Internet terminal, no- smoking rooms* ⊟*AE, DC, MC, V* ⦵*CP.* ✛*4D*

$$$$ 🏨 **Hilton Queen of Sheba.** The imaginary palace King Solomon built for the queen is what Hilton International set out to construct with this imposing example of grandeur: a palatial entrance capped with a pillared dome rises between two turrets, with a wing of more than 200 rooms on either side. Khaki-color curtains cover the windows of the 40-foot-high lobby, and Italian mosaics of biblical animals cover the floor. The queen must have loved cats—images of them are every- where. The bedrooms have gold-framed mirrors, taupe-and-orange carpeting, Egyptian-motif black-and-taupe bedspreads and curtains, and marble bathrooms with hand-painted murals. Rooms on even- numbered floors have balconies (some with Jacuzzis) facing the sea or the marina. Opened in late 1999, the 14-floor hotel was developed by Itzhak Tshuva (who recently snapped up Manhattan's Plaza Hotel) and designed by the Romanian-born architect Shlomo Gertner. Trans- parent gold-cage elevators offer views of the atrium as they rise. **Pros:** prime location, close to both seafront and shops; stunning views of the Eilat Bay and mountains. **Cons:** late-night music from the board- walk can be disturbing to rooms on lower floors; lines for the dining room at dinner are sometimes annoyingly long. ⊠*North Beach, Box 2228* ☎*08/630–6666* 🖷*08/630–6677* ⊕*www.hiltonworldresorts.com* ↪*479 rooms, 20 suites* ♨*In-room: safe. In-hotel: 4 restaurants, bar, pools, gym, spa, children's programs (ages 3–10), laundry service, Internet terminal, no-smoking rooms* ⊟*AE, DC, MC, V* ❘○❘*CP.* ⊹*4C*

$$$ 🏨**King Solomon's Palace.** Solomon's entire court could easily have been
★ accommodated at this venerable member of Isrotel's chain. It's a huge and comfortably utilitarian family hotel with an expansive lobby furnished in beige wicker with gray upholstery. The staff attends to guests' every need, and everything runs like clockwork. The commodious dining room is open market–style and serves Chinese and other foods. Breakfast selections are vast, and eating on the leafy, shaded terrace is a pleasure. Palm-fringed pools (one with a 50-meter slide), overlook the Lagoon, and the children's "house" offers all-day entertainment. Garden-terrace suites have their own hot tubs. **Pros:** one of Eilat's most child-friendly hotels, with a jamboree, arts-and-crafts workshops, computer rooms, games, and activities; rooftop lounge with free Internet access. **Cons:** not on the beachfront; noisy; food is uninspired. ⊠*Promenade, North Beach* ☎*08/636–3444* 🖷*08/633–4189* ⊕*www.isrotel.co.il* ↪*398 rooms, 22 suites* ♨*In-room: safe, refrigerator. In-hotel: restaurant, room service, bar, pools, gym, spa, children's programs (ages 2–10), laundry service, no-smoking rooms* ⊟*AE, DC, MC, V* ❘○❘*CP.* ⊹*3C*

$$ 🏨**Le Meridien.** Enter this dandy hotel, and the first thing you'll see
★ through its glass walls is a breathtaking view of the shimmering sea and Jordanian mountains beyond. This all-suite lodging (rooms house four to six guests) has a refined air. The spacious lobby lounge has a bar and a dance floor (there's a quiet lobby as well), and waiters sing in the pub at night. Parents can keep an eye on their children in the Kids' Club via a closed-circuit system transmitted to their in-room TV. The spa offers the last word in beauty and health treatments, and there's a beach exclusively for hotel guests. **Pros:** lovely views; a short walk from the Mall Hayam shopping area. **Cons:** late-night music from the hotel's club may disturb some guests; small, rocky beachfront; no concierge desk. ⊠*Arava Rd., Box 2120* ☎*08/638–3333* 🖷*08/638–3300* ⊕*www.fattal.co.il* ↪*246 suites* ♨*In-room: safe, refrigerator. In-hotel: 2 restaurants, room service, bar, pool, gym, spa, beachfront, children's programs (ages 3–10), laundry service, no-smoking rooms* ⊟*AE, DC, MC, V* ❘○❘*CP.* ⊹*4B*

$$ 🏨**The Orchid.** Teak furnishings from the Far East, and high wood beams characterize this Oriental-theme hotel on the quiet South Beach, which also has opulent luxury villas with extraordinary views of Eilat Bay, many of them with private Jacuzzis. The pool offers views of the mountains and a small waterfall. **Pros:** just across from the aquarium; free shuttle to downtown Eilat; good kosher Thai restaurant. **Cons:** you have to wait for a gold cart to take you up the steep hill to the rooms; if you visit during the winter, bear in mind that the rooms are unheated. ⊠*South Beach, Box 994, Eilat* ☎*08/636–0360* 🖷*08/637–5323* ⊕*www.orchidhotel.co.il* ↪*168 rooms, 16 villas* ♨*In-room: safe, refrigerator. In-hotel: 2 restaurants, room service, bar, 2 pools, spa, laundry service, Internet terminal.* ⊟*AE, DC, MC, V.* ⊹*6A*

8

$$$$
★

☆ **Princess.** The southernmost hotel in Israel (it's five minutes from the Egyptian border), the Princess has a light-filled reception area facing a two-story sheer rock cliff through a soaring glass wall; the public spaces are dazzlingly white with gold trim. The pool area is a country club in itself, where squiggle-shape pools connected by bridges afford views of charcoal-gray mountains across the bay. Down at the serene beach, reached by a tunnel under the road, two jetties lead to the water, and sun-tanning beds beckon. The spa in this self-contained resort is ultramodern. **Pros:** great new Moscow–New York nightclub; a free shuttle into town for sightseeing. **Cons:** far from the action in Eilat; mobbed with kids during summer vacation. ✉ *Rte. 90 (Eilat–Taba Rd.), Box 2323* ☎ *08/636–5555* 📠 *08/637–6333* ⊕ *www.eilatprincess. com* ⤳ *355 rooms, 65 suites* ♿ *In-room: safe. In-hotel: 2 restaurants, room service, bar, tennis courts, pools, gym, spa, beachfront, children's programs (ages 3–10), laundry service, Internet terminal, parking (free), no-smoking rooms* ▭ *AE, DC, MC, V* ⦿ *CP.* ✛6A

$$$$
Fodor's Choice
★

☆ **Royal Beach.** At the jewel in the Isrotel chain's crown, guests discover a magical blend of comfort, glamour, and sophistication. Opened in 1994, across the Promenade from the beach, the Royal Beach has a serene lobby that beckons with cushy, smoky-green leather couches. Three-story glass windows bring graceful bamboo and palm trees inside. A large terrace—crammed with multicolored flowers, overhead fans, and kilim rugs—faces the Bay of Eilat, providing especially stunning views at sundown. Rooms are decorated in warm blue; all have comfortable sofas and chairs, and a balcony. Suites come with whirlpool tubs. For the best views, ask for a higher floor. **Pros:** nice pool graced by palm trees and waterfalls; excellent seaside location. **Cons:** laissez-faire staff; apart from the suites, the rooms are small. ✉ *North Beach* ☎ *08/636–8888* 📠 *08/636–8811* ⊕ *www.isrotel.co.il* ⤳ *363 rooms, 19 suites* ♿ *In-room: safe, Wi-Fi. In-hotel: 4 restaurants, room service, bar, pools, spa, beachfront, children's programs (ages 3–10), laundry service, no-smoking rooms* ▭ *AE, DC, MC, V* ⦿ *CP.* ✛4D

$$

☆ **Sheraton Moriah Eilat.** The hotel faces the beach from the promenade near the marina, and everything is within walking distance. A decorator's touch is needed in the lobby and reception area. That being said, the pleasant dining room was renovated in 2004, and the western wing got a makeover a year later. The rooms, along outside corridors, have carpets in shades of blue and white, dark-blue bedspreads, and gold-and-blue curtains. Most rooms face the sea or pool, and 14 have in-room hot tubs. American tour groups and French visitors are partial to this Sheraton. The fourth-floor business lounge has fax and Internet facilities. **Pros:** the beachfront location, in the middle of the promenade, couldn't be better; extensive kids' activities. **Cons:** within earshot of the beachfront discos; Internet is expensive. ✉ *Promenade, Box 135, Eilat* ☎ *08/636–1111* 📠 *08/633–4158* ⊕ *www.sheraton.com* ⤳ *299 rooms, 7 suites* ♿ *In-room: safe, refrigerator, Wi-Fi. In-hotel: 2 restaurants, room service, bar, pools, spa, beachfront, children's programs (ages 4–10), laundry service, Internet terminal, no-smoking rooms* ▭ *AE, DC, MC, V* ⦿ *CP.* ✛4C

$$ ⚏**Yam Suf.** Near the Coral Beach, this swank Isrotel hotel (formerly known as the Ambassador) is made up of three wings: an L-shape, three-floor wing still called the Ambassador, where the rooms (all with balconies) face the sea; the Garden Wing, comprising two three-floor buildings with rooms and suites that have private gardens; and the Diver's Wing, which faces the Manta Dive Center and has nine rooms that can each accommodate four guests. The hotel's entrance, facing the Eilat Mountains, is up a palm-lined drive; inside, the decor is ultra-modern and lively. The color scheme of the guest rooms is particularly attractive, with marine blue, khaki, and sunny yellow tones. Just across the road is the beach and a seafood restaurant. **Pros:** great beach for snorkeling; very close to the aquarium and the Last Refuge fish restaurant. **Cons:** bland food; not within walking distance to central Eilat. ⊠*Rte. 90 (Eilat–Taba Rd.)* ☎*08/638–2222* 📠*08/638–2200* ⊕*www.isrotel.co.il* ⇆*237 rooms, 14 suites* ⚸*In-room: safe, refrigerator. In-hotel: restaurant, bar, pool, gym, spa, diving, children's programs (ages 3–10), laundry service, Internet terminal, no-smoking rooms* ▭*AE, DC, MC, V* ⏍*CP.* ⚓*6A*

NIGHTLIFE AND THE ARTS

For an overview of local events, pick up a copy of the detailed leaflet "Events and Places of Interest," available at the tourist information office. For the coming week's arts and entertainment information, check out Friday's *Jerusalem Post* magazine, or the *Herald Tribune*'s *Haaretz Guide,* both of which carry listings for Eilat.

BARS AND CLUBS

Most hotels in Eilat have a piano bar (some with space for cutting loose), and many have dance clubs; all are open to the public. Pubs abound; top bands perform at several, and at many you can even get a decent meal. Other dancing options are beach parties, where bronzed bodies groove to recorded music all night; keep an eye out in town for English-language posters listing times and places. Admission is free. On Friday night, join Eilatis who gather at the Aqua Sport beach at sunset.

At the Princess Hotel, **Moscow-New York** (⊠*Eilat–Taba Rd.* ☎*08/636–5555*) tops the disco bill, with mirrored walls, fluted columns, and a checkered dance floor. **Platinum** (⊠*Promenade, North Beach* ☎*08/636–3444*), at King Solomon's Palace hotel, has laser light shows and well-known DJs. Good bands are the claim to fame at the very popular **Three Monkeys Pub** (⊠*Royal Beach Promenade* ☎*08/636–8888*) club.

★ ISRAELI FOLK DANCING

At the **Etzion Gaver School** (⊠*entrance on Argaman St.* ☎*052/352–9588* 🎫*NIS 22*) you can learn how to folk dance on Monday, Wednesday, and Saturday night starting at 9 (call ahead to verify times).

LOCAL HOSPITALITY

Have a cup of tea with **Mrs. Faye Morris** (☎*08/637–2344*), the amiable former U.S. consul in Eilat, and meet her crocodile.

If you call ahead, PM **Nurit Goren** (☎*052/392–0884*) will take groups (minimum of 10) around Kibbutz Elot, which is 3 km (2 mi) north of

After a day at the beach, secure a seat with a waterside view at one of Eilat's many restaurants.

Eilat, to meet longtime members, listen to some gossip, and enjoy coffee and homemade jam and cake.

MUSIC FESTIVALS

★ Two of the country's most important music events have long taken place in Eilat. Both festivals feature internationally acclaimed musicians. Check with the tourist office for details. **Music by the Red Sea,** a series of chamber music concerts, takes place in late December. The **Red Sea Jazz Festival** (⊕ *redseajazzeilat.com*) is held in Eilat's cargo port in late August.

THEATER

☽ **WOW** (⊠ *Royal Gardens Hotel* ☎ *08/638–6701* ⊕ *www.isrotel.co.il*
★ ⚏ *NIS 105*) is a 1½-hour show (performances are daily 11 AM–9 PM) with vaudeville sketches, magicians, jugglers, and acrobats flying over the audience—all in a 3-D video-art setting. The best of its kind in Israel.

WINE TASTINGS

For an early evening sampling of "Private Collection" Carmel wines produced in the Shomron region, drop by Eilat's oldest wine shop, **Ha-Martef** (⊠ *Sheba shopping center [Canion Shva]* ☎ *08/637–2787*). Owner Itzik Ben Adiva will happily bring you up to date on Israel's burgeoning viniculture scene in his modest, jam-packed shop. It's in the Industrial Area close to Eddie's Hideaway and next to Lisa Fish— look for wall-size murals of women treading grapes. Ha-Martef is open Sunday through Thursday, 8 to 2 and 5 to 8.

SPORTS AND THE OUTDOORS

Many of the activities outlined below can be arranged through your hotel or a travel agency. Several tour operators maintain desks in hotel lobbies and will take reservations there.

BEACHES

★ Eilat's beautiful **beachfront**—the North Beach and the South Beach—is operated by beach managers who ensure the cleanliness of their section and provide open-air showers and (for a fee) deck chairs. Look for beaches with the large white sign that says A PUBLIC, AUTHORIZED SWIMMING ZONE, along with the wooden lifeguard huts on stilts; lifeguards are usually on duty until 4 or 5 in the afternoon. The beaches are free, and many turn into clubs after nightfall, with thatched-roof restaurants and pubs, contemporary music, and dancing. Beach No. 2, at the Sheraton Moriah, and Beach No. 3, on the northern promenade near the Dan Hotel, are particularly pleasant.

Families favor North Beach, which runs northeast from the intersection of Durban and Arava streets up to the marina and the bridge. Here you can go paragliding or rent paddle boats or a "banana" (a plastic boat towed by a motorboat). Farther along, after the bridge and opposite the Queen of Sheba, Royal Beach, Dan, and Herod's hotels, lies a beautifully landscaped series of beaches. Young people tend to hang out at the southernmost beaches, near the dive centers (south of the port, along the Eilat–Taba Road). The southern beaches share the coast with the Underwater Observatory and the Coral Reserve.

The Eilat municipality has in recent years made a number of beaches wheelchair-accessible. The best is opposite the Neptune Hotel, where a wheelchair path leads from the promenade to the water's edge.

BIRD-WATCHING

★ **International Birding and Research Center** (✉*Entrance to Eilat, at Dor gas station* ☎*08/633–5339 or 052/337–7714* ⊕*www.birdsofeilat.com*). Over a billion birds migrate annually through these skies to and from Africa, and bird-watching enthusiasts come for the spectacle. The birding center holds Thursday lectures at 6 PM at Le Meridien Hotel and also organizes Jeep bird-watching tours.

BOATING AND WATER SPORTS

There are boat-rental and water-sports facilities at both Eilat's marina (near the Bridge) and Coral Beach, south of the port on the Eilat–Taba Road (Route 90).

The **Red Sea Sports Club** (✉*Bridge House* ☎*08/633–3666* ✉*Coral Beach* ☎*08/637–0688* ⊕*www.redseasports.co.il*) rents paddleboats, canoes, and mini-speedboats. It also offers water-skiing lessons, parasailing, and cruises to Taba (4 hours, NIS 155). You can also charter a 150-horsepower speedboat piloted by a water-ski instructor for about NIS 300 per half-hour.

★ You've got to get out on the water if you're in Eilat; choose from an array of water-ski, Jet-ski, banana-ride, or parasailing adventures. **Aqua Sport International Red Sea Diving Center** (✉*Coral Beach* ☎*08/633–4404* ⊕*www.aqua-sport.com*) rents windsurfing equipment and provides lessons (NIS 75 per hour), and also rents Jet Skis (NIS 30 per 10 minutes), skippered speedboats (NIS 60 per half-hour), laser dinghies (NIS 40 per hour), and catamarans (NIS 50 per hour).

DESERT TOURS

Camel Ranch (☎*08/637–0022* ⊕*www.camel-ranch.co.il*) has tours that venture in the desert to explore mountain and canyons that leave daily at 4:30. The ranch is closed on Sunday.

HORSEBACK RIDING

Texas Ranch (⊠*Coral Beach, Rte. 90* ☎*08/637–6663 or 08/637–9685*) takes riders on trails through Wadi Shlomo (Solomon's Valley) and into the desert. The sunset rides are particularly popular. The cost is NIS 165; call ahead to reserve a horse. Children over 12 who know how to ride are welcome on the trails, and younger children may ride in the ring (NIS 80 for 30 minutes).

RAPPELLING

Jeep Sea (⊠*Bridge House, near the marina* ☎*08/633–0133* ⊕*www. weekend.co.il/eilat/jeepsi*), which specializes in desert tourism, runs rappelling (known in Israel as snappelling) trips for both novices and experienced rappellers. Call ahead to reserve.

SCUBA DIVING AND SNORKELING

★ In Eilat you'll find everything from beginner's courses to expert PADI (Professional Association of Diving Instructors) 5-star dive centers; **snorkeling and scuba diving** are extremely popular activities here. Eilat Bay is located at the northern tip of a coral reef that extends from the equator.

Aqua Sport International Red Sea Diving Center (⊠*Coral Beach* ☎*08/633–4404* ⊕*www.aqua-sport.com*) is a British-owned company that for over 45 years has been operating diving courses and three-day diving cruises to Sinai.

Ⅽ Families (ages 8 and over) have fun "snuba"-diving at **Caves Reef** (☎*08/637–2722* ⊕*www.snuba.co.il*), south of the Underwater Observatory. In this snorkeling-diving hybrid, you breathe through tubes connected to tanks carried in a rubber boat. The price, NIS 200 per person, includes instruction, a practice session, and a guided underwater tour that goes no deeper than 20 feet. Reserve in advance.

Coral Beach Nature Reserve (⊠*Eilat–Taba Rd., Coral Beach* ☎*08/637–6829* ◪*NIS 23* ☉*Daily 9–5*) is a veritable utopia for qualified divers who want to get close to the region's fabulous fish and corals. Facilities include hot showers, lockers, and a small restaurant.

Lucky Divers (⊠*5 Simtat Zukim, near the Mul Yam Shopping Center* ☎*08/632–3466* ⊕*www.luckydivers.com*) is Eilat's only PADI Gold Palm 5-star Diving Center, which for 25 years has been offering all manner of dive courses.

At the Ambassador hotel, **Manta Diving Club** (⊠*Eilat–Taba Rd., Coral Beach* ☎*08/637–6569* ⊕*www.redseasports.co.il*) is an excellent diving center.

TENNIS AND SQUASH

The two squash courts at the **Dan Hotel** (☎*08/636–2222*) are available to guests and nonguests for NIS 45 for 40 minutes.

Courts at the **Sport Hotel Country Club** (✉ *North Beach* ☎ *08/630–3333*) are open to guests of the several Isrotel properties at the hourly rate of NIS 40; you can rent rackets and balls.

SHOPPING

Eilat is a tax-free zone; all items are exempt from VAT (Value-Added Tax) and/or purchase tax. Articles such as bathing suits and jewelry sold in chain stores are less expensive in Eilat branches, as are items that are price-controlled, like gas, beer, cigarettes, and alcohol.

SHOPPING CENTERS AND MALLS

One of Eilat's two shopping malls, **Mul Yam** (✉ *Arava Rd. and Yotam St.*) is at the entrance to town and is noted for made-in-Israel products. Here you can stroll along with the chattering crowd, stop for a drink of freshly squeezed orange or carrot juice, and perhaps pick up a lottery ticket at the stand outside the Israel Jewelery Exchange shop. Then check out such stores as **Intima** for women's soft and sexy lingerie; **Gottex** for famous swimwear; **Honigman** for women's sweaters, shirts, and skirts; and **Fox** for cheeky casual clothing for adults and children. There's also a bookstore, drugstore, and several coffee shops. Outside the mall, on the Promenade going west, are one-after-the-other tacky but fun stalls selling hats, T-shirts, and earrings. Also, a branch of **Rockport** sells Teva sandals and other shoes.

The two sections of **Kanion Adom and Shalom Plaza** (✉ *HaTmarim Blvd.*) are connected by a café-filled passage. You'll find a variety of shops, but this is on a smaller scale than Mul Yam. There is a notable absence of tacky souvenir and gift shops.

HOTEL BOUTIQUES

On the western side of the Marina Bridge, Eilat's luxury hotels stand tall and splendid. On the ground level of each hotel, along the beachside promenade, is one boutique shop after another. You'll find at least 40 stores and lots of restaurants, pubs, and coffeehouses—Cafe Aroma, which is open 24/7, is a good bet for a chocolate croissant, Greek salad, or orange cake. If you'd rather sun and play during the day, you'll still have plenty of time to shop at night—these places are open until 9 PM or later (except Friday night). Here's a sampling of some of the best.

At Herod's Palace hotel, **Cardo** (☎ *08/638–0000*) is an intriguing marketplace carrying unusual paintings, sculptures, Judaica, old-style objets d'art, Moroccan furnishings such as painted and inlaid mirrors, boxes and frames, gifts, and wall hangings. Stop at **Emporium** (☎ *08/633–9495*) on the Promenade near Herod's Palace to browse familiar designer names, such as DKNY, Polo, and Calvin Klein. **H. Stern** (✉ *Queen of Sheba hotel* ☎ *08/633–1525*) has an excellent reputation for high-quality gold and diamond pieces, pearls, and also a small selection of silver sculptures by the well-known artist Frank Meisler. **Laline** (✉ *Promenade near Queen of Sheba hotel* ☎ *08/633–5713*) features Israeli-made soap, body-care products, and candles. Look for Breitling timepieces at **Padani** (✉ *Royal Beach hotel* ☎ *08/636–8872*). Shop at **Red Sea Sportswear** (☎ *08/633–0825*) for the latest in swim and surf wear. You'll find everything from resort wear and cosmetics to T-shirts, jewelry, and toys at **Royal Beach Rotunda** (✉ *Royal Beach Hotel* ☎ *08/636–8811*).

8

HAI BAR NATURE RESERVE

35 km (21½ mi) north of Eilat on Rte. 90, between Kibbutz Yotvata and Kibbutz Samar. Look for the sign for Hai Bar and Predator Center, opposite entrance to Kibbutz Samar. Drive 1½ km (1 mi) to entrance.

The Hai Bar Nature Reserve makes a good day trip from Eilat and can be combined with a visit to the Timna Park. The reserve consists of a 12-square-km (4½-square-mi) natural habitat for biblical-era animals and birds and the Predator Center. The reserve was created not only as a refuge for animals that were almost extinct in the region but also as a breeding ground for animals set free in the Negev. Opened to the public in 1977, the area re-creates the ancient savanna landscape of acacia trees and includes a salt marsh. Roaming around are stripe-legged wild asses, addaxes, gazelles and ibex, and the Arabian oryx (antelope). Ostriches come prancing over, ready to stick their heads into your car windows. Try to be here in the morning, when the animals are most active. You need a car and a CD player if you want a "guided tour"; you rent the CD for a few shekels and off you go. It takes about 45 minutes.

The 20-square-km (7¾-square-mi) **Predators Center** houses local birds and beasts of prey: foxes, wolves, leopards, and striped hyenas. As you watch the hyena, notice that its front legs are stronger than its rear legs, enabling it to carry heavy prey a long distance. The birds of prey hang out in gigantic cages, where you'll see, among other species, the only lappet-face vultures left in Israel, with average wingspans of about 10 feet. In the pitch-black **Nightlife Room,** watch nocturnal animals who are active when we sleep: owls, desert hedgehogs, scorpions, and Egyptian fruit bats. ⊠ *Rte. 90, 35 km (21 mi) north of Eilat* ☎ *08/637–3057 or 08/637–6018* ⊕ *www.redseadesert.com* ⊠ *NIS 39 (Predator Center only, NIS 23)* ⊙ *Sun.–Thurs. 8:30–5, Fri. and Sat. 8:30–3:30.*

NEED A BREAK? If you're looking for fantastic kibbutz-made ice cream, stop by Yotvata Rest Inn (☎ *08/635-7229*), next to a gas station on Rte. 90 between the Hai Bar Reserve and Timna Park (40 km [25 mi]) north of Eilat. The kibbutz of the same name is across the way, and their dairy products are much loved by Israelis: cheeses, chocolate milk, yogurt, puddings, and ice cream (try the pitaya, or dragonfruit, flavor). Hot dishes (chicken or beef) and sandwiches are available as well. There's also a tourist information center at the entrance. Open 24 hours.

TIMNA PARK

Fodor'sChoice ★ *From Hai Bar Nature Reserve, return to Rte. 90 south toward Eilat. Turn right after 15 km (9 mi) at sign for Timna Park and Timna Lake. A 3-km (2-mi) access road (which passes Kibbutz Elifaz) leads to entrance booth.*

This desert park is a lunarlike landscape interspersed with amazing geological shapes and ancient archaeological sites, surrounded by beautifully colored cliffs in a range of shades from sandy beige to rich red and dusky black. The granite Timna Mountains (whose highest peak is 2,550 feet) encompass the park's spectacular collection of rock formations and canyons. Millions of years of erosion have sculpted shapes of amazing beauty, such as the red-hued Solomon's Pillars (created by rare patterns of erosion, *not* by the biblical king) and

the 20-foot-high freestanding Mushroom. The late-afternoon hours provide unusual light for spectators and photographers alike.

People have also left their mark here. South of the Pillars are the remains of a small **temple** built in white sandstone by Egyptians who worked the mines 3,400 years ago, during the Egyptian New Kingdom (the time of Moses); the temple was dedicated to the cow-eared goddess Hathor. In the temple, archaeologists have discovered a snake made of copper (*nehushtan* in Hebrew)—according to Numbers 21:4–9, Moses made a serpent in the wilderness to heal people suffering from snake bites, and the snake remains a symbol of healing to this day. Near the temple, a path and stairway lead up to the observation platform overlooking the valley. Above the platform is a rock-cut inscription whose hieroglyph you can see clearly with the aid of a sighting telescope. It shows Ramses III offering a sacrifice to Hathor.

When you arrive, ask for the explanatory pamphlet, which shows the driving route in red. Because of the park's size (60 square km [23 square mi]), we suggest driving from sight to sight and exploring each on foot; some of the sights are several kilometers apart. A small building just inside the entrance screens a multimedia video (with a revolving stage and 360-degree screen) detailing humanity's 6,000-year-old relationship with the Timna area, starting with the ancient Egyptians who established the world's oldest known copper mine here. Wall panels explain the valley's fascinating geological makeup.

Experienced hikers can pick up a map detailing various serious hikes that take from 7 to 10 hours to complete. They're best done in winter (summer daytime heat exceeds 100 degrees). Watch out for old mine shafts, take adequate water, and *be sure* to let the staff at the gate know you are going, and when you plan to return. You can also rent bikes and paddleboats near the small lake. Multimedia sunset stargazing tours, accompanied by actors and darbooka-playing musicians, run through July and August. ⊠ *Rte. 90* ☎ *08/631–6756* ⊕ *www.timna-park.co.il* ☞ *NIS 38* ⊙ *Sat.–Thurs. 8–4, Fri. 8–1.*

NEED A BREAK? Here's a surprise in the desert landscape, right in Timna Park: a lake (man-made). Nearby is **Solomon's Khan**, a rest house with goodies and refreshing drinks for the worn-out traveler. ⊠ *Timna Park* ☎ *08/631–7850.*

OFF THE BEATEN PATH **Mt. Yoash.** This fine lookout along the border road with Egypt is an easy trip from Eilat. Notice the huge storage tanks as you drive along Route 12; they belong to the Eilat–Ashkelon oil pipeline. After you pass the tanks, you enter the Eilat Mountains Nature Reserve, with Nahal Shlomo, a dry riverbed, on your left. Drive 12 km (7½ mi) into the reserve and turn left at the orange sign for Mt. Yoash; then drive another 1 km (½ mi), bearing right up a rough, steep, and winding stone road. Park and take in knockout views of the alternating light and dark ridges of the Eilat Mountains; the cities of Eilat and Aqaba; the mountains of Edom, behind Aqaba; the start of the Saudi Arabian coastline and the Nahal Geshron gorge, emptying into the Red Sea at Taba; and the plain of Moon Valley and the mountains of Sinai, in Egypt. A beautiful two-hour hiking trail begins in the parking lot. The Jordanian army operated a strategic lookout here until 1949, when it was taken by Israeli forces during the War of Independence. To get to Mt. Yoash, leave Eilat from the junction of Route 90 (Arava Rd.) and Yotam Boulevard, traveling west on Yotam (which becomes Route 12), with a tourist center on the left.

SIDE TRIP TO PETRA

By Benjamin Balint

Poet Dean Burgon called Petra, the ancient city of dazzling facades tucked into the mountains of southern Jordan, the "rose-red city, half as old as time." Petra is about two hours north of Eilat, and four hours south of the capital Amman. Its boulevards, temples, and splendid tombs (800 in all) secreted among the high cliffs, evoke incomparable mystery and grandeur. Once inaccessible to all but an intrepid few, it is now easier to reach and has become an increasingly popular destination since the Israel-Jordan border was opened in 1994.

Petra (called Rekem in the Dead Sea Scrolls) lies in the biblical region of Edom. According to Genesis, the Edomites were descendants of Esau, Jacob's brother and rival. Edom's fertile land was a magnet that desert dwellers couldn't ignore, but the Edomites were careful to keep it exclusive. When Moses led the Israelites to the Promised Land and asked to pass through Edom, he was denied.

By the 7th century BC, a new group had arrived from Arabia: the Nabateans. It is their spectacular tombs and carved monuments that draw travelers to Petra today. With a wealthy empire that at its height stretched from Damascus to the Sinai, the Nabateans controlled the region's trade routes, their caravans bearing frankincense and myrrh, Indian silks, and African ivory. Most of Petra's famous tombs—which fuse Graeco-Roman, Egyptian, and Mesopotamian styles–were carved during the first century AD, before the Nabatean kingdom was subsumed into the Roman Empire. Although the combination of a necropolis and a capital city may seem strange today, this custom was common among ancient peoples, who established cemeteries at the entrances to many of their capitals. The presence of tombs of the rich and powerful near the city's major monuments was perhaps part of a cult of the dead. When travelers came to the city, they would leave offerings at the tombs to ensure the success of their journeys.

Gradually, Christianity replaced the old religion, and churches were built in Petra. By this time, the rise of sea trade precipitated Petra's decline, as ancient traders learned that they could use prevailing winds to hasten ships across the sea. Some Arabian goods began to come to Egypt and its Mediterranean ports via the Red Sea. It didn't help that a series of earthquakes left a ruinous mark on the city.

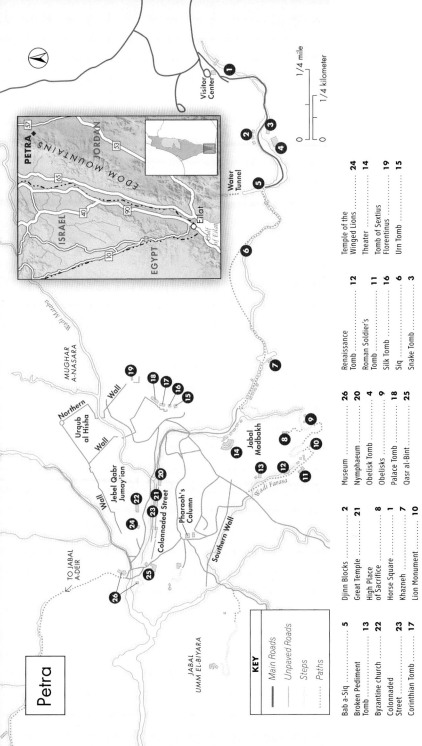

Petra

KEY

▬▬ Main Roads	
── Unpaved Roads	
─── Steps	
········ Paths	

Bab a-Siq	**5**
Broken Pediment Tomb	**13**
Byzantine church	**22**
Colonnaded Street	**23**
Corinthian Tomb	**17**

Djinn Blocks	**2**
Great Temple	**21**
High Place of Sacrifice	**8**
Horse Square	**1**
Khazneh	**7**
Lion Monument	**10**

Museum	**26**
Nymphaeum	**20**
Obelisk Tomb	**4**
Obelisks	**9**
Palace Tomb	**18**
Qasr al-Bint	**25**

Renaissance Tomb	**12**
Roman Soldier's Tomb	**11**
Silk Tomb	**16**
Siq	**6**
Snake Tomb	**3**

Temple of the Winged Lions	**24**
Theater	**14**
Tomb of Sextius Florentinus	**19**
Urn Tomb	**15**

PETRA PLANNER

When to Go

Summer temperatures hit 100 degrees, but it can get cold, rainy and snowy in January and February. In all seasons, sturdy shoes are essential for the rocky, uneven terrain. If traveling during the Muslim holy month of Ramadan, some services may be cut. Check with your hotel or the tourist office ahead of time.

Visitor Information

Petra's visitor center, located right next to the entrance of the site, has brochures and a computerized information service about Jordan as well as a well-stocked souvenir shop. You can also arrange a local guide for a basic two-hour Petra tour here for a flat fee of JD 15.

Contacts Petra visitor center (📠 *03/215–6029*).

Touring Petra

A number of operators run tours to Petra that you can reserve in advance. These are a good option if you want to see the highlights without having to worry about logistics. ⊕ www.petraisrael.com offers good tips on arranging tours to Petra from Israel.

Getting Here and Around

Air Travel: El Al and Royal Jordanian Airlines both fly to Amman, Jordan's capital, from Tel Aviv's Ben-Gurion Airport. This option has limited appeal, as you must be at the airport two hours before flight time for the 15-minute flight, then drive three hours from Amman to Petra.

Twice a week, Arkia airlines offers one-day guided tours in which you fly from Tel Aviv to Eilat at 6:30 AM, drive to Petra in an air-conditioned bus, spend three hours walking through Petra, and take a return flight arriving in Tel Aviv at 9 PM. The rate per person is $265 (⊕ *www.arkia.com*).

Bus Travel: There is no direct bus service from the Arava side of the border to Petra. There are two buses a day from Aqaba to Petra at a cost of JD 1.75 but there is no specific timetable.

Public buses also run between Petra and Amman (Mujema Al Janoub, or the South Bus Station). They depart when full. Three private bus companies offer air-conditioned service between Petra and Amman: **Alpha** (📠 *06/582–7623*).; **Jett** (📠 *06/569–6151*); and **Trust** (📠 *06/581–3449*)

Car Travel: A parking area on the Israeli side of the border makes it possible to drive a rental car here, but only cars registered to their drivers can be taken into Jordan. For those taking longer trips, rental cars are available in Aqaba and Petra. Hidab Hotel can book rental cars from local agencies. There is an Avis agency in the Moevenpick Hotel in Petra and in Aqaba. The Hertz office in Petra is located next to the Palace Hotel on the main street of Wadi Musa.

Taxi Travel: Shared taxis are available on the Jordanian side of the Arava border to take you into Aqaba, where you can rent a car or take the bus to Petra if the scheduling is right. A shared taxi to Aqaba costs about JD 5, which is divided among all passengers; a private taxi from the border to Petra or from Aqaba to Petra is JD 40–JD 45, but be prepared to negotiate.

If your time in Petra is limited, consider taking the direct although costlier route by taxi from the Arava border rather than sharing a taxi to Aqaba and taking the bus.

Crossing the Border

The closest border crossing to Petra is at Eilat; cross the border early in the morning to avoid waiting in line behind large tour groups and aim to be in Petra before noon. When crossing back from Jordan to Israel, bring JD 5 for the Jordanian exit tax.

Americans need a visa to enter Jordan. It can be bought on the spot for about NIS 88 everywhere except at the Allenby Bridge crossing. If you plan to enter Jordan at the Allenby Bridge, you'll need to obtain your visa ahead of time at the Jordanian Embassy in Tel Aviv or in your country of origin. Remember to bring a passport photo.

Most visitors take a taxi to the Jordan border from Eilat (10 minutes, NIS 30), walk across, and catch a taxi to Petra on the other side (about JD 40). The Arava border crossing, just north of Eilat in Israel, is open Sunday–Thursday 6:30 AM–10 PM, Friday and Saturday 8–8. The crossing is closed on the religious holidays Yom Kippur and Id el Fitr. There is a border tax of NIS 88 on the Israeli side. Two other border crossings might be convenient under certain circumstances. The Allenby Bridge crossing (known in Jordan as the Hussein crossing, four hours' drive from Petra) is about 45 minutes from Jerusalem. The Beit She'an border crossing (five hours' drive from Petra) is approximately 40 minutes from Tiberias.

Before traveling to Jordan, make sure to check your government's travel advisory and always exercise caution.

Money Matters

The Jordanian unit of currency is the dinar, abbreviated JD. The exchange rate at press time was approximately JD .7 to the U.S. dollar. You can change money at the Moevenpick, next to the entrance to Petra.

WHAT IT COSTS					
	¢	$	$$	$$$	$$$$
Restaurants	under JD 3	JD 3–JD 4	JD 4–JD 5	JD 5–JD 7	over JD 7
Hotels	under $35	$35–$50	$50–$65	$65–$110	over $110

Restaurant prices are in Jordanian Dinar, for one main course at dinner. Hotel prices are in U.S. dollars, for two people in a standard double room in high season.

Planning Your Time

Petra is open daily from 6 AM to 7 PM; the city is gated and has an entrance fee of JD 21 for a one-day visit, with a discount for multiple entries.

An overnight (two-day) trip to Petra will allow you to see many of the area's highlights. Begin early in the afternoon at the Horse Square, and walk through the narrow and mysterious Siq to the Khazneh (the treasury), Petra's most magnificent facade. Be sure to take a peek through a slit in the rock at the end of the Siq for an awe-inspiring view.

From there, continue along a route that was once the city's main street, lined with monuments from Petra's glory days. End with a walk along the Colonnaded Street to The Basin for a rewarding lunch. Although the route back is the same, the sun striking the rocks at different angles in the late afternoon reveals new beauty. In the evening, take a moment to enjoy the sunset from a hotel balcony or rooftop terrace.

On the second day, you can return to the Khazneh and explore other sites. Afterward, spend a little time souvenir shopping in the town of Wadi Musa before heading back to Eilat.

8

After Petra's takeover by the Muslims in 633, alliances and crossroads changed and the world lost interest in the area. The Crusaders built fortifications among the ruins in the 11th century, but after their 1189 surrender to the Muslim warrior Saladin, the city sank into oblivion. Only the local Bedouins knew it. It was not until 1812 that Swiss explorer Johann Ludwig Burckhardt rediscovered Petra, providing the Western world with its first contemporary description of the marvels of the ancient city. It is now a United Nations World Heritage Site.

TOP ATTRACTIONS

㉓ Colonnaded Street. The Romans built the main street of Petra in the early 1st century BC. In typical Roman style, it became the city's major thoroughfare, suitable for both commerce and grand ceremonial processions. After the Roman annexation of the Nabatean kingdom, the street was restored, as noted in an inscription dated AD 114 and dedicated to Emperor Trajan. The original marble paving stones as well as remains of statues of deities still stand, including Hermes and Tyche. In 363 an earthquake devastated Petra and the entire surrounding region, and the street never returned to its former glory.

㉑ Great Temple. No one can say for sure who was worshipped at this temple, or if it was the seat of the city's government. But the dozens of columns that adorn its courtyards, beautifully restored in recent years by archaeologists from Brown University, attest to its ancient grandeur; it even had its own theater, which some scholars believe may have been a meeting hall for Petra's rulers.

❶ Horse Square. Horses used to be the conveyance of choice for the approximately 1-km (1/2-mi) trip to Petra's main antiquities. You can still hire horses for the first 800 yards before the path narrows to become the Siq.

❼ Khazneh. The Siq opens suddenly onto Petra's most famous monument,
★ known in English as the Treasury. This 130-foot-high structure displays a splendid frontage graced by a number of mythological figures adopted by the Nabateans from Greek and Roman worship. Castor and Pollux (who after their death became the two brightest stars in the constellation Gemini), Amazons, Gorgons, eagles, and other creatures march across the Khazneh's rosy facade. Between the columns of the *tholos* (the rounded section above the tympanum) are the remains of a female deity holding a cornucopia; she is believed to be al-Uzza, the patroness of Petra and the Nabatean version of Aphrodite, goddess of love.

The Arabic name for this monument means "treasury"—its full name is Khaznet Fara'un, the Pharaoh's Treasury. It was assumed by archaeologists to be a tomb, but legends of treasures allegedly secreted within have drawn grave robbers to this place for centuries. The urn carved at the top of the tholos was thought to be the hiding place for the hoard. The Bedouin have been taking potshots at it for generations in the hopes of dislodging its contents, a practice whose results are still visible.

㉗ Qasr al-Bint. This structure's full name, which translates as the "Palace of the Daughter of Pharaoh," stems from a legend that the pharaoh's daughter promised she would marry the man who could channel water to the city where she lived. When she had to choose between two

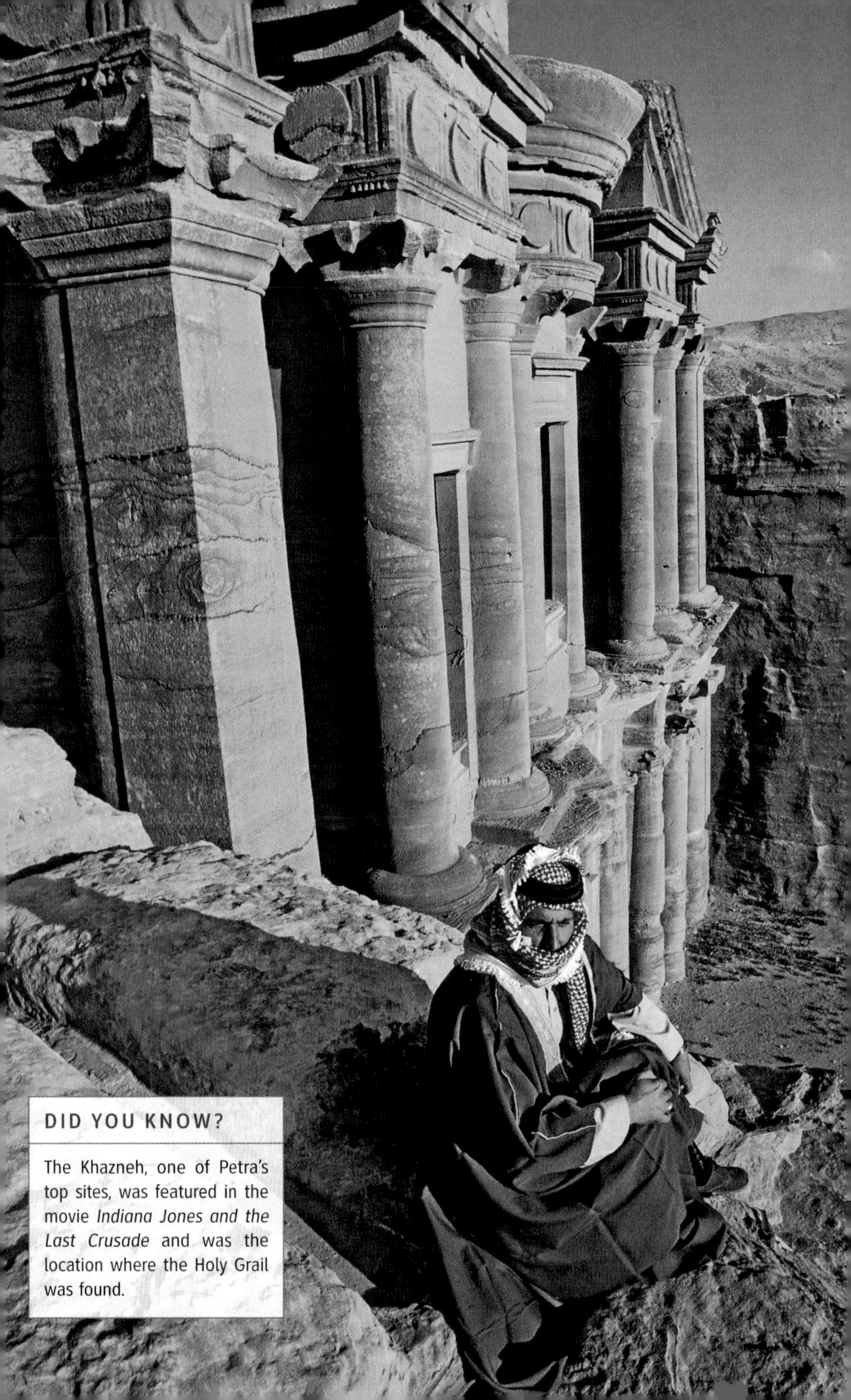

DID YOU KNOW?

The Khazneh, one of Petra's top sites, was featured in the movie *Indiana Jones and the Last Crusade* and was the location where the Holy Grail was found.

winners, she asked each how he had managed his appointed task. The one whose answer she preferred won her hand. In fact, the structure was the most important temple in Petra, built in the early 1st century AD. As in the Temple of the Winged Lions, the identity of the deity worshipped here isn't known, but a statue depicting him or her—perhaps Dushara, the greatest deity of the Nabatean pantheon—certainly stood in the temple's inner sanctum. A giant marble hand, part of a colossal statue, was discovered here in 1959.

⑥ Siq. The main entrance to Petra, in ancient times as in ours, is through the Siq (meaning "cleft"), a 1200-meter narrow canyon between towering walls of astonishing red and purple-hued stone. Nabatean paving stones are still visible along the way. Votive niches, some of which contain inscriptions dating from the 2nd and 3rd centuries AD, show that this road was as much a ceremonial path as a passageway. One niche is carved into a small outcropping of rock near one of the paved patches; it's unusual in that it faces away from the approach and may have been designed to bestow a blessing on those leaving the city. Film buffs may recall Harrison Ford riding through this area in *Indiana Jones and the Last Crusade.*

⑭ Theater. This semicircular amphitheater is a clear sign of the extent to which the Nabateans, like most other peoples of this region, had adopted Roman culture. The Nabateans apparently had no qualms about building a theater in a cemetery; their stone masons even cut into some of the existing tombs (the remains of which you can see at the back of the rock-cut theater) to do so. The capacity of the theater has been estimated at 7,000.

WORTH NOTING

⑤ Bab a-Siq. The Gate of the Cleft opens onto the Siq, the canyon-lined passageway leading to the main sights. From here you can spot the remains of a Nabatean water tunnel, built to divert flood waters from coursing through the narrow cleft and flooding the necropolis. A dam, constructed for the same purpose in the second half of the 1st century AD, was restored by the Jordanians after particularly serious flooding some years ago.

⑬ Broken Pediment Tomb. One of a series of facades carved into the western face of Jabal Madhba, this tomb is characterized by the broken-off gable of its roof, supported by four pilasters topped with Nabatean capitals.

㉒ Byzantine Church. Richly decorated with mosaics in the style of the period, this church (discovered by the American archaeologist Kenneth Russell, and excavated in the 1990s) appears to have been destroyed by fire soon after its construction, perhaps in a severe earthquake that took place in AD 551. The remains, including a spectacular mosaic floor, have undergone only partial conservation. One hundred and forty papyrus scrolls were found here.

⑰ Corinthian Tomb. Set among some of Petra's finest tombs is one named for the large number of Corinthian capitals, now badly deteriorated, that once decorated its facade.

❷ Djinn Blocks. The function of these three large structures is unclear; they may have been connected to Nabatean worship, perhaps symbolizing one of their deities. In Arabic, *djinn* refers to malevolent spirits, a common theme in Arab folklore.

❽ High Place of Sacrifice. An ancient flight of stairs cut into the rock—
★ and restored by the Jordanian Department of Antiquities—leads to the summit of Jabal Madhbah, or the Mount of the Altar. Its peak, besides offering spectacular views of Petra below, contains a rectangular court surrounded on three sides by benches in the triclinium style of the Roman dining room; in the center of the court is a raised block of stone, on which the priest may have stood. To the west are two altars accessed by steps, in front of which is a channel into which the blood of the sacrificial animal may have pooled.

❿ Lion Monument. Surface runoff fed this fountain on the path to the High Place via a channel leading to the lion's mouth, from which water once streamed.

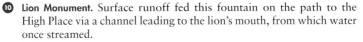

★ **Monastery (Ad Deir).** After the Treasury, this is Petra's second most impressive monument. Larger than the Treasury (it stands 170 feet wide), but less impressively ornate, it is reached at the end of a winding uphill 4-km (2½-mi) trail. An inscription was discovered nearby referring to "the symposium of Obodas the God." From this inscription, archeologists deduced that the Monastery was built 2,000 years ago as a meeting place for members of the cult of Obodas. Either tomb or temple, it holds a large chamber cut deep into the mountainside, and offers sweeping views of the adjacent gorges.

㉖ Museum. Petra's museum, which has restrooms, is in the same building as The Basin restaurant. Displays include a small number of Nabatean artifacts, such as jewelry and pottery.

⑳ Nymphaeum. Dedicated to the water nymphs, this fountain was used for both refreshment and worship. The fountains of the two-story structure were fed by a water channel that continued along Petra's main street.

❹ Obelisk Tomb. This upper story of a two-story tomb is named for the four freestanding obelisks that decorate its facade. The lower story, the Triclinium tomb, was so named because three walls of the empty room are lined with triclinia, a Latin word for this kind of bench. Sacred memorial feasts to honor the dead were held here.

❾ Obelisks. On the terrace below the High Place stand two obelisks hewed from the bedrock, examples of a common method of representing deities in the ancient Near East. Some scholars believe them to be representations of Dushara and al-Uzza; others believe they are simply the remains of quarrying activity.

18 Palace Tomb. This unfinished tomb is one of the few in Petra not carved entirely out of the rock. Many of the tomb's constructed segments have fallen away, so it's hard to ascertain its original dimensions. At the base of the Palace Tomb are the remains of the northern city wall, built after the 1st century BC.

12 Renaissance Tomb. This tomb, bearing a pediment with three urns, bears a resemblance to the Tomb of Sextius Florentinus, in the main part of the city. It may have been created around the same time, the first third of the 1st century AD.

> ### WORD OF MOUTH
>
> "Hint: if you have any Israeli shekels left over, spend them in Petra on food, souvenirs, etc. In the hotel they only wanted dinars or dollars, but in historic Petra, EVERY vendor was happy to take shekels—just make sure you know the exchange rate before you leave Israel!"
> —Pitzikat

11 Roman Soldier's Tomb. The headless figure in the niche of this unusual tomb's facade is dressed in typical Roman military garb, while the friezes and floral capitals appear more typical of Nabatean architecture before the Roman annexation. Directly opposite the Roman Soldier's Tomb is a triclinium; the rubble in between was probably once a colonnaded courtyard connecting the two edifices.

16 Silk Tomb. The striations of natural color in the Silk Tomb's rock make it one of Petra's finest and certainly make it easy to spot it. They flow across the facade like a multicolor silk scarf blowing gently in the wind.

3 Snake Tomb. No outward decoration marks this tomb, but 12 burial niches are carved into the floor inside. The name comes from a rough wall relief that shows two snakes attacking what may be a dog. Notice also the horse and rider relief above it.

24 Temple of the Winged Lions. This impressive building overlooking the Colonnaded Street takes its name from the sculptures that serve as capitals for its columns. The identity of the deity worshipped within is unknown, but votive figurines suggest that it may have been Isis, Egyptian goddess of the heavens and patroness of fertility. An inscription dates the construction of the temple to around AD 27, during the reign of Aretas IV.

19 Tomb of Sextius Florentinus. This is one of the few Petra monuments that can be dated with certainty: the name of this Roman governor of Arabia who died in office in AD 128 appears in the Latin inscription over the tomb's doorway.

15 Urn Tomb. Named for the vase-like decoration at the top of its pediment, this is the largest of the royal tombs. It is supported by a series of vaults at its lower level, dubbed *al makhamah* (the law court) by the locals for some long-forgotten reason; the upper level was called *a-sijn* (the prison). Although originally carved around 70 AD, according to an inscription within, Petra's Byzantine Christians turned the Urn Tomb into a church in AD 446.

WHERE TO EAT AND STAY

Dining in the town closest to the antiquities site of Petra—Wadi Musa—ranges from simple, inexpensive fare to the very elegant and pricey, with little in between. Both dining experiences, however, have one thing in common: courteous service and a welcoming spirit. Don't be put off by the plainness of the center-village eateries mentioned here. The locals enjoying their meal at the next table will remind you that the best fare is often to be had at such restaurants.

Petra has many lodging options. You can choose from luxurious to money-saving accommodations; both can be found adjacent to or near the site. The hotels closest to the site obviously provide the most convenient access to Petra and save you taxi money. A short car drive away in Wadi Musa are several good hotels, with some on the ridge above Wadi Musa. Taybet Zeman, in the village of Taybeh 9 km (5½ mi) from Petra, is the farthest from the site, but its uniquely authentic flavor is well worth the ride. All rooms have a private bath unless otherwise indicated.

$$–$$$
MIDDLE EASTERN
✕ **Al-Arabi.** This is a reliable place for a quick, inexpensive lunch, where diners can get a substantial meal, including mixed grill (their specialty), shawarma, barbecued meats, and hummus. The interior is very simple but bright. Look for the red sign on the left as you walk uphill. ✉ *Main St., Wadi Musa* ☎ *03/215–7661* ▭ *AE, MC, V.*

$$$
MIDDLE EASTERN
✕ **The Basin.** This buffet restaurant owned by the Crowne Plaza Hotel is in the antiquities site of Petra at the end of the Colonnaded Street. It serves hummus, baba ghanoush, and a variety of salads. It may not be the most imaginative meal you'll ever have but the shaded patio offers a pleasant midday break. ✉ *Petra* ☎ *03/215–6266* ▭ *AE, MC, V.*

$$$
MIDDLE EASTERN
✕ **Petra Zeman.** The specialty here is *maklouba,* a chicken-and-rice dish which the locals call "upside down" because servers seem to enjoy the diners' reaction as they turn the pot upside down with a flourish on the serving tray at the table. This is also a great place to try the Jordanian national dish, *mansaf*—lamb in a tangy yogurt sauce served over rice. Dessert, here and everywhere in town, means a tiny cup of strong coffee spiced with *hel* (cardamom) and a dish of baklava, or one of the many kindred versions of this Middle Eastern honey-and-pistachio sweet. ✉ *Main St., Wadi Musa* ☎ *79/513–5513* ▭ *AE, MC, V.*

$$$$
▭ **Crowne Plaza Petra.** The Crowne Plaza is conveniently adjacent to Petra's entrance. Next door is the Petra Cave, the hotel's bar-disco-thèque, with nightly live Arabic and Western music, and "hubbly-bubblies"—water-pipes—for those who want to try smoking tobacco the traditional Middle Eastern way. Many of the rooms were recently renovated. **Pros:** excellent location; great pool; stunning views from many rooms. **Cons:** old furnishings; small rooms. ✉ *Tourism St., Wadi Musa* ☎ *03/215–6266* 🖷 *03/215–6977* ▭ *147 rooms, 3 suites, 31 hillside chalets* ♿ *In-room: Internet, safe. In-hotel: 3 restaurants, bar, pool, tennis court, gym, Internet terminal* ▭ *MC, V.*

$$$$
▭ **Marriott Petra.** This excellent three-floor hotel is located on the ridge above Petra, somewhat farther away than the other hotels, though free shuttle service to the Petra entrance is available. Most rooms offer spectacular views of the Petra Valley below. A marble-floor lobby and high atrium of white stone arches greets you. Guests can take advantage

8

of the spa with Turkish bath and sauna, and visit the Bedouin tent behind the hotel. **Pros:** stunning sunset views; Petra's best Italian restaurant, open nightly. **Cons:** 15-minute drive to Petra entrance; do not change Israeli currency. ✉*Taybeh Rd., Wadi Musa* 🕿*03/215–6407* 🖷*03/215–7096* ⊕*www.marriott.com/hotels* ⛵*99 rooms, 1 suite* ⛅*In-hotel: 2 restaurants, bar, pool, spa, Wi-Fi* ▭*MC, V.*

$$$$ 🏨**Moevenpick.** Located just steps from the entrance to Petra, this five-floor, Swiss-run hotel has comfortable rooms with blond-wood furnishings and gold-framed mirrors. A beautiful interior courtyard with arabesques, a fountain, and palm trees, is the ideal place for an afternoon coffee, after which you can enjoy the sunset from the roof garden, or take a refreshing dip in the outdoor pool. **Pros:** the hotel's Al Iwan restaurant is the best in Wadi Musa; the breakfast buffet is excellent. **Cons:** no views to speak of; bedding only changed every second day. ✍*Box 214, Wadi Musa* 🕿*03/215–7111* 🖷*03/215–7112* ⊕*www. moevenpick-petra.com* ⛵*183 rooms* ⛅*In-hotel: 2 restaurants, bar, pool, gym* ▭*AE, DC, MC, V.*

$$$$ 🏨**Taybet Zeman.** Nine kilometers (5½ mi) from Petra, on the outskirts of the town of Taybeh, this unique lodging was once a Bedouin village. Abandoned for years, it was eventually revamped into a hotel that has every modern amenity but has been designed to steep guests in aspects of Bedouin culture that have all but disappeared. Rooms are spacious and decorated in authentic Bedouin style with throw rugs and wall hangings—a colorful counterpoint to the natural stone walls. At the hotel's souk (market) you can watch handcrafted items being made. The central courtyard has a spice garden, and its yields are served in the hotel's excellent restaurant, where the menu mixes Eastern and Western favorites. The buffet is worth a trip in itself. The hotel has one wheelchair-accessible room. **Pros:** on a ridge high above Petra, the hotel offers an incomparable view of the mountains of Edom, especially from the Diwan, its garden terrace; excellent service. **Cons:** not within walking distance to the entrance to Petra; no air-conditioning in many rooms. ✉*Queen Ranya St., Wadi Musa* 🕿*03/215–0111* 🖷*03/215–0101* ⛵*105 rooms* ⛅*In-hotel: 2 pools, restaurant, laundry* ▭*AE, MC, V.*

NIGHTLIFE AND THE ARTS

A **candle-lit tour** of Petra is one of the city's unique attractions. A stroll through the Siq as shadows play on the canyon walls is a dramatic way to discover aspects hidden by day. Music is played on traditional instruments such as the *rababa*, and stories are told in front of the Khazneh at the end of the walk. Tours depart at 8:30 PM. Check for availability at the Petra visitor center.

SHOPPING

Petra's handicraft specialty is the work of its "sand artists"—artisans who fill bottles with sand in a variety of hues and complex designs. They can customize the purchase by writing a name or other text in the sand. The artists work and sell their unique wares in shops in Wadi Musa, as well as in the Siq.

HEBREW VOCABULARY

Many people in Israel speak at least one other language, in addition to Hebrew, and most can get by in English. So the chances of getting too lost for words are slim. At the same time, your traveling experience can be enriched by having at least a few words to share in conversation or to use while touring and shopping, even at the local grocery store. Here are some basic words and expressions that may be of use during your stay. Please note that the letters "kh" in this glossary are pronounced like the "ch" in chanuka or the Scottish loch.

ENGLISH	HEBREW TRANSLITERATION	PRONUNCIATION

GREETINGS AND BASICS

Hello/good-bye/peace	Shalom	shah-**lohm**
Nice to meet you	Na'im me'od	nah-**eem** meh-**ohd**
Good morning	Boker tov	boh-ker **tohv**
Good evening	Erev tov	eh-rev **tohv**
Good night	Layla tov	lahy-lah tohv
How are you?	Ma shlomekh?	mah shloh-**maykh**
How are you? (to a man)	Ma shlomkha?	mah shlohm-**khah**
How are you?	Ma nishma?	mah-nee-**shmah**
Fine	Beseder	beh-**say-dehr**
Everything is fine	Hakol beseder	hah-kohl beh-**say-dehr**
Is everything okay?	Hakol beseder?	hah-kohl beh-**say-dehr**
Very well	Tov me'od	tohv-meh-**ohd**
Excellent/terrific	Metzuyan	meh-tzoo-**yahn**
Send regards!	Timsor dash!	teem-sohr **dahsh** `
Thank you	Toda	toh-**dah**
Thank you very much	Toda raba	toh-dah rah-**bah**
See you again	Lehitra'ot	leh-heet-rah-**oht**
Yes	Ken	kehn
No	Lo	lo
Maybe	Oolai	**oo**-ligh
Excuse me/Sorry	Slicha	slee-**khah**
Again/Could you repeat that?	Od pa'am	ohd pah-**ahm**

ENGLISH	HEBREW TRANSLITERATION	PRONUNCIATION

DAYS

Today	Hayom	hah-**yohm**
Tomorrow	Machar	mah-**khahr**
Yesterday	Etmol	eht-**mohl**
Sunday	Yom Rishon	yohm ree-**shohn**
Monday	Yom Sheni	yohm sheh-**nee**
Tuesday	Yom Shlishi	yohm sh-**leeshee**
Wednesday	Yom Revi'i	yohm reh-**vee**
Thursday	Yom Chamishi	yohm kha-mee-**shee**
Friday	Yom Shishi	yohm shee-**shee**
Saturday, Sabbath	Shabbat	yohm shah-**bat**

NUMBERS

1	Echad	eh-**khad**
2	Shtayim	shtah-**yeem**
3	Shalosh	shah-**lohsh**
4	Arba	ah-**rbah**
5	Chamesh	chah-**maysh**
6	Shesh	shehsh
7	Sheva	**sheh**-vah
8	Shmoneh	**shmoh**-neh
9	Teisha	**tay**-shah
10	Esser	**eh**-sehr
11	Achad esreh	ah-**chahd** eh-**sreh**
12	Shteim esreh	sht**aym** eh-**sreh**
20	Esrim	eh-**sreem**
50	Chamishim	khah-mee-**sheem**
100	Me'a	may-**ah**
200	Ma'tayim	mah-**tah**-yeem

ENGLISH	HEBREW TRANSLITERATION	PRONUNCIATION

USEFUL PHRASES

ENGLISH	HEBREW TRANSLITERATION	PRONUNCIATION
Do you speak English?	Ata medaber anglit?	ah-ta meh-dah-ber ahng-**leet**
I don't understand (man)	Ani lo mevin	a-**nee** loh meh-**veen**
I don't understand (woman)	Ani lo m'vina	a-**nee** m'veena
I don't know (man)	Ani lo yodea	a-nee loh yoh-**day**-ah
I don't know (woman)	Ani lo yodaat	a-nee loh yoh-**dah**-aht
I am lost (man)	Ani avud	a-nee ah-**vood**
I am lost (woman)	Ani avuda	a-nee ahvoo-**dah**
I am American	Ani Amerika'i	ah-nee ah-mer-ee-**kah**-ee
I am British	Ani Briti	ah-**nee bree**-tee
I am Canadian	Ani Canadi	ah-**nee** kah-**nah**-dee
What is the time?	Ma hasha'a?	mah hah-shah-**ah**
Just a minute	Rak rega	rahk **reh**-gah
Minute, moment	Rega	**reh**-gah
Now	Achshav	ahkh-**shahv**
Not yet	Od lo	ohd loh
Later	Achar kach	ah-**khahr** kahkh
I would like	Hayiti mevakesh	hah-**yee**-tee m-vah-**kehsh**
Where is..?	Eifo..?	**ay**foh
The central bus station	Hatachana hamerkazit	hah-tah-khah-**nah** hah-mehr-kah-**zeet**
The bus stop	Tachanat ha'autobus	tah-khah-**naht** hah-oh-toh-**boos**
The train station	Tachanat harakevet	tah-khah-**naht** hah-rah-**keh-veht**
The city center	Merkaz ha'ir	mehr kahz hah-**eer**
The post office	Hado'ar	hah-**doh**-ahr

ENGLISH	HEBREW TRANSLITERATION	PRONUNCIATION
A pharmacy	Beit mirkachat	bayt meer-**kah**-khaht
A public telephone	Telefon tziburi	teh-leh-**fohn** tzee-boo-**ree**
A good restaurant	Mis'ada tova	mee-sah-**dah toh-vah**
The rest rooms	Hasherutim	hah-shay-roo-**teem**
Right	Yemina	yeh-**mee**-nah
Left	Smola	s-**moh**-lah
Straight ahead	Yashar	yah-**shar**
Here	Kan	kahn
There	Sham	shahm
Do you have a (vacant) room?	Yesh lachem cheder (panui)?	yehsh lah-**chehm khed**-ehr (pah-**nooy**)
Is it possible to order a taxi?	Efshar lehazmin monit?	ehf-**shahr** leh-hahz-**meen** moh-**neet**
Taxi	Monit	moh-**neet**
A little	k'tzat	keh-**tzaht**
A lot	harbe	hahr-**beh**
Enough	maspik	Mah-**speek**
I have a problem	Yesh li ba'aya	yehsh lee bah-**yah**
I don't feel well (man)	Ani lo margish tov	ah-**nee** loh mahr-**geesh** tohv
I don't feel well (woman)	Ani lo margisha tov	ah-**nee** loh mahr-**gee**-**shah** tohv
I need a doctor (man)	Ani tzarich rofe	ah-**nee** tzah-**reech** roh-**feh**
I need a doctor (woman)	Ani tzricha rofe	ah-**nee** tzree-**khah** roh-**feh**
Help	Ezra	Eh-**zrah**
Fire	Dleika	duh-leh-**kah**

DINING

ENGLISH	HEBREW TRANSLITERATION	PRONUNCIATION
I would like	Hayiti mevakesh	hah-**yee**-tee m-vah-**kehsh**
Some water, please	Mayim, bevakasha	mah-**yeem** beh-vah-kah-**shah**

ENGLISH	HEBREW TRANSLITERATION	PRONUNCIATION
Bread	Lechem	**leh**-khehm
Soup	Marak	mah-**rahk**
Meat	Bassar	bah-**ssahr**
Chicken	Off	ohf
Vegetables	Yerakot	yeh-rah-**koht**
Dessert	Kinuach	kee-**noo**-ahkh
Cake	Ooga	**oo**-gah
Fruit	Perot	peh-**roht**
Coffee	Cafe	kah-**feh**
Tea	Te	teh
fork	Mazleg	mahz-**lehg**
spoon	Kapit	kah-**peet**
knife	Sakin	sah-**keen**
plate	Tzalachat	tzah-**lah**-chaht
Napkin	Mapit	mah-**peet**
Food	Ochel	**oh**-khehl
Meal	Arucha	ah-roo-**khah**
Breakfast	Aruchat boker	ah-roo-**khaht boh**-ker
Lunch	Aruchat tzaharayim	ah-roo-khaht tzah-hah-**rah**-yeem
Dinner	Aruchat erev	Ahroo-**khaht eh**-rehv
Do you have a menu in English?	Yesh tafrit be'anglit?	yehsh tahf-**reet** beh- ahng-**leet**
A pita filled with felafel	Manat felafel	mah-naht feh-**lah**-fehl
Without hot sauce	Bli charif	blee khah-**reef**
It's tasty, delicious	Zeh ta'im	zeh tah-**eem**
I don't like the taste	Zeh lo ta'im li	zeh loh tah-**eem** lee
The check, please	Cheshbon, bevakasha	Khehsh-bohn beh-vah-kah-**shah**

ENGLISH	HEBREW TRANSLITERATION	PRONUNCIATION

SHOPPING

ENGLISH	HEBREW TRANSLITERATION	PRONUNCIATION
Do you have..?	Yesh lecha..?	yesh leh-khah
Milk	Chalav	khah-**lahv**
(Orange) Juice	Mitz (tapuzim)	meetz (tah-poo-**zeem**)
Butter	Chem'a	khem-**ah**
Cream cheese	Gevina levana	geh-vee-**nah** leh-vah-nah
Hard cheese	Gevina tzehuba	gevee-**nah** tzeh-**hoo**-bah
Sausage	Naknik	Nahk-**neek**
Jelly	Riba	**ree**-bah
Sugar	Sukar	**soo**-kahr
Ice cream	Glida	**glee**-da
Map	Mapa	**mah**-pa
Cigarettes	Sigariyot	see-gahr-ee-**yoht**
Telephone card (for public phones)	Telecart	teh-leh-**kahrt**
That one, please	Et zeh, bevakasha	eht zeh, beh-vah-kah-**shah**
May I see it?	Efshar lir'ot?	ehf-**shahr** leer-**oht**
How much does it cost?	Kama zeh oleh?	**kah**-ma zeh **ohleh**
That's expensive!	Yakar!	yah-**kahr**
No, it's too expensive	Lo, zeh yakar midai	loh, zeh yah-**kahr** meed-**igh**
Too big	Gadol midai	gah-dohl meed-**igh**
Too small	Katan midai	kah-tan meed-**igh**
Perhaps there is a discount ?	Yesh hanacha oolai	Yehsh hah-na-**khah** oo-ligh oo-**ligh**
I'll take it	Ani ekach et zeh	ah-nee eh-**kakh** eht zeh

PALESTINIAN ARABIC VOCABULARY

Arabic is spoken by all Arab citizens of Israel, (about 20% of the Israeli population) and in the West Bank and Gaza. The areas where you're most likely to hear Arabic are East Jerusalem, Jaffa, and Nazareth, and in the popular sites of the West Bank, Bethlehem and Jericho (when these are open to travelers). Many people in these areas speak some English, but a little Arabic will come in handy with some vendors and taxi drivers or when you are in more rural areas and villages. It helps to have a written address for a taxi ride as well. You may run into small differences in dialect and accent between villages and cities, but for the most part Palestinians dialects are similar.

Some letters in Arabic do not have English equivalents. This glossary tries to approximate Arabic sounds. The letter 'r' is always rolled. When you see 'gh' at the start of a word, pronounce it like a French 'r', lightly gargled at the back of the throat. Any double letters should be extended: 'aa' is pronounced as an extended 'ah'; 'hh' is an extended 'h' sound; 'ss' is an extended hiss.

ENGLISH	ARABIC TRANSLITERATION	PRONUNCIATION
GREETINGS AND BASICS		
Hello/ peace be upon you	salamou alaikom	sah-**lah**-moo aah-**lay**-kom
(reply) Hello/ and peace be upon you	wa aalaikom essalaam	wah aah-**lay**-kom **ehss**-sah-**ahm**
Good-bye	maa issalameh	**maah** is-**ah-lah**-meh
Mr./ Sir	sayyed	**sigh**-yed
Mrs./ Madam	sayyida	**sigh**-yee-dah
Miss	anisseh	**ah**-niss-say
How are you? (man speaking)	keif hhalak	kayf **hah**-luck
How are you? (woman speaking)	keif hhalik	kayf **hah**-lik
Fine, thank you	bi kheir elhhamdilla	bee **khayr** el-**ham**-dihl-lah
Pleased to meet you	tsharrafna	tshahr-**ruhf**-nah
Please (man)	min fadlak	min **fahd**-lahk
Please (woman)	min fadlik	min **fahd**-lik
Thank you	shokran	shohk-rahn
God willing	Inshallah	ihn-**shahl-lah**
Yes	aah or naam	aah or naahm

ENGLISH	ARABIC TRANSLITERATION	PRONUNCIATION
No	la	lah
I'm Sorry (man)	mit assif	miht **ass**-sef
I'm Sorry (woman)	mit assfeh	miht **ass**-feh

DAYS

Today	eliom	el-**yohm**
Tomorrow	bokra	bok-rah
Yesterday	embarehh	ehm-**bah**-rehh
Sunday	il ahhad	**il ah**-had
Monday	Ittinein	it-tee-**nayn**
Tuesday	ittalata	it-tah-**lah**-tah
Wednesday	il 'arbaa	il **ahr**-bah-**aah**
Thursday	il khamees	il khah-**mees**
Friday	iljumaa	il zhum-**aah**
Saturday	issabet	**iss-sah**-bet

NUMBERS

1	wahed	**wah**-hed
2	tinein	tee-**nayn**
3	talati	tah-**lah**-tee
4	arbaa	**ahr**-bah-aah
5	khamseh	**khahm**-seh
6	sitteh	**sit**-teh
7	sabaa	sub-**aah**
8	tamanyeh	tah-**mah**-nee-**yeh**
9	tisaa	**tiss**-aah
10	aashara	**aah**-shah-rah
11	ihhdaaesh	ihh-**dah**-ehsh
12	itnaaesh	it-**nah**-ehsh
20	ishreen	iish-**reen**
50	khamseen	khahm-**seen**
100	meyyeh	**may**-yeh

ENGLISH	ARABIC TRANSLITERATION	PRONUNCIATION
200	mitein	**mee**-tain

USEFUL PHRASES

Do you speak English?	btihki inglizi?	btih-**kee** in-**glee**-zee?
I don't understand (man)	mish fahem	mish **fah**-him
I don't understand (woman)	mish fahmi	mish **fah**-meh
I don't know (man)	mish aarif	mish **aah**-ref
I don't know (woman)	mish aarfi	mish **aahr**-fee
I'm lost (man)	ana dayih	ah-nah **dah-yeh**
I'm lost (woman)	ana dayaa	ah-nah **dah**-ye-aah
I am American (man)	ana amriki	ah-nah ahm-**ree-kee**
I am American (woman)	ana amrikiyya	ah-nah ahm-**ree-key-**yah
I am British (man)	ana baritani	ah-nah bah-**ree-tah-nee**
I am British (woman)	ana baritaniya	ah-nah bah-**ree-tah-nay**-yah
What is this?	eish hada?	aysh **hah**-dah?
What time is it?	Addeish el wa'ed?	Ahd-**daysh**-el **wah**-ed
Where is?	wein?	wayn?
The train station	mahattit iltrain	mah-**huht-tit il-train**
The bus station	mahattit el buss	mah-**huht**-tit el **buhss**
The intracity bus station	mahattit el bus eddakheli	mah-huht-**tit el** buhss **ed**-dah-**khe-lee**
The taxi station	mujammaa el takasi	moo-**jam**-maah el tah-**kah**-see
The airport	el matar	el mah-**tahr**
The hotel	el oteil	el **ooh**-tayl
The cafe	el ahwi	el ah-**weh**
The restaurant	el mataam	el **matt-aahm**
The telephone	el tiliphon	el tih-lih-**fohn**
The hospital	el mostashfa	el moos-**tash**-fah

ENGLISH	ARABIC TRANSLITERATION	PRONUNCIATION
The post office	el bareed	el bah-**reed**
The rest room	el hammam	el huhm-**mahm**
The pharmacy	el saydaleyyeh	el sigh-dah-**lay-yeh**
The bank	el bank	el bahnk
The embassy	el safara	el sah-fah-**rah**
Right	yameen	yah-meen
Left	shmal	shmahl
Straight ahead	doughri	doo-ghree
I would like a room	beddi ghorfi	bed-dee **ghor-fih**
A little	shway or aleel	shway or ah-leel
A lot	kteer	kteer
Enough	bikaffi	bee-kaf-fee
I have a problem	aandi moshkili	aahn-dee **moosh**-keh-lee
I am ill	ana mareed	ah-nah mah-reed
I need a doctor	beddi daktor	bed-**dee** dac-**tor**
Help	saadoonee	**saah-doo**-nee
Fire	naar or harika	naahr or hah-**ree**-kah
Caution/ look out	entebeh or owaa	in-teh-beh or ohw-**aah**

DINING

I would like	beddi	behd-dee
Water	mayy	muhyy
Bread	khobez	kho-bihz
Vegetables	khodra	khod-rah
Meat	lahhmi	**lahh**-meh
Fruits	fawakeh	fah-**wah**-keh
Cakes/ Sweets	helou/ halaweyyat	**heh**-loo/ hah-lah-**way-yaht**
Tea	shay	shahy
Coffee	ahwi	ah-weh
A fork	shokeh	show-keh

ENGLISH	ARABIC TRANSLITERATION	PRONUNCIATION
A spoon	maala a	**maah**-lah ah
A knife	sikkeen	sick-**keen**
A plate	sahin	sah-hin

SHOPPING

I would like to buy	beddi ashtri	bed-**dee** ahsh-tree
cigarettes	sagayer or dokhkhan	sah-**gah**-yer or dokh-**khahn**
a city map	khareeta lal madeeni	khah-**ree**-tah lahl mah-**dee**-nee
a road map	khareeta lal tareek	khah-**ree**-tah lahl tah-**reek**
How much is it?	addaish ha o	**ad**-daysh **ha** oh
It's expensive	ghali	**ghah**-lee

Travel Smart
Israel

WORD OF MOUTH

"I may add that the weather can get quite cold, especially in Jerusalem (due to its elevation). You'll definitely need sweaters, and probably either a lined raincoat or wool coat."

—W9London

"Please go to Israel, it was one of the best trips of my life."

—P_M

GETTING HERE & AROUND

■ AIR TRAVEL

The least expensive airfares to Israel are often priced for round-trip travel and must be purchased well in advance. Airlines generally allow you to change your return date for a fee; most low-fare tickets, however, are nonrefundable.

Flights to Israel tend to be least expensive from November through March, except for the holiday season at the end of December. Prices are also higher during the Jewish New Year's holidays (usually in September) and during Passover (usually in April).

Flying time from New York to Israel is approximately 11 hours; from Los Angeles, it's about 18 hours (including the usual stopover in Europe or New York). International passengers are asked to arrive at the airport three hours prior to their flight time in order to allow for security checks.

From North America, the New York City area's international airports offer the highest number of nonstop flights, with El Al Airlines, Continental, and Delta providing service. Direct flights via El Al are also available from Los Angeles and Toronto. Major European carriers—including Air France, Alitalia, British Airways, Czech Airways, Iberia, KLM, Lufthansa, Olympic, Swissair, Turkish Airways, and Virgin Atlantic—have daily flights from the United States and on to Israel with stopovers in their domestic hub airports.

Because Israel is only 1/16 the size of California, it's often more efficient to drive within the country than fly. The exception is traveling to the resort city of Eilat, which is 360 km (224 mi) south of Tel Aviv on the Gulf of Eilat. There are flights every day from Tel Aviv and every other day from Haifa.

Reconfirmation obligations differ from airline to airline (and change from time to time); be certain to check with your carrier for all legs of your journey.

Airline Security Issues Transportation Security Administration (⊕ *www.tsa.gov*) has answers for almost every question that might come up.

Air Travel Resources in Israel El Al Customer Care Department (☏ *03/977–1111*).

AIRPORTS

Israel's main airport, Ben Gurion International Airport (TLV) is a few miles southeast of Tel Aviv. The airport has towering interior walls adorned with sixth-century Byzantine mosaics that were discovered during construction. A soothing fountain lies in the center of the departure hall, surrounded by leather and chrome armchairs. A food court serves Middle Eastern cuisine and fast-food favorites. From Sde Dov Airport (SDV), about 4 km (2½ mi) north of the city center, domestic airlines fly to Eilat, and to Haifa or Rosh Pina in the north.

Charter flights between Europe and the southern resort town of Eilat land at Ovda Airport (VDA) (which operates only late September through May) or Eilat Airport (ETH).

Airport Information Ben Gurion International Airport (☏ **6663 or 03/975–5555* ⊕ *www.iaa.gov.il*). **Eilat Airport** (☏ *08/636–3838 or 1700/705–022* ⊕ *www.iaa.gov.il*). **Ovda Airport** (☏ *08/637–5880* ⊕ *www.iaa.gov.il*). **Sde Dov Airport** (☏ *03/698–4500* ⊕ *www.iaa.gov.il*).

GROUND TRANSPORTATION

The quickest and most convenient way to get to and from the airport is by taxi. Taxis are always available directly outside the arrivals hall. Fares are NIS 140 to Tel Aviv and NIS 280 to Jerusalem. From the airport, trains depart for Tel Aviv every 25 minutes. They will take you to the city in 25 minutes for NIS 13. Trains continue on to Herzliya, Netanya, Haifa, Akko, and Nahariya. Direct train service to Jerusalem won't commence until 2012.

The Nesher shuttle service takes you to Jerusalem for NIS 50. The 10-passenger *sherut* taxis (limo-vans) depart whenever they fill up. The main disadvantage is that if you're the last passenger to be dropped off, you may tour the city for an hour while the driver discharges the other passengers. To get to Ben Gurion Airport from Jerusalem the same way, call Nesher to book a place, preferably a day in advance. A "special" taxi (as opposed to a shared sherut) costs about NIS 220, with a 25% surcharge after 9 PM and on Saturday and holidays.

When departing for the airport from central Tel Aviv by car or taxi at rush hour (7–9 AM, 5–7 PM), the roads can get clogged so allow 45 minutes for a trip that would otherwise take only about 20 minutes.

Taking the bus from Ben Gurion Airport to Jerusalem has become tedious. You need to board the Egged local shuttle (line #5, fare NIS 4.80) for a 10-minute ride to the Airport City commercial complex, and wait there for the Jerusalem-bound Egged bus (line #947, fare NIS 21). It runs to Jerusalem's Central Bus Station approximately every 30 minutes during the day, less frequently in the evening.

Contacts Egged (☎ *03/694–8888 or *2800* ⊕ *www.egged.co.il/Eng*). **Nesher** (☎ *599/500–205; 02/625–3233 or 02/623–1231 in Jerusalem*).

FLIGHTS

The national carrier, El Al Israel Airlines, is known for maintaining some of the world's strictest security standards. It is not necessarily the cheapest carrier, especially from the United States. Continental and Delta often have cheaper fares. Within Israel, Arkia Israeli Airlines has flights from Tel Aviv to Eilat and Rosh Pina. Israir Airlines has service from Tel Aviv and Haifa to Eilat.

To Israel Continental Airlines (☎ *800/523–3273 for U.S. reservations, 800/231–0856 for international reservations* ⊕ *www.continental.com*). **Delta Airlines** (☎ *800/221–1212 for U.S. reservations, 800/241–4141 for international reservations* ⊕ *www.delta.com*). **El Al Israel Airlines**

(☎ *212/768–9200 or 800/223–6700 in the U.S.; *2250 or 03/977–1111 in Israel* ⊕ *www.elal.co.il*).**Royal Jordanian Airlines** (☎ *03/516–5566 for information* ⊕ *www.rja.com.jo*).

Within Israel Arkia Israeli Airlines (☎ **5758 general reservations and information or 03/690–3712* ⊕ *www.arkia.com*). **Israir Airlines** (☎ *877/477–2471 or 1-700/505–777* ⊕ *www.israirairlines.com*).

▮ BIKE TRAVEL

Biking has really taken off in Israel, and over the past few years an estimated 100,000 have hit the trails. With mountains, deserts, and wooded hills, this small country is ideal for bicycling. Off-road adventure tours take you to remote archeological sites and other places not reachable by car. Keep in mind, though, the going can get rough due to the extreme heat much of the year, the winding and hilly roads, and aggressive drivers. Biking is best enjoyed from September to June. Trains don't accept bikes, but buses do.

Israel Bike Trails has a Web site with comprehensive bike trail information listing elevations and level of difficulty. Biking maps in English are hard to find. Serious bikers use the Israel Hiking and Touring Maps published by the Society for the Protection of Nature. At this writing, only one in this series (#20, Eilat Mountains) has been published in English.

Bike Contacts Israel Bike Trails (⊕ *www. israelbiketrails.com*). **Society for the Protection of Nature** (☎ *03/638–8719*).

▮ BOAT TRAVEL

Ferries shuttle passengers between Israel and Greece and Cyprus. Service is quite limited with the Cyprus-based Varianos Travel providing the only reliable departures. The weekly ferry between Haifa and Limassol, Cyprus operates between May and October. Cabins for two range from $450 to $625, including all meals on the 11-hour crossing.

Ferry Contacts Varianos Travel
(☎ 357/2268–0500 ⊕ www.varianostravel.com).

▌BUS TRAVEL

Buses can take you almost anywhere in Israel. All routes are run by Egged, except in metropolitan Tel Aviv, where Dan provides some competition. Buses in Israel are clean, comfortable, modern, and air-conditioned. Inter-city bus fares vary according to the distance traveled. During weekday rush hours allow time for long lines at the obligatory security checks to enter the bus station. Buses are often overcrowded on Saturday nights after Shabbat and always on Sunday mornings when it looks like the entire Israeli army is returning to base after a weekend at home.

The central bus station in Tel Aviv looks like the work of a mad scientist. The stark concrete building has multiple entrances on several levels, endless corridors, and a confusing array of platforms. It's all topped off by dozens of kiosks selling fast food and cheap merchandise. By contrast, Jerusalem's central bus station is clean, well organized, and easy to navigate. There's a pleasant food court, an ATM, and branches of some of the country's best-known stores.

Although the buses resemble those in most other countries, there are a few quirks. When you're in Jerusalem, remember that Buses 1 and 2, which service the Western Wall area, are used primarily by the ultra-Orthodox population. It's generally accepted that women should sit separately in the rear of the bus. Women should never sit in an empty seat next to an ultra-Orthodox man, and shouldn't be offended if a man would rather stand than sit beside them in an empty seat. (And in case you're wondering, ultra-Orthodox women generally accept this arrangement.)

Bus service is available between Jerusalem and Tel Aviv. Egged bus line #405 runs from the Tel Aviv Central Bus Station, and line #480 from the Arlozorov Street terminal, each with two to five departures per hour, depending on the time of day (fare NIS 18.50). There is a similar service to Jerusalem from most major cities, terminating at the Central Bus Station. The two small bus stations in East Jerusalem are the termini for private, Palestinian-operated bus lines, with daily service to West Bank towns such as Bethlehem and Jericho.

FARES

For both local and long-distance travel, drivers accept payment in shekels. Drivers on the long-distance buses will grumble when they have to make change for a bill over NIS 50, so make sure to have smaller denominations. Unless you're running to catch a bus, it's almost always faster to buy your ticket at the station. On city buses you don't need exact change.

For travel between major cities and within each city, Egged offers good rates on packs of 10 or more tickets and monthly passes that give you an unlimited number of rides. These may be purchased at any city bus station or on the bus. These are particularly good for children and senior citizens, who get large discounts. Children under age five ride free whether or not they occupy their own seat.

The fare on all routes is NIS 5.70; you need local currency. There are no transfers.

Phone reservations usually are not accepted in Israel. It's best to buy tickets ahead at the bus stations if you plan to travel between cities on Thursday night or the weekend, including Saturday night and Sunday morning. The exception is for buses traveling from Tel Aviv or Jerusalem to Eilat. Make your reservations as early as you can, as last-minute travelers may have to stand in the aisle.

SCHEDULES

All bus service is available Sunday to Thursday from 5:30 AM to 12:30 AM. Keep in mind that most public transportation ceases to run on Shabbat, which lasts from sundown Friday afternoon to sundown Saturday evening. The exception is a few lines in Tel Aviv and Haifa.

Every large bus station has an information booth where you'll generally be able to find schedule and platform information in English. Bus maps in English are virtually non-existent—just tell the clerk where you want to go and you'll probably get a hand-written map.

Jerusalem buses do not automatically stop at every bus stop; you need to signal the driver. Bus schedules are available at the city's Central Bus Station (the western end of Jaffa Street). Some commercial maps show bus routes. Buses are predictably crowded at certain times of day, and often take circuitous routes.

TOURS

Egged operates Route 99, a two-hour circle tour of Jerusalem for visitors. Its distinctive red double-decker buses are equipped with audio explanations in several languages (individual headphones). The route begins at the Central Bus Station at the city's western entrance, and its 29 stops include the Machaneh Yehuda market, the edge of the downtown, Mt. Scopus, City of David, Dung Gate, Mt. Zion, Jaffa Gate, City Hall (Safra Square), King David Hotel (and other hotels en route), Haas Promenade, Jerusalem (Malcha) Mall, the railway station at the Biblical Zoo, Mt. Herzl, Yad Vashem, Israel Museum, the Knesset, and the Supreme Court. Departures are Sunday–Thursday at 9 AM, 11 AM, 1:30 PM, 3:45 PM, and 6 PM (the last tour does not operate Nov.–Feb.). On Friday and the eves of Jewish holidays, the last bus leaves at 1:30 PM. The cost is NIS 60 for one full trip, NIS 80 for a one-day ticket (unlimited transfers), and NIS 110 for an unlimited two-day ticket; children's discounts are available.

Bus Information Dan (☎ 03/639–4444 ⊕ www.dan.co.il/english/default.asp). **East Jerusalem Bus Station** (✉ Sultan Suleiman St., opposite Damascus Gate, East Jerusalem ☎ 054/449–3088). **Egged** (☎ 03/694–8888 or *2800 ⊕ www.egged.co.il/eng.). **Jerusalem Central Bus Station** (✉ 224 Jaffa Rd., Romema ☎ 03/694–8888).

▌ BY CAR

The Hebrew word for a native-born Israeli is *sabra,* which literally refers to a prickly cactus with sweet fruit inside. You'll meet the sweet Israeli if you get lost or have automotive difficulties—helping hands are quick to arrive—but behind the wheel, Israelis are prickly, aggressive, and honk their horns far more than their Western counterparts. Try not to take it personally.

Some travelers will feel more comfortable hiring a driver, and there are plenty of ways to find someone reliable. Ask for recommendations at your hotel. Every hotel has taxi drivers that serve their guests and most are familiar with all parts of the country and will be happy to quote you a daily rate. For one day, the rate should be around NIS 700.

Israel's highways are numbered, but most people still know them simply by the towns they connect: the Tiberias–Nazareth Road, for example. Intersections and turnoffs are similarly indicated, as in "the Eilat Junction." Orange signs indicate tourist sites; national parks signs are on brown wood.

ADDRESSES

In Israel, streets are generally named after famous people or events, meaning that almost every community has a Herzl Street and a Six-Day War Street. Don't worry about the "boulevard" or "alley" attached to many street names—Israelis just use the proper name. You won't find a Jabotinsky Street and a Jabotinsky Alley in the same city. What you might encounter, because there are too many famous people and not enough streets, is a street that will change names after a couple of blocks. Street numbers follow the standard format, with odd numbers on one side and even numbers on the other. Larger apartment buildings often have several entrances marked by the first three or four letters of the Hebrew alphabet.

If you know history, you'll have an easier time finding your way around Jerusalem's neighborhoods. In Baka the streets are named after the biblical tribes, in Rehavia it's medieval Jewish scholars, and in Old Katamon the brigades who fought in Israel's War of Independence are honored with street names.

There are four towns in Israel that have functioning Old Cities dating from either biblical times (Jerusalem), the Crusader period (Akko and Jaffa), or the Middle Ages (Tzfat). Streets and alleys in these areas have names, but often not numbers.

GASOLINE

Gas stations are to be found at regular intervals along the country's major highways, except in the Negev. On highways they're generally always open, while those in the city tend to close at midnight. Prices are standardized, so it doesn't matter which station you choose. Most offer both full- and self-service pumps. If you go the full-service route, ask for a *kabbalah* (receipt). Attendants do not expect to be tipped. Most rental cars take unleaded gas, which at press time costs NIS 6.50 per liter. Most stations accept international credit cards.

PARKING

In Tel Aviv, Jerusalem, and Haifa parking laws are stringently enforced. Expect a ticket of NIS 150 on your windshield if you've overstayed your welcome at a paid parking spot. Cars will be towed if parked in a no-parking zone. Pay attention to the curb. Parking is forbidden where the curb is painted red. In downtown areas, parking is permitted only where there are blue and white stripes on the curb or where there are meters. Meters cost NIS 4.60 per hour and accept 5, 2, and 1 shekel coins. Pay-and-display cards may also be used and are for sale at post offices, kiosks, and lottery booths.

Sound complicated? Stick to parking lots. Covered and open parking lots are plentiful in the major cities, and cost NIS 15 per hour or NIS 70 per day.

RENTAL CARS

In Jerusalem, a combination of walking and taking cabs or a guide-driven tourist limo-van is often more time-effective—and, in the case of the former, more cost-effective—than a rental car. This has become especially true of late with the increase in traffic and the confusion caused by road construction. Exceptions are the more distant West Jerusalem sights and panoramic overlooks, which have plenty of free parking. On the east side, a rental car is often more of a bother than a boon, and cabs are the way to go.

Rental rates in Israel start at around $50 per day and $200 per week for an economy car with unlimited mileage. The cars here are generally smaller than similar American models and may be standard shift, not automatic. Minivans and four-wheel-drive vehicles are very popular and should be reserved well in advance, especially during high season.

Drivers must be at least 24 years old. Your own driver's license is acceptable in Israel, but an International Driver's Permit is still a good idea. This international permit is universally recognized, so having one in your wallet is extra insurance against problems with the local authorities.

Your insurance coverage does not extend to areas outside the borders of Israel. Most companies do not allow their cars to cross into the Palestinian Authority.

Rental Agencies Avis (☎ 800/638–4016). **Best** (☎ 800/220–015 ⊕ www.best-car.co.il). **Eldan** (☎ 800/938–5000 ⊕ www.eldan.co.il). **Sixt** (☎ 70/050–1502 In Israel ⊕ www.sixt.co.il).

ROAD CONDITIONS

Israel's highway system is very modern, and has signs in English as well as Hebrew and Arabic. Route 6, the main north–south toll road, can save significant time on longer journeys. The highway starts at the Maahaz Junction south of Kiryat Gat and ends about 75 km (50 mi) north at the Iron Junction between Hadera and Afula. Electronic sensors read your license plate number and transmit the bill, according to the distance you travel, to your rental-car company. Expect to pay around NIS 60 to drive the length of the highway.

Route 1 is the chief route to Jerusalem from both the west (Tel Aviv, Ben Gurion Airport, Mediterranean coast) and the east

(Galilee via Jordan Valley, Dead Sea area, Eilat). The road from Tel Aviv is a divided highway that presents no problems except at morning rush hour (7:30–9), when traffic backs up at the entrance to the city. For this reason, some drivers prefer Route 443—via Modi'in—which leaves Route 1 just east of the Ben Gurion Airport, and enters Jerusalem from the north (most convenient for East Jerusalem locations). Route 1, which enters Jerusalem under the new Bridge of Strings, is more convenient for Givat Ram, West Jerusalem, downtown, and Talbieh.

Jerusalem, Haifa, and Tel Aviv are all clogged with traffic during the workday. Many of Jerusalem's streets were not built to accommodate cars. Don't drive in the city center if you're not comfortable negotiating narrow spaces or parking in tight spots.

If you're driving through the Negev, watch out for camels that can come loping out of the desert and onto the road. In the winter rainy season, sudden flash floods sometimes cascade through the *wadis* (streambeds that are usually dry) with little warning, washing out roads. It's best to postpone your desert trip if there's heavy rain in the forecast.

The desert can be unbelievably hot, even in the winter. It's a good idea to carry extra water—both for yourself and for your car—while driving at any time of year.

ROADSIDE EMERGENCIES

In case of an accident or roadside emergency, call either the police or Shagrir, the national breakdown service. English-speaking assistance is generally available.

The local representative of AAA is Memsi. Should anything happen to your rental car, call your rental company for roadside repair or replacement of the vehicle.

Automobile Associations Memsi (☎ 03/564–1111 in Tel Aviv, 02/625–0661 in Jerusalem).

Emergency Services Police (☎ 100). **Shagrir** (☎ 03/557–8888).

RULES OF THE ROAD

More Israelis have been killed by car accidents than in all of the nation's wars combined. Use extra caution when driving a car in Israel. By law, drivers and all passengers must wear seat belts at all times. Don't drink and drive. Police crack down on drunk driving; the legal blood-alcohol limit is .05%. It's against the law to use a cell phone while driving.

Speed limits vary little across Israel: motorways (represented with blue signs) have speed limits of either 90 or 100 kph (56 or 62 mph). The exception is Route 6, where the limit is 110 kph (68 mph). Highways with green signs have speed limits of 80 or 90 kph (50 or 56 mph). Urban roads are 50 or 60 kph (31 or 37 mph).

Headlights must be turned on in daylight when driving on intercity roads from November through April 1. A flashing green traffic light indicates that the red stop light is about 3 seconds away and you should come to a halt.

Children ages nine and under must be seated in age-appropriate car seats, and children under 14 are not allowed in the front seat.

▌ LIGHT RAIL TRAVEL

Jerusalem's controversial new light rail is years behind schedule. The revised date for the opening of its first line is sometime in 2010, but at this writing the downtown area and arterial roads elsewhere along the route are a mess of construction. Once it's on track, the rail could serve visitors traveling from Downtown via the Central Bus Station to the area of Mt. Herzl in West Jerusalem. For an optimistic (but not updated) vision of the project, visit its Web site, *www.rakevetkala-jerusalem.org.il*.

▌ TAXI TRAVEL

Taxis are an affordable way to get around. If you need to get somewhere fast or are unfamiliar with the area, a taxi is your best bet, and you can hail one on the street or request one by phone. On the whole, drivers are knowledgeable, cheerful, and like to practice their English with tourists.

Taxis are white sedans with a yellow sign on the roof. The sign lights up to indicate availability. According to law, taxi drivers must use the meter (you need to be firm when you request this) unless you hire them for the day or for a trip out of town, for which there are set rates. If you're pressed to take the cab at a set price, you can ask your hotel staff for an estimate of the cost of your journey. In such a case, agree on the price before you begin the journey and assume that the driver has built in a tip. In the event of a serious problem with the driver, report his cab number (on the illuminated plastic sign on the roof) or license-plate number to the Ministry of Tourism or the Ministry of Transport.

Certain shared taxis or minivans have fixed rates and run fixed routes, such as from Tel Aviv to Haifa or from the airport to Jerusalem; such a taxi is called a *sherut* (as opposed to a "special," the term used for a private cab). Some sheruts can be booked in advance.

Eight- or ten-seat sheruts are also an option if you're coming to Jerusalem from Tel Aviv. They operate from outside Tel Aviv's New Central Bus Station seven days a week, departing when they fill up (fare NIS 20). They end their journey with stops opposite the Jerusalem Central Bus Station and near Zion Square in the downtown area. A "special" cab costs about NIS 270, with a 25% surcharge after 9 PM and on Saturday and holidays.

Taxi Contact Nesher (☎ *599/500–205; 02/625–3233 or 02/623–1231 in Jerusalem*).

Jerusalem Taxi Contacts Hapalmach (☎ *02/679–2333 or 02/679–3333*). **Hapisgah** (☎ *02/642–1111 or 02/642–3333 except on Sat.*). **Ha'ooma/Habira** (✉ *1 Harav Kook St., near Zion Sq., Downtown* ✉ *Central Bus Station, Romema* ☎ *02/538–9999*). **Rehavia** (☎ *02/625–4444 or 02/622–2444*). **Smadar** (☎ *02/566–4444*).

Eilat Taxi Contacts Taba (☎ *08/633–3339*). **London** (☎ *08/996–3789*). **Massada Taxis** (☎ *08/642–2222*). **Netz Taxis** (☎ *08/627–0808*).

▌ TRAIN TRAVEL

It takes 75 min to travel between Tel Aviv and Jerusalem by train. It's a good alternative at rush hour, but about 50 minutes slower than the bus at other times. It's a comfortable ride, and many just do it for fun, or for the attractive scenery. The train leaves the Malcha Station (near the big Jerusalem Mall) almost every hour, with a first stop close by at the Biblical Zoo. It terminates at Tel Aviv Savidor Station (popularly known as Arlozorov Street terminal), with connections to Haifa and the north. Service ends midafternoon on Friday (because of the Sabbath), and resumes about two hours after dark on Saturday. (A similar schedule applies to Jewish religious holidays.) The adult fare to or from Tel Aviv is NIS 20 one-way, and NIS 36 round-trip.

Other cities—including Ashkelon, Beersheva, Beit Shemesh, Haifa, Akko, and Nahariya—can reached by train, but with service geared more toward commuters.

There are no different classes of service. All carriages are clean, spacious, and comfortable with well-upholstered seats. Sandwiches, snacks, and cold drinks are always available.

All train stations post up-to-date schedules in English. Complete schedules are also available on the Web site of the Israel Railway Authority. Tickets may be purchased at the ticket office in the station. There's no train service on Saturdays or Jewish holidays.

Purchase your train tickets with cash or credit card at the station ticketing booth before you board.

Reservations are not accepted for train travel.

Information Israel Railways (☎ *03/577–4000 or *5770 from any phone in Israel* ⊕ *www.rail.co.il*).

ESSENTIALS

■ COMMUNICATIONS

INTERNET

Many hotels in Israel have connections for laptops, and larger hotels typically offer wireless access. Ask about the price, as some charge as much as $20 per day for the privilege. You can also find Internet access at the Tel Aviv and Jerusalem central bus stations and in many cafés. Jerusalem has free Wi-Fi Internet access in the downtown area, on Emek Refaim Street, and at Safra Square. Ben Gurion Aiport and the Eilat Airport also offer free Wi-Fi.

Contacts Cybercafes (⊕ *www.cybercafes. com*) lists over 4,000 Internet cafés worldwide.

PHONES

Israel's phone numbers have seven digits, except for certain special numbers that have four to six digits. Double-check the number if you don't get an answer. Toll-free numbers in Israel begin with 177, 1800, 1700, or 1888. When calling an out-of-town number within Israel, be sure to dial the zero that begins every area code.

The country code for Israel is 972. When dialing an Israeli number from abroad, drop the initial 0 from the local area code. The country code for Jordan is 962. When dialing from Israel, dial 00962 and the area code 3 before land line numbers in Petra; for Amman, use 00962 and the area code 6. When dialing within Jordan, add a 0 before the area code.

CALLING WITHIN ISRAEL

Making a local call in Israel is quite simple. All public telephones use phone cards that may be purchased at newspaper kiosks and post offices. Pick up the receiver, insert the card in the slot, dial the number when you hear the tone, and the number of units remaining on the card will appear on the screen. One unit equals two minutes.

The area codes for dialing between cities within Israel are Jerusalem (02); Tel Aviv (03); Netanya and Herzliya (09); Haifa, Galilee, Tiberias, Zfat, and Nazareth (04); Eilat and the Negev (08).

Pay phones are found in shopping malls, bus stations, gas stations, and at booths on main streets. On public phones, the number you're dialing appears on a digital readout; to its right is the number of units remaining on your card.

Dial 144 for directory or operator assistance. Operators all speak English. Dial 188 for an international operator.

CALLING OUTSIDE ISRAEL

When calling internationally direct from Israel, first dial the international access code and then the country code. The international access code for the United States and Canada is 001, and the country code for each is 1.

You can make international calls using a telecard from a public phone. A call from Israel to most countries costs about 25¢ per minute.

By dialing Israel's toll-free numbers (1800 or 177) and the number of your long-distance service, you can link up directly to an operator in your home country. This service works from all public phones and most hotel rooms.

Access Codes AT&T Direct (☎ *180/949–4949*). **MCI WorldPhone** (☎ *180/940–2727*). **Sprint International Access** (☎ *180/938–7000*).

MOBILE PHONES

If you have a multiband phone (some countries use different frequencies than what's used in the United States) and your service provider uses the world-standard GSM network (as do T-Mobile, Cingular, and Verizon), you can probably use your phone abroad. Roaming fees can be steep, however: 99¢ a minute is considered reasonable. And overseas you normally pay the toll charges for incoming calls.

It's almost always cheaper to send a text message than to make a call, since text messages have a very low set fee (often less than 5¢).

If you just want to make local calls, consider buying a new SIM card (note that your provider may have to unlock your phone for you to use a different SIM card) and a prepaid service plan in the destination. You'll then have a local number and can make local calls at local rates.

■**TIP➔** If you travel internationally frequently, save one of your old mobile phones or buy a cheap one on the Internet; ask your cell phone company to unlock it for you, and take it with you as a travel phone, buying a new SIM card with pay-as-you-go service in each destination.

It is significantly cheaper to rent a cell phone at Ben Gurion Airport than to use your cell phone from abroad. Rental booths are in the arrivals hall.

Several Israeli cell-phone rental companies offer tourists a phone for 65¢ per day. ATS offers free incoming calls; local calls inside Israel at 24¢ per minute and 33¢ per minute to the U.S. If you order the phone in advance, it will be waiting for you on the day of your arrival.

Contacts ATS (☎50/571–3972 ⊕ www.ats israel.com). **Cellular Abroad** (☎800/287–5072 ⊕ www.cellularabroad.com) rents and sells GMS phones and sells SIM cards that work in many countries.

Mobal (☎888/888–9162 ⊕ www.mobalren tal.com) rents mobiles and sells GSM phones (starting at $49) that will operate in 140 countries. Per-call rates vary throughout the world.

Planet Fone (☎888/988–4777 ⊕ www. planetfone.com) rents cell phones, but the per-minute rates are expensive.

■ CUSTOMS AND DUTIES

For visitors with nothing to declare, clearing customs at Ben Gurion Airport requires simply following the clearly marked green line in the baggage claims hall. Lines are generally short, with no more than a five-minute wait. Customs inspectors rarely examine luggage. The red line for those with items to declare is next to the green line. Those over 17 may import into Israel duty-free: 250 cigarettes or 250 grams of tobacco products; 2 liters of wine and 1 liter of spirits; ¼ liter of eau de cologne or perfume; and gifts totaling no more than $200 in value. You may also import up to 15 kg of food products, but no fresh meat.

Pets are not quarantined if you bring a certificate issued by a government veterinary officer in your country of origin issued within seven days prior to travel. The certificate must state that the animal has been vaccinated against rabies not more than a year and not less than one month prior to travel. Dogs and cats less than three months old will not be admitted. At least 48 hours prior to arrival, pet owners must send a fax to the Ramla Quarantine Section stating the name of the owner, animal species, age, flight number, and approximate arrival time.

Information in Israel Israel Customs Authority (☎02/666–3784 ⊕ www.mof.gov. il/customs/eng). **Ramla Quarantine Station** (☎03/968–8963 ☎03/960–5194).

U.S. Information U.S. Customs and Border Protection (⊕ www.cbp.gov).

■ EATING OUT

Seafood is a specialty in many restaurants in Eilat, Haifa, and Tel Aviv. Mediterranean dishes such as hummus and warmed pita bread are staples. A variety of skewered grilled meats accompanied by mounds of french fries and a salad of chopped tomatoes and cucumbers is served at neighborhood restaurants known as a *steakiya*. These days you can also sample just about any national cuisine you want—Thai, Italian, Indian, Chinese, French, Indonesian, Japanese, even American—in any of the larger cities.

While "kosher" once meant "boring," the number of inventive kosher restaurants is growing. Restaurants certified as kosher by the local rabbinate in every city are required to display a dated and signed Hebrew certificate. The weekend editions of the *Jerusalem Post* and *Ha Aretz* newspapers both carry extensive restaurant listings and note kosher restaurants.

MEALS AND MEALTIMES

Hotels serve a huge, buffet-style breakfast called *arukhat boker*, comprising a variety of breads and rolls, eggs, oatmeal, excellent yogurt, cheeses, vegetable and fish salads, and such American-style breakfast foods as pancakes and granola. You can find the same spread at many cafés. Outdoor coffee shops serving salads, sandwiches, cakes, and delicious coffee abound. Every city and small town has modestly priced restaurants that open in midmorning and serve soup, salad, and grilled meats.

Many restaurants offer business lunch specials or fixed-price menus, but à la carte menus are most common. A service charge (*sherut*) of 10%–15% is sometimes levied and should be noted separately on your bill.

Because Friday is not a workday for most Israelis, Thursday night is the big night out at the start of the weekend, when cafés and restaurants fill up quickly.

PAYING

Credit cards are widely accepted in restaurants, but always check first. Tips of between 12% and 15% can be paid in cash only. If you are dining in a smaller town or village, make sure you have sufficient cash with you, as credit cards are sometimes not accepted.

RESERVATIONS AND DRESS

Dress in Israeli restaurants is generally casual.

WINES, BEER AND SPIRITS

Wine has deep roots in Israeli culture. Israel is one of the earliest wine-producing areas in the world, and the symbol of Israel's Ministry of Tourism is a cluster of grapes borne on a pole by two men. Wineries built during the 19th century are still producing wine today, and a plethora of boutique wineries have sprung up in the past five years. Dalton, Ben Ami, Golan, and Carmel's Rothschild Series are good bets. As for spirits, those with a taste for Greek *ouzo* may enjoy the comparable, local *arak*. Sabra is a locally produced chocolate- and orange-flavored liqueur.

The local brews in Israel are Maccabi (lager) and Goldstar (bitter), while Carlsberg, Heineken, and Tuborg are popular imports. Beer is most commonly available by the bottle, but some bars serve it on draught.

▌ELECTRICITY

The electrical current in Israel is 220 volts, 50 cycles alternating current (AC); wall outlets take Continental-type plugs, with two round prongs.

If your appliances are dual-voltage, you'll need only an adapter. Don't use 110-volt outlets marked FOR SHAVERS ONLY for high-wattage appliances such as blow-dryers. Most laptops operate equally well on 110 and 220 volts and so require only an adapter.

▌EMERGENCIES

Israel has an extremely sophisticated emergency response system and a very high percentage of citizens who are trained medics. If you find yourself in any kind of medical or security emergency in a public place, the professional and citizen response will be instantaneous.

To obtain police assistance at any time, dial 100. For emergency ambulance service, run by Magen David Adom, dial 101. To report a fire, dial 102. Emergency calls are free at public phones.

MEDICAL CENTERS

Emergency rooms in major hospitals are on duty 24 hours a day in rotation; the schedule is published in the daily press. In an emergency, call Magen David Adom to find out which hospital is on duty that day for your specific need (orthopedic or gastric, for example). Be sure to take your passport with you. There will be a fee.

EILAT AND THE NEGEV
Two hospitals serve the Negev, Soroka in Beersheva, and Yoseftal in Eilat; both have English-speakers on staff. Each has a 24-hour emergency room (bring your insurance documents). Both may be approached for emergency dental problems.

JERUSALEM
The privately run Terem Emergency Care Center in Jerusalem offers first aid and full medical attention, 24 hours a day, at its Romema clinic, and more limited hours at its other two Jerusalem locations.

A private dental clinic offers emergency service Sunday and Monday 8–6, Tuesday–Thursday 8–8, and Friday 8–1. Call first: when the office is closed, the call is automatically transferred to an on-call dentist, who will treat urgent cases after hours.

The major hospitals in Jerusalem are Hadassah Ein Kerem, Sha'arei Zedek near Mt. Herzl, Bikur Holim downtown, and Hadassah Mt. Scopus.

PETRA
There is a private clinic in Wadi Musa next to the Arab Bank. The closest hospital is the Queen Rania Hospital, 7 km south of Wadi Musa. It has a 24-hour emergency service and English is spoken.

TEL AVIV
Ichilov Hospital, which is in north Tel Aviv, is about a 10-minute drive (depending on traffic) from the heart of downtown. They have a 24-hour emergency room. Be sure to bring your passport with you. You will be provided with all records in English for your insurance providers at home. If you need an ambulance, you can call 101 to reach Magen David Adom.

Foreign Embassies U.S. Embassy (⌷ *71 Hayarkon St., Tel Aviv* ☎ *03/519–7575).*

General Emergency Contacts Magen David Adom (⌷ *2 Alkalai St., Tel Aviv* ☎ *101 for emergencies; 02/652–3133 in Jerusalem; 03/546–0111 in Tel Aviv).*

Eilat and the Negev Hospital Contacts Soroka Hospital (Beersheva) (⌷ *Hanessi'im St.* ☎ *08/640–0111).* **Yoseftal Hospital (Eilat)** (⌷ *Yotam St.* ☎ *08/635–8011).*

Jerusalem Hospital Contacts Bikur Holim (⌷ *Strauss St., Downtown* ☎ *02/646–4111, 02/646–4113 emergency room).* **Hadassah Ein Kerem Hospital** (⌷ *Ein Kerem* ☎ *02/677–7111 (including emergency room), 02/677–9444 children's emergency room).* **Hadassah Mt. Scopus** (☎ *02/584–4111 or 02/584–4333).* **Sha'arei Zedek** (⌷ *Mt. Herzl* ☎ *02/655–5111, 02/655–5509 emergency room).* **Terem Emergency Care Center** (⌷ *Bet Yahav, 80 Yirmiyahu St., Romema* ☎ *1–599–520–520 general line, 02/509–3333 Romema main branch).*

Petra Hospital Contacts The Petra Medical Clinic (⌷ *Tourism St., next to the Arab Bank* ☎ *03/215–6694).* **Queen Rania Hospital** (⌷ *Queen Rania Rd.* ☎ *03/215–06345).*

Tel Aviv Hospital Contact Ichilov Hospital (⌷ *6 Weizmann St., Center City* ☎ *03/697–4444).*

∎ HEALTH

No vaccinations are required to visit Israel. The country has one of the world's most advanced health care systems. Most doctors at emergency clinics and hospitals in Israel speak English. Emergency and trauma care is among the best in the world.

It is safe to drink tap water and eat fresh produce after it's been washed, but take care when buying food from outdoor stands; make sure the food is hot and cooked in front of you. Imodium and Pepto-Bismol are available over the counter at every pharmacy.

Heat stroke and dehydration are real dangers if you're going to be outdoors for any length of time: a sun hat and sunblock are musts, as is plenty of bottled water (available even in the most remote places) to guard against dehydration. Take at least 1 liter per person for every hour you plan to be outside. Use sunscreen with SPF 30 or higher. Most supermarkets and pharmacies carry sunscreen in a wide range of SPFs, but it is much more expensive than in the United States.

U.S. brands of mosquito repellent with DEET are available in pharmacies and supermarkets. Wear light, long-sleeved clothing and long pants particularly at dusk when mosquitoes like to attack.

Yad Sarah is a nationwide voluntary organization that lends medical equipment and accessories such as wheelchairs, crutches, and canes. There is no charge, but a contribution is expected. It's open Sunday–Thursday 8–7 and Friday 8–noon. Equipment can be returned elsewhere in the country.

OVER-THE-COUNTER REMEDIES

At the pharmacy (*beit mirkachat*) it is very easy to find many of the same over-the-counter remedies as you would at home. Everyday pain relievers such as Tylenol and Advil are widely available. Medication can be obtained from pharmacies, which are plentiful. Fluent English is spoken in the majority of pharmacies. Locally produced medication is fairly inexpensive, but expect to pay more for drugs that are imported.

The daily press publishes the addresses of pharmacies on duty at night, on Saturday, and on holidays. This information is

also available from Magen David Adom. In Jerusalem, SuperPharm Nayot is open Sunday–Thursday 8:30 AM–midnight, Friday 8:30 AM–3 PM, and Saturday one hour after the Sabbath ends until midnight. Its downtown location has slightly shorter hours.

In Eilat, the Michlin Pharmacy will deliver to your hotel and is open Sunday–Thursday 8–2 and 4–8:30, Friday 8–3. Superpharm is open daily 9:30 AM–1 AM. There are also pharmacies in Arad, Beersheva, and Mitzpe Ramon. There are no 24-hour pharmacies in Petra.

Health Contacts Michlin Pharmacy (⊠ *Opposite Central Bus Station, Eilat* ☎ *08/637-2434*). **Modern Pharmacy** (⊠ *Tourism St., Petra* ☎ *03/215-6444*). **Petra Pharmacy** (⊠ *Tourism St.* ☎ *03/215-6999*). **SuperPharm** (⊠ *5 Burla St., Nayot, Jerusalem* ☎ *02/649-7555* ⊠ *3 Hahistadrut St., Downtown, Jerusalem* ☎ *02/624-6244* ⊠ *Kanion Mul Yam, Eilat* ☎ *08/634-0880*). **Yad Sarah** (⊠ *124 Herzl Blvd., Bet Hakerem* ☎ *02/644-4444*).

❙ HOURS OF OPERATION

Sunday is a regular workday in Israel. All government offices and most private offices and travel agencies are closed on Friday as well as for all Jewish religious holidays. Businesses are generally open by 8:30 AM in Israel.

Although hours can differ among banks, almost all open by 8:30 Sunday–Thursday. Most close at 12:30 and then reopen on Monday and Thursday from 4 to 7 PM. Banks are closed on Jewish religious holidays and on Friday and Saturday except in Muslim areas, where they're closed Friday only. In Christian areas they're open Saturday morning and closed Sunday.

Museums don't have a fixed closing day, so although they're usually open 10–6, and often on Saturday mornings, confirm the schedule before you go.

Most local pharmacies close at 7 PM. Large chain stores, such as Superpharm and Newpharm, are usually open until 10 PM. In most cities a few drugstores are open all night, on a rotating basis. Daily listings can be found in English-language newspapers.

Shops generally open at 9 or 9:30; neighborhood grocery stores usually open around 7. A few shops still close for a two- or three-hour siesta between 1 and 4. Most stores do not close before 7 PM; supermarkets are often open later, and in large cities, there are all-night supermarkets. Arab-owned stores usually open at 8 and close in late afternoon. Mall hours are 9:30–9:30 Sunday–Thursday. Friday, the malls that close for Shabbat shut down about two hours before sundown and reopen two hours after sunset on Saturday evening. Outside Jerusalem, some malls keep regular hours on Saturday, while others stay closed.

▮ MAIL

The post office does it all: handles regular and express letters, sends and receives faxes, accepts bill payments, sells phone cards and parking cards, handles money transfers, and offers quick-delivery service. Nearly every neighborhood has a post office, identified by a white racing deer on a red background. English is almost always spoken. The main branches are usually open from 8 until 6 or 7, and small offices are usually open Sunday–Tuesday and Thursday 8–12:30 and 3:30–6, Wednesday 8–1:30, and Friday 8–noon. In Muslim cities the post office is closed Friday, in Christian towns it's closed Sunday, and in Jericho it's closed Saturday.

It takes about 7–12 days for mail to reach the United States from Israel.

In mailing addresses, the abbreviation M.P. stands for Mobile Post (M.P. Gilboa, for example). You'll see this as part of the address in more rural areas.

Tourists who want to receive mail at a local post office should have it addressed to "Poste Restante" along with the name of the town. Such mail will be held for pickup free of charge for up to three months. Mail delivery from Israel is reliable.

SHIPPING PACKAGES

Most stores offer shipping to international destinations. If you choose to send your purchases home yourself, you'll find all the supplies you need at any local post office, but be prepared to wait in a long line for service. Be sure to bring picture ID with you. Boxes and labels are available in various sizes, and you may insure your package. Parcels are generally secure when mailed from Israel. To Canada and the United States, it takes approximately two weeks by air and up to three months by surface mail. Quicker, more expensive alternatives are FedEx and UPS.

Express Services EMS Service (☎ 03/538–5909 ⊕ www.israelpost.co.il). **FedEx** (☎ 1700/700–339 ⊕ www.fedex.com/il). **UPS** (☎ 1800/834–834 ⊕ www.ups.com/content/il/en/contact/index.html).

▮ MONEY

Israel is a moderately priced country compared to Western Europe, but it's more expensive than many of its Mediterranean neighbors. Tourist costs, calculated in dollars, are little affected by inflation. Prices are much the same throughout the country. To save money, try the excellent prepared food from supermarkets (buy local brands), take public transportation, eat your main meal at lunch, eat inexpensive local foods such as falafel, and stay at hotels with kitchen facilities and guest houses. Airfares are lowest in winter.

Sample prices: cup of coffee, NIS 10; falafel, NIS 10; beer at a bar, NIS 20; canned soft drink, NIS 10; hamburger at a fast-food restaurant, NIS 18; short taxi ride, about NIS 30–NIS 35; museum admission NIS 32; movie, NIS 35.

Prices throughout this guide are given for adults. Substantially reduced fees are almost always available for children, students, and senior citizens.

■ TIP→ Banks never have every foreign currency on hand, and it may take as long as a week to order. If you're planning to exchange funds before leaving home, don't wait till the last minute.

Currency Conversion Google (⊕ www. google.com). **Oanda.com** (⊕ www.oanda.com). **XE.com** (⊕ www.xe.com).

ATMS AND BANKS
Your own bank will probably charge a fee for using ATMs abroad; the foreign bank you use may also charge a fee. Nevertheless, you'll usually get a better rate of exchange at an ATM than you will at a currency-exchange office or even when changing money in a bank. And extracting funds as you need them is a safer option than carrying around a large amount of cash.

■ TIP→ PIN codes with more than four digits are not recognized at ATMs in many countries. If yours has five or more, remember to change it before you leave.

The main branches of all the banks—Hapoalim, Leumi, Discount, First International—are in Jerusalem's downtown area, but they are arguably the last resort for changing money. Several times a week they have morning hours only (different banks, different days), they give relatively low rates of exchange, and it usually involves waiting in line and having the clerk fill out paperwork.

Banks in the Negev towns and Eilat have their own hours and closing days, which vary. ATM machines (called "caspomats" in Israel) are generally not enclosed but rather installed in a wall, usually next to a bank.

The automated teller machine, known locally as a *kaspomat*, is very common in Israel. Look for machines that have stickers stating that they accept foreign credit cards or that have a PLUS, NYCE, or CIRRUS sign. All have instructions in English. Almost all ATMs now have protective shields around the keypad to prevent anyone seeing your PIN.

With a debit card, the ATM machine will give you the desired amount of shekels and your home account will be debited at the current exchange rate. Note that there may be a limit on how much money you are allowed to withdraw each day and that service charges are usually applied. Make sure you have enough cash in rural areas, villages, and small towns where ATM machines may be harder to find.

The banks and the exchange bureaus in the downtown Jerusalem and Jewish neighborhoods close early on Friday, and only reopen on Sunday morning.

CREDIT CARDS
Throughout this guide, the following abbreviations are used: **AE**, American Express; **DC**, Diners Club; **MC**, MasterCard; and **V**, Visa.

It's a good idea to inform your credit-card company before you travel, especially if you're going abroad and don't travel internationally very often. Otherwise, the credit-card company might put a hold on your card owing to unusual activity—not a good thing halfway through your trip. Record all your credit-card numbers—as well as the phone numbers to call if your cards are lost or stolen—in a safe place, so you're prepared should something go wrong. Both MasterCard and Visa have general numbers you can call (collect if you're abroad) if your card is lost, but you're better off calling the number of your issuing bank, since MasterCard and Visa usually just transfer you to your bank; your bank's number is usually printed on your card.

If you plan to use your credit card for cash advances, you'll need to apply for a PIN at least two weeks before your trip. Although it's usually cheaper (and safer) to use a credit card abroad for large purchases (so you can cancel payments or be reimbursed if there's a problem), note that some credit-card companies *and* the banks that issue them add substantial percentages to all foreign transactions, whether they're in a foreign currency or not. Check on these fees before leaving home, so there won't be any surprises when you get the bill.

■ TIP➔ Before you charge something, ask the merchant whether or not he or she plans to do a dynamic currency conversion (DCC). In such a transaction the credit-card *processor* (shop, restaurant, or hotel, not Visa or MasterCard) converts the currency and charges you in dollars. In most cases you'll pay the merchant a 3% fee for this service in addition to any credit-card company and issuing-bank foreign-transaction surcharges.

Dynamic currency conversion programs are becoming increasingly widespread. Merchants who participate in them are supposed to ask whether you want to be charged in dollars or the local currency, but they don't always do so. And even if they do offer you a choice, they may well avoid mentioning the additional surcharges. The good news is that you *do* have a choice. And if this practice really gets your goat, you can avoid it entirely thanks to American Express; with its cards, DCC simply isn't an option.

All hotels, restaurants, and shops accept major credit cards. Israelis use credit cards even for $5 purchases. Plastic is also accepted at banks for cash advances, although some banks will accept one card but none of the others. For cash advances using a Visa card, go to the Israel Discount Bank or Bank Leumi; with a MasterCard go to Bank Hapoalim or the United Mizrahi Branch. All of the credit-card companies give an exchange rate that can be up to 5% better than the rate commonly used by banks.

Before you leave home, you must have a Personal Identification Number (PIN) to withdraw cash while overseas. Even if you already have a PIN, check with your credit-card company to make sure that it will work in Israel. Again, the norm for PINs in Israel is four digits. If the PIN for your account has a different number of digits, you must change your number

before you leave for Israel. Most credit cards offer additional services, such as emergency assistance and insurance. Call and find out what additional coverage you have.

Reporting Lost Cards American Express (☎ 800/528–4800 in the U.S. or 336/393–1111 collect from abroad ⊕ www.americanex press.com). **Diners Club** (☎ 800/234–6377 in the U.S. or 303/799–1504 collect from abroad ⊕ www.dinersclub.com). **Master-Card** (☎ 800/627–8372 in the U.S. or 636/722–7111 collect from abroad ⊕ www. mastercard.com). **Visa** (☎ 800/847–2911 in the U.S. or 410/581–9994 collect from abroad ⊕ www.visa.com).

CURRENCY AND EXCHANGE

Israel's monetary unit is the New Israel Shekel, abbreviated NIS. There are 100 agorot to the shekel. The silver one-shekel coin is the size and shape of an American dime, but thicker. Smaller-value bronze coins are the half-shekel and the 10-agorot coin (both of which are larger than the shekel), and the less-used 5-agorot coin. There is also a 2-shekel round coin (silver); a 5-shekel hexagonal coin (silver), and a similar-size 10-shekel coin (bronze center, silver rim). Paper bills come in 20-, 50-, 100-, and 200-shekel denominations.

Dollars are widely accepted at hotels and shops—less so at restaurants. As of this writing, the exchange rate was about 3.80 shekels to the U.S dollar.

Banks charge a fee to exchange your money. In Israel, the best rates are at ATMs or at the myriad of currency-exchange shops (typically marked "Change") in and around the central areas of the large cities. In Jerusalem you'll find these around Zion Square and the Ben Yehuda Street open mall, inside Jaffa Gate, and at a few strategic locations elsewhere in the city (Jerusalem Mall, German Colony neighborhood, Jewish Quarter).

■ TIP➔ Even if a currency-exchange booth has a sign promising no commission, rest assured that there's some kind of huge, hidden fee. (Oh . . . that's right. The sign didn't say no *fee*.). And as for rates, you're almost always better off getting foreign currency at an ATM or exchanging money at a bank.

▌PACKING

Israel is a very casual country, and comfort comes first. For touring in the hot summer months, wear cool, easy-care clothing. If you're coming between May and September, you won't need a coat, but you should bring a sun hat that completely shades your face and neck. Take one sweater for cool nights, particularly in the hilly areas and the desert. Also take long pants to protect your legs and a spare pair of walking shoes for adventure travel. A raincoat with a zip-out lining is ideal for October to April, when the weather can get cold enough for snow (and is as likely to be warm enough in the south for outdoor swimming). Rain boots may also be a useful accessory in winter. Pack a bathing suit for all seasons. Note that many religious sites forbid shorts and sleeveless shirts for both sexes; and women should bring modest dress for general touring in religious neighborhoods.

Along with the sun hat, take plenty of sunscreen, insect repellent, and sunglasses in summer. Essentials such as contact-lens solution and feminine hygiene supplies are available everywhere, but are very expensive.

▌PASSPORTS AND VISAS

U.S. citizens, even infants, need only a valid passport to enter Israel for stays of up to 90 days. Make sure your passport is valid for at least six months after your travel date or you won't be permitted entry. No health certificate or inoculations are required.

Israel issues three-month tourist visas free of charge at the point of entry when a valid passport is presented. Some countries, particularly those in the Middle East, refuse to admit travelers whose passports carry an Israeli visa entry stamp. If you're concerned about regional mobility, you can ask the customs officer at your point of entry to issue a tourist visa on a separate piece of paper; you can also apply for a second passport and include a letter with the application explaining that you need the passport for travel to Israel. Be advised that it is not unheard of for Israeli customs officers to stamp passports despite requests not to do so; if you plan to travel repeatedly between Israel and those Arab states still hostile to Israel, a second passport is advisable.

Notarized consent from parents is required for children under 18 traveling alone, with one parent, or in someone else's custody.

▌RESTROOMS

Public restrooms are plentiful in Israel and similar in facilities and cleanliness to those in the United States. At gas stations and some parks, toilet paper is sometimes in short supply, so you might want to carry some with you. No public sinks, except those at hotels, have hot water, but most dispense liquid soap. Occasionally you may be asked to pay one shekel at some facilities.

Find a Loo The Bathroom Diaries (⊕ *www.thebathroomdiaries.com*) is flush with unsanitized info on restrooms the world over—each one located, reviewed, and rated.

▌SAFETY

For the latest governmental travel advisories regarding travel to and within Israel, check with the U.S. State Department. The Israel Ministry of Tourism includes a section in its Web site with a non-alarmist perspective on visiting Israel during periods of unrest. For the latest local news, check the English-language papers *Ha Aretz* or the *Jerusalem Post*, available online.

General Information and Warnings Israel Ministry of Tourism (⊕ *www.goisrael.com*).

U.S. Department of State (⊕ *www.travel. state.gov*).

On-line News Ha Aretz (⊕ *www.haaretzdaily. com*). Jerusalem Post (⊕ *www.jpost.com*).

▍TAXES

A Value-Added Tax is charged on all purchases and transactions except tourists' hotel bills and car rentals paid in foreign currency (cash, traveler's checks, or foreign credit cards). Upon departure, you are entitled to a refund of this tax on purchases made in foreign currency of more than $100 on one invoice; but the refund is not mandatory, and not all stores provide VAT return forms. Stores so organized display TAXVAT signs and give 5% discounts.

Keep your receipts and ask for a cash refund at Ben Gurion Airport. Change Place Ltd. has a special desk for this purpose in the duty-free area. If you leave from another departure point, the VAT refund will be sent to your home address.

As of this writing, Israel has no departure tax.

▍TIME

Israel is 2 hours ahead of Greenwich Mean Time. Normally, New York and Montréal are 7 hours behind, California is 10 behind. From late March until early September, Israel operates on Daylight Saving Time. When the Daylight Saving Times do not match, the time difference is reduced by one hour.

Time Zones Timeanddate.com (⊕ *www.time anddate.com/worldclock*).

▍TIPPING

There are no hard-and-fast rules for tipping in Israel. Taxi drivers do not expect tips, but a gratuity for good service is in order. If you have negotiated a price, assume the tip has been built in.

If a restaurant bill does not include service, 15% is expected—round up if the service was particularly good, down if it was dismal. Hotel bellboys should be tipped a lump sum of NIS 10–NIS 20, not per bag. Tipping is customary for tour guides, tour-bus drivers, and chauffeurs. Bus groups normally tip their guide NIS 20–NIS 25 per person per day, and half that for the driver. Private guides normally get tipped NIS 80–NIS 100 a day from the whole party. A small tip is expected by both the person who washes your hair and the stylist—except if one of them owns the salon. Leave NIS 10 per day for your hotel's housekeeping staff, and the same for spa personnel.

▍TOURS

SIGHTSEEING GUIDES

Guides are organized through tour companies and must be licensed by the Ministry of Tourism. Freelance guides may approach unaccompanied travelers near the Jaffa Gate in the Old City of Jerusalem. These guides are not licensed, so it's impossible to know whether the tour they're offering is worthwhile or if they're planning on taking you to the souvenir stall of their best friend. It's best to ignore them and walk on.

GUIDE-DRIVEN LIMOUSINES

Modern, air-conditioned limousines and minibuses driven by expert, licensed guides are not only a good value for a family, but also a great way to see the country for anyone whose budget can bear it. At this writing, the cost was $650 per day. An additional $150–$200 per night is charged for the driver's expenses if he or she sleeps away from home. Half-day tours are also available.

Contacts Guided Limousine Tours (☎ *03/642–1649* ⊕ *www.glt.co.il*). **Superb Limousine Services** (✉ *Ben Gurion Airport* ☎ *03/973–1780* ⊕ *www.superb.co.il*).

SPECIAL-INTEREST TOURS

ART

U.S.-based Gil Travel, which has an office in Tel Aviv, offers a nine-night tour for "art lovers, artists and friends." Recent itineraries include the latest exhibits at the country's top museums, studio visits with local artists, and a chance to take in the best of Israeli music, opera, and dance.

Contacts Gil Travel (☎ *03/642-1649* ⊕ *www.giltravel.com/special-art-lovers.html*).

BIKING

The Jerusalem Cyclists Club can give you advice about local conditions and recommend routes. They organize one-day tours from Jerusalem on occasional Saturdays. The Green Wheelers Mountain Biking Group offers Friday and Saturday tours in the Judean Hills, Carmel, and Galilee areas. For Saturday tours in Tel Aviv and Jaffa, try the Tel Aviv Bicycle Club. Walkways runs country-wide 7-, 10-, and 14-day trips with professional guides. These tours combine cycling and hiking along biblical paths around the Carmel area, the coastal plain, the Galilee, the Red Sea, the Sinai Desert, as well as Petra in Jordan. Walkways handles all logistics, including round-trip transfer to the airport.

■TIP→ Most airlines accommodate bikes as luggage, provided they're dismantled and boxed.

Contacts Green Wheelers Mountain Biking Group (☎ *054/944-539* ⊕ *www.geocities.com/Ron5506*). **Jerusalem Cyclists Club** (☎ *02/643-8386*). **Tel Aviv Biker's Association** (☎ *03/566-9667* ⊕ *bike.org.il/taba/page12e.html*). **Walkways** (☎ *02/534-4452* ⊕ *www.inisrael.com/walkways/main.htm*).

BIRD-WATCHING

Spring is the best time for bird-watching in Israel. Eilat, in southern Israel, hosts an annual Spring Migration Festival every March. The Kibbutz Lotan Center for Birdwatching offers three-day birdwatching tours for small groups during the winter and spring around Eilat and

Lotan. Many people report spotting more than 100 species.

Contacts Kibbutz Lotan Center for Bird-watching (☎ *08/635-6935*).

HIKING

Israel is a hiker's paradise. Terrains range from desert to forest to mountains. Israel Extreme can make up an itinerary for you, while Women Walkers arranges hiking tours of Israel exclusively for women.

The Society for the Protection of Nature in Israel, or SPNI, an important environmentalist lobby in Israel, runs a dozen regional "field schools" across the country, and conducts city walks and nature hikes, often trekking off the beaten path. SPNI no longer offers English-speaking tours, but for nature hikes, where the experience and the camaraderie often matter more than the explanations, you might want to consider it. Many tours are family-oriented, but require you to have your own vehicle.

Contacts Israel Extreme (☎ *052/647-8474* ⊕ *www.israelextreme.com*). **Society for the Protection of Nature in Israel** (☎ *03/638-8666* ⊕ *www.aspni.org*). **Woman Walkers** (⊕ *www.womenwalkers.com*).

JORDAN

Geographical Tours offers, among other services, three-day jeep tours of Jordan.

Contact Geographical Tours (✉ *Begin Rd. 82, Tel Aviv* ☎ *03/563-9000* ⊕ *www.geotours.co.il*).

WINE

See the Wines of Israel feature in Chapter 5.

Contacts Amiel Tours (☎ *03/538-8444* ⊕ *www.amiel.com*).

▌ VISITOR INFORMATION

The Israel Ministry of Tourism has a toll-free information line and Web site.

Contacts Israel Ministry of Tourism
(☎ 888/774-7723 ⊕ www.tourism.gov.il).
Israel Government Tourism Office (⊕ www.goisrael.com).

In the U.S. (✉ 800 2nd Ave., 16th fl.,
New York, NY ☎ 212/499-5650 ✉ 6380
Wilshire Blvd., Suite 1718, Los Angeles, CA
☎ 323/658-7463).

ONLINE TRAVEL TOOLS
Contacts Focus Multimedia Online
Magazine (⊕ www.focusmm.com.au/israel/
is_anamn.htm). Israel Ministry of Foreign
Affairs (⊕ www.mfa.gov.il). Israel National
Parks (⊕ www.parks.org.il/parkseng). Israel
Tourism Guide (⊕ www.index.co.il/tourism).
Knesset (⊕ www.knesset.gov.il/index.html).

INDEX

A

Aaronson, Aaron, *325*
Abouhav Synagogue, *415–416*
Absalom's Pillar, *100*
Acre. ⇨ *See* Akko
Ad Deir, *503*
Addresses, *522–523*
Adelina ✕, *346*
Agamin ⊤̄, *484*
Air travel. ⇨ *See* Plane travel
Akhziv Beach, *349*
Akko, *336–349*
Al-Aqsa Mosque, *78–80*
Albert Promenade, *458*
Alpaca Farm, *459, 4561*
Amirim Holiday Village ⊤̄,
  423
Ammonite Wall, *459*
Ancient Katzrin Park, *442–443*
Andromeda's Rock, *234–235*
Apartment and house rent-
  als, *29*
Aqua Sport International Red
  Sea Diving Center, *491*
Aquariums, *479–480*
Aqueduct (Akko region), *345*
Arad, *187–189*
Arava Road, *193*
Archaeology sites
  Akko, 342
  Avdat, 456
  Beit She'an, 366–367
  Benyamina, 336
  Bethsaida, 402
  Caesarea, 309–311
  digs, 469
  Eilat and the Negev, 456
  *Haifa and the Northern Coast,
    309–311, 321–322, 336, 342*
  Hammat Tiberias, 394–396
  Jericho, 174–175
  *Jerusalem, 62–63, 73, 84–85,
    91, 93, 100*
  *Jerusalem and the Dead Sea
    region, 174–177, 188–189,
    209*
  Katzrin, 442–443
  *lower Galilee, 360–361, 366–
    367, 394–396, 402*
  Megiddo, 360–361
  *Nahal Me'arot Nature Reserve,
    321–322*
  Qumran, 175–177
  Tel Arad, 188–189
  Tel Aviv, 233
  Tel Bet Shemesh, 204
  Tel Dan, 436
  Tel Hatzor, 428–429
  Tel Maresha, 207–208
  *upper Galilee and the Golan,
    428–429, 436, 442–443*
Archaeological seminars, *209*
Archery, *461*
Area G (excavation site), *93*

Aromantica ✕, *347*
Art galleries and museums
  Ein Hod, 319, 321
  *Haifa and the Northern Coast,
    294, 296, 297, 319, 321,
    334–335*
  *Jerusalem, 108, 110, 113, 115,
    159–160*
  South Bat Shlomo, 334–335
  *Tel Aviv, 223, 225, 227, 232,
    235*
  Tzfat (Safed) and environs, 416
  *upper Galilee and the Golan,
    416*
Art tours, *536*
Artists' Colony, *416*
Artists' retreats
  Ein Hod, 319–321
  Tzfat (Safed) and environs, 416
Arts. ⇨ *See* Nightlife and the
  arts
Astronomy tours, *468*
Atlit detention camp, *307, 309*
ATMs, *532*
Auberge Shulamit ✕, *427*
Avdat, *456*
Avenue of the Righteous, *109*
Azrieli Towers, *226*

B

Bab a-Siq, *502*
Baha'i Founder's Shrine and
  Gardens (Akko), *343*
Baha'i Shrine and Gardens
  (Haifa), *288, 292*
Banana Land (water park), *175*
Banias Nature Reserve,
  436–438
Banias Spring, *437*
Banias Cave, *437*
Banias Waterfall, *438*
Banking hours, *530*
Banks, *532*
Baptist Church (Nazareth), *370*
Bar Shva-esray (dance club),
  151
Bar Yochai, Rabbi Shimon,
  tomb of, *422*
Bar'am National Park, *424–425*
Bars and lounges
  Eilat and the Negev, 473, 489
  *Haifa and the Northern Coast,
    304–305*
  Jerusalem, 150–151
  Rosh Pina, 428
  *Tel Aviv, 265–266, 268, 269,
    271–273*
  *upper Galilee and the Golan,
    424*
Baseball, *277*
Basilica of the Agony, *94, 97*
Basilica of the Annunciation,
  370–372
Basketball, *435*

Bat Gamlin beaches, *305*
Bat Ha'ikar ✕, *316*
Bauhaus Foundation Museum,
  223
Beaches, *33, 35*
  Eilat and the Negev, 480, 491
  *Jerusalem and the Dead Sea
    region, 177–178, 186, 198,
    199*
  *Haifa and the Northern Coast,
    305, 307, 314–315, 318, 349*
  lower Galilee, 394, 404
  Tel Aviv, 275–276
  Tiberias, 394
Bed-and-breakfasts, *29*
Bedouin culture, *470–471, 474*
Bedouin life tours, *190, 468*
Beersheva, *470, 471–473, 475*
Beit Alfa, *365*
Beit Gordon, *406*
Beit She'an, *366–368*
Beit She'an National Park,
  366–367
Beit She'arim, *358, 360*
Beit Yannai beach, *318*
Belvoir fortress, *368–369*
Ben-Gurion, David
  desert home, 452–453
  grave site, 454
Benyamina, *335–336*
Benyamina Winery, *335*
Ben-Yehuda Street (Jerusalem),
  111
Bet Aaronson, *325*
Bet Bialik, *226*
Bet Guvrin, *207–209*
Bet Guvrin caves, *208*
Bet Shemesh, *204*
Bet Ticho, *113, 115*
Bet Ussishkin Museum, *436*
Bethlehem, *209–216*
Bethsaida, *402*
Betzet Beach, *349*
Bialik, Chaim Nachman, *226*
Bialik Street (Tel Aviv), *226*
Biankini Beach, *177*
Bible Lands Museum, *102*
Biblical life tours, *468*
Bicycling, *520*
  Eilat and the Negev, 461
  Jerusalem, 155
  mountain, 461
  tours, 536
Binyamin Pool, *325*
Bio Ramon, *457–458*
Bird-watching
  Eilat and the Negev, 469, 491
  tours, 469, 536
Blue Beach, *394*
Boat and ferry travel, *520–521*
  *Haifa and the Northern Coast,
    288*
Boating and sailing
  Eilat and the Negev, 491
  Kiryat Shmona, 433

Tel Aviv, 276
upper Galilee and the Golan,
  433
Bograshov Beach, *275*
Bridge of Strings, *105*
Broad Wall, *85*
Broken Pediment Tomb, *502*
Burnt House, *84*
Bus tours, *522*
Bus travel, *521–522*
Haifa and the Northern Coast,
  288
Business hours, *530–531*
Byzantine Church (Nahariya),
  346
Byzantine Church (Petra),
  502–503
Byzantine street (Caesarea),
  310

C

Caesarea, *309–315*
Caesarea Beach Club, *314*
Caesarea Museum of Antiqui-
  ties, *310–311*
Cafeneto ✕, *459*
Camel tours, *466*
Camping, *29*
Cana, *376–377*
Cana Wedding Church, *377*
Capernaum, *400–402*
Car rentals, *15, 523*
Car travel, *14, 522–524*
Jerusalem and the Dead Sea
  region, 187, 193
Cardo, *86*
Carmel Caves, *321–322*
Carmel Forest Spa Resort 🏨,
  301
Carmel Market, *223*
Carmel Wine Cellars, *333*
Carmelite Monastery (Haifa),
  294–295
Carmelite Monastery
  (Mukhraka), *323–324*
Caro Synagogue, *416*
Carpentry, *458–459*
Casemate Wall (Masada), *183*
Castles. ⇨ *See* Fortresses
Catacombs (Beit She'arim),
  358, 360
Caverns
Haifa and the Northern Coast,
  296, 321–322
Jerusalem and the Dead Sea
  region, 175–176, 178,
  202–204, 208
upper Galilee and the Golan,
  437
Cemeteries
Jerusalem, 99, 107, 110–111
Kibbutz Kinneret, 406
Tzfat (Safed) and environs, 417
Chagall, Marc, *102*
Chagall Windows, *102*
Chamber of the Holocaust, *88*
Children, activities for, *32–33*

Eilat and the Negev, 33, 455,
  459, 461, 470–471, 474,
  479–488, 485, 490, 492
Jerusalem, 32, 104–106, 108,
  127, 128, 130, 139, 141,
  144, 146
Jerusalem and the Dead Sea
  region, 175, 193, 199,
  200–201, 203
Haifa and the Northern Coast,
  33, 296–297, 307, 310–311,
  312, 313–314, 316, 321–322,
  342–343, 349, 350
lower Galilee, 362, 364–365,
  372–373, 385, 391, 404, 405
Tel Aviv, 32, 238
upper Galilee and the Golan,
  420, 421, 427–428, 436,
  442–443
Children's Memorial, *109*
Christian holidays, *215, 384*
Christian hospices, *29*
Christmas, *215*
Church of All Nations, *94, 97*
Church of Mary Magdalene, *99*
Church of St. Catherine, *210,*
  213
Church of St. Gabriel, *372*
Church of St. John the Baptist,
  110
Church of the Holy Sepulcher,
  62, 74–77
Church of the Multiplication,
  398
Church of the Nativity, *210–211*
Church of the Primacy of St.
  Peter, *398–399*
Church of the Transfiguration,
  385
Church of the Visitation, *110*
Churches. ⇨ *See also* Convents;
  Monasteries and abbeys
Bethlehem, 210–211, 213, 215
Cana, 377
Haifa and the Northern Coast,
  294–295, 346
Jerusalem, 62, 74–77, 82–83,
  94, 97, 99–100, 110, 154
Jerusalem and the Dead Sea
  region, 183, 200, 210–211,
  213, 215
Kursi, 402
Latrun, 200
lower Galilee, 370–372, 377,
  385, 398–399, 402
Masada, 183
Mount of Beatitudes, 399
Mt. Tabor, 385
music in, 154
Nahariya, 346
Nazareth, 370–372
Petra, 502–503
Tabgha, 398–399
Tel Aviv, 236
Citadel Park (Tzfat), *417*
Clandestine Immigration and
  Naval Museum, *295–296*

Cliff rappelling. ⇨ *See*
  Rappelling
Clock Tower Square (Jaffa), *235*
Colleges and universities,
  454–455
Colonnaded Street (Petra), *500*
Convents, *64, 82, 100*
Coral Beach Reserve, *480*
Coral World Underwater
  Observatory and Aquarium,
  479–480
Corinthian Tomb, *503*
Credit cards, *7, 532–533*
Crusader City, *310*
Crusader Vaults and Halls, *339*
Crypt of St. John, *342*
Currency exchange, *288, 532,*
  533–534
Customs, *527*

D

Daliyat el Carmel, *323*
Dan Eilat 🏨, *485*
Dance, *36*
Eilat and the Negev, 489
folk, 489
Jerusalem, 152
Tel Aviv, 230, 273
Dance clubs
Eilat and the Negev, 489
Haifa and the Northern Coast,
  349
Jerusalem, 151–152
lower Galilee, 393
Nahariya, 349
Tel Aviv, 265–266, 270,
  271–273
Tiberias, 393
Daniel Alsberg (shop), *164*
David, King, tomb of, *89*
David Citadel 🏨, *139*
David Intercontinental 🏨, *263*
Davidson Visitors Center, *63*
Dead Sea bath and beauty
  products, *199*
Dead sea, bathing in, *197*
Dead Sea region. ⇨ *See also*
  Jerusalem and the Dead Sea
  region
Dead Sea Scrolls, *104–106,*
  175–177
Degania, *405–406*
Degania Alef, *405–406*
Desert Home 🏨, *460*
Desert precautions, *448*
Desert Sculpture Park, *458*
Desert tours, *492*
Detention camp, *307, 309*
Diaspora Museum, *237*
Dining, *7, 15, 16, 30–31,*
  527–528. ⇨ *See also* Restau-
  rants; Under cities and areas
Diving. ⇨ *See* Scuba diving and
  snorkeling
Djinn Blocks, *503*
Dogs Beach, *276*
Dolphinarum Beach, *275*
Dome of the Rock, *62, 78–80*

Dominus Flevit Church, *99–100*
Dor Beach, *307*
Dormition Abbey, *88–89*
Druze people, *324*
Dudim (Lovers') Cave, *179*
Dugit Beach, *404*
Duties, *527*

E

Ecce Homo Convent of the Sisters of Zion, *64, 82*
Ecotourism, *469*
Eilat and the Negev, *12, 446–506*
beaches, *480, 491*
Beersheva and the northern Negev, *470–474, 475, 477*
border crossings, *499*
children, activities for, *33, 455, 459, 461, 470–471, 474, 479–488, 485, 490, 492*
Eilat and environs, *477–493*
emergencies, *529*
festivals, *490*
guided tours, *460, 465–469, 492, 498*
heart of the Negev, *451–461, 470–477*
hotels, *449, 454–455, 460–461, 473, 484–489, 505–506*
money matters, *409*
nightlife and the arts, *473, 489–490, 506*
orientation, *447*
outdoor activities and sports, *461, 465–469, 490–492*
Petra and environs, *496–506*
price categories, *449, 499*
restaurants, *449, 454, 459–460, 472, 481–484, 505*
safety and precautions, *448*
shopping, *461, 473, 475, 493*
timing the visit, *448, 449, 498, 499*
transportation, *448, 498*
visitor information, *449, 498*
Ein Avdat, *455*
Ein Avdat National Park, *455*
Ein Avdat Observation Point, *455*
Ein Bokek, *189–193, 199–200*
Ein Camonim ✕, *419*
Ein Gedi, *178–179, 186–187*
Ein Gedi Spa, *186*
Ein Hod, *319–321*
Ein Kerem, *102, 104*
Ein Kiniya, *441*
Einot Zukim, *177*
Electoral system of Israel, *106*
El-Jazzar Mosque, *339–340*
Electricity, *528*
Elijah's Cave, *296*
Ella Valley, *206–207*
El-Mahmoudiye Mosque, *235*
Emergencies, *528–529*
and car travel, *524*
Eretz Israel Museum, *237–238*

Eshkol, Levi, *107*
Ethnography Center of Acre, *340*
Ethiopian Monastery, *82*
Etiquette for visitors, *16–17, 384*

F

Festivals and seasonal events
Eilat and the Negev, 490
Ginosar, 397
Jerusalem, 153
lower Galilee, 355, 366, 394, 397, 404
Tel Aviv, 230
Tiberias, 294
Tzfat (Safed) and environs, 421
upper Galilee and the Golan, 421
Film, *37*
Haifa and the Northern Coast, 305
Jerusalem, 153
First Aliya Museum, *325, 333*
Flea Market (Tel Aviv), *232–233*
Folk dancing, *489*
Folk-music clubs, *152, 489*
Football, *277*
Fortresses
lower Galilee, 368–369
upper Galilee and the Golan, 438, 440
Founders' Monument and Fountain, *226*

G

Galei Galil Beach, *349*
Galilee region. ⇨ *See* Lower Galilee; Upper Galilee and the Golan
Gallerina, *334–335*
Gallery, The, *321*
Gamla Nature Reserve, *444*
Gan-Garoo, *364–365*
Gan Hashelosha National Park, *364*
Gan Meir (Tel Aviv), *226*
Ganei Yehoshua (Hayarkon Park), *238*
Garden of Gethsemane, *94, 97*
Garden Tomb, *97*
Gardens
Akko, 343
Haifa and the Northern Coast, 288, 292, 343
Jerusalem, 94, 97
Gas stations, *523*
General Exhibition (Tzfat), *416*
German Colony (Haifa), *292–294*
German Colony (Jerusalem), *113, 129, 145–146*
Ghetto Fighters Museum, *343*
Ginger Asian Kitchen and Bar ✕, *481–482*
Ginosar, *396–397*

Glass Museum, *188*
Golan Archaeological Museum, *442*
Golan Beach, *404*
Golan Heights, *436–444.* ⇨*See also* Upper Galilee and the Golan
Golan Heights Winery, *443*
Golani Junction, *377*
Golf, *315*
Golgotha, *75*
Gordon Beach, *275*
Great Temple, *500*
Greek sites and artifacts, *437*
Grotto of the Nativity, *211*
Grottoes of Rosh Hanikra, *350*
Guides, *535–536*
Gutmann, Nahum, *231–232*
Gutmann Museum, *231–232*

H

Ha'Ari Synagogue, *416–417*
Haas Promenade (Jerusalem), *115*
Ha'atzmaut Square (Netanya), *315*
Habimah National Theater, *226–227*
Hadassah Hospital, *102*
Haggay Observation Point, *452*
Hai Bar Nature Reserve, *494*
Haifa and the Northern Coast, *12, 282–350*
Akko to Rosh Hanikra, 336–350
banks and exchanging services, 288
beaches, 305, 307, 314–315, 318, 349
children, activities for, 33, 296–297, 307, 310–311, 312, 313–314, 316, 321–322, 342–343, 349, 350
guided tours, 309, 322, 346
history, 293, 337
hotels, 285, 301, 303–304, 307, 313–314, 317, 320, 334, 344–345, 347–349
internet, 288
medical assistance, 288, 315, 346
nightlife and the arts, 304–305, 321
orientation, 283
outdoor activities and sports, 305–306, 307, 312–313, 314–315, 318, 322, 345, 349
price categories, 285
restaurants, 285, 298–301, 307, 312–313, 316, 319–320, 322, 323, 333–334, 343–344, 346–347, 350
safety and precautions, 337
shopping, 306, 318, 321, 323, 345
timing the visit, 284, 285, 337

transportation, *284, 288, 306, 319, 322, 323, 325, 337*
visitor information, *288, 315, 325, 339, 346*
Wine Country and Mt. Carmel, 318–336
Haifa Museum of Art, *296*
Haifa Zoo, *296–297*
Hameiri House, *417*
Hametzizim Beach, *275*
Hameyasdim, *325*
Hammat Gader, *404–405*
Hammat Tiberias, *394–396*
Haram Esh-Sharif, *62, 72–73, 80*
Harmony ⊤̄, *134, 136*
Hatzor Hayain Wine Bar, *473*
Hatzor Museum, *429*
Hayarkon Park, *238*
Health and fitness clubs
Jerusalem, *155*
Tel Aviv, *276*
Health concerns, *529–530*
Hebrew language, *507–512*
Hecht Museum, *297*
Helena ✕, *312–313*
Helena Rubinstein Pavilion, *227*
Herb Farm on Mount Gilboa ✕, *365*
Hermon River (Banias) **Nature Reserve,** *436–438*
Herod, King, *84–85, 174, 181*
Herodian amphitheater, *309–310*
Herodian Quarter, *84–85*
Herod's Palace ⊤̄, *486*
Herod's port, *310, 311*
Herzl, Theodor, *107*
Herzl Museum, *107*
Herzog, Chaim, *107*
Hezekiah's Tunnel, *90–91*
Hidden Waterfall, *179*
High Place of Sacrifice, *503*
Hiking
Eilat and the Negev Desert, *461, 465*
lower Galilee, *384*
tours, *536*
Hilton Beach, *275*
Hinnom Valley, *115–116*
Hisham's Palace, *174–175*
History
of Haifa and the Northern Coast, *293, 337*
of Israel, *48–52, 380–381*
of Jerusalem, *85, 95*
of Tel Aviv, *227*
of Tiberias, *388*
Hod Hamidbar ⊤̄, *192*
Hof HaShaket Beach, *305*
Hof Shonit Beach, *314*
Holidays, *38–40*
Christian, *215, 384*
cuisine for, *122–123*
Holocaust History Museum, *108*
Holocaust memorials, *88, 108–110*

Holy Sepulcher Church, *62, 74–77*
Horse Square (Petra), *500*
Horseback riding
Eilat and the Negev, *492*
Heifa and the Northern Coast, *318*
Jerusalem, *155*
upper Galilee and the Golan, *424*
Hospitality visits, *489*
Hot springs
Hammat Gader, *405*
Hammat Tiberias, *396*
Hotel Montefiore ⊤̄, *259*
Hotels, *7, 15, 29*
price categories, *15, 57, 134, 169, 221, 256, 355, 411, 449, 499*
House rentals, *29*
Hula Nature Reserve, *429–430*

I

Ice-skating, *435*
Ilana Goor Museum, *235*
Ima ✕, *126–127*
Inbal ⊤̄, *139*
Independence Hall Museum, *223, 225*
Independence Park, *116*
Inn of the Good Samaritan, *171*
International Birding and Research Center, *491*
Internet, *288, 526*
Isfiya, *322*
Israel Air Force Museum, *475*
Israel Bible Museum, *417–418*
Israel Museum, *104–106*
Israeli folk dancing, *489*
Itineraries, *41–46*

J

Jaffa, *232–236, 250, 252*
Jaffa Port, *233*
Janco-Dada Museum, *319*
Jazz clubs, *152*
Jeep tours, *424, 461, 466, 536*
Jericho, *172, 174–175*
Jerusalem, *12, 54–164*
cafés, *131*
Center City, *111–116, 119, 124–129, 134, 136–138*
children, activities for, *32, 104–106, 108, 127, 128, 130, 139, 141, 144, 146*
City of David, *90–91, 93*
emergencies, *529*
exploring, *59–116*
festivals, *153*
German Colony, *113, 129, 145–146*
guided tours, *92*
Hebron Road and environs, *145–146*
history, *85, 95*
holy places, *66–81*

hotels, *57, 133–149*
Jewish Quarter, *83–86*
Mount of Olives and East Jerusalem, *94, 97, 99–101, 147–149*
nightlife and the arts, *149–154*
Old City, *59–62, 82–83, 129–130, 147*
orientation, *55*
outdoor activities and sports, *155–157*
price categories, *57, 117, 134*
restaurants, *57, 117–133*
safety and precautions, *57*
Seam Line, *147–149*
shopping, *157–164*
street markets, *159*
Talbieh and King David Street, *130, 132–133, 138–141*
timing the visit, *56, 57*
Tower of David and Mt. Zion, *86–89*
transportation, *56*
visitor information, *56*
West Jerusalem, *101–111, 133, 141, 143–144*
Jerusalem and the Dead Sea region, *12, 166–216*
beaches and pools, *177–178, 186, 198, 199*
Bethlehem, *209–216*
children, activities for, *175, 193, 199, 200–201, 203*
guided tours, *169, 190*
hotels, *169, 187, 189, 191–193, 199, 203–204, 215–216*
Masada and the Dead Sea, *171–200*
orientation, *167*
outdoor activities and sports, *199*
price categories, *169*
restaurants, *169, 175, 186–187, 189, 190–191, 202, 215*
safety and precautions, *172, 175, 178, 210*
shopping, *199–200, 204, 216*
timing the visit, *168, 169*
transportation, *168*
West Bank, *212*
West of Jerusalem, *200–209*
Jerusalem Archaeological Park, *62–63, 73*
Jerusalem Beach, *275*
Jesus, sites associated with
Bethlehem, *209, 211, 213*
Cana, *376*
Capernaum, *400–402*
Ginosar, *396–397*
Jericho, *172*
Jerusalem, *62, 63–64, 65, 74–77, 87–88, 97*
Jerusalem and the Dead Sea region, *172, 209, 211, 213*
Kursi, *402–403*
lower Galilee, *369–373, 376, 377–386, 396–397, 398–399, 400–402*

Mount of Beatitudes, 399
Mt. Tabor, 377, 385
Nazareth, 369–373
Tabgha, 398–399
Jewish cemetery (Jerusalem), 99
Jewish shrines. ⇨ *See also*
  Synagogues
Bethlehem, 213, 215
Haifa and the Northern Coast, 296
Jerusalem, 62, 63–64, 70–71, 74–77
Mt. Meron, 422
upper Galilee and the Golan, 422
Jezreel and Jordan Valleys, 357–369
Jogging, 394
Jordan, tours of, 536
Jordan River, 402

K

Kabbalah, 415
Kafriat Shaket, 475
Kalia Beach, 177
Katzrin, 442–444
Kayaking
  lower Galilee, 402
  upper Galilee and the Golan, 434
Kedumim Square (Tel Aviv), 233
Kfar Kama, 386
Kfar Tavor, 385
Khazneh monument, 500
Kibbutz guest houses, 29
Kibbutz Kinneret Cemetery, 406
Kibbutz life, 363
Kibbutz Lochamei Hagetao't, 343
Kibbutz Mitzpe Shalem, 178
Kibbutz Sde Boker, 452–453
Kibbutzim, history of, 363
Kidron Valley, 100
Kikar Hameginim, 418
Kikar Magen David (Tel Aviv), 227–228
King Albert Square (Tel Aviv), 228
King Solomon's Palace 🍽️, 487
Kings City, 480
Kinneret, 397, 405–406
Kinneret Swim, 394
Kiryat Sanz Beach, 318
Kiryat Shmona, 430, 432–434
Klezmer Festival, 421
Knesset, 106–107
Kochav Hayarden National Park, 368
Korazim, 399–400
Kursi, 403–404

L

L.A. Mayer Museum for Islamic Art, 110
La Crepe Jacob ✕, 347

Language, 16–17
  Hebrew vocabulary, 507–512
  Palestinian Arabic vocabulary, 513–517
Last Refuge ✕, 482
Last Supper, Room of, 87–88
Latrun, 200–202
Latrun Armored Corps Museum, 200–201
Le Meridien (Eilat) 🍽️, 487
Le Meridien (Ein Bokek) 🍽️, 192–193
Light rail travel, 524
Limousine tours, 535
Lion Monument, 503
Little Jerusalem ✕, 127
Lochamei Hageta'ot, 343
Lodging, 7, 15, 28. ⇨ *See also*
  Hotels
Lovers' Cave, 179
Lower Galilee, 12, 352–406
  beaches, 394, 404
  children activities for, 362, 364–365, 372–373, 385, 391, 404, 405
  festivals and seasonal events, 355, 366, 394, 397, 404
  guided tours, 382–383
  hotels, 355, 366, 368, 374–375, 390–393, 400, 403–404, 405
  Jezreel and Jordan Valleys, 357–369
  Nazareth and the Galilee Hills, 369–386
  nightlife and the arts, 393
  orientation, 353
  outdoor activities and sports, 384, 394, 402
  price categories, 355
  restaurants, 355, 365, 373, 385, 389–390, 403
  shopping, 394
  Tiberias and the Sea of Galilee, 386–406
  timing the visit, 354, 355
  transportation, 354, 384
  walking tours, 354, 366
Lunagal (water park), 404

M

Ma'alot Olei Hagardom, 418
Ma'ayan Harod, 362
Machaneh Yehuda, 111–112, 159
Mail and shipping, 332, 531
Maimonides, Moses, 388
Makhtesh Ramon, 457–461
Manara Cable Car, 430
Mané Katz Museum, 297
Manger Square, 213
Mann Auditorium, 228
Marketplace (Daliyat el Carmel), 323
Markets, 34
  Akko, 342
  Jerusalem, 159
  Nazareth, 373

Tel Aviv, 232–233, 280
Mary, Virgin
  birthplace, 375–376
  Magnificat site, 110
  tomb, 100–101
Marzipan Museum, 385
Masada, 171–200
Mashabim Junction, 452
Me'a She'arim, 116
Meal plans, 7
Megiddo, 360–361
Meir, Golda, 107
Meir Ba'al Ha-Ness, Rabbi, tomb of, 396
Merom Golan, 441
Messa ✕, 247
Metulla, 434–435
Mikhmoret beach, 318
Mikveh (Masada), 183
Military Cemetery, 110–111
Mineral Beach, 178
Mineral pools, 177–178, 186
Mini Israel, 201
Mitzpe Gadot, 444
Mitzpe Ramon, 457–461
Mitzpe Revivim, 451–452
Mona ✕, 127
Monasteries and abbeys
  Daliyat el Carmel, 323–324
  Haifa and the Northern Coast, 294–295, 323–324
  Jerusalem, 82, 88–89
  Jerusalem and the Dead Sea region, 200
  Kursi, 403
  Latrun, 200
  lower Galilee, 403
  Petra, 503
  Tel Aviv, 233–234
Money matters, 17, 531–534
  Eilat and the Negev, 409
Montefiore's Windmill, 112–113
Mosques
  Akko, 339–340
  Jerusalem, 78–80
  Tel Aviv, 235
Mt. Bental Observatory, 441–442
Mt. Gilboa, 361–362, 364–366
Mt. Hermon, 440–441
Mt. Herzl National Memorial Park, 107
Mt. Herzl Military Cemetery, 110–111
Mt. Meron, 422–424
Mount of Beatitudes, 399
Mount of Olives, 94, 97, 99–101
Mount of Olives Observation Point, 97, 99
Mount of Temptation, 174
Mt. Tabor, 387, 385–386
Mt. Yoash, 495–496
Mt. Zion, 86–89
Muhammad, Prophet, 78–79
Mukhraka, 323–324

Museum of Bedouin Culture, 470–471
Museum of Hungarian Speaking Jewry, 418
Museum of the Underground Prisoners, 340–341
Museums. ⇨ *See also* Art galleries and museums
Aaronson, 325
Air Force, 475
in Akko, 340–341, 343
archaeology, 63, 84, 88, 99, 102, 104–106, 182, 297, 307, 310–311, 406, 429, 442
Bedouin culture, 470–471
Bible, 417–418
in Caesarea, 310–311
in Degania Alef, 406
Diaspora, 237
in Eilat and the Negev, 470–471, 475, 503
in Ein Hod, 319, 321
ethnography, 340
farming, 432
glass, 188
in Haifa and the Northern Coast, 294–295, 296, 297, 298, 307, 319, 321, 325, 333, 334–335, 340–341, 343
Herzl, 107
Holocaust, 88, 108–110
hours, 530
Hungarian Jewry, 418
immigrants to Palestine, 294–295, 325, 333
Israeli history, 237–238, 239, 294–295, 325
Israeli independence, 223, 225
in Jerusalem, 63, 84, 88, 99, 102, 104–106, 107, 108–110, 113, 115
in Jerusalem and the Dead Sea region, 182, 188, 200–201
Jerusalem history, 84, 88, 99
in Katzrin, 442
in Kiryat Shmona, 432
in lower Galilee, 385, 406
maritime history, 294–295, 297
marzipan, 385
military, 200–201
in Mt. Tabor, 385
in Nahsholim-Dor, 307
natural history, 406, 436
in Petra, 503
prison, 340–341
Roman artifacts, 310–311
in Rosh Pina, 426
science, 297
in South Bat Shlomo, 334–335
in Tel Aviv, 223, 225, 227, 231–232, 235, 237–238, 239
in Tel Dan, 436
in Tel Hatzor, 429
in Tzfat (Safed) and environs, 416, 417–418
Tzfat (Safed) history, 417

in upper Galilee and the Golan, 416, 417–418, 426, 429, 432, 436, 442
Warsaw Ghetto uprising, 343
in Zichron Ya'akov, 325, 333
Music, classical, 36
Eilat and the Negev, 473, 490
festivals, 397, 404, 490
Ginosar, 397
Haifa and the Northern Coast, 305, 321
Jerusalem, 153–154
Kiryat Shmona, 432
lower Galilee, 368, 397
Tel Aviv, 274
upper Galilee and the Golan, 432
Music, popular, 36–37. ⇨ *See also* Dance clubs; Folk-music clubs; Jazz clubs
Muza ✕, 189

N

Nahal Ayoun Nature Reserve, 435
Nahal David, 178–179
Nahal Me'arot Nature Reserve, 321–322
Nahalat Binyamin Pedestrian Mall, 225
Nahalat Shiva, 113
Nahariya, 345–349
Nahsholim-Dor, 306–307, 309
Nahsholim-Dor Museum, 307
National Maritime Museum, 297
National Museum of Science and Technology (Technoda), 297
National Reserves Authority, 322
National Solar Energy Center, 454
National Water Carrier, 397
Nature reserves
Eilat and the Negev, 480, 494
Haifa and the Northern Coast, 321–322
Jerusalem and the Dead Sea region, 178–179
upper Galilee and the Golan, 429–430, 435–438, 444
Naturescent (shop), 461
Nazareth, 369–375
Nazareth Village, 372–373
Negev Brigade Memorial, 475
Negev Desert. ⇨ *See* Eilat and the Negev
Neot Kedumim, 202
Netanya, 315–318
Neve Midbar Beach, 178
Neve Midbar spa, 472
Nightlife and the arts, 36–37
Nimrod's Fortress, 438, 440
North Beach, 491

Northern Coast. ⇨ *See* Haifa and the Northern Coast
Number 7 *Simtat Plonit*, 229–230
Number 23 *Yefet Street*, 236
Nymphaeum fountain, 503

O

Obelisks, 503
Observatory Tower, 480
Off-road vehicles, 434
Ohel Ya'akov, 325
Old Caesarea Diving Center, 315
Old Rosh Pina office, 426
Opera, 37, 274
Outdoor activities and sports. ⇨ *See* specific sports; under cities and areas

P

Packing for the trip, 534
Palace Tomb, 504
Palaces
Jericho, 174–175
Masada, 183
Palestinian Arabic language, 513–517
Palmach Museum, 239
Pan, 437
Paragliding, 318
Parks, national
Eilat and the Negev, 455
Jerusalem, 107
Jerusalem and the Dead Sea region, 207–208
lower Galilee, 358, 360–361, 362, 364, 366–367, 368–369, 394–396, 399–400
upper Galilee and the Golan, 424–425
Passports, 534
Pater Noster Convent, 100
Peki'in, 424
Performing arts, 36–37
Petra, 496–506
emergencies, 529
Pisan Harbor, 341
Pivko Village ✕, 348–349
Plane travel, 519–520
Pools of Bethesda, 82–83
Precautions. ⇨ *See* Desert precautions; Safety and precautions
Predator Center, 494
Prehistoric cultures
Carmel Caves, 321–322
Megiddo, 360–361
Price categories
dining, 15, 57, 117, 169, 221, 239, 285, 355, 411, 449, 499
Eilat and the Negev, 449, 499
Haifa and the Northern Coast, 285
Jerusalem, 57, 117, 134

Jerusalem and the Dead Sea region, 169
lodging, *15, 57, 134, 169, 221, 256, 285, 355, 411, 449, 499*
lower Galilee, 355
Petra, 499
Tel Aviv, 221, 239, 256
upper Galilee and the Golan, 411
Princess ⌐, *488*
Pubs
Jerusalem, 150
Katzrin, 444
Rosh Pina, 428
Pundak Ha Dov (bar), *305*

Q

Qasr al-Bint, *500, 502*
Qumran, *175–178*

R

Rabin, Yitzhak, *228–229*
Rabin Square (Tel Aviv), *228–229*
Rachel's Tomb, *213, 215*
Ralli Museum, *311*
Ramparts, The (Akko), *341–342*
Ramparts Walk (Jerusalem), *87*
Rappelling, *461, 492*
Refectory (Akko), *342*
Renaissance Tomb, *504*
Renne ✕, *301*
Restaurants, *7, 15, 16, 30–31, 527–528.* ⇨ *See* under cities and areas
price categories, *15, 57, 117, 169, 221, 239, 285, 355, 411, 449, 499*
Restrooms, *534*
Robinson's Arch, *63*
Rockefeller Museum of Archaeology, *99*
Rokach House, *232*
Roman aqueduct (Caesarea), *311, 314–315*
Roman Catholic church, *399*
Roman Inn ⌐, *460*
Roman sites and artifacts
Avdat, 456
Beit She'an, 367
Benyamina, 336
Caesarea, 309–311, 313
Eilat and the Negev, 456, 500, 504
Gamla, 444
Haifa and the Northern Coast, 309–311, 336
Jerusalem, 84, 85, 100
Jerusalem and the Dead Sea region, 182, 183, 208
lower Galilee, 367, 375–376
Masada, 182, 183
Petra, 500, 504
upper Galilee and the Golan, 444
Zippori, 375–376

Roman Camps, *182, 183*
Roman Soldier's Tomb, *504*
Roman theater (Beit She'an), *367, 368*
Roman theater (Benyamina), *336*
Roman theater (Caesarea), *309*
Roman theater (Petra), *502*
Roman theater (Zippori), *375–376*
Room of the Last Supper, *87–88*
Rosh Hanikra, *336, 350*
Rosh Pina, *425–428*
Rothschild Boulevard (Tel Aviv), *225*
Royal Beach ⌐, *488*
Rubin Museum, *225*
Rubin, Reuven, *225*
Running and jogging, *394*

S

Safed. ⇨ *See* Tzfat (Safed) and environs
Safety and precautions, *17, 534–535*
Eilat and the Negev, 448
Haifa and the Northern Coast, 337
Jerusalem, 57
Jerusalem and the Dead Sea region, 172, 175, 178, 210
Sailing. ⇨*See* Boating and sailing
St. Anne's Church, *82–83*
St. Gabriel's Church, *372*
St. John, Crypt of, *342*
St. Peter's Monastery, *233–234*
San Antonio Roman Catholic Church, *236*
Santahanna apse, *208*
Sara's Gift Shop, *306*
Saul, King, *362*
Schwartz Hotel, *426*
Scots Hotel ⌐, *392*
Scuba diving and snorkeling
Caesorea, 315
Eilat and the Negev, 491, 492
Haifa and the Northern Coast, 315, 349
Nahariya, 349
Sde Boker College, *454–455*
Sea View (Mitzpe Hayamin) ⌐, *420*
Seaside Promenade (Netanya), *316*
Sermon on the Mount, site of, *399*
Shalvata ✕, *253*
Shapira Quarter (Tel Aviv), *230*
Shazar, Zalman, *107*
Sheinkin Street (Tel Aviv), *229*
Shepards' Fields, *215*
Sheraton Tel Aviv Hotel and Towers ⌐, *262*
Shopping, *17, 34.* ⇨ *See also* under cities and areas
hours, *531*

Sidonian Burial Caves, *208*
Silk Tomb, *504*
Simtat Plonit (Tel Aviv), *229–230*
Siq, *502*
Sira (dance club), *151–152*
Sironit Beach, *318*
Skiing, *441*
Skydiving, *307*
Snake Path, *182*
Snorkeling. ⇨*See* Scuba diving and snorkeling
Soccer, *277*
Solomon, King, *395*
Sorek Cave, *202–204*
Souk (market; Akko), *342*
Souk (market; Nazareth), *373*
South Bat Shlomo, *334–335*
Southern Steps, *63*
Spas
Eilat and the Negev, 472
Jerusalem and the Dead Sea region, 177, 178, 198, 199
Sports. ⇨ *See* specific sport; Under cities and areas
Squash, *156, 492–493*
Stardust (bar), *150*
Stations of the Cross, *63–64*
Stella Maris Church, *294–295*
Stone of Unction, *75*
Succah in the Desert ⌐, *460*
Summit Park, *234*
Suzanne Dellal Center for Dance and Theater, *230*
Swimming
Eilat and the Negev, 461
Haifa and the Northern Coast, 325
Jerusalem, 156
Jerusalem and the Dead Sea region, 197
Tel Aviv, 277
Symbols, *7*
Synagogues
Bar'am, 425
Beit Alfa, 365
Capernaum, 401–402
Ein Gedi, 186
Hammat Tiberias, 396
Jerusalem and the Dead Sea region, 183, 186
Katzrin, 442–443
Korazim, 400
lower Galilee, 365, 396, 400, 401–402
Masada, 183
Rosh Pina, 426
Tzfat (Safed) and environs, 415–417
upper Galilee and the Golan, 415–417, 425, 426, 442–443
Zichron Ya'akov, 325

T

Tabgha, *397–399*
Tabitha School, *236*
Tabor Winery, *385*

Taxes, *535*
Taxis, *524–525*
*Haifa and the Northern Coast,
288*
Technion (research center), *298*
Tel Arad, *188–189*
Tel Aviv, *12, 218–280*
beaches, 275–276
*Center City, 223–230, 244–249,
256–260, 262*
children, activities for, 32, 238
emergencies, 529
festivals, 230
Herzliya Pituach, 263–264
history, 227
hotels, 221, 253–264
Jaffa, 232–236, 250, 252
*Neveh Tzedek, 230–236,
249–250, 262–263*
*nightlife and the arts, 230,
264–274*
*outdoor activities and sports,
274–277*
price categories, 221, 239, 256
restaurants, 221, 239–253
shopping, 277–280
street markets, 232–233, 280
*Tel Aviv Port and Northern Tel
Aviv, 236–239, 252–253*
timing the visit, 220, 221
transportation, 220
visitor information, 221
walking tours, 221
Tel Aviv Museum of Art, *225*
Tel Azekah, *206*
Tel Baruch Beach, *275*
Tel Beer Sheva, *475–476*
Tel Bet Shemesh, *204*
Tel Dan Nature Reserve,
435–436
Tel Hai, *430, 432*
Tel Hai Courtyard Museum, *432*
Tel Hatzor, *428–429*
Tel Maresha, *207–208*
Tel Megiddo National Park,
360–361
Tel Yizre'el, *361*
Telephones, *526–527*
Telul Abu 'Alayiq, *174*
Temple Mount, *62, 72–73*
Temple of the Winged Lions, *504*
Tennis
Eilat and the Negev, 492–493
Jerusalem, 156–157
Theater, *37*
Caesarea, 314
Eilat and the Negev, 473, 490
*Haifa and the Northern Coast,
314*
Jerusalem, 154
Tel Aviv, 226–227, 228, 230, 274
Tiberias, *386–394*
Tiberias Hot Springs, *396*
Tikotin Museum of Japanese
Art, *294*
Time, *535*
Time Trek, *310*

Timing the visit, *15*
Timna Park, *494–496*
Tipping, *16, 535*
Tishbi Estate Winery, *335–336*
Tomb of David, *89*
Tomb of Moses Maimonides,
388
Tomb of Rabbi Shimon Bar
Yochai, *422*
Tomb of Sextius Florentinus, *504*
Tomb of the Virgin, *100–101*
Tour operators, *535–536*
Tower of David, *86–89*
Tower of David Museum, *88*
Train travel, *525*
*Haifa and the Northern Coast,
288*
Transportation, *14. ⇨ See also*
under cities and areas
Trappist Abbey of Latrun, *200*
Tree-planting projects, *376*
Turkish Bathhouse, *342–343*
Tzfat (Safed) and environs,
413–430
Tzuk Farm, *207*

U

Underwater Archaeological
Center, *307*
Underwater Observatory, *480*
Upper Galilee and the Golan,
12, 408–444
*children, activities for, 420, 421,
427–428, 436, 442–443*
Golan Heights, 436–444
guided tours, 424
*hotels, 411, 419–420, 422–424,
427–428, 429, 433, 444*
*nightlife and the arts, 421, 428,
433, 444*
orientation, 409
*outdoor activities and sports,
421, 433–434, 435, 441*
price categories, 411
*restaurants, 411, 419, 422, 425,
427, 432, 441, 443*
shopping, 421, 428
timing the visit, 410, 411
transportation, 410
*Tzfat (Safed) and environs,
413–430*
Upper Hula Valley, 430–436
visitor information, 411
Upper Hula Valley, *430–436*
Uri Buri ✕, *344*
Urn Tomb, *504*

V

Valley of the Communities,
109–110
Value-added tax, *535*
Vered Ha-Galil Guest Farm ⛺,
400
Via Dolorosa, *63–64, 65*
Villa Provence ⛺, *349*
Visas, *534*

Visitor information, *537. ⇨ See
also* under cities and areas

W

Walking
lower Galilee, 354, 366, 394
Tel Aviv, 221
Warren's Shaft, *91, 93*
Water Cistern (Masada), *183*
Water sports
Eilat and the Negev, 491
lower Galilee, 394
Waterfalls
*Jerusalem and the Dead Sea
region, 178–179*
Negev, 455
*upper Galilee and the Golan,
438*
Waterskiing, *277*
Way of Suffering (Way of the
Cross), *63–64, 65*
West Bank, *212*
Western Palace (Masada), *183*
Western Wall, *64, 70–71*
Western Wall Tunnel, *64*
Wilderness of Zin, *452*
Wildlife preserves. ⇨ See
Nature reserves
Wine festivals, *332*
Wine touring and tastings,
330–331, 332, 490, 536
Wineries, *328–332*
Eilat and the Negev, 454
*Haifa and the Northern Coast,
333, 335–336*
*Jerusalem and the Dead Sea
region, 189, 205*
lower Galilee, 385
*upper Galilee and the Golan,
443*
Wohl Archaeological Museum,
84

Y

Yad Layeled, *343*
Yad Vashem, *108–110*
Yatir Winery, *189*
Yefe Nof Street (Haifa), *294*
Yefet Street (Jaffa), *236*
Yehuda Hanassi, Rabbi, *375–376*
Yemin Moshe, *116, 130, 132–133*
YMCA, *113*

Z

Zachariah's Tomb, *100*
Zichron Ya'akov, *324–325,
333–334*
Zippori, *375–376*
Zoological Gardens, *108*
Zoos
Eilat and the Negev, 457–458
*Haifa and the Northern Coast,
296–297*
Jerusalem, 108
lower Galilee, 364–365

546 <   **Photo Credits**

Photo Credits: 1, *Mikhail Levit/Shutterstock.* 2 (top left), *erela, Fodors.com member.* 2 (top right), *RJun, Fodors.com member.* 2 (center left), *GeneZ, Fodors.com member.* 2 (center right), *rooneyroo, Fodors.com member.* 2 (bottom left), *Keith_Marks, Fodors.com member.* 2 (bottom center), *leahzzzz85, Fodors.com member.* 2 (bottom right), *GeneZ, Fodors.com member.* 5, *Israel images/Alamy.* **Chapter 1: Experience Israel:** 8–9, *John Norman/Alamy.* 10, *David Shankbone/wikipedia.* 11 (left), *Israel Ministry of Tourism.* 11 (right), *Odelia Cohen/Shutterstock.* 12 (top right), *Israel Ministry of Tourism.* 12 (top left), *PhotoStock-Israel/Alamy.* 12 (bottom left), *Israel Ministry of Tourism.* 12 (bottom right), *kavram/Shutterstock.* 16 and 17 (left), *Israel Ministry of Tourism.* 17 (right), *Israel Ministry of Tourism.* 18 (left), *Bomshtein/Shutterstock.* 18 (top center), *David Shankbone/wikipedia.* 18 (bottom center), *Israel Ministry of Tourism.* 18 (top right), *Amit Erez/iStockphoto.* 18 (bottom right), *Israel Ministry of Tourism.* 19 (top left), *Arkady Mazor/Shutterstock.* 19 (bottom left), *Mikhail Levit/Shutterstock.* 19 (top center), *Judy Balint.* 19 (bottom center), *wikipedia.org.* 19 (right), *Judy Balint.* 20 and 21, *Elan Fleisher/age fotostock.* 22 and 23 (left), *Israel Ministry of Tourism.* 23 (right), *Mordechai Meiri/Shutterstock.* 24, *Gisella Caroti.* 25 (left), *phogel/Flickr.* 25 (right), *Mikhail Levit/Shutterstock.* 26, *Bantosh/wikipedia.* 27 (left), *David Masters/Flickr.* 27 (right), *Benjamin Balint.* 28, *Ariy/Shutterstock.* 29, *InterContinental Hotels and Resorts.* 30, *Pina BaRosh Wine Bar.* 31 (left and right), *Avi Ganor.* 32, *Noam Armonn/iStockphoto.* 33 (left), *hoyasmeg/Flickr.* 33 (right), *Elisei Shafer/Shutterstock.* 34, *Israel Ministry of Tourism.* 35, *Jonathan Nackstrand/Shutterstock.* 37, *Gadi Dagon.* 37, *ogimogi/Flickr.* 38, *Noam Armonn/Shutterstock.* 39 (left), *Vitaliy Berkovych/Shutterstock.* 39, *Howard Sandler/Shutterstock.* 40, *Ella/Shutterstock.* 47, *Kord.com/age fotostock.* 48 (top left), *Lebrecht Music and Arts Photo Library/Alamy.* 48 (bottom left and right), *wikipedia.org.* 49 (top left), *The London Art Archive/Alamy.* 49 (top center), *wikipedia.org.* 49 (bottom left), *Mikhail Levit/Shutterstock.* 49 (right), *Israel Ministry of Tourism.* 50 (left), *North Wind Picture Archives/Alamy.* 50 (top right), *The Print Collector/Alamy.* 50 (bottom right) and 51 (top left and bottom left), *wikipedia.org.* 51 (right), *Israel images/Alamy.* 52 (left), *wikipedia.org.* 52 (top right), *INTERFOTO Pressebildagentur/Alamy.* 52 (bottom right), *Robert Judges/Alamy.* **Chapter 2: Jerusalem:** 53, *Nicole_pappas, Fodors.com member.* 58, *Eyal Nahmias/Alamy.* 66 (left), *Israel Ministry of Tourism.* 67 (center), *Elan Fleisher/age fotostock.* 67 (right), *Israel Ministry of Tourism.* 68 (left), *Israel images/Alamy.* 68 (top right), *Mikhail Levit/Shutterstock.* 68 (bottom right), *Jason Moore/Alamy.* 69, *North Wind Picture Archives/Alamy.* 70, *Mikhail Levit/Shutterstock.* 71 (top), *Israel Ministry of Tourism.* 71 (bottom), *Mikhail Levit/Shutterstock.* 72, *Israel images/Alamy.* 73 (top left), *Mikhail Levit/Shutterstock.* 73 (top right), *wikipedia.org.* 73 (bottom), *TNT Magazine/Alamy.* 74, *Joel Carillet/iStockphoto.* 75 (top), *David Sanger Photography/Alamy.* 75 (bottom), *Alvaro Leiva/age fotostock.* 77 (top), *Mikhail Levit/Shutterstock.* 77 (bottom), *Israel Ministry of Tourism.* 78, *ARCO/J Erichsen/age fotostock.* 79 (top), *Corbis.* 79 (bottom), *Joshua Haviv/iStockphoto.* 80, *Terry J Alcorn/iStockphoto.* 81, *Robin Laurance/age fotostock.* 83, *moris kushelevitch/Alamy.* 89, *Alvaro Leiva/age fotostock.* 98, *ARCO/J Erichsen/age fotostock.* 101, *Kord.com/SuperStock.* 104, *Israel Ministry of Tourism.* 109, *Eitan Simanor/Alamy.* 122, *Howard Sandler/Shutterstock.* 123 (top), *8828810875/Shutterstock.* 123 (bottom), *Adem Demir/Shutterstock.* 137, *Hemis.fr/SuperStock.* 142 (top), *The Inbal Jerusalem Hotel.* 142 (left bottom and right bottom), *The David Citadel Hotel, Jerusalem.* 151, *Israel Ministry of Tourism.* 158, *Chadica/Flickr.* 161, *Dallas & John Heaton/age fotostock.* **Chapter 3: Around Jerusalem and the Dead Sea:** 165, *markdewd, Fodors.com member.* 166 and 167 (left), *Paul Prescott/Shutterstock.* 167 (right), *phardt, Fodors.com member.* 170, *Joseph Calev/Shutterstock.* 176, *R. Matina/age fotostock.* 179, *ARCO/J Erichsen/age fotostock.* 180, *Israel images/Alamy.* 181, *Gisella Caroti.* 182 (top), *Israel images/Alamy.* 182 (bottom), *Roger Cracknell 18/Israel/Alamy.* 183 (top left), *Hanan Isachar/Alamy.* 183 (bottom left), *Israel images/Alamy.* 183 (top right), *Ppja/wikipedia.org.* 183 (center right), *PhotoStock-Israel/Alamy.* 183 (bottom right), *Israel images/Alamy.* 184, *Terence Mendoza/Shutterstock.* 185 (top), *David Shankbone/wikipedia.org.* 185 (bottom), *Israel images/Alamy.* 194, *Steve Vidler/SuperStock.* 195, *Hemis.fr/SuperStock.* 197 (top), *Images&Stories/Alamy.* 197 (bottom), *Yvette Cardozo/age fotostock.* 198, *Bruno Morandi/SuperStock.* 198, *Eitan Simanor/Alamy.* 206 and 211, *Israel images/Alamy.* 214, *Jon Arnold Images Ltd/Alamy.* **Chapter 4: Tel Aviv:** 217 and 218, *Israel Ministry of Tourism.* 219 (top), *Dmitry Pistrov/iStockphoto.* 219 (bottom), *Israel Ministry of Tourism.* 222, *Gadi Dagon.* 228, *Israel Ministry of Tourism.* 229 and 231, *LOOK Die Bildagentur der Fotografen GmbH/Alamy.* 234, *Dave Houser/ImageState/photolibrary.com.* 242, *Arkadiy Yarmolenko/Shutterstock.* 243 (top), *Paul Cowan/Shutterstock.* 243 (bottom), *Andrea Skjold/Shutterstock.* 246, *rooneyroo, Fodors.com member.* 251, *LOOK Die Bildagentur der Fotografen GmbH/Alamy.* 252, *Israel Ministry of Tourism.* 261 (top), *InterContinental Hotels and Resorts.* 261 (bottom left), *Hotel Montefiore, Tel Aviv.* 261 (bottom right), *Sheraton Tel Aviv Hotels & Towers.* 262, *Eddie Gerald/Alamy.* 267, *Gadi Dagon.* 268 (top left), *Israel images/Alamy.* 268 (top right), *Israel Ministry of Tourism.* 268 (bottom right), *Benjamin Balint.* 269 (top left), *Israel Ministry* *of Tourism.* 269 (top right and bottom right), *Avi Ganor.* 270 (top left), *PhotoStock-Israel/Alamy.* 270 (top right and bottom right), 272, and 275 , *Eddie Gerald/Alamy.* 278, *Kevin Galvin/Alamy.* **Chapter 5: Haifa and the Northern Coast:** 281, *Russell Kord/Alamy.* 282, *erela, Fodors.com member.* 283 (top), *Nathan Chor/Shutterstock.* 283 (bottom), *Paul Prescott/Shutterstock.* 286, *Arkady Mazor/Shutterstock.* 289, *GeneZ, Fodors.com member.* 295, *Eitan Simanor/Alamy.* 296, *Rafael Ben-Ari/Alamy.* 302, *Israel images/Alamy.* 314, *mgplessner, Fodors.com member.* 317, *Vitaliy Berkovych/Shutterstock.* 326 (left), *Eddie Gerald/Alamy.* 326-27, *Rina Nagila.* 328 (top left), *Bernard Edelstein.* 328 (bottom left), *Golan Heights Winery.* 328 (right), *Eddie Gerald/Alamy.* 329 (top), *Sea Horse Winery.* 329 (bottom), *Clos de Gat.* 330 (top left), *Daniel P. Acevedo/age fotostock.* 330 (bottom left), *Clos de Gat.* 330 (right), *Carmel Winery.* 331 (top), *Galil Mountain Winery.* 331 (center and bottom), *Carmel Winery.* 332, *Pina BaRosh Wine Bar.* 345, *R. Matina/age fotostock.* 348, *Eddie Gerald/Alamy.* **Chapter 6: Lower Galilee:** 351, *Jon Arnold Images Ltd/Alamy.* 352, *erela, Fodors.com member.* 353 (left), Noam Armonn/iStockphoto. 353 (right), *Israel Ministry of Tourism.* 356, *Mary Lane/iStockphoto.* 361, *Jon Arnold Images Ltd/Alamy.* 364, *Israel images/Alamy.* 367 and 373, *Israel Ministry of Tourism.* 374, *Alexandre Grigoriev/Shutterstock.* 378-79 (top), *Jon Arnold/age fotostock.* 378 (bottom), *Israel Ministry of Tourism.* 380 (top and bottom), *www.wga.hu.* 381 and 382 (top left), *Israel Ministry of Tourism.* 382 (bottom left and right) and 383 (top left), *Israel images/Alamy.* 383 (top center), *Tomasz Parys/ Shutterstock.* 383 (top right and bottom right), *Israel images/Alamy.* 383 (bottom left), *Israel Ministry of Tourism.* 384, *Paul Prescott/Shutterstock.* 390 and 395, *Israel images/Alamy.* 398, *Johnny Stock-shooter/age fotostock.* 401, *Tomasz Parys/Shutterstock.* **Chapter 7: Upper Galilee:** 407, *Israel images/ Alamy.* 408, *wikipedia.org.* 409 (top), *Yory Frenklakh/Shutterstock.* 409 (bottom), *Israel Ministry of Tourism.* 412, *PhotoStock-Israel/Alamy.* 418, *Helio San Miguel.* 421, *Eddie Gerald/Alamy.* 426, *PhotoStock-Israel/Alamy.* 434, *Niall Benvie/Alamy.* 439, *Keith_Marks, Fodors.com member.* 440, *Israel images/Alamy.* 443, *Israel Ministry of Tourism.* **Chapter 8: Eilat and Negev:** 445, *Keith_Marks, Fodors. com member.* 446 (top), *Yory Frenklakh/Shutterstock.* 446 (bottom), *zepperwing, Fodors.com member.* 447 (left), *Paul Prescott/Shutterstock.* 447 (right), *urosr/Shutterstock.* 450, *Paul Prescott/Shutterstock.* 453, *Eddie Gerald/Alamy.* 458, *Israel Ministry of Tourism.* 462, *Josef F. Stuefer/Shutterstock.* 464 (top), *Israel images/Alamy.* 464 (bottom), *Alan Keohane/age fotostock.* 465, *Israel images/Alamy.* 466 (top left), *James Margolis/iStockphoto.* 466 (top right), *Bomshtein/Shutterstock.* 466 (bottom), *Ester Inbar/wikipedia.org.* 467 (top), *kavram/Shutterstock.* 467 (bottom), 467, *blickwinkel/Alamy.* 468 (left), *Israel Ministry of Tourism.* 468 (right), *Eddie Gerald/Alamy.* 469 (top), *Yvette Cardozo/ Index Stock Imagery/photolibrary.com.* 469 (center), *Kibbutz Lotan.* 469 (bottom), *ARCO/D. Usher/ age fotostock.* 476, *RIEGER Bertrand/Hemis photolibrary.com.* 481, *Elisei Shafer/Shutterstock.* 490, *Benjamin Balint.* 501, *RIEGER Bertrand/age fotostock.*

ABOUT OUR WRITERS

Benjamin Balint, a writer based in Jerusalem, has lived in Israel for six years. His work has appeared in the *Wall Street Journal*, *Haaretz*, *Commentary*, and *Policy Review*. In addition, he's an editorial writer for the *Jerusalem Post*. Ben updated the Eilat and the Negev chapter, and wrote our "Tel Aviv After Dark" and "Adventures in the Negev" features.

Judy Lash Balint is an award-winning, Jerusalem-based writer and researcher, and the author of *Jerusalem Diaries: In Tense Times* and *Jerusalem Diaries II: What's Really Happening in Israel*, as well as dozens of articles. She updated Travel Smart Israel and wrote "Israel and the Performing Arts." Judy is the communications coordinator at the Jerusalem Center for Public Affairs and blogs at *jerusalemdiaries.blogspot.com*.

Sarah Bronson, who grew up in Boston, is a freelance writer and editor based in Jerusalem. Her work has appeared in the *New York Times*, and the *Washington Times*, and she frequently writes about Israeli tourism for New York's *Jewish Week*. She can be reached through her blog at *chayyeisarah.blogspot.com*.

American-born **Phyllis Glazer** is one of Israel's top food personalities. She's worked for the Associated Press, the *Los Angeles Times*, and *Bon Appétit*. The author of five cookbooks, she gives green cooking workshops in her eco-kitchen in Tel Aviv. Phyllis contributed to "Quintessential Israel," "If You Like," and "Israeli Cuisine."

Born in Montréal, **Judy Stacey Goldman** has lived in Israel for the past 30 years, where she works as a professional tour guide. She's also co-authored three books on cuisine in Jerusalem and Tel Aviv. Judy updated the Haifa and the Northern Coast chapter, contributed to "Israeli Cuisine," and wrote "Street Food in Israel" and "Holiday Foods in Israel." Contact Judy at *judebob@netvision.net.il*.

Shelly Paz is the tenth generation of her family to live in Jerusalem. She writes for the *Jerusalem Post* and has been covering political, local and tourist events for Israeli and foreign media outlets for almost a decade.

Lisa Perlman grew up in Australia but settled in Israel over 20 years ago. She's worked as a journalist and a spokesperson. Lisa wrote "Israel's Best Markets" and "Israel with Kids."

Mike Rogoff, a professional tour guide and writer, has been exploring the byways of Israel with visitors of all persuasions since the early 1970s. South African–born and Jerusalem-based, Mike is a recipient of the Israel government's Guide of the Year award, and has contributed to *Fodor's Israel* since 1985. He updated Jerusalem and wrote the "Jesus in the Galilee" and "Jerusalem: Keeping the Faith" features. Contact Mike at *rogoff@netvision.net.il*.

Adeena Sussman is a food writer, recipe developer, and cooking instructor who has written about Israeli food and wine for publications including *Gourmet* and *Hadassah*. Based in New York, she contributed "The Wines of Israel," "Top Attractions," and "Top Experiences." Adeena's Web site is *adeenasussman.com*.

Miriam Feinberg Vamosh, from New Jersey, is a longtime tour educator. She's an editorial staff writer at *Ha'aretz* English edition, and an editor for the Israel Antiquities Authority and the Israel National Commission for UNESCO. Miriam is also the author of six books on Israel's history and heritage. She updated our Tel Aviv chapter.

Gil Zohar, who was born in Toronto and moved to Jerusalem in 1982, is a journalist writing for the *Jerusalem Post* and other publications. He's also a professional tour guide who likes to weave together the Holy Land's multiple narratives. Gil updated the Lower Galilee and Around Jerusalem and the Dead Sea chapters. Contact him at *gkezwer@rogers.com*.